Signed by the Author

SEBRING

We recognize that some words, model names and designations
mentioned in this book are the property of the trademark holder.
We use them only for identification purposes.

Library of Congress Cataloging-in-Publication Data Available
ISBN: 0-9649722-0-4

Printed in Hong Kong

Book and cover design:
Tom Morgan and Brenda Eno at Blue Design

10 9 8 7 6 5 4 3 2 1

David Bull Publishing
115 Mt. Auburn Street
Cambridge, MA 02138
617-354-8500

Cover photo top: Drivers sprint to their cars to start the 1968 race.

Cover photo bottom: Chris Amon leaps into his Ferrari at the start
of the 1969 race. He co-drove with Mario Andretti to second place.

Photo page 4: Phil Hill reaches for his seat cushion during a driver change
and night pit stop for the Shelby American team. Hill went on to finish
sixth with co-driver Jo Schlesser.

Photo this page: Safety had not yet become a concern at Sebring. The
flagman stands only a few feet from the number-12 Ferrari 315S of
Alfonso de Portago and Luigi Musso and the number-51 MGA of Dave
Ash/Gus Ehram/J. Van Driel. Spectators in the background line the edge
of the track with no barrier protection.

SEBRING

THE OFFICIAL HISTORY OF AMERICA'S GREAT SPORTS CAR RACE

KEN BRESLAUER

DAVID BULL PUBLISHING

CAMBRIDGE

TABLE OF CONTENTS

FOREWORD BY DAN GURNEY

In the world of motor racing there exist a few, magical words that evoke a wealth of images and emotions in drivers and racing fans the world over: Monte Carlo, Indianapolis, Le Mans, the Nurburgring and Sebring, the sports car capital and road-racing Mecca of the United States. When I hear "Sebring" I smell orange blossoms, I see brilliant sunsets and horrendous rain storms, modest motels, giant scrap World War II airplanes, and team owners in blazers and ties. My ears are ringing with names like Castellotti, Moss, Fangio, Shelby, Phil Walters, Phil Hill, Bruce McLaren, Jim Hall, Derek Bell, Mark Donohue, Alec Ulmann and many, many more. All the classic cars of my youth assemble in front of my inner eye with their colors and style and sounds: Ferrari, Cunningham, OSCA, Jaguar, Corvette, Cobra and Porsche.

Sebring always had a unique character and I am tickled pink that the old place is still there and still functioning after all these years. What makes it extra special in my heart, of course, is the fact that my own career as a driver and race car manufacturer is so closely linked with the place. I drove my first big sports car race there in 1958 and my last in 1970 together with the late Frenchman, Francois Cevert. As a manufacturer and team owner, two of our biggest successes took place there, our back-to-back wins in '92 and '93 with our GTP Toyota Eagle with Juan Fangio II and Andy Wallace driving.

What made my first pilgrimage to Sebring so memorable was not so much the race itself as the trip by car from Los Angeles together with Skip Hudson and my hero of those days, Phil Hill. Phil gave us young, eager and determined future racers a ride in his old Packard.

It was a long, adventurous journey across the country spanning many days. Whenever I flew to Sebring in subsequent years and looked down on the countryside below from the comfort of my airplane seat I remembered with nostalgia and wonder the enthusiasm of those early days.

In 1959 as a member of the Ferrari team, I had tremendous difficulty fitting into the tight little cockpit of the Ferrari due to my size. I actually exhausted both legs on my first driving stint. It was like squatting for an hour and forty-five minutes while trying to hold my body down on the brakes with everything at an angle. I wore a hole through my shoe and could not walk when I first got out of the car for a driver change. As fortune would have it, Phil Hill and Olivier Gendebien's Ferrari broke down while Chuck Daigh and I managed to work ourselves into the lead. As those two drivers were the stars of the day, the Ferrari team manager called us in and handed our car over to them. They held the lead and all four of us shared in the victory.

In the early sixties I drove Porsches long before the Germans became the dominant power in sports car racing. Jo Bonnier and I were constantly trying to sneak our little 1.6 liter air-cooled engine past bigger machines. We often came close, but never could do it. Still the races were enjoyable, as were those in the Cobras with Carroll Shelby's gang of wonderful characters. My co-driver, Bob Johnson, had a terrific accident hitting a stationary, no-lights Alfa at night, going 120 mph, which sent him to the hospital and ended his career. In 1966 I had a one-minute lead over the field with one minute and thirty seconds to go in

In 1960, Dan Gurney and Stirling Moss drove this Camoradi-prepared Maserati T61, to a six-lap lead before transmission failure ended their day.

the race after twelve grueling hours driving a Ford Mk II 427. Then the camshaft broke...and my heart with it. I pushed the car about 300 yards and got across the finish line in second place behind Ken Miles. But I was disqualified as the rule book stated that a car had to finish on its own and not the driver's power. Once in a while I come across a video of that race on ESPN's "Glory Days" and I marvel at the muscle power and determination of that young man pushing that monster toward the chequered flag, and the disappointment of that day comes back fresh and strong and immediate.

When our red and white GTP Toyota Eagle drove by the pits for the last time at the 1992 12 Hour race before crossing the finish line in first, I was very moved. I felt like a proud and exhausted parent. We had tried before with our GTU and GTO cars and now finally AAR had done it, we had won America's premier road racing event. It made us incredibly proud.

Sebring is now - as it was then, a Spring ritual for all road racers around the world. For the young and starry-eyed who go there on a shoestring for the very first time, as well as for the established and proven who want to race against the best. While the track has modernized to keep up with the times, it has not been swallowed up by commercialism like so many others, but has managed to retain its soul and its links to the past. It attracts a special kind of fan, too, who looks at the event as a traditional happening that should not be missed.

Not long ago, I read in one of former president Carter's biographies that he and his family used to go to Sebring in the early sixties, camp out along the track and enjoy themselves. A history as colorful and genuine as Sebring's should be valued and cherished, and as long as there are road racers, I am sure it will.

Dan Gurney and Jerry Grant's Ford Mk II dominated the 1966 Sebring race—until the heartbreaking last lap.

An emotional victory for Dan Gurney as a team owner in 1992.

Dan Gurney

8

I N T R O D U C T I O N

Nestled among the orange groves and cattle ranches of Florida's outback is an American sports tradition. In this unlikely location is America's oldest permanent sports car circuit and the site of the legendary 12 Hours of Sebring International Grand Prix of Endurance.

Who would have thought that Alec Ulmann's dream of bringing international road racing to America would flourish in this remote location? The legends of sports car racing have gathered at Sebring for five decades. The 12-hour race has been the site of incredible finishes, improbable winners and more than its share of tragedy. The race itself has died many deaths, only to be reborn again and again.

Sebring has been refined and remodeled over the years, but it's still the same old Sebring. It is tough, and surviving Sebring is the definition of endurance.

The purpose of this book is to document the incredible history of America's most important international sports car race, including a detailed statistical history located in the Appendix. It is designed to be a definitive reference for motorsports historians and an entertaining history for auto racing enthusiasts around the world.

View of the pit area just before the start of the 1954 race.

B E F O R E   S E B R I N G :
The Origins of Postwar American Sports Car Racing

The beginning of sports car racing in North America can be traced back to the Automobile Racing Club of America (ARCA), which began holding road races in the early 1930s. A small organization of affluent racing enthusiasts, ARCA was more of a social club than a true racing organization. Most ARCA events were club races held in relatively obscure locations. The race at the New York World's Fair in 1940 represented a significant move up to a major venue of international stature. Unfortunately, the onset of the war ended ARCA's momentum and that race proved to be its last event.

World War II forced the cessation of racing activity worldwide

Sam Colliers's Jaguar
XK120 at the inaugural
Palm Beach Shores Road
Race on January 3, 1950.
He placed sixth.

Sam Collier refuels his Culver Cadet at the Sebring Airport as Bob Gegen looks on. This photo was taken in March 1950, when the two SCCA officials flew to Sebring at Alec Ulmann's suggestion to look over the facility as a possible site for a sports car endurance race.

Below: On February 27, 1949 one of the first sports car races to be held at an airport took place at the Ft. Lauderdale-Davie Airport in conjunction with a NASCAR roadster event. The winner was Tom Demetry driving an MG TD (at left receiving his trophy). Sam Collier finished second, followed by Bob Gegen and George Rand.

and it wasn't until 1948 that sports car racing was revived in the United States with the Watkins Glen Grand Prix in New York, staged by the Sports Car Club of America (SCCA). Many of those involved were originally members of ARCA.

The pioneers of American sports car racing were heavily influenced by racing in Europe. Primarily wealthy businessmen from the northeast United States, many of whom had winter homes in Florida, they all shared a goal of bringing international road racing competition to America. Most had traveled to Europe and seen the popularity of road racing, especially the glamorous spectacle at Le Mans, France.

Among these pioneers were the Collier brothers, Sam and Miles, of the Collier real estate and financial empire in southwest Florida. Miles had raced in the 24 Hours of Le Mans in 1939 (and would do so again in 1950 with brother Sam), and his interest in foreign automobiles and international competition inspired his efforts in the United States.

Auto racing flourished in the United States at the time, but it comprised mainly dirt track races featuring championship [Indy] cars, sprint cars and midgets-all open-wheel cars built exclusively for racing. Most competition, including the Indianapolis 500, was sanctioned by the American Automobile Association (AAA) Contest Board, which concentrated on oval track racing.

The National Association of Stock Car Automobile Racing (NASCAR) was still in its infancy, sanctioning stock car races primarily in the southern United States.

In 1950 sports car racing was still virtually unknown in America, as were marques such as Jaguar, Aston Martin, Ferrari and Maserati. Although the Watkins Glen road races

were successful, and events at Bridgehampton, Long Island; Elkhart Lake, Wisconsin; and Pebble Beach, California were attracting large crowds, sports car racing had yet to gain acceptance in America.

Alec Ulmann was an official with the SCCA who longed to see sports car racing take its rightful place alongside other major sports. He was an ardent proponent of an international event that would become as prestigious as Le Mans.

Ulmann was born in Russia in 1903, and came to the United States in 1922 with his family after two years of prep school in Switzerland. He studied engineering at MIT and Harvard and upon graduation went into the aviation industry. Although aviation provided his main source of income, his first love was automobiles. At every possible opportunity, he made trips to famous European circuits such as Le Mans, Nurburgring, Monza and Monaco. He was a member of

Before the Palm Beach Shores Road Race 1951. John Fitch won in the number-1 Ferrari 340 America. Tom Cole is in the Chrysler Allard J2 (4), Phil Walters is in the Cadillac Healey (7), and Fred Wacker is in his famous "8 Ball" Cadillac Allard.

ARCA and among the first members of its successor, the SCCA.

In January 1950, Ulmann had helped officiate the Palm Beach Shores Road Race, a landmark event in the history of American sports car racing. Designed to emulate the Monaco circuit, the race was to run along the waterfront in West Palm Beach, Florida, past a marina and through the outskirts of an exclusive residential area. Originally called the Around the Houses Road Race, city officials got cold feet only weeks before the event. Fearing liability from accidents, organizers canceled the race.

The SCCA found another location on Palm Beach Shores, a new development on the south end of Singer Island, just across the inlet from Palm Beach and the homes of such legendary sports car pioneers as Briggs Cunningham and Jim Kimberly.

The race was a major success, but the limitations and safety concerns of running on public roads were obvious (see Appendix for detailed results).

Airports were a logical location for sports car racing-expansive tarmacs with few obstructions, and there were plenty of seldom-used airfields around the country. The Strategic Air Command, at the urging of General Curtis LeMay, would later promote a series of SCCA races at military bases around the United States. The largest such event took place at MacDill Air Force Base near Tampa, Florida in 1953.

In 1949, Bill France, Sr., founder of NASCAR and later the Daytona International Speedway, promoted a race at the Ft. Lauderdale-Davie Airport (now the site of Broward Community College). Included on the schedule of events was a short race for sports cars. The field was made up primarily of MGs, but it ranks as one of the first postwar sports car races held on an airfield.

Ulmann's intent was to find a suitable venue for America's first international sports car endurance race. He, too, believed an airport circuit would be most logical.

The Sebring Airport would soon realize Alec Ulmann's dream.

Porsche made its first major impact on American racing during the Kiwanis Trophy event at the Palm Beach Shores Road Race on December 8, 1951. The beautiful aerodynamic Glockler Porsche driven by importer Max Hoffman was leading by more than two laps when its engine failed early in the race.

Miles Collier drove his Ford Riley Special in the Palm Beach Shores race, but was disqualified.

Left: Victory celebration as Deshon and Koster accept the trophy for winning the Sam Collier Memorial. Car owner Vic Sharpe stands on the left and Alec Ulmann is in the background wearing a white cap.

1950

Alec Ulmann prepares to give the command to start America's first sports car endurance race on December 31, 1950.

The Sebring Airport, originally known as Hendricks Field, was first recommended for use as a racing circuit by Alec Ulmann. He helped stage the Watkins Glen Road Race in 1948 and 1949 and the Palm Beach Shores Road Race in January 1950, but he longed for an American endurance classic of the same stature as Le Mans.

Ulmann was in the aviation business and had visited the huge facility five miles southeast of Sebring several times. A seldom-used airport such as Hendricks Field was a logical location for a sports car race. The generally favorable climate and close proximity to many sports car racers living on Florida's east coast were prime factors in choosing Sebring.

The Sebring Airport was in a remote location in Highlands County. Used as a B-17 training base during World War II, the Airport offered little scenery beyond the abandoned military barracks, aging aircraft, and dilapidated hangars and warehouses.

At Ulmann's invitation, road racing pioneer Sam Collier and SCCA Florida Region Director Bob Gegen flew to Sebring in the spring of 1950 to begin planning a race for later in the year.

They mapped out a 3.5-mile circuit and set plans for the first Sebring race to be held on New Year's Eve. Ulmann planned a "Little Le Mans" endurance race to be run on a complicated handicapping system called the Index of Performance (see Appendix for a detailed explanation). The course included airport runways and narrow asphalt roads within the former military base.

Sadly, Sam Collier was killed during the running of the Watkins Glen race of September 1950. Thus, in his honor the first Sebring race was officially named the Sam Collier Memorial Grand Prix of Endurance.

Collier's contributions to road racing in America were numerous. An original member of the Automobile Racing Club of America, which attempted to revive road racing in America during the 1930s, Collier had competed at Le Mans and shared Ulmann's desire for a

The Sebring race course
included roadways
through the Sebring
Airport industrial area.
Here the Ferrari 166
driven by Bill Spear and
George Roberts, Jr. leads
the Allard Cadillac of
Erwin Goldschmidt and
Tommy Cole.

great international event to be held in America.

It was decided that the first Sebring race was to be a six-hour
race. Sanctioned by the SCCA, it would be the first sports car endurance race ever held in the United States and run in strict accordance
with international rules.

Having secured the support of local firefighters the Sebring Firemen, Inc., in sponsoring the event and providing valuable local man-
power, Ulmann was ready to send out entry forms. The response was
excellent, and many of the top sports cars in America were entered.

Among the top drivers entered were Jim Kimberly, Briggs
Cunningham (who had raced at Le Mans earlier in the year), Luigi
Chinetti (who won at Le Mans in 1949), Fred Wacker, Phil Walters,
Bill Spear and Tommy Cole. Among the field of cars were Ferrari,
Aston Martin, Jaguar, Allard, MG and Fiat entries. Almost all were
still oddities in the United States.

Vic Sharpe of Tampa, Florida, drove his little Crosley Hot Shot
to Sebring to watch the race and bring some spare parts for Tommy
Cole, who was co-driving a Allard Cadillac with Erwin Goldschmidt.

It was Cole who approached Sharpe about borrowing the Crosley
for a spin around the circuit. He timed himself with his wristwatch,
then used a slide rule to calculate how the Crosley could do on the
complicated handicapping system. As he expected, the tiny 724cc
Crosley would have an excellent chance of winning.

Since Sharpe was not an eligible SCCA driver, Ralph (Bob) Deshon
and Fred (Fritz) Koster were chosen to drive the Crosley. Sharpe
agreed to have the bumpers and windshield removed to reduce weight.
An old piece of plexiglass found near a runway was used as a small
windscreen. The Crosley managed only a few practice laps the night

before the race during a heavy rain.

Ulmann knew the value of good publicity, and he aggressively promoted the race to key media people. He also invited the governor of Florida and several other VIP types to help raise the stature of the sport, which was far from front page news back in 1950.

The field of 28 cars lined up for the Le Mans start. Grid positions were determined by engine displacement—the cars with the largest engines were placed at the front of the field, and those drivers drew lots for their actual starting position. Consequently, the tiny Crosley drew the 28th and last spot.

The crude Sebring circuit was marked by hay bales and a few signs. The pits were merely wooden tables. It was certainly a modest beginning.

A small crowd estimated at 2,800 arrived on a chilly winter day for what would be remembered as the most important event in American sports car racing history.

The Sam Collier Memorial Grand Prix started at 3 P.M. on December 31, 1950.

While the Crosley was certainly one of the slowest cars on the track, it settled into a consistent lap speed and quickly took the lead on the handicapping index.

The famous Le Mans start: Drivers run to their cars to begin the Sam Collier six-hour Memorial Grand Prix of Endurance. Note the unfortunate driver running back to the starting line. He was caught out while making last-minute adjustments to his car.

The Robert Keller/Paul Farago Fiat and the Kimberly/Marshall Lewis Ferrari 166 were the top contenders for the handicap win, while the Fred Wacker/Frank Burrell Cadillac-Allard was leading the field on distance.

By mid-race, the Crosley had established a solid lead over the Fiat, with the Bill Spear/George Roberts and Kimberly/Lewis Ferraris in contention. Only three cars had dropped out of the race. John Van Driel was leading class in his MG TC, driving the entire race solo.

Racing into the night provided a rather unique experience for drivers and spectators alike. Never before had such a sports car race been contested in the United States.

With an hour remaining, the Kimberly/Lewis Ferrari began turning even faster lap speeds, pressing the Crosley for the lead on handicap. Using a suitcase as a pitboard, Koster was instructed to speed up, and much to the Ferrari's surprise, the Crosley began lapping the track four MPH faster than before!

The Crosley held off the charging Ferrari to win the Sam Collier

The Spear/Roberts, Jr. Ferrari 166 leads the MG TD of Herbert Brundage and Hobart Cook in front of a hangar remaining from when the Sebring Airport was the Hendricks Field military base. This hangar still stands at turn one.

A flagman stands right on the edge of the course as two Ferraris battle for position. The Liugi Chinetti/Alfredo Momo 195S (17) leads the 166 driven by Jim Kimberly and Marshall Lewis.

Memorial Grand Prix. The lone American car had done the impossible and recorded the first of many Sebring upsets. Koster and Deshon shared the trophy in victory circle, then handed the car back to Sharpe, who drove it back to Tampa the following morning.

It was many weeks later that everyone learned the Crosley had been heavily damaged in an accident several weeks before the race and had been repaired only days before its trip to Sebring!

Following the race, Deshon wrote to Sharpe: "Just wanted to thank you for the wonderful afternoon at the expense of your Crosley. I can't remember when I ever had a better time. Except for the laughing I did during the race I can't think of ever having a more relaxing ride. I hope the Hot Shot is none the worse for wear. I learn now that Fritz was using the gear shift hoping to speed up a bit. I'm afraid the Crosley was quite content with whatever speed it had decided to maintain and that was that…Think how a stripped Crosley would go!"

The Kimberly/Lewis Ferrari finished second (although they were 19 laps ahead of the Crosley on distance), followed by the Keller/Farago Fiat and the Spear/Roberts Ferrari. The Wacker/Burrell Allard covered the most distance, finishing eighth on handicap. Luigi Chinetti, winner at Le Mans in 1949, drove the most distance without relief, finishing the six-hour race in seventh place.

The first Sebring race received international coverage and was considered a huge success. It would return in 1952 as a 12-hour race sanctioned by the American Automobile Association.

The Sebring legend had been born.

The Crosley Hot Shot that won the first Sebring race, driven by Ralph Deshon and Fritz Koster. The winner was determined by a handicapping formula, and not by overall distance completed during the six-hour race.

Alec Ulmann was convinced
that an international endurance race in North America would suc-
ceed. The Collier race had provided the valuable first step toward
that goal. Since then, however, Ulmann had severed his ties with
the SCCA in a bitter political dispute over the future of road racing in America.

The first Sebring 12-hour race was to be sanctioned by the Contest
Board of the American Automobile Association (AAA), which primarily sanctioned oval track events, including the Indianapolis 500.

Not by coincidence, the SCCA scheduled a 12-hour race at the
Vero Beach Airport, 60 miles east of Sebring, for the weekend before Ulmann's race.

The Sebring circuit was expanded from the 3.5-mile configura-
tion used for the Collier race to a new 5.2-mile circuit, the longest in
North America. It was a very fast circuit as well, utilizing two long
concrete airport runways and asphalt roads within the old military
base complex. Hay bales and peach baskets marked the circuit. A
crude timing stand was erected in front of the airport office. Much
of the circuit was off limits to spectators, although there was virtually no way to control them.

Ulmann and his wife Mary vigorously promoted the race, setting up an office at Sebring's famous Harder Hall hotel, and enlisted the help of Reggie Smith as race secretary and Joe Lane as
timing and scoring chief. Both would remain with Ulmann for two
decades. The Sebring Firemen, Inc., again provided a great deal of
local support. Sebring resident, Forrest Howard, was named race
chairman and Ford Heacock, another prominent local resident, was
chosen as co-chairman.

Ulmann initially predicted 75 entries and a crowd approaching
50,000. He would fall far short on both counts, but the race itself
would be regarded as a huge success.

In 1952 sport cars were still a rarity in the U.S., but the first
Sebring race represented the finest gathering of road racing cars

Left: The start of the first

12 Hours of Sebring.

and drivers in postwar history. The Vero Beach event (see Appendix for detailed results) the previous week did have an adverse effect on the Sebring entry, as several cars suffered mechanical problems that could not be repaired in time for another 12-hour grind. In addition, the Goldschmidt Allard lost its transmission on the way to the Sebring circuit, while practice eliminated several other cars.

The new Cunningham cars were entered but could not be prepared in time, although Briggs Cunningham did enter a Siata Crosley for George Huntoon and Phil Stiles, and Cunningham himself co-drove Bill Spear's Ferrari 340 America. Other cars, such as the Jim Kimberly/Marshall Lewis Ferrari 166MM (overall winner of the Vero Beach race) withdrew because of the possible political ramifications of competing in the AAA-sanctioned race. This, no doubt, kept other teams away.

Despite the underlying politics, many of road racing's early pioneers entered. Walt Hansgen, Cunningham, Spear, George Schrafft

The drivers' meeting before the start of the first 12 Hours of Sebring. This was the only year the pit area was located in front of the airport office between turns one and two.

and many others were instrumental in the evolution of American sports car racing. They recognized the importance of the Sebring event and supported Ulmann in his efforts to bring professional sports car racing to America.

SEBRING INTERNATIONAL GRAND PRIX
OF ENDURANCE

PARTICIPANT'S PASS

Sebring Air Terminal
Sebring, Florida
MARCH 15, 1952
12 Noon to 12 Midnight

As the American affiliate of the Fédération Internationale de l'Automobile, the world-governing body of motor racing, the AAA sanction made this event especially significant. The race was to be run under the strict rules of Le Mans, as this race was listed on the international calendar of events.

The first 12 Hours of Sebring race attracted its first international entry, the French Deutsch-Bonnet team. These beautiful front-drive cars with their tiny air-cooled Panhard engines were entered for the purpose of winning the Index of Performance, considered at that time of equal importance to an overall victory.

Scheduled to start at noon on March 15, the race was delayed over an hour by heavy rains, which pelted the old military base for

The Morgan Plus 4 driven by Bob Wilder and Gus Ehrman finished ninth. Behind is the Deutsch-Bonnet Panhard of Steve Lansing/Wade Morehouse/Rene Bonnet that won the Index of Performance and finished seventh overall.

The winning Kulok/Gray Frazer Nash on the expansive airport runway section of the 5.2-mile Sebring circuit.

most of the morning. Finally the skies cleared and drivers and cars lined up for the Le Mans start. The course was altered slightly on one runway to bypass a large pool of standing rainwater.

At 1:05 P.M., Russ Boss lowered the starter's flag, signaling the start of the first 12 Hours of Sebring. The 32 drivers sprinted to their cars and the usually quiet Sebring Airport roared to life.

With a crowd of 7,000 looking on, the Jaguar XK120 of Charles Schott and Morris Carroll was first off the line but the blue and white Spear/Cunningham Ferrari led the first lap, followed by the Frazer Nash LM driven by Harry Gray and Larry Kulok.

Four cars dropped out in the first 20 laps, with the rough circuit taking its toll on many entries. Bob Gegen spun in the esses after his Aston Martin DB2's rear suspension collapsed. He forever referred to that turn as "where the Martin lost its Aston."

The Cunningham-entered Siata expired on the 31st lap, but Cunningham had his team stay for the duration of the race in case other teams needed his tires and wheels. Such was the spirit of competition at this first Sebring 12-hour race.

Teams before the first 12 Hours of Sebring in 1952. On the left, the Index of Performance-winning Deutsch-Bonnet Panhard (25) and its sister car. On the right, the overall-winning Frazer Nash.

The diverse field of cars competing for the 12 hours at the un-likely site of the Sebring Airport provided a truly unique experience for all those in attendance.

The Spear/Cunningham Ferrari led the first three hours and built a two-lap lead before an axle let go, handing the lead to the Frazer Nash. The Schott/Carroll Jaguar was in second, followed by the Grier/Collins Allard J2 Ford, which expired a short time later when its automatic transmission seized, much to the dismay of team man-ager Rene Dreyfus.

The Bandini Crosley was another potential giant killer to expire. Fitted with a McAfee Engineering Crosley engine, the car went from 21st to 8th position before the universal joint let go.

This Ferrari 340 America driven by Bill Spear and Briggs Cunningham led the first 51 laps before an axle let go.

The French DBs, as intended, led the Index of Performance, and were a real crowd-pleaser with their two-cylinder engines sounding like "buzz saws" to the curious spectators. The Dick Irish/Robert Fergus Siata 1400GS was putting up a strong battle, second on Index and challenging for third overall.

The leading Frazer Nash was not immune to trouble, losing its clutch during the fifth hour. The remainder of the race would be a struggle for Gray and Kulok.

The race was not without its bizarre moments, which would become a Sebring trademark. The Steven Spitler/Roger Wing Morris Minor ran out of gas near turn one, which meant the driver had to push the car nearly five miles back to the pits by himself (help was forbidden by the rules). When Wing finally returned to the pits, he was greeted by applause from the sympathetic crowd. After refueling, Spitler returned the car to action, only to run out of gas again on the circuit—it seems his gas tank had a leak! The car eventually won its class, the drivers beeping their horn at the faster cars, much to the delight of the spectators.

The race progressed during the night without major incident as the Frazer Nash held its lead and finished with a comfortable six-lap margin of victory, averaging 62.8 MPH. The Jaguar of Schott/Carroll finished second, one lap ahead of the Siata driven by Fergus and Irish.

Fourth went to the Ferrari 166MM of Robert O'Brien and Richard Cicurel, with the Chuck Wallace/Dick Yates Jaguar XK120 fifth. Sixth went to the surprising MG Mk II driven by Dave Ash and John Van Driel. This highly-modified, aluminum-bodied car with a Mercedes swing rear axle put on a great show and could be considered one of the first "specials" to run at Sebring.

The number-23 Jaguar XK120 driven by Schott/Carroll exiting the hairpin turn. It finished second, and is followed here by the third-place Irish/Fergus Siata and the Deutsch-Bonnet of Bonnet and Cook.

The remarkable DB won the Index of Performance and finished seventh overall, with builder Rene Bonnet finishing the race after Steve Lansing (on his honeymoon) and Wade Morehouse did most of the driving. A Volkswagen that featured a standard VW chassis with a special streamlined body took 11th place overall.

George Sanderson drove the entire race solo in his Crosley Hot Shot, finishing 16th. A total of 17 cars managed to finish the race.

The winning Frazer Nash Le Mans Replica, which had been delivered to owner Stuart (Duke) Donaldson from England only a few days earlier, was prepared by famed mechanic Frankie Del Roy. Its 2.0-liter Bristol BMW engine performed beautifully and was clearly the fastest car on the track once the Spear Ferrari retired. Drivers Kulok and Gray, although experienced pilots, were virtually unheard from again.

Following the awards ceremony, which took place in the back of a flatbed truck the morning after the race, Ulmann announced there would definitely be a Sebring race the following March.

Ulmann's dream had been realized, if not quite on the grand scale he had first envisioned. Work started immediately for the second annual race.

Larry Kulok (partially behind flag) and Harry Gray accept congratulations for winning the first 12 Hours of Sebring.

With the help of the AAA, Sebring's 12-hour race became the inaugural event of the first FIA Sports Car World Championship for manufacturers. Ulmann's persistent lobbying and the success of the 1952 inaugural helped Sebring join the elite company of races such as Le Mans and the Targa Florio.

Despite some consideration of making Sebring a 24-hour race, the 12-hour "noon to midnight" format would remain the same. The SCCA had decided not to repeat the Vero Beach endurance event, electing instead to stage a race at MacDill Air Force Base in Tampa two weeks before Sebring (see Appendix for detailed results).

Ulmann scored a major achievement for Sebring by signing Shell Oil as sponsor of the event. Ulmann was far ahead of his time in marketing, and over the next two decades he would bring numerous corporate sponsors to Sebring.

Minor improvements were made to the Sebring circuit, including wooden pit stalls and better night markers. A few small grandstands were built, and a scoreboard was constructed so spectators could better follow both the overall standings and class battles. Admission to the race was $2.

A superb field of entries was filed for the Sebring race, most notably the John Wyer-led Aston Martin team from England. Drivers were Peter Collins, Reg Parnell, George Abacassis and motorcycle racing veteran Geoffrey Duke. The Aston Martin team was among the best the world had to offer at the time, and Ulmann did everything to ensure their satisfaction.

Wyer, however, was initially disappointed with the Sebring circuit. As he wrote in *The Motor*: "Quite frankly, we were somewhat dismayed [with Sebring]. Only three days before the race, the circuit was completely unmarked, and the runways seemed even wider and more featureless than usual… It seemed almost impossible that the drivers would find their way round, particularly in the dark. Gradually, the course was marked out and began to look more like a racing circuit… By the second practice the course had begun to look

The second-place Aston Martin DB3 driven by Reg Parnell and George Abecassis makes a pit stop early in the race.

like a very presentable racing circuit and, in that magical way, had begun to acquire real atmosphere."

Wyer's observations were prophetic in that Sebring would become world famous, and in some respects infamous, for its unique atmosphere.

During the Aston Martin team's visit Briggs Cunningham—the consummate ambassador for the sport—made great efforts to welcome them and assisted them in any way possible, including loaning them passenger cars.

Cunningham fielded the only serious American threat. His namesake C4R with its V-8 Chrysler engine was clearly among the fastest, and his team of drivers was a force to be reckoned with. Phil Walters and John Fitch co-drove the C4R at Sebring and had both raced with Cunningham at Le Mans.

Phil Walters had also campaigned successfully on oval tracks using the name Ted Tappett, which he had first pressed into service to bluff his way into the driver's seat of a midget car at a Long Island dirt track. Because the AAA frowned on its drivers competing in other sanctioning bodies' events, the alias allowed Walters to race undetected.

John Fitch arrived at Sebring fresh from his win in the C4R at MacDill two weeks earlier. He was among the first American road racing stars to compete overseas, and during his career he achieved international successes in races as far afield as Italy's Mille Miglia, England's Tourist Trophy and Mexico's La Carrera Panamericana.

View of the start/finish line along the front straight before the race. Jim Kimberly is seen looking over his Ferrari 225S.

Top Ferrari entries included the Bill Spear 225S entry with co-driver Phil Hill, a West Coast driver with impressive credentials. Jim Kimberly entered his Ferrari 225S with Marshall Lewis as co-driver, while Ed Lunken entered a Ferrari 166MM. Peter and Robert Yung, originally from China, entered a Ferrari 225S.

Several Allards were entered, although they proved quite fragile on the tough Sebring circuit. Jaguar was represented by several privateers, while the smaller displacement classes would be contested between MG, OSCA and Siata entries.

The defending Sebring champion Frazer Nash was entered as well, although it would not be a factor this year. Other notable entries included the Excaliburs designed by famed industrial designer Brooks Stevens and powered by a Willys engine. The French Deutsch-Bonnet team returned, looking for another Index of Performance win.

The practice sessions were not kind to some competitors, as at least seven cars suffered mechanical problems and were unable to start. In final practice Erwin Goldschmidt's Healey-Cadillac blew an engine, which had to be replaced with a motor from a spectator's automobile.

Beautiful weather and a crowd of over 12,000 were on hand March 8, 1953, for the start of the first ever FIA world championship sports

A practice pit stop for Jim Kimberly's Ferrari 225S before the 1953 race.

The winning drivers of the first-ever FIA World Championship sports car race, John Fitch (wearing driver's helmet) and Phil Walters (far right) celebrate their 1953 Sebring victory in a Cunningham C4R. This photo appeared in *Esquire* magazine with an article written by Fitch.

car endurance race. Key people from the world of racing were present, including Tony Hulman, owner of the Indianapolis Motor Speedway, Arthur Herrington, AAA president, and dozens of sponsors and manufacturers' representatives from America and abroad.

A total of 51 cars made it to the starting line for the noon start. Famed world land speed record holder George E. T. Eyston was the chief starter. The cars were lined up according to engine displacement, the bigger cars in front.

As soon as the second annual Sebring 12-hour race started, it quickly became obvious it would be a battle between the Cunningham and the Aston Martin team as they traded the lead during the first hour.

After managing to build a one-minute lead, Duke's Aston Martin DB3 collided with the Jaguar XK120 coupe driven by Norm Christianson. Both cars had to retire, handing the lead to the Cunningham.

Other incidents during the race illustrated the hazards of the Sebring circuit. Tall grass along the circuit created a vision problem for both the drivers and officials. Tony Cumming's Allard J2X Cadillac pulled off the course with flaming brakes, only to have the grass catch fire and burn the car. Another early victim was Spear's Ferrari. Suffering from brake problems, it went off course and struck the foundation of an old building hidden by the grass.

Oil drums filled with sand, used to mark portions of the circuit, also caused problems. Several cars suffered significant damage after striking them, including the remaining Aston Martin.

The final four hours were an excellent nighttime duel, with the Aston Martin closing within 30 seconds of the Cunningham. The night driving provided plenty of adventures for Fitch, as he wrote in *Esquire* magazine: "Frankly, I was lost during the first laps in the moonless evening, twice missing a fast bend for a slow one (luckily not the reverse) on the airport stretch. In the same vein, a tiny Siata dived out of a turn between the barrels, perhaps thinking that the formidable Cunningham, bearing down with 5-1/2 liter thunder, did not see him. It did."

As it turned out, the Cunningham and drivers Fitch and Walters were simply too powerful for the Aston Martin, averaging nearly 75 MPH en route to an historic Sebring victory.

Jaguars took third and fourth, with Sherwood Johnston/Bob Wilder finishing third, followed by Bob Gegen and 1952 co-win-

In-car photos of a practice session that appeared with John Fitch's Sebring article in *Esquire*.

ner Harry Gray. Briggs Cunningham and Bill Lloyd drove an OSCA MT4 to fifth overall, followed by the Ferrari 166MM of Lunken and Hassen.

The Deutsch-Bonnet team again won the Index of Performance, finishing 11th overall with Rene Bonnet and Wade Morehouse driving. The runner-up Aston Martin also took second on Index.

The win by an American car in the first ever world championship race for sports cars was certainly a surprise, but one that would not be repeated at Sebring for 12 years.

The American magazine *Autosport* reported: "Those of us who remember the beginnings of professional football were impressed by the parallel between those early pro games and the International Grand Prix Road Race staged at Sebring this year... from a second rate event in 1952, it has moved to the top rank of American sports car events and may well be called America's response to Le Mans."

The international motoring press was quite enthusiastic about the inclusion of an American event in the world championship. Despite problems with both corner flagging and timing, and the fact that the Sebring Airport circuit was crude (with an occasional airplane landing on the circuit while the race was in progress!), it was hoped by all in attendance that Sebring would become a regular fixture of the sports car championship.

The Aston Martin drivers (right) seem disappointed to receive their second-place trophy after finishing a lap down to the Fitch/Walters/Cunningham C4R. Reg Parnell is being interviewed by Hemp Oliver while George Abecassis looks on.

1954

If Sebring reached the big leagues of motor racing in 1953, then the 1954 race quickly elevated it to legendary status. The storybook third annual 12 Hours of Sebring was the first of many incredible finishes at the Florida airport circuit.

Entries for the 1954 race were outstanding. Never before had American race fans been able to witness such a stellar international lineup of cars and drivers. Leading the way was the Lancia team with four D-24s, and a group of legendary drivers including Juan Manuel Fangio, Alberto Ascari and Piero Taruffi. One of these Lancias had recently won the Mexican road race.

In Alec Ulmann's book *The Sebring Story*, he recounts the day when the Lancia team requested a police escort through the town of Sebring to protect world champion Fangio from the mobs of admirers. Ulmann assured the team manager that "the Great Manuel could walk through the middle of Sebring with a big sign stating that he was Juan Manuel Fangio, the World Racing Champion, and not a single one of the local inhabitants would turn an eye, let alone walk up to him!"

Indeed, the American public knew little about sports car racing, but Sebring would be the place an entire generation would come to know as the mecca for sports car competition.

The defending champion Cunningham C4R was back with Briggs Cunningham and Sherwood Johnston driving. Cunningham also entered a Ferrari 375 for John Fitch and Phil Walters and an OSCA MT4 for Stirling Moss and Bill Lloyd. Moss was under contract with Jaguar and was forbidden to drive any car of comparable size, so he drove the little 1.5-liter OSCA.

Aston Martin returned with three cars, one of which was assigned to American drivers Carroll Shelby and Chuck Wallace, a fine gesture on the part of team manager John Wyer.

American in Paris Harry Schell brought his beautiful Ferrari 250MM with the flamboyant Marques de Portago as co-driver. Bill Spear entered his Ferrari 375 with Phil Hill as his co-driver.

Jaguar was well represented with no less than 11 entries, and Donald Healey brought his surprisingly strong cars from England to contest the world championship event.

Most teams and officials were lodged at Harder Hall, Sebring's landmark hotel, which for one week every year would be the international headquarters for famous drivers and their entourage of the rich and famous.

Opposite: Bill Lloyd (left) and Stirling Moss celebrate their come-from-behind victory. Not until the fourth hour was their car in the top 10. By the eighth hour they were in third place and finally took the lead with only 54 minutes remaining.

The James Simpson/

George Colby OSCA

MT4 finished fourth.

This period in sports car racing offered tremendous diversity, with many unusual makes and some true "specials" appearing at America's showcase sports car event. A Chevrolet Corvette made its first ever international competition appearance, but was withdrawn without reason after the first official practice session. An Offenhauser-powered Aston Martin appeared as well before clutch problems caused it to withdraw. Perhaps the most unusual non-starter was the Rex, designed by the son of boat racer Gar Wood. The little car was powered by a 325cc Mercury Marine engine!

Miles Collier entered a Bandini Crosley for drivers Bret Hannaway and "John Marshall". After his brother Sam was killed Collier had promised his family that he would no longer race. But instead he used the pseudonym John Marshall so his family wouldn't know and drove anyway.

Heavy rains the day before the race flooded parts of the circuit, but clearing skies and cool temperatures greeted race day. With a crowd estimated at 14,000 on hand, a lineup of 59 cars was ready for the start.

The race progressed as many had predicted—the beautiful red Lancias dueling with each other while the Hill/Spear Ferrari challenged and led briefly. The factory Austin-Healey driven by George Huntoon and Lance Macklin also remained close to the leaders.

The Sebring circuit, however, was unlike any in the world, and far more demanding than the Lancia team had anticipated. Their top two entries retired early—first Fangio at three hours, then Ascari at five hours. The Porfiro Rubirosa/Gino Valenzano Lancia D24 had lost first and second gears, thanks mainly to the driving of Rubirosa, a millionaire playboy who had been named part of the Lancia team as a publicity stunt only a few weeks earlier.

By mid-race, the Fitch/Walters Ferrari was trailing the Taruffi/Robert Manzon Lancia with the Huntoon/Macklin Austin-Healey taking third. The Rubirosa/Valenzano Lancia was far back in 10th.

The Lancias were not the only team having problems. By the seventh hour, all three Ferraris had dropped out along with the Cunningham and all three Aston Martins. Half of the Jaguar contingent had also retired.

The number-56 OSCA driven by Stirling Moss and Bill Lloyd spins at the Webster turn while being chased by the Carpenter/Van Driel Kieft-Bristol (97) and the Makins/Bott OSCA (65). Moss and Lloyd carried on to record a stunning upset win.

The Austin-Healey soon moved to second place behind the leading Lancia. Briggs Cunningham's OSCA MT4, driven by Moss and Lloyd, was now in third, but several laps behind the leader. This car had not even broken into the top 10 until the fourth hour, but had moved steadily up as Moss put on a spectacular show of cornering for the spectators.

As the race entered the 11th hour, the OSCA moved into second as the Austin-Healey began to suffer mechanical problems.

Suddenly, with a five-lap lead and 54 minutes remaining, the leading Lancia pulled off and Taruffi began pushing the car down the long back straight. Flashbulbs from photographers and a trailing

official's car illuminated Taruffi's gallant effort on the otherwise pitch black night. When Taruffi finally reached the pits, it was obvious the Lancia's engine had seized. The car was subsequently disqualified because it had left the pits after a previous stop without the use of the electric starter, and it had crossed the finish line under power other than its own.

With Moss at the wheel, the OSCA took the lead and recorded one of the biggest upsets in the history of endurance racing. The sole surviving Lancia made a gallant attempt to gain ground in the final hour with Valenzano at the wheel, finishing five laps behind in second.

Macklin and Huntoon held on for third in their Austin-Healey while two other OSCA entries finished fourth and fifth. Of the top 12 finishers, 9 were under 2.0 liters. Only 25 of the 59 starters managed to finish the race, and the OSCA's average speed of 72.8 MPH was less than the previous year's winner.

To add icing to the cake, the OSCA MT4 also won the coveted Index of Performance, with the Otto Linton/Harry Beck OSCA MT4 second.

The media was thrilled with the quality of competition and the incredible drama that a race of such length could produce. However, Sebring was criticized for its poor facilities and organization. As Robert Cumberford reported for *Road & Track* magazine: "Sebring can only be given a low rating in such categories as crowd control, pit policing and general safety measures. There were but seven flagmen available for the entire 12 hours on the 5.2-mile course."

Despite the event's many problems, it had established itself in three years as America's famous international sports car race. The stage was now set for many more years of great racing.

Less than a month after the 1954 Sebring race, Miles Collier died suddenly. Miles and his brother Sam were America's great road racing pioneers, and it is unfortunate that neither lived to see Sebring blossom into one of the world's great motor racing events.

Juan Manuel Fangio prepares to lead the Lancia team out for a first look at the Sebring circuit.

1955

The Maserati 300S
of Bill Spear and
Sherwood Johnston
finished third in 1955.

The 1955 Sebring race was memorable for its furious duel between Ferrari and Jaguar, and a rather bizarre beginning and end.

Many improvements were made to the Sebring circuit for the 1955 race including a walkover bridge, new fencing, better course barriers and improved pit structures. Amoco signed as race sponsor, a relationship which would last several years.

An estimated 20,000 spectators turned out for the fourth Sebring, and they were not to be disappointed. More than 100 cars were officially entered, with many of the world's top drivers on hand.

A new D-type Jaguar, which only a few weeks earlier set speed records at the NASCAR performance trials on Daytona Beach, was entered by Briggs Cunningham for Mike Hawthorn and Phil Walters. Cunningham also entered an OSCA MT4 for Bill Lloyd and George Huntoon and his Offy powered C6R for himself and John Bennett.

Allen Guiberson entered a Ferrari 750S Monza for Carroll Shelby and Phil Hill, two of America's leading road racing drivers. U.S. Ferrari representative Luigi Chinetti entered a Ferrari 750S for Harry Schell and Piero Taruffi. Maserati 300S entries included a factory ride for Gino Valenzano and Cesare Perdisa and another entered by Bill Spear and co-driver Sherwood Johnston.

Jim Kimberly entered his Ferrari 375 Plus with Ed Lunken as co-driver and Alfonso de Portago joined Umberto Magliloi in a Ferrari 750S, but neither would be a factor in the race.

Austin-Healey returned to Sebring, this time with Stirling Moss among the team's drivers. Chet Flynn entered a Mercedes-Benz 300SL and even a Ford Thunderbird was on the starting grid.

The smaller displacement classes featured a wide variety of teams, including a factory Renault and Porsche effort and several OSCA, Lotus, MG and Morgan entries.

The start of the race was an embarrassing comedy of errors and near disasters. A record 80 cars lined up for the start, but when the signal was given for the Le Mans start, six reserve entries decided to start at the back of the pack as well. The timing and scoring staff headed by Joe Lane was in near panic when the six mystery cars passed by. They were quickly flagged off the course, but moments later an ambulance was dispatched to the scene of an accident involving the Renault 1063 of Louis Pons, only to crash with Bob Said's Ferrari 750S.

Meanwhile, first off the line was the Hawthorn/Walters Jaguar, followed by the Ferrari of Hill and Shelby. These cars were never

Left: Lance Macklin and
Stirling Moss drove this
Austin-Healey 100S to
a sixth-place finish.

more than seven minutes apart the entire 12 hours. Only the Schell/Taruffi Ferrari and the Valenzano/Perdisa Maserati were able to mount any kind of challenge during the early stages of the race.

By the ninth hour it was clearly a two-car race between the Hawthorn/Walters Jaguar and the Shelby/Hill Ferrari. The Jaguar had held a slight advantage for most of the race, losing the lead only for four laps due to a pit stop.

As the 12 hours neared conclusion, the race announcer was incorrectly reporting that the Ferrari had taken the lead. In the confusing final minutes, the Ferrari was flagged the winner. Then the Hawthorn/Walters Jaguar was called to victory lane, but it had run out of fuel on its cool down lap. Finally, Walters and Hawthorn arrived in victory lane to receive their awards, but doubts remained about the official results and Allen Guiberson filed a protest. At an AAA review the following week in New York, where chief timer Joe Lane presented the lap charts, the Jaguar was officially declared the winner. The margin was 25.4 seconds over the Ferrari, an amazingly close finish after 12 grueling hours.

Phil Hill and Carroll Shelby placed second in this Ferrari 750S Monza in 1955. They were only 25.4 seconds behind the Hawthorn/Walters Jaguar at the finish, and during the entire 12 hours they were never separated from the winning Jaguar by more than 7 minutes.

Walters became Sebring's first two-time winner, while Briggs Cunningham recorded his third consecutive win as a car owner. Years later Walters would remark that this Sebring was his most memorable race. "It was an absolute sprint from start to finish. While the previous year showed a conservative pace could 'save' the car, we ran flat-out."

The winning D-type Jaguar of Mike Hawthorn and Phil Walters led all but four laps in 1955.

Although finishing second overall, Hill and Shelby did win the Index of Performance, edging out the Lloyd/Huntoon OSCA MT4, which finished seventh overall, two laps behind the Austin-Healey of Moss/Lance Macklin. Finishing third was the Spear/Johnston Maserati, two laps down and one lap ahead of the Valenzano/Perdisa Maserati.

Baron Von Hanstein and Herbert Linge piloted a Porsche 550 Spyder to eighth overall. Ray Crawford, driving a Kurtis-Kraft Lincoln, drove the entire race solo (with special permission from the AAA) to finish 13th overall.

Despite the confusion at the finish, the international motorsports media were pleased with America's round of the sports car championship. *Auto Age* reported: "Whatever the reason for the confusion, the race as a whole was one of the most exciting ever seen on these shores, and the organizers and drivers alike should be very proud of their efforts. Sebring is really big-time stuff."

Sebring was still in its infancy, but Ulmann had visions of making it a spectacle on the same scale as Le Mans. As reported in *Speed Age* magazine: "Prior to the start there was an impressive little ceremony when the flags of the nations that were represented at Sebring were raised above the pits. The atmosphere at this time was getting more and more like Le Mans, and all that was lacking was the line of gendarmes marching down pit to their positions and the background noise of an amusement park… based on the pattern set by the last two Sebring enduros, the 1956 race should be one of the most glamorous sports events anywhere in the world."

The terrible tragedy at Le Mans a few months later, in which over 80 spectators died, would cause the AAA to withdraw from auto racing. This forced Ulmann to reorganize and create a new promoting and sanctioning body called the Automobile Racing Club of Florida (ARCF) exclusively for his 12-hour event.

An exuberant Briggs Cunningham at the microphone with winning drivers Phil Walters and Mike Hawthorn. It was Cunningham's third-straight Sebring win as a car owner.

1956

Looking back at the entries for the 1956 race, one can appreciate the international importance of Sebring. It is difficult to imagine so many legendary names gathered at such an unlikely place. Sebring was without question second only to Indianapolis on the American motor racing calendar, and to this day ranks second only to Le Mans in sports car racing fame.

Entered at Sebring in 1956 were Juan Manuel Fangio, Jean Behra, Stirling Moss, Hans Herrmann, Eugenio Castellotti, Luigi Musso, Duncan Hamilton, Ivor Bueb, Peter Collins and Mike Hawthorn—to name just a few. American drivers included Phil Hill, Masten Gregory, Carroll Shelby, stock car racing pioneer Red Byron and Indianapolis winners Bob Sweikert and Troy Ruttman.

Of course, the showcase of the 1956 Sebring race was the appearance of Scuderia Ferrari and its lead drivers Fangio, Castellotti, Musso and Harry Schell. They were the clear favorites with their beautiful 860 Monzas.

Jaguar offered the most serious challenge to Ferrari with nine D-type entries, most notably the fuel-injected Hawthorn/Desmond Titterington entry, which had set the fastest laps during practice.

Aston Martin fielded three factory cars with an all-star cast of drivers and Porsche returned with a strong offering led by the Herrmann/Wolfgang Von Trips 550 Spyder. The Maserati factory sent two 300S entries and Lotus Engineering entered a new Mk XI for Colin Chapman and Len Bastrup. Unfortunately, the Lotus crashed in practice and was unable to start.

Of particular interest was the first appearance of a factory-supported Chevrolet Corvette team headed by John Fitch. Three cars were entered under the name Raceway Enterprises, but General Motors provided a retinue of mechanics, experts and other officials from Detroit. The team had set up shop at Sebring in February before the race and tested had extensively. The unproven Corvettes were given little chance to win their class, let alone win overall.

More improvements had made Sebring a very acceptable circuit for competitors, although far behind the standards of most European tracks. The wide runway portions and ample runoff areas made it a relatively safe for the drivers, but it was torturous for the cars.

A large crowd of 25,000 turned out, and the race was broadcast live on radio throughout the United States. Hundreds of journalists descended on the small central Florida town, which could hardly handle the influx of race fans that temporarily tripled its population.

Scuderia Ferrari captured its first Sebring victory in 1956. The number-17 Ferrari 860 Monza was driven by Juan Manuel Fangio and Eugenio Castellotti. The Arnolt-Bristol (67) was driven by John Ryan.

43

The race was now officially professional, with a $10,000 purse posted in addition to the traditional orange blossom wreaths and the Amoco Trophy.

Race officials were now more strict about accepting entries and a maximum of 65 cars would be allowed to start this and most future Sebring races.

The race started under perfect weather conditions as 59 drivers sprinted to their cars in the traditional Le Mans start. What a thrill it was for the race fans as the Fitch Corvette was first off the line and into the lead! Its glory was short-lived, however, as Hawthorn swept into the lead at turn one.

The Hawthorn/Titterington Jaguar led the first 25 laps and then traded the lead several times with Fangio/Castellotti. Stirling Moss also challenged early, putting his Aston Martin DB3S as far up as second place.

The race evolved into a furious Ferrari versus Jaguar battle for several hours. Further back, several interesting class battles were developing as well, especially in D class, where Maserati, Aston Martin and Austin-Healey were all quite competitive.

Attrition was high; 17 cars did not even reach the three-hour mark. Early retirements included the Collins/Moss Aston Martin, one of the factory Corvettes and the Bueb/Hamilton Jaguar D-type. Carlos Menditeguy was seriously injured when his Maserati 300S rolled in the esses during the third hour.

As the pace continued, the brakes in the fuel-injected Jaguar soon began to fade, and Hawthorn could not keep pace. Fangio effortlessly (or so it seemed) took command and the hard-pressed Jaguar retired

The number-1 Corvette of John Fitch and Walt Hansgen won its class and finished ninth overall, a major accomplishment for an American manufacturer at Sebring in 1956.

Amoco billboards throughout Florida and the Southeast advertised the 1956 12 Hours of Sebring.

162 with terminal brake problems. From there Fangio/Castellotti kept a steady two-lap cushion over the team car of Musso/Schell. The winning Ferrari averaged 84.07 MPH and became the first car to cover 1,000 miles in 12 hours at Sebring.

Musso and Schell finished second and the Jaguar of Sweikert and Ensley finished third. It was Sweikert's first sports car race, and he proved to the many doubters that an oval track specialist could adapt quickly to road racing.

The Shelby/Salvadori Aston Martin DB3S took the fourth position, winning their class by one lap over the fifth-place Maserati 300S of Taruffi/Behra. Porsche took an important class win with a sixth overall finish for Herrmann/Von Trips. That team's 550 Spyder also captured the important Index of Performance. The Deutsch-Bonnet HBR5 of Paul Armagnac/G. Mercader held the Index lead but ran out of fuel during the 10th hour, still managing a class win and 16th overall.

The Fitch/Hansgen Corvette took ninth overall and first in B class, a monumental achievement that would inspire Chevrolet to pursue a more serious effort for 1957.

The only to team to survive intact was the three-car MG team led by David Ash, which finished the race in team formation.

An interesting sidelight was the performance of Hap Dressel and Bill Woodbury in their AC Ace, which was in everyday use prior to the race. It was driven to Sebring for the race, finished the 12 hours, and then driven back to Virginia to go back into use as Dressel's everyday car.

The husband-and-wife team of M.R.J. and Peggy Wyllie drove this Lotus Mk IX to a 24th-place finish.

The D-type Jaguar of Mike Hawthorn and Desmond Titterington led for several hours in 1956 before retiring with brake failure.

When it comes to driving prowess, so often the hype does not live up to reality. Such was not the case for Fangio's appearance at Sebring. The media marveled at his flawless driving style and his consistent, smooth handling of the powerful Ferrari on Sebring's incredibly difficult course. Even though he was near the end of his career, the world champion had proven himself again and helped Ferrari earn its first Sebring victory and produce the first one-two sweep ever by a manufacturer. It also helped Ferrari lead the manufacturers world championship standings.

Jeff Cooper wrote in *Road & Track* magazine: "Sebring has come a long way in five years…. It has developed into a truly great sporting event of intercontinental stature, and the only contest in the U.S. in which we can observe the masters at work."

BLEACHER SEAT
The Florida International Twelve-Hour
Grand Prix of Endurance   Section   9
for the AMOCO Trophy.   Row   L
March 23, 1957   Seat   8
Sebring, Florida
Price $1.76 Fed. Tax   .18 Sta. Tax   .06 Total $2.00

The return of Juan Manuel Fangio, this time driving for Maserati, and the new Corvette SS were the big stories at Sebring in 1957.

Entries were again superb for the Florida International 12 Hour Grand Prix for the Amoco Trophy, which was now the official name of the race. Fangio and Jean Behra were assigned to the powerful new Maserati 450S, which had led the first world championship race of the year in Argentina before retiring. Maserati teammates Stirling Moss and Harry Schell were in the proven 300S, with Carroll Shelby and Roy Salvadori assigned to a third 300S.

Scuderia Ferrari countered with the Peter Collins/Maurice Trintignant and Alfonso de Portago/Luigi Musso 315S. Phil Hill and Von Trips were entered in a Ferrari 290. Five other privately entered Ferraris were in the field.

Le Mans winners Ivor Bueb and Mike Hawthorn were at the wheel of a D-type Jaguar. Briggs Cunningham entered two D-types, one for Russ Boss and Walt Hansgen and the other he would share with Lloyd.

The star of the 1957 Sebring race, however, was the beautiful new Corvette SS designed by Zora Duntov and scheduled to be driven by John Fitch and Piero Taruffi. The prototype Corvette was the greatest American road racing effort to date. The SS Corvette featured a magnesium alloy body, de dion-type rear axle, tubular space frame, inboard rear brakes and fuel injection. A second test car, with a plain white fiberglass body, was used in practice.

With a huge crowd of curious spectators and journalists on hand during the two days of practice, the test mule took to the Sebring circuit. Practice times for the Corvette were quite fast, but the highlight came when the legendary Fangio (quickest in practice at 3:24.5 in the Maserati), was invited to take the wheel of the SS. As described by Bernard Cahier in *Road & Track*: "With his typical grin on his face, Fangio took off for his first time out in the car. Within three laps, the Old Maestro, who seemed to be enjoying himself immensely as I watched him on a curve, had accomplished the fantastic time of 3:27.4.

The Maserati team in the

pits before the start of

the 1957 race.

Juan Manuel Fangio won back-to-back victories in 1956 and 1957. Here he celebrates with 1956 co-driver Eugenio Castellotti. Writer Bernard Cahier is at left.

He was justly greeted by warm applause. The Americans could well cheer about that performance, since Fangio had proven to them that if masterly driven, the new Corvette could hold its own with the best from Europe."

"Fantastico," said Fangio. "I could have gone two seconds faster if I had tried."

Another Corvette with similar body styling was entered by Lindsey Hopkins and driven by Paul O'Shea and Pete Lovely, with two other stock-appearing Corvettes in the field.

Other notable drivers entered were oval track stars Pat O'Connor and Bobby Unser, who would go on to win three Indianapolis 500 races.

In the smaller displacement categories, Sebring had its usual top-flight field, including Porsche, MGA, Renault, AC Ace, Austin-Healey and Triumph entries all eager for a class win.

The Chevrolet Corvette SS was General Motors' first serious attempt at road racing. Seated next to driver Piero Taruffi is Chevrolet chief engineer Ed Cole.

Perfect weather and an astounding crowd—at least 39,000—were on hand race day. The circuit at that time sandwiched the large gathering into a relatively small area in and around the paddock area. Much of the circuit's airport runway sections were not accessible, and the large area inside the track (now known as Green Park) was off-limits to spectators.

The Collins Ferrari jumped into the lead, but all eyes were on the Corvette SS, which came by in sixth after the first lap. Fitch then had to pit three times in the next 23 laps with brake and ignition problems and the car was withdrawn. Most experts agreed, however, that the design showed much promise.

Meanwhile, the Fangio/Behra Maserati took command on the 20th lap, passing the Collins Ferrari. They would never give up the lead as the V8 Maserati proved it was as reliable as it was fast.

The Collins/Trintignant Ferrari could not keep pace and the Jaguars were suffering brake problems. Later, the Hill/Von Trips Ferrari retired with engine failure. The Gendebien/Greenspun Ferrari held a comfortable lead among the GT cars, but it too retired at mid-race.

The Salvadori/Shelby Maserati was disqualified on its 68th lap for a refueling infraction. A dejected Carroll Shelby roamed up and down the pit area the rest of the race, apologizing for the mistake made by the normally efficient Maserati crew.

Early in the third hour, Bob Goldich lost control in the esses, rolling his Arnolt Bristol. He was pronounced dead at the scene, Sebring's first racing fatality. The two remaining Arnolt Bristol cars were subsequently withdrawn.

Fangio and Behra easily held the lead for the final 10 hours. Bernard Cahier wrote: "Around the time of the halfway mark I went to various

The start of the 1957 12 Hours of Sebring viewed from above the pits. The small displacement cars are gridded at the back of the field. From left to right: A Stanguellini Bialbero (56), three Renault Dauphines (66, 65, 64), three Lotus 11s (61, 60, 59) a Cooper Climax (58), and three Alfa Romeo Giulietta SVs (55, 54, 52).

The Ferrari 290MM of Masten Gregory and Lou Brero finished a close fourth.

corners, most notably the hairpin. There it was amazing to see how tranquilly Fangio or Behra were taking these turns, and yet they were gaining constantly on all others, which in most cases were starting to have brake troubles… Hawthorn's car sounded good, but he looked very hot, and so did Moss, who signaled me he was very thirsty. Next time around, in true 'Tour de France Cyclist' fashion I handed him a bottle of Coca-Cola, to the greatest delight of the crowd, which also appreciated Moss' polite gesture of handing back the empty on the next lap."

Fangio and Behra finished with a two-lap margin over the Moss/Schell Maserati. The Jaguar of Hawthorn and Bueb finished third, just ahead of the Masten Gregory/Lou Brero Ferrari 290MM. The Boss/Hansgen Jaguar, running with virtually no brakes the final hour, held on for fifth.

The Art Bunker/Chuck Wallace Porsche RS finished eighth over-all, winning its class and the Index of Performance. The Kunstle/Miles Porsche RS took 9th overall.

Only 38 cars managed to finish the race, among them the Corvette of Dick Thompson/Gaston Andrey, entered by Fitch, taking a hard-earned 12th overall.

The victory of Fangio and Behra was the most dominating thus far in Sebring history, and Fangio became the first driver to win two consecutive Sebring races. The team broke all records, averaging 85.36 MPH and covering 1,024 miles.

Ulmann's race was growing bigger every year, and plans were announced to make further improvements to the circuit. The remarkable 12 Hours of Sebring was already being called a legendary event, but it did have its critics.

The Jaguar D-types of Pierce Woods and Bobby Unser (10) and Jack Ensley and Pat O'Connor lead the number-19 Maserati of Juan Manuel Fangio and Jean Behra out of the esses toward the big bend. Note the mailboxes on the edge of the track and junk cars in what is now known as Green Park.

1957 (AMOCO) SEBRING
RACE
CHAIRMAN

The Dick Thompson/ Gaston Andrey Corvette about to be overtaken by the second-place Maserati 300S of Stirling Moss and Harry Schell.

Limited hotel rooms (at five times regular rates), rather crude track facilities and middle-of-nowhere location were common complaints. But Sebring had inspired a religious following, and *everyone* in sports car racing *had* to be at Sebring in March. It seemed that every little detail, barely noticed anywhere else, was magnified at Sebring. Every bizarre incident, inconceivable anywhere else, was somehow common at Sebring.

From the downtown technical inspection to its loyal following of Palm Beach's rich and famous, there was nothing like it in the motor racing world.

Pinkie Windridge wrote in *Sports Car*: "It would be possible to go on and on mentioning personalities and incidents from Sebring… the hard-fought victory won by the MG team, barely able to finish the number 50 MG because paint from a funnel had clogged the gas lines; or the somewhat comical sight of Ernie Erickson in his yellow coveralls, pushing the matching D Jag along the back straight? What about the Corvette garage, which looked like the Flint assembly line at lunch hour… or Denise McCluggage and her crazy polka dot helmet. Perhaps the worst memory is the way we all went on that orange juice kick, or maybe the way a hungover Hawthorn looked when accepting his trophy."

The Ferrari 290MM of Phil Hill and Wolfgang Von Trips awaits final adjustments before the start in 1957. Engine failure ended its race after six hours.

Sebring again attracted a quality field of cars and drivers to its seventh annual endurance classic. Prime contenders for Sebring's world championship event were Ferrari and Aston Martin, while Jaguar and Porsche entries were rated long shots. The new 3-liter limit for FIA championship cars certainly favored the Ferrari team, which brought three 250TRs. Ferrari drivers included American star Phil Hill, Peter Collins, Mike Hawthorn, Wolfgang Von Trips, Olivier Gendebien and Luigi Musso.

Aston Martin fielded two new DBR1s for drivers Stirling Moss, Tony Brooks, Carroll Shelby and Roy Salvadori. They were very quick in practice and were rated strong contenders, although their reliability was uncertain.

Three factory Porsche entries included drivers Jean Behra, Harry Schell and Edgar Barth. Lotus also entered three factory cars, which turned in suspiciously slow practice laps, leading many to believe they would be quite competitive in the race.

Jaguar entries included three D-types and two Listers. Among the drivers were Masten Gregory, Ron Flockhart, Briggs Cunningham and Ivor Bueb.

The smaller displacement classes were again very competitive, with OSCA, AC Cars and Triumph among the manufacturers making the trek to Sebring for a chance at an international victory in America.

The Sebring race was now well known internationally as a car-killing event, with both pace and preparation the keys to surviving the brutal 5.2-mile circuit. As *Sports Car Illustrated* reported: "Sebring is the toughest test in the world on brakes and gears. As of now, it's also no daisy-dance for the drivers; for them it is the toughest twelve hours they can spend behind the wheel."

There were many improvements made at Sebring for 1958. A large portion of the circuit was widened and resurfaced. Other major changes included the new MG pedestrian bridge, constructed over the esses, leading spectators to a new viewing area at the Webster turn. In addition, a new drive-over bridge sponsored by Martini &

Underway at the start of the 1958 12 Hours of Sebring. At the fore is the winning Ferrari 250TR (14), its sister car (15), two Lister Jaguars (11 and 10), two Aston Martin DBR1s (24 and 25) and GT Coupe (26), another TR250 (16) and Jaguar D-type (9).

Rossi was constructed leading into the paddock. Both would remain Sebring landmarks for many years.

Another record crowd—at least 45,000—was on hand enjoying the beautiful weather and the astounding array of cars and drivers. As reported in *Motor Trend*: "Sebring is the mecca for American sports motorists every year on the weekend nearest the vernal equinox. It's the only event of the year in which we can see everything that is newest and best in equipment, handled by the international masters of the road. There are no klunkers at Sebring and few drivers are not in the distinguished category… A close look at Sebring sets the aficionado up for the year with an appraisal of the competing marques."

After a false start by some overanxious drivers, the 65 starters got away without major incident, and Moss took the lead for Aston Martin followed by the Hawthorn Ferrari 250TR and the second Aston Martin DBR1 driven by Salvadori.

It was a disastrous start for the Jaguars, with the Archie Scott-Brown Lister dropping out on the third lap after a collision with the Ferrari 250TR driven by Gendebien. Three laps later the Ed Crawford Lister blew an engine. The three D-types all expired by the third hour, which eliminated every Jaguar entry.

Moss and Brooks had set a blistering pace, lapping all but four cars, but retired with transmission failure after leading the first 70 laps and setting the fastest lap. The lead was inherited by the Hill/Collins Ferrari 250TR, with Musso/Gendebien and Von Trips/Hawthorn in contention. The Ferrari 250TR entry driven by John Von Neumann and Richie Ginther trailed in fourth, keeping the running order in numerical order (numbers 14, 15, 16, 17) for nearly five hours.

Porsche, usually known for its reliability, lost three of its RS entries by mid-race, leaving only the Schell/Seidel RS in operation.

The race continued without major incident, and a sweep of the

Stirling Moss and Tony Brooks had led the first 70 laps and lapped all but four cars before their Aston Martin DBR1 dropped out with a broken gearbox.

A spectator's view of the pit area and front straight as the drivers line up for the Le Mans start. Note the driver in short pants.

top three positions by the Ferrari factory was prevented only after the Hawthorn/Von Trips Ferrari 250TR and the independent Neumann/Ginther car expired in the final two hours.

Hill and Collins ended up with a one-lap victory over Musso and Gendebien, averaging a record 86.67 MPH. Seven laps behind was the third-place Porsche RS of Schell and Seidel, which finished second on Index of Performance behind the amazing de Tomaso OSCA 750S entry. The little 748cc OSCA finished eighth overall, easily winning its class.

Team Lotus recorded three finishes in the top ten positions, led by the fourth place Weiss/Tallakson entry. Only one American car finished in the top 30, that being the Chevrolet Corvette driven by Richard Doane and future Indianapolis winner Jim Rathmann, which won its class with a 12th-place finish. An Alfa Romeo Veloce took a class victory and 18th overall, and an AC Ace captured class honors as well.

As usual, the motor racing press was quick to praise the quality of the Sebring entries and criticize the obvious drawbacks. Jeff Cooper wrote in *Sportscar Quarterly*: "It's not an easy race to appreciate. Twelve solid hours of race-watching is a long haul, and facilities are not such as to entertain the casual spectator... But, if automobiles and driving are your passions, it's paradise enow."

The star of Sebring '58 was the fabulous Ferrari 250TR. The blood-red machines from Modena would dominate three of the next four Sebring races.

Olivier Gendebien and Luigi Musso finished second in this Scuderia Ferrari-entered 250TR, one lap behind the sister car of Phil Hill and Peter Collins.

1959

OFFICIAL PROGRAM #1
MARCH 21, 1959

12-HOUR FLORIDA INTERNATIONAL GRAND
PRIX OF ENDURANCE FOR THE AMOCO TROPHY
SEBRING, FLORIDA
PROMOTED BY **AUTOSPORT** BRITAIN'S MOTOR SPORTING WEEKLY

For the first time, weather would be a key factor in the running of the 12 Hours of Sebring. The entire race weekend was plagued by heavy rains and the track surface was flooded in many sections of the 5.2-mile circuit.

The entries were again led by the heavily favored Scuderia Ferrari, which set up shop in downtown Sebring at the Oldsmobile dealership. Three new factory 250TRs, lighter and more powerful than the previous year, were piloted by such greats as Jean Behra, Phil Hill, Dan Gurney and Olivier Gendebien. Other Ferrari entries included the 1958 Le Mans winner, a 250TR/58 driven by Pedro Rodriguez and Paul O'Shea.

The Porsche factory returned to Sebring with two RSK entries, joining several strong independent teams. Joakim Bonnier and Wolfgang Von Trips led the cast of Porsche drivers.

The only other serious threats to Ferrari appeared to be the lone Aston Martin DBR1 entered for Roy Salvadori and Carroll Shelby, and the Lister Jaguar piloted by Stirling Moss and Ivor Bueb. Briggs Cunningham also entered two Lister Jaguars, hoping to improve on their disastrous performance of the previous year.

The field of smaller displacement cars was very strong at Sebring and included several notable drivers. Among them was Walter Cronkite in a Lancia Appia Zagato, who also assisted in the national radio coverage from Sebring.

With heavy rains pelting the circuit during most of the three days of practice, tragedy struck early when a mechanic for the AC Bristol team was killed driving one of the team cars to the track. The following day Edwin Lawrence was killed when his Maserati rolled eight times at the hairpin and then caught fire.

Barrett Clark wrote on the *1959 Sounds of Sebring* album: "Everybody was miserable all week, constantly soaked to the skin, cold and tired. But the drivers seemed to respond to this meteorological double-cross by taking an increased interest in the race. Everybody was anxious… lots of teams showed up at the practice sessions and most drivers took turns plowing through the lakes that abounded the course."

Rain also caused other problems. It was discovered before the race that the fuel supplied by the promoter was full of contaminants, mainly water and rust. This caused teams to tear down carburetors and engines.

Race day arrived with clear skies, but more rain was in the forecast. No doubt this was the reason for the smaller crowd compared to previous years.

Left: The Ferrari 250TR/59 of Jean Behra and Cliff Allison drives through the heavy rain that plagued Sebring in 1959.

Salvadori took command at the start, leading the first four laps until Behra took his Ferrari out front, trading the lead briefly with Gurney's Ferrari. The Shelby/Salvadori DBR1 Aston Martin retired with transmission problems on the 32nd lap. Another early retirement due to transmission trouble was the Hill/Gendebien Ferrari 250TR/59, which exited in the fourth hour. Moss stayed close to the leading Ferraris, and then took the lead on the 96th lap, only to be disqualified for a refueling infraction. He had run out of fuel on the circuit and had accepted a ride back to the pits.

This made it a duel between the two leading Ferraris, with the third-place Porsche several laps behind. To make matters more difficult, heavy rains began to fall after the fifth hour, flooding several turns and the pit lane.

Gurney and Chuck Daigh, who had guided the Ferrari into the lead, were replaced by Ferrari team manager Tavone with Hill and Gendebien (rules allowed drivers to be transferred to another car on the same team). Gurney was actually pleased to be pulled from the car, as it was terribly uncomfortable for the tall Californian.

The skies began to clear as darkness approached, producing the glorious Sebring sunset that is part of this great race tradition. Bernard Cahier wrote in *Road & Track*: "When the rain stopped we were

Jean Behra and Cliff Allison drove this Ferrari 250TR/59 to second place in 1959.

OSCA team mechanics prepare a 187S to be started by Ricardo Rodriguez in the 1959 race.

treated to one of the most beautiful sunsets we had ever seen. The crowd, which had dwindled considerably in the deluge, was much taken with the sight and for a short time the speeding cars were ignored… it was a scene taken straight from a Hollywood Technicolor extravaganza and, had the race been done to a movie script, the flag would have fallen at this moment and the clean-cut winner would have won the girl and paid off the mortgage on the farm."

From this point, the race provided little excitement. Hill and Gendebien took the number-7 Ferrari 250TR/59 to a one-lap victory over Behra/Cliff Allison at a race average of 81.46 MPH, the slowest Sebring in three years. Finishing third was the Bonnier/Von Trips Porsche followed by Don Sesslar/Bob Holbert in another RSK, each recording wins in their respective classes.

Lance Reventlow and E.D. Martin finished sixth in a Ferrari 250TR/58, while the beautiful Ferrari California 250GT driven by Richie Ginther and Howard Hively took 9th overall and first in the GT class.

The rain produced a slower pace that resulted in all but 16 of the 65 starters finishing, the best finishing percentage to date at Sebring's brutal circuit. With the rain-soaked eighth annual 12 Hours of Sebring concluded, Ulmann set his sights on promoting America's first Formula One race, scheduled to take place at Sebring in December.

1 9 5 9   F O R M U L A   O N E   R A C E

The final Formula One World Championship race of the 1959 season took place at Sebring on December 12. Alec Ulmann had lobbied to host this event, the first of its kind in the United States since the modern world championship began in 1950.

While Sebring's spring endurance race had grown to become America's second biggest motor sports event, behind only Indianapolis, the first Grand Prix of the United States would fall far short of expectations. The December date and slim field of cars on the huge 5.2-mile circuit proved to be a box office failure.

The championship had come down to a three-way battle between Jack Brabham and Bruce McLaren of the Cooper team and Tony Brooks of Ferrari. The field also included Phil Hill, Maurice Trintignant and Stirling Moss. A total of 18 cars were on the starting grid, with Moss the fastest qualifier. The field included a Kurtis Kraft Offenhauser midget for Indianapolis veteran Rodger Ward.

Attrition for the grand prix cars was high at Sebring, and by the 10th lap of the 42-lap race, eight cars had retired. McLaren and Brabham were battling most of the race, but a dramatic finish was in store for America's first Grand Prix.

Jack Brady described the incredible final minutes in *Road & Track*: "McLaren took the winner's flag while startled officials, and the Cooper pits, tried to account for Brabham's absence. The ten-

Left: An exhausted Jack Brabham pushes his Cooper T51 Climax toward the finish line and a world driving title at Sebring in 1959.

Below: Postcard showing the start of the 1959 U.S. Grand Prix at Sebring.

Walt Hansgen is greeted by photographers after winning a preliminary race to the 1959 U.S. Grand Prix, driving a Jaguar Mk II.

The Ferrari Dino 246s of Tony Brooks (2) and Cliff Allison (3) and Phil Hill (5) before the race.

1 9 5 9   F O R M U L A   O N E   R A C E

sion grew almost unbearable as Trintignant followed McLaren across the line a second later...Brabham, by this time, was in sight. Bent nearly double over the Cooper, he was pushing for all he was worth. Brooks' Ferrari slipped past while he was still seconds from the finish line, for third. Crowd control by this time had degenerated to the nonexistent point with two of seven finishers still on the course. Innes Ireland and Henry Blanchard were dodging spectators to finish... As Brabham approached the finish line it appeared that he wouldn't be able to get through the dense crowd. Parting barely enough to let the Cooper and its exhausted driver through, the crowd closed on him again as he fell to the ground beside the car. The new world champion had pushed his car over a quarter mile. A faulty fuel system had caused the remainder of his rapidly dwindling gas to drain from the tank."

The spectacular finish in an otherwise uneventful race was among the most thrilling in grand prix racing history (See Appendix for complete results).

Due to the poor crowd, the race was moved to Riverside, California, in 1960 before finding a permanent home at Watkins Glen the following year.

Although the race was a financial failure, credit must be given to Ulmann, who helped bring Formula One to the United States.

Bruce McLaren accepts the first-place trophy at America's first Formula One World Championship race, held at Sebring

After the dismal weather of March 1959 and a disappointing crowd at the inaugural Formula One World Championship race in December, Alec Ulmann was hopeful a new decade would bring better results. Unfortunately, the 1960 12 Hours of Sebring would produce a new set of problems for Ulmann.

The official sponsor and fuel of Sebring was Amoco, but several factory teams had exclusive agreements with other brands of fuels. This created serious political problems which eventually led to a boycott by Porsche and Ferrari factory teams.

Entries were therefore somewhat disappointing compared with recent years, but in reality there were several factory cars entered under the guise of a private team. Porsche sold ("loaned" would perhaps be more accurate) one of its factory cars to Joakim Bonnier the week before the race, avoiding a conflict with British Petroleum. And unlike the official Ferrari factory team, the independent NART Ferrari entries were not obligated to use Shell fuel.

In addition to the fuel problem, rumors were circulating that this was to be the last Sebring 12-hour and that Ulmann was moving the race to a new site elsewhere in Florida (Miami, Bartow or Daytona Beach, to name a few). This rumor, in various forms, would become a Sebring tradition, with nearly every race in the '60s and '70s rumored to be the last.

The 65-car field featured four new Maserati T61s, nine Ferraris, three new Porsche RS60 quasi-factory cars and the usual array of smaller displacement machines to contest for class honors. This race was also the first scored with the use of computers, a fact that might seem rather amusing today, especially considering the bulky IBM computers took up two entire pit stalls. And 1960 was the first year that support races were held before the 12-hour race. Jim Hall won the Formula Junior race and Paul Richards was victorious in the four-hour GT race.

A crowd somewhat smaller than what promoter Ulmann had hoped for arrived race day to see the anticipated Maserati-Ferrari duel. A

Left: Corvettes had the largest engines at Sebring in 1960, so they were gridded at the front of the field for the start.

The Jack Nethercutt/
Pete Lovely Ferrari
250TR/59 finished third
in 1960.

tragic accident occurred at the beginning of the race. Jimmy Hughes, driving a Lotus Elite, lost control at the hairpin and slid into the escape road. A *Tampa Tribune* photographer, George Thompson, was in the path of the car and a last-second effort by Hughes to avoid hitting him failed. Hughes struck the photographer and rolled over several times. Both men were killed.

It was obvious from the start that Maserati would be the manufacturer to beat, although reliability was the key question. The Dan Gurney/Stirling Moss Camoradi USA T61 built a huge lead through the first half of the race, eventually leading by over 30 miles. The Chuck Daigh/Richie Ginther Ferrari 250TR/60 and the Graham Hill/Joakim Bonnier Porsche RS60 followed.

Transmission failure in the eighth hour spelled doom for the Maserati effort. Since both the top Ferrari and the Hill/Bonnier Porsche had earlier retired with engine failure, the lead was inherited by the Porsche RS60 of Olivier Gendebien and Hans Herrmann.

It was a classic case of driving a steady endurance pace and waiting for the leaders to break. It paid off as Gendebien and Herrmann ended with a nine-lap victory over the Bob Holbert/ Roy Schechter/Howard Fowler RS60.

It was the first major international endurance win by Porsche, and the first at Sebring by a rear-engine car. The next five finishers, all Ferraris, finished within three laps of each other. Pete Lovely and Jack Nethercutt were third in a 250TR, fol-

Briggs Cunningham (seated) and Alec Ulmann look over Sebring's new computerized scoring system. This marked the first time computers were used to score a race, and the enormous IBM machines took up two entire pit stalls.

lowed by Augie Pabst and Ed Hugus in a 250GT.

OSCA scored its usual Index of Performance win with a brilliant 12th overall finish for Jack Gordon and John Bentley's OSCA 187N. Alfa Romeo, Lola and Arnolt-Bristol produced notable class wins, but the race in general received generally negative reviews in the racing press.

The only Corvette to finish in the top 25 was driven by Chuck Hall and Jim Fritts. A second Corvette driven by Briggs Cunningham and John Fitch was eliminated when it rolled at the Webster turn early in the race.

The fuel problems would be resolved before next year's race, and more important, the quality of racing would improve.

Sequence of the start of the 1960 12 Hours of Sebring showing the winning number-42 Porsche RS60. These photos appeared in a short-lived magazine called *On the Grid*.

Early in the race the Lotus Elite driven by Jim Hughes overshot the hairpin and struck a *Tampa Tribune* photographer before rolling over. Both Hughes and the photographer were killed.

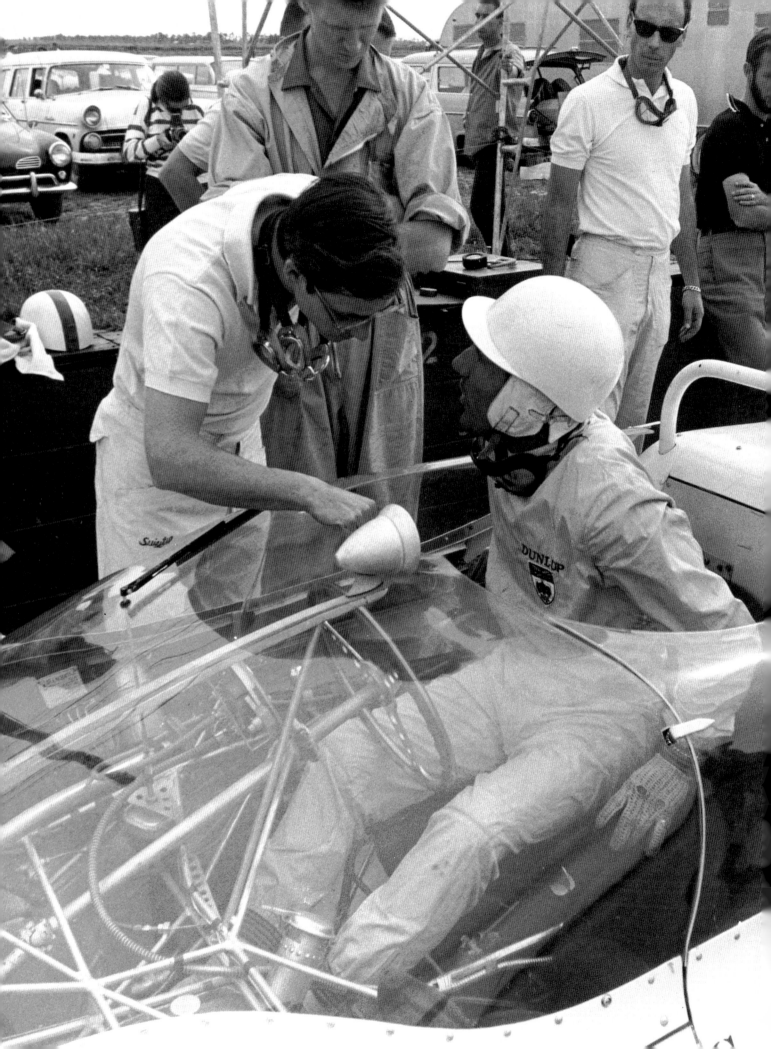

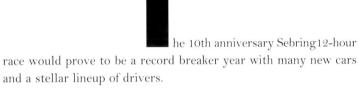

The 10th anniversary Sebring 12-hour race would prove to be a record breaker year with many new cars and a stellar lineup of drivers.

Entries included the heavily-favored Ferrari factory team and several well-financed independent Ferrari entries. Only Porsche and Maserati were considered contenders. Phil Hill, Olivier Gendebien, Richie Ginther, Wolfgang Von Trips and Pedro and Ricardo Rodriguez were among the drivers for Ferrari, while Graham Hill, Stirling Moss, John Fitch, Bruce McLaren and Briggs Cunningham were aboard Maserati entries.

Porsche drivers included Dan Gurney, Edgar Barth, Joakim Bonnier, Roger Penske and Bob Holbert.

Austin-Healey and BMC fielded their usual efficient teams to compete for class honors, while Lola, OSCA and Arnolt-Bristol entries rounded out a tough field of smaller displacement cars.

It was obvious in practice that records would be broken as several Ferrari and Maserati entries were well below the existing record for the 5.2-mile circuit. The new rear-engine Ferrari driven by Ginther and Von Trips was the sensation of Sebring '61, recording laps several seconds under the existing record. Maserati, too, was quick in practice but questions about reliability would again haunt Camoradi's entries.

Alitalia, the Italian airline, was the new Sebring sponsor, replacing Amoco. Ulmann was far ahead of his time in marketing the Sebring classic. Few events, including Indianapolis, could boast the extensive sponsorships by major international companies that Ulmann had procured. As usual, everyone who was anybody found their way to Sebring for the road racing society event of the year.

Warm weather greeted the big crowd of about 43,000 on hand for the start of what proved to be a Ferrari romp.

Masten Gregory took his Maserati T63 into the early lead but the Maserati T61 Stirling Moss was to drive failed to start at the line, requiring a six-minute battery repair. Moss then began a spec-

Left: Stirling Moss (in car) consults with co-driver Masten Gregory during practice for the 1961 race.

tacular drive from last, two laps down, to fifth, before turning the car over to Graham Hill.

The sprint-like pace of the race, unusual for Sebring at that time, took its toll on the field. The Maserati threat fizzled early and two of the three Porsche RS61 entries retired, leaving the outcome to an inter-team Ferrari battle.

The Ginther/Von Trips Ferrari 246SP led until its steering failed. The drivers were then assigned to the Mairesse/Baghetti Ferrari and gave chase to Hill and Gendebien, who had taken the lead in the sixth hour from the Rodriguez brothers.

The two factory Ferraris stayed close, with Hill and Gendebien holding on for a three-lap victory aboard their 250TR, the third Sebring win for both drivers and Gendebien's third straight, a Sebring record that has never been duplicated. The Mairesse/Baghetti/Ginther/Von Trips Ferrari took second, followed by Pedro and Ricardo Rodriguez.

The sixth-place Porsche RS61 of Holbert and Penske managed both a class win and the Index of Performance title, while two factory MGA entries produced a one-two finish in class.

The GT class win went to the Ferrari 250GT driven by Allen Eager and Denise McCluggage, a female driver who was among the best road racers in America.

The race was plagued by timing and scoring problems, which resulted in the race results being revised several times before the final finishing order was declared official several weeks after the race.

With Ferrari taking seven of the top 10 positions, there was little doubt which manufacturer would dominate the 1961 sports car World Championship season.

Now a decade old, Sebring continued to be a fixture in American motor racing culture. Thousands made the annual trek to the small town, which could hardly accommodate such a huge event. As reported in *Sports Car Graphic*: "Five days before the race itself, cars begin to appear in the quiet little town. They come on trailers, on huge haulers, on tow-bars behind passenger cars and some arrive under their own power...

Right: The Corvettes of Bob Johnson / David Morgan (left) and Don Yenko / Ben Moore pass beneath the pedestrian bridges. Note the spectators.

The Ferrari 250TR/61 of Mairesse/Baghetti/ Ginther/Von Trips finished in second place, three laps behind the 250TR/61 of Phil Hill and Olivier Gendebien.

Gulf Crest Gasoline restores clean engine performance

Try a tank-ful!

DUNLOP FLY

SEBRING, FLORIDA

MARTINI & ROSSI

"Garages, both public and private are pre-empted for the racing machinery. Work goes on around the clock and unfortunate is the private citizen who blows an engine or needs repairs on mundane equipment, for garage space, even filling station space, is nil for the week. Tourists passing through are well advised to take alternate routes if they expect to stop in central Florida for the night—every available bed, even spares in the city jail, are booked long in advance.

"Even so, Sebring is not for sleeping. The aura of orange blossoms that normally pervades the air is supplemented by the sharp smell of burned castor and exhaust fumes; all day and far into the small hours of the morning comes the close or distant sound of engines."

Ferrari was again the star of the show at Sebring in 1962. The 10-lap victory margin by Joakim Bonnier and Lucien Bianchi was the largest yet. The race, however, was one of the most controversial in Sebring history.

Ferrari was again the obvious prerace favorite, but there was a large contingent of cars to make the race more than interesting. Porsche, Alfa Romeo, Chaparral and a Briggs Cunningham-entered Jaguar XKE and Cooper Maserati promised to produce a good race.

As usual, the Sebring field included some unique entries such as Daytona 500 winner Marvin Panch in a Holman-Moody-prepared Ford Falcon Challenger and Indianapolis 500 winner Rodger Ward in the "Nickey Nouse" Corvette entered by Nickey Chevrolet of Chicago.

The entries also included flamboyant Frank Mabry, Jr., the first black driver to enter Sebring. The NAACP used the publicity surrounding Mabry's entry in a preliminary GT race to pressure many of the central Florida hotels and restaurants to end their "white only" practice. The ARCF issued a statement promising that Mabry would receive equal treatment and race fans of all colors would be welcome at Sebring. Mabry qualified for the race but wrecked his Austin-Healey Sprite in a highway accident near the track and ended up in the hospital, unable to start the race.

The now traditional field of 65 cars took starter Jesse Coleman's command for the famous Le Mans start. The Ferrari 250TR of Innes Ireland and Stirling Moss led most of the early laps, battling the NART-entered Ferrari Dino 246 of Pedro and Ricardo Rodriguez. The Cooper Maserati of Bruce McLaren and Roger Penske also led briefly in the hotly contested early laps.

The Rodriguez brothers' Ferrari expired with engine problems, but a second NART Ferrari Dino 246 with Bob Grossman and Alan Connell, later joined by Pedro Rodriguez, challenged for the lead until it retired with transmission problems.

The race took a dramatic turn when the Moss/Ireland car was

The Ferrari GTO driven by Phil Hill and Olivier Gendebien in the pits late in the 1962 race. It finished second overall and first in the GT category.

flagged off the track while holding a two-lap lead near the midway point. The car had been disqualified for a refueling infraction that actually took place on the 73rd lap when Ireland made a pit stop that included refueling. Rules permitted refueling every 20 laps, but the car had last stopped for fuel 18 laps earlier. The infraction was reported by a pit marshal and then relayed to the chief steward, who disqualified the leader.

Moss and Ireland were furious. Apparently the pit official had cut the gas cap tape and indicated to the team they could legally refuel at that point.

"I am disgusted with Sebring", said Moss, who had had incredibly bad luck at Sebring since his upset win in 1954. "I had nearly a three-lap lead and the car was running perfectly. The trouble with Sebring is that they try to copy Le Mans, which is the worst race in the world."

While confusion reigned among officials and the NART team, Jo

Denise McCluggage, shown here pushing her OSCA S1000, was America's first great female sports car driver and is now a noted motorsports journalist.

Bonnier and Lucien Bianchi inherited the lead and were never seriously challenged in their Ferrari 250TR. Their winning Ferrari was a rebodied version of the chassis that had won the previous year.

Phil Hill and Olivier Gendebien finished second and won the important GT category, earning championship points for Ferrari. A Porsche RSK managed to win the Index of Performance with a third-place finish at the hands of F. Rand/Bruce Jennings/Bill Wuesthoff. The George Hammil/Fabrizio Serena Ferrari 250GT took fourth, followed by the McLaren/Penske Cooper Maserati.

The American-built Chaparral driven by Jim Hall, Hap Sharp and Ronnie Hissom captured sixth and a class win.

John Bentley and Jack Gordon gave OSCA yet another Sebring class win, while the Alfa Romeo Veloce of Art Swanson/Bob Richardson/Ross Durant took an impressive GT class victory.

While Sebring was on the verge of perhaps its most glorious period, Ulmann was quite displeased at the scheduling of a three-hour race in Daytona the month before, and made his feelings known to the FIA. Ulmann was especially appalled that a sports car race on a banked track at a facility built for stock car racing would even be considered for an international sports car event.

Ulmann was fully aware that it was Bill France's goal to make Daytona the site of a 24-hour race to be held annually during Daytona's famed speed weeks. Although the race would become a reality, it never attracted the fan interest or achieved the international stature of Sebring. As Ulmann later stated: "Admittedly, there was nothing wrong in establishing a second or even third championship race in the United States...but [for the FIA] to authorize a race six weeks before the traditional date of Sebring in the same state seemed altogether wrong. This resulted in diluting spectator interest, as can be witnessed by the acres of empty stands at Daytona."

The 12 hours was already a motor racing tradition that could never be duplicated. As John Christy wrote in *Sports Car Graphic:* "If it ever went smoothly, it wouldn't be Sebring. Stuffy, disorganized, aggravating, dirty and hard on equipment, Sebring is all of that but is also exciting, at times wildly so, a brutal test and one of three or four of the most interesting races in the world. And as usual, we're looking forward with both dread and anticipation to the next one."

Stirling Moss and Innes Ireland dominated in this Ferrari 250TR/61 and stretched out a three-lap lead before their controversial disqualification for a refueling infraction.

By 1963, Sebring was virtually a household name. The race was broadcast live across the country on radio and highlights were televised nationally on the ABC network. There was a popular board game sold nationally called "Road Racing on the Famous Sebring Track," the Sounds of Sebring record albums were popular sellers, slot car sets were named after Sebring and even Elvis Presley made a movie in which he often refers to racing at the 12 Hours of Sebring.

The gathering of drivers at Sebring in 1963 is considered among the finest ever at any event in American motorsports history. The unusually diverse field included A.J. Foyt, Fireball Roberts, Phil Hill, Briggs Cunningham, Bruce McLaren, Graham Hill, Roger Penske, Dan Gurney...just about every notable name in racing at that time. In addition, a new generation of drivers who would soon make their mark in sports car racing were at Sebring, including Mark Donohue, Bob Tullius, Jim Hall, Don Yenko and Jerry Titus.

Sebring was also fast earning its reputation as a party. Crowds arrived early and camped at the track. Tents and campfires sprung up throughout the huge airport and industrial park, which was strewn with abandoned airplanes and dilapidated buildings.

James Crow wrote in *Road & Track:* "Sebring is an anomaly: an unlikely circuit in an unlikely location... The Sebring 12–hour race is, however, equal to more than the sum of its parts. The town is surprisingly cosmopolitan, a neat little green-lawned resort spot catering to Northerners who appreciate its winter warmth. The airport circuit, though completely flat, has been developed until its facilities are unsurpassed in the United States. And the race itself is America's premier sports car race.

"For U.S. sports car drivers, it's one of the major goals, one in which participation indicates a certain status symbol of having 'arrived.' For manufacturers and distributors it's a now-established advertising medium that means something to the prospective buyer."

Left: The only traffic jam in Sebring—the wild start of the 1963 race.

The Ferrari factory returned as the overwhelming favorite to win its third straight Sebring race. There was little doubt nothing could challenge Ferrari for the overall win, but plenty of new and exciting machinery was on hand. Carroll Shelby's Ford-powered Cobras were the most popular and America's great hope, but they were virtually untested for an event such as Sebring.

Jim Hall's Chaparral entries, powered by Chevrolet engines, survived last-minute body changes to meet the rather confusing FIA rules. They also proved fast but unreliable.

The huge crowd certainly got a thrill when Phil Hill led the first lap driving a Shelby Cobra, but the NART-entered Ferrari 330TR/LM of Pedro Rodriguez and Graham Hill then moved into the lead.

Three Corvettes thunder down the front straight. A.J. Foyt and Jim Hurtubise drove the number-5 car, which is shown here leading the Ed Towlher/Duncan Black/ Don Yenko car number 2.

On the 14th lap, the Chaparral took the lead but its engine expired on the next lap, giving the lead back to the Rodriguez/Hill entry, followed closely by the two Ferrari 250P factory entries.

The top three Ferraris exchanged the lead during pit stops throughout the middle portions of the race, with the John Surtees/ Lodovico Scarfiotti 250P taking the lead permanently in the eighth hour. They finished with a one-lap margin over Willy Mairesse/ Nino Vaccarella/Lorenzo Bandini, becoming the first Sebring winners since 1954 to also win the Index of Performance (1963 was the last year of the Index).

The top six positions were all occupied by Ferraris, with the Rodriguez/Hill entry taking third and the Penske/Augie Pabst Ferrari GTO fourth.

The Jaguar XKE of Ed Leslie and Frank Morrill took seventh overall while Bruce McLaren and Walt Hansgen were a lap behind in another Jaguar XKE. Bob Holbert and Don Wester took an impressive class win in a Porsche Abarth Carrera. Not to be overlooked was the Triumph team, which scored a popular class victory.

The Cobras were fast, but as expected they lacked the durability to compete at a tough circuit like Sebring. Four of the six Cobras that started the race failed to finish. The Ken Miles/Phil Hill/Lew Spencer car, suffering brake problems for most of the race, finished

The Ferrari 330TRI/LM

of Pedro Rodriguez and

Graham Hill finished

third. Ferraris swept the

top six positions in 1963.

11th. Dan Gurney drove his Cobra solo the first six hours of the race until a steering problem took him out of contention. Hill took over the car after repairs and struggled to 29th overall.

Despite the disappointing performance, Shelby's Cobras would return next year at Sebring and produce a very different ending.

The Shelby Cobra driven

by Phil Hill, Ken Miles

and Lew Spencer.

The seven Chevrolet Corvettes entered also failed to seriously challenge the established European makes. The best finish among them was 16th place by the Delmo Johnson/David Morgan entry.

The overwhelming performance by Ferrari would soon be challenged by American muscle, and Sebring would be the battleground for spectacular races over the next three years.

1964

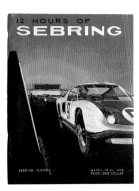

The 1964 running of the 12 Hours of Sebring featured a serious American challenge for the first time in over a decade. The Ford-powered Shelby Cobras were out to win the manufacturers world championship for GT cars, and the stage was set for a duel with Ferrari.

The Ferrari versus Cobra era has been well documented by racing historians. In reality, the Cobras were never a match against Ferrari on Sebring's tough 5.2-mile circuit in terms of an overall win. Three factory rear-engine prototypes along with several strong independent efforts made sure the red cars from Modena would dominate.

Carroll Shelby and his Cobra team believed Sebring would be a key race to earn points toward the GT title, and five cars, including the new streamlined coupe, were entered. Leading drivers enlisted for the effort included Dan Gurney, Phil Hill, Bob Holbert, Dave MacDonald, Ken Miles (in the 7-liter Cobra prototype) and a young-ster named John Morton, who would earn his fame at Sebring 30 years later.

The Chevrolet Corvette Grand Sports entries were another strong American effort with drivers Roger Penske, Jim Hall, A.J. Foyt and others. A variety of Porsche and Alfa Romeo entries promised to battle for class wins.

In 1964 Sebring began to use official qualifying sessions for the first time to determine how the cars would line up for the Le Mans start, instead of gridding them based on engine displacement. This was done to help weed out cars too slow to race competitively and make the Le Mans start a bit safer. It also brought an extra measure of excitement and prestige to the event. Fastest in qualifying was the John Surtees/Lorenzo Bandini Ferrari 330P.

The largest crowd in Sebring history was on hand to witness the outstanding lineup of cars and drivers. The Jim Hall/Roger Penske Corvette Grand Sport led the first lap, but after that, it was total Ferrari domination.

Left: A jubilant victory

lane celebration for the

Ferrari team.

The factory Ferraris traded the lead with the Surtees/Bandini 330P setting the pace early. The Graham Hill/Joakim Bonnier 330P Ferrari took the lead near the mid-race point until transmission problems eventually ended their challenge.

A frightening accident took place late in the event when the class-leading Cobra driven by Bob Johnson slammed into the rear of the Alfa Romeo 1600 TZ driven by Consalvo Sansei. The Alfa was running slowly in front of the pits with no tail lights, and the impact shot the car into a concrete wall, where it burst into flames. Sansei was trapped in the car, but driver Jocko Maggiacomo ran from the pit area and pulled him to safety in one of the most heroic acts in Sebring history.

In the final hours the Ludovico Scarfiotti/Nino Vaccarella and Mike Parkes/Umberto Maglioli 275Ps exchanged the lead several times, following typically chaotic Ferrari pit stops, described here by Steve Smith in *Car and Driver* magazine: "The Ferrari pit stops were riotous mayhem. One mechanic peered into a tailpipe just in time to get a 10,000 rpm blip of exhaust in his face. Once, with two

Ferraris in the pit at the same time, two mechanics came galloping around each car from opposite sides, collided, dropped all their tools, then got into an argument about who owned which tools...and the driver who was screaming for something to clean off his windshield, got a chamois flung at him so hard it wrapped around his helmeted head like a turban."

The deciding lead change came in the final 20 minutes as the Scarfiotti/Vaccarella car entered the pits with clutch problems. The Parkes/Maglioli Ferrari emerged with a one-lap win over Scarfiotti/Vaccarella in what appeared to be a predetermined "team ordered" finish.

Ferrari dominated the race as expected, but the Cobras accomplished their goal of earning maximum points. The Holbert/MacDonald Cobra coupe finished fourth overall and first in GT. Lew Spencer and Bob Bondurant took fifth in another Cobra, with Phil Hill and Jo Schlesser making it a sweep of the GT top three for Shelby American.

Richard Poe reported in *Sports Car* on the typically Sebring event that followed the race: "While Ferrari got the publicity, the Cobras

John Surtees and Lorenzo Bandini drove this Ferrari 330P to third place. Qualifying was first introduced in 1964, and Surtees won the pole and later set the fastest lap during the race.

Briggs Cunningham and Lake Underwood finished ninth driving this Porsche 904. It was the highest–finishing of the 10 Porsches that competed in 1964.

A nighttime pit stop in 1964 for the Shelby Cobra of Lew Spencer and Bob Bondurant. They finished fifth behind the Bob Holbert/Dave MacDonald Cobra Coupe GT and ahead of the sixth-place Phil Hill/ Jo Schlesser Cobra.

were busy collecting those valuable points for the FIA World Championship for GT cars...On the theory that the 12-hour race is for GT points, Shelby had the [winning] Cobra coupe pushed to victory circle. Mr. Ulmann was nearly apoplectic. The Ferrari finally was pushed to the appointed place of honor in a scene that was rapidly going from confusion to chaos. And I imagine that Carroll laughed all the way back to California."

A NART-entered Ferrari GTO took seventh with the Briggs Cunningham/Lake Underwood Porsche 904 ninth overall and first in class. Also of note was the class win by the Chuck Stoddard/Jim Kaser Alfa Romeo 1600 TZ, well ahead of a Lotus Cortina co-driven by Jim Clark.

The excitement created by the Cobra team produced a spectacular race for those in attendance at Sebring in 1964, and a rematch was eagerly anticipated for next year.

T he excitement that preceded this Sebring race was greater than any of the previous 13 endurance classics.

The enormous crowd that arrived on race day caused traffic to be backed up for several miles, and undoubtedly thousands of race fans missed the start waiting in line.

As usual, a prestigious field of drivers was on hand. The Cobras, new Ford GT40s and Ferrari were the favorites, although there were many other contenders. The two-car Chaparral team was a crowd favorite, although few really believed the Chevrolet-powered open-cockpit car with an automatic transmission could survive 12 brutal hours on Sebring's 5.2-mile circuit. Nonetheless, builder and driver Jim Hall displayed a quiet confidence before the race.

The Ferrari factory was not officially entered, unhappy with rules that allowed outright sports/racing cars (giving American "specials" such as the Chaparral a much better chance to win overall), but there were plenty of privately entered cars on hand to keep their Sebring win streak alive.

"It looked like a Ferrari-less Sebring," wrote John Christy in *Sports Car Graphic*, "until something called the Ferrari Owners Racing Association appeared on the scene—supposedly composed of loyal Ferrari owners determined to uphold the name of the marque. All this enthusiasm and loyalty seemed to capture the imagination of Graham Hill, Pedro Rodriguez, Willy Mairese, Mauro Bianchi, Giancarlo Baghetti and Umberto Maglioli, together with a slew of small, dark mechanic types in Italian Army brown coveralls, none of whom could speak a word of English. All the marque-loyal enthusiasts were in charge of the strangest looking assortment of Ferraris ever seen in one place. Had they all been painted red, it would have been an awesome array of 275LMs, 275Ps and 330Ps, but these were painted every shade from metallic blue through copper-bronze to bright green."

Porsche had a strong lineup of 904s and Shelby American fielded four Cobra GT Coupe entries. Two Ford GT40s for drivers Bruce

Left: Torrential rains flooded the pits during the 1965 race.

Richie Ginther dashes to his Ford GT40 for the Le Mans start. Note the spectator "sky-ride" in the background.

McLaren, Ken Miles, and Richie Ginther plus a Lotus Ford with Dan Gurney and Jerry Grant driving rounded a very strong field.

The smaller displacement classes were always well subscribed at Sebring, and 1965 was no different. Factory teams from Standard Triumph, Austin-Healey, British Motor Corp. and Alfa Romeo were on hand to contest for class wins.

The Chaparral displayed stunning speed in practice and qualifying, breaking the existing Sebring record by nine seconds. The McLaren/Miles Ford was also well below the track record, while the fastest Ferrari was nearly 12 seconds slower than the Chaparral.

A hot, humid day was on tap as the drivers lined up for the start. The Miles/Ginther Ford GT 40 and the Gurney/Grant Lotus Ford challenged the Chaparrals early in the race, but both dropped out early with mechanical problems. Only the McLaren/Miles Ford appeared to be a threat to the two Chaparrals.

Early in the race, Charlie Rainville spun in turn one and struck two spectators standing near a snow fence (hardly enough protection from an out-of-control car). While they were not seriously injured, it foreshadowed tragic events to come the following year.

At the five-hour mark, ominous skies suddenly appeared and turned into a torrential downpour, the worst ever seen at Sebring. Within a few minutes, the driving rainstorm had flooded the circuit, especially the pit area and back straight. Water up to three feet deep in some areas made driving virtually impossible. Smaller displacement cars were passing more powerful cars with ease, while others were stranded out on course. Many drivers were blinded by the rain and became completely lost on Sebring's expansive airport runway straights.

In the pit area, rainwater accumulated and made pit stops nearly impossible. Tires could be seen floating down pit lane. Despite the

conditions, Ulmann and the ARCF race officials had no intentions of stopping the race. Ironically, it would not rain at Sebring again on race day for another 26 years.

The monsoon slowed the race tremendously, but the open-cock-pit Chaparral somehow survived and continued to hold its lead. Its sister car, driven by Ronnie Hissom and Bruce Jennings, suffered from electrical problems that the Chaparral crew worried might also affect the leading car.

The John Fulp/Roger McCluskey Ferrari 330P, The Ed Lowther/ Bob Natgel/Sid Sinkel Cobra roadster and the Peter Gregg/George

Barber Porsche 904 were all victims of mechanical problems by mid-race. The factory Porsches continued their steady pace but were too far behind to challenge for an overall victory.

The circuit dried almost as fast as it flooded, and by sunset track conditions were almost normal. It didn't seem possible that the Chaparral could survive such a difficult race, but it went on to record one of the most popular wins in American road racing history. It was an American car, driven by American drivers, the first time that had happened at Sebring since 1953, when the Cunningham C4R claimed victory.

Jim Hall and Hap Sharp were greeted in a festive victory lane by a mob of race fans, a Sebring tradition. Their victory was considered a major upset by virtually everyone. They finished with a four-lap margin over the McLaren/Miles Ford. Hall's prerace confidence could be explained by their extensive testing, even skipping the season-opening Daytona endurance race in favor of a test session at Sebring.

The only Ferrari in the top five was the David Piper/Tony Maggs 275LM, which finished three laps ahead of the Jo Schlesser/Bob Bondurant Cobra. The Lake Underwood/Gunther Klass Porsche 904 took fifth. Alfa Romeo and MG took important class wins, but all other performances were overshadowed by the Chaparral.

Jerry Grant and Dan Gurney led early in the 1965 race driving this Lotus Ford before suspension problems ended their run.

1966

Sebring 1966 is considered among the greatest sports car endurance races of all time. Unfortunately, it will forever be known as Sebring's most tragic event.

From the standpoint of entries, this was another spectacular race. Ford and Ferrari were again the favorites. Among the Ferrari entries were a factory Dino 206/S for Ludovico Scarfiotti and Lorenzo Bandini and a 330P3 with Mike Parkes and Bob Bondurant driving. Mario Andretti and Pedro Rodriguez were aboard a NART-entered 330P2.

Ford had plenty of power on hand in an all-out effort to defeat Ferrari, entering a Mk II for Dan Gurney and Jerry Grant to go along with the X-1 roadster special for Ken Miles and Lloyd Ruby. Nine Ford GT40s were entered, plus three Cobras.

There was more American-made muscle as well. Jim Hall was back with two Chaparrals and Roger Penske was among those who entered Corvettes.

The smaller displacement classes in the field were very competitive and included factory teams from Austin-Healey, Alfa Romeo and Triumph. Porsche was represented by three factory cars and a large contingent of private entries.

Improvements to the circuit included a new driveover bridge into Green Park, opening up that area of the circuit to spectators for the first time, and in the paddock, bright orange and green covered pits. The first ever Sports Car Club of America (SCCA) Trans-Am race was held at Sebring the day before the 12-hour race, with Jochen Rindt winning in an Alfa Romeo followed by Bob Tullius in a Dodge Dart. Although this race is a footnote in Sebring's legendary history, the Trans-Am series continues three decades later as America's oldest sports car racing series.

At the start of the 15th annual 12 Hours of Sebring, the field roared into the sweeping left-hand first turn, all except the fastest qualifying Gurney/Miles Ford, which sat alone on the grid, unable to start. Gurney finally got the Ford started just as the field was

Left: The Shelby
American Ford team
turned one of the many
hangars located around
the Sebring circuit into a
first-rate raceshop.

89

about to complete the first lap. He then carved his way through the field in one of the most spectacular drives ever seen at Sebring, taking the lead on the 24th lap.

At about the three-hour mark, the Comstock Racing Ford GT40 driven by Canadian Bob McLean lost control at the big bend approaching the hairpin, rolling over several times before striking a telephone pole and bursting into flames. McLean was killed and the car was destroyed.

The Gurney/Grant Ford continued to lead, followed by the Bondurant/Parkes Ferrari and the Miles/Ruby Ford. Walt Hansgen and Mark Donohue also remained near the leaders in the Holman-Moody Mk II. Both Chaparrals retired early and the Graham Hill/Jackie Stewart Ford GT40 was strong until engine failure ended their run.

The Bondurant/Parkes Ferrari retired in the eighth hour with transmission problems, leaving the two Shelby American Fords to battle for the overall win.

With about two hours remaining, Mario Andretti and Porsche 906 driver Don Wester were involved in a terrible accident that re-

Start of the 1966 12 Hours of Sebring. The Ford Mk II of Dan Gurney and Jerry Grant (2) would not fire for several minutes, but eventually fought its way through the pack and into the lead.

sulted in the deaths of four spectators. Among the fatalities was Patricia Heacock, wife of a prominent Sebring businessman and race official. Wester was badly injured in the crash.

"I was dueling back and forth with the Ferrari driven by Mario Andretti," said Wester from his hospital room. "I noticed earlier he seemed to be having brake problems. He was on and off the course. So when we came out of the hairpin, I let him go."

Andretti described the fateful incident: "I had just pulled away from the Porsche when I tried to gear down from fourth to third. But something snapped in the gear box. I went into first and locked my wheels. Then I went into a terrible spin. It felt like I spun 1,000 times, but I didn't think I hit [Wester]."

Andretti's Ferrari spun off the course, then came back into Wester's path. "All of a sudden I saw this cloud of dust," said Wester. "I figured he had gone off the track again. Then he hit me. There wasn't anything I could do."

Wester's Porsche was punted off the circuit by the errant Ferrari near the Webster turn (named after a manufacturing company located at that part of the circuit) where several people were watching the race. While the four victims were in an "unauthorized" area, it was a tragic event that drew worldwide criticism.

Andretti continued to the pit area, but didn't learn of the tragic results of his mishap for another 30 minutes.

The row of old warehouses along the short straight leading to the Webster turn was often occupied by spectators who sat only a few feet from the circuit with no protection. Old curbing, concrete blocks, pipes, storage tanks and even trees were along the side of

View of the famous esses and MG bridge during the 1966 race.

A mechanical failure in the Mario Andretti/ Pedro Rodriguez Ferrari 330P2 triggered the tragic accident with the Don Wester/Scooter Patrick Porsche 906 at the Webster turn.

the circuit, a hazard to any unfortunate driver who went off course in that area.

With the race clearly a Ford romp, it appeared Dan Gurney was on the way to his second Sebring win as he took over for his co-driver Jerry Grant with a half hour remaining. As is so often the case at Sebring, however, the final minutes proved to be a drama beyond what even a Hollywood screenwriter could dream up.

Gurney held a comfortable lead over the Miles/Ruby Ford as he started his 228th and final lap. As he powered the Ford down the long concrete back straight toward the timing turn, the engine suddenly seized. Gurney coasted to a stop about 250 yards from the finish line and then decided to push the car the remainder of the distance. With less than a minute left in the race, however, it would be impossible for Gurney to push his ailing Ford across the finish ahead of his fast-approaching teammates. The Miles/Ruby Ford swept by to take the checkered flag from starter Jesse Coleman as a stunned crowd watched in disbelief.

Miles and Ruby celebrated in victory lane, winning America's premier sports car race, leading only the last lap!

To make matters worse for Gurney, he was disqualified for pushing the car, moving the Hansgen/Donohue Ford into second place, 12 laps behind the winners.

Peter Revson and Skip Scott finished third in a Ford GT40 followed by the Hans Herrmann/Joe Buzzetta Porsche 906. The only Ferrari in the top five was the Dino of Bandini/Scarfiotti. The Ed Lowther/Bob Gross Cobra took a class win with a 10th place finish, just behind the Penske Corvette of Ben Moore/George Wintersteen, which won the GT category.

The tragedy and the litigation that followed convinced Ulmann that a move to a new venue was essential for the survival of the event. He agreed to move to the newly constructed Palm Beach International Raceway, 85 miles to the southeast of Sebring on the outskirts of West Palm Beach. The announcement was made official in the summer of 1966, but the plans quickly fell apart when heavy rains delayed the completion of the new track. It is likely, however,

A broken camshaft in Dan Gurney and Jerry Grant's Ford Mk II ended their dominating run just 250 yards from the finish line.

that this was more of a bluff by Ulmann to get the Sebring Airport Authority to agree to assist in making major improvements to the circuit.

The most significant change was the deletion of the Webster turn, site of that terrible accident. It was replaced with the new Green Park chicane. More safety improvements, including better run-off protection for drivers, were also made before the 1967 event. There has not been another fatal accident during the 12 Hours of Sebring since McLean's 1966 accident.

Tragedy seemed to follow the 1966 Sebring race. Co-winner Ken Miles and second-place finisher Walt Hansgen were killed only months after Sebring in testing accidents.

There were other criticisms of the Sebring event. Police using electric cattle prods for crowd control, a near riot at the location of the McLean accident, price gouging by local merchants, poor traffic control and other problems forced Ulmann to make many changes in the race organization.

In addition, a rivalry had developed between Ulmann and Daytona International Speedway owner Bill France. Daytona hosted its first 24-hour sports car race in February 1966, further pressuring Ulmann to upgrade the Sebring circuit.

This Porsche 906 driven to fourth place by Hans Herrmann and Joe Buzzetta was the top finishing non-Ford in 1966.

1967

Don Yenko and Dave Morgan drove this Corvette to first place in the GT Class at Sebring in 1967 and 10th overall.

Ferrari had soundly defeated Ford at Daytona to open the season, but decided to bypass Sebring in order to prepare for Le Mans. In reality, Ferrari not only feared they could not compete with Ford at Sebring (although they didn't need the points since Ford was not going to compete in all the European events), but they also feared legal action resulting from the tragic Sebring events of 1966.

Indeed, Ferrari had already been named in one lawsuit, and there were also problems between the Sebring promoter and the Italian manufacturer. Ulmann was not willing to "assist" Ferrari or NART, its North American arm, like some other event promoters. Appearance money was an issue that few people were willing to acknowledge even existed at the time.

In the end, Ulmann could not convince Enzo Ferrari to send his factory cars to Sebring. Even the NART team withdrew its entries, leaving a host of private teams to challenge Ford.

The race appeared to be a virtual lock for Ford despite their dismal performance at Daytona. Only Jim Hall's Chaparrals appeared capable of challenging Ford, with Phil Hill and Mike Spence slated to drive the winged 2F. Just two days before the race, Hill was rushed to the hospital with appendicitis, so Hall entered as a co-driver. Porsche had an outstanding entry but would be a long shot for an overall win.

Mario Andretti was now driving for Ford, assigned to drive the new MkIV with Bruce McLaren. The MkIV was an aerodynamically refined version of the J-car, which had been tested extensively in the weeks before Sebring. A.J. Foyt and Lloyd Ruby were assigned a Ford MkII.

Andretti was the fastest qualifier in the unusually small 58-car field, setting a new track record, helped in part by the new chicane, which was faster than the old Webster turn it replaced. This was the first major change to the circuit since 1952.

At the start, the Alfa Romeo T33 of Andrea de Adamich and

Left: The Ford team in the pits before the 1967 race. They swept to a one-two finish with Mario Andretti and Bruce McLaren driving the number-1 car to victory at a record speed.

Finishing third in 1967 was this Porsche 910 driven by Gerhard Mitter and Scooter Patrick.

Teodoro Zeccoli led the first lap, then the factory Fords took over, followed by the Chaparral 2F with Hall and Spence aboard. After leading some laps in the first few hours, the Chaparral retired and the Andretti/McLaren Ford was on the way to a record-setting journey.

The private Ferrari teams suffered a disastrous day, with six of the seven entries dropping out in the first four hours.

There was little drama as the race headed toward its conclusion. Never had any car dominated so easily. Andretti and McLaren finished with an all-time record 12-lap margin and averaged 102.9 MPH, the first team to average more than 100 MPH for the entire 12 hours.

There was, however, drama in the battle for second place. The Foyt/Ruby Ford held a comfortable margin when it suffered engine failure with about 30 minutes remaining. The third place Gerhard Mitter/Scooter Patrick Porsche 910 was several laps behind and began a furious race against the clock, but fell just eight seconds short of taking second place.

Porsche entries occupied half of the top 10 by the end of the race, including the third-place showing by Mitter and Patrick in a

Denise McCluggage (shown here in her signature polka-dot helmet) and Pinkie Rollo finished 17th in this Ferrari 275GTB Spyder.

908. Maglioli and Vaccarella drove a Ford GT40 to fifth and Robert Kirby teamed with Alan Johnson to win the GT class in a Porsche 911S.

It was a disappointing race in terms of entries and attendance, and there was little racing after the first few hours. Rule changes on the horizon pointed toward even more lackluster international sports car racing.

The race continued to receive generally negative publicity, some of it a carryover from the unfortunate accidents of 1966, but most because of Ulmann's reluctance to further modernize the aging circuit. This fueled rumors of Sebring's demise and many believed the 1968 race would be the last.

Jim Hall and Mike Spence led briefly in the high-winged Chaparral 2F during the 1967 race and were running a solid fourth when they were sidelined by a faulty electrical system.

New FIA rules had a negative effect on the 12 Hours of Sebring and all endurance races in 1968. The FIA dictated that big bore cars were no longer part of the Manufacturers Championship, with the emphasis placed on smaller displacement cars (3 liters or less). The decision-makers in Europe apparently had had enough of American cars winning at Sebring and Le Mans.

The smallest crowd in several years arrived on an overcast day to watch what surely would be a Porsche parade. Ford and Ferrari fielded entries but there appeared to be little hope they could contend against the Porsche 907, which sported a "short-tail" version for the Sebring race.

Although Porsche had not won overall at Sebring since 1960, the manufacturer had dominated various classes for several years and the cars seemed bulletproof on Sebring's tough circuit. The make's enviable finishing percentage in endurance races would continue to flourish in future years at Sebring.

A SCCA Trans-Am race was included within the 12 hours, helping to boost the starting grid. At the time, the race was criticized for the number of GT and Trans-Am cars in the field, but this event is now considered unique in Sebring history for its two-races-in-one format.

The Trans-Am class featured the Roger Penske-prepared Sunoco Chevrolet Camaros with drivers Mark Donohue and Craig Fisher competing against arch-rival Ford. Shelby Racing fielded two Mustangs with Jerry Titus and Ronnie Bucknum in the lead car.

In qualifying, the Porsche 907 driven by Hans Herrmann was fastest. Actor James Garner fielded a pair of Chevrolet-powered Lolas, one of which qualified near the top of the grid with Scooter Patrick driving. The two J.W. Engineering Ford GT40s with Brian Redman, Jacky Ickx, David Hobbs and Paul Hawkins driving were considered contenders, but reliability was questionable.

Left: Drivers sprint to their cars to start the 1968 race.

The race started as predicted, with the Porsches pulling out to a safe lead and then toying with various challengers, wearing them down. The Scooter Patrick/Dave Jordan Lola challenged early but was sidelined by mid-race with engine failure. The Hobbs/Hawkins Ford GT40 was in contention until an accident with the all-female AMC Javelin of Janet Guthrie (later to become the first woman to race at Indianapolis) and Liane Engeman.

The Hans Herrmann/Jo Siffert Porsche 907 makes a pit stop on the way to a dominating win in 1968.

One of the most popular cars in the race was the turbine-powered Howmet driven by its creator, Ray Heppenstall. It was fast, but it needed to stop for kerosene fuel every hour. Ultimately, its suspension could not withstand the tough Sebring circuit and it retired after running as high as third.

While two of the four factory Porsche 907 entries dropped out early in the race, the remaining two dominated the final half of the race. Hans Herrmann and Jo Siffert drove to a 11-lap victory in one of the most dominating wins in Sebring history. The Vic Elford/Jochen Neerspasch 907 finished in second place.

The Porsche effort was impressive. The eight-cylinder 2.2-liter engines in the light 907 chassis produced speeds nearly equal to the 7-liter Fords of the previous year. Meanwhile, a Porsche 911S driven by Alan Johnson and Alan Kirby took a GT class win with seventh overall.

The Penske two-car Chevrolet Camaro team produced stunning results with a third and fourth overall, winning the Trans-Am portion of the race. Mark Donohue and Craig Fisher drove the top Penske entry.

The Ronnie Bucknum/Jerry Titus Mustang took fifth overall, followed by the GT class-winning Chevrolet Corvette of David Morgan and Hap Sharp. MG took two class wins and Lancia cap-

The Howmet Turbine car was fast but proved fragile. It ran as high as third before dropping out when its suspension broke.

tured a class win as well, its best showing at Sebring since 1954.

Although the race was considered a disappointment, Ulmann announced after the race that he had been assured by the FIA that the 12 Hours of Sebring would continue to be part of the world championship at least through 1971. He would be rewarded with three outstanding races in the next three years, and Sebring was on the way to yet another resurgence in its roller coaster history.

It should be remembered that 1968 was a rather tumultuous year in American history, and Sebring's young crowd reflected that. The local community was beginning to dread the race week and the vandalism and public drunkenness that accompanied this enormous sports event. Some merchants even refused to open while the race fans were in town.

There was a remarkable contrast at Sebring, which had a generation gap of its own. The ARCF Club, located in the paddock, remained an exclusive gathering place that still attracted the rich and famous Palm Beach crowd and key politicians. ARCF officials wore their blazers and sipped cocktails.

"What makes this race so desirable is that the Palm Beachers and those who come down from New York have a chance to mingle with the many Europeans and South Americans," said Mary Ulmann. "Here at Sebring, the beautiful people gather with many of their European friends, several titled people amongst them, and preside over the Florida 12 Hour International Grand Prix of Endurance."

Across the circuit in Green Park, college students on spring break partied, virtually oblivious to the race.

The unruly Sebring spring break tradition was really no different from the notorious crowds at Watkins Glen during the United States Grand Prix, or any other major sporting event. This aspect of Sebring, however, went uncontrolled into the 1970s and nearly led to the demise of the event.

Mark Donohue, Roger Penske and Craig Fisher celebrate their Trans-Am class win at the 1968 race.

The Penske Camaro driven by Mark Donohue and Craig Fisher makes a pit stop. They recorded an impressive third-place finish overall in 1968, and a first in the Trans-Am category.

1969

This edition of the 12 Hours of Sebring turned out to be one of the most exciting yet, with a surprising result.

Sebring was beginning what might be termed a comeback after two disappointing years. The crowd was one of the largest yet, anticipating the return of the Ferrari factory team. Porsche and Alfa Romeo also entered factory teams, all of which showed potential for an overall win. Roger Penske's Chevrolet Lola, which had won at Daytona, was also a threat. England's John Wyer entered a pair of aging Ford GT40s and James Garner entered two Chevrolet Lolas.

Chris Amon was the fastest qualifier in a Ferrari 312P, the new 3-liter prototype he would share with Mario Andretti. Penske's Lola was second fastest, followed by the Gerhard Mitter/Udo Schutz Porsche 908.

The field of 70 cars, the largest number of starters since 1955, took the starter's flag under beautiful blue skies. It was to be Sebring's last Le Mans-style start, due to safety concerns.

The Porsche 908 of Brian Redman and Jo Siffert led early, battling Mark Donohue and Ronnie Bucknum in the Penske Lola. The Alfa Romeo effort suffered a disastrous start, with all three T-33/3 entries retiring in the first hour. Another early retirement was the Lola driven by Scooter Patrick.

After the Donohue/Bucknum Lola suffered terminal mechanical problems in the fourth hour, the race quickly became a classic Porsche versus Ferrari duel. Virtually all the contenders stayed on the same lap and the pace was at a record speed. The Joe Buzzetta/Kurt Ahrens Porsche 908 and the Mitter/Schutz 908 each held the lead, but the Redman/Siffert car withdrew with suspension problems.

Several of the top Porsche entries began making extended pit stops for chassis repairs, allowing the Andretti/Amon Ferrari to take the lead. Almost unnoticed was the progress of the Jacky Ickx/Jackie Oliver Ford GT40, which had steadily moved up through the field.

With just under two hours remaining there were now four different makes in the top four positions. The lead Ferrari with Andretti

Left: Chris Amon leaps into his Ferrari at the start of the 1969 race. He co-drove with Mario Andretti to second place.

Another view of
Sebring's last Le Mans
start in 1969. The Ferrari
312P of Mario Andretti
and Chris Amon (25) is
flanked by the Lola
Chevrolet Mk III of Mark
Donohue and Ronnie
Bucknum.

driving was forced to make a pit stop
with overheating problems that had
plagued it earlier in the race. The
11-minute stop was enough to give
the Ickx/Oliver Ford the lead. The
Ferrari, with Amon now driving,
turned up the pace in an attempt to
regain the lead but Ickx responded with faster lap times himself.

To add further drama to the incredibly close race, the leading
Ford had to pit for a tire change in the final half hour, bringing the
Ferrari within 30 seconds.

The Ford's upset victory was assured when the Ferrari ran out
of gas and lost a lap coasting to the pits to refuel. John Wyer's Gulf-
sponsored Ford had pulled off a major upset, winning at a record
average speed of 103.363 MPH. The car had its engine changed the
night before the race and the team had quietly speculated the car

The 1969 winning
Jacky Ickx/Jackie Oliver
Ford GT40 heads into
the esses.

could not last the full distance. The winning Ford qualified only 12th fastest and didn't even reach the top four until the seventh hour. It was the last overall win recorded by an American car at Sebring.

Andretti and Amon finished one lap behind. Porsche took five of the next six positions with Stommelen/Buzetta/Ahrens third. The Lothar Motschenbacher/Ed Leslie Lola finished sixth after a bearing failure late in the race while running third.

Dick Smothers of the popular Smothers Brothers television show finished eighth, co-driving with Fred Baker in a Porsche 906E. The top-finishing GT car was the Chevrolet Camaro driven by Don Yenko and Bob Grossman.

The year concluded at Sebring with an SCCA Continental event in December. It was the first time Ulmann had attempted to promote a second event at Sebring since the Formula One race 10 years earlier. The race was won by David Hobbs before a sparse crowd.

The decade of the '60s was truly spectacular at Sebring, but the event's future looked uncertain.

The Corvette of Tony DeLorenzo and Jerry Thompson finished 24th in 1969.

The Ferrari team celebrates its spectacular win.

1970

Despite a broken ankle,

actor Steve McQueen

helped Peter Revson

drive a Porsche 908 to

second place behind

Mario Andretti's Ferrari

in the closest finish ever.

Just 22 seconds separated

Andretti and Revson at

the checkered flag.

Sebring's third decade opened with a spectacular race culminating in a dramatic finish. Mario Andretti and Arturo Merzario drove their Ferrari 512S to a 68-mile lead, the largest in Sebring history, only to see it suddenly disappear with transmission failure. The race then really began, and Andretti would come back to star in what is now regarded as the greatest finish in Sebring history.

The entries at Sebring in 1970 were among the finest ever. Ferrari fielded four new 512S models, looking for its first international sports car win since April 1967. Ferrari had not won at Sebring since 1964.

Porsche entered four 917s, two of which were fielded by J.W. Engineering, which had orchestrated the Ford upset at Sebring the previous year.

Alfa Romeo and Matra also brought factory-prepared entries, and the GT field was equally impressive with a huge field of Corvettes and Camaros. Smaller displacement classes were not as diverse as previous years, as emphasis by automotive manufacturers was on the "muscle cars."

With the heavy factory involvement at Sebring in 1970, the driver lineup was outstanding. Andretti, Jacky Ickx, Pedro Rodriguez, Dan Gurney, Hans Herrmann, Nino Vaccarella, Mike Parkes and Vic Elford were but a few of the many international stars on hand.

Andretti was the fastest qualifier in the number-25 Ferrari 512S, with the Porsche 917 of Brian Redman and Jo Siffert second-fastest.

A crowd of 67,000–the largest in Sebring history–gathered for what looked to be one of the finest races in years, and those who stayed until the end were not disappointed.

For reasons of safety the traditional Le Mans start had been abandoned. As drivers' restraint systems improved, it became increasingly difficult for them to buckle in securely and get underway quickly. The dash to the cars had become impractical.

Ironically, Sebring's first rolling start was nearly a disaster. The crush of fans against the fencing near the hairpin caused the fence to collapse during the pace lap, only a short distance from the edge of the circuit. Fortunately, there were no injuries and the race started on schedule.

The early stages of the race represented yet another classic Porsche versus Ferrari confrontation. An amazing 12 lead changes in the first 100 laps gave race fans a sprint-style version of endurance racing.

Attrition was particularly high due to the combination of warm and humid weather and the rough Sebring circuit. The concrete runway sections of the circuit had deteriorated over the years and the asphalt sections were both rough and narrow. Sixteen cars dropped out in the first two hours, and by the halfway mark 11 more had retired, including two Porsche 917s and two Ferrari 512S entries.

When the Ickx/Peter Schetty Ferrari retired in the eighth hour with engine failure, the Andretti/Merzario car took a commanding lead. The Redman/Siffert Porsche retired with suspension problems, giving the Ferrari team a huge cushion over the nearest Porsche.

Andretti and Merzario eventually built a 13-lap lead, with the next positions occupied by the Ignazio Giunti/Vaccarella Ferrari 512S and the Leo Kinnunen/Rodriguez Porsche 917. An interesting battle ensued further back with the Porsche 908 driven by Peter Revson and actor Steve McQueen (driving with a cast on his leg) moving steadily up to fourth.

On its 227th lap, disaster struck the Ferrari team when their lead car retired with a broken transmission. The Rodriguez/Kinnunen Porsche 917 (with Siffert now joining them) inherited the lead, followed by the Giunti/Vaccarella Ferrari.

The Ferrari team manager decided to put Andretti in the Giunti/Vaccarella Ferrari with 55 minutes remaining. During the Ferrari's pit stop, the McQueen/Revson Porsche 908 moved into second, setting the stage for a spectacular finish.

With less than 20 minutes remaining, the leading Porsche 917 was forced to pit with suspension problems, giving the lead to the under-powered but persistent Porsche 908 with Revson driving.

The crowd went wild over the 3-liter Porsche with its celebrity drivers on the verge of an incredible upset. Revson, the heir to the Revlon cosmetic fortune, was certainly an accomplished driver, but he could not match the speed the Ferrari 512S was capable of, especially with Andretti at the wheel.

Andretti quickly passed Revson and took the lead, but the Ferrari was running dangerously low on fuel and he would have to stop in the final three minutes for a quick splash in order to finish the race. Andretti brought the Ferrari in the pits and quickly returned to the race, only seconds ahead of Revson. He won

The winning Ferrari

512S, driven by Ignazio

Giunti, Nino Vaccarella

and Mario Andretti,

makes a late pit stop.

by a margin of 22.1 seconds, the closest finish ever at the 12 Hours of Sebring.

Andretti was mobbed by his team as he pulled into victory lane. Revson and McQueen (on crutches) were also congratulated for their incredible drive to second place. Their crew had not changed a tire or brake pad on their Porsche during the entire race.

The trio of Andretti, Giunti and Vaccarella averaged 107.029 MPH, breaking the race record and ending Ferrari's six-year winless streak at Sebring.

Andretti would later describe the win as perhaps the most rewarding race of his career. "I guarantee you I never drove so hard in my life. McQueen did a good job but Peter [Revson] was fantastic. It was a balls-out race right from the start and you got to give Nino [Vaccarella] and Giunti lots of credit. They kept the car up there and I drove it for 55 minutes."

Ted West described the postrace scene in *Sports Car Graphic:* "What a beautiful celebration there was, with everyone delighted, the entire Ferrari crowd gone mad, Giunti laughing and joking, fine Nino Vaccarella kissing Mario and crying great Italian tears like the grand man he is, and Mario lifting the huge bottle of champers high over his head for the crowd and looking happier than I have ever seen him look!"

The Masten Gregory/Toine Hezemans Alfa Romeo T33-3 recorded third place, while the Rodriguez/Kinnunen/Siffert Porsche 917 was fourth. The Matra-Simca 650 driven by Henri Pescarolo and Johnny Servoz-Gavin finished fifth, and the NART-entered Ferrari 312P of Mike Parkes and Chuck Parsons was sixth.

Tony DeLorenzo and Dick Lang drove a Chevrolet Corvette to 10th overall and first in the GT class, with Peter Gregg and Pete Harrison winning the under-2-liter GT category in a Porsche 911.

Sebring 1970 was truly a historical event, and Ulmann again proved his race was still the most important sports car race in America. But it also marked the beginning of the end as the FIA gave Ulmann just one more year to upgrade the aging facility.

In December 1970, Ulmann promoted another SCCA Continental series race. Won by Mark Donohue, the race was again a financial failure and Ulmann would never again attempt to promote a race at Sebring other than the traditional 12-hour classic.

Peter Revson and actor Steve McQueen drove this Porsche 908 to a surprising second place finish in 1970.

1971

It was generally acknowledged that 1971 was likely to be the last 12 Hours of Sebring.

Despite the fabulous success of the 1970 race, the Sebring circuit was simply out of date, barely meeting FIA standards. Adding to the doubtful future of the race was the Federal Aviation Administration (FAA), which decreed that beginning in 1972 the active airport runways could no longer be shut down for the race. That meant either massive changes to the airport/industrial park circuit had to be made, or a completely new track had to be built elsewhere.

Since Ulmann leased the track from the Sebring Airport Authority, he had little incentive to finance massive improvements on property he didn't own and for a sport that was encountering numerous problems.

Sports car racing had changed dramatically over the 20 years since Ulmann first founded racing at Sebring. European manufacturers were beginning to take a closer look at the incredible cost of fielding factory teams and the huge expense of sending them to Sebring and other overseas circuits. Many top sports car drivers were going on to Indianapolis cars or other forms of racing, and the public was beginning to take more interest in oval track racing in general and NASCAR stock car racing in particular.

Ulmann had a huge following of corporate sponsors who had subsidized his event over the years, but they too were beginning to spread out their budgets in other forms of racing, and even other sports.

Porsche and Ferrari were again set to do battle at Sebring in 1971, resuming their often bitter battle for the Manufacturers Championship. Alfa Romeo was now a serious contender, making it a three-way battle for the overall win at the 20th annual Sebring 12-hour classic.

Two-time winner Mario Andretti returned to Sebring, again driving for Ferrari, this time in a 312PB teamed with Jacky Ickx. This was the lone factory entry, although there were several independent Ferrari teams, including Mark Donohue and David Hobbs in a Penske-prepared 512M.

The GT field was again strong at Sebring, though heavily slanted toward Chevrolet with 18 Corvettes and Camaros in the starting field.

Mark Donohue won the pole position with a speed of 123.440 MPH, setting a new record on the 5.2-mile circuit, one of the world's fastest road courses. The crowd, perhaps sensing this could be their last chance to see racing at Sebring, turned out in record numbers.

Left: The 1971 winning Porsche 917 driven by Vic Elford and Gerard Larrousse heads toward the esses. Note the poor condition of the track surface.

"Sebring's gate successes culminated this year," wrote Joe Whitlock in *Sports Car Graphic*. "Traffic was backed for four miles at the gate when Florida Governor Reubin Askew waved the starting flag... Sebring, despite becoming a magnificent montage that nobody seems to be able to bring into focus, epitomizes purism in sports car racing in this country... The final go on the old Sebring course shaped up beautifully."

The race showed some similarities to the previous year, including very high attrition. Fifteen of the 57 starters failed to make it to the halfway point.

Donohue and co-driver Hobbs led the first hour, challenged by the Porsche 917K of Derek Bell and Jo Siffert. After taking the lead, Siffert ran out of fuel and was then penalized four laps for accepting a ride back to the pits on a spectator's motorcycle to retrieve fuel.

By the third hour the Andretti/Ickx Ferrari had taken the lead. Pedro Rodriguez and Jackie Oliver led briefly in their Porsche 917K and now were battling the Donohue/Hobbs Ferrari for second.

After the four-hour mark, Rodriguez and Donohue collided in a controversial incident that Donohue claimed was intentional. Both cars were forced to make lengthy pit stops for repairs, putting them out of contention for the win.

Building a three-lap lead, the Andretti/Ickx Ferrari retired on the 117th lap with a seized gearbox. This gave the lead to the Alfa Romeo T33 driven by Nani Galli and Rolf Stommelen, with the Porsche 917 of Vic Elford and Gerard Larrousse now in second place. But time was on the side of the more powerful Porsche.

Elford and Larrousse chased down the Alfa Romeo and pulled away to a three-lap margin by the end of the 12 hours, giving Porsche its first victory at Sebring since 1968.

Alfa Romeo took the next two positions, followed by both J.W. Engineering 917Ks and the Donohue/Hobbs Ferrari, which had battled

back gallantly after spending an hour in the pits for repairs.

John Greenwood and Dick Smothers finished seventh overall and first in the GT category aboard their Chevrolet Corvette. They were followed by the Ferrari 312P driven by Luigi Chinetti, Jr. and George Eaton. Finishing ninth overall and first in the under-2-liter GT category was the Porsche 911T of Bert Everett and James Locke.

After the race Ulmann announced a plan to build a new circuit, but he still had to find the financing. Selling stock was one possibility, but time was running out. While the FIA told Ulmann that he might be given a one-year extension, most journalists were convinced this was the end.

Whitlock added in his *Sports Car Graphic* article: "Ulmann seems to think a new layout could employ the same pit area and more than likely turn out to be a better Sebring. It's probably just as well. The OLD Sebring is old and pocket-marked. Windstripped and faded. Resigned to menopause."

Jeff Scott echoed those thoughts in *Auto Racing*: "...it appears America's most renowned sports car track will not offer again the world's finest international competition...It's a sad thought. Like saying goodbye to a temperamental but remarkably talented old friend...It would be pathetic to see this classic but demanding track fade into the scrapbooks."

Actor James Garner talks with driver Mark Donohue before the 1971 race. Donohue finished sixth in a Ferrari 512M and went on to win the Indianapolis 500 the following year.

The obituary had already been written in virtually every international motor sports publication: After two decades of promoting America's premier sports car race, Alec Ulmann decided 1972 *really* was the final 12 Hours of Sebring.

Because Ulmann had not been able to improve the Sebring facilities to the satisfaction of the FIA, he was notified that the race would not be on the 1973 FIA international calendar. It was a testament to his skill in motorsports politics that the race had survived as long as it had; the FIA had been threatening to drop it since 1969. Although there was still talk of a new circuit being built, Ulmann knew it was not to be. Though many agreed that it was time to abandon the old Sebring course, everyone respected this tough track, for it was a true test of endurance.

Sebring was an institution in American racing. Drivers, teams, officials and race fans had developed a love-hate relationship with the event. The facility simply had not kept up to international standards, and the town of Sebring could not accommodate the increasingly larger crowds. But they kept coming back every year.

Ironically, Daytona International Speedway canceled its plans for a 24-hour race in 1972, running instead a six-hour event as strongly urged by the FIA. Daytona's sports car races still had not attracted the fans or international interest that Bill France had hoped, and rumors circulated that Daytona would abandon sports car racing.

Alec and Mary Ulmann went about the business of promoting their last event as if it were just another year, though there was much sadness knowing it was the end of a glorious era of American sports history.

A fine field of cars turned out for Sebring's farewell, as did the huge contingent of national and international journalists.

Ferrari was the overwhelming favorite in 1972. Alfa Romeo entered four cars, but there was no Porsche factory effort. It was the last official appearance by Ferrari at Sebring for 23 years. In the future, the legendary Italian manufacturer would concentrate on Formula One racing.

Left: The Ferrari 312PB driven by Ronnie Peterson and Tim Schenken leads the starting field through the chicane on the pace lap. On the right is the Alfa Romeo T33 of Rolf Stomelen / Peter Revson / Andrea de Adamich (31)

Mario Andretti was the fastest qualifier for the third time of his career at Sebring, driving a Ferrari 312PB he would share with Jacky Ickx.

Andretti and Ickx led the first 63 laps before teammates Brian Redman and Clay Regazzoni took the lead in another 312PB. Ronnie Peterson and Tim Schenken were running third in the other factory Ferrari. Meanwhile, three of the four Alfa Romeo entries had dropped out with mechanical problems before the halfway mark.

By the ninth hour, the three factory Ferraris built a 10-lap margin over the lone remaining Alfa Romeo of Toine Hezemans and Nino Vaccarella. The race so far had proven to be somewhat uneventful, with the exception of an incident involving hot-tempered Peter Revson, who was disqualified for unsportsmanlike conduct while driving a factory Alfa Romeo. Revson was accused of passing under a yellow flag, making an obscene gesture and flipping the hat off race official Charles Earwood. Revson appealed the decision, but his disqualification was upheld.

With two hours remaining, the leading Ferrari caught fire due to an electrical short. Regazzoni abandoned the blazing car on course, where it was destroyed by the fire. The Andretti/Ickx Ferrari then took the lead and despite a severe oil leak managed a two-lap margin

The Ferrari 365GTB4 driven by Luigi Chinetti, Jr. and Bob Grossman to an eighth-place in 1972.

Sebring founder Alec Ulmann (l) and famed racing journalist Chris Economaki talk during a practice session in 1972.

of victory over Peterson and Schenken. The Hezemans/Vaccarella Alfa Romeo finished 24 laps behind in third.

Andretti became Sebring's third three-time winner, joining Olivier Gendebien and Phil Hill. Ickx became a two-time Sebring champion and helped Ferrari take its ninth overall win.

Dave Heinz and Bob Johnson drove a Chevrolet Corvette to fourth overall and first in the GTO category. Floridians Peter Gregg and Hurley Haywood finished fifth, winning GTU. The Camaro driven by Vince Gimondo and Bill Dingman claimed a class win, as did a Chevron driven by Robert Fisher and Bruce Ponder.

Many not-so-flattering tributes appeared after the race. ABC television broadcast a documentary titled *Requiem for a Racetrack—The Last 12 Hours of Sebring*, in which narrator Jackie Stewart blasted the safety conditions of the circuit. In reality, only one driver fatality could even remotely be blamed on the track in over 20 years of racing—a record no other international road racing circuit could claim.

Sports Illustrated, which covered the race religiously during the 1950s and early '60s, returned to do its obituary on the race, as did many other publications.

Although their era had ended on somewhat of a sour note, Alec and Mary Ulmann made significant and lasting contributions to sports car competition. Bringing professional international sports car competition to the United States, then introducing Formula One, certainly were major accomplishments. More than anyone in American racing history, Alec Ulmann realized the significance of international competition. His ability to promote brought international recognition to the remote town of Sebring and made sports car racing a major league sport.

The Ulmanns made Sebring a magic name in auto racing. Daytona's Bill France, Sr. tried to duplicate Sebring's sports car success, but achieved only disappointment. To this day, Sebring remains the pinnacle of American sports car racing, but it will always lack the international flavor that only Alec and Mary Ulmann could orchestrate.

The Ulmanns left Sebring a few days after the 1972 race, and the ARCF was officially dissolved. Sebring was dead...or was it?

The field for the last Sebring race that was promoted by Alec Ulmann and sanctioned by the FIA begins the pace lap.

1973

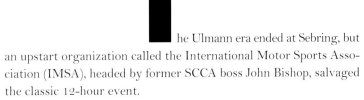

The Ulmann era ended at Sebring, but an upstart organization called the International Motor Sports Association (IMSA), headed by former SCCA boss John Bishop, salvaged the classic 12-hour event.

The timing was perfect. Sanctioning Sebring would be a major coup for IMSA toward international recognition of its GT sports car racing series. Ulmann's right-hand man for two decades, Reggie Smith, was enlisted to help promote the race, forming SARA (Sebring Auto Racing Association) to replace the now-retired ARCF organization.

These events occurred in only a few weeks in late 1972. Scheduled as part of the IMSA Camel GT series and not an FIA World Championship event of international stature, the 12 Hours of Sebring was nevertheless saved and a new era was on the horizon.

The first IMSA-sanctioned 12 Hours of Sebring was a far cry from the Ulmann era. Gone were the international teams, drivers, celebrities, sponsors and journalists. The crowd was less than half the size of the previous year's.

"I wish them all the luck, but Sebring will never be Sebring again," said Ulmann. Many years later he would return to Sebring with a far different perspective.

The entire event was more informal, but no less competitive than previous years. In retrospect, the 1973 race was one of the finest gatherings of GT production race cars ever in North America. Entries totaled the second largest ever at Sebring.

Tony DeLorenzo won the pole position in a Chevrolet Corvette at a speed nearly 18 MPH slower than the previous year's speed by a Ferrari prototype. There were over a dozen cars easily capable of winning, however, and those in attendance were pleased with a return to cars that spectators could readily identify with.

Peter Gregg and Hurley Haywood, winners at Daytona's revived 24-hour race in February, came to Sebring in a brand-new Porsche Carrera RSR that was delivered to Dave Helmick the week before

Left: Hurley Haywood

(arms raised) and Peter

Gregg celebrate their

win at the 1973 12

Hours of Sebring.

the race. Another Carrera with Milt Minter and Mike Keyser driving also looked to be a contender. A huge field of Chevrolet Corvettes and Camaros, Ford Mustangs and Porsche 911s promised plenty of close racing.

The early stages of the race featured a battle between the DeLorenzo/Steve Durst Corvette and another Corvette driven by Sebring veterans Jerry Thompson and Dave Heinz. The pace proved too much for the American muscle cars, however, and the Gregg/Haywood Porsche took the lead on lap 86.

Fighting off a challenge from the Keyser/Minter Porsche late in the race, Gregg, Haywood and Helmick drove to a one-lap victory, ushering in a new era of sports car racing at Sebring. Both Gregg and Haywood would go on to become international road racing legends.

Following the second place Minter/Keyser Porsche was the Ron Grable/John Greenwood/Mike Brockman Corvette and another Porsche Carrera driven by Elliott Forbes-Robinson and Gray Egerton.

The GTU class win went to the Porsche 911S driven by Steve Behr, Don Lindley and Brian Goellnicht.

The winning team averaged 97.854 MPH and earned a modest $8,150 in prize money. Of the 72 starters, 41 cars managed to finish.

The general media all but ignored the running of the 1973 12 Hours of Sebring, citing the lack of famous names in the race. What they didn't consider was that Sebring had taken that difficult first step on the way back to international recognition.

Sebring's race had survived many a crisis over the years, but it could not overcome the circumstances of world politics that consumed America in early 1974. The OPEC oil embargo and ensuing fuel shortage forced cancellation of the 12 Hours of Sebring, and it seemed

Sebring's famous sunset serves as a backdrop for this 1973 photo.

The second-place Porsche Carrera RSR driven by Milt Minter and Michael Keyser lifts a wheel exiting the hairpin.

that endurance racing had suddenly become a frivolous sport that could never justify its existence in a nation dealing with a fuel shortage emergency.

When the first signs of a fuel shortage appeared, Sebring and IMSA officials proposed shortening the race to 1,200 kilometers as a token means of conserving fuel (Daytona had canceled its 24-hour race). Objections then came from the local community. Residents of Highlands County feared race fans would come to town and use up the region's fuel allocations (even though the allocations factored in the arrival of the race crowd). The decision was made to cancel the race.

On the third weekend in March 1974, about 2,000 race fans showed up anyway. The Sebring tradition simply would not die.

This Porsche Carrera RSR driven by Gray Egerton and Elliott Forbes-Robinson finished fourth in 1973.

With the fuel crisis subsiding, Sebring returned to the IMSA schedule in 1975. The track, however, was in a terrible state of disrepair. The neglect of the past two years had added to the already poor conditions.

The asphalt portion was rough and covered with potholes. The pit structure was dirty and dilapidated, and the MG bridge had fallen down with only the stairway supports remaining. Abandoned airplanes parked at the airport circuit for future salvage were strewn around the spectator area. Fencing was falling down, and there were virtually no restroom facilities. It was an eerie sight to see this famous venue in such disrepair, resembling the Indianapolis Motor Speedway in 1945 after years of inactivity during World War II.

Stirling Moss helped produce a documentary on the history of Sebring in 1974. Titled *Sebring—The Glory Years*, the film gave a brief history of the circuit and included an interview with Alec Ulmann.

Veteran Corvette racer John Greenwood took over promotion of the race, but not before last-minute legal maneuvering with a partner (who was to have promoted a huge rock concert at the same time). The FAA was also imposing strict regulations on the use of the airport runways, and a long-term solution had yet to be reached.

The Sebring entry list was highlighted by the appearance of the BMW factory team and a NART-entered Ferrari Boxer. Of course, there was a plethora of Porsches and Corvettes. So many entries flooded the IMSA headquarters that a special qualifying race was added to the schedule to keep the starting field to a reasonable number of starters.

The variety of production cars entered was certainly a plus. IMSA race fans wanted to see cars compete that were the same as they drove to the track. Despite the absence of an event the prior year, the crowd was larger than in 1973, an encouraging sign. And when the crowd arrived, it started to look like the same old Sebring. As Bruce Czaja wrote in *AutoWeek:* "Suddenly, as if nothing had changed, it was the Sebring of old...The pits and paddock were filled beyond

Left: The winning BMW CSL makes a pit stop late in the 1975 race. At the last minute Ronnie Peterson was forbidden to race at Sebring by the FIA, so Allan Moffat substituted for him. Peterson's name remained on the car's door.

The BMW factory team dominated Sebring in 1975. Hans Stuck and Sam Posey led early in this car, while its sister car eventually won the race.

capacity, the midway and its many attractions was going full force to add to the carnival atmosphere and the college students were out in droves to enjoy their time in the sun...Once again it was Sebring, in all her glory."

The BMW team featured two CSL models for drivers Hans Stuck, Sam Posey, Brian Redman and Allan Moffat (replacing Ronnie Peterson, who was not allowed to participate by the FIA, although his name remained on the side of the car).

The BMW strategy was to send out one car as a rabbit, forcing the Corvettes and Porsches to keep pace and then hopefully break. The second car, running a more conservative pace, would then take the win. This strategy, devised by team manager Jochen Neerspasch, was hardly novel, but it worked exactly as planned.

Hans Stuck won the pole position and Peter Gregg qualified the Porsche Carrera he would share with Hurley Haywood to the second grid position.

The "Spirit of Sebring Corvette" driven by promoter Greenwood and Jerry Thompson took the lead early, then the Stuck/Posey BMW took the lead. As planned, they drove at an all-out pace. By the fourth hour, both the Greenwood Corvette and the Gregg/Haywood Porsche (damaged in an accident with an errant Corvette) had retired.

Redman and Moffat took their BMW into the lead on lap 68, and shortly after the halfway point, the Stuck/Posey BMW retired. Three laps ahead of the George Dyer/Jacques Bienvenue Porsche Carrera, the leading BMW was comfortably headed for the German manufacturer's first major international win. Posey and Stuck each drove a stint in the eventual winner, and all four factory drivers celebrated the win.

The Dyer/Bienvenue Porsche finished second and another Carrera, driven by John Graves, John O'Steen and Dave Helmick, took third. Milt Minter and Eppie Wietzes managed sixth in their Ferrari BB512, while Alberto Naon, Tony Garcia and John Freyre won the GTU class in a Porsche 911S. It was a tough race on equipment, and fewer than half of the 69 starters managed to finish.

Porsches occupied 14 of the top 17 positions, but BMW captured the headlines with its impressive win. More important, Sebring proved once again that it was still the biggest sports car race in America.

The Ferrari Boxer driven to sixth place at Sebring in 1975 by Milt Minter and Eppie Wietzes.

1976

Preparing for the start of the 1976 race. Al Holbert and Michael Keyser drove this Porsche Carrera RSR to a two-lap victory margin.

It looked to be another battle between Porsche, Corvette and BMW at Sebring in 1976. Few changes had been made to the aging circuit, and the race still was not recognized by the FIA as an international event. Still, Sebring was the premier event on the IMSA schedule, and a huge entry was received for the race.

As it had in the early years, Sebring also attracted an odd assortment of entries. Part-time amateur racers had a good chance to make the starting grid, and models such as the BMW 2002, Mazda RX-2, Datsun 240Z, Volkswagen Scirocco, MGB, Pontiac Astre and Austin Marina would be competing with the likes of Pantera, Lotus Elan, Porsche Carrera, BMW CSL and Chevrolet Corvette.

Promoter John Greenwood led the qualifying by setting a new track record in his "Spirit of Sebring '76" Corvette. The favorites, however, were the two BMW CSL factory cars entered for drivers Hurley Haywood, Peter Gregg, David Hobbs and NASCAR star Benny Parsons.

Porsche had strength in numbers with a huge contingent of entries, the fastest of which was the Carrera of Michael Keyser and Al Holbert, son of Bob Holbert, who had recorded five class wins at Sebring during the 1960s.

With another large crowd on hand, Greenwood led the first 15 laps of the race, after which the Hobbs/Parsons BMW took the lead. They held the lead until the 63rd lap, when the Holbert/Keyser Porsche moved in front with Keyser at the wheel. Only a few minutes later, Keyser was hit from behind in the hairpin and a pit stop to repair damaged exhaust pipes was necessary, dropping them three laps behind the new leader, the Porsche Carrera driven by Jim Busby and Carl Shafer.

The Busby/Shafer Porsche led past the midway point, building a lead of more than a lap, but then lost a wheel on course. Repairs were made but they fell out of contention. The Bob Hagestad/Jerry Jolly Porsche became the fifth new leader of the race, holding the lead for nearly two hours until an electrical problem handed the lead back to the Holbert/Keyser Porsche, which had battled back from its earlier deficit.

With the BMW team now out of contention, and the remainder of the top Porsche teams hindered by earlier mechanical problems,

The number-61 Brumos entry of Jim Busby and Carl Shafer battling the Carrera driven by Roberto Quintanilla and Roberto Gonzalez. They went on to finish eighth and third, respectively. Porsche would dominate Sebring for several years, with the durable Carrera providing many wins.

the Holbert/Keyser Porsche Carrera won with a two-lap margin over John Gunn and Carson Baird in another Porsche Carrera. Roberto Quintanilla teamed with Roberto Gonzalez to take fourth followed by the Hagestad/Jolly entry.

Porsche dominated with the seventh place Gregg/Haywood BMW as the lone non-Porsche in the top 15. Florida State Senator David McClain won the GTU class co-driving a Porsche 911S with Dave White.

Holbert and Keyser averaged 99.667 MPH on the way to the victory.

Although big names won the race, this period in Sebring's history had become the era of the weekend warrior. A totally stock Mazda Cosmo was driven all the way from New Jersey, finishing the 12 hours with Tom Davey and Tom Reddy driving, then drove back home the next day. Thrill show stunt driver Tim Chitwood joined Vince Gimondo for a 16th-place finish in a Camaro.

Sebring was another box office success in 1976, but crowd control again became a major problem. A small portion of the crowd was unruly and sometimes destructive. Alcohol and drug use added to the problem. College students on spring break and motorcycle gangs traveling south from their traditional week in Daytona combined to make Sebring a party of incredible proportions. The thousands of fans with their campfires and cookouts caused a thick layer of smoke to blanket the raceway, adding to the rather bizarre sights and sounds that made Sebring famous—and infamous.

Start of the 1976

12 Hours of Sebring.

PADDOCK ADMISSION
ADMIT ONE | **Complimentary**
MARCH 17 thru 19, 1977
SEBRING '77
IMSA - 12 HOUR CAMEL G. T. CHALLENGE RACE
A JOHN GREENWOOD RACE COURSE, INC. PROMOTION
00612

Although this race marked the 25th anniversary of the 12-hour classic, Sebring reached the low point in its history. The circuit was in worse condition than ever and the quality of entries was its poorest.

Promoter John Greenwood had announced a plan to build a new circuit on property a few miles from the current location. It would include an oval track and drag strip, and construction was to start as soon as financing was in place. This attempt at building a new circuit, like those proposed by Ulmann five years earlier, would never materialize.

The die-hard road racing fans continued to come to Sebring every spring because it was clearly the most important sports car race in America, yet sports car racing was rapidly losing out in popularity to NASCAR, and to a lesser extent Indy car racing.

In 1977, the Porsche-dominated field was led in qualifying by the new turbocharged Porsche 934 driven by Peter Gregg and Jim Busby. The Interscope Racing Porsche 934 of Danny Ongais, Hurley Haywood and Ted Field qualified second fastest, followed by the Greenwood Corvette.

The Chevrolet Monza of Jim Trueman, teamed with veterans Don Yenko and Jerry Thompson, qualified sixth while the Ferrari Daytona of John Morton and actor Bobby Carradine qualified 10th. There were few other non-Porsche contenders.

A total of 72 cars started the race under beautiful Florida skies. As usual, the tough Sebring circuit took its toll early, with 18 cars retiring in the first three hours.

The first eight hours of the race were dominated by the Gregg/Busby Porsche, which built a five-lap lead and looked invincible. Following a routine pit stop, however, the leading Porsche lost a wheel and Gregg slowly guided it back to the pits. Damage to the oil cooler and suspension forced a prolonged stop, giving the lead to the Porsche Carrera RSR of George Dyer and Brad Frisselle.

Gregg and Busby returned to the race after repairs and began a strong run to recapture the lead. Another flat tire and other minor mechanical problems, however, ended any hopes of catching the Dyer/Frisselle team.

The race concluded with Dyer and Frisselle five laps ahead of Diego Febles and Hiram Cruz in another Porsche Carrera, which had fought its way

Diego Febles and Hiram Cruz piloted this Porsche Carrera to second place in 1977.

from the 11th starting position to second place. The Busby/Gregg 934 managed third, one lap ahead of Gary Belcher and John Gunn in a Porsche 934.

The Porsche 911S of Fritz Hochreuter, Gerhard Hirsch and Rainer Brezinka won the GTU class, just ahead of another 911S driven by Ray Mummery, Jack Refenning and Joe Hamilton.

Porsche swept the top 11 overall positions and the top seven positions in the GTU class. Endurance racing had become somewhat lackluster as no other make could come close to matching the reliability of Porsche.

Crowd control, always a concern at Sebring during the 1970s, became a major issue in the media. No longer just a "fun-loving party crowd" in the spirit of the 1960s, the unruly Green Park section had become even more infamous than Watkins Glen's "Bog" and the "Snake Pit" at Indianapolis. Local law enforcement officials could hardly control the situation. A notorious adult magazine published a pictorial on the happenings off the track at Sebring, adding to the community outrage.

Meanwhile, competitors were demanding improved safety features and the FAA was pressuring the Sebring Airport Authority to rule on the use of the airport runways. There was yet again speculation in the racing industry that Sebring had run its last race.

John Greenwood became increasingly frustrated by the many obstacles in promoting the 12 Hours of Sebring. It must be remembered that the raceway was not a year-round racing facility at the time, and the Sebring Airport Authority managed the property for most of the year. It was therefore logical that promoters were reluctant to make significant improvements to a facility they could utilize for only a few days during the year.

Jim Busby and Peter Gregg drove this Porsche 934 to third place in 1977.

1978

Sebring promoter

Charles Mendez

(center) celebrates his

1978 victory with Brian

Redman (right) and Bob

Garretson (left). Their

Porsche 935 beat the

935 driven by Hurley

Haywood and Bob

Hagestad by 92 seconds.

A new promoter arrived on the scene at Sebring in 1978. Tampa businessman and race car driver Charles Mendez formed Sebring Motorsports, Inc., to take over promotion of the race after lengthy negotiations with the Sebring Airport Authority.

Mendez immediately embarked on an improvement program that brought the circuit back to FIA standards. New paving, safety barriers and other measures made the aging raceway much cleaner and safer. Also on the new promoter's staff was David Cowart, another veteran competitor who greatly contributed to Sebring's revival.

Mendez increased involvement with the local community, improving relations that had been strained during the Greenwood era.

"One would think, with literally hundreds of thousands of dollars being poured into the economy of a town as small as Sebring in a week's time, that the race would be welcomed with open arms," wrote Mark Yeager in *Formula* magazine. "Not so in Florida, not until this year, at least. As an example of just how far the attitude changes reached, the majority of the Florida Highway Patrol and Sheriff's deputies hired for crowd control were actually courteous to people this year. Some of them were actually observed smiling—a complete turnaround from their apparent Gestapo attitude of previous years."

Mendez and his Sebring Motorsports, Inc. brought Coca-Cola in as a title sponsor, and corporate involvement grew steadily in the ensuing years. Increased advertising and promotion of the event resulted in the largest crowd since the Ulmann era.

The field of entries improved greatly as well, with more internationally known drivers appearing due to the establishment of the new World Challenge for Endurance Drivers. This new championship included several major international sports car races such as Sebring and Le Mans. It also helped produce a wider variety of makes and models. While the race was still a Porsche-dominated field, the 1978 race was the beginning of a remarkable resurgence for the famous circuit.

The new Porsche 935 made its first appearance at Sebring with eight entries, six of which qualified in the top 10. The 935 would eventually surpass the Ferrari 250TR as the most dominant endurance racing car in Sebring history.

The McLaren BMW 320i team took the pole position in qualifying and David Hobbs set a new track record, an astounding 8 MPH faster than the existing record. The Bob Hagestad/Hurley Haywood Porsche 935 was third on the grid while the Dick Barbour Racing team qualified both their 935s in the top five. Peter Gregg qualified

the Brumos Porsche 935 fourth fastest.

A total of 76 cars started Sebring in 1978. Although the McLaren BMW led the first lap, the remainder of the race would be a battle between three Porsche 935s. Early retirements included Peter Gregg, who ended upside down on top of a dirt embankment on the 11th lap. The Dick Barbour/Rolf Stommelen/Manfred Schurti Porsche 935 withdrew with suspension problems early, as did the fastest qualifying Corvette, driven by Dave Heinz, Michael Keyser and R.V. Shulnburg. Ludwig Heimrath's Porsche 935 retired with a blown engine after just five laps.

The Hagestad/Haywood Porsche led most of the first six hours, although the Hal Shaw, Jr./Tom Spalding Porsche 935 was close behind. Also in contention was the surviving Dick Barbour entry driven by promoter Mendez with Brian Redman and Bob Garretson. Redman was making his first start since a terrible accident the previous year in a Can-Am race. Garretson, meanwhile, hadn't driven in a major race in over 10 years. This odd trio of drivers would take the lead on lap 154 when the Haywood/Hagestad Porsche had to pit with a broken brake caliper.

After the brake repairs, the Haywood/Hagestad Porsche gave a furious chase and nearly caught the Barbour team, but a turbocharger failure again set them back. From there, Redman, Mendez and Garretson managed to hold off the Hagestad/Haywood Porsche to score the upset win by a margin of just 92 seconds. The Shaw/Spalding Porsche finished third, giving the new Porsche 935 a clean sweep of the top three.

John Paul, Sr. and Bonky Fernandez won the GTO class in a Porsche Carrera and the GTU category was won by Francisco Romero and Ernesto Soto driving a Porsche 911. The eighth-place BMW CSL of Walt Bohren and Kenper Miller was the highest finishing non-Porsche, while a Buick Skylark driven by veterans Gene Felton and Vince Gimondo finished ninth, first in the new American Challenge category.

Mendez had brought new life to Sebring and won his own race in the process. The coming years would show a steady climb back to international prominence for the 12 Hours of Sebring.

Road-racing legend Peter Gregg rolled his Porsche 935 early in the 1978 race. He is shown here being helped out of the car by SCCA corner workers.

1979

12 HRS. Sebring 1979

The tumultuous decade of the '70s ended at Sebring with yet another Porsche parade.

There was little doubt regarding the outcome as 46 of the 72 Sebring starters were Porsches, and Porsche 935s occupied the top 11 starting positions. The fastest qualifier was Rolf Stommelen in one of the three Dick Barbour Racing entries. His co-drivers were Barbour and Rick Mears, who two months later would score the first of his four Indianapolis 500 wins.

Another large crowd was on hand for the 27th running of the 12 Hours of Sebring. The Swap Shop Porsche 935 driven by car owner Preston Henn and former winners Peter Gregg and Hurley Haywood led for most of the first two hours. Al Holbert and John Paul, Sr. then took the lead, which they would hold until the eighth hour when transmission failure handed the lead to the Porsche 935 driven by Bob Akin, Rob McFarlin and Roy Woods, who started from the ninth position and ran a steady pace throughout the day.

The Charles Mendez/Brian Redman/Paul Miller entry was rapidly moving through the field after brake problems earlier in the race had dropped their Porsche back to 54th position. They eventually moved into second, only a lap behind Akin/McFarlin/Woods, but simply ran out of time.

The Akin/McFarlin/Woods Porsche 935 averaged 103.446 MPH, slightly slower than the previous year's winner.

Bob Garretson, Gary Belcher and Bob Bondurant finished third, followed by the pole-winning Porsche of Barbour/Stommelen/Mears.

The Porsche Carrera driven by Bonky Fernandez, Tato Ferrer and Chiqui Soldevila won the GTO class. Rusty Bond and Ren Tilton scored the GTU class win in a Porsche 911. The new Mazda RX-7, which had been so successful in its debut at Daytona, was not competitive at Sebring due to a huge weight penalty imposed by IMSA.

The all-female driving team of Janet Guthrie, Bonnie Henn and Lyn St. James managed a 17th place finish in the only Ferrari entered in the race and one of only three non-Porsches in the top 20.

The Porsche domination was complete, taking a sweep of the top 10 for the second time in three years. Three of the top four finishers were Porsches owned by Dick Barbour.

While other tracks, including Daytona, were having trouble attracting race fans for sports car races, Sebring was flourishing. As Tom Kowaleski wrote in *Road & Track:* "Going to Sebring is a bit like reading an old magazine. At first glance you're struck with a wealth of memories. The more you look the more you remember.

The Porsche 935 driven by Charles Mendez / Brian Redman / Paul Miller (94) takes the inside line entering turn one at the beginning of the 1979 race. It finished in second place. The Whittington brothers 935 (5) is on the left.

Déjá vu. And soon you begin to think, 'Those were the good old days, weren't they?'

"That's Sebring all right. With the exception of relocating the chicane in 1967, the 5.2–mile course is exactly as it was 27 years ago when Alec Ulmann's dream became reality. A new coat of paint and a new sponsor's name on the main tower and pit buildings may have freshened appearances somewhat, but grass still grows in the cracks of the wide, flat airport runways that Cunningham, Moss, Fangio and Hill did battle on. The World War II airport terminal and tower continue to stand as if frozen in time, so much so that you expect to see a squad of leather-helmeted pilots rush out to their planes at any moment. And Sebring, after all these years, is still a happening—a mid-March gathering in warm Florida sun for avid race fans, college students on break and a rag-tag collection of party people who wouldn't know a Porsche Turbo from a Porsche Speedster. Sebring is indeed a place to come back to, to relive the grand old days."

The Bob Garretson/ Gary Belcher/Bob Bondurant Porsche 935 heads down one of Sebring's long airport straights during the 1979 race. The car finished in third place.

1980

This Porsche 935 was driven by Bobby Rahal, Bob Garretson and Kees Nierop to seventh place in 1980.

The best field of cars and drivers in nearly 10 years was on hand at Sebring in 1980. Although Porsche was again an overwhelming favorite, a variety of cars made for some interesting competition, especially in the GTO and GTU classes. And there was promise of even more variety in the future as IMSA announced that the Grand Touring Prototype class (GTP) would return beginning in 1981.

John Fitzpatrick set a new track record in winning the pole position, qualifying at a speed of 121.517 MPH in a Barbour Racing Porsche 935 K3. The 935s were at the pinnacle of their long reign in endurance racing, having won Le Mans the previous year in addition to Sebring and Daytona since 1978.

Tragedy struck at Sebring during a practice session when Floridian Manuel Quintana was killed in a single-car accident. His Porsche 911 apparently spun in oil and flipped over. It was the first fatality at Sebring since the disastrous 1966 race.

The largest field since 1955 started before another impressive crowd. Sebring was once again attracting a large contingent of state and national media, which had all but abandoned the race back in 1973. And the atmosphere was beginning to resemble the great years of the 1950s and '60s. Sebring was still America's version of Le Mans. Daytona continued struggling to attract spectators to its 24-hour race, and other American road racing circuits simply could not boast the great tradition and international following of Sebring's 12-hour classic.

The early stages of the race featured a battle between the Fitzpatrick/Barbour Porsche and the Bayside Racing Porsche 935 of Peter Gregg, Hurley Haywood and Bruce Leven. The Barbour Porsche led most of the first three hours, then the Bayside Porsche took the lead, which it held until lap 145, when transmission problems surfaced.

With the Barbour Porsche back in the lead, Ted Field and Danny Ongais aboard the Interscope Racing Porsche 935 moved into second but could not challenge the leader. Fitzpatrick and Barbour finished with a three-lap margin, covering 1,315.6 miles, the most since 1972.

Dick Barbour Racing became only the second private team to win three consecutive races at Sebring, joining Briggs Cunningham's racing team (1953-55).

The three Whittington brothers, Don, Bill and Dale, finished third, followed by John Paul, Sr., Al Holbert and Preston Henn in another Porsche 935.

Bob Tullius and Bill Adam scored an impressive win in the GTO class aboard the Group 44 Triumph TR8. They finished sixth overall and 14 laps ahead of the second-place GTO Porsche Carrera.

A Mazda RX-7 finished ninth overall and won the GTU class with Roger Mandeville, Jim Downing and Brad Frisselle driving. It was both the first non-Porsche to win the GTU class and the first Japanese-manufactured car to win at Sebring.

Three Porsches battle for position exiting the chicane in 1980. Porsche dominated Sebring, winning 13 consecutive races.

1981

Sports car racing was rapidly gaining in popularity in the early 1980s, and manufacturers and corporate sponsors were returning at a rapid rate, anticipating an exciting new era as IMSA's new Grand Touring Prototype (GTP) class began to materialize.

American road racing was in need of stars, however, and it received a major setback in November 1980 when Peter Gregg committed suicide on a lonely section of beach near Ponte Vedra Beach, Florida. Gregg was America's best–known international road–racing driver and the owner of the Brumos Porsche dealership in Jacksonville, Florida, which had become famous for its competitive road–racing progam.

Although new cars and drivers were on the horizon, Sebring would still be the domain of the reliable Porsche 935 in 1981.

John Fitzpatrick won the pole position for the second straight year, again driving a Porsche 935 K3. The 12 fastest cars in qualifying were all Porsche 935s, with a Chevrolet Monza being the fastest non-Porsche in the 78-car field.

A rather crude-looking Alfa Romeo Chevron entered by Del Russo Taylor was the first and only true GTP car to appear at Sebring in 1981, but GTP cars would soon dominate the IMSA series.

Fitzpatrick and Busby led for much of the first five hours, but transmission problems would eventually result in an early retirement. The race was very competitive, with six cars exchanging the lead 11 times. Brian Redman, Bob Garretson and Bobby Rahal drove their Daytona-winning Porsche 935 K3 to second place, but Garretson flipped exiting the hairpin in an encounter with a slower car.

Hurley Haywood, Al Holbert and Bruce Leven also led briefly in the Bayside Porsche 935, but eventually lost seven laps repairing suspension problems. The Porsche 935 K3 of Roy Woods, Ralph Kent Cooke and Skeeter McKitterick took the lead near the halfway point and led for three hours before suspension problems from an accident caused a lengthy pit stop. Marty Hinze, Milt Minter and

Bill Whittington then took the lead briefly, before the Haywood/ Holbert/Leven Porsche stormed back from a seven-lap deficit to retake the lead with under three hours remaining.

The Haywood/Holbert/Leven Porsche 935 finished with a three-lap margin of victory over Woods/Cooke/McKitterick. Hinze/ Minter/ Whittington finished third, five laps behind the winners.

Haywood and Holbert, who each won their second Sebring classic, were the new stars of American sports car racing. Both would go on to score three wins at Le Mans and earn numerous other honors.

Finishing fifth overall was the GTO class winner, a Porsche Carrera driven by Dennis Aase, Chuck Kendall and Pete Smith. A Mazda RX-7 driven by Walt Bohren and Lee Mueller won the GTU class.

The Sebring circuit, though much improved in recent years, was still incredibly tough. As Betty Jo Turner wrote in *Porsche Panorama:* "[Sebring] is the oldest professional international sports car race in America. It is also the meanest, most brutal endurance test ever devised for racing cars in this country and always has been. Those 12 hours of blowing sand and disintegrating concrete are half as long and twice as hard as 24 hours at Daytona.

"It is a marathon of exhaustion for drivers and crew and a pounding torture test for cars. Nearly every human being—driver, mechanic, reporter and spectator alike—eventually turns away from the circus din of screaming healthy cars and silent broken ones, looks up into the soft vernal Florida night and wonders why. There aren't any cosmic answers to questions like that, but it has something to do with the human drive to meet and master tough jobs no matter how crazy they are. And a lot to do with how good it feels when it stops."

Marty Hinze, Bill Whittington and Milt Minter led momentarily, but finished third in 1981 in this Porsche 935.

1982

The Chevrolet-March represented the new IMSA GTP class. Bobby Rahal, Jim Trueman and Mauricio DeNarvaez drove the car to second place in 1982.

The 1982 race marked the 30th anniversary of the 12 Hours of Sebring and a near-record crowd of 63,000 was in attendance for a huge celebration of America's legendary international sports car race.

Racing journalist Tom Tucker wrote before the race: "If the Daytona 500 and the Indianapolis 500 are the Super Bowls for stock car and Indy car racing, then the 12 Hours of Sebring is the Mecca of sports car racing in the United States. One look through the colorful 30-year history of the Sebring track provides ample evidence of the nostalgia and spirit which has made the 12 Hours of Sebring."

America's most prominent road racing star, Al Holbert, said: "I can remember listening to Sebring on the radio in the '50s when my dad [Bob] was running there. It's rough on machinery. It may be outdated. Sometimes chunks of concrete come up during the race and damage your car. But, for me, it's fun to drive. It's a nifty track. There are hazards, but they are outweighed by the challenge of winning and the knowledge that you're running at a place with so much history."

The powerful new GTP cars were beginning to make their mark at Sebring. Bobby Rahal was the fastest qualifier in a Chevrolet March, setting a new track record with a lap average of 127.289 MPH. John Fitzpatrick qualified second in his Porsche 935 K3, with the previous year's winning team of Al Holbert/Hurley Haywood/Bruce Leven taking the third position on the grid in an updated Porsche 935.

Rahal's record lap in qualifying was significant because speeds were now exceeding the qualifying records set by the Porsche 917 and the Ferrari 312PB in the early '70's. Despite changes to the circuit, the next 10 years would see incredible speeds at Sebring as GTP cars continued to be refined with remarkable technology and materials.

The practice and qualifying sessions were not without their humorous moments. Actor James Brolin, driving a Porsche 924, ran over a wild boar on the runway section of the circuit. That evening, the team roasted the unfortunate victim for dinner. Such was Sebring: anything could happen—and usually did.

This Sebring race was especially tough on equipment. After four hours, nearly one-third of the 67-car field had retired. Fitzpatrick flipped his Porsche on the seventh lap and several other contenders suffered problems in the early stages of the race.

The Porsche 935 K3 of Ted Field and Danny Ongais appeared to be a leading contender early, as did the Bobby Rahal/Jim Trueman/Mauricio DeNarvaez Chevrolet March and the Whittington brothers' Porsche 935, which led for nearly three hours before its engine expired.

The race turned into a battle of the wounded, as virtually every contender was running with some type of major problem.

John Paul, Sr. and Jr., despite the engine in their Porsche 935 losing a cylinder with two hours remaining, held on for the victory, less than a lap ahead of the Rahal/Trueman/DeNarvaez Chevrolet March (the highest finish by an American engine since the Ford win 13 years earlier), which raced the final nine hours with only third gear. The Porsche 935 of Terry Wolters, M.L. Speer and Charles Mendez finished third.

Diego Febles, Tato Ferrer and Chiqui Soldevila won the GTO class driving a Porsche Carrera RSR to fourth place overall. Amos Johnson, Roger Mandeville and Jeff Kline won the GTU class driving a Mazda RX-7 to sixth.

The Pauls had become the first father-son team to win the 12 Hours of Sebring. It was the same tube-frame Porsche 935 they had driven to victory a few weeks earlier at Daytona's 24-hour race.

Sports car racing, always the domain of the wealthy sportsman, would unfortunately attract a number of competitors financed by illegal activities. Unknown at the time was that John Paul, Sr. was deeply involved in the drug trade.

Paul had constructed an elaborate underground marijuana-growing facility in north Georgia, and he would eventually be convicted on numerous drug charges and attempted murder. John Paul, Jr. would serve prison time for much lesser charges and eventually resume his driving career.

The Whittington brothers, winners at Le Mans in 1979 and one of IMSA's leading teams during this period, would also be implicated in drug activity. Don and Bill Whittington were both sentenced to prison time.

Randy Lanier, a little-known amateur driver from Davie, Florida, would suddenly rise to the top of the American road racing scene and win the IMSA championship in 1984. He, too, ended up in prison. Certainly only a very small number of drivers to race at Sebring were involved in these activities, but the high-spending, high-living 1980s had its dark side in the world of sports car racing.

Charles Mendez had promoted his best race yet at Sebring, but the FAA had issued an edict demanding the end of racing on the main airport runways. His five-year contract with the Sebring Airport Authority was up for renewal, and changes were in store yet again at Sebring.

The father-and-son team of John Paul, Sr. and Jr. captured the 1982 race driving this Porsche 935. The Pauls held off the faster Chevrolet March GTP car of Bobby Rahal, Jim Trueman and Mauricio DeNarvaez, which had run the last nine hours using only third gear.

1983

In 1983, Jim Mullen (left), Wayne Baker (center) and Kees Nierop drove their GTO-class Porsche 934 from 14th starting position to Sebring's biggest upset victory.

After five years of promotion by Charles Mendez, the Sebring Airport Authority took over promotion of the 12 Hours of Sebring in 1983.

The long-running battle with the FAA was resolved with the first major change to the circuit since the Webster turn was deleted in 1967. A large section of the airport runways was bypassed by a new asphalt section, shortening the circuit length to 4.75 miles, still the longest in North America.

Among the many old–timers and dignitaries in attendance was race founder Alec Ulmann, who returned as Grand Marshal and was impressed with the improvements that had been made at Sebring since his departure in 1972.

The major changes to the circuit, however, were overshadowed by the largest and most diverse entry in Sebring history, which produced the most stunning upset ever.

A total of 84 cars started the 12 Hours of Sebring in 1983, including a large array of exotic new GTP cars such as the Jaguar XJR-5, Chevrolet Lola T-600, Chevrolet March 83G, Aston Martin Nimrod and Cosworth Grid S1. There were also plenty of trusty old Porsche 935s and a large array of GT cars, including Mazda RX-7s, Porsche 911s and even a Ford Pinto.

Despite all the new GTP cars on hand, a proven Porsche 935 driven by John Paul, Jr. won the pole position. His co-drivers were Michael Andretti and Derek Bell. The Group 44 Jaguar XJR-5 driven by Bob Tullius and Bill Adam qualified second fastest.

The race quickly evolved into one of the wildest endurance races ever witnessed. With eight different leaders and 23 lead changes (both Sebring records), no team held the lead very long before some type of mechanical problem occurred.

The Tullius/Adam Jaguar XJR-5 traded the lead early with the Porsche 935 of Hurley Haywood and Al Holbert. Marty Hinze, Randy Lanier and Terry Wolters moved their Chevrolet March up into the lead in the third hour with the Bob Akin/Dale Whittington/John O'Steen Porsche 935 K3 challenging as well.

The large field of cars created an embarrassing problem for race officials as the fuel supply was running low. The only remedy was to put the race under yellow flag conditions to allow a fuel truck to cross the track (it was too heavy to use the drive-over bridge) and deliver fuel to the paddock area.

In the fifth hour, both the Jaguar and the pole-winning Porsche retired with engine failure. Just after the halfway mark, the Hinze/

Left: In 1983 the Mazda RX-7 of Pete Halsmer and Rick Knoop led until brake failure late in the race ended its charge. It was the first time a Japanese manufacturer led a major international endurance race.

Whittington/Lanier entry retired, giving the lead back to the Bob Akin team. They built a two-lap lead over the Haywood/Holbert Bayside Porsche, which was suffering from nagging electrical problems.

The Cosworth Grid driven by Milt Minter and Skeeter McKitterick had moved up through the field, as had the Mazda RX-7 driven by Pete Halsmer and Rick Knoop, which had fought its way from the 16th starting position.

With just two hours remaining, the leading Akin/O'Steen/Whittington Porsche was unable to restart after a pit stop, apparently due to water in the fuel. The Halsmer/Knoop Mazda then took the lead while the other contenders were suffering from a variety of mechanical problems.

The GTO class Mazda tried desperately to hold the lead, but with just over an hour remaining, suspension and brake failure ended its hopes. This development gave the lead to the Minter/McKitterick Grid, but they were forced to make frequent pit stops due to severe handling problems and surrendered the lead to the Bayside Porsche of Haywood and Holbert.

Incredibly, the Bayside Porsche continued to suffer from electrical problems, including no headlights, and it was forced to pit with 30 minutes remaining. Taking the lead was the Porsche 934 driven by Wayne Baker, Jim Mullen and Kees Nierop, running steadily from the 14th starting position. The crowd went wild in disbelief as a GTO class Porsche appeared headed for an amazing upset.

In the final minutes, the leading Porsche began to encounter handling problems and was running low on fuel. Wayne Baker was driving the car but he was unaware that he was leading overall (and his crew purposely did not tell him). The Whittington/Akin/O'Steen Porsche closed to within 94.8 seconds when the checkered flag came out to end the wildest 12-hour classic ever at Sebring.

Baker, thinking he had won only the GTO class, was ready to pull into the paddock after the race when his crew told him to head for victory lane. It was the first time in IMSA history a GTO class car had won overall. The winning Porsche had a remarkable history. It had actually started life in 1979 as a Porsche 911 chassis. It eventually was converted to a Porsche 935 K3 and won the 24 Hours of Daytona in 1981. In 1982 it was totally rebuilt as a 934.

Baker explained the upset win in simple terms: "We built this car to take punishment. You can't spend endurance races in the pits. The whole idea of endurance races is to endure. It's amazing how people

Fastest qualifier in 1983 was this Porsche 935 driven by Michael Andretti, Derek Bell and John Paul, Jr. Paul took the pole with an average speed of 118.779 MPH.

Pit stop for the Porsche 934 driven by Wayne Baker, Jim Mullen and Kees Nierop en route to their stunning victory at Sebring in 1983.

come into these kinds of races and duke it out for the first six hours when you have to last 12 hours."

The Akin/Whittington/O'Steen Porsche 935 won the GTP class with its second-place finish and was followed by the Haywood/Holbert Porsche. Finishing fourth was a Chevrolet Monza driven by Don Courtney, Luis Sereix and Brent O'Neill in one of the unheralded performances of the race.

The Aston Martin Nimrod driven by Lyn St. James, Drake Olson and Reggie Smith finished fifth, just ahead of the GTU class-winning Mazda RX-7 of Jack Dunham, Jeff Kline and Jon Compton.

A bizarre footnote to the 1983 race was the appearance of a driver named Christopher Wilder, who finished 27th place in a Porsche 911S. Wilder would later become the focus of a national manhunt as police discovered his involvement in several murders in south Florida. Wilder led police on a chase across the country which eventually ended in his death.

The successful 1983 race was further proof that Sebring had returned to its previous glory after a tough decade of change. No other American sports car race could boast the huge crowd that attended Sebring, and the future was indeed bright. Still, it was Sebring's past that seemed to be its biggest draw.

Didier Braillon wrote in *Grand Prix International:* "Sebring reeks of nostalgia. There are numerous reminders of the fifties and sixties everywhere. In the few hangars that remain, DC6s, Lockheed Super Constellations and various other relics in varying forms of decay remind us that Sebring was once a prosperous and busy airfield...Another distinguishing feature of this weird but appealing track is that there are no grandstands for spectators. Instead, the traditionally large crowd brings its own stands: everyone simply climbs onto the roofs of their motorhomes."

1984

With the prototypes gaining reliability, a repeat win by a GT car was highly improbable, but another upset was in store at Sebring '84.

For the second straight year, a major change was made to the circuit. The back straight was moved out several hundred feet, allowing the paddock area to expand. This change increased the circuit length to 4.86 miles. Other improvements included track resurfacing, improved lighting, expansion of press facilities and a general clean-up of the spectator area.

A record number of entries was received for the 1984 12 Hours of Sebring, with several GTP cars highlighting the 81-car starting field. The front row included fastest qualifier Brian Redman in a Jaguar XJR-5 and the Porsche March 83G, which had won at Daytona with South Africans Sarel Van der Merwe, Graham Duxbury and Tony Martin driving. Another Jaguar driven by Bob Tullius and Doc Bundy qualified fourth fastest behind the Porsche 935 of Bob Akin, Hans Stuck and John O'Steen.

The Jaguar team dominated the early stages of the race, but by the fourth hour it was the legendary A.J. Foyt, co-driving with Derek Bell and Bob Wollek, taking the lead in a Porsche 935.

Running in the lead for nearly five hours, the Foyt/Bell/Wollek Porsche eventually built a two-lap lead, but that disappeared when an extended pit stop was required to repair a broken front suspension. Akin, Stuck and O'Steen then took the lead with the Chevrolet March of Randy Lanier, Marty Hinze and Bill Whittington in second and on the same lap.

The race then began to resemble the previous year as virtually every contender was battling mechanical problems. The Akin Porsche had to pit with a damaged wheel hub, while the Lanier/Whittington/Hinze March was plagued by a variety of minor problems. This put the Porsche 935 driven by Mauricio DeNarvaez, Hans Heyer and Stefan Johansson into the lead.

DeNarvaez had rented the car from the Joest Racing team in Germany, where it was actually in a museum when called back into service. The team was a last-minute entry for Sebring (Johansson and Heyer had never even seen the Sebring circuit before) and their victory was yet another major upset at America's premier sports car race. The team started from the 16th qualifying position, further back than any winning car since qualifying began in 1964.

The winning Porsche 935 finished with a two-lap lead over the Lanier/Whittington/Hinze Chevrolet March. Foyt, Wollek and Bell managed to finish third.

A Chevrolet Camaro driven by Gene Felton, Billy Hagen and NASCAR driver Terry Labonte won the GTO class, finishing an impressive eighth overall. The GTU honors went to the Mazda RX-7 of Jack Baldwin, Robert Reed and Ira Young.

By the mid-1980s, the IMSA series was heading toward an exciting and prosperous era. Several manufacturers were constructing cars for the series, most notably Porsche, which was building a version of its 956 model for U.S. customers. In Europe, sports car racing was also on the upswing with renewed interest in the FIA World Sports Car Championship.

Sebring was a major part of the renewed interest in sports car racing. Betty Jo Turner wrote in *Porsche Panorama:* "After years of decline serious enough to raise questions of safety and sanction, the ancient circuit is in a graceful period of renewal. The addition of a tenth of a mile to the previous 4.75–mile course has provided smoother runway straights and a paddock double its previous size...The character is still there though. This is the place where the likes of Jaguar, Ferrari, Maserati, Porsche and a marvelous variety of lesser known exoticars have slugged it out over the years and it doesn't take much imagination to hear the ghosts of wonderful old cars roaring down the long back straight."

Sunset over the front straight at Sebring in 1984.

1985

Wally Dallenbach, Jr. and John Jones gave Roush Racing the GTO win in 1985 driving this Ford Mustang. They placed sixth overall.

In 1985 Sebring would attract probably its finest international entry since the end of the Ulmann era.

For the first time, Sebring now offered total prize money exceeding $100,000, with the winning team earning over $20,000. Further improvements were made at the circuit, including the paving of paddock roads, improved media facilities and a new scoreboard.

Porsche would be attempting to win its tenth consecutive Sebring classic in 1985, and this year marked the debut of the Porsche 962 at Sebring. With the 935 no longer competitive, the 962 (a derivative of the proven 956 racing abroad) would help continue the manufacturer's dominance in international sports car racing.

The Sebring entry in 1985 was very strong. Qualifying was led by Porsche 962s, which took the top two positions. Hans Stuck won the pole with a lap of 131.574 MPH in the car he would share with Bob Akin and Jim Mullen. Al Unser, Jr., Derek Bell and Al Holbert were second fastest in qualifying aboard the Holbert Racing Lowenbrau Porsche 962. A March chassis with Chevrolet, Buick and Porsche engines qualified in the top 10 along with two Jaguar XJR-5s and a Corvette GTP.

Beautiful weather helped attract a huge crowd for the start of the 33rd 12 Hours of Sebring. The Buick March of John Paul, Jr., Ken Madren and Wayne Pickering led the first three laps, then the Akin/Stuck/Mullen Porsche 962 took the lead.

On the 30th lap, the BF Goodrich/Busby Racing Porsche 962 driven by Jochen Mass, Jim Busby and John Morton took the lead and methodically built a commanding margin. Several contenders retired with mechanical failure, including the pole-winning Akin Porsche 962 and the Lanier/Whittington Chevrolet March. The Holbert Porsche was setting the fastest laps but was involved in an accident early in the race and then lost a wheel, putting it several laps behind.

The attrition of this Sebring race would prove to be the worst ever. After five hours, nearly half the field had retired, most with suspension or engine failure (only 36% of the starters would manage to finish the race).

A frightening mishap in the seventh hour ended the hopes of the leading Busby/Morton/Mass Porsche. With Busby driving, the

Al Unser, Jr., Derek Bell and Al Holbert finished second in 1985 driving this Porsche 962.

Porsche 962 ran over a large piece of debris on the race circuit approaching the first turn. The object cut through the bottom of the car, nearly causing serious injury to Busby. After leading for over six hours, the Porsche was too damaged to continue.

The lead then went to the Porsche 962 driven by A.J. Foyt and Bob Wollek. Entered by Preston Henn, owner of the Thunderbird Swap Shop in Ft. Lauderdale, the Porsche qualified only 13th but moved up quickly through the field. Despite losing a wheel on course and gearbox problems late in the race, Foyt and Wollek held on to win by a margin of four laps over the hard–charging Holbert/Bell/ Unser, Jr. Porsche.

The win by Foyt made him one of only five drivers to win Le Mans, Sebring and Daytona. It also marked the last win of his stellar career, which was highlighted by four wins in the Indianapolis 500.

Another Busby/BF Goodrich Porsche 962 managed third place with Pete Halsmer, Rick Knoop and Dieter Quester driving. The Jaguar XJR-5 of Bob Tullius and Chip Robinson finished fourth, followed by the Mazda Argo driven by Jim Downing and John Maffucci, winners of the new GTP Lights class.

Wally Dallenbach, Jr. and John Jones teamed to win the GTO class driving a Roush Racing Ford Mustang. Scoring an upset win in the GTU class was the Porsche 911 driven by Gary Auberlen, Pete Jauker and Adrian Gang.

The legendary A.J. Foyt won at Sebring in 1985, co-driving this Porsche 962 with Bob Wollek.

1986

The 1986 race would be the last to utilize the expansive concrete runways of the Sebring Airport. As the longest road course in North America, the runways allowed cars to reach maximum velocity, making Sebring one of the world's fastest circuits. The runways were also quite rough, the surface being the same concrete poured in 1941 for the Hendricks Field military base.

The runway section had never been accessible to spectators, however, and the FAA was again demanding that the race no longer use the active runways or adjacent airport property. A grant from the state would allow the Sebring Airport Authority to redesign the circuit after the 1986 race so it no longer used the runways. It also allowed for the construction of shorter test circuits that could be used simultaneously, adding greatly to the year-round revenue of the facility.

As the last race on the runways, it would certainly be the fastest. In qualifying, Whitney Ganz toured the circuit at an average speed of 133.134 MPH in a Buick March, the fastest lap ever recorded at Sebring International Raceway. The Holbert Racing Lowenbrau Porsche 962 was the second fastest qualifier.

Mazda's RX-7 dominated IMSA GTU competition during the 1980s. This 1986 photo shows Roger Mandeville and Danny Smith on their way to a GTU class win and an eighth overall.

The new BMW GTP team suffered a disastrous practice at Sebring, with one car destroyed by fire and another, driven by Bobby Rahal, becoming airborne and flipping over several times. Rahal was unhurt but the car was destroyed. The team later withdrew.

A field of 76 cars and a large crowd were in attendance on a clear but cold day for the first Sebring race that was to be televised live nationally on the TBS network. A total of 29 GTP and Lights cars among the large entry made this a very impressive field.

The Holbert Porsche 962 of Derek Bell/Al Unser, Jr./Al Holbert battled with the A.J. Foyt/Drake Olson Porsche during the early stages of the race. Early retirements included both Jaguar XJR-7 entries and the Bayside Porsche 962.

By mid-race the Lowenbrau Porsche was engaged in a furious battle with the Coke Porsche 962 of Bob Akin, Hans Stuck and Jo Gartner. Just before the seventh hour, a blown turbocharger forced the Lowenbrau Porsche to pit for over 30 minutes. At about the same time the Foyt/Olson Porsche retired with suspension problems from an incident on course. This gave the lead to the Akin/Stuck/ Gartner Porsche, and they cruised virtually unchallenged the remainder of the race.

The winning Porsche came limping into victory lane on

three wheels, having lost its left front wheel on the last lap. It hardly mattered, however, as they finished with an eight-lap margin over the John Morton/Jim Busby/Darin Brassfield Porsche 962. Holbert/ Bell/Unser, Jr. managed a third-place finish.

Except for the wheel problem, it was a flawless race for the Akin team as they averaged 115.852 MPH for the 12 hours, covering 1,394.82 miles (both all-time records). The Sebring win was the second for both Akin and Stuck. Sadly, Gartner would be killed two months later at Le Mans, ending a very promising career.

The GTO class produced a controversial finish between the two Roush Ford Mustangs. Olympian Bruce Jenner and Scott Pruett were paired in one car, while NASCAR stars Ricky Rudd and Bill Elliott were in the second car. Rudd and Elliott led for much of the race, but their transmission began to fail in the final hour. Jenner, in the pits, displayed a pit board (the radios in both cars were not working) instructing his teammate to make a pit stop, but he had mistakenly displayed it to Rudd, who came into the pits, losing valuable time needlessly.

The Pruett/Jenner Mustang ended up winning the GTO class by a margin of only 10 seconds, in part due to Jenner's mistake.

The GTP Lights class was won by Jim Rothbarth, Mike Meyer and Jeff Kline, driving a Mazda Royale to sixth place overall. Roger Mandeville and Danny Smith drove their Mazda RX-7 to the GTU class win.

A controversy centering on accusations of improprieties in the use of tickets by some members of the Sebring Airport Authority followed the 1986 race and made headlines. Race Director Ron Jestes and his entire race staff later resigned in a dispute with the Sebring Airport Authority.

The fastest average lap speed ever recorded during qualifying at Sebring was 133.134 MPH, set by this Buick March driven by Whitney Ganz in 1986.

1987

The biggest change ever to occur to the Sebring circuit took place before the 1987 race.

The Sebring Airport Authority hired veteran race official Charles Earwood as race director. Along with race officials John Burns, Tres Stephenson and engineer Charles Connell, Earwood would oversee the massive changes to the circuit that would finally take the race off the airport runways.

The circuit now curved sharply to the left just past the old hangar (turn one), with a new stretch of road leading to a carrousel turn, which replaced the esses. After the chicane, another new section of track bypassed the active airport runways before reconnecting with the old circuit at the back straight. The track length now measured 4.11 miles, still the longest in North America.

Other improvements were made to the safety barriers and track surface. While the improvements were significant, the character of Sebring was preserved. As Bill Lovell wrote in *AutoWeek:* "The old place has changed. New management has come in with a large broom, and plenty of heavy equipment as well. The circuit itself is new, and shorter. Gone are the endless concrete runways... In their place is a tighter, 4.–11 mile ribbon of mostly asphalt, with a turn one enclosed like a street course. Sebring is all different now—and nothing, really, has changed."

The updated Sebring circuit received positive reviews from the motorsports community, but entries for the 12-hour classic were disappointing. With an expanded IMSA schedule, teams could now afford to skip the Daytona and Sebring endurance races and still contend for the season championship. Only nine GTPs entered Sebring, eight of them Porsche 962s. The field also included 19 GTP Lights and a huge field of GT cars.

The expense of competing in endurance races was obviously greater than sprint races, but the tradition, prestige and publicity of winning Sebring was paramount, one reason why internationally famous drivers are attracted to sports car endurance races such as Sebring.

Temporary street circuits were flourishing in several cities in the late 1980s, and much of the available marketing and sponsorship money was going to these events instead of to the permanent circuits such as Sebring. Events at West Palm Beach, Tampa and Miami, among others across the nation, boasted what proved to be grossly inflated attendance figures. The street race trend would be short-lived, however, as nearly every temporary circuit would be defunct within five years, leaving a trail of bankrupt race promoters across the country.

There was little doubt that the 1987 Sebring race would be a

battle of Porsche 962s. Chip Robinson won the pole position in the Holbert Lowenbrau Porsche. The Bayside Racing Budweiser Porsche with drivers Jochen Mass and Bobby Rahal qualified second. These two cars would dominate the 74-car field, with only the Porsche driven by Price Cobb and Vern Schuppan offering a challenge early in the race. The Porsche driven by Danny Sullivan, A.J. Foyt and Hurley Haywood was eliminated in a pit lane accident.

Holbert, still looking for his third win at Sebring after coming so close the past five years, and co-driver Robinson began to pull away from the Rahal/Mass Porsche. But with just two hours remaining, the Holbert team was forced to pit and change the turbocharger. Even though the crew accomplished this difficult task in only nine minutes, it was enough time for the Rahal/Mass team to take the lead.

Holbert and Robinson were unable to make up the deficit, and Rahal and Mass took the victory by a margin of two laps. They averaged 101.859 MPH, slowed by over two hours of caution laps to retrieve disabled cars from the circuit.

A Chevrolet Camaro driven by Greg Pickett and Tommy Riggins won the GTO class, finishing fifth overall. A Porsche Fabcar driven by John Higgins, Charles Monk and Howard Cherry won the GTP Lights class. A Mazda RX-7 driven by Bob Reed and Al Bacon won the GTU class, finishing 17th overall after starting 43rd.

Start of the 1987 12 Hours of Sebring. The Jochen Mass/Bobby Rahal Porsche 962 leads the 962 of Al Holbert and Chip Robinson.

1988

Sarel Van der Merwe and

Elliot Forbes-Robinson

put their Corvette

GTP sixth on the grid

but engine failure ended

their race at the

halfway point

It had been 16 years since Sebring was part of the FIA World Championship for sports cars. In fact, no American event had appeared on the schedule since the mid-1970s. The IMSA and FIA Group C sports car series were both flourishing. Unfortunately, there was no serious effort between the two organizations to unify their championships.

The highly successful Mercedes-Benz Group C effort would never appear in North America. What a sight it would have been to see the "Silver Arrows" screaming into turn one at Sebring!

One team that did cross the Atlantic to compete in the IMSA series was the TWR Jaguar team. This created a great deal of excitement at Sebring in 1988 as Porsche appeared to finally have a serious challenger. The Jaguar team had won earlier in the year at Daytona and brought an all-star cast of drivers to Sebring, including John Nielsen, Jan Lammers, Martin Brundle and Danny Sullivan.

The 65-car field was led in qualifying by Chip Robinson in a Porsche 962, who won the pole for the second straight year, breaking the track record by seven MPH. Price Cobb and James Weaver claimed the second position on the grid in the Dyson Porsche 962, while Jaguar took the third and fifth positions. The defending champion Bayside team was fourth fastest, this time with Hans Stuck and Klaus Ludwig driving. Rounding out the top six was the Chevrolet Corvette GTP driven by Sarel Van der Merwe and Elliott Forbes-Robinson.

During a practice session, Californian Bob Copeman was killed in a single-car accident. He apparently lost control of his Porsche 911 and struck the barriers at turn one.

Despite the strong field, the race would be decided before the halfway point. One of the new Jaguars lasted less than two hours and the pole-winning Porsche of Holbert and Robinson dropped out with engine failure in the fifth hour. The DNF of the Holbert Porsche marked the end of Al Holbert's fabulous driving career. Later in the year he was killed when the plane he was piloting crashed in Columbus, Ohio.

Although the Dyson Porsche 962 was a contender the first six hours, the Ludwig/Stuck team drove a perfect race in the same car that had won the previous year. They easily pulled away to a dominating nine-lap victory. Averaging 108.782 MPH, the winners earned a record $53,000 of the quarter-million-dollar purse. Hans Stuck became only the fourth driver to win Sebring three times, joining Phil Hill, Mario Andretti and Olivier Gendebien.

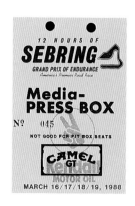

Porsche took the top five positions and stretched its incredible win streak at America's premier sports car race to 13. The Joest Racing team of John Winter, Frank Jelinski and Paolo Barilla finished second, followed by Cobb and Weaver in their Porsche. The surviving Jaguar managed a disappointing seventh-place finish.

Wally Dallenbach, Jr. and John Jones, winners of the GTO class three years earlier in a Ford, teamed to win the class again, this time in a Chevrolet Corvette. They finished with only a one-lap margin over the Lincoln-Mercury XR4Ti of Lyn St. James, Deborah Gregg and Pete Halsmer.

The GTP Lights class win went to the Buick Tiga of Tom Hessert and David Loring. Amos Johnson and Dennis Shaw won the GTU class in a Mazda RX-7.

In IMSA sprint races following Sebring, the Electramotive Nissan team was nearly unbeatable, but they had not yet been tested in an endurance race. They had their sights set on Sebring in 1989.

This Buick Tiga driven by Tom Hessert and David Loring won the GTP Lights class at Sebring in 1988.

1989

The Jaguar XJ-9 driven by Price Cobb and John Nielson ran a strong second place despite brake problems.

The Electramotive Nissan team entered Sebring for the first time in 1989. Nissan was coming off a remarkable year when it won eight straight sprint races, but it did not compete in any endurance races. Few experts gave them much chance to survive the brutal Sebring race in their first ever 12-hour test.

The Nissan team captured the front row in qualifying with Geoff Brabham setting a new track record with a speed of 127.747 MPH to take the pole. Arie Luyendyk qualified second fastest, followed by the Jaguar XJR-9 of Price Cobb and John Nielsen. The Porsche 962C driven by Derek Bell, John Andretti and Bob Wollek could only manage the fifth fastest time.

With the largest crowd in Sebring history looking on, the Brabham/Robinson Nissan ZXT-GTP took the lead and began to set a blistering sprint-like pace. The second Nissan, driven by Arie Luyendyk, retired after only 14 laps with suspension failure, leading many to believe it was only a matter of time before the leading Nissan expired.

Brabham and Robinson, later joined by Luyendyk, continued to build their lead over the Cobb/Nielsen Jaguar, which was forced to make a long pit stop for brake repairs. Even though the leading Nissan nearly lost a wheel late in the race, they never let up from their torrid pace.

In one of the most dominating performances in Sebring history, the Nissan easily survived the 12 hours at an average speed of 112.742 MPH. Brabham, Robinson and Luyendyk led 316 of 330 laps and finished with a two-lap margin of victory.

The race ranks as one of the most significant in IMSA history. It was the first overall win ever for a Japanese manufacturer in a major endurance race and represented the end of the Porsche dynasty at Sebring.

The Cobb/Nielsen Jaguar XJR-9 finished second in a brilliant run that was overshadowed by the historic Nissan win. James Weaver and Dominic Dobson finished third in the Bayside Porsche 962C. Fourth place went to the MOMO Porsche 962C of Gianpiero Moretti, Massimo Sigala, Michael Roe and Derek Bell.

The GTP Lights class was won by Dan Marvin and Bob Lesnett driving the Huffaker Racing Pontiac Spice. Dorsey Schroeder and Wally Dallenbach, Jr. won the GTO class in a Mercury Cougar XR7. The GTU class winner was the Pontiac Fiero of George Robinson, Johnny Unser and Bart Kendall, also fielded by the Huffaker team.

Sebring still proudly lived up to its reputation as the ultimate test of endurance racing. As Jonathan Ingram wrote in *On Track:* "The Sebring course remains after all these years a demanding test of man and chassis, although it's no longer possible to get lost in the dark and find one's self racing an airplane. Since its downsizing in 1987 to eliminate the use of active runways at the Sebring Airport, the circuit has become one of medium-speed corners and medium-length straights...Combined with the traffic of the GTO/GTU cars and the many transitions in pavement from old, old concrete to new asphalt to old asphalt and back again, the track gives a car and driver maximum workout. In the past, the drivers have complained that Sebring's concrete washboard left them irregular for a week. Alas there was a new angle on an old story when Dieter Quester passed a kidney stone—an event believed to have occurred on the runways that encircle the pits."

The 1980s brought great change to Sebring. The circuit had improved significantly, and the town of Sebring had grown dramatically. Sports car racing appeared as healthy as ever, and despite no American manufacturers being involved in GTP racing, its popularity was near that of the mid-1960s. No other sports car event in North America could boast the tradition and mystique of Sebring's 12-hour classic, let alone the huge crowds that continued to migrate to the famous Florida circuit every March. Sebring entered its fifth decade stronger than ever.

Dorsey Schroeder and Wally Dallenbach, Jr. won the GTO class and finished eighth overall in 1989 driving this Mercury Cougar XR7.

Sebring's fifth decade of racing began with one of the most competitive endurance races ever. Six cars would exchange the lead 19 times, and three cars would finish the race on the lead lap for the first time in Sebring history.

The defending champion Nissan team came into the race as the favorite, although Jaguar and Porsche entries were proven contenders. Dan Gurney's All American Racers Toyota team was also showing some promise, although reliability was questionable.

The cost of sports car racing had rapidly escalated the past few years, and those teams without factory support or a major sponsor were rapidly dropping out of the sport. Thus, the car count had dropped significantly in recent years at Sebring, with only 49 cars qualifying for the race in 1990. The days of the "weekend warrior" were certainly numbered.

Chip Robinson drove the Nissan ZXT-GTP he would share with Geoff Brabham to the pole position, while the Bayside Porsche 962C to be driven by Bob Wollek, Dominic Dobson and Sarel Van der Merwe qualified second fastest. The Nissan of Derek Daly and Bob Earl started third on the grid next to the Nielsen/Cobb Jaguar XJR-12.

The Bayside Porsche led for most of the first hour, with both factory Nissans and the Jones/Lammers/Wallace Jaguar staying close. A privately entered Nissan driven by John Paul, Jr. and Kevin Cogan led briefly early in the race, as did the Dauer Porsche driven by Hans Stuck and Raul Boesel.

The Bayside Porsche and the Cobb/Nielsen Jaguar retired in the third hour with engine failure, while the Joest Porsche driven by Bob Wollek, Henri Pescarolo and John Winter moved up from the eighth starting position to take the lead on the 114th lap.

Two major developments in the always dramatic nighttime hours changed the race's outcome. The Brabham/Robinson Nissan was forced to pit for radiator repairs, dropping them six laps behind. Then,

Left: Twilight at Sebring

in 1990.

Pit stop for the Chip

Robinson/Geoff

Brabham/Derek Daly

Nissan GTP-ZXT, which

finished second in 1990.

with less than three hours remaining, the Joest Porsche collided with a slower GTU car entering the pit straight. Both cars were badly damaged and unable to continue. The extended caution period to clean up the debris was one of six full course cautions amounting to nearly three hours, slowing the race average considerably.

With the Joest Porsche eliminated, the Daly/Earl Nissan took a more comfortable lead, although the Jones/Wallace/Lammers Jaguar was within one lap. Brabham, meanwhile, was accomplishing one of the greatest drives in Sebring history, setting record laps trying to overcome the huge deficit.

With the leading Nissan slowing the pace in the final minutes, Brabham was able to pass the second-place Jaguar (running low on fuel) on the last lap, bringing his Nissan to the same lap as Daly and Earl.

Daly and Earl held on for the victory by a margin of just 87.8 seconds over the Brabham/Robinson Nissan (Daly also drove the second-place car, making him the first ever to drive in both the first- and second-place cars). It was the first time the same team had taken the top two overall positions at Sebring since 1972.

Fourth place went to the Porsche 962 of John Hotchkis Jr. and Sr. and James Adams. Six different makes finished in the top 10 positions.

The Roush team swept the top two positions in the GTO class with Robby Gordon, Lyn St. James and Calvin Fish driving their Mercury Cougar XR7 to sixth overall, eight laps ahead of the Schroeder/Jones Cougar.

The GTP Lights class was won by the Buick Spice driven by Tom Hessert and Charles Morgan. GTU honors went to the Leitzinger Nissan 240SX driven by David Loring, Butch Leitzinger and Chuck Kurtz, 13 laps ahead of its nearest competitor.

A major development in the history of Sebring International Raceway would take place following the 1990 race as the Sebring Airport Authority would lease the facility to a private promoter for the first time since 1982.

1991

This year opened yet another new era for Sebring International Raceway. Floridian Mike Cone, owner of a large highway construction firm who had purchased IMSA in 1988, negotiated a long-term lease with the Sebring Airport Authority. Sebring International Raceway would now be privately promoted and managed on a year-round basis for the first time in its history.

Cone immediately embarked on a massive improvement program, drastically changing the circuit. Under the supervision of Cone and Raceway Director Tres Stephenson, nearly the entire asphalt section of the track was widened and resurfaced. More important, a portion of the track was reconfigured to place a manufacturing warehouse on the outside of the circuit. It also meant that for the first time in 40 years of racing at Sebring, the entire circuit would be accessible to spectators.

The new circuit also allowed the raceway to be totally separate from the neighboring Sebring Airport and Industrial Park.

Additional improvements included a new drive-over bridge into the paddock, pit lane improvements and new viewing berms for spectators at several locations around the circuit. The paddock tower, a fixture at Sebring since the late 1950s, was remodeled and new suites were added above the pits.

Several safety improvements were made, including the removal of all telephone poles along the warehouse straight, new tire barriers, better run-off areas and improved markers and lighting for night driving.

The changes were met with great enthusiasm, and the improved short course was rated among the finest test courses in North America.

Another change in 1991 was the weather. For the first time in 26 years, heavy rains would plague the 12 Hours of Sebring.

Nissan again led the field in qualifying with Geoff Brabham lapping the new 3.7-mile circuit at a speed of 121.354 MPH in his Nissan NPT-90. Porsche, Jaguar and Toyota entries occupied the next three grid positions with a Chevrolet Spice qualifying seventh fastest.

The 46-car field started under threatening skies, and it didn't take long for the rain to begin. The two Joest Porsches traded the lead early in the race, but on the 81st lap it became a battle between the two Nissan entries. Geoff Brabham, his brother Gary, and Derek Daly exchanged the lead several times with the team car of Chip Robinson, Bob Earl and Julian Bailey.

As the rain intensified, flooding parts of the circuit, full course cautions were required several times. Over three hours of the race

were run with the pace car in front of the field.

Leading entering the final hour, the Brabham/Daly/Brabham Nissan appeared headed for victory, but as often is the case at Sebring, the final hour would provide plenty of surprises. With 39 minutes remaining, Daly hit the wall at turn three and damaged a tire. While in the pits, the Robinson/Earl/Bailey Nissan moved into the lead. But with 16 minutes remaining, Robinson was forced to pit with electrical problems, handing the lead back to Brabham/Daly/Brabham. They finished with a one-lap margin of victory over their teammates.

Joest Porsches took the next two positions, followed by the Jaguar of Davy Jones, Raul Boesel and John Nielsen (a second Jaguar had been destroyed in practice).

It was the third consecutive Sebring win for Nissan and the first time two brothers drove the winning car.

Charles Morgan and Jim Pace won the GTP Lights class in a Buick Kudzu, finishing seventh overall. Robby Gordon and Max Jones won the GTO class in a Roush Ford Mustang, two laps ahead of the Nissan 300ZX driven by Steve Millen, Jeremy Dale and Johnny O'Connell. The GTU class victory went to the Nissan 240SX of Bob Leitzinger and David Loring.

The Nissan NPT-90 makes its way through the heavy rain at Sebring in 1991. Chip Robinson, Bob Earl and Julian Bailey drove the car to second place.

1992

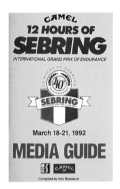

The 40th anniversary of the 12 Hours of Sebring turned out to be one of the great races in its history. The largest crowd ever to attend the legendary race witnessed a truly historic result.

Toyota was beginning to dominate sprint races as Nissan had done the previous three years, although Dan Gurney's 4-cylinder Toyotas were unproven in endurance racing. Nissan was still the favorite at Sebring, while Porsche, Jaguar, Chevrolet and Mazda were long shots at best.

The race week started on a tragic note: During practice for a supporting race, driver Mark Kent was killed when he lost control of his BMW and crashed entering turn three.

Juan Fangio II led qualifying in the Toyota Eagle Mk III he would share with Andy Wallace.

Beautiful weather ensured this race would be run at a record pace, and from the very start both Nissan and Toyota treated Sebring like a sprint race. The lead was exchanged 13 times in the first four hours, and the record crowd and national television audience were treated to a very competitive endurance race.

Late in the afternoon, the Nissan NPT-91A of Chip Robinson, Bob Earl and Arie Luyendyk retired with engine failure, handing the lead to the Nissan NPT-91A driven by last year's winners, Geoff Brabham, Gary Brabham and Derek Daly. The Fangio/Wallace Toyota Eagle Mk III was in second place, followed by the Joest Porsche 962C of Gianpiero Moretti/Massimo Sigala/Oscar Larrauri/Bernd Schneider.

The race was decided at sunset when the leading Nissan entered the pits for what was supposed to be a routine stop, but the Nissan was unable to get its headlights working. The crew worked frantically, but by the time they had solved the problem, the Toyota was five laps ahead.

The Toyota was unchallenged the final four hours, but continued its torrid pace to record the first endurance victory for the manufacturer. They averaged 110.724 MPH and earned a record $70,500 out of a purse totaling $325,000. The 20 lead changes were the second most recorded at the 12 Hours of Sebring.

The winning team shared a special historical significance with Sebring. Fangio's legendary uncle won Sebring in 1956 and 57. For Andy Wallace, the win completed his prestigious triple crown, having won at Le Mans, Daytona and now Sebring.

The win was especially meaningful to team owner Dan Gurney (who had won in 1959 and suffered the heartbreak of the 1966 race).

He best understood the significance of winning at Sebring: "This race has enormous historical significance. It's so hard to win this race—it's so rough and demanding. The feeling of being able to put it in the record books is great—they'll be able to tell their grandchildren about this one. It's a fabulous feeling to win America's greatest road race."

Jim Downing, Howard Katz and Tim McAdam won the GTP Lights class in a Mazda Kudzu. The Oldsmobile Cutlass team of Irv Hoerr, Darin Brassfield, Paul Gentilozzi and George Robinson won the GTS class, while the Leitzinger team swept the GTU category for the third straight year as John Paul Jr. and David Loring drove their Nissan 240SX to victory and an eighth-place overall finish.

The race marked the end not only of the Nissan domination (they would never win another IMSA GTP race), but the beginning of the end for the entire GTP concept. Nissan, Jaguar and Mazda would withdraw from sports car prototype racing in the coming year, leaving Toyota unchallenged. The cost of GTP racing could no longer be justified by manufacturers or afforded by private teams.

The 12 Hours of Sebring, the crown jewel of sports car racing in North America, was one of only a handful of sports car races that was profitable, hence the shrinking IMSA schedule. It was obvious major changes to the sport were needed.

Juan Fangio II and Andy Wallace scored a historic and emotional win for team owner Dan Gurney in 1992. As a driver, Gurney had won Sebring in 1959 but suffered terrible disappointments with mechanical failures in the years that followed.

1993

Coming off perhaps its most successful race ever, Sebring would host one of its more disappointing races in 1993. For the second time in three years, heavy rains would plague the race.

The field of cars was weak, with one privately entered Nissan offering the only serious challenge to the Toyota team. The GTP fields had been shrinking the past year and the tremendous cost of racing GTPs had taken its toll. The FIA Group C championship had completely fallen apart, leaving sports car racing in disarray worldwide.

IMSA wisely announced this would be the last year of the GTP class. A new concept called World Sports Cars would be the headline attraction beginning in 1994. It was designed to be much more cost effective than the GTP class, and allow private teams to compete equally with factory supported teams.

Sebring is an established motorsports tradition, and that perhaps explains the huge crowd that attended the event in 1993 despite the negative factors.

As expected, Toyota dominated qualifying. Juan Fangio II set a new track record with a speed of 125.5 MPH in the Dan Gurney All American Racers Toyota Eagle Mk III he would again share with Andy Wallace. Rocky Moran and P.J. Jones, winners at Daytona's 24-hour race, qualified second fastest in the other Toyota Eagle Mk III.

Rain began to fall about 30 minutes into the race and it never stopped, periodically reaching torrential levels.

After three hours the race was red-flagged, stopping the 12 Hours of Sebring for the first time in its history. The race resumed one hour and nine minutes later but the weather conditions had hardly improved.

The Toyotas continued to trade the lead but the Nissan NPT-90 driven by Derek Bell, Gianpiero Moretti and John Paul, Jr. was only three laps behind. During the night hours, John Paul, Jr. began driving incredible laps despite the terrible conditions, and eventually moved into second when the Moran/Jones Toyota was forced to make a long pit stop.

The rains subsided slightly during the final two hours, but the leading Toyota was unstoppable. Fangio and Wallace repeated their triumph of the previous year in the exact same car. It was the slowest race at Sebring since the first race in 1952, with an average speed of only 70.699 MPH due to the rain.

The starting field gets ready to roll in 1993 with Dan Gurney's Toyota team on the front row.

The Moretti/Bell/Paul Jr. Nissan finished two laps behind in second, followed by the Moran/Jones Toyota. Finishing fourth overall and first in the GTS category was the Nissan 300ZX of Steve Millen, John Morton and Johnny O'Connell. The GTP Lights victory went to the Acura Spice of Parker Johnstone, Dan Marvin and Ruggero Melgrati.

The Invitational GT class was won by the new Porsche 911 LM Turbo driven by Hurley Haywood, Hans Stuck and Walter Rohrl. The GTU category win went to the Mazda RX-7 driven by Dick Greer, Peter Uria, Mike Mees and Al Bacon.

With the demise of the GTP class, sports car racing was certainly heading toward an uncertain future, but Sebring would always be a premier event. As Robert Cumberford wrote in *Automobile*, "We won't see the like of the Nissans, Toyotas, and Jaguars at Sebring again for quite some time, and the new World Sports Cars won't be as fast at first. No matter; the race is always going to be worth attending, whatever the cars. After all, with the Indy 500 and the Pikes Peak hill-climb, it is one of only three classic American motor races...it has attracted most of the world's best drivers. And some of the most improbable."

Juan Fangio II, Andy Wallace and the All American Racers crew celebrate their second consecutive Sebring win in 1993.

This Mazda Kudzu

finished third in 1994

with Jim Downing,

Wayne Taylor and Tim

McAdam driving.

A new era of sports car competition began at Sebring in 1994 with the introduction of the open-cockpit World Sports Car category, replacing the GTP formula. This transition year brought a unique field of cars to Sebring and gave production-based GT cars a legitimate chance to win the race overall, something that had not happened at Sebring since 1983.

With the high-tech but expensive GTP cars now a thing of the past, speeds dropped dramatically at Sebring. The GTS class Nissan 300ZX driven by Paul Gentilozzi, which had won overall at Daytona, was the fastest qualifier (at a speed nearly 15 MPH slower than the Toyota set the previous year). An Oldsmobile Spice was the fastest World Sports Car.

The 48-car field, including 10 World Sports Cars (most converted from GTP cars), started under beautiful Florida skies. The race proved to be more competitive than most had predicted. The Bob Schader/ Jeremy Dale/Ruggero Melgrati Oldsmobile Spice led for much of the first three hours with the Steve Millen/Johnny O'Connell/John Morton Nissan 300ZX and the Irv Hoerr/Darin Brassfield/R.K. Smith/ Tommy Riggins Oldsmobile also taking the lead.

The Chevrolet Spice driven by Derek Bell, Andy Wallace and James Weaver moved up from the eighth starting position to challenge for the lead. Wallace had started the race in a Toyota Spice entered by actor Craig T. Nelson, but joined the Auto Toy Store team when the car retired early in the race.

On the 91st lap, the Schader/Dale/Melgrati Oldsmobile retired with engine failure. The Gentilozzi/Leitzinger Nissan also was forced to quit with mechanical problems, making the race a battle between the GT Nissan of Millen/O'Connell/Morton and the Chevrolet Spice World Sports Car piloted by Wallace/Bell/Weaver. Despite a failing clutch, fading brakes, and problems with heat and exhaust fumes tiring the driver, the Spice ran a remarkable race, keeping pace with the Nissan.

The Nissan proved stronger, however, and became the first GT car to win overall at Sebring since 1983.

Millen, O'Connell and Morton averaged just over 100 MPH as the Clayton Cunningham-prepared Nissan scored a rare Daytona-Sebring endurance sweep. Morton's victory came 30 years after his first Sebring start.

Five different cars led the race and there were 19 lead changes. Finishing third overall and second in the World Sports Car class behind the Bell/Wallace/Weaver Chevrolet Spice was the Mazda Kudzu driven by Jim Downing, Wayne Taylor and Tim McAdam. Fourth overall went to the Chevrolet Spice driven by Andy Evans, Ross Bentley and Butch Leitzinger, which set the fastest race lap.

Finishing 10th overall was NASCAR driver Ken Schrader and Scott Lagasse in a Chevrolet Consulier Intruder.

The GTU class battle went down to the wire as the Porsche 911 RSR driven by Mark Sandridge, Joe Varde and Nick Ham edged the Nissan 240SX driven by Jim Pace, Butch Hamlet and Barry Waddell by only 19 seconds.

The 1994 12 Hours of Sebring proved to be better than most had anticipated, and the announcement that Ferrari would soon return to sports car racing was a major indication that better races were ahead.

This GT-class Nissan 300ZX won in 1994 with John Morton, Steve Millen and Johnny O'Connell driving.

1995

The second-place
Chevrolet Spice of Andy
Wallace, James Weaver
and Derek Bell heads
into the hairpin.

The return of Ferrari after a 23-year absence at America's premier sports car race, plus the largest field of entries in seven years, helped make this one of the most memorable Sebring races ever. Ferrari's magic name in the world of motorsports had dropped out of sports car racing in the mid-1970s in favor of Formula One competition. Its return to Sebring marked a significant achievement for the new IMSA World Sports Car Championship.

Ferrari made a
triumphant return to
Sebring in 1995.

The Scandia Ferrari 333SP driven by Michele Alboreto and Mauro Baldi set the fastest qualifying time, followed by the Oldsmobile Spice with Jeremy Dale, Jay Cochran and Fredrik Ekblom driving. Another Ferrari fielded by the Euromotorsports team and a second Ferrari from the Scandia team rounded out the top four in qualifying.

The Ferraris took command early in the race with Andy Evans, Fermin Velez and Eric Van de Poele in a 333SP leading most of the first hour. For the third time in the past five years, weather became a major factor at Sebring. Heavy rains hit the track in the second hour and returned later in the afternoon. Six different cars had led laps when the race was red-flagged due to flooding on various parts of the circuit. It was only the second time in history the race was stopped.

When the race was resumed after an hour, a furious duel developed between the Derek Bell/Andy Wallace/Jan Lammers Auto Toy Store Chevrolet Spice, which hounded the leading Ferrari of Velez/Evans/Van de Poele for the remainder of the race.

Although the Chevrolet Spice closed to within ten seconds of the

leading Ferrari at one point, a late race pit stop dropped them back. Evans, Velez and Van de Poele won with an 86.59-second margin, the third closest race in Sebring history. It was the 10th win by Ferrari at Sebring, but the first in 23 years.

The Auto Toy Store team's second-place finish was their second straight runnerup result. It was also Derek Bell's third straight second-place finish, and his eighth top-five finish at Sebring without a win.

The Jim Downing/Jim Pace/Butch Hamlet Mazda Kudzu finished third, although it crashed heavily on the last lap. The Alboreto/Baldi Ferrari managed a fourth place finish, while the Nissan 300ZX that had won overall the previous year captured fifth (first in the GTS-1 class), again driven by Steve Millen, John Morton and Johnny O'Connell. They finished two laps ahead of the Porsche 911 Turbo driven by Hans Stuck and Bill Adam.

The GTS-2 class was won by Charles Slater, Joe Cogbill and Bill Auberlen driving a Porsche 911. A Porsche 962 Spyder fielded by Konrad Racing won the Le Mans WSC class.

The 1995 race tied a Sebring record with 23 lead changes, a record that probably would have been broken if not for the red flag period. The average speed was only 80 MPH due to the heavy rains.

Following the race, the chicane was replaced with the new Fangio Chicane, making room for a new entrance road to the Sebring Airport. This change shortened the track length to 3.6 miles.

The sun breaks through following a heavy rain that stopped the 1995 race, only the second time in history that the 12 Hours was temporarily halted.

SEBRING 12 HOUR SPORTS CAR RACE

A F T E R W O R D

If only the weathered and cracked runways of old Hendricks Field could talk. They've heard everything from the rumble of B-17s to the scream of Ferrari 333SPs some 50 years later. Legends such as Fangio, Moss, Hill, Gurney, Foyt and Andretti, to name only a few, have all raced on this historic expanse of tarmac, and though the track has since been modernized, their spirit and greatness can still be felt.

As the famous circuit heads toward a new century, racing fans continue to make the pilgrimage to Sebring every March. At a time when new tracks seem like motorsports shopping malls—lots of glitz and glamor but no substance—Sebring remains a place people remember. Its evokes a sense of nostalgia and never ceases to create drama, thrills and heartbreak. Over the years, Sebring has endured despite frequent controversy, a merry-go-round of race organizers and sanctioning bodies, misgivings about track conditions, and the perennial threat that this year's event will be the last. Sebring is a tradition. And there's only one thing tougher than starting a tradition—ending it.

SEBRING INTERNATIONAL RACEWAY

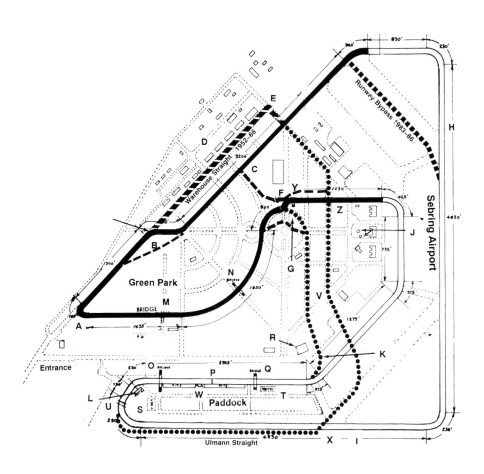

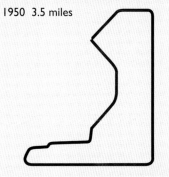

1950 3.5 miles

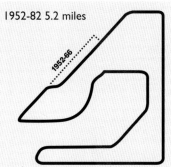

1952-82 5.2 miles

1952-66

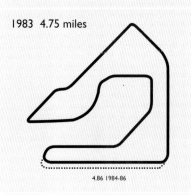

1983 4.75 miles

4.86 1984-86

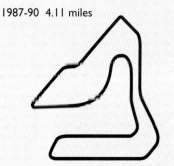

1987-90 4.11 miles

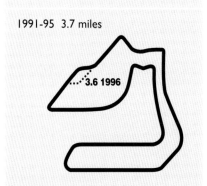

1991-95 3.7 miles

3.6 1996

SEBRING INTERNATIONAL RACEWAY LANDMARKS

A Hairpin (1952 – present)
B Chicane (1967-95) replaced with Fangio Chicane in 1996
C Cunningham Corner (1991– present)
D Warehouse Row
E Webster Turn (1952-66)
Γ Collier Curve (1991 – present)
G Carrousel (1987-90)
H North South runway
I Ullmann Straight/East West runway
J Water Tower
K New Turn One (1987 – present)
L Timing Trailer
M Green Park pedestrian bridge (1966 – present)

N Green Park vehicle bridge (1965 – present)
O Paddock pedestrian bridge (replaced Martini & Rossi vehicle bridge in 1987)
P Start-Finish Line
Ω Paddock pedestrian bridge (1955 – present)
R Blue Hangar
S Fuel depot
T Medical Center
U Paddock vehicle bridge (1991 – present)
V Bishop Bend (1991 – present)
W Pit Race Control Tower
X Le Mans Curve (1991 – present)
Y MG Bridge (1958-73)
Z Tower Turn (1991 – present)

GRANDSTANDS: Viewing grandstands have been located at various locations around the circuit. Most notable were those along the front straight in front of the pits from 1954-75 and at the Hairpin from the late 1950s to the mid-1970s. A small grandstand is presently located at turn one.

PIT STRUCTURE: The original pit was a primitive wooden structure built in 1954-55. Concrete pit stalls were constructed in the late 1950s and expanded upon throughout the 1960s. Enclosed suites above the pits were added in the late 1980s and early 1990s. The Control Tower, originally known as the Jaguar Tower, was built in 1957 and remodeled in 1991.

VIEWING HILLS: Spectator viewing hills were added beginning in 1991 at several turns around the circuit.

SCOREBOARDS: Manual scoreboards were located on top of the pit structure during the 1950s and 60s. An electronic scoreboard extended out from the pits over pit lane from the early 60s until 1990. A scoreboard has been located at the Hairpin since 1983. A clock was located on the Innver House tower along the front straight during the 1960s.

AN EXPLAINATION OF THE INDEX OF PERFOMANCE AND RACE RESULTS CHARTS

A tremendous amount of research has gone into each 12 Hours of Sebring results chart on the following pages. Much of the data has been compiled using the original lap charts and official records. A driver is listed only if he actually drove the car during the race. Complete first names are listed when possible. Engine displacement and entrant/sponsor information is generally shown as it was listed on the official entry form.

INDEX OF PERFORMANCE: The Index of Performance prizes were awarded 1952-63 for cars showing the best coefficient performance based on the following Formula:

$$\text{Coefficient of Performance} = \frac{D}{d}$$

Where d is the prescribed qualifying distance for each car (which is different for each actual car displacement) and D is the total miles covered by the entrant. d in miles is arrived at as follows:

$$d = .23 \ \frac{3000 \times C}{(C + 350)} \ \times .62 = \ \dots \text{miles}$$

Where C is the exact individual cubic centimeter capacity of the entry (if bored and stroked indicated present displacement) (1 cubic inch = 16.4 cubic centimeters). The winning cars' displacements were checked after the race. *For supercharged, multiply by 2.*
EXAMPLE:
Minimum distance to qualify = d miles

$$d = .23 \ \frac{3000 \times C}{(C + 350)} \ \times .62 \quad \text{Where C = Displacement in cc.}$$

$$\text{e.g. } 1000 \text{ cc } d = .23 \ \frac{3000 \times 1000}{(1000 + 350)} \ \times .62$$

$$= .23 \times 2222.2 \times .62 = \frac{\text{Minimum Miles}}{316.7} \qquad \frac{\text{Minimum Miles}}{52.8}$$

The car that exceeded its minimum mileage by the largest percentage was the winner. This percentage was computed by dividing the actual mileage covered by the minimum mileage prescribed. The more powerful the engine being driven, the greater number of miles they were handicapped. This formula was derived from the Le Mans scoring method, but adjusted for the shorter distance/time at Sebring.

MAKES AND MODELS: Every effort has been made to list the exact model/type of every entrant to compete at Sebring. Chassis numbers of winning cars are based on manufacturer data and were not officially recorded by the race organizers or the sanctioning body.

FINISH POSITION: It is important to note that for the years 1952-72, non-finishers are always placed behind finishers in the final standings, regardless of the number of laps. From 1973 to present, final positions are determined solely by the number of laps completed.

QUALIFYING POSITIONS: Sebring used the "Le Mans start" from 1950-69, then a rolling pace car start was used beginning in 1970. Qualifying lap times are shown for 1970-95.

CLASS: All finishers from 1952-72 are shown with class and finish positions within class. Non-finishers 1952-72 are not assigned a class position. Exact class specifications often change from year to year, and were sometimes quite complicated. Basic abbreviations are shown below:

BASIC CLASS ABBREVIATIONS:

P	=	Prototype
S	=	Sports
GT	=	Grand Touring
X	=	Prototype/Experimental
U	=	Under (specified engine displacement)
O	=	Over (specified engine displacement)
L	=	Lights GTP
A	=	American Challenge
T	=	Touring
W	=	World Sports Car
TA	=	Trans Am

NON-STARTERS: DNS (Did Not Start) cars listed are generally limited to those entries which were officially entered, and in most cases, actually appeared at the circuit.

HOURLY STANDINGS: Have been compiled from official lap charts. The eventual winning car is listed in bold face type. Qualifying times for the top ten are listed beginning in 1970.

DNF Codes (Did Not Finish): Listed with official reason out as follows:

e	=	engine
b	=	brakes
a	=	accident
k	=	electrical/ignition
t	=	transmission/clutch
x	=	axle/rearend
s	=	suspension/steering wheel
f	=	fuel
u	=	unknown
m	=	mechanical, not specified
w	=	withdrew
DNS	=	Did Not Start
DISQ	=	Disqualified

ATTENDANCE: Estimated based on race reports and coverage. Official figures are seldom released.

1950

**1950 SEBRING WINNER —
Crosley Hot Shot**
Built by Crosley Motors, Inc.
Cincinnati, OH ./ Entered by Vic
Sharpe, Tampa, FL/Engine: 724cc
Crosley

**Drivers: Fritz Koster /
Ralph Deshon**

SAM COLLIER MEMORIAL SEBRING GRAND PRIX OF ENDURANCE
SIX HOURS / DECEMBER 31, 1950

FIN.	DRIVERS	NO.	MAKE / TYPE	DISP.	ENTRANT	CLASS	LAPS +1	INDEX
1	Fritz Koster / Ralph Deshon	19	Crosley Hot Shot	724	Victor Sharpe, Jr., Tampa, FL	H-1	89	1.0854
2	Jim Kimberly / Marshall Lewis	55	Ferrari 166	1995	Jim Kimberly, Chicago, IL	E-1	108	1.0385
3	Robert Keller / Paul Farago	20	Fiat 1100 MM	1086	Richard Haynes, Boca Raton, FL	G-1	95	1.0326
4	Bill Spear / George Roberts, Jr.	10	Ferrari 166	1995	William Spear, Manchester, NH	E-2	106	1.0102
5	John T. Van Driel	1	MG TC	1250	John F. Van Driel, Irvington, NJ	F-1	95	1.0000
6	Frank O'Hare / William Milliken	3	MG TC	1250	Frank O'Hare, Rochester, NY	F-2	94	.9894
7	Luigi Chinetti / Alfredo Momo	17	Ferrari 195S	2340	Briggs Cunningham, Palm Beach, FL	D-1	104	.9811
8	Fred Wacker / Frank Burrell	8	Allard Cadillac	5424	Fred G. Wacker, Chicago, IL	B-2	109	.9479
9	Rowland Keith / Robert Wilder	25	MG TC	1098	Robert Wilder, Palmer, MA	G-2	89	.9570
10	Jean Davidson / George Weaver	21	Allard Cadillac	5424	Jean Davidson, Clarkville, MD	B-2	109	.9479
11	J.W. Ferguson	24	Morris Minor	1140	J.W. Ferguson, Toronto, Ontario	F-2	89	.9438
12	Phil Walters / Bill Frick	16	Cadillac-Healey	5400	Briggs Cunningham, Palm Beach, FL	B-3	109	.9397
13	D.C. Viall / Red Charlwood	22	MG TD	1250	D.C. Viall, Alexandria, VA	F-4	89	.9368
14	Karl Brocken / Larry Whiting	5	Morris Minor	918	Karl Brocken, Milwaukee, WI	G-3	80	.9091
15	Bob Gegen	12	Morris Minor	918	Robert Gegen, Miami, FL	G-4	80	.9091
16	George Rand / George Marshall	9	Aston Martin DB2	2580	William Spear, Manchester, NH	D-2	97	.8981
17	Briggs Cunningham	18	Aston Martin DB2	2580	Briggs Cunningham, Palm Beach, FL	D-3	97	.8981
18	John Fitch / Colby Whitmore	23	Jaguar XK120	3442	John C. Fitch, White Plains, NY	C-1	93	.8829
19	B. Thomas	14	Morris Minor	918	Frankie Watts, Miami, FL	C-5	79	.8768
20	Delvan Lee / Harry Gray	15	Allard Cadillac	5425	Cal Connell, Detroit, MI	B-4	97	.8435
21	John Bentley / Paul O'Shea	30	Simca 8	1221	John Bentley, New York, NY	F-5	79	.8315
22	E. McIntosh / Mel Doyle	33	Jaguar XK120	3442	J.L. Cooke, Toronto, Ontario	C-2	90	.8108
23	C. Wheaton / R. Dillnutt	29	Aston Martin DB2	2580	J.C. Gilher, Toronto, Ontario	D-4	85	.7870
24	Hubert Brundage / Hobart Cook	32	MG TD	1250	Hubert L. Brundage, Miami, FL	DNF-u	67	.7052
25	Tom Braun / Charles Hassan	35	Jaguar XK120	3442	Charles D. Thompson, Cincinnati, OH	DNF-u	54	.4865
26	Erwin Goldschmidt / Tommy Cole	34	Allard Cadillac	5422	A.E. Goldschmidt, New York, NY	DNF-disq.	50	.4425
27	H.O. Beeler / James Cunningham	27	Allard Mercury	3918	H.O. Beeler, Houston, TX	DNF-e	39	.3482
28	Kurt Hildebrand	11	Volkswagen Spl.	1131	Kurt Hildebrand, Chicago, IL	DNF-e	8	.0860

Average Speed: 64.9 mph (#8)
Attendance: 2,800
Weather: Clear and cold

1952

1952 SEBRING WINNER —
Frazer Nash Le Mans Replica
Built by AFN Ltd., England /
Entered by Stuart Donaldson, New
York, NY. Chassis No. 421/100/
160; Engine: 3.0 Bristol/
BMW — No. SNS/1/37
**Drivers: Larry Kulok,
Harry Gray**

1ST ANNUAL 12 HOURS OF SEBRING / MARCH 15, 1952

POS.	DRIVERS	NO.	MAKE	DISP.	ENTRANT	CLASS	LAPS
1	Larry Kulok / Harry Gray	9	Frazer Nash LM	1991	Stuart Donaldson, New York, N.Y.	E-1	145
2	Charles Schott / Morris Carroll	23	Jaguar XK120	3442	Charles Schott, Brookside, N.J.	C-1	139
3	Dick Irish / Robert Fergus	1	Siata 1400 GS	1500	Robert Fergus, Columbus, Ohio	F-1	138
4	R. O'Brien / Richard Cicurel	57	Ferrari 166MM	1995		E-2	137
5	Chuck Wallace / Dick Yates	89	Jaguar XK120	3442	Jack Pry Ltd., Washington, D.C.	C-2	137
6	Dave Ash / John Van Driel	4	MG Mk II Spl.	1390	John Van Driel, Mt. Vernon, N.Y.	F-2	133
7	Steve Lansing / Wade Morehouse / R. Bonnet	25	Deutsch-Bonnet Panhard	745	Deutsch-Bonnet Autos, France	H-1	130
8	Dick Thompson / Bill Kinchloe	2	MG TD	1250	Dick Thompson, Washington, D.C.	F-3	129
9	Gus Ehrman / Bob Wilder	7	Morgan Plus 4	2088	Gus Ehrman, Greenwich, Conn.	D-1	128
10	Walt Hansgen / Randy Pearsall	52	MG TD	1250		F-4	128
11	Hubert Brundage / I. Brundage	10	Volkswagen Spl.	1190	H.L. Brundage, Miami, Fla.	F-5	128
12	Frank O'Hare / Frank Allen	5	MG TD	1250		F-6	125
13	Rene Bonnet / Hobart Cook	24	Deutsch-Bonnet Panhard	745	Deutsch-Bonnet Autos, France	H-2	101
14	George Schrafft / David Vial	40	Crosley	725		H-3	94
15	Roger Wing / Steven Spitler	26	Morris-Minor	980	John Gifford Motors, Washington, D.C.	G-1	75
16	George Sanderson	50	Crosley Hot Shot	725	George Sanderson, Mt. Kisco, N.Y.	H-4	72
17	Johnnie Rodgers / Fred Dagavar	13	Jaguar XK120	3442	Fred Dagavar, Pelham Manor, N.Y.	C-3	64
18	J. Greenwood / Paul Ceresole	47	Cisitalia Spyder	1050		DNF-u	105
19	Bob Grier / Myke Collins	11	Allard J2 Ford	4500	Bob Grier, New York, N.Y.	DNF-t	73
20	Otto Linton / T.L. Scatchard	39	Siata Crosley	1500	Otto Linton, Exton, Pa.	DNF-e	67
21	N. Patton / Bruce Bailey	34	MG TD	1250		DNF-u	63
22	Beau Clarke / Charles Hassan	51	Bandini Crosley	867		DNF-x	55
23	Bill Spear / Briggs Cunningham	8	Ferrari 340 America	4100	Bill Spear, Chicago, Ill.	DNF-x	51
24	Paul Ramos / Tony Cumming	12	MG TC-S	2500		DNF-e	43
25	Gary McDonald / B. Kennedy	45	Jaguar XK120	3442		DNF-e	37
26	George Huntoon / Phil Stiles	22	Siata Crosley	870	Briggs Cunningham, West Palm Beach, Fla.	DNF-e	31
27	Dave Hirsch / Bob Gegen	38	Aston Martin DB2	2600	Dave Hirsch, New York, N.Y.	DNF-x	29
28	James Simpson / George Colby	28	Ferrari 166MM	1995		DNF-f	26
29	Jim Keeley / J. Norcross	29	MG TC	1381		DNF-e	20
30	Joe Ferguson	18	Siata 1400 GS	1500	R. Belfield, New York, N.Y.	DNF-e	14
31	C. Sarle	43	MG TD	1250		DNF-e	4
32	Rex Easton	54	Mercury	4700		DNF-e	1
DNS	A.E. Goldschmidt / Bret Hannaway	98	Allard J2X Cadillac	5424	A.E. Goldschmidt, New York, N.Y.	transmission	
DNS	Fritz Koster / Alfons Koster	31	Porsche 1500 Super	1486		withdrawn	
DNS	Paul O'Shea / Tommy Cole	17	Allard J2X Cadillac	5424		transmission	
DNS	Jim Kimberly / Marshall Lewis	55	Ferrari 166MM	2715	Jim Kimberly, Chicago, Ill.	withdrawn	
DNS	Phil Walters / John Fitch	21	Cunningham C4R	5425	Briggs Cunningham, W. Palm Beach, Fla.	withdrawn	
DNS	Frank Bott / Rees Makins	14	Cisitalia Spyder	1050		withdrawn	

INDEX OF PERFORMANCE

1. #25 Deutsch-Bonnet 1.125
2. #1 Siata 1400 GS 1.028
3. #9 Frazer Nash LM 1.012
4. #4 MG Spl 994
5. #10 Volkswagen Spl 990
6. #2 MG TD 976
7. #52 MG TD 970

Average Speed: 62.8 mph
Distance: 754 miles
Margin of Victory: 6 laps
Leaders: **#8** 1-51, **#9** 52-145
Fastest Qualifier: None — Le Mans type start
Fastest Race Lap: #8 Bill Spear (unofficial)
Attendance: 7,000 (est.)
Weather: Heavy rains delayed start 1 hour 5 min. Partly cloudy and warm most of race.

1952 HOURLY STANDINGS — TOP 10

POS.	1 HR.	2 HRS.	3 HRS.	4 HRS.	5 HRS.	6 HRS.	7 HRS.	8 HRS.	9 HRS.	10 HRS.	11 HRS.	Finish
1	8	8	8	**9**	**9**	**9**	**9**	**9**	**9**	**9**	**9**	**9**
2	**9**	**9**	**9**	11	11	57	57	57	1	23	1	23
3	28	1	11	23	23	1	1	1	23	57	23	1
4	89	23	89	89	89	23	89	89	57	1	57	57
5	11	89	23	1	57	89	23	23	89	89	89	89
6	24	25	1	57	1	4	4	4	25	4	4	4
7	1	11	57	25	25	25	25	25	4	25	25	25
8	12	4	25	4	4	2	2	2	7	2	2	2
9	23	12	4	51	52	10	7	7	2	10	10	7
10	4	57	51	2	39	7	10	52	10	7	7	52

1953

**1953 SEBRING WINNER —
Cunningham C4R**
Built and entered by Cunningham
Cars, West Palm Beach, FL. Chassis No. 5216; Engine: 5.7 liter, 8
cyl. Chrysler
Drivers: John Fitch, Phil Walters

2ND ANNUAL 12 HOURS OF SEBRING / MARCH 8, 1953

POS.	DRIVERS	NO.	MAKE	DISP.	ENTRANT	CLASS	LAPS
1	John Fitch / Phil Walters	57	Cunningham C4R	5425	Briggs Cunningham, West Palm Beach, Fla.	B-1	173
2	Reg Parnell / George Abecassis	30	Aston Martin DB3	2920	Aston Martin, Ltd., England	D-1	172
3	Sherwood Johnston / Bob Wilder	74	Jaguar C	3442	A.H. Feverbacher, St. Louis, Mo.	C-1	162
4	Bob Gegen / Harry Gray	311	Jaguar C	3442	David Hirsch, New York, N.Y.	C-2	155
5	Briggs Cunningham / Bill Lloyd	59	OSCA MT4	1342	Briggs Cunningham, West Palm Beach, Fla.	F-1	153
6	Ed Lunken / Charles Hassan	49	Ferrari 166MM	1995	Ed Lunken, Cincinnati, Ohio	E-1	153
7	Chuck Wallace / Chuck Sarle	38	Jaguar XK120	3442	Jack Pry, Ltd., Washington, D.C.	C-3	151
8	Peter Yung / Robert Yung	45	Ferrari 225S	2715	Peter S. Yung, New York, N.Y.	D-2	148
9	James Simpson / George Colby	91	OSCA MT4 1100	1092	James Simpson, Chicago, Ill.	G-1	146
10	Russ Boss / Jake Kaplan	28	Jaguar XK120M	3442	J. Kaplan, Providence, R.I.	C-4	144
11	Rene Bonnet / Wade Morehouse	25	Deutsch-Bonnet Panhard	745	Hobart Cook, Woodbury, N.Y.	H-1	143
12	Walt Hansgen / Don McKnought	18	Jaguar XK120 coupe	3442	Walt Hansgen, Westfield, N.J.	C-5	142
13	Dave Ash / Frank Ahrens	4	MG Spl.	1389	David Ash, Mount Ivy, N.Y.	F-2	135
14	Phil Smyth / Bob Said	50	Frazer Nash MM	1971	W. Kalaczkowski, Forest Hills, N.Y.	E-2	134
15	Jim Shields / Bob McKinsley	53	MG TD	1250	James Shields, Kessington, Md.	F-3	132
16	William Wellenberg / Bill Wonder	42	MG TD	1381	Wm. Wellenberg, Jr., Flushing, N.Y.	F-4	132
17	Fred Dagavar / Al Garz	29	Jaguar XK120	3442	Fred Dagavar, Pelham Manor, N.Y.	C-6	132
18	Harry Beck / Charles Devaney	63	Siata Spyder	724	Paul Hessler, Wilmington, Del.	H-2	132
19	Fred Allen / Robert Longworth	44	MG Spl.	1250	Fred F. Allen, Rochester, N.Y.	F-5	127
20	T.L. Scatchard / H.B. Wessells	56	Siata Spyder	724	Thomas Scatchard, Philadelphia, Pa.	H-3	127
21	Paul Farago / Lou Torco	27	Siata Spyder	1100	Robert T. Keller, Wilmington, Del.	G-2	123
22	George Schrafft / Jim Hamlett	111	Crosley Palm Beach Spl.	726	George Schrafft, Palm Beach, Fla.	H-4	119
23	Mike Rothschild / Jack Nile	55	Morgan Plus 4	2088	Mike Rothschild, New York, N.Y.	D-3	119
24	Arnold Stubbs / Jack McAfee	32	Allard J2X Cadillac	6000	Jack Burkhard, Los Angeles, Calif.	B-2	116
25	Rees Makins / Frank Bott	6	OSCA roadster	1342	Rees T. Makins, Chicago, Ill.	F-6	115
26	George Huntoon / Phil Stiles	15	Jaguar C	3442	Jack Sheppard, Tampa, Fla.	C-7	114
27	Walter von Schonfeld / Rene Soulas	64	Maserati A6GCS	1978	W. von Schonfeld, Nutley, N.J.	E-3	110
28	Allan Patterson / H.L. Brundage	14	MG Spl.	1250	Al Patterson, Coconut Grove, Fla.	F-7	99
29	Morris Carroll / Randy Pearsall	16	Jaguar XK120	3442	George Tilp, Short Hills, N.J.	C-8	94
30	Walter Gray / Dale Duncan	51	Allard J2X Oldsmobile	5000	Walter Gray, Kansas City, Mo.	C-9	94
31	Roger Wing / Steven Spitler	37	Morris Minor	918	Jack Pry, Ltd., Washington, D.C.	G-3	93
32	Paul Ceresole / Logan Hill	11	Cisitalia Spyder	1091	Paul Ceresole, Concord, Mass.	G-4	88
33	Hal Ullrich / Dick Irish	2	Excalibur J Willys	2700	Brooks Stevens, Milwaukee, Wisc.	D-4	86
34	Charles Schott / John Van Driel	23	Jaguar XK120	3442	Charles Schott, Brookside, N.J.	C-10	63
35	Jim Kimberly / Marshall Lewis	5	Ferrari 225S	2715	Jim Kimberly, Chicago, Ill.	DNF-t	95
36	Ray Leibensperger / Howard Class	61	MG Spl.	1972	Ray Leibensperger, Allentown, Pa.	DNF-u	78
37	William Eager / Otto Linton	39	Siata Spyder	721	Speedcraft Ent., Exton, Pa.	DNF-e	63
38	Phil Hill / Bill Spear	8	Ferrari 225S	2715	Bill Spear, Palm Beach, Fla.	DNF-b	56

39	Norm Christianson / Austin Conley	19	Jaguar XK120 coupe	3442	Austin Conley, N. Arlington, N.J.	DNF-a	56
40	Geoff Duke / Peter Collins	31	Aston Martin DB3	2920	Aston-Martin, Ltd., England	DNF-a	52
41	A.E. Goldschmidt / Paul O'Shea	98	Healey-Cadillac	5442	A.E. Goldschmidt, New York, N.Y.	DNF-x	45
42	John Bennett / Charles Moran	58	Frazer Nash TF	1971	Briggs Cunningham, West Palm Beach, Fla.	DNF-x	28
43	Ralph Deshon / Don Quackenbush	26	Crosley Spl.	748	Ralph Deshon, Byram, Ct.	DNF-s	25
44	Tony Cumming	66	Allard J2X Cadillac	4031	Paul Ramos, New York, N.Y.	DNF-f	20
45	Masten Gregory	36	Allard J2X Chrysler	5428	Masten Gregory, Kansas City, Mo.	DNF-t	16
46	Tony Bonadies	1	Frazer Nash LM	1971	Stuart Donaldson, New York, N.Y.	DNF-e	10
47	Beau Clarke	97	Allard J2X Cadillac	5441	Mark Deitsch, Columbus, Ohio	DNF-e	9
48	Ralph Knudson	3	Excalibur J Willys	2700	Brooks Stevens, Milwaukee, Wisc.	DNF-e	4
49	Johnnie Rogers	9	Frazer Nash LM	1971	Stuart Donaldson, New York, N.Y.	DNF-e	2
50 dq	Bill Cook / John Marshall	24	Deutsch Bonnet Panhard	745	Hobart Cook, Woodbury, N.Y.	Disq.—pit violation	
51 dq.	Fritz Koster / George Deponte	48	Maserati A6GCS	1988	Fritz Koster, Sayville, N.Y.	Disq.—pit violation	
DNS	Larry Kulok / Harry Gray	21	Porsche 1500 Super	1488	Larry Kulok, New York, N.Y.	transmission	
DNS	Tommy Cole / Bill Lloyd	65	Ferrari 340 America	4100	William Lloyd, Green Farms, Ct.	engine	
DNS	Miles Collier / Cameron Argetsinger	75	Jaguar XK120	3442	C. Argetsinger, Burdett, N.Y.	engine	
DNS	George Sanderson / N. Coscoros	17	Crosley Hot Shot	724	George Sanderson, Mt. Kisco, N.Y.	engine	
DNS	F.R. Pearsall / William Eager	41	Cisitalia Spyder	1090	F. Randolf Pearson, Westfield, N.J.	engine	
DNS	Rene Bonnet	33	Deutsch-Bonnet Gordini	800	Rene Bonnet, France	withdrew	
DNS	Dick Thompson / Bill Kinchloe	12	Nash Healey Roadster	3900	Dick Thompson, Washington, D.C.	withdrew	

INDEX OF PERFORMANCE
1. #25 Deutsch-Bonnet 1.212
2. #30 Aston Martin DB3 . . . . 1.171
3. #91 OSCA 1.131
4. #59 OSCA 1.128
5. #63 Siata Spyder 1.127
6. #57 Cunningham C4R 1.113
7. #74 Jaguar C 1.095

Average Speed: 74.96 mph
Distance: 899.6 miles
Margin of Victory: 1 lap
Lap Leaders: #57 1-6, 8-18, 52-173; #31 7, 19-32; #30 33-51
Fastest Qualifier: None—Le Mans type start
Fastest Race Lap: Not recorded
Attendance: 12,500 (est.)
Weather: Partly cloudy and mild

1953 HOURLY STANDINGS — TOP 10

POS.	1 HR.	2 HRS.	3 HRS.	4 HRS.	5 HRS.	6 HRS.	7 HRS.	8 HRS.	9 HRS.	10 HRS.	11 HRS.	Finish
1	31	31	31	57	30	57	57	57	57	57	57	57
2	57	57	57	30	57	30	30	30	30	30	30	30
3	30	8	30	5	5	74	74	74	74	74	74	74
4	5	30	8	8	74	311	311	311	311	311	311	311
5	8	5	5	74	311	38	49	49	49	59	59	59
6	74	8	311	311	38	49	38	59	59	38	49	49
7	98	74	74	38	49	5	59	38	38	49	38	38
8	311	311	36	49	18	59	45	45	45	45	45	45
9	36	38	38	31	8	45	28	91	28	28	91	91
10	38	36	49	59	59	91	91	18	18	91	28	28

1954

1954 SEBRING WINNER — OSCA MT-4b
Built by Officine Specializzate Construzione Automobili, Italy / Entered by Briggs Cunningham, Palm Beach, FL. Chassis No. 1137; Engine: 1400/2 AD 1.5 liter, 4 cyl. OSCA
Drivers: Stirling Moss, Bill Lloyd

3RD ANNUAL 12 HOURS OF SEBRING / MARCH 7, 1954

POS.	DRIVERS	NO.	MAKE	DISP.	ENTRANT	CLASS	LAPS
1	Stirling Moss / Bill Lloyd	56	OSCA MT4	1452	Briggs Cunningham, West Palm Beach, Fla.	F-1	168
2	Porfirio Rubirosa / Gino Valenzano	39	Lancia D-24	3300	Scuderia Lancia Co., Italy	C-1	163
3	Lance Macklin / George Huntoon	29	Austin-Healey 100	2660	Donald Healey Ltd., England	D-1	163
4	James Simpson / George Colby	91	OSCA MT4	1452	James Simpson, Wadsworth, Ill.	F-2	163
5	Otto Linton / Harry Beck	61	OSCA MT4	1342	Speedcraft Enterprises, Exton, Pa.	F-3	161
6	W.K. Carpenter / John Van Driel	97	Kieft Bristol	1996	W.K. Carpenter, Montchanin, Del.	E-1	158
7	Richard Cicurel / Jim Pauley	41	Siata 208S	1996	Richard Cicurel, Bronxville, N.Y.	E-2	155
8	Rees Makins / Frank Bott	65	OSCA MT4 1100	1092	Rees Makins, Chicago, Ill.	G-1	152
9	Jake Kaplan / Russ Boss	15	Jaguar XK120	3442	Jacob Kaplan, Warwick, R.I.	E-3	151
10	Fernando Segura / Bojanich	49	Porsche 550 Spyder	1488	Fernando Segura, Argentina	F-4	144
11	Fred Allen / Gus Ehrman	54	Kieft MG	1465	Fred Allen, Pittsford, N.Y.	F-5	144
12	Richard Toland / Charles Devaney	62	Denzel VW roadster	1488	Richard Toland, Wayne, Pa.	F-6	142
13	A.F. Young / Jack Morton	9	Jaguar XK120	3442	A.F. Young, Jr., West Palm Beach, Fla.	C-2	142
14	Fred Dagavar / Henry Fanelli	18	Jaguar XK120	3442	Fred Dagavar, Pelham Manor, N.Y.	C-3	141
15	H.L. Brundage / James Simpson	50	Porsche 550 Spyder	1488	H.L. Brundage, Miami Springs, Fla.	F-7	141
16	Walter Gray / Charles Hall	2	Allard J2X Oldsmobile	5062	Walter Gray, Kansas City, Ks.	B-1	141
17	Jim Feld / Robert Gary	32	Excalibur Willys	2635	Brooks Stevens, Milwaukee, Wisc.	D-2	141
18	Howard Hanna / R. Williams	46	Porsche 550 Spyder	1488	Howard Hanna, Newtown Sq., Pa.	F-8	136
19	Ken Heavlin / C.J. Davis	74	Deutsch-Bonnet Panhard	749	C.J. Davis, Ypsilanti, Mich.	H-1	129
20	John Bentley / Guy Atkins	67	Siata Fiat	1089	John Bentley, New York, N.Y.	G-2	127
21	Austin Conley / Norm Christianson	66	Siata Fiat	1089	Austin Conley, N. Arlington, N.J.	G-3	126
22	Carlton Wilson / B. Kennedy	64	Jaguar XK120	3442	Carlton Wilson, West Palm Beach, Fla.	C-4	124
23	Charles Schott / Dave Michaels	12	Jaguar XK120	3442	Charles Schott, Brookside, N.J.	C-5	111
24	Alan Patterson / Jim Hendricks	35	Triumph TR2	1991	Alan Patterson, Miami, Fla.	E-4	103
25	George Moffett / Bob Said	57	OSCA MT4	1452	George Moffett, Mt. Kisco, N.Y.	F-9	102
26	Ken Lesko / Al Garz	19	Jaguar XK120	3442	Fred Dagavar, Pelham Manor, N.Y.	DNF-b	134
27	Phil Walters / John Fitch	5	Ferrari 375	4552	Briggs Cunningham, West Palm Beach, Fla.	DNF-e	104
28	Briggs Cunningham / Sherwood Johnston	1	Cunningham C4R	5454	Briggs Cunningham, West Palm Beach, Fla.	DNF-e	104
29	Victor Herzog / Steve Lansing	99	Kieft MG	1467	A.E. Goldschmidt, New York, N.Y.	DNF-u	88
30	Alberto Ascari / Gigi Villoresi	37	Lancia D-24	3300	Scuderia Lancia Co., Italy	DNF-b	87
31	John Schmidt / Jack German	17	Jaguar XK120	3442	John Ellwood, Daytona Beach, Fla.	DNF-u	82
32	Chuck Wallace / Carroll Shelby	25	Aston Martin DB3S	2922	Aston Martin Ltd., England	DNF-x	77
33	Don McKnought / William Eager	42	Maserati A6GCS	1988	Don McKnought, Cranford, N.J.	DNF-u	67
34	Gleb Derujinsky / Don Underwood	100	Kieft MG	1467	Gleb Derujinsky, New York, N.Y.	DNF-u	65
35	Conrad Janis / James Daly	14	Jaguar XK120	3442	Conrad Janis, New York, N.Y.	DNF-u	65
36	Bill Spear / Phil Hill	7	Ferrari 375	4522	William Spear, Palm Beach, Fla.	DNF-x	60
37	James Graham / J. Stimpson	48	Porsche 550 Spyder	1488	James Graham, Rye, N.Y.	DNF-f	57
38	Juan Fangio / Eugenio Castellotti	36	Lancia D-24	3300	Scuderia Lancia Co., Italy	DNF-t	51

39	Larry Kulok / Harry Gray	44	Frazer Nash LM	1971	George B. McClellan, Douglaston, N.Y.	DNF-e	50
40	William Brewster / Henry Rudkin	58	OSCA MT4	1452	William Brewster, Essex, Conn.	DNF-t	47
41	Luigi Musso / Gatta	40	Maserati A6GCS	1988	Maserati Co., Milano, Italy	DNF-b	47
42	James Lewis Brundage+ / James Orr	30	Austin-Healey 100	2660	H.L. Brundage, Miami Springs, Fla.	DNF-e	36
43	Walt Hansgen / Paul Timmins	11	Jaguar C	3442	Walt Hansgen, Westfield, N.J.	DNF-e	28
44	Franklin Curtis	59	MG Spl.	1444	Howard Hanna, Newton Square, Pa.	DNF-u	27
45	Harry Schell / Alfonso de Portago	22	Ferrari 250MM	2953	Harry Schell, Paris, France	DNF-x	26
46	Peter Collins / Pat Griffith	24	Aston Martin DB3S	2922	Aston Martin, Ltd., England	DNF-b	26
47	Sparacino / Ray Osborne	8	Jaguar XK120	3442	A.F. Young, Jr., West Palm Beach, Fla.	DNF-u	25
48	Reg Parnell / Roy Salvadori	23	Aston Martin DB3S	2922	Aston Martin Ltd., England	DNF-k	24
49	Bret Hannaway / John Marshall	70	Bandini Crosley	749	Miles Collier, Palm Beach, Fla.	DNF-e	21
50	William Wellenberg / Bill Wonder	26	Austin-Healey 100	2719	William Wellenberg, Flushing, N.Y.	DNF-e	20
51	Mike Rothschild / George Hunt	33	Healey Riley	9488	Mike Rothschild, New York, N.Y.	DNF-u	17
52	Roger Wing / Karl Brocken	69	Siata Crosley	749	Isabell Haskell, Palm Beach, Fla.	DNF-u	17
53	George Schrafft / Phil Stiles	72	Crosley Palm Beach Spl.	748	George Schrafft, Palm Beach, Fla.	DNF-x	16
54	Hal Ullrich	31	Excalibur Willys	2635	Brooks Stevens, Milwaukee, Wisc.	DNF-f	10
55	A.E. Goldschmidt	98	Allard JR Cadillac	5441	A.E. Goldschmidt, New York, N.Y.	DNF-e	9
56	Joseph Giubardo	27	Austin-Healey 100	2719	Joseph Giubardo, Valley Stream, N.Y.	DNF-u	3
57	Dick Irish	28	Excalibur Willys	2704	Brooks Stevens, Milwaukee, Wisc.	DNF-e	1
58	Piero Taruffi / Robert Manzon	38	Lancia D-24	3300	Scuderia Lancia Co., Italy	Disq.	161
59	J.G. Bennett / Traver McKenna	10	Jaguar C	3442	Frank Miller, Larchmont, N.Y.	Disq.	113
DNS	Randy Pearsall / George Tilp	20	Aston Martin DB2 Offy	2980	George Tilp, Short Hills, N.J.	transmission	
DNS	William Wood / John Moncur	75	Rex Mercury Marine	325	William Wood, Detroit, Mich.	failed inspection	
DNS	A.F. Young / Jack Morton	8	Chevrolet Corvette	3840	A.F. Young, West Palm Beach, Fla.	withdrew	
DNS	Kerner / Max Goldman	68	OSCA-S	750	C.J. Davis, Ypsilanti, Mich.	withdrew	

INDEX OF PERFORMANCE

1. # 56 OSCA MT4 . . . . 1.235
2. # 61 OSCA MT4 . . . . 1.201
3. # 91 OSCA MT4 . . . . 1.198
4. # 65 OSCA MT4 . . . . 1.174
5. # 29 Austin-Healey 100S 1.125
6. # 97 Kieft-Bristol 1.122
7. # 41 Siata-Fiat 1.101

Average Speed: 72.8 mph
Distance: 873.6 miles
Margin of Victory: 5 laps
Lap Leaders: **#37** 1, 3-4, 25-41; **#36** 2, 5-11, 18-24; **#7** 42-51; **#38** 12-17, 52-161; **#56** 162-168
Fastest Qualifier: None — Le Mans type start
Fastest Race Lap: #37 Alberto Ascari (unofficial)
Attendance: 14,000 (est.)
Weather: Clear and cold

+Killed in highway accident leaving track

1954 HOURLY STANDINGS — TOP 10

POS.	1 HR.	2 HRS.	3 HRS.	4 HRS.	5 HRS.	6 HRS.	7 HRS.	8 HRS.	9 HRS.	10 HRS.	11 HRS.	Finish
1	38	37	38	38	38	38	38	38	38	38	38	**56**
2	37	36	36	37	37	5	5	29	29	29	**56**	39
3	36	38	37	5	5	29	29	**56**	**56**	**56**	29	29
4	7	7	25	29	29	91	**56**	91	91	39	91	91
5	22	1	7	25	91	**56**	91	61	61	91	39	61
6	1	25	29	91	**56**	1	1	97	39	97	61	97
7	24	29	91	**56**	25	97	97	39	97	41	97	41
8	23	91	5	42	42	57	61	65	65	65	41	65
9	25	5	10	1	1	61	65	41	41	15	65	15
10	40	10	1	97	97	41	39	2	19	19	15	49

179

1955

1955 SEBRING WINNER —
Jaguar D-type
Built by Jaguar Cars, Ltd. /
Entered by Briggs Cunningham,
West Palm Beach, FL. Chassis No.
XKD406; Engine: 3.5 liter, fuel
injected, 6 cyl. Jaguar No. E2003-9
Drivers: Mike Hawthorn,
Phil Walters

4TH ANNUAL 12 HOURS OF SEBRING / MARCH 13, 1955

POS.	DRIVERS	NO. MAKE	DISP.	ENTRANT	CLASS	LAPS
1	Mike Hawthorn / Phil Walters	19 Jaguar D	3442	Briggs Cunningham, W. Palm Beach, Fla.	C-1	182
2	Phil Hill / Carroll Shelby	25 Ferrari 750S Monza	2999	Allen Guiberson, Dallas, Tex.	D-1	182
3	Bill Spear / Sherwood Johnston	35 Maserati 300S	2989	Bill Spear, W. Palm Beach, Fla.	D-2	180
4	Gino Valenzano / Cesare Perdisa	36 Maserati 300S	2989	Maserati Factory / Cunningham Co.	D-2	178
5	Piero Taruffi / Harry Schell	28 Ferrari 750S Monza	2999	Luigi Chinetti, New York, N.Y.	D-4	177
6	Stirling Moss / Lance Macklin	44 Austin-Healey 100S	2660	Donald Healey Motor Co., England	D-5	176
7	Bill Lloyd / George Huntoon	64 OSCA MT4	1492	Briggs Cunningham, W. Palm Beach, Fla.	F-1	168
8	Baron Von Hanstein / Herbert Linge	68 Porsche 550 Spyder	1498	Porsche Factory / Cunningham Co.	F-2	166
9	Carlos Braniff / Javier Velazquez	63 OSCA MT4	1492	Carlos Braniff, Mexico	F-3	166
10	Charles Wallace / Dick Thompson	15 Jaguar XK140	3442	Jack Pry, Washington, D.C.	C-2	163
11	Robert Davis / Candy Poole	61 Porsche 550 Spyder	1498	R.H. Davis, Ft. Lauderdale, Fla.	F-4	163
12	Russ Boss / Jake Kaplan	14 Jaguar C	3442	Jake Kaplan, Providence, R.I.	C-3	162
13	Ray Crawford+	5 Kurtis Kraft Lincoln	5196	Ray Crawford, Elmonte, Calif.	B-1	161
14	Ed Crawford / John Urbas	70 Porsche 1500 Super	1488	Ed Crawford, Northfield, N.Y.	F-5	161
15	William Brewster / Charles Rutan	45 Austin-Healey 100S	2660	William Brewster, Essex, Conn.	D-6	160
16	Bill Cook / George Rand	40 Austin-Healey 100S	2660	Bill Cook, Woodbury, L.I., N.Y.	D-7	156
17	Loyal Katskee / Roger Wing	12 Jaguar C	3442	Loyal Katskee, Omaha, Neb.	C-4	155
18	John Panks / Ernie Erickson	60 Arnolt-Bristol	1971	S.H. Arnolt, Inc., Warsaw, Ind.	E-1	154
19	B. Murphy / Sam Hanks	4 Kurtis Kraft Buick	5420	B. Murphy, Culver City, Calif.	B-2	153
20	M.R.J. Wyllie / Leech Cracaft	17 Jaguar XK140	3442	Dr. M. Wyllie, Allison Park, Pa.	C-5	152
21	Harry Woodnorth / Howard Hively	31 Mercedes-Benz 300SL	2996	R. Makins, Ft. Lauderdale, Fla.	D-8	152
22	Joseph Guibardo / Fred Wolf	38 Austin-Healey 100S	2660	J. Guibardo, Valley Stream, N.Y.	D-9	152
23	Paul O'Shea / Fritz Koster	81 Porsche 550 Spyder	1089	Porsche / Hoffman, New York, N.Y.	G-1	152
24	Bill Wonder / William Wellenberg	39 Austin-Healey 100S	2660	Wm. Wellenberg, Flushing, N.Y.	D-10	151
25	S.H. Arnolt / Bob Goldich	59 Arnolt-Bristol	1971	S.H. Arnolt, Inc., Warsaw, Ind.	E-2	151
26	Dr. Dolph Vilardi / Robert Grossman	18 Jaguar XK140	3442	Dolph Vilardi, Suffern, N.Y.	C-6	149
27	Mike Rothschild / Harold Kunz	55 Morgan Plus 4	1988	M.G. Rothschild, E. Orange, N.J.	E-3	149
28	Jim Feld / Bob Ballinger	48 Excalibur Willys	2638	Brooks Stevens, Milwaukee, Wis.	D-11	148
29	Rene Dreyfus / Bob Grier	58 Arnolt-Bristol	1971	S.H. Arnolt, Inc., Warsaw, Ind.	E-4	148
30	John Weitz / Gordon Mackenzie	52 Morgan Plus 4	1991	John Weitz, New York, N.Y.	E-5	145
31	John Penn / William Weirdon	84 Siata Fiat	1089	John Penn, Westerfield, N.J.	G-2	145
32	Bob Wilder / Rowland Keith	43 Austin-Healey 100S	2660	J. Fergusson, Toronto, Canada	D-12	143
33	John Norwood / Don Vitali	57 Arnolt-Bristol	1971	John Norwood, Rye, N.Y.	E-6	141
34	Guy Atkins / Traver McKenna	69 Porsche 1500 Super LM	1488	Guy Atkins, Pt. Washington, N.Y.	F-6	141
35	Chet Flynn / Luis Gonzalez	32 Mercedes-Benz 300SL	2996	Chet Flynn, Caracas, Venezuela	D-13	139
36	H.L. Brundage / Howard Fowler	75 Porsche 356 coupe	1290	H. Brundage, Miami Springs, Fla.	F-7	139
37	Fred Scherer / Don Davis	9 Ford Thunderbird	4786	Fred Scherer, Skokie, Ill.	C-7	138
38	Dave Ash / Duncan Black	76 MG TF	1250	Dave Ash, New York N.Y.	F-8	137
39	John Ryan / Buel Kinne	77 MG TF	1250	John Ryan, Miami, Fla.	F-9	135
40	Fred Van Beuren / E. Towle	8 Van Beuren Special	4842	Fred Van Beuren, Mexico City	C-8	131
41	Jackie Cooper / Roy Jackson-Moore	42 Austin-Healey 100S	2660	Jackie Cooper, New York, N.Y.	D-14	131
42	Evans Hunt / Howard Hanna	67 Porsche 550 Spyder	1498	Evans Hunt, Newton Square, Pa.	F-10	130
43	P. Morewood / G. Derujinsky / M. Gregory	50 Ferrari Mondial 500	1985	Ecurie Yankee, New York	E-7	124
44	E.C. Miller / Curtis Attaway	88 Renault 1063	748	Int. Auto Sales Co., Chicago, Ill.	H-1	124
45	Walt Gray / Paul Ceresole	3 Allard J2X Le Mans	5600	Walt Gray, Kansas City, Kansas	B-3	104

46	Thomas Friedmann / Karl Brocken	54 Maserati A6GCS	1988	T.A. Friedmann, Milwaukee, Wis.	DNF-t 129
47	Jean Pons / P. Herbert	87 Renault 1063	748	Renault Co. Paris, France	DNF-e 121
48	Norman Christianson / Don McKnought	72 Porsche 550 Spyder	1498	Norman Christianson, Roselle, N.J.	DNF-b 119
49	Austin Conley / LeRoy Thorpe	82 Siata Fiat	1089	Austin Conley, N. Arlington, N.J.	DNF-u 112
50	John Schmidt / Jack German	51 Triumph TR2	1991	John F. Ellwood, Ormond Beach, Fla.	DNF-u 111
51	N.J. Scott / R.W. Samuelson	78 Lotus Mk IX	1098	Bobbie Burns, Houston, Tex.	DNF-a 109
52	Ernie McAfee / Howard Wheeler	24 Ferrari 750S	2999	William Doheny, Los Angeles, Calif.	DNF-u 99
53	Jim Pauley / Dave Michaels	100 Siata 208S	1996	James E. Pauley, Stamford, Conn.	DNF-t 96
54	Chuck Daigh / Sterling Edwards	29 Ferrari 750S	2997	Manfredo Lippman, Guatemala	DNF-e 88
55	Otto Linton / Hal Stetson	73 OSCA MT4	1452	Speedcraft Ent., Exton, Pa.	DNF-u 83
56	Fred Dagavar / Al Garz	16 Jaguar XK120	3442	Fred Dagavar, Pelham Manor, N.Y.	DNF-e 73
57	Dick Irish / Isabelle Haskell	83 Siata Fiat	1089	Isabelle Haskell, Andover, England	DNF-e 67
58	Richard Toland / Howard Hanna	71 Denzel VW roadster	1290	Richard Toland, Wayne, Pa.	DNF-u 61
59	Robert Fergus / Harly Watts	41 Austin-Healey 100	2660	Robert Fergus, Columbus, Ohio	DNF-u 60
60	Walt Hansgen / William Eager	74 OSCA MT4	1342	George Tilp, Short Hills, N.J.	DNF-x 58
61	Briggs Cunningham / J.G. Bennett	37 Cunningham C6R Offy	2942	Briggs Cunningham, W. Palm Beach, Fla.	DNF-t 54
62	Alfonso de Portago / Umberto Maglioli	26 Ferrari 750S	2999	M. de Portago, Madrid, Spain	DNF-t 53
63	Hal Ullrich	47 Excalibur Willys	2638	Brooks Stevens, Milwaukee, Wis.	DNF-e 50
64	Gus Ehrman / Fred Allen	46 Austin-Healey 100S	2660	Fred Allen, Pittsford, N.Y.	DNF-e 47
65	Sidney Oakes / Lady Greta Oakes	49 Austin-Healey 100	2719	Sir Sydney Oakes, Nassau, Bahamas	DNF-a 44
66	Sandy McArthur / Paul Gougleman	89 Bandini Kiekhaeffer	690	Sandy McArthur, Chicago, Ill.	DNF-t 34
67	Phil Stewart / Ted Boynton	66 OSCA MT4	1491	Philip Stewart, Chicago, Ill.	DNF-u 33
68	Harry Chapman / W.G. Bell	65 OSCA MT4	1491	Harry Chapman, Tucson, Ariz.	DNF-u 18
69	Jim Kimberly / Ed Lunken	7 Ferrari 375 Plus	4890	James Kimberly, Chicago, Ill.	DNF-x 18
70	Julio Polo / Pancho Croquer	33 Mercedes-Benz 300SL	2996	Pancho Croquer, Venezuela	DNF-f 17
71	Porfirio Rubirosa / Cal Niday	53 Ferrari 500 Mondial	1990	Porfirio Rubirosa, Dominican Republic	DNF-a 14
72	A. Rosenberger / Charles Cowdin	2 Nash-Healey LM	4140	A. Rosenberger, Milwaukee, Wis.	DNF-t 14
73	Bret Hannaway	85 Kieft Fiat	1098	Bret Hannaway, New York, N.Y.	DNF-e 10
74	Jack McAfee	11 Ferrari 375MM	4500	Tony Parravao, Inglewood, Calif.	DNF-f 5
75	Jack Ensley	1 Kurtis Kraft Cadillac	5842	Jack Ensley, Indianapolis, Ind.	DNF-e 3
76*	Bob Said	27 Ferrari 750S	2999	Ecurie Yankee, New York, N.Y.	DNF-a* 3
77	Louis Pons	86 Renault 1063	748	Renault Co., France	DNF-a 2
78	John Shakespeare	10 Ferrari 375MM	4522	J.W. Shakespeare, Centralia, Ill.	DNF-k 0
79	Frank Miller / George Rabe	79 Lotus Mk IX	1098	Frank Miller, Larchmont, N.Y.	—Disq.—pushed across finish line
80	John Bentley / Jim McGee	80 Abarth Fiat	1098	John Bentley, Port Washington, N.Y.	—Disq.—refueling on course

NOTE: Six reserve entries also started the race without authorization and were immediately flagged off the course.

  *Bob Said's Ferrari collided with an ambulance which was on the course en route to an accident.

  +Ray Crawford received special permission from AAA to drive solo.

INDEX OF PERFORMANCE

1. #25 Ferrari 750S Monza 1.239
2. #64 OSCA MT4 . . . . 1.235
3. #19 Jaguar D 1.229
4. #44 Austin-Healey 100S 1.224
5. #68 Porsche 550 Spyder 1.220
6. #63 OSCA MT4 . . . . 1.220

Average Speed: 79.3 mph

Distance: 946.4 miles

Margin of Victory: 25.4 seconds

Fastest Qualifier: None—Le Mans type start

Fastest Race Lap: #19 Mike Hawthorn (unofficial)

Lap Leaders: #19 1-182 except lap 32 led by #28

Attendance: 20,000 (est.)

Weather: Clear and warm, cold in evening

1955 HOURLY STANDINGS — TOP 10

POS.	1 HR.	2 HRS.	3 HRS.	4 HRS.	5 HRS.	6 HRS.	7 HRS.	8 HRS.	9 HRS.	10 HRS.	11 HRS.	Finish
1	19	19	19	19	19	19	19	19	19	19	19	19
2	28	28	28	28	28	28	36	36	25	25	25	25
3	25	25	25	25	25	25	25	25	36	36	35	35
4	26	24	24	36	35	36	28	28	28	28	36	36
5	35	35	36	35	36	44	35	35	35	35	28	28
6	24	36	26	24	44	35	44	44	44	44	44	44
7	36	26	35	44	29	29	61	64	64	64	64	64
8	44	44	44	5	5	61	64	61	63	68	63	68
9	50	50	29	64	61	64	54	63	54	63	68	63
10	5	5	5	29	64	63	63	68	68	61	15	15

1956

**1956 SEBRING WINNER —
Ferrari 860 Monza**
Built and entered by Scuderia
Ferrari, Italy. Chassis No.
0604M; Engine: 3.4 liter,
4 cyl. Ferrari
**Drivers: Juan Fangio,
Eugenio Castellotti**

5TH ANNUAL 12 HOURS OF SEBRING / MARCH 24, 1956

POS.	DRIVERS	NO.	MAKE	DISP.	ENTRANT	CLASS	LAPS
1	Juan Fangio / Eugenio Castellotti	17	Ferrari 860 Monza	3422	Scuderia Ferrari, Italy	C-1	194
2	Luigi Musso / Harry Schell	18	Ferrari 860 Monza	3422	Scuderia Ferrari, Italy	C-2	192
3	Bob Sweikert / Jack Ensley	14	Jaguar D	3442	Jack Ensley, Indianapolis, Ind.	C-3	188
4	Roy Salvadori / Carroll Shelby	27	Aston Martin DB3S	2992	David Brown & Sons, Ltd., England	D-1	187
5	Piero Taruffi / Jean Behra	24	Maserati 300S	2992	Officine Alfieri Maserati Co., Italy	D-2	186
6	Hans Herrmann / Wolfgang Von Trips	41	Porsche 550 Spyder	1496	Porsche KG, Germany	F-1	182
7	Jack McAfee / Pete Lovely	43	Porsche 550 Spyder	1496	John Edgar Enterprises, Hollywood, Calif.	F-2	179
8	Alfonso Mena / Santiago Gonzales	16	Jaguar D	3442	Alfonso Gomez Mena, Cuba	C-4	176
9	John Fitch / Walt Hansgen	1	Chevrolet Corvette	5180	Raceway Enterprises, Dundee, Ill.	B-1	176
10	Porfirio Rubirosa / Jim Pauley	33	Ferrari 500 Mondial	1996	Porfirio Rubirosa, Dom. Rep.	E-1	172
11	Phil Stiles / George Huntoon	31	Austin-Healey 100S	2660	Ship & Shore Motors, Palm Beach, Fla.	D-3	168
12	Briggs Cunningham / J.G. Bennett	11	Jaguar D	3442	Briggs Cunningham, West Palm Beach, Fla.	C-5	168
13	Bob Ballinger / Phil Stewart	39	Arnolt-Bristol	1971	S.H. Arnolt Co., Warsaw, Ind.	E-2	158
14	George Marshall / Hubert Brundage	66	Porsche 550 Spyder	1496	Porsche KG, Germany	F-3	158
15	Max Goldman / Ray Crawford	6	Chevrolet Corvette	4346	Raceway Enterprises, Dundee, Ill.	C-6	157
16	Paul Armagnac / G. Mercader	58	Deutsch-Bonnet HBR5	745	Ecurie Jeudy Bonnet, France	H-1	155
17	Ted Boynton / J.E. Peterson	40	Arnolt-Bristol	1971	S.H. Arnolt Co., Warsaw, Ind.	E-3	154
18	J.H. Dressel / Bill Woodbury	37	AC Ace	1991	J.H. Dressel, Arlington, Va.	E-4	154
19	William Kinchloe / Steve Spitler	50	MGA	1489	Hambro Automotive Co., N.Y.	F-4	151
20	Dave Ash / Gus Ehrman	49	MGA	1489	Hambro Automotive Co., N.Y.	F-5	151
21	Leech Cracaft / Red Byron	55	Cooper T-39 Climax	1098	Cooper Car Co., England	G-1	147
22	Fred Allen / John Van Driel	51	MGA	1489	Hambro Automotive Co., N.Y.	F-5	139
23	Don Davis / Bob Gatz	3	Chevrolet Corvette	4346	Carl Beuhler III, U.S.A.	C-7	136
24	M.R.J. Wyllie / Peggy Wyllie	54	Lotus Mk IX	1097	Dr. M.R.J. Wyllie, Allison Park, Pa.	G-2	99
25	Reg Parnell / Tony Brooks	28	Aston Martin DB3S	2992	David Brown & Sons, Ltd., England	DNF-e	169
26	Mike Hawthorn / Desmond Titterington	8	Jaguar D	3442	Jaguar of New York Dist., Inc.	DNF-b	162
27	Alfonso de Portago / Jim Kimberly	19	Ferrari 857S	3422	Scuderia Ferrari, Italy	DNF-e	137
28	John Ryan	67	Arnolt-Bristol	1971	John Ryan, Chicago, Ill.	DNF-f	133
29	Chester Flynn / George Reed	22	Mercedes Benz 300SL	2996	Chester Flynn, New York, N.Y.	DNF-e	126
30	Bill Spear / Sherwood Johnston	10	Jaguar D	3442	Jaguar of New York Dist., Inc.	DNF-e	127
31	Russ Boss / Jake Kaplan	12	Jaguar D	3442	Jake Kaplan, New York, N.Y.	DNF-b	120
32	Ed Hugus / John Bentley	56	Cooper T-39 Climax	1098	Cooper Car Co., England	DNF-k	117
33	Lance Macklin / Archie Scott-Brown	29	Austin-Healey 100S	2660	Donald Healey Motor Co., England	DNF-k	110
34	Ed Crawford / Herbert Linge	42	Porsche 550	1496	Porsche KG, Germany	DNF-w	108
35	Roy Jackson-Moore / E. Forbes-Robinson	30	Austin-Healey 100S	2660	Donald Healey Motor Co., England	DNF-t	90
36	Mike Rothschild / George Hunt	35	Morgan Plus 4	1991	Morgan Motors, England	DNF-t	87
37	William Greenspun / Bruce Kessler	32	Ferrari 250MM	2975	William Greenspun, New York, N.Y.	DNF-e	82
38	Robert Burns / Norman Scott	47	Maserati 150S	1484	Allen Guiberson, Dallas, Tex.	DNF-t	77
39	S.H. Arnolt / Bob Goldich	38	Arnolt-Bristol	1971	S.H. Arnolt Co., Warsaw, Ind.	DNF-s	77

40	Sam Weiss / Lou Brero	15	Jaguar D	3442	A.A. Brown, England	DNF-t	68
41	Ivor Bueb / Duncan Hamilton	9	Jaguar D	3442	Jaguar of New York Dist., Inc.	DNF-b	63
42	Phil Hill / Masten Gregory	20	Ferrari 857	3500	George Tilp, Short Hills, N.J.	DNF-e	61
43	Stirling Moss / Peter Collins	26	Aston Martin DB3S	2922	David Brown & Sons, Ltd., England	DNF-t	51
44	Ralph Miller / H. Fenner	63	Lotus Mk IX	1097	Ralph Miller, U.S.A.	DNF-e	49
45	Troy Ruttman / Howard Hively	2	Ferrari 375 Plus	4954	Howard Hively, Cincinnati, Ohio	DNF-t	48
46	Cesare Perdisa / Carlos Menditeguy	25	Maserati 300S	2992	Officine Alfieri Maserati Co., Italy	DNF-a	39
47	Loyal Katskee / Roger Wing	62	Jaguar D	3442	Loyal Katskee, Omaha, Neb.	DNF-a	39
48	William Brewster / Bill Rutan	64	Austin-Healey 100S	2660	William Brewster, Essex, Conn.	DNF-t	39
49	Gerard Laureau / Hal Ullrich	59	Deutsch-Bonnet HBR	745	Brooks Stevens, Milwaukee, Wisc.	DNF-e	36
50	Curtis Attaway / Ralph Parkinson	52	Cooper T-39 Climax	1098	Robert Brown, Wilkes-Barre, Pa.	DNF-e	26
51	Harry Kite / Francois Crouzet	60	Deutsch-Bonnet HBR	745	Harry Kite Co., Ohio	DNF-a	25
52	Ernie Erickson / Charles Hassan	7	Chevrolet Corvette	4346	Ernie Erickson, Chicago, Ill.	DNF-e	22
53	A. de Tomaso / Isabell Haskell	48	Maserati 150S	1484	Alejandro de Tomaso, Argentina	DNF-t	15
54	Bill Lloyd / Karl Brocken	46	Maserati 150S	1484	William E. Lloyd, New Canaan, Conn.	DNF-t	13
55	Mauricio Marcotulli	57	OSCA S1000	1082	Touring Club of Venezuela	DNF-x	11
56	Jean Lucas	61	Renault 1063	748	Ecurie Lafayette, France	DNF-t	8
57	Julio Polo	34	Ferrari 500 Mondial	1996	Touring Club of Venezuela	DNF-a	8
58	Dale Duncan	5	Chevrolet Corvette	4346	Raceway Enterprises, Dundee, Ill.	DNF-x	3
59dq	Joe Sheppard / William Smith	53	Lotus Mk IX	1097	Joe Sheppard, Tampa, Fla.	Disq.	60
DNS	Colin Chapman / Len Bastrup	45	Lotus Coventry Climax	1490	Lotus Engineering, England	accident	
DNS	Charles Wallace / Duncan Black	23	Mercedes-Benz 300SL	2996	Jack Pry, Washington, D.C.	withdrew	
DNS	Paul O'Shea / Dick Thompson	21	Mercedes-Benz 300SL	2996	George Tilp, Short Hills, N.J.	oil leak	
DNS	John Weitz / Manuel Bos	36	Morgan Plus 4	1991	John Weitz, New York, N.Y.	accident	
DNS	Jim Kimberly / Ed Lunken	3	Ferrari 121 LM	4400	Jim Kimberly, Chicago, Ill.	transmission	
DNS	Rees Makins / Frank Bott	44	OSCA MT4	1485	Automobile OSCA SpA, Italy	withdrew	

INDEX OF PERFORMANCE

1. #41 Porsche 550 Spyder 1.347
2. #43 Porsche 550 Spyder 1.325
3. #17 Ferrari 860 Monza 1.310
4. #58 Deutsch-Bonnet 1.302
5. #18 Ferrari 860 Monza 1.289
6. #27 Aston-Martin DB3S 1.274
7. #14 Jaguar D 1.269

Average Speed: 84.07 mph
Distance: 1,008.8 miles
Margin of Victory: 2 laps
Fastest Race Lap: #8 Mike Hawthorn 89.5 mph
Fastest Qualifier: None—Le Mans type start
Lap Leaders: #8 1-25, 41-65, 71-80, 91-116, 129-135;
#17 26-40, 66-70, 81-90, 117-128, 136-194
Attendance: 25,754
Weather: Clear and warm

1956 HOURLY STANDINGS — TOP 10

POS.	I HR.	2 HRS.	3 HRS.	4 HRS.	5 HRS.	6 HRS.	7 HRS.	8 HRS.	9 HRS.	10 HRS.	11 HRS.	Finish
1	18	17	8	17	17	17	17	17	17	17	17	17
2	26	26	24	8	8	8	18	18	18	18	18	18
3	17	8	17	18	18	18	8	8	8	8	14	14
4	9	9	18	19	28	19	28	28	28	14	27	27
5	18	18	19	28	19	28	19	14	14	27	24	24
6	24	24	28	24	24	14	14	19	19	24	41	41
7	25	19	24	14	27	24	24	27	27	41	43	43
8	19	28	20	10	14	10	27	24	24	43	16	16
9	15	15	9	11	10	27	41	41	41	28	1	1
10	20	25	15	27	11	41	43	43	43	16	8	33

1957

**1957 SEBRING WINNER —
Maserati 450S**
Built and entered by Officine
Alfieri Maserati Co., Italy. Chassis
No. 4501; Engine: 4.5 liter, V-8 cyl.
Maserati
Drivers: Juan Fangio, Jean Behra

6TH ANNUAL 12 HOURS OF SEBRING / MARCH 23, 1957

POS.	DRIVERS	NO.	MAKE	DISP.	ENTRANT	CLASS	LAPS
1	Juan Fangio / Jean Behra	19	Maserati 450S	4454	Maserati Co., Italy	S1-1	197
2	Stirling Moss / Harry Schell	20	Maserati 300S	2991	Maserati Co., Italy	S2-1	195
3	Mike Hawthorn / Ivor Bueb	5	Jaguar D	3810	Jaguar Cars, North America, N.Y.	S1-2	193
4	Masten Gregory / Lou Brero	15	Ferrari 290MM	3490	George Tilp, Short Hills, N.J.	S1-3	193
5	Walt Hansgen / Russ Boss	7	Jaguar D	3810	B.S. Cunningham, New York, N.Y.	S1-4	188
6	Peter Collins / Maurice Trintignant	11	Ferrari 315S	3809	Scuderia Ferrari, Italy	51-5	187
7	Alfonso de Portago / Luigi Musso	12	Ferrari 315S	3809	Scuderia Ferrari, Italy	S1-6	186
8	Art Bunker / Chuck Wallace	44	Porsche RS	1498	Jack Pry Motors, Washington, D.C.	S4-1	185
9	Pierre Kunstle / Ken Miles	45	Porsche RS	1498	Jean Kunstle, Carmel, Calif.	S4-2	184
10	Howard Hively / Richie Ginther	28	Ferrari 500TRC	1996	T. Buell, Denver, Colo.	S3-1	179
11	Colin Chapman / Joe Sheppard / D. Dungan	59	Lotus 11	1097	Lotus Engineering, England	S5-1	174
12	Dick Thompson / Gaston Andrey	4	Chevrolet Corvette	4638	John Fitch, Stamford, Ct.	G1-1	173
13	Harry Beck / Hal Stetson / Otto Linton	47	OSCA MT4	1492	Scuderia OSCA, Italy	S4-3	170
14	Jan de Vroom / George Arents / D. Cunningham	31	Ferrari 500TRC	1996	Jan de Vroom, New York, N.Y.	S3-2	169
15	John Kilborn / Jim Jeffords / Dale Duncan	3	Chevrolet Corvette	4638	Lindsey Hopkins, Miami, Fla.	G1-2	168
16	Paul O'Shea / Pete Lovely	2	Chevrolet Corvette	4638	Lindsey Hopkins, Miami, Fla.	S1-7	166
17	J. Fernandez / J. Droulers	36	AC Ace	1971	A.C. Cars Ltd., England	G3-1	161
18	Tom Hallock / Max Goldman	58	Cooper Climax	1098	Cooper Car Co., England	S5-2	159
19	E. Pennybacker / Robert Oker	34	Triumph TR3	1991	Standard Motor Co. Ltd., England	G3-2	159
20	Jake Kaplan / Charlie Rainville	55	Alfa Romeo Giulietta SV	1290	J. Kaplan, Providence, R.I.	G5-1	158
21	Mike Rothschild / R. Johns	33	Triumph TR3	1991	Standard Motor Co. Ltd., England	G3-3	156
22	Hap Dressel / Don Cullen / W. Woodbury	35	AC Ace	1971	A.C. Cars Ltd., England	G3-4	154
23	A. Miller / Abe Leavens / Rowland Keith	49	MGA	1486	Hambro Auto Co., New York, N.Y.	G4-1	154
24	Red Crise / Alan Markelson	52	Alfa Romeo Giulietta SV	1290	Sir Sidney Oakes, Nassau	G5-2	153
25	Fred Windridge / George Reed / R. Gilbert	18	Mercedes-Benz 300SL	2996	C. Kreisler, New York, N.Y.	G2-1	153
26	Gil Geitner / Ray Cuomo	25	Austin-Healey Special	2680	Hambro Auto Co., New York, N.Y.	G2-2	151
27	Dave Ash / Gus Ehrman / J. Van Driel	51	MGA	1486	Hambro Auto Co., New York, N.Y.	G5-2	150
28	Harry Behm / Carl Haas / Sandy McArthur	56	Stanguellini Bialbero	750	Behm Motors, Oshkosh, Wisc.	S6-1	149
29	Bob Grier / Bob Kennedy	32	Morgan 4/4	1991	Robert Grier, New York, N.Y.	S3-5	147
30	J. Cook / Ralph Durbin / L. Karber	71	Arnolt Bristol	1971	J. Cook, Detroit, Mich.	G3-6	146
31	H. von Hanstein / Herbert Linge	40	Porsche Carrera	1498	Porsche KG, Germany	G4-3	144
32	Victor Merino / Luis Pedrerra / R. Rosales	61	Lotus 11	1097	Puerto Rico Auto Club	S5-3	141
33	Chet Flynn / Ed Hugus	17	Mercedes-Benz 300SL	2996	Chet Flynn, New York, N.Y.	G2-3	138
34	Maurice Michy / M. Foulgoc	64	Renault Dauphine	845	Renault Co., France	G6-1	138
35	Gilberte Thirion / Nadege Ferrier	65	Renault Dauphine	845	Renault Co., France	G6-2	138
36	Steve Spitler / William Kinchloe	50	MGA	1489	Hambro Auto Co., New York, N.Y.	G4-4	137
37	Paul Frere / Jean Lucas	66	Renault Dauphine	845	Renault Co., France	G6-3	134
38	Lou Comito / Richard Kessler / R. Rubin	54	Alfa Romeo Giulietta SV	1290	Lou Comito Centerville, N.Y.	G5-3	42
39	Norman Scott / Frank Bott	42	Porsche RS	1498	N.J. Scott, Houston, Texas	DNF-t	168

40	Hans Herrmann / Jack McAfee	41	Porsche RS	1498	Porsche KG, Germany	DNF-t	165
41	John Mull / Ed Mull	72	AC Ace	1971	A.C. Car Co. Ltd., England	DNF-x	146
42	Ed Lunken / Charles Hassan	29	Ferrari 500	1986	E. Lunken, Cincinnati, Ohio	DNF-f	143
43	Olivier Gendebien / Gene Greenspun	16	Ferrari 250GT	2996	H. Kullen, Baltimore, Md.	DNF-e	111
44	Phil Hill / Wolfgang Von Trips	14	Ferrari 290MM	3490	Scuderia Ferrari, Italy	DNF-e	106
45	Roy Jackson-Moore / E. Forbes-Robinson	24	Austin-Healey 100/6	2680	Hambro Auto Co., New York, N.Y.	DNF-e	105
46	Phil Stiles / John Bentley	23	Austin-Healey 100/6	2680	Hambro Auto Co., New York, N.Y.	DNF-e	98
47	M.R.J. Wyllie / Peggy Wyllie / Charles Moran	74	Lotus 11	1486	Charles Moran, Rye, N.Y.	DNF-e	89
48	Lance Reventlow / W. Pollack	27	Maserati 200S	1998	Lance Reventlow, Beverly Hills, Calif.	DNF-e	88
49	Jay Chamberlain / Ignacio Lozano	60	Lotus 11	1097	Lotus Engineering Co., England	DNF-f	77
50	G. Storr / Hal Ullrich	63	Deutsch-Bonnet HBR	846	Graham Shaw, Columbia, S.C.	DNF-e	67
51	Jim Kimberly / Ted Boynton	26	Maserati 200S	1998	Jim Kimberly, Chicago, Ill.	DNF-t	58
52	Joakim Bonnier / Giorgio Scarlatti	22	Maserati 300S	2991	A.V. Dayton, Kansas City, Mo.	DNF-e	55
53	John Weitz / Robert Gary	38	Arnolt Bristol	1997	S.H. Arnolt, Warsaw, Ind.	DNF-w	51
54	Jack Ensley / Pat O'Connor	8	Jaguar D	3442	Jack Ensley, Indianapolis, Ind.	DNF-x	50
55	Bob Ballinger / J.E. Peterson	39	Arnolt Bristol	1997	S.H. Arnolt, Warsaw, Ind.	DNF-w	49
56	S.H. Arnolt / Bob Goldich*	37	Arnolt Bristol	1997	S.H. Arnolt, Warsaw, Ind.	DNF-a	40
57	Jim Pauley / William Helborn	30	Ferrari 500	1996	W. Helborn, New York, N.Y.	DNF-e	38
58	Alfonso Mena / Ernie Erickson	9	Jaguar D	3442	Alfonso Gomez Mena, Cuba	DNF-e	37
59	Ed Crawford / Phil Stewart	43	Porsche RS	1498	E. Crawford, Northfield, Ill.	DNF-x	35
60	Pierce Woods / Bobby Unser	10	Jaguar D	3442	R.V. Milosevich, U.S.A.	DNF-x	33
61	Piero Taruffi / John Fitch	1	Chevrolet Corvette SS	4638	Lindsey Hopkins, Miami, Fla.	DNF-s	23
62	Lloyd Ruby	46	Maserati 150S	1498	B. Burns, Wichita Falls, Texas	DNF-e	20
63	J. Roberts	70	Triumph TR3	1991	Standard Motor Co., England	DNF-t	10
64	Briggs Cunningham	6	Jaguar D	3800	Briggs Cunningham, New York, N.Y.	DNF-e	2
65dq	Roy Salvadori / Carroll Shelby	21	Maserati 300S	2991	Maserati Co., Italy	Disq.	68
DNS	Taruffi / Moss / Fitch / Fangio	0	Chevrolet Corvette SS	4638	Special practice car not officially entered		
DNS	Jim Pauley / D. Vitales	69	Ferrari 250GT	2996	J. Pauley, Stamford, Ct.	reserve	
DNS	J. Von Neuman / Pete Lovely	73	Porsche RS	1498	J. Von Neuman, Los Angeles, Calif.	reserve	
DNS	Howard Hanna / H. Brown	75	Deutsch-Bonnet	846	H. Hanna, Broomall, Pa.	reserve	

*Killed in race accident at esses. Remaining two Arnolt Bristol entries withdrew.

INDEX OF PERFORMANCE

1. #44 Porsche RS 1.360
2. #45 Porsche RS 1.359
3. #59 Lotus Mk XI 1.349
4. #20 Maserati 300S 1.326
5. #19 Maserati 450S 1.306

Average Speed: 85.36 mph
Distance: 1,024.4 miles
Margin of Victory: 2 laps
Fastest Race Lap: #19 Juan Fangio 92.5 mph
Fastest Qualifier: None — Le Mans type start
Lap Leaders: #11 1-19; #19 20-197
Attendance: 39,126
Weather: clear and hot

1957 HOURLY STANDINGS — TOP 10

POS.	1 HR.	2 HRS.	3 HRS.	4 HRS.	5 HRS.	6 HRS.	7 HRS.	8 HRS.	9 HRS.	10 HRS.	11 HRS.	Finish
1	11	19	19	19	19	19	19	19	19	19	19	19
2	19	20	11	20	20	15	15	20	12	20	20	20
3	20	11	20	11	11	5	20	5	5	5	5	5
4	12	12	15	17	14	12	5	15	20	15	15	15
5	15	15	14	15	15	11	14	16	15	7	7	7
6	14	14	12	5	5	7	7	7	7	11	11	11
7	16	5	5	7	7	14	16	11	11	41	12	12
8	5	7	7	14	12	20	11	12	41	12	44	44
9	7	16	16	16	16	16	12	41	12	44	45	45
10	8	22	26	28	28	28	41	42	42	45	28	28

1958

**1958 SEBRING WINNER —
Ferrari 250TR**
Built and entered by Scuderia
Ferrari, Italy. Chassis No. 0704;
Engine: 3.0 liter, V-12 Ferrari
Drivers: Phil Hill, Peter Collins

7TH ANNUAL 12 HOURS OF SEBRING / MARCH 22, 1958

POS.	DRIVERS	NO.	MAKE	DISP.	ENTRANT	CLASS	LAPS
1	Phil Hill / Peter Collins	14	Ferrari 250TR	2953	Scuderia Ferrari, Italy	D-1	200
2	Luigi Musso / Olivier Gendebien	16	Ferrari 250TR	2953	Scuderia Ferrari, Italy	D-2	199
3	Harry Schell / Wolfgang Seidel	41	Porsche RS	1587	Porsche K.G., Germany	E-1	193
4	Sam Weiss / Dave Tallakson	56	Lotus 11	1096	Team Lotus, England	G-1	179
5	Paul O'Shea / Bruce Kessler / David Cunningham	22	Ferrari 250GT	2953	N.A.R.T., New York, N.Y.	9-1	179
6	Colin Chapman / Cliff Allison	55	Lotus 11	1096	Team Lotus, England	G-2	179
7	George Arents / George Reed / Dan O'dell	21	Ferrari 250GT	2953	N.A.R.T., Coconut Grove, Fla.	9-2	175
8	A. de Tomaso / I. de Tomaso/ R. Ferguson	60	OSCA S750	748	O.S.C.A., Bologna, Italy	H-1	175
9	Jay Chamberlain / Bill Frost	54	Lotus 11	1096	Team Lotus, England	G-3	175
10	H. von Hanstein / Herbert Linge / John Cuevas	43	Porsche GT	1498	Porsche K.G., Germany	6-1	174
11	Porfirio Rubirosa / Jean Malle / W. Helburn	30	Ferrari 500TR	1998	Porfirio Rubirosa, Palm Beach, Fla.	E-2	172
12	Richard Doane / Jim Rathmann	1	Chevrolet Corvette	4632	Richard Doane, Dundee, Ill.	10-1	170
13	Hal Stetson / Otto Linton / Harry Beck	47	OSCA MT4	1491	O.S.C.A., Bologna, Italy	F-1	170
14	Gil Geitner / Phil Stiles / Harold Kunz	27	Austin-Healey 100	2639	Hambro Automotive Corp., New York, N.Y.	9-3	169
15	Luke Stear / M. Norris	72	AC-Bristol Ace	1971	A.C. Cars Ltd., England	E-3	168
16	F. Fuller / Art Tweedale / T. Briggs	39	AC-Bristol Ace	1971	A.C. Cars Ltd., England	E-4	166
17	William Kinchloe / F. Monroe	28	Austin-Healey 100	2639	Hambro Automotive Corp., New York, N.Y.	9-4	166
18	Fred Van Beuren / Javier Velasquez	50	Alfa Romeo Veloce	1290	Fredrick T. Van Beuren, Mexico	5-1	164
19	R. Milo / George McClure / Duncan Forlong	37	AC-Bristol Ace	1971	A.C. Cars Ltd., England	7-1	163
20	Mike Rothschild / W. Kimberly / B. Lott	34	Triumph TR3	1991	Standard Motor Co., England	7-2	160
21	Carl Haas / Alan Ross / Charles Dietrich	53	Stanguellini Sports	1098	Behm Motors, Oshkosh, Wisc.	G-4	160
22	Bill Love / Roy Jackson-Moore / George Crowder	38	AC-Bristol Ace	1971	A.C. Cars Ltd., England	E-5	159
23	Gus Ehrman / Ray Cuomo	29	Austin-Healey 100	2639	Hambro Automotive Corp., New York, N.Y.	9-5	159
24	Charlie Rainville / Jake Kaplan	52	Alfa Romeo Veloce	1290	Jake Kaplan, Providence, R.l.	5-2	157
25	Bob Holbert / Charles Wallace / S. Hudson	46	Porsche RS	1498	Marshall Motors, Miami, Fla.	F-2	153
26	J. Roberts / L. Heuss / G. Spaulding	35	Triumph TR3	1991	Standard Motor Co., England	7-3	153
27	Alfonso Mena / Abelardo Carraras / Jorge Galtes	71	Ferrari 500TR	1998	Scuderia Cuba, Havana, Cuba	E-6	151
28	Bill Milliken / M. Ripley / Cameron Argetsinger	78	Elva Mk II	1096	Ripley Motor Co., Ithaca, N.Y.	G-5	151
29	H. Brown / Richard Toland	61	Deutsch-Bonnet coupe	749	Richard Toland, Devon, Pa.	H-2	151
30	John Brumby / Frank Aldhous / Ray Martinez	63	Fiat Abarth Zagato	747	Baron de Graffenried, Switzerland	H-3	150
31	Charles Kissinger / Willie West / Alfonso Thiele	64	Fiat Abarth Zagato	747	Baron de Graffenried, Switzerland	3-1	148
32	Harry Fry / Lew Rappaport	80	Fiat Abarth Zagato	747	Dr. Harry Fry, Miami, Fla.	3-2	145
33	Dick Thompson / Fred Windridge	2	Chevrolet Corvette	4632	Richard Thompson, Washington, D.C.	10-2	144
34	Dan Gurney / Howard Hanna	62	Deutsch-Bonnet coupe	749	Howard Hanna, Broomall, Pa.	H-4	143
35	Max Goldman / Ralph Durbin	40	Arnolt Bristol Bolide	1971	S.H. Arnolt, Warsaw, Ind.	7-4	141
36	Robert Oker / H. Hurtley	33	Triumph TR3	1991	Standard Motor Co., England	7-5	131
37	Lou Comito / Alan Markelson / Bob Pfaff	51	Alfa Romeo Veloce	1290	Louis Comito, Centerport, N.Y.	5-3	126
38	Charles Moran / Paul Ceresole	49	Lotus Le Mans	1475	Charles Moran, Jr., Rye, N.Y.	F-3	110
39	Norman Scott / Frank Bott	74	Porsche RS	1498	N.J. Scott, Jr., Houston, Tex.	F-4	109

40	Bob Kennedy / Tom Payne / C. Sherman	36	Morgan roadster	1991	Richard Kennedy, Detroit, Mich.	7-6	76
41	John Bentley / Bill Bradley	58	Elva Mk lll	1096	Elva Engineering Co., England	G-6	71
42	John von Neumann / Richie Ginther	17	Ferrari 250TR	2953	Ferrari of Calif., Hollywood, Ca.	DNF-t	168
43	Mike Hawthorn / Wolfgang Von Trips	15	Ferrari 250TR	2953	Scuderia Ferrari, Italy	DNF-t	159
44	Gaston Andrey / Bill Lloyd	31	Ferrari 500TR	1998	Mike Garber, Hamden, Ct.	DNF-x	125
45	Denise McCluggage / Ruth Levy	65	Fiat Abarth Zagato	747	Alfred Momo, Woodside, N.Y.	DNF-t	116
46	B. Martin / Frank Baptista / W. Warren	57	Elva Mk III	1096	Elva Engineering, Hollywood, Ca.	DNF-u	114
47	Art Bunker / Godin de Beaufort	14	Porsche RS	1498	Art's Sports Motors, Kansas City, Mo.	DNF-t	106
48	Jean Behra / Edgar Barth	42	Porsche RS	1587	Porsche K.G., Germany	DNF-t	105
49	Dale Duncan / Joakim Bonnier / Jack Hinkle	7	Maserati 300S	2983	A.V. Dayton, Tulsa, Ok.	DNF-t	90
50	Stirling Moss / Tony Brooks	24	Aston Martin DBR1	2922	David Brown Ltd., England	DNF-t	90
51	John Fitch / Ed Martin	19	Ferrari 250TR	2953	H. Kullen, Baltimore, Md.	DNF-e	85
52	Alfonso Mena / Jan deVroom / A. Carraras	79	Ferrari 500TR	1998	Alfonso Gomez Mena, Havana, Cuba	DNF-e	69
53	Charles Kurtz / J. Karmer / Dean Patterson	77	Elva Mk III	1096	Avant Corp., Pittsburgh, Pa.	DNF-t	68
54	Carroll Shelby / Roy Salvadori	25	Aston Martin DBR1	2922	David Brown Ltd., England	DNF-t	62
55	Ken Miles / Jean Kunstle	45	Porsche RS	1498	John P. Kunstle, Carmel, Ca.	DNF-t	59
56	Chet Flynn / Ed Hugus	23	Ferrari 250TR	2953	Chester Flynn, New York, N.Y.	DNF-a	58
57	Masten Gregory / Ron Flockhart	9	Jaguar D	2986	Ecurie Ecosse, Edinburgh, Scotland	DNF-e	55
58	Bob Said / M. Rivera / A. Morewood	81	Ferrari 500TR	1998	Scuderia Central America, El Salvador	DNF-b	43
59	Augie Pabst / James Jeffords	3	Chevrolet Corvette	4632	James Jeffords, Milwaukee, Wisc.	DNF-x	27
60	Ivor Bueb / Ninah Sanderson	8	Jaguar D	2986	Ecurie Ecosse, Edinburgh, Scotland	DNF-e	22
61	Briggs Cunningham / Russ Boss	12	Jaguar D	2986	Alfred Momo, Woodside, N.Y.	DNF-e	16
62	John Dalton / George Constantine	26	Aston Martin GT coupe	2922	David Brown Ltd., England	DNF-w	15
63	Jim Kimberly / Pete Lovely	32	Maserati 200S	1996	Jim Kimberly, Chicago, Ill.	DNF-t	14
64	Ed Crawford	11	Lister Jaguar	2986	Alfred Momo, Woodside, N.Y.	DNF-e	6
65	Archie Scott-Brown	10	Lister Jaguar	2986	Alfred Momo, Woodside, N.Y.	DNF-a	3
DNS	Manfredo Lippman / G. Giron	4	Mercedes Benz 300SL	2996	Scuderia Central America, El Salvador	withdrew	
DNS	Samuel Alvarez / Miguel Rivera	5	Mercedes Benz 300SL	2996	Scuderia Central America, El Salvador	withdrew	
DNS	M.R.J. Wyllie / Chuck Dietrich	48	Elva	1476	Dr. M.J. Wyllie, Allison Park, Pa.	accident	

INDEX OF PERFORMANCE

1. #60 OSCA 750S 1.470
2. #41 Porsche RS 1.408
3. #56 Lotus 11 . . . . 1.389
4. #55 Lotus 11 . . . . 1.389
5. #14 Ferrari 250TR 1.360
6. #54 Lotus 11 . . . . 1.356
7. #16 Ferrari 250TR 1.353

Average Speed: 86.67 mph
Distance: 1,040 miles
Margin of Victory: 1 lap
Fastest Race Lap: #24 Stirling Moss 93.6 mph
Fastest Qualifier: None — Le Mans type start
Lap Leaders: #24 1-70; #14 71-200
Attendance: 45,763
Weather: Clear and warm

1958 HOURLY STANDINGS — TOP 10

POS.	1 HR.	2 HRS.	3 HRS.	4 HRS.	5 HRS.	6 HRS.	7 HRS.	8 HRS.	9 HRS.	10 HRS.	11 HRS.	Finish
1	24	24	24	24	14	14	14	14	14	14	14	14
2	25	25	25	14	24	15	15	15	15	15	16	16
3	15	15	15	15	17	16	16	16	16	16	41	41
4	14	17	14	17	15	17	17	17	17	17	56	56
5	17	14	42	16	16	42	41	41	41	56	22	22
6	19	42	17	42	42	41	31	56	56	41	55	55
7	42	19	16	41	41	46	22	55	55	55	21	21
8	41	41	41	25	7	31	56	31	22	22	54	60
9	7	16	19	7	46	22	42	22	21	21	60	54
10	8	7	44	19	19	56	55	21	60	60	43	43

1959

**1959 SEBRING WINNER —
Ferrari 250TR**
Built and entered by Scuderia
Ferrari, Italy. Chassis No. 0766;
Engine: 3.0 liter, V-12 Ferrari
**Drivers: Phil Hill, Olivier
Gendebien, Dan Gurney,
Chuck Daigh**

8TH ANNUAL 12 HOURS OF SEBRING / MARCH 21, 1959

POS.	DRIVERS	NO.	MAKE	DISP.	ENTRANT	CLASS-POS.	LAPS
1	Phil Hill / Olivier Gendebien / Dan Gurney / Chuck Daigh	7	Ferrari 250TR/59	2953	Scuderia Ferrari, Modena,Italy	D-1	188
2	Jean Behra / Cliff Allison	9	Ferrari 250TR/59	2953	Scuderia Ferrari, Modena,Italy	D-2	187
3	Joakim Bonnier / Wolfgang Von Trips	31	Porsche RSK	1588	Porsche Auto Co., Germany	E-1	184
4	Bob Holbert / Don Sesslar	34	Porsche RSK	1498	Cyrus L. Fulton, Lancaster, Ohio	F-1	182
5	John Fitch / Edgar Barth	32	Porsche RSK	1498	Porsche Automobile Co., Germany	F-2	181
6	E.D. Martin / Lance Reventlow	12	Ferrari 250TR/58	2953	E.D. Martin, Columbus, Ga.	D-3	174
7	James Johnston / Ed Lunken / Gaston Andrey	14	Ferrari 250TR/58	2953	James Johnston, Cincinnati, Ohio	D-4	174
8	Ken Miles / Jack McAfee	35	Porsche RSK	1588	Precision Motors, Los Angeles, Calif.	F-3	173
9	Richie Ginther / Howard Hively	70	Ferrari 250GT California	2953	Scuderia Ferrari, Modena, Italy	GT9-1	171
10	Ernie Erickson / Ed Hugus	37	Porsche RSK	1498	Chester Flynn, New York, N.Y.	F-4	170
11	Huschke von Hanstein / Godin de Beaufort	33	Porsche Carrera	1598	Porsche Auto Co., Germany	GT6-1	164
12	Walt Hansgen / Dick Thompson	3	Lister Jaguar	2986	Briggs Cunningham, Green Farms, Ct.	D-5	164
13	Lloyd Casner / Jim Hunt	19	Ferrari 500TRC	1994	N.A.R.T., New York, N.Y.	E-3	164
14	Roy Jackson-Moore / James Cook / Bobbie Burns	25	AC Bristol	1971	A.C. Cars Ltd., Surrey, England	GT7-1	164
15	B. Cunningham / L.Underwood / S. Moss / R. Boss	4	Lister Jaguar	2986	Briggs Cunningham, Green Farms, Ct.	D-6	164
16	Charlie Rainville / Jake Kaplan	44	Alfa Romeo Veloce	1290	Jake Kaplan, Providence, R.I.	GT5-1	162
17	Paul Armagnac / Gerald Laureau	59	Deutsch-Bonnet HBR4	750	Deutsch-Bonnet Co., France	H-1	162
18	A. de Tomaso / D. McCluggage / R. Rodriguez	60	OSCA 187S	750	Alejandro de Tomaso, Argentina	H-2	161
19	Frank Baptista / Arthur Tweedale / Charles Wallace	48	Elva Mk IV	1098	Elva Engineering Co., England	G-1	160
20	Alfonso Mena / Juan Fernandez	15	Ferrari 250GT	2953	Auto Sport Club, Havana, Cuba	GT9-2	160
21	Colin Chapman / Pete Lovely / Jay Chamberlain	45	Lotus Elite	1216	Team Lotus, England	GT5-2	160
22	Arch Means / Ross Wees / Charles Kurtz	24	AC-Bristol	1971	A.C. Cars Ltd., Surrey, England	GT7-2	159
23	William Jordan / Charles Dietrich	49	Elva Mk IV	1098	Elva Engineering Co., England	G-2	158
24	Lonnie Rix / Ed Rahal	23	AC-Bristol	1971	A.C. Cars Ltd., Surrey, England	GT7-3	158
25	Ralph Durbin / Max Goldman	26	Arnolt-Bristol Bolide	1971	S.H. Arnolt, Warsaw, Ind.	GT7-4	155
26	Archibald McNeill / Mike Rothschild	22	Morgan Plus 4	1991	Fergus Motors, New York, N.Y.	GT7-5	155
27	Gus Ehrman / Ray Saidel	28	MGA	1586	Hambro Auto Corp., New York, N.Y.	GT6-2	155
28	Bill Rutman / Ray Cuomo / Paul Richards	64	Fiat Abarth Monza	747	Roosevelt Auto Inc., Washington, DC	H-3	152
29	Remo Cattini / Lanzo Cussino	62	Fiat Abarth Monza	747	Roosevelt Auto Co., Inc., New York, N.Y.	H-4	150
30	George Schrafft / Jim Jeffords / R. Kuhn	65	Fiat Abarth Monza	747	George F. Schrafft, New York, N.Y.	GT3-3	149
31	Hugh Sutherland / Phil Stiles	54	Austin-Healey Sprite	948	Hambro Auto Corp., New York, N.Y.	GT4-1	149
32	Mario Poltronieri / Alfonso Thiele / John Norwood	63	Fiat Abarth Monza	747	Roosevelt Auto Co. Inc., Washington, DC	GT3-4	147
33	Charles Moran / George Rand	40	Lotus Le Mans	1475	Charles Moran, Jr., Rye, N.Y.	F-5	145
34	Jim Parkinson / John Dalton	29	MGA	1586	Hambro Auto Corp., New York, N.Y.	GT6-3	145
35	Harry Blanchard / Skip Callahan	51	Lancia Appia Zagato	1090	Harry C. Blanchard, Greenwich, Ct.	GT5-3	144
36	Ed Leavens / Harold Kunz	53	Austin-Healey Sprite	948	Hambro Auto Corp., New York, N.Y.	GT4-2	142
37	Bill Wood / Henri Perrier	58	Deutsch-Bonnet HBR4	750	Deutsch Bonnet Co., France	H-7	141
38	Fred Hayes / John Christy / John Colgate	55	Austin-Healey Sprite	948	Hambro Auto Corp., New York, N.Y.	GT4-3	141
39	Lou Comito / Wynn Kramarsky / Bob Plaff	43	Alfa Romeo Veloce	1290	Louis Comito, Centerport, N.Y.	GT5-4	140

40	Peter Baumberger / Walter Cronkite / Warren Rohlfs	52	Lancia Appia Zagato	1090	Charles Kreisler, New York, N.Y.	GT5-5 140
41	Jim Hall / Hap Sharp / Red Byron	18	Maserati 250S	2500	Carroll Shelby, Dallas, Tex.	E-4 138
42	Bob Grossman / Bob Rubin	42	Alfa Romeo Veloce	1290	Robert Grossman, West Nyack, N.Y.	GT5-6 134
43	Frank Lieb / Smokey Drolet	80	Turner	948	Turner Sports Cars, Ltd., England	GT4-4 128
44	Tom Flemming / Bill Schade	47	Lotus 11	1096	Team Lotus, England	G-4 123
45	Ray Pickering / Jack Flaherty / Sherman Decker	30	MGA	1586	Hambro Auto Corp., New York, N.Y.	GT6-4 121
46	George Reed / Don O'dell	16	Ferrari Berlinetta 250GT	2953	RRR Enterprises, Homewood, Ill.	GT9-3 110
47	Ricardo Rodriguez / Bruce Kessler	56	OSCA S950	954	Automobile OSCA, Bologna, Italy	G-5 106
48	John Bentley / Robert Samm	20	Triumph TR3	1991	Standard Triumph Motor Co., New York, N.Y.	GT7-6 98
49	Gil Geitner / Rod Carveth	10	Ferrari 250TR/58	2953	N.A.R.T., New York, N.Y.	DNF-a 130
50	Charles Kolb / Fred Moore / Gene Hobbs	21	Triumph TR3	1991	Standard Triumph Motor Co., New York, N.Y.	DNF-e 128
51	William Entwistle / Robert Hanna	27	Lotus Mk 15	1962	Autosport, Ltd., Canada	DNF-k 126
52	Frank Campbell / Carl Haas / Jay Middleton	38	OSCA S1500	1491	Automobile OSCA, Bologna, Italy	DNF-k 115
53	Sandy McArthur / Rob Rollason	66	Stanguellini 750 Sport	748	Sandy McArthur, Lake Forest, Ill.	DNF-a 97
54	Howard Hanna / Richard Toland	57	Deutsch-Bonnet coupe	850	Deutsch Bonnet Co., France	DNF-e 82
55	Robert Publicker / Rees Makins	61	OSCA 187S	749	Automobile OSCA, Bologna, Italy	DNF-k 82
56	Phil Hill / Olivier Gendebien	8	Ferrari 250TR/59	2953	Scuderia Ferrari, Modena, Italy	DNF-t 77
57	Pedro Rodriguez / Paul O'Shea	11	Ferrari 250TR/58	2953	Mexican Nat'l. Auto Club, Mexico	DNF-e 66
58	Jay Chamberlain / Sam Weiss	46	Lotus Elite	1216	Team Lotus, England	DNF-e 65
59	Anton von Dory / Roberto Mieres	36	Porsche RSK	1498	Count von Dory, Argentina	DNF-e 34
60	M.R.J. Wyllie / Skip Lange / Peggy Wyllie	50	Elva Mk IV	1098	M.J. Wyllie, Allison Park, Pa.	DNF-a 34
61	Roy Salvadori / Carroll Shelby	1	Aston Martin DBR1	2992	David Brown Aston-Martin, England	DNF-t 32
62	Fred Van Beuren / Javier Velasquez	41	Alfa Romeo Veloce	1290	Fred T. Van Beuren, Mexico	DNF-a 31
63	Jean Lucas	39	Cooper Monaco 1500	1500	Los Amigos Racing, Paris, France	DNF-e 20
64	Joe Sheppard	17	Aston Martin DB2/4	2992	Joe Sheppard, Tampa, Fla.	DNF-e 11
65dq	Stirling Moss / Ivor Bueb	2	Lister Jaguar	2986	The Lister Corp., Cambridge, Eng.— disq.	98
DNS	Edwin P. Lawrence* / J. Cook / R. Durbin	5	Maserati 300S	2996	Rallye Motors, Glen Cove, N.Y.	accident
DNS	Briggs Cunningham / Lake Underwood	73	Porsche RSK	1498	Briggs Cunningham, Green Farms, Ct.	withdrew
DNS	Sydney Oakes / Greta Oakes / P. Bethel	78	Austin-Healey Sprite	948	Sir Sydney Oakes, Nassau, Bahamas	reserve
DNS	Art Bunker	72	Porsche RSK	1498	Art Bunker Motors, Kansas City, Mo.	reserve
DNS	Ross Durant, Jr. / George Peck	75	Alfa Romeo Veloce	1290	Ross Durant, Jr., Clearwater, Fla.	reserve

*Killed in practice accident at the Hairpin.

INDEX OF PERFORMANCE

1. #59 Deutsch-Bonnet 1.361
2. #60 OSCA 187S 1.352
3. #34 Porsche RSK 1.338
4. #31 Porsche RSK 1.333

Average Speed: 81.466 mph
Distance: 977.6 miles
Margin of Victory: 1 lap
Fastest Race Lap: #9 Jean Behra 92.857 mph
Fastest Qualifier: None — Le Mans type start
Weather: Cloudy, heavy rains, cool.
Lap Leaders: #1 1-4; #9 5-14,18-60, 77-95; #7 15-17,105-188; #8 61-76; #2 96-104
Attendance: 41,000 (est.)

1959 HOURLY STANDINGS — TOP 10

POS.	1 HR.	2 HRS.	3 HRS.	4 HRS.	5 HRS.	6 HRS.	7 HRS.	8 HRS.	9 HRS.	10 HRS.	11 HRS.	Finish
1	9	9	9	2	2	8	9	7	7	7	7	7
2	1	2	2	9	9	9	7	9	9	9	9	9
3	2	8	7	7	7	7	31	31	31	31	31	31
4	7	7	8	8	8	31	34	34	34	34	34	34
5	8	11	11	11	31	2	32	32	32	32	32	32
6	11	1	3	31	34	34	10	10	12	12	14	12
7	10	10	10	10	10	10	12	12	14	14	12	14
8	3	3	31	34	32	32	14	14	35	35	35	35
9	34	31	34	32	14	12	70	3	3	70	70	70
10	4	4	4	3	3	14	3	70	70	37	37	37

1960

**1960 SEBRING WINNER —
Porsche RS60**
Built by Porsche / Entered by
Joakim Bonnier, Sweden, for
Porsche factory. Chassis No.
718042; Engine: 1.6 liter, 4 cyl.
(rear engine) Porsche
**Drivers: Hans Herrmann,
Olivier Gendebien**

9TH ANNUAL 12 HOURS OF SEBRING / MARCH 26, 1960

POS.	DRIVERS	NO.	MAKE	DISP.	ENTRANT	CLASS-POS.	LAPS
1	Hans Herrmann / Olivier Gendebien	42	Porsche RS60	1587	Joakim Bonnier, Stockholm, Sweden	9S-1	196
2	Bob Holbert / Roy Schechter / Howard Fowler	44	Porsche RS60	1498	Brumos Porsche, Jacksonville, Fla.	9S-2	187
3	Jack Nethercutt / Pete Lovely	8	Ferrari 250TR/59	2996	Jack Nethercutt, Los Angeles, Calif.	12S-1	186
4	Augie Pabst / Ed Hugus	10	Ferrari 250GT	2996	N.A.R.T., New York, N.Y.	12S-2	185
5	George Reed / Alan Connell	17	Ferrari 250GT California	2953	RRR Motors, Homewood, Ill.	12S-3	185
6	Fritz Dorey / William Sturgis	12	Ferrari 250GT	2996	William Sturgis, Gardnerville, N.Y.	12S-4	183
7	George Arents / Bill Kimberly	11	Ferrari 250GT	2996	N.A.R.T., New York, N.Y.	12S-5	183
8	Georgio Scarlatti / Fabrizio Serena	16	Ferrari 250GT California	2953	Scuderia Serenissima, Italy	12G-1	179
9	Joe Sheppard / Dick Dungan	72	Porsche Carrera	1498	Camoradi USA Team, Miami, Fla.	9G-1	177
10	B. Publicker / D. McCarthy / G. Constantine	14	Ferrari 250GT California	2996	Robert Publicker, Ft. Lauderdale, Fla.	12S-6	174
11	Jan Bootz / Godin de Beaufort	80	Porsche Carrera	1587	Count Karl de Beaufort, Holland	9G-2	172
12	John Bentley / Jack Gordon	63	OSCA 187N	746	Automobile OSCA, Italy	5S-1	170
13	Rees Makins / George Koehne	47	OSCA MT4	1491	Automobile OSCA USA, Morton Grove, Ill.	9S-3	169
14	Max Goldman / Ralph Durbin	31	Arnolt-Bristol	1971	S.H. Arnolt, Inc., Chicago, Ill.	10G-1	169
15	Gil Geitner / Lou Spencer	20	Austin-Healey 3000	2912	British Motor Car Co., New York, N.Y.	12G-2	167
16	Chuck Hall / Bill Fritts	6	Chevrolet Corvette	4639	RRR Motors, Homewood, Ill.	14G-1	167
17	Charles Voegle / Peter Ashdown / Rolf Roth	85	Lola Climax	1098	Charles Voegle, Switzerland	7S-1	167
18	F. Van Beuren / Javier Velazquez / A. Velasquez	54	Alfa Romeo Veloce	1290	Fredrico Van Beuren, Mexico	8G-1	166
19	Don Horn / Tom O'Brien	50	Alfa Romeo Veloce	1290	Louis Comito, Centerport, N.Y.	8G-2	166
20	Bud Hulsey / Harry Washburn	36	AC-Bristol	1971	A.C. Cars Ltd., England	10G-2	166
21	Bob Grossman / Mike Rothschild	54	AC-Bristol	1971	A.C. Cars Ltd., England	10G-3	166
22	Bud Seaverns / Jim Johnson / W. Bradley	33	Arnolt-Bristol	1971	S.H. Arnolt, Inc., Chicago, Ill.	10G-4	165
23	John Fulp / David Cunningham	65	OSCA 187S	749	Luigi Chinetti Motors, New York, N.Y.	5S-7	162
24	Fred Hays / Ed Leavens	39	MGA	1588	British Motor Corp. Ltd., New York, N.Y.	9G-3	160
25	Jay Chamberlain / C.W. Evans	55	Lotus Elite	1220	Lotus Cars USA, N. Hollywood, Calif.	8G-3	158
26	Jim Jeffords / William Wuesthoff	3	Chevrolet Corvette	4639	Camoradi USA Team, Miami, Fla.	14G-2	157
27	Cameron Argetsinger / Bill Milliken	48	Alfa Romeo Veloce	1290	Cameron Argetsinger, Watkins Glen, N.Y.	8G-4	156
28	Tony O'Sullivan / Peter Procter	77	AC-Bristol	1971	Tony O'Sullivan, Venezuela	10G-5	151
29	Jim Parkinson / Jim Flaherty	40	MGA	1588	British Motor Corp. Ltd., New York, N.Y.	9G-4	148
30	Ross Durant / R. Richardson / Lou Comito	51	Alfa Romeo Veloce	1290	Ross Durant, Jr., Clearwater, Fla.	8G-5	143
31	Charles Kessinger / Jim Gardner	52	Alfa Romeo Veloce	1290	Dr. Roy Martinez, Burbank, Calif.	8G-6	143
32	Fred Gamble / Leon Lilley	4	Chevrolet Corvette	4639	Camoradi USA Team, Miami, Fla.	14G-2	143
33	Jack Sears / Peter Riley	18	Austin-Healey 3000	2912	British Motor Corp. Ltd., New York, N.Y.	12G-6	141
34	Charlemagne Tower / Duncan Black	26	Daimler SP250	2549	Charlemagne Tower, IV, New York, N.Y.	12S-7	137
35	Delmo Johnson / David Morgan	5	Chevrolet Corvette	4639	Johnson Chevrolet Co., Dallas, Texas	14G-3	134
36	Dean Patterson / John Masterson	37	Elva Courier	1588	Elva Dist. USA, Kensington, Md.	9S-4	131
37	Ed Costley / Pete Harrison	60	Elva Mk IV	1098	Edgar M. Costley, Atlanta, Ga.	7S-2	131
38	Paul Richards / Ray Cuomo	66	Fiat Abarth	747	Roosevelt Automobiles, Washington, D.C.	5S-3	115
39	Tom Payne / Bob Gary	32	Arnolt-Bristol	1971	S.H. Arnolt Co., Chicago, Ill.	10G-6	99

40	Charlie Kolb / Chuck Wallace	68	Elva Courier	1971	Elva Dist. USA, Kensington, Md.	9S-5	92
41	John Sprinzel / John Lumkin	61	Austin-Healey Sprite	948	Donald Healey, Warwick, England	6S-1	62
42	David Causey / L.W. Stear	24	Maserati T61	2890	David F. Causey, Carmel, Ind.	DNF-t	169
43	Walt Hansgen / Ed Crawford	25	Maserati T61	2890	Jaguar Dist. of N.Y., Woodside, N.Y.	DNF-t	149
44	Stirling Moss / Dan Gurney	23	Maserati T61	2843	Camoradi USA Team, Miami, Fla.	DNF-t	136
45	Pedros Von Dorey / Anton Von Dorey	46	Porsche RSK	1498	Anton Von Dorey, Argentina	DNF-e	133
46	Pedro Rodriguez / Ricardo Rodriguez	28	Ferrari Dino 196S	2000	N.A.R.T., New York, N.Y.	DNF-t	126
47	Richie Ginther / Chuck Daigh	7	Ferrari 250TR/60	3000	N.A.R.T., New York, N.Y.	DNF-e	123
48	Joakim Bonnier / Graham Hill	43	Porsche RS60	1587	Joakim Bonnier, Stockholm, Sweden	DNF-e	84
49	Art Swanson / George Waltman	53	Alfa Romeo Veloce	1290	Racing Assoc. of New England, Brookline, Mass	DNF-e	70
50	Frank Schroeder / Robert Mazzi	35	AC-Bristol	1971	A.C. Cars Ltd., England	DNF-x	61
51	James Forno / H.B. Williamson	30	Morgan Plus 4	1991	Morgan Motors, Ltd., England	DNF-w	60
52	Frank Bott	57	Lotus Elite	1220	Lotus Cars USA, N. Hollywood, Calif.	DNF-w	57
53	Fred Spross / John Colgate	19	Austin-Healey 3000	2912	British Motor Car Co., New York, N.Y.	DNF-a	54
54	Dick Thompson / Fred Windridge	2	Chevrolet Corvette	4639	Jaguar Dist. of N.Y., Woodside, N.Y.	DNF-a	41
55	Denise McCluggage / Pinkie Windridge	65	OSCA 187S	749	Camoradi USA Team, Miami, Fla.	DNF-e	34
56	John Cuevas / Ulf Norinder	41	Porsche Carrera	1588	Quiver Enterprises, Miami, Fla.	DNF-e	33
57	Carlo Abate / Giovanni Balzarini	15	Ferrari 250GT	2953	Scuderia Serenissima, Milan, Italy	DNF-u	28
58	Briggs Cunningham / John Fitch	1	Chevrolet Corvette	4639	Jaguar Dist. of N.Y., Woodside, N.Y.	DNF-a	27
59	Al Penn / Steve Wilder	67	Bandini Fiat	747	Racemasters, New York, N.Y.	DNF-e	27
60	Hap Sharp / Jim Hall	27	Cooper-Maserati	2479	Hap Sharp, Midland, Texas	DNF-e	26
61	Charlie Rainville / Jake Kaplan	49	Alfa Romeo Veloce	1290	Jacob Kaplan, Warwick, R.I.	DNF-e	16
62	Jim Hughes*	56	Lotus Elite	1220	Lotus Cars, USA, N. Hollywood, Calif.	DNF-a	5
63	Colin Escott	38	MGA	1588	British Motor Corp., New York, N.Y.	DNF-e	3
64	Carroll Shelby	22	Maserati T61	2843	Camoradi USA Team, Miami, Fla.	DNF-e	2
65	Ernie Erickson	45	Porsche RSK	1498	Carl Erickson Co., Chicago, Ill.	DNF-e	1
DNS	Bob Grimes / Paul Hill	73	Elva Mk IV	1098	Elva Dist. USA, Kensington, Md.	reserve	
DNS	Howard Hanna / Richard Toland	74	Deutsch-Bonnet	851	Howard Hanna, Broomall, Pa.	reserve	
DNS	Otto Linton / E. Ginther	75	OSCA 187N	748	John Miles, Phoenixville, Pa.	reserve	
DNS	Mel Siegel / Dr. Harry Fry	79	Austin-Healey 3000	2912	London Motors, Inc., Miami, Fla.	reserve	
DNS	Paul O'Shea / H.N. York	81	Mercedes-Benz 300SL	2993	Lewis Engineering Co., Alliance, Ohio	reserve	
DNS	Jim Rathmann / Lloyd Casner	21	Maserati T61	2843	Camoradi USA Team, Miami, Fla.	reserve	

*Killed in race accident at Hairpin escape route.

INDEX OF PERFORMANCE

1. #63 OSCA 187N 1.4306
2. #42 Porsche RS60 . . . . 1.4300
3. #44 Porsche RS60 . . . . 1.3754
4. #65 OSCA 187S 1.3619
5. #72 Porsche Carrera 1.3019
6. #85 Lola Climax 1.2923
7. #8 Ferrari 250TR 1.2702

Average Speed: 84.927 mph
Distance: 1,019.2 miles
Margin of Victory: 9 laps
Fastest Race Lap: #44 Stirling Moss 94.996 mph
Fastest Qualifier: None—Le Mans type start
Lap Leaders: #8 1-3; **#23** 4-136; **#42** 137-196
Attendance: 37,000 (est.)
Weather: Clear and cool

1960 HOURLY STANDINGS — TOP 10

POS.	1 HR.	2 HRS.	3 HRS.	4 HRS.	5 HRS.	6 HRS.	7 HRS.	8 HRS.	9 HRS.	10 HRS.	11 HRS.	Finish
1	23	23	23	23	23	23	23	23	**42**	**42**	**42**	**42**
2	25	7	7	7	7	24	**42**	**42**	44	44	44	44
3	7	25	25	25	24	**42**	44	44	24	17	10	8
4	8	28	28	28	25	44	24	24	17	10	8	10
5	28	43	43	24	**42**	25	17	17	12	8	17	17
6	43	44	24	**42**	44	7	25	10	11	12	12	12
7	44	**42**	**42**	44	28	17	10	12	10	11	11	11
8	**42**	46	44	12	12	10	12	11	8	24	16	16
9	46	12	12	10	10	12	11	8	16	16	72	72
10	12	8	10	17	17	11	8	16	72	72	14	14

1961

**1961 SEBRING WINNER —
Ferrari 250TR/61**
Built and entered by Scuderia
Ferrari, Italy. Chassis No. 0790;
Engine: 3.0 liter, 12 cyl. Ferrari
**Drivers: Phil Hill, Olivier
Gendebien**

10TH ANNUAL 12 HOURS OF SEBRING / MARCH 25, 1961

POS.	DRIVERS	NO.	MAKE	DISP.	ENTRANT	CLASS-POS.	LAPS
1	Phil Hill / Olivier Gendebien	14	Ferrari 250TR/61	2953	Sefac Automobili Ferrari, Modena, Italy	S-12-1	208
2	W. Mairesse / G. Baghetti / R. Ginther / W. Von Trips	15	Ferrari 250TR/61	2953	Sefac Automobili Ferrari, Modena, Italy	S-12-2	205
3	Pedro Rodriguez / Ricardo Rodriguez	17	Ferrari 250TR/60	2953	N.A.R.T., New York, N.Y.	S-12-3	204
4	Hap Sharp / Ronnie Hissom	10	Ferrari 250TR/59	2996	Hap Sharp, Midland, Tex.	S-12-4	201
5	Jim Hall / George Constantine	22	Ferrari Dino 246S	2461	N.A.R.T., New York, N.Y.	S-11-1	199
6	Bob Holbert / Roger Penske	51	Porsche RS61	1498	Brumos Co., Jacksonville, Fla.	S-9-1	199
7	Bob Donner / Don Sesslar / Ernie Erickson	47	Porsche RSK	1587	Bob Donner, Colorado Springs, Colo.	S-9-1	198
8	George Reed / Bill Sturgis	16	Ferrari 250TR/59	2953	McCook Window Co., McCook, Ill.	S-12-5	194
9	Ludwig Heimrath / Francis Bradley / Peter Ryan	39	Porsche RS61	1597	Eglinton Caledonia Motors, Toronto, Ontario	S-9-3	187
10	Denise McCluggage / Allen Eager	12	Ferrari 250GT	2953	D. McCluggage, New York, N.Y.	GT-11/12-1	182
11	Bob Johnson / David Morgan	4	Chevrolet Corvette	4638	Johnson Chevrolet, Dallas, Tex.	GT-13/15-1	181
12	Allen Newman / Gaston Andrey / R. Publicker	18	Ferrari 250GT Calif.	2953	N.A.R.T., New York, N.Y.	GT-12-2	180
13	Charles Kurtz / Millard Ripley	64	Lola Climax	1098	Lola America, Kenilworth, Ill.	S-7/8-1	179
14	Jim Parkinson / Jack Flaherty	44	MGA	1588	British Motor Corp. (USA), New York, N.Y.	GT-8/9-1	174
15	Joe Buzzetta / Glenn Carlson	66	Austin-Healey Sprite	994	Donald Healey, Warwick, England	B-6/7-1	175
16	Peter Riley / John Whitmore	43	MGA	1588	British Motor Corp. (USA), New York, N.Y.	GT-8/9-2	173
17	Peter Proctor / P. Harper / Bob Olthoff	42	Sunbeam Alpine	1592	J. Brabham Motors Ltd., Surrey, England	GT-8/9-3	173
18	Briggs Cunningham / Walt Hansgen	31	Maserati T60	1989	Momo Corp., New York, N.Y.	S-10-1	171
19	Bill Helborn / John Fulp / Skip Hudson	37	Ferrari Dino 196S	1989	N.A.R.T., New York, N.Y.	S-10-2	171
20	George Peck / R. Richardson / John Hoffman	71	OSCA Sport 750	749	Clearwater Motors, Clearwater, Fla.	S-5-1	171
21	Ralph Durbin / Max Goldman	32	Arnolt-Bristol	1971	S.H. Arnolt, Warsaw, Ind.	GT-10-1	166
22	Tom Payne / Bob Gary	33	Arnolt-Bristol	1971	S.H. Arnolt, Warsaw, Ind.	GT-10-2	166
23	Bud Gates / Chuck Rickert	83	Chevrolet Corvette	4638	Bud Gates, Inc., Indianapolis, Ind.	GT-13/15-2	164
24	Bud Seaverns / Ray Cuomo	87	Arnolt-Bristol	1971	S.H. Arnolt, Warsaw, Ind.	GT-10-3	163
25	Ed Leavens / John Colgate	65	Austin-Healey Sprite	994	Donald Healey, Warwick, England	B-6/7-2	161
26	Hector Rebaque / Fred Van Beuren / Carlos Sales	60	Alfa Romeo Giulietta	1290	Autosport S.A., Mexico City, Mexico	GT-7/8-1	156
27	Al Rogers / Jim Bailey	30	Morgan 4/4	1991	Salter Auto Imports, Shaker Heights, Ohio	GT-10-4	155
28	Art Swanson / Ross Durant, Jr.	58	Alfa Romeo SV	1290	Arthur A. Swanson, Brookline, Mass.	GT-7/8-2	155
29	Don Parsons / Jack Rashin	29	Triumph TR3	1991	Suburban Foreign Cars, Montgomery, Ala.	GT-10-5	154
30	Filippo Theodoli / Fred Barrette	55	Sunbeam Alpine	1592	Filippo Theodoli, New York, N.Y.	GT-10-6	153
31	George Waltman / H.B. Williamson	28	Triumph TR3	1991	George Waltman, Bayside, N.Y.	GT-10-7	153
32	Don Yenko / Ben Moore	1	Chevrolet Corvette	4638	Yenko Chevrolet, Cannonsburg, Pa.	GT-13/15-3	151
33	Tom O'Brien / Allan Jacobson	59	Alfa Romeo Veloce	1290	Thomas M. O'Brien, Wycoff, N.J.	GT-7/8-3	151
34	Ed Gelder / John Dennis	46	Elva Courier	1588	Carl Haas Automotive, Chicago, Ill.	GT-9-4	149
35	Paddy Hopkirk / Peter Jopp	40	Sunbeam Alpine	1592	Rootes Motors, Inc., New York, N.Y.	GT-9-5	149
36	Don Horn / Edward Tucker	45	Elva Courier	1588	Carl Haas Automotive, Chicago, Ill.	GT-9-6	144
37	Ed Sprinzel / Paul Hawkins / Cyril Simson	67	Austin-Healey Sprite	994	John Sprinzel, London, England	B-6/7-3	144
38	George Robertson / Bill Warren / Ben Burroughs	3	Chevrolet Corvette	4638	Red Vogt, Daytona Beach, Fla.	GT-13/15*	133
39	Harry Theodoracopulos / Lou Comito	57	Alfa Romeo Zagato	1290	Lou Comito, Centerport, N.Y.	GT-7/8*	103

40	James Calhoun / Marvin Dee	80	Fiat Abarth Monza	982	Abarth DFL Co., Chicago, Ill.	S-6/7*	101
41	Dave Causey / Luke Stear	25	Maserati T61	2890	Rallye Motors, Inc., Glen Cove, N.Y.	DNF-u	
42	Hans Herrmann / Edgar Barth	50	Porsche RS61	1682	Porsche Auto, Stuttgart, Germany	DNF-e	
43	Dr. F. Taylor / Harry Washburn	68	Fiat Abarth Monza	982	Abarth DFL Co., Chicago, Ill.	DNF-e	
44	Charles Hall / Allan Ross	63	Lola Climax	1098	Lola America, Kenilworth, Ill.	DNF-k	
45	Ed Hugus / Allan Connell	26	Ferrari Dino 246S	2461	N.A.R.T., New York, N.Y.	DNF-x	
46	Dan Gurney / Joakim Bonnier	49	Porsche RS61	1682	Porsche Auto, Stuttgart, Germany	DNF-t	
47	David Cunningham / R. Price	69	OSCA S1000	850	N.A.R.T., New York, N.Y.	DNF-x	
48	Walt Hansgen / Bruce McLaren	20	Maserati T63	2890	Momo Corp., New York, N.Y.	DNF-u	
49	Robert Bucher / Sherman Decker	8	Aston Martin DB4-GT	3670	David Ash, West Nyack, N.Y.	DNF-e	
50	Chuck Cassel / Bob Dusinberrie / D. Lane	48	Porsche RSK	1587	Automovilista, Santaneca Motors	DNF-u	
51	Frank Laughton / R. Bowers / Tony O'Sullivan	36	AC-Bristol	1971	A.C. Cars Ltd., Surrey, England	DNF-u	
52	John Bentley / Henry Grady / Eugene Beach	70	Begra Saab	748	Begra Competition Cars, Clearwater, Fla.	DNF-c	
53	Fabrizio Serena / George Arents	11	Ferrari 250GT	2953	N.A.R.T., New York, N.Y.	DNF-x	
54	Howard Hanna / F. Manley / Paul Hagan	72	Deutsch-Bonnet HBR5	701	YBH Sales & Service, Edgemont, Pa.	DNF-e	
55	Bob Grossman / Duncan Black	7	Aston Martin DB4-GT	3670	David Ash, West Nyack, N.Y.	DNF-s	
56	John Kilborn / Ray Reardon	2	Chevrolet Corvette	4638	Yenko Chevrolet, Cannonsburg, Pa.	DNF-e	
57	Stirling Moss / Masten Gregory	24	Maserati T63	2997	Camoradi International, London, England	DNF-s	
58	Richie Ginther / Wolfgang Von Trips	27	Ferrari 246SP	2417	Sefac Automobili Ferrari, Modena, Italy	DNF-s	
59	L. Wilson / Vince Tamburo	41	Sunbeam Alpine	1592	Rootes Motors, Inc., New York, N.Y.	DNF-e	
60	John Fitch / Dick Thompson	21	Maserati T61	2890	Momo Corp., New York, N.Y.	DNF-t	
61	Graham Hill / Stirling Moss	23	Maserati T61	2997	Camoradi International, London, England	DNF-e	
62	Augie Pabst / Bill Wuesthoff	38	Porsche RS60	1597	Porsche Car Import, Northbrook, Ill.	DNF-s	
63	Leo May / Jim Johnson	35	AC-Bristol	1971	A.C. Cars Ltd., Surrey, England	DNF-a	
64	Pete Lovely	9	Ferrari 250TR/59	2996	Jack Nethercutt, Los Angeles, Calif.	DNF-e	
65dq	Jake Kaplan / Charlie Rainville	56	Alfa Romeo SS	1290	Jake Kaplan, Warwick, R.I.	Disq.	
DNS	Jack Moore / Bob Johnson	5	Chevrolet Corvette	4638	Glen Campbell Chevrolet, Williamsville, N.Y.	withdrew	
DNS	Jim Rathmann / Charlie Kolb	19	Asardo Pontiac Spl.	2590	Asardo Co., Rockledge, Fla.	withdrew	
DNS	Robert Hathaway / Fred Spross	84	AC-Bristol	1991	A.C. Cars, Surrey, England	reserve	
DNS	Herb Swan / Ed Johnson	86	Porsche RSK	1598	Lester Castings, Bedford, Ohio	reserve	

*Non-classified finisher
Note: Lap totals not available for non-finishers.

INDEX OF PERFORMANCE

1. #51 Porsche RSK 1.46362
2. #47 Porsche RSK 1.44458
3. #71 OSCA 1.43060
4. #14 Ferrari 250TR 1.42201
5. #15 Ferrari 250TR 1.40150
6. #17 Ferrari 250TR 1.39309
7. #22 Ferrari V6 Dino 1.38430

Average Speed: 90.13 mph
Distance: 1,081.6 miles
Margin of Victory: 2 laps
Fastest Race Lap: Stirling Moss 96.9 mph
Fastest Qualifier: None — Le Mans type start
Lap Leaders: **#24** 1-4; **#17** 5-25, 59-121; **#27** 26-58; **#14** 122-210
Attendance: 43,431
Weather: Clear and warm

1961 HOURLY STANDINGS — TOP 10

POS.	1 HR.	2 HRS.	3 HRS.	4 HRS.	5 HRS.	6 HRS.	7 HRS.	8 HRS.	9 HRS.	10 HRS.	11 HRS.	Finish
1	17	27	27	17	17	14	14	14	14	14	14	14
2	27	23	17	14	14	17	15	15	15	15	15	15
3	14	17	14	20	20	15	17	17	17	17	17	17
4	20	14	20	15	15	10	10	10	10	10	10	10
5	23	20	15	10	10	16	22	22	22	22	22	51
6	24	15	26	26	26	50	16	51	51	51	51	22
7	15	24	10	16	16	22	51	16	16	16	16	47
8	49	10	51	50	50	51	39	47	47	47	47	16
9	10	26	24	48	22	26	47	39	39	39	39	39
10	26	50	22	22	39	39	18	12	12	12	12	12

1962

1962 SEBRING WINNER —
Ferrari 250TR/61
Built by Ferrari / Entered by
SSS Republica de Venezia, Italy.
Chassis No. 0792; Engine: 3.0
liter, 12 cyl. Ferrari
Drivers: Joakim Bonnier,
Lucien Bianchi

11TH ANNUAL 12 HOURS OF SEBRING / MARCH 24, 1962

POS.	DRIVERS	NO.	MAKE	DISP.	ENTRANT	CLASS-POS.		LAPS
1	Joakim Bonnier / Lucien Bianchi	23	Ferrari 250TR/61	2953	SSS Republica di Venezia, Italy	SP11/12	1	206
2	Phil Hill / Olivier Gendebien	24	Ferrari 250GTO	2953	N.A.R.T., New York, N.Y.	GT11/12	1	196
3	F. Rand / Bruce Jennings / Bill Wuesthoff	59	Porsche RS60	1498	Porsche Imports, Chicago, Ill.	SP8/9	1	195
4	George Hammil / Fabrizio Serena	25	Ferrari 250GT	2953	N.A.R.T., New York, N.Y.	GT11/12	2	190
5	Bruce McLaren / Roger Penske	21	Cooper Maserati	2989	Briggs Cunningham, New York, N.Y.	SP11/12	2	190
6	Jim Hall / Hap Sharp / Ronnie Hissom	10	Chaparral	3988	Chaparral Cars, Midland, Tex.	C/M13	1	189
7	Dan Gurney / Bob Holbert	48	Porsche Abarth Carrera	1588	Porsche S.E., Switzerland	GT9	1	188
8	Ed Hugus / George Reed	28	Ferrari 250GT	2953	G. McKelvy, Pittsburgh, Pa.	GT11/12	3	187
9	Paul Straehle / Edgar Barth	49	Porsche Abarth Carrera	1588	Porsche S.E., Switzerland	GT9	1	182
10	J.Guichet / Alfonso Thiele / M. Bianchi	76	Fiat 850S Abarth	982	Abarth Corse, Italy	BP6/7	1	180
11	Art Swanson / R. Richardson / Ross Durant	63	Alfa Romeo Veloce	1290	Durant-Swanson, Clearwater, Fla.	GT7/	1	178
12	Massimo Priolo / Carlo Facetti	60	Alfa Romeo Veloce	1290	Scuderia Ambrosina, Italy	GT7/8	2	178
13	Peter Ryan / Bob Fulp	36	Ferrari Dino 248SP	2458	N.A.R.T., New York, N.Y.	SP11/12	3	176
14	Briggs Cunningham / John Fitch	14	Jaguar XKE	3875	Briggs Cunningham, New York, N.Y.	GT13		176
15	Peter Harper / Peter Proctor	41	Sunbeam Alpine	1598	Rootes Motors, England	GT9	3	173
16	John Sears / Andrew Hedges	52	MGA	1588	Ecurie Safety Fast, England	GT9	4	172
17	Jim Parkinson / Jack Flaherty	51	MGA	1588	Ecurie Safety Fast, England	GT9	5	171
18	Duncan Black / M.R.J. Wyllie	2	Chevrolet Corvette	5360	Grady Davis, Pittsburgh, Pa.	GT14/15	1	171
19	Don Yenko / Ed Lowther	1	Chevrolet Corvette	5360	Grady Davis, Pittsburgh, Pa.	GT14/15	2	169
20	John Whitmore / Bob Olthoff / F. Morrell	53	MGA	1588	Ecurie Safety Fast, England	GT9	6	169
21	Delmo Johnson / David Morgan	4	Chevrolet Corvette	5360	Johnson Chevrolet, Dallas, Tex.	GT14/15	3	169
22	Harry Theodoracopulos / Giancarlo Sala	61	Alfa Romeo Veloce	1290	Scuderia Ambrosiana, Italy	GT7/8	3	168
23	Jack Gordon / John Bentley	79	OSCA Sport 750	749	Automobile OSCA, Italy	SP5	1	167
24	Lin Coleman / Pat Corrigan	83	Porsche 356 coupe	1588	Brumos Porsche, Jacksonville, Fla.	GT9	7	165
25	Mark Donohue / Jay Signore	55	TVR	1588	TVR Cars Limited, England	GT9	8	163
26	Ludwig Heimrath / Jerry Palivka	46	Porsche RSK	1597	Eglinton Cal. Motors, Canada	SP8/9	2	158
27	Howard Hanna / Richard Toland	80	DB Panhard	701	Fran-Am Racing Team, Los Angeles, Calif.	SP5	2	158
28	Frank Manley / Eitum Newcomer	81	DB Panhard	701	Fran-Am Racing Team, Los Angeles, Calif.	SP5	3	157
29	Newton Davis / Peter Pulver	68	Lotus Elite	1216	Duchess Auto, New York	GT7/8	4	155
30	George Waltman / Nick Cone	37	Triumph TR4	2138	George Waltman, New York	GT11/12	4	154
31	Harry Washburn / Bill Fuller	7	Chevrolet Corvette	5360	Fuller Murray Race Cars, Oakdale, La.	GT14/15	4	153
32	Joe Sheppard / Tom Payne	43	Sunbeam Alpine	1598	Rootes Motors, England	GT9	9	151
33	Freddie Barrette / Filippo Theodoli	44	Sunbeam Alpine	1598	Rootes Motors, England	GT9	10	150
34	C. Hayes / Carl Haas / Charles Dietrich	27	Ferrari 250GT	2953	N.A.R.T., New York, N.Y.	GT11/12	5	147
35	Alton Rodgers / James Bailey	39	Morgan Plus 4SS	1991	Alton Rodgers, Niles, Ohio	GT10	1	143
36	Jocko Maggiacomo / Marvin Panch	9	Ford Falcon Challenger	3990	Holman-Moody, Charlotte, N.C.	C/M13	2	107
37	Paul Richards / Charlie Kolb	62	Alfa Romeo Zagato	1290	Martini-Rossi Racing, New York	GT7/8	5	101
38	Bob Grossman / Allen Connell / P. Rodriguez	35	Ferrari Dino 246S	2498	N.A.R.T., New York, N.Y.	DNF-t		168
39	Pat Piggott / Jerry Grant	5	Chevrolet Corvette	5360	Don Campbell, Seattle, Wash.	DNF-f		148

40	Chuck Daigh / Chuck Hall	11	Chaparral	3988	Chaparral Cars, Midland, Tex.	DNF-s	127
41	S. Tavano / Colin Davis	22	Ferrari 250GT	2953	SSS Republica di Venezia, Italy	DNF-e	119
42	Ben Warren / Allan Ross / Art Tweedale	73	Elva Mk VI Sports	1096	Elva Cars Ltd., England	DNF-e	115
43	Bob Donner / Don Sesslar	45	Porsche RSK	1597	Rennod Race Cars, Colorado Springs, Colo.	DNF-t	108
44	Pedro Rodriguez / Ricardo Rodriguez	34	Ferrari Dino 246	2498	N.A.R.T., New York, N.Y.	DNF-e	97
45	Charlie Rainville / W. Ballard	65	Alfa Romeo Veloce	1290	Jake Kaplan, Providence, R.I.	DNF-e	96
46	Steve McQueen / John Colgate	72	Austin-Healey Sprite	1098	Donald Healey, England	DNF-e	71
47	Johnny Allen / George Robertson	3	Chevrolet Corvette	5360	Red Vogt, Daytona Beach, Fla.	DNF-e	59
48	Don Hulette / Burk Wiedner	69	Lotus Elite	1216	Don Hulette, Los Angeles, Calif.	DNF-f	59
49	Ray Cuomo / Jake Jacobs	56	TVR	1588	TVR Cars Ltd., England	DNF-e	56
50	Dick Kingham / Bob Kingham	40	AC Bristol	1972	Richard Kingham, Winter Haven, Fla.	DNF-x	52
51	Everet Smith / Harold Whims	47	Elva Courier	1585	Elva Cars Ltd., England	DNF-e	46
52	Enus Wilson / Ernie Grimm / J.C. Kilborn	33	Maserati T61	2890	Enus Wilson, Jr., Oklahoma City, Ok.	DNF-e	45
53	George Constantine / Gaston Andrey	20	Ferrari 250TR/59	2993	John T. Bunch, New Canaan, Ct.	DNF-x	40
54	Rafael Rosales / Victor Merino	74	Elva Mk VI Sports	1096	Elva Cars Ltd., England	DNF-e	37
55	Rodger Ward / Bob Johnson	6	Chevrolet Corvette	5360	Ronnie Kaplan, Chicago, Ill.	DNF-s	34
56	Robert Publicker / Spencer Litchie	58	OSCA GT1600	1600	N.A.R.T., New York, N.Y.	DNF-e	33
57	Walt Hansgen / Dick Thompson	32	Maserati T64	2890	Briggs Cunningham, New York, N.Y.	DNF-s	30
58	Ken Miles / Lew Spencer	42	Sunbeam Alpine	1598	Rootes Motors, England	DNF-e	25
59	Peter Bolton / Mike Rothschild	54	TVR	1588	TVR Cars Ltd., England	DNF-x	23
60	John Todd / W.B. Todd	15	Warwick-Buick Spl.	3518	Scuderia Light Blue, U.S.A.	DNF-e	20
61	Nino Vaccarella	30	Maserati T64	2890	SSS Republica di Venezia, Italy	DNF-t	16
62	K.Gorstead / Oliver Schmidt	75	DeTomaso	1100	Oliver Schmidt, Chicago, Ill.	DNF-s	16
63	Denise McCluggage	77	OSCA S1000	1000	N.A.R.T., New York, N.Y.	DNF-a	10
64	Chuck Cassel	50	Porsche 356 coupe	1587	Continental Motors, Ft. Lauderdale, Fla.	DNF-t	4
65dq	Stirling Moss / Innes Ireland	26	Ferrari 250TR/61	2953	N.A.R.T., New York, N.Y.	Disq.*	128
DNS	Charles Dietrich / Dr. J.W. Baxter	29	Ferrari 250GT	2957	RRR Motors, Homewood, Ill.	reserve	
DNS	Guido Lollobrigida / P. Ronchieri	31	Maserati	3000	Sorocaima Racing Team, Miami, Fla.	withdrew	
DNS	James Binford / Howard Cole	38	Triumph TR4	2138	James Binford, Houston, Tex.	reserve	
DNS	Paul Lund / Jack Walsh	57	Porsche Carrera	1582	Paul Lund, Boston, Mass.	reserve	
DNS	Tim Mayer / Millard Ripley	66	Lotus Elite	1216	Team Lotus, England	withdrew	
DNS	Harvey Snow / Sy Kaback	71	Lotus 23	1098	Team Lotus, England	withdrew	
DNS	Mac Knight / B. Bescanson	78	OSCA	850	Merrimac Racing, Pompano Beach, Fla.	reserve	

*Disqualified while leading for fueling infraction which occurred on lap 73.

INDEX OF PERFORMANCE

1. #59 Porsche RS60 . . . . 1.4342
2. #76 Fiat Abarth 1.4234
3. #23 Ferrari 250TR 1.4083
4. #79 OSCA 1.4034
5. #48 Porsche 1.3715
6. #80 DB Panhard 1.3510
7. #81 DB Panhard 1.3425

Average Speed: 89.142 mph
Distance: 1,071.2 miles
Margin of Victory: 10 laps
Fastest Race Lap: Pedro Rodriguez, 97.263 mph
Fastest Qualifier: None — Le Mans type start
Lap Leaders: #26 1-12, 20-34, 45-68, 89-128*; #34 13-19, 69-88; #21 35-44; #23 129-206
Attendance: 45,000 (est.)
Weather: Partly cloudy and warm.

1962 HOURLY STANDINGS — TOP 10

POS.	1 HR.	2 HRS.	3 HRS.	4 HRS.	5 HRS.	6 HRS.	7 HRS.	8 HRS.	9 HRS.	10 HRS.	11 HRS.	Finish
1	26	21	26	26	34	26	26	23	23	23	23	23
2	34	34	34	34	26	23	23	21	35	35	24	24
3	21	26	21	21	23	35	21	35	24	24	59	59
4	23	35	23	23	35	21	35	24	59	59	25	25
5	35	20	35	35	22	22	24	59	21	25	21	21
6	20	23	22	22	21	24	59	14	25	21	10	10
7	32	22	20	24	24	59	10	10	10	10	48	48
8	22	45	24	45	59	10	25	25	48	48	28	28
9	30	24	45	11	10	25	14	48	28	28	49	49
10	24	11	59	59	25	14	28	49	49	49	76	76

1963

1963 SEBRING WINNER —
Ferrari 250P
Built and entered by Scuderia
Ferrari, Italy. Chassis No. 0810;
Engine: 3.0 liter, 12 cyl. Ferrari
**Drivers: John Surtees,
Lodovico Scarfiotti**

12TH ANNUAL 12 HOURS OF SEBRING / MARCH 23, 1963

POS.	DRIVERS	NO.	MAKE	DISP.	ENTRANT	CLASS-POS.		LAPS
1	John Surtees / Lodovico Scarfiotti	30	Ferrari 250P	2953	S.E.F.A.C., Modena, Italy	PRTO	1	209
2	Willy Mairesse / Nino Vaccarella / L. Bandini	31	Ferrari 250P	2953	S.E.F.A.C., Modena, Italy	PRTO	2	208
3	Pedro Rodriguez / Graham Hill	18	Ferrari 330TRI/LM	3998	N.A.R.T., New York, N.Y.	PRTO	3	207
4	Roger Penske / Augie Pabst	24	Ferrari GTO	2998	Mecom Racing Team, Houston, Texas	12	1	203
5	Carlo Abate / Juan Bordeu	26	Ferrari GTO	2953	Republic of Argentina, Buenos Aires, Argentina	12	2	196
6	Richie Ginther / Innes Ireland	25	Ferrari GTO	2953	Rosebud Racing Team, Victoria, Texas	12	3	196
7	Ed Leslie / Frank Morrill	23	Jaguar XKE	3785	Kjelle Qvale, San Francisco, Calif.	13	1	195
8	Bruce McLaren / Walt Hansgen	20	Jaguar XKE	3785	Briggs Cunningham, New York, N.Y.	13	2	194
9	Bob Holbert / Don Wester	44	Porsche Abarth Carrera	1966	Porsche System Eng. Ltd., Stuttgart, Germany	10	1	193
10	Edgar Barth / Herbert Linge	43	Porsche Abarlh Carrera	1966	Porsche System Eng. Ltd., Stuttgart, Germany	10	2	193
11	Phil Hill / Lew Spencer / Ken Miles	12	Ford Cobra	4727	Ed Hugus, Pittsburgh, Pa.	14/15	1	192
12	Bobby Olthoff / Ronnie Bucknum	33	Austin-Healey 3000	2912	Donald Healey Motors, England	PRTO	4	187
13	Joakim Bonnier / John Cannon	28	Ferrari GTO	2953	N.A.R.T., New York, N.Y.	12	4	186
14	David Piper / Ed Cantrell	29	Ferrari GTO	2953	David Piper, England	12	5	186
15	Chuck Cassel / Don Sesslar	58	Porsche Abarth Carrera	1592	Porsche Car Imports, Chicago, Ill.	9	1	185
16	Delmo Johnson / David Morgan	3	Chevrolet Corvette	5360	Johnson Chevrolet Co., Dallas, Texas	14/15	2	182
17	Jeff Stevens / Johnny Allen	6	Chevrolet Corvette	5360	Dixie Motor Co., McDonough, Ga.	14/15	3	181
18	Charles Hayes / Doug Thiem	32	Ferrari GTO	2953	N.A.R.T., New York, N.Y.	12	6	179
19	Bill Kimberly / Paul Richards	21	Jaguar XKE	3785	Briggs Cunningham, New York	13	3	177
20	Victor Merino / Rafel Rosales	46	Porsche GT	1487	Puerto Rico Racing Team	9	3	176
21	Tommy Spychiger / Teddy Pilette	61	Abarth 1300 Simca	1288	Abarth Corse, Torino, Italy	7/8	1	173
22	Peter Bolton / Mike Rothschild	36	Triumph TR4	2138	Standard Triumph Motor Co., New York	11	1	172
23	Art Riley / Nick Cone	49	Volvo P1800	1780	Art Riley, Franklin Square, New York	10	3	170
24	Charles Gates / V. Diehl / Robert Cole	38	Triumph TR4	2138	Standard Triumph Motor Co., New York	11	2	168
25*	Ed Lowther / Duncan Black / Don Yenko	2	Chevrolet Corvette	5360	I.G. Davis, Pittsburgh, Pa.	14/15	4	167
26	Paddy Hopkirk / Don Morley	34	Austin-Healey 3000	2912	Donald Healey Motor Co., England	PRTO	5	166
27	Ed Wilson / Ralph Salyer / Bob Hall	40	Triumph Prototype	1898	Keymo Motors, Miami, Fla.	PRTO	6	165
28	Arch McNeill / Wm. Clarens / Alton Rogers	42	Morgan Plus 4	2138	Morgan Motor Co., Malvern, England	11	3	164
29	Dan Gurney / Phil Hill	15	Ford Cobra	4727	Shelby American, Venice, Calif.	14/15	5	163
30	Art Swanson / Ross Durant / R. Richardson	59	Alfa Romeo Zagato	1290	Swanson-Durant, Clearwater, Fla.	7/8	2	163
31	Dave Jordan / Jerry Titus	54	Sunbeam Alpine	1592	Sports Car Graphic, Hollywood, Calif.	9	3	162
32*	John Colgate / Clive Baker	69	Austin-Healey Sprite	1089	Healey Motor Co., England	PRTO	7	161
33	Norman Namerow / Peter Lerch / V. Atwell	63	Abarth 1300 Simca	1288	Canada Track & Traffic Magazine, Canada	7/8	3	160
34*	Harry Heuer / Bob Fulp	27	Ferrari 248SP Dino	2645	N.A.R.T., New York, N.Y.	PRTO	8	160
35	Bob Tullius / Dana Kellner / Lew Spencer	37	Triumph TR4	2138	Standard Triumph Motor Co., New York	11	4	158
36	F. Theodoli / William Kneeland	55	Sunbeam Alpine	1592	Filippo Theodoli, New York, N.Y.	9	4	155
37	George Waltman	39	Triumph TR4	2138	Genser Forman Dist., New York	11	5	154
38	John Bentley / Jack Gordon	67	Lotus Elite	1216	Duchess Auto Company, Millerton, N.Y.	7/8	4	151
39	Lee Lilley / Ed Graham	66	Lotus Elite	1216	Lee Lilley, Miami, Fla.	7/8	5	149

40	B. Flemming / Don Bauman / Ray Heppenstall	57	OSCA GT1600	1592	N.A.R.T., New York, N.Y.	9	5	139
41	Jocko Maggiacomo / Peter Jopp	11	Ford Cobra	4727	Holman & Moody, Charlotte, N.C.	14/15	6	117
42	Jerry Grant / Don Campbell	7	Chevrolet Corvette	5360	Alan Green Chevrolet Co., Seattle, Wash.	14/15	7	46
43	Ralph Salyer / Roy Kumnick	4	Chevrolet Corvette	5360	Ralph Salyer, Hammond, In.	DNF-e		120
44	Briggs Cunningham / John Fitch	22	Jaguar XKE	3785	Briggs Cunningham, New York, N.Y.	DNF-t		112
45	Edmund Hessert, Jr. / H. Swartz	50	Sabra	1703	Autocars Co., Haifa, Israel	DNF-t		90
46	A.J. Foyt / Jim Hurtubise	5	Chevrolet Corvette	5360	Nickey Chevrolet, Chicago, Ill.	DNF-e		84
47	Hans Herrmann / Mauro Bianchi	62	Abarth 1300 Simca	1288	Abarth Corse, Torino, Italy	DNF-e		83
48	Mike Parkes / Lorenzo Bandini	19	Ferrari 330LM	3867	S.E.F.A.C., Modena, Italy	DNF-f		72
49	Grant Clark / Gordon Browne	68	Austin Cooper	1088	Frederick Royston, Philadelphia, Pa.	DNF-e		71
50	Linley Coleman / Charlie Kolb	45	Porsche GT	1966	Brumos Porsche Corp., Jacksonville, Fla.	DNF-t		67
51	Bob Grossman / Ray Cuomo	60	Abarth 1300 Simca	1288	Abarth Corse, Torino, Italy	DNF-e		62
52	Ken Miles / Lew Spencer	16	Ford Cobra	4727	Shelby American, Venice, Calif.	DNF-s		56
53	Ronnie Hissom / Hap Sharp / Bob Donner	10	Chaparral	4999	Chaparral Cars, Midland, Texas	DNF-s		56
54	Dave McDonald / Fireball Roberts	14	Ford Cobra	4727	Shelby American, Venice, Calif.	DNF-x		52
55	Alton Rogers / Richard Holquist	41	Morgan Plus 4	2138	Morgan Motor Co., Malvern, England	DNF-e		45
56	Jim Parkinson / Jack Flaherty	47	MGB	1790	Ecurie Safety Fast, Abingdon, England	DNF-e		45
57	Piero Frescobaldi / G.P. Biscaldi	64	Abarth 1300 Simca	1288	Abarth Corse, Torino, Italy	DNF-e		41
58	Robert Publicker / Burrell Besancon	56	OSCA GT1600	1592	Robert Publicker, Ft. Lauderdale, Fla.	DNF-r		41
59	Howard Hanna / Richard Toland	71	Rene Bonnet Djet	996	Howard Hanna, Newtown Sq., Pa.	DNF-e		35
60	Denise McCluggage / Cris Carlisle	48	MGB	1790	Ecurie Safety Fast, Abingdon, England	DNF-e		32
61	George Reed, Jr.	17	Ford Cobra	4727	George Reed, Jr., Midlothian, Ill.	DNF-k		22
62	Jim Hall	9	Chaparral	4999	Chaparral Cars, Midland, Texas	DNF-e		15
63	Dick Thompson	1	Chevrolet Corvette	5360	I. Grady Davis, Pittsburgh, Pa.	DNF-t		14
64	Mark Donohue	51	TVR	1622	R.M. Imports, New York	DNF-e		7
65	George McClure	53	TVR	1622	R.M. Imports, New York	DNF-e		7
DNS	Harry Heuer / Jeff Houghton	8	Pontiac	5340	Meisterbrau Racing, Chicago, Ill.	reserve		
DNS	Anatoly Arutunoff / William Pryor	35	Lancia	2458	Oklahoma A.R.C., Kansas City, Okla.	reserve		
DNS	Dick Semko / George McClure	52	TVR	1622	RM Imports, New York, N.Y.	reserve		
DNS	Georgio Bassi / Giancarlo Facetti	70	ASA RB600	1032	Scuderia A.S.A., Italy	reserve		

*Classified Finisher (not running at end of race)

INDEX OF PERFORMANCE

1. #30 Ferrari 250P 1.42893
2. #31 Ferrari 250P 1.42209
3. #18 Ferrari 330TR 1.38648
4. #24 Ferrari GTO 1.38628
5. #43 Porsche Carrera 1.37068

Average Speed: 90.391 mph
Distance: 209 laps, 1 086.8 miles
Fastest Race Lap: #30 John Surtees, 97.805 mph
Fastest Qualifier: None — Le Mans type start
Margin of Victory: 1 lap
Lap Leaders: #12 1; #18 2-13, 15-70, 79-145; #9 14; #30 71-78, 146-209
Weather: Partly cloudy and cold
Attendance: 43,398

1963 HOURLY STANDINGS — TOP 10

POS.	1 HR.	2 HRS.	3 HRS.	4 HRS.	5 HRS.	6 HRS.	7 HRS.	8 HRS.	9 HRS.	10 HRS.	11 HRS.	Finish
1	18	18	18	18	30	18	18	18	30	30	30	30
2	12	24	30	30	18	30	30	30	18	18	31	31
3	24	30	31	31	31	31	31	31	31	31	18	18
4	15	15	15	15	24	24	24	24	24	24	24	24
5	19	12	24	24	15	15	23	20	2	26	26	26
6	25	31	19	19	23	20	2	2	27	2	23	25
7	16	19	26	20	27	27	20	26	26	20	25	23
8	14	14	27	26	20	23	26	27	20	23	43	20
9	30	20	20	23	26	2	27	44	25	25	20	44
10	28	23	28	27	2	26	43	23	23	27	44	43

1964

**1964 SEBRING WINNER —
Ferrari 275P**
Built and entered by Scuderia
Ferrari, Italy. Chassis No. 0812;
Engine: 3.3 liter, 12 cyl. Ferrari
**Drivers: Mike Parkes, Umberto
Maglioli**

13TH ANNUAL 12 HOURS OF SEBRING / MARCH 21, 1964

POS.	DRIVERS	NO.	MAKE	DISP.	ENTRANT	CLASS-POS.	LAPS
1	Mike Parkes / Umberto Maglioli	22	Ferrari 275P	3286	S.E.F.A.C.-Ferrari, Modena, Italy	PT 13-1	214
2	Lodovico Scarfiotti / Nino Vaccarella	23	Ferrari 275P	3286	S.E.F.A.C.-Ferrari, Modena, Italy	PT 13-2	213
3	John Surtees / Lorenzo Bandini	21	Ferrari 330P	3967	S.E.F.A.C.-Ferrari, Modena, Italy	PT 13-3	212
4	Bob Holbert / Dave MacDonald	10	Ford Cobra coupe	4727	Shelby American Corp., Venice, Calif.	GT 14-1	209
5	Lew Spencer / Bob Bondurant	12	Ford Cobra	4727	Shelby American Corp., Venice, Calif.	GT 14-2	205
6	Jo Schlesser / Phil Hill	14	Ford Cobra	4727	Ford of France, Paris, France	GT 14-3	203
7	Pedro Rodriguez / David Piper / Mike Gammino	30	Ferrari GTO	2953	N.A.R.T., New York, N.Y.	GT 12-1	201
8	Harold Keck / Robert Scott	80	Ford Cobra	4727	Hellerton Motors, Bethlehem, Pa.	GT 14-4	195
9	Briggs Cunningham / Lake Underwood	37	Porsche 904	1984	B.S. Cunningham, Los Angeles, Calif.	PT 10-1	194
10*	Dan Gurney / Bob Johnson	11	Ford Cobra	4727	Shelby American Corp., Venice, Calif.	GT 14-5	191
11	Joe Buzzeta / Ben Pon	43	Porsche 2000GS LM	1966	Porsche System Engineering, Germany	GT 10-1	191
12	Chuck Cassel / Don Sesslar	45	Porsche Abarth Carrera	1966	Carl W. Lindell, Inc., Ft. Lauderdale, Fla.	GT 10-2	190
13	Charles Stoddard / Jim Kaser	53	Alfa Romeo 1600TZ	1570	Scuderia Sant Ambroeus, Milano, Italy	GT 9-1	188
14	Thomas Hitchcock / Zourab Tchkotoura	15	Ford Cobra	4727	Thomas Hitchcock, New York, N.Y.	GT 14-6	187
15	Bob Grossman / Dick Thompson	29	Ferrari GTO	2953	N.A.R.T., New York, N.Y.	GT 12-2	186
16	Skip Hudson / Jerry Grant	9	Chevy Corvette Stingray	5360	Nickey Chevrolet Co., Chicago, Ill.	GT 15-1	183
17	Ed Leslie / Jack Dalton	47	MGB	1787	Kjelle Qvalle, San Francisco, Calif.	GT 10-3	180
18	Roger Penske / Jim Hall	4	Chevrolet Corvette GS	6183	McKean Chevrolet, Inc., Philadelphia, Pa.	PT 15-1	177
19	Don Wester / Bruce Jennings	42	Porsche 2000GS LM	1966	Porsche System Engineering, Germany	PT 10-2	175
20	Edgar Barth / Herbert Linge	41	Porsche 718 RS Spyder	1982	Porsche System Engineering, Germany	PT 10-3	173
21	Jim Clark / Ray Parsons	59	Lotus-Cortina	1558	Robert Scott, Jr., Grosse Point, Mich.	GT 9-2	171
22	Jim Adams / Merle Brennan	48	MGB	1787	Kjelle Qvale, San Francisco, Calif.	GT 10-4	170
23	A.J. Foyt / John Cannon	2	Chevrolet Corvette GS	6183	Mecom Racing Team, Houston, Texas	PT 15-2	168
24	Thomas Fleming / Otto Linton / Jim Diaz	62	Abarth Simca	1267	Ray Heppenstall, Glenside, N.Y.	GT 8-1	165
25	John Colgate / Clive Baker	61	Austin-Healey Sprite	1275	Donald Healey Motor Co., Warwick, England	PT 8-1	164
26*	Roberto Bussinello / Consalvo Sanesi	55	Alfa Romeo 1600TZ	1570	Scuderia Sant Ambroeus, Milano, Italy	GT 9-3	160
27	Larry Perkins / William Eve	82	Ferrari GTO	2953	Larry Perkins, Cocoa Beach, Fla.	GT 12-3	158
28	Harry Heuer / Don Yenko / Ed Cantrell	32	Ferrari GTO	2953	Angels Aviation Racing Team, Calif.	GT 12-4	154
29	Charlie Rainville / Paul Richards	69	Alpine Renault	1002	Autosport International, New York, N.Y.	PT 7-1	153
30	Howard Hanna / Richard Toland	65	Rene Bonnet Djet 2	1109	Automobiles Rene Bonnet, France	GT 7-1	153
31*	John Ryan / William Bencker	39	Porsche 904	1984	John E. Ryan, Griffin, Ga.	PT 10-4	147
32	Delmo Johnson / David Morgan	3	Chevrolet Corvette GS	6183	Johnson Chevrolet Co., Dallas, Texas	PT 15-3	144
33*	Jose Rosinski / Mauro Bianchi	68	Alpine Renault M63	1002	Automobiles Alpine, Paris, France	PT 7-2	140
34	W.S. McKelvy / Richard Holquist	63	Abarth Simca	1267	Scuderia Bear, Pittsburgh, Pa.	GT 8-2	139
35	Ed Lowther / George Wintersteen	18	Ford Cobra	4727	Ed Hugus, Pittsburgh, Pa.	GT 14-7	138
36*	Art Riley / Nick Cone	51	Volvo P1800	1780	Volvo Imports, Inc., N.J.	PT 10-5	136
37*	Richie Ginther / Ronnie Bucknum	36	Porsche 904	1984	Precision Motor Cars, Beverly Hills, Calif.	PT 10-6	129
38	Newton Davis / Paul Layman	84	Lotus Elite	1216	Duchess Auto Company, Millerton, N.Y.	GT 8-3	124
39	Ed Hugus / William McLaughlin / E. Wilson	5	ISO Chevy Corsa	5453	William McLaughlin, Tulsa, Okla.	PT 15-4	110

40	George Waltman / Ted Lawrence	34	Triumph TR4	2138	Genser Forman Triumph Dist., N.J.	GT 11-1	79
41	Graham Hill / Joakim Bonnier	24	Ferrari 330P	3967	Maranello Concessionaires, Italy	DNF-t	139
42	Ralph Noseda / Jeff Stevens	16	Ford Cobra	4727	Ralph Noseda, Miami, Fla.	DNF-u	138
43	George Reed / Dan Gerber	19	Ford Cobra	4727	George Reed, Jr. Midlothian, Ill.	DNF-f	117
44	Carlo Abate / Jean Guichet	31	Ferrari GTO	2953	S.E.F.A.C.-Ferrari, Modena, Italy	DNF-u	113
45	Victor Merino / Jorge Torruellas	44	Porsche Abarth Carrera	1966	Porsche Car Import, Chicago, Ill.	DNF-e	101
46	Filippo Theodoli / Gianni Bulgari / C. Sanesi	56	Alfa Romeo 1600TZ	1570	Scuderia Sant Ambroeus, Milano, Italy	DNF-e	93
47	Ken Miles / John Morton	1	Ford Cobra prototype	7000	Shelby American Corp., Venice, Calif.	DNF-e	81
48	Charles Dietrich / Bill Wuesthoff	54	Alfa Romeo 1600TZ	1570	Scuderia Sant Ambroeus, Milano, Italy	DNF-t	70
49	Bob Tullius / Paul Richards	70	Alpine Renault	1002	Autosport Int'l., New York, N.Y.	DNF-t	66
50	Graham Shaw / Tiny Lund / Charles Hayes	17	Ford Cobra	4727	Graham Shaw, Columbia, S.C.	DNF-b	62
51	Richard Boo / George Robertson, Jr.	6	Chevy Corvette Stingray	5360	George Robertson, Jr., Locust Grove, Calif	DNF t	52
52	John Bentley / Lyle Witmer	52	Porsche Carrera	1588	K Chambliss, Eau Galle, Fla.	DNF-e	52
53	Paddy Hopkirk / Grant Clark	33	Austin-Healey 3000	2912	Donald Healey Motor Co., Warwick, England	DNF-a	49
54	Godin de Beaufort	38	Porsche 904	1984	Count de Beaufort, Holland	DNF-f	48
55	Hap Sharp / Ronnie Hissom	40	Porsche 904	1984	Hap Sharp, Midland, Texas	DNF-t	45
56	Walt Hansgen / Augie Pabst	20	Lola-Chevrolet coupe	4638	Mecom Racing Team, Houston, Texas	DNF-e	44
57	Pedro Rodriguez / John Fulp	25	Ferrari 330P	3967	N.A.R.T., New York, N.Y.	DNF-e	40
58	Hugh Dibley / R.G. Rossler	57	Lotus Elan	1558	Stirling Moss Auto Racing Team, England	DNF-a	39
59	Art Tattersall / Gunnar Engelin	49	Volvo P1800	1780	Volvo Imports, Inc., N.J.	DNF-a	31
60	Charles Kolb / Tom O'Brien	28	Ferrari 250LM	2953	N.A.R.T., New York, N.Y.	DNF-a	30
61	John Christy / Dave Jordan	50	Volvo P1800	1780	Volvo Imports, Inc., N.J.	DNF-e	29
62	Jim Parkinson	46	MGB	1787	Kjelle Qvalle, San Francisco, Calif.	DNF-a	15
63	Al Rogers	35	Morgan 4/4	2138	Nuclear Electronic Lab, Walnut Creek, Calif.	DNF-e	12
64	Al Pease	67	Austin-Healey Sprite	1099	Donald Healey Motor Co., Warwick, England	DNF-x	9
65	Donald Kearny	64	Triumph Spitfire	1147	Donald F. Kearney, Clearwater, Fla.	DNF-e	7
66	Bill Haenelt	85	Alpine Renault	1108	Autosport Int'l., New York, N.Y.	DNF-e	2
DNS	Charles Kolb / Charlie Rainville	27	Ferrari prototype	3967	Fong Racing Associates, Atlanta, Ga.	reserve	
DNS	Claude Maurel / Georges Bonnet	66	Rene Bonnet Djet 2	1109	Automobiles Rene Bonnet, France	reserve	

*Classified finishers (not running at finish)

Average Speed: 92.2 mph
Distance: 1,112.8 miles
Fastest Race Lap: #21 John Surtees, 100.539 mph
Fastest Qualifier: #21 John Surtees, 3:04.2 = 101.62 mph
Attendance: 48,000 (est.)
Weather: Mostly sunny and warm

Leaders: #4 1; #21 2-3, 13-32, 36-97, 108-121, 135-151; #25 4-12; #22 33-34, 186-195, 206-214; #23 35, 152-185, 196-205; #24 98-107, 122-134

1964 HOURLY STANDINGS — TOP 10

POS.	1 HR.	2 HRS.	3 HRS.	4 HRS.	5 HRS.	6 HRS.	7 HRS.	8 HRS.	9 HRS.	10 HRS.	11 HRS.	Finish
1	21	21	21	21	21	21	24	21	21	23	**22**	**22**
2	24	24	24	24	24	24	21	23	23	**22**	23	23
3	**22**	**22**	23	**22**	23	23	23	**22**	**22**	21	21	21
4	23	23	**22**	23	**22**	**22**	**22**	11	11	11	11	10
5	4	11	4	11	4	11	11	24	10	10	10	12
6	11	4	11	4	11	41	14	10	12	12	12	14
7	10	25	10	10	10	14	10	12	14	14	14	30
8	2	10	2	41	41	10	12	14	30	30	30	80
9	14	41	41	2	14	12	2	30	80	80	80	37
10	25	14	14	14	2	2	41	2	2	37	37	11

1965

**1965 SEBRING WINNER —
Chaparral 2A**
Built and entered by Chaparral
Cars, Midland, Texas. Chassis No.
01; Engine: 5.4 liter, 8 cyl.
Chevrolet
Drivers: Jim Hall, Hap Sharp

14TH ANNUAL 12 HOURS OF SEBRING / MARCH 27, 1965

POS.	DRIVERS	NO.	MAKE	DISP.	ENTRANT	CLASS-POS.		LAPS
1	Jim Hall / Hap Sharp	3	Chaparral 2A	5370	Chaparral Cars, Midland, Tex.	S	1	196
2	Bruce McLaren / Ken Miles	11	Ford GT 40	4727	Al Dowd, Santa Monica, Calif.	PT-14/15	1	192
3	David Piper / Tony Maggs	31	Ferrari 275LM	3300	David Piper(Auto Racing Ltd.),London, Eng.	PT-11/13	1	190
4	Jo Schlesser / Bob Bondurant	15	Ford Cobra GT coupe	4727	Shelby American, Inc., Venice, Calif.	GT-14	1	187
5	Lake Underwood / Gunther Klass	40	Porsche 904	1966	Porsche Automobile Co., Stuttgart, Germany	GT-10	1	185
6	Ben Pon / Joe Buzzetta	39	Porsche 904	1966	Porsche Automobile Co., Stuttgart, Germany	GT-10	2	185
7	Bob Johnson / Tom Payne	14	Ford Cobra GT coupe	4727	Shelby American, Inc., Venice, Calif.	GT-14	2	185
8	Umberto Maglioli / Giancarlo Baghetti	33	Ferrari 330 P	3980	Kleiner Racing Ent., Austin, Texas	S	2	184
9	Herbert Linge / Gerhard Mitter	38	Porsche 904/8	1981	Porsche Automobile Co., Stuttgart, Germany	PT-7/10	1	184
10	Scooter Patrick / Dave Jordan	41	Porsche 904	1966	Precision Motors, Beverly Hills, Calif.	GT-10	3	183
11	Walt Hansgen / Mark Donohue	29	Ferrari 275 LM	3300	Mecom Racing Team, Houston, Texas	PT-11/13	2	183
12	Tom O'Brien / Ed Hugus / Paul Richards	32	Ferrari 275P	3300	Ed Hugus, Pittsburgh, Pa.	PT-11/13	3	182
13	Ed Leslie / Allen Grant	12	Ford Cobra GT coupe	4727	Shelby American, Inc., Venice, Calif.	GT-14	4	178
14	George Wintersteen / Peter Goetz / Milton Diehl	2	Chevrolet Corvette GS	6200	George Wintersteen, Villanova, Pa.	PT-14/15	2	175
15	Rauno Aaltonen / Clive Baker	61	Austin-Healey Sprite	1292	Donald Healey Motor Co., Warwick, Eng.	PT-7/10	2	175
16	Jean Rolland / Bernard Consten	58	Alfa Romeo TZ-C	1570	Autodelta S.p.A., Milan, Italy	GT-9	1	175
17	Warwick Banks / Paul Hawkins	34	Austin-Healey 3000	2990	Donald Healey Motor Co., Warwick, Eng.	GT-12	1	175
18	Paddy Hopkirk / Timo Makinen	62	Austin-Healey Sprite	1292	Donald Healey Motor Co., Warwick, Eng.	PT-7/10	3	175
19	Graham Shaw / Dick Thompson	17	Ford Cobra roadster	4727	Shaw Racing Team, Columbia, S.C.	GT-14	4	173
20	Briggs Cunningham / John Fitch / William Bencker	44	Porsche 904	1966	Briggs Cunningham, Newport Beach, Calif.	GT-10	4	173
21	Jim Adams / Lew Spencer / Phil Hill	16	Ford Cobra GT coupe	4727	Shelby American, Inc., Venice, Calif.	GT-14	5	173
22	Ronnie Hissom / Bruce Jennings	4	Chaparral 2A	5370	Chaparral Cars, Midland, Texas	S	3	173
23	Willy Mairesse / Mauro Bianchi	81	Ferrari 275P	3300	Fong Racing Assoc., Atlanta, Ga.	PT-11/13	4	171
24	Roberto Bussinello / Andrea de Adamich	56	Alfa Romeo TZ-C	1530	Autodelta, S.p.A., Milan, Italy	GT-9	2	170
25	Merle Brennen / Frank Morrell	49	MGB	1801	British Motor Corp., Abingdon, England	PT-7/10	4	169
26	Andrew Hedges / Roger Mac	68	MG Midget	1139	British Motor Corp., Abingdon, England	GT-7/8	1	168
27	Teodoro Zeccoli / Bruno Deserti	57	Alfa Romeo TZ-C	1570	Autodelta, S.p.A., Milan, Italy	GT-9	3	167
28	Jack Ryan / Ted Tidwell	43	Porsche 904	1966	R.B.M. Motors, Griffin, Ga.	GT-10	5	163
29	Ed Barker / Duane Fuerhelm / Mike Rothschild	67	Triumph Spitfire	1147	Standard Triumph, Inc., New York, N.Y.	GT-7/8	2	163
30	Bob Tullius / Charles Gates	66	Triumph Spitfire	1147	Standard Triumph, Inc., New York, N.Y.	GT-7/8	3	162
31	Dave McClain / Leland Dieas	54	Porsche 356SC	1582	David H. McClain,Tampa, Fla.	GT-7/8	4	158
32	Brad Pickard / Alan Pease	48	MGB 1800	1801	British Motor Corp., Abingdon, England	GT-10	6	151
33	Dick Boo / George Robertson, Jr.	5	Chevy Corvette Stingray	5360	George Robertson, Jr., Locust Grove, Ga.	GT-15	1	145
34*	Bob Grossman / Skip Hudson	26	Ferrari 330P	3980	Scuderia Bear, Pittsburgh, Pa.	PT-11/13	5	143
35	Al Rogers / George Waltman	60	Turner Specialle	1498	Turner Cars, Ltd., Wolverhampton, England	PT-7/10	5	143
36	Delmo Johnson / David Morgan / Ed Sevadvian	1	Chevrolet Corvette GS	6780	Ridgeway Racing, Inc., Arlington, Texas	PT-14/15	3	137
37*	Graham Hill / Pedro Rodriguez	30	Ferrari 330 P	3980	Mecom Racing Team, Houston, Texas	S	4	133
38	Peter Pulver / Newton Davis / Lance Pruyn	59	Lotus Elan	1558	Dutchess Auto, Inc., Millerton, N.Y.	GT-9	4	127
39*	Charlie Rainville / Mike Gammino	9	Grifo A3C coupe	5359	Bizzarrini Automobili, Livorno, Italy	S	5	122

Pos.	Drivers	No.	Car	Disp.	Entrant	Class/Status		Laps
40	K.H. Sellers / Frank Manley	69	Alpine Renault A110	1108	Societe des Automobiles Alpine, Paris, France	GT-7/8	5	99
41	M. Barry Martin / Craig Hill	37	Triumph TR4	2138	M. Barry Martin, Montreal, Canada	GT-11	1	95
42	Howard Hanna / Richard Toland	71	Rene Bonnet Djet	1108	Howard Hanna, Newtown Sq., Pa.	GT-7/8	6	95
43	Dave Hull / Bob Kingham / Milo Vega	25	Jaguar XKE	3781	Jaguar Cars, Inc., Winter Haven, Fla.	GT-13	1	59
44	John Fulp / Charlie Kolb	27	Ferrari 330P	3980	John Fulp, Anderson, S.C.	DNF-t		104
45	Peter Gregg / George Barber, Jr.	45	Porsche 904	1966	Peter Gregg, Jacksonville, Fla.	DNF-s		99
46	Ed Lowther / Bob Nagel	18	Ford Cobra roadster	4727	Ed Lowther, McMurray, Pa.	DNF-u		93
47	John Walsh / G. Brown / Peter Keith	52	Ginetta G4	1729	Ginetta Cars, Ltd., England	DNF-e		82
48	Sherman Decker / Oscar Koveleski	21	Cooper Ford Monaco	4727	Greenwich Autos, Greenwich, Ct.	DNF-e		70
49	Gaston Andrey / Chuck Stoddard	55	Alfa Romeo TZ-C	1570	Autodelta S.p.A., Milan, Italy	DNF-a		66
50	George Reed / Daniel Gerber	20	Ford Cobra roadster	4797	Gerber-Payne Ford, Fremont, Mich.	DNF-a		64
51	Don Yenko / John Bushell	6	Chevrolet Corvette	5360	Ken Hablow, Chestnut Hill, Mass.	DNF-s		61
52	John Cannon / Jack Saunders	22	Lola T-70 Ford	4727	Mecom Racing Team, Houston, Tex.	DNF-e		55
53	Fred Baker / Bill Kirtley	70	Alpine Renault A110	1108	Fred J. Baker, Mound, Minn.	DNF-e		53
54	Art Riley / Nick Cone	51	Volvo P1800	1780	Art Riley, Franklin Sq., N.Y.	DNF-a		51
55	John Norris / Roger Heftler	64	Lotus Elite	1226	Crespi Motors, N. Miami Beach, Fla.	DNF-s		46
56	Dan Gurney / Jerry Grant	23	Lotus Ford	4727	All American Racers, Santa Ana, Calif.	DNF-f		43
57	Phil Hill / Richie Ginther	10	Ford GT 40	4727	Ken Miles, Hollywood, Calif.	DNF-s		37
58	Arthur Swanson / Bob Ennis	46	Abarth Simca	1946	Arthur A. Swanson, Boston, Mass.	DNF-t		36
59	Chuck Cassel / David Lane	42	Porsche 904	1966	Carl W. Lindell Co., Ft. Lauderdale, Fla.	DNF-x		36
60	Peter Clarke / Skip Scott	35	Ferrari GTO	2953	Peter Clarke, London, Eng.	DNF-t		35
61	Richard Holquist / Millard Ripley	63	Abarth Simca	1288	Scuderia Bear, Pittsburgh, Pa.	DNF-a		27
62	Richard Robson / Art Baggely	28	Jaguar XKE	3781	Richardson Robson Jr., Titusville, Fla.	DNF-e		26
63	John Bentley / Ray Cuomo	53	Beach Mk8	1594	Comp. Components, Inc., Clearwater, Fla.	DNF-s		16
64	Silvio Moser	8	Grifo A3C coupe	5359	Bizzarrini Automobili, Italy	DNF-a		16
65	Chuck Tannlund	82	MG Midget	1108	British Motor Corp., England	DNF-e		7
66	Peter Bolton	65	Triumph Spitfire	1147	Standard Triumph, New York, N.Y.	DNF-a		5
DNS	John Wagstaff / J.H. Porter	47	Abarth Simca	1996	Faza Motorsport, Ridgefield, Ct.	reserve		
DNS	Anatoly Arutunoff / William Pryor	36	Lancia Flaminia	2458	A.R.C.O., Inc., Nashville, Tenn.	reserve		
DNS	Jack Wybenga / Harry Jackson	7	Chevrolet Corvette Stingray	5360	Jack Wybenga, Hyattsville, Md.	reserve		
DNS	Peter Harrison / Linley Coleman	19	Ford Cobra roadster	4727	Arthur Harrison, Clearwater, Fla.	reserve		

*Classified Finisher (not running at end of race)

Average Speed: 84.72 mph
Distance: 1019.2 miles
Margin of Victory: 4 laps
Fastest Race Lap: #3 Jim Hall, 104.41 mph

Fastest Qualifier: #3 Jim Hall, 2:57.6 = 105.41 mph
Lap Leaders: #10 1; #3 9-33, 43-196; **#23** 2-8, 34-42
Attendance: 60,000 (est.)
Weather: Partly cloudy and hot, heavy rainstorm during race.

1965 HOURLY STANDINGS — TOP 10

POS.	1 HR.	2 HRS.	3 HRS.	4 HRS.	5 HRS.	6 HRS.	7 HRS.	8 HRS.	9 HRS.	10 HRS.	11 HRS.	Finish
1	3	23	3	3	3	3	3	3	3	3	3	3
2	23	3	30	30	30	30	30	11	11	11	11	11
3	4	4	4	11	11	11	11	30	31	31	31	31
4	30	11	11	27	27	27	31	31	15	15	15	15
5	11	30	27	15	15	31	4	15	39	29	39	40
6	27	29	15	14	14	4	15	33	29	39	40	39
7	29	27	32	12	26	15	33	4	40	40	14	14
8	21	14	14	31	4	14	12	12	38	32	33	33
9	32	15	12	32	38	12	26	38	32	33	32	38
10	2	26	38	38	12	26	32	14	4	38	38	41

1966

1966 SEBRING WINNER —
Ford X-1 (spl. roadster)
Built and entered by Shelby
American, Los Angeles, California.
Chassis No. 110; Engine: 7.0 liter,
8 cyl. Ford
Drivers: Ken Miles, Lloyd Ruby

15TH ANNUAL 12 HOURS OF SEBRING / MARCH 26, 1966

POS.	DRIVERS	NO.	MAKE	DISP.	ENTRANT	CLASS	POS.	LAPS
1	Ken Miles / Lloyd Ruby	1	Ford X-1 roadster	7010	Shelby American, Los Angeles, Calif.	SP13	1	228
2	Walt Hansgen / Mark Donohue	3	Ford Mk ll	7010	Holman-Moody, Charlotte, N.C.	SP13	2	216
3	Peter Revson / Skip Scott	19	Ford GT40	4727	Essex Wire Corp., Pa.	S12	1	213
4	Hans Herrmann / Joe Buzzetta / Gerhard Mitter	52	Porsche 906	1991	Porsche Auto, Stuttgart, Germany	SP9	1	209
5	Lorenzo Bandini / Ludovico Scarfiotti	46	Ferrari Dino 206/S	1996	S.E.F.A.C., Modena, Italy	SP9	2	206
6	Charles Voegele / Jo Siffert	49	Porsche 906	1991	Charles Voegele, Switzerland	SP9	3	206
7	George Follmer / Peter Gregg	54	Porsche 904	1966	Porsche Auto, Stuttgart, Germany	S9	1	205
8	Ed Hugus / Lake Underwood	50	Porsche 906	1991	Ed Hugus, Pittsburgh, Pa.	SP9	4	204
9	Ben Moore / George Wintersteen	9	Chevrolet Corvette Stingray	6997	Roger Penske, Philadelphia, Pa.	GT13	1	201
10	Bob Grossman / Ed Lowther	6	Ford Cobra roadster	7010	Scuderia Bear, Pittsburgh, Pa.	S13	1	197
11	Don Yenko / Harold Whims / David Morgan	8	Chevrolet Corvette Stingray	6997	Harold C. Whims, Jr., Carrboro, N.C.	GT13	2	197
12	A.J. Foyt / Ronnie Bucknum	4	Ford Mk ll	7010	Holman-Moody, Charlotte,N.C.	SP13	3	192
13	Richard Holquist / Bruce Jennings	23	Ford GT40	4727	Scuderia Bear, Pittsburgh, Pa.	S12	2	189
14	Giacomo Russo / Gaston Andrey	63	Alfa Romeo TZ/2	1570	Autodelta S.p.A., Milan, Italy	S8	1	189
15	Ray Cuomo / Bob Said / John Addison	80	Ford Cobra roadster	4727	Tom Payne, Ann Arbor, Mich.	S13	2	188
16	Jacques Duval / Horst Kroll	56	Porsche 904	1966	Jacques Duval, St. Bruno, Canada	S9	2	188
17	Roger Mac / Peter Manton / Andrew Hedges	59	MGB	1798	British Motor Corp., England	GT9	1	178
18	Timo Makinen / Paul Hawkins	67	Austin-Healey Sprite	1293	Donald Healey Motor Co., England	SP7	1	175
19	Bill Pendleton / Steve Froines	41	Triumph TR4A	2182	Standard Triumph Motor Co., New York, N.Y.	GT10	1	172
20	Jack Ryan / Linley Coleman	51	Porsche 911	1991	R.B.M., Atlanta, Ga.	GT9	2	168
21	Fred Baker / Bill Kirtley	65	Alpine Renault M65	1296	Fred J. Baker, Mound, Minn.	S7	1	168
22	John Bentley / H. Byrne / Arthur Latta	7	Ford Cobra roadster	7010	Space Science Service, Orlando, Fla.	S13	3	166
23	E. Richard Gilmartin / Mike Rothschild	40	Triumph TR4A	2182	Standard Triumph Motor Co., England	GT10	2	162
24	Kenneth Sellers / Robert Shaw	69	Alpine Renault A110	1108	Capt. Kenneth Sellers, Charleston S.C.	S6	1	162
25	Fred Opert / William McKemie	58	Elva Courier Mk IV	1840	Carl Haas Automobiles, Chicago, Ill.	S9	3	153
26	R. Craig Hill / Ludwig Heimrath	42	Triumph TR4A	2182	Standard Triumph Motor Co., New York, N.Y.	GT10	3	151
27	Howard Hanna / Morrow Decker	68	Matra MB8S	1108	Howard Hanna, Newtown Square, Pa.	S6	2*	148
28	Bob Kingham / Milo Vega	92	Triumph TR4A	2182	John Kingham, Winter Haven, Fla.	GT10	4	131
29	Rauno Aaltonen / Clive Baker	66	Austin-Healey Sprite	1293	Donald Healey Motor Co., England	SP7	2	121
30	Richard Robson / W. Buckman / R. Rogers	32	Jaguar XKE	3784	Richard B. Robson, Titusville, Fla.	GT12	1	82
31	Pedro Rodriguez / Mario Andretti	26	Ferrari 330P2	4400	N.A.R.T., New York, N.Y.	DNF-a		188
32	Scooter Patrick / Don Wester	48	Porsche 906	1991	Precision Motor Cars, Beverly Hills, Calif.	DNF-a		182
33	Mike Parkes / Bob Bondurant	27	Ferrari 330P3	4000	S.E.F.A.C., Modena, Italy	DNF-t		172
34	Paddy Hopkirk / Peter Manton / Andrew Hedges	44	MGB prototype	2009	British Motor Corp., England	DNF-e		157
35	Briggs Cunningham / John Fitch / David Jordan	47	Porsche 904	1966	Briggs S. Cunningham, Lido Sound, Calif.	DNF-e		148
36	John Whitmore / Frank Gardner	25	Ford GT40	4727	Alan Mann Racing Ltd., England	DNF-t		146
37	Graham Hill / Jackie Stewart	24	Ford GT40	4727	Alan Mann Racing Ltd., England	DNF-e		142
38	Albert Ackerly / Arch McNeill	85	MGB	1798	Continental Cars, Ltd., Memphis, Tenn.	DNF-e		137
39	Gerhard Mitter / Gunther Klass	53	Porsche 906	1991	Porsche Auto, Stuttgart, Germany	DNF-e		120

40	Dieter Glemser / Udo Schutz	55	Porsche 904	1966	Porsche Auto, Stuttgart, Germany	DNF-t	114
41	Eppie Wietzes / Craig Fisher	17	Ford GT40	4727	Comstock Racing Team, Toronto, Canada	DNF-w	96
42	Herb Wetanson / Millard Ripley	57	Porsche 904	1966	Wetanson & Riley, Ithaca, N.Y.	DNF-t	94
43	Charlie Kolb / Buck Fulp	87	Porsche 8 Spyder	1991	Keymo Motors Corp., Miami, Fla.	DNF-e	87
44	Bob McLean+ / Jean Oulette	18	Ford GT40	4727	Comstock Racing Team, Toronto, Canada	DNF-a	83
45	Terry Kohler / Walt Biddle	82	Ford GT350 Mustang	4727	Terry Kohler, Sheboygan, Wisc.	DNF-t	71
46	Arthur Swanson / Robert Ennis	33	Ferrari 275LM	3285	Arthur Swanson, Roxbury, Mass.	DNF-e	70
47	Dick Thompson / Dick Guldstrand	10	Chevrolet Corvette GS rdstr.	6997	Roger Penske, Philadelphia, Pa.	DNF-a	65
48	Bernard Consten / Luciano Bianchi	69	Alfa Romeo TZ/2	1570	Autodelta S.p.A., Milan, Italy	DNF-t	61
49	Jack Slottag / Larry Perkins	35	Ferrari GTO	2953	Jack Slottag, Orlando, Fla.	DNF-e	61
50	Bob Tullius / Charles Gates	39	Triumph TR4A prototype	2182	Standard Triumph Motor Co., New York, N.Y.	DNF-f	47
51	Peter Sutcliffe / Innes Ireland	21	Ford GT40	4727	Peter Sutcliffe, England	DNF-e	47
52	Jim Hall / Hap Sharp	11	Chaparral 2D	5355	Chaparral Cars, Midland, Tex.	DNF-s	35
53	Masten Gregory	20	Ford GT40	4727	Essex Wire Corp., Pa.	DNF-e	30
54	Joakim Bonnier / Phil Hill	12	Chaparral 2D	5355	Chaparral Cars, Midland, Tex.	DNF-e	27
55	R. Colombosian	60	Lotus Elan	1594	Autolab Imports, Waburn, Mass.	DNF-e	25
56	Teodoro Zeccoli	61	Alfa Romeo TZ/2	1570	Autodelta S.p.A., Milan, Italy	DNF-e	22
57	Sam Posey	64	Alfa Romeo TZ/2	1570	Filippo Theodoli, Rome, Italy	DNF-e	16
58	Edgar Schantz	89	Abarth Simca 1300	1288	Sherman S. Smith, Newark, N.J.	DNF-t	13
59	Roger West	84	MGB	1798	Roger West, Birmingham, Ala.	DNF-u	7
60	Donna Mae Mimms	37	Yenko Stinger Corvair	2690	McMillan Ring Free Oil Co., N. Y., N.Y.	DNF-e	1
61dq	Dan Gurney / Jerry Grant	2	Ford Mk II	7010	Shelby American, Los Angeles, Calif.	Disq.	227
62dq	William Wonder / Bob Brown	22	Ford GT40	4727	William Wonder, Long Island, N.Y.	Disq.	100
63dq	Al Costner	43	Morgan Super Sport	2138	Fergus Import Motors, New York, N.Y.	Disq.	35
64dq	Ross MacGrotty	36	Yenko Stinger Corvair	2690	MacGrotty Chevrolet, Flushing, N.Y.	Disq.	25
DNS	David Hull / Bob Kingham	31	Jaguar XKE	3784	Jaguar Cars of Winter Haven, Fla.	withdrew	
DNS	Emie Croucher / Pete Glenn	86	MGB	1798	Ken Chambliss, Smyrna, Ga.	reserve	
DNS	Ben Warren / John Scott / Don Russell	16	Ford GT350 Mustang	4727	Ben Warren, Mebane, NC	reserve	
DNS	Don Kearney / Michael Reina	83	Ford GT350 Mustang	4727	Michael Reina, Clearwater, Fla.	reserve	
DNS	Pierre Noblet / Franco Bernabei	15	DeTomaso 858	4734	DeTomaso Automobili, Italy	withdrew	

+ Killed in race accident approaching Hairpin
*Not running at finish

Average Speed: 98.631 mph
Distance: 1,185.6 miles
Fastest Race Lap: #2 Dan Gurney 107.09 mph

Fastest Qualifier: #2 Dan Gurney, 2:54.6 = 107.22 mph
Lap Leaders: #24 1; #27 2-23; #2 24-227; #1 228

1966 HOURLY STANDINGS — TOP 10

POS.	1 HR.	2 HRS.	3 HRS.	4 HRS.	5 HRS.	6 HRS.	7 HRS.	8 HRS.	9 HRS.	10 HRS.	11 HRS.	Finish
1	27	2	2	2	2	2	2	2	2	2	2	1
2	1	1	1	27	27	27	1	1	27	1	1	3
3	2	27	27	1	1	1	27	27	1	26	3	19
4	24	24	24	26	26	26	26	26	26	48	19	52
5	26	26	26	25	25	48	46	25	48	3	52	46
6	3	25	25	46	46	53	25	46	3	19	46	49
7	11	46	46	48	48	46	48	48	19	52	26	54
8	25	19	3	24	24	25	52	52	52	27	54	50
9	4	52	19	19	19	52	24	19	50	46	49	9
10	46	18	48	52	52	50	50	50	49	49	50	6

**1967 SEBRING WINNER —
Ford Mk IV**
Built and entered by Ford,
Dearborn, Michigan. Chassis No.
J4; Engine: 7.0 liter, 8 cyl. Ford
**Drivers: Mario Andretti,
Bruce McLaren**

16TH ANNUAL 12 HOURS OF SEBRING / APRIL 1, 1967

POS.	-DRIVERS	NO.	MAKE	DISP.	ENTRANT	CLASS-POS.	LAPS
1	Mario Andretti / Bruce McLaren	1	Ford Mk IV	7010	Ford Motor Co., Dearborn, Mich.	P-13-1	238
2	A.J. Foyt / Lloyd Ruby	2	Ford Mk II	7010	Ford Motor Co., Dearborn, Mich.	P-13-2*	226
3	Gerhard Mitter / Scooter Patrick	36	Porsche 910	1991	Porsche System Eng., Ltd., Germany	P-9-1	226
4	Hans Herrmann / Jo Siffert	37	Porsche 910	1991	Porsche System Eng., Ltd., Germany	P-9-2	223
5	Umberto Maglioli / Nino Vaccarella	19	Ford GT 40	4736	Brescia Corse Team, Brescia, Italy	S-12-1	223
6	Dieter Spoerry / Rico Steinemann	40	Porsche 906E	1991	Squadra Tartaruga, Switzerland	P-9-3	218
7	Jo Buzzetta / Peter Gregg	38	Porsche 906	1991	Porsche System Eng., Germany	P-9-4	215
8	Bob Grossman / William McNamara	17	Ford GT40	4736	Autosport Int., London, England	S-12-2	214
9	Robert Kirby / Alan Johnson	46	Porsche 911S	1991	Bursch Tuned Exhaust, Pasadena, Calif.	GT-9-1	197
10	Don Yenko / Dave Morgan	8	Chevrolet Corvette Stingray	7261	Sunray DX Oil Co., Tulsa, Ok.	GT-13-1*	195
11	Paddy Hopkirk / Andrew Hedges	30	MG prototype	2004	British Motor Corp., Abingdon, England	P-10-1	189
12	Timo Makinen / John Rhodes	48	MGB	1824	British Motor Corp., Abingdon, England	GT-9-2	188
13	Rauno Aaltonen / Clive Baker	59	Austin-Healey Sprite	1293	Donald Healey Motors, Warwick, England	P-7-1	187
14	Leo Cella / Sandeo Munari / Umberto Maglioli	56	Lancia 1300	1298	H.F. Squadra, Torino, Italy	P-7-2	187
15	Fred Opert / John Pauly / Bill Bowman	72	Porsche 911S	1991	Valvoline-Opert Racing, Paramus, N.J.	GT-9-3	186
16	Fred Van Beuren / Paul Jett	18	Shelby American GT 350	4788	Dos Caballos Racing, Houston, Tex.	GT-12-1	185
17	Denise McCluggage / Pinkie Rollo	25	Ferrari 275 GTB Spyder	3285	Northern Vermont Racing, Warren, Vt.	GT-12-2	185
18	Alec Poole / Carson Baird / Roger Enever	58	Austin-Healey Sprite	1293	Donald Healey Motors, Warwick, England	P-7-3	183
19	Ray Heppenstall / Bill Seeley / Bob Nagel	15	Howmet Sprint	4727	Howmet Corp., Conshohocken, Pa.	P-12-1	181
20	Sepp Greger / Hans Kater	41	Porsche 911S	1966	Sepp Greger, Munich, Germany	GT-9-4	181
21	George Drolsom / Bill Campbell	47	Porsche 904	1998	George Drolsom, Jacksonville, Fla.	S-9-1	180
22	Bob Bailey / Phil Groggins / John Kelly	43	Porsche 356 coupe	1998	B & B Motors, Burnt Hills, N.Y.	S-9-2	170
23	Liane Engeman / Janet Guthrie	62	Matra DJet 5S	1108	Ring Free Oil Racing, New York City	GT-6-1	163
24	Laszlo Siegmund / George Liebl	51	Volvo P1800	1823	Viper Racing, Inc., Hartford, Ct.	S-9-3	159
25	Suzy Dietrich / Donna Mae Mims	63	ASA Prototype	1307	Ring Free Oil Racing, New York City	P-8-1	159
26	Joe Welch / George Wintersteen	4	Chevrolet Corvette	6997	Roger Penske Racing, Philadelphia, Pa.	GT-13-2	157
27	Billy Turner / M.D. Smith	68	Austin-Healey Sprite	1098	Maj. Billy Turner, Eglin AFB, Fla.	S-7-1	155
28	Brad Brooker / Tom Yeager	16	Shelby American GT 350	4727	Brad Brooker, Wichita Falls, Kans.	GT-12-3	152
29	Buell Owen / Tim Burr	29	Triumph TR4A	2138	Tim Burr, Little Rock, Ark.	GT-10-1	150
30	Anatoly Arutunoff / William Pryor	54	Alfa Romeo Conrero	1587	A.R.CO., Inc., Nashville, Tenn.	GT-8-1	142
31	Bob Kingham / Milo Vega / John Witt	28	Triumph TR4A	2182	Milo Vega, Tampa, Fla.	GT-10-2	139
32	Richard Kondrack / Michael Pickering	60	Triumph Spitfire	1147	Richard G. Kondrack, Sanford, Fla.	GT-6-2	135
33	Hugh Kleinpeter / Mike Rothschild	53	Beach Mk 8	1598	Competition Components, Clearwater, Fla.	P-8-2	123
34	Richard Robson / R. Rodgers / William Buchman	21	Jaguar XKE	3792	Richard Robson,Titusville, Fla.	GT-12-4	117
35	Anita Taylor / Smoky Drolet	57	Alpine Renault KLG	1298	Nisonger-KLG Challenger, Miami, Fla.	S-7-2	77
36	Udo Schutz / Rolf Stommelen / G. Van Lennep	39	Porsche 906	1991	Porsche System Eng., Germany	DNF-a	156
37	Mike Spence / Jim Hall	6	Chaparral 2F	7000	Chaparral Cars, Midland, Tex.	DNF-e	145
38	Or Costanzo / Dave McClain / Gene Guy	9	Chevrolet Corvette Stingray	6997	O. Costanzo, Tampa, Fla.	DNF-a	141
39	Ed Hugus / John Cannon	42	Porsche 906	1991	Ed Hugus, Pittsburgh, Pa.	DNF-e	138

40	R. Mouat / Wilton Jowett, Jr.	69	Chevrolet Corvette	5358	Wilton Jowett, Upper Marlboro, Md.	DNF-e	130
41	Bruce Jennings / Bob Johnson / Jim Hall	5	Chaparral 2D	7000	Chaparral Cars, Midland, Tex.	DNF-k	128
42	Ed Lowther / Dick Thompson	11	Ford GT 40	4736	J.W. Engineering, England	DNF-e	119
43	Jean Guichet / Pedro Rodriguez	32	Ferrari Dino	1998	Pedro Rodriguez, Mexico	DNF-a	101
44	John Ryan / Bill Benker	45	Porsche 911S	1991	RBM Motors, Griffin, Ga.	DNF-a	93
45	Andrea de Adamich / Teodoro Zeccoli	65	Alfa Romeo T33	1995	Autodelta, Milan, Italy	DNF-s	84
46	Wilbur Pickett / T.J. Kelly / Whit Tharin	27	Triumph TR4A	2138	Joseph C. Hines, Statesboro, Ga.	DNF-e	77
47	William Wonder / Ray Caldwell	14	Ford GT 40	4736	William Wonder, Locust Valley, N.Y.	DNF-e	71
48	David Piper / Richard Attwood	20	Ferrari 365 P2/3	4380	David Piper Racing, England	DNF-t	65
49	Albert Mueller / Gunther Klass	34	Ferrari Dino	1998	Scuderia Filipinetti, Italy	DNF-s	65
50	Gary Magwood / Raymond Gray	49	MGB	1798	Canadian Auto Racing, Canada	DNF-s	59
51	Fred Baker / Charles Kolb	44	Porsche 906	1998	Baker Racing Team, Miami, Fla.	DNF-e	51
52	Roberto Bussinello / Nanni Galli	66	Alfa Romeo T33	1995	Autodelta, Milan, Italy	DNF-k	36
53	Bobby Allison / Roger West	70	Shelby American GT 350	4727	Treadwell Ford Racing, Ala.	DNF-a	26
54	Paul Richards	71	Shelby American GT 350	4727	Ring Free Oil Racing, New York City	DNF-e	22
55	Ricardo Rodriguez	23	Ferrari 275 LM	3285	Federico De Lachia, Mexico	DNF-e	18
56	Jon Williams	33	Ferrari Dino	1998	Scuderia Brescia Corse, Brescia, Italy	DNF-e	5
57	George Waltman	55	OSCA Berlinetta	1589	George Waltman, New York, N.Y.	DNF-e	4
58	Ed Crawford	35	Ferrari Dino	1998	Baker Racing Team, Miami, Fla.	DNF-t	0
DNS	Roger McCluskey / Buck Fulp	12	Lola T-70 Chevy Mk3	5361	John R. Fulp, Anderson, S.C.	withdrew	
DNS	Howard Brown / Howard Hanna	61	Matra D Jet 5S	1108	Howard Hanna, Edgemont, Pa.	withdrew	
DNS	Pedro Rodriguez	26	Ferrari P3	4000	N.A.R.T., New York, N.Y.	withdrew	

*Not running at finish

Average Speed: 102.923 mph
Distance: 1,237.6 miles
Margin of Victory: 2 laps
Fastest Race Lap: #6 Mike Spence, 111.032 mph
Fastest Qualifier: #1 Mario Andretti, 2:48.0 = 111.428 mph
Lap Leaders: #65 1; #1 2-35, 46-55, 71-238; #6 36-45, 56-70
Margin of Victory: 12 laps (Car #2 finished 1 lap behind but was disqualified)
Attendance: 54,000 (est.)
Weather: Partly cloudy and warm.
Fastest Race Lap: #2 Dan Gurney 107.09 mph

1967 HOURLY STANDINGS — TOP 10

POS.	1 HR.	2 HRS.	3 HRS.	4 HRS.	5 HRS.	6 HRS.	7 HRS.	8 HRS.	9 HRS.	10 HRS.	11 HRS.	Finish
1	1	1	6	1	1	1	1	1	1	1	1	1
2	2	20	1	2	6	6	6	2	7	2	2	2
3	20	6	2	6	2	2	2	36	36	36	36	36
4	6	2	20	5	5	5	37	19	19	19	37	37
5	5	5	5	38	36	11	36	37	37	37	19	19
6	11	11	11	36	11	36	38	40	40	40	40	40
7	36	36	36	37	37	37	19	6	38	17	38	38
8	37-38	11	19	40	5	38	17	38	17	17		
9	38	38	37	19	38	38	40	39	8	8	8	46
10	44	44	34	40	40	19	42	17	46	46	46	8

1968

**1968 SEBRING WINNER —
Porsche 907 (short tail)**
Built and entered by Porsche,
Stuttgart, Germany.
Chassis No. 907.023; Engine: 2.2 liter, 8 cyl. Porsche
**Drivers: Hans Herrmann,
Jo Siffert**

17TH ANNUAL 12 HOURS OF SEBRING / MARCH 23, 1968

POS.	DRIVERS	NO.	MAKE	DISP.	ENTRANT	CLASS-POS.	LAPS
1	Hans Herrmann / Jo Siffert	49	Porsche 907	2200	Porsche Automobile Co., Stuttgart, Germany	10/P-1	237
2	Vic Elford / Jochen Neerpasch	51	Porsche 907	2200	Porsche Automobile Co., Stuttgart, Germany	10/P-2	227
3	Mark Donohue / Craig Fisher	15	Chevrolet Camaro	4956	Roger Penske Racing, Philadelphia, Pa.	12/T-1	221
4	Joseph Welch / Bob Johnson / Craig Fisher	16	Chevrolet Camaro	4956	Roger Penske Racing, Philadelphia, Pa.	12/T-2	217
5	Jerry Titus / Ronnie Bucknum	31	Ford Mustang	4727	Shelby Racing, Torrance, Calif.	12/T-3	217
6	David Morgan / Hap Sharp	3	Chevrolet Corvette	6997	Sunray DX Oil Company, Tulsa, Ok.	13/GT-1	208
7	Alan Johnson / Robert Kirby	59	Porsche 911S	1991	Don Burns VW, Garden Grove, Calif.	9/GT-1	208
8	Gregg Loomis / Pete Harrison / Jack Ryan	60	Porsche 911S	1991	Gregg Loomis, Atlanta, Ga.	9/GT-2	204
9	Jacques Duval / Horst Kroll	61	Porsche 911S	1991	Jacques Duval, Montreal, Canada	9/GT-3	203
10	Andrew Hedges / Paddy Hopkirk	44	MGC	2968	British Motor Company, Abingdon, England	11 /P-1	195
11	John McComb / Paul Richards	33	Ford Mustang	4727	John McComb, Hutchinson, Kans.	12/T-4	195
12	Peter Revson / Skip Scott	24	AMC Javelin	4752	Javelin Racing Team, Milwaukee, Wisc.	12/T-5	193
13	Jean Hanrioud / Sylvain Garant	62	Porsche 911S	1991	Jean Pierre Hanrioud, Paris, France	9/GT-4	190
14	Rafaele Pinto / Gigi Taramazzo / Claudio Maglioli	72	Lancia Fulvia HF	1401	H.F. Squadra, Torino, Italy	8/P-1	187
15	Jerry Truitt / Randy Canfield	74	MG Midget	1293	Donald Healey Motor Co., Ltd., Warwick, England	8/S-1	185
16	Ed Nelson / David Piper	30	Ford GT 40	4727	Edward Nelson Racing, London, England	12/S-1	184
17	Marius Amyot / Francois Favreau / Andre Samson	38	Ford Mustang	4727	Gagnon Spring, Inc., Montreal, Canada	12/T-6	184
18	Gary Rodriguez / Richard McDaniel	66	MGB	1845	British Motor Company, Abingdon, England	9/GT-5	183
19	Dale Keenan / Daniel Torpy	80	Chevrolet Corvette	5359	William H. Laughlin, Alexandria, Va.	13/GT-2	171
20	Rico Steinemann / Dieter Spoerry	58	Porsche 910	1991	Squadra Tartaruga, Zurich, Switzerland	9/P-1	168
21	John Moore / Jim Murphy	19	Chevrolet Camaro	4956	H.R.H. Corp., Annandale, Va.	12/T-7	168
22	Richard Cline / Michael Pickering	52	Triumph GT6	1998	Richard B. Cline, Sanford, Fla.	9/GT-6	168
23	David McClain / Dick Boo	20	Chevrolet Camaro	4956	Padrick Chevrolet, Ft. Pierce, Fla.	12/T-8	164
24	Rajah Rodgers / Richard Robson	84	Jaguar XKE	3772	Coquina Motors, Titusville Fla.	12/GT-1	161
25	Jim Corwin / Fred Pipin	18	Chevrolet Camaro	4956	James Corwin, New Buffalo, Mich.	12/T-9	161
26	Charlie Rainville / Bruce Jennings	23	Mercury Cougar	4788	Squadra Course Verona, Romulus, Mich.	12/T-10	159
27	Or Costanzo / Dave Heinz / William Harris	7	Chevrolet Corvette	6997	Slaton Chevrolet, Ft. Lauderdale, Fla.	13/GT-3	158
28	Joie Chitwood / Dick Hoffman / Dave Horchler	17	Chevrolet Camaro	4956	Joie Chitwood, Jr., Tampa, Fla.	12/T-11	158
29	David Hobbs / Paul Hawkins	29	Ford GT40	4727	J.W. Engineering, England	12/S-2	157
30	Bob Bailey / Jim Locke	64	Porsche 906	1991	B&B Motors, Burnt Hills, N.Y.	9/S-1	157
31	Chris Waldron / James Gammon / Ben Scott	67	MGB	1798	Waldron Motors, Boca Raton, Fla.	9/GT-7	148
32	Janet Guthrie / Liane Engeman	26	AMC Javelin	4752	G&H Engineering, Bloomingburg, N.Y.	12/T-12	144
33	Arthur Cohn / Don Pickett / Tony Lilly	95	Beach Prototype	1498	Arthur Cohn, Clearwater, Fla.	8/P-2	140
34	Donna Mae Mims / Mike Summers	85	Yenko Stinger	2690	Best Sports Cars, Syracuse, N.Y.	11 /P-3	130
35	Clive Baker / Mike Garton	73	Austin-Healey Sprite	1293	Donald Healey Motor Co., Ltd., Warwick, England	8/P-3	125
36	Bruce Hollander / Hugh Kleinpeter / Ray Mummery	27	Ford Shelby GT 350	4740	Port of Entry Motors, Miami, Fla.	12/GT-2	98
37	Norberto Mastandra / Ralph Noseda	14	Chevrolet Camaro	4956	Mar Shipping, Miami, Fla.	DNF-t	132
38	Ed Lowther / Dick Thompson / Ray Heppenstall	76	Howmet TX Turbine	2997	Howmet Corp., New York	DNF-s	125
39	Scooter Patrick / Dave Jordan	9	Lola T-70 Chevy Mk lll	4997	American International, Los Angeles, Calif.	DNF-e	103

40	Jerry Grant / Skip Scott	25	AMC Javelin	4752	Javelin Racing Team, Milwaukee, Wisc.	DNF-e	90
41	Earl Sylvia / Dave Domizi / Robert Fogle	68	Lotus 47	1594	Dyno Racing, Fairfield, Ct.	DNF-a	81
42	Richard Kondracki / Fred Andrews	96	Triumph Spitfire	1147	Richard P. Cline, Sanford, Fla.	DNF-a	72
43	Bert Everett / Claudio Maglioli	71	Lancia Zagato	1401	H.F. Squadra, Torino, Italy	DNF-u	67
44	Allan Moffat / Horst Kwech	32	Ford Mustang	4727	Shelby Racing, Torrance, Calif.	DNF-e	63
45	Michael de Udy / Hugh Dibley	11	Lola T-70 Chevy Mk III	4997	Michael de Udy, London, England	DNF-u	61
46	Milo Vega / John Witt / John Cameron	86	Triumph TR4A	2138	John Cameron, Hightstown, N.J.	DNF-e	59
47	Bill Boye / Billy Yuma	21	Chevrolet Camaro	4956	Bill Boye Racing, Vero Beach, Fla.	DNF-e	55
48	Jim Dittmore / Bob Tullius	47	Triumph TR250K	2498	Leyland Motor Corp., Teaneck, N.J.	DNF-s	49
49	Jerry Thompson / Tony DeLorenzo	4	Chevrolet Corvette	6997	Sunray DX Oil Company, Tulsa, Ok.	DNF-x	48
50	Gerhard Mitter / Rolf Stommelen	48	Porsche 907	2200	Porsche Automobile Co., Stuttgart, Germany	DNF-e	46
51	Sepp Greger / Malte Huth	63	Porsche 911E	1991	Sepp Greger, Munich, Germany	DNF-e	46
52	Al Unser / Lloyd Ruby	81	Chevrolet Camaro	4956	Samadco Ltd. / Smokey Yunick, Daytona Beach, Fla.	DNF-e	43
53	Pedro Rodriguez / Don Yenko	2	Chevrolet Corvette	6997	Sunray DX Oil Company, Tulsa, Ok.	DNF-e	43
54	Malcolm Starr / George Wintersteen	37	Ford Mustang	4727	Starr Racing, Montclair, N.J.	DNF-e	43
55	Wilton Jowett / Claude Cardwell	12	Chevrolet Camaro	4956	Wilton T. Jowett, Sr., Marlboro, Md.	DNF-e	40
56	Joakim Bonnier / Sten Axelsson	10	Lola T-70 Chevy Mk III	4997	Ecurie Bonnier, Geneva, Switzerland	DNF-k	40
57	Mauro Bianchi / Henri Grandsire	42	Renault Alpine	3000	Societe Alpine, Paris, France	DNF-e	39
58	Jacky Ickx / Brian Redman	28	Ford GT40	4727	J.W. Engineering, England	DNF-t	36
59	Alfredo Atencio / Armando Capriles	55	Porsche 906E	1991	Raceco, Miami, Fla.	DNF-a	35
60	G. Ortega / John Gunn	39	Ferrari 275 LM	3285	Raceco, Miami, Fla.	DNF-e	33
61	Fred Van Beuren / Ruben Novoa	36	Ford Mustang	4727	Dos Caballos Racing, Tex.	DNF-t	25
62	Karl Foitek	56	Porsche 910	1991	Valvoline Oil Company, Zurich, Switzerland	DNF-a	16
63	Sam Posey	34	Ford Mustang	4727	Mathews Racing Team, Fresno, Calif.	DNF-b	16
64	Lothar Motschenbacher	8	Lola T-70 Chevy Mk III	4997	American International, Los Angeles, Calif.	DNF-t	12
65	Bob Grossman	35	Ford Mustang	4727	Randy's Auto Body, Clifton, N.J.	DNF-u	11
66	Billy Hagan	22	Mercury Cougar	4788	Billy Hagen, Lafayette, La.	DNF-e	10
67	Lodovico Scarfiotti	50	Porsche 907	2200	Porsche Automobile Co., Stuttgart, Germany	DNF-e	7
68	Arthur Mollin	93	TVR 1800	1798	Arthur Mollin Racing, Port Washington, N.Y.	DNF-s	6
DNS	Ed Hugus / Chuck Dietrich	69	Lotus BMW	1599	Elsco BMW, Jacksonville, Fla.	withdrew	
DNS	E. Nearburg / Paul Jett	70	Lotus BMW	1599	Elsco BMW, Jacksonville, Fla.	withdrew	
DNS	Dieter Oest / Sam Feinstein	91	Porsche Carrera	1966	Dieter Oest, Philadelphia, Pa.	reserve	

Average Speed: 102.512 mph
Fastest Qualifier: #19 Hans Herrmann, 2:49.4 = 119,51 mph
Distance: 1,232.2 miles
Lap Leaders: #49 1-8, 32-36, 45-72, 81-237; **#9** 9-31, 37-44; **#29** 73-80
Margin of Victory: 10 laps
Attendance: 42,000 (est.)
Fastest Race Lap: #9 Scooter Patrick, 110.759 mph
Weather: Cool and partly cloudy.

1968 HOURLY STANDINGS — TOP 10

POS.	1 HR.	2 HRS.	3 HRS.	4 HRS.	5 HRS.	6 HRS.	7 HRS.	8 HRS.	9 HRS.	10 HRS.	11 HRS.	Finish
1	9	9	49	49	49	49	49	49	49	49	49	49
2	49	49	29	29	51	51	51	29	51	51	51	51
3	29	29	51	51	29	29	29	51	15	15	15	15
4	28	51	15	15	58	15	58	58	16	16	16	16
5	51	48	32	58	15	58	15	15	31	31	31	31
6	30	42	31	16	16	16	76	16	3	3	3	3
7	42	76	58	31	76	76	16	31	59	59	59	59
8	2	30	6	3	31	31	31	3	23	60	60	60
9	48	31	76	76	23	3	3	59	58	58	61	61
10	31	32	23	23	3	59	59	23	61	61	44	44

1969

**1969 SEBRING WINNER —
Ford GT40**
Built by Ford / Entered by J.W.
Automotive Engineering, England.
Chassis No. 1075; Engine: 4.9 liter,
8 cyl. Ford
Drivers: Jacky Ickx, Jackie Oliver

18TH ANNUAL 12 HOURS OF SEBRING / MARCH 22, 1969

POS.	DRIVERS	NO.	MAKE	DISP.	ENTRANT	CLASS-POS.	LAPS
1	Jacky Ickx / Jackie Oliver	22	Ford GT 40	4942	J.W. Automotive Engineering Ltd., England	S/12-1	239
2	Mario Andretti / Chris Amon	25	Ferrari 312P	3000	Ferrari SpA SEFAC, Modena, Italy	P/11-1	238
3	Rolf Stommelen / Joe Buzzetta / Kurt Ahrens	27	Porsche 908	2996	Porsche System Eng., Stuttgart, Germany	P/11-2	235
4	Alex Soler-Roig / Rudy Lins	44	Porsche 907	1996	Escuderia Nacional SC, Barcelona, Spain	P/9-1	233
5	Gebhard Mitter / Udo Schutz	29	Porsche 908	2996	Porsche System Eng., Stuttgart, Germany	P/11-3	232
6	Ed Leslie / Lothar Motschenbacher	11	Lola Chevrolet Mk III	4956	American Internat'l Racing, Los Angeles, Calif.	S/12-2	229
7	Vic Elford / Dick Attwood	30	Porsche 908	2996	Porsche System Eng., Stuttgart, Germany	P/11-4	228
8	Dick Smothers / Fred Baker	45	Porsche 906E	1996	Smothers Bros. Racing Team, Hollywood, Ca.	P/9-2	215
9	Ricardo Rodriguez / Charlie Kolb	37	Ferrari Dino	2400	N.A.R.T.,Greenwich,Ct.	P/10-1	215
10	Don Yenko / Bob Grossman	5	Chevrolet Camaro	6997	Best Photo Service, Syracuse, N.Y.	GT/13-1	209
11	Armando Capriles /Alfredo Atencio	46	Porsche 906E	1996	Escuderia Mahana, Venezuela	P/9-2	203
12	Gerard Lamousse / Andre Wicky / Jean Sage	52	Porsche 911T	1991	Wicky Racing Team, Switzerland	GT/9-1	201
13	Bob Bailey / Jim Locke	47	Porsche 911T	1991	P.A.R.T., Towson, Md.	GT/9-2	199
14	Dick Lang / Gib Hufstaeder	2	Chevrolet Corvette Stingray	7000	Troy Promotions, Inc., Troy, Mich.	GT/13-2	196
15	Andrew Hedges / Paddy Hopkirk	35	MGC	2982	British Leyland Motor Corp., England	P/11-5	195
16	Jim Netterstrom / Bruce Jennings / Mike Downs	90	Porsche 911	1991	P.A.R.T., Towson, Md.	GT/9-3	195
17	Peter Gregg / Dr. Wilbur Pickett	53	Porsche 911	1991	Wilbur Pickett, MD, Daytona Beach, Fla.	T/9-1	192
18	Claudio Maglioli / Rafaele Pinto	65	Lancia Fulvia	1600	Algar Enterprises, Inc., Rosemont, Pa.	P/8-1	191
19	Robin Ormes / Norberto Mastandrea	94	Chevrolet Camaro	4956	Freeport Bahama Racing Team, Bahamas	T/12-1	189
20	Jim Baker / Paul Richards / Clive Baker	71	Austin-Healey Sprite	1293	Ring Free Oil Racing Team, Atlanta, Ga.	P/7-1	184
21	Or Costanzo / Dave Heinz	4	Chevrolet Corvette	7000	O. Costanzo, Tampa, Fla.	GT/13-3	184
22	Vince Gimondo / John Tremblay	17	Chevrolet Camaro	4956	Bruce Behrens Racing Ent., Winter Park, Fla.	T/12-2	182
23	Janet Guthrie / Donna Mae Mims / Liane Engeman	72	Austin-Healey Sprite	1293	Ring Free Oil Racing Team, Atlanta, Ga.	P/7-2	182
24	Tony DeLorenzo / Gerald Thompson	1	Chevrolet Corvette	7000	Troy Promotions, Inc., Troy, Mich.	GT/13-4	181
25	Rick Stevens / Robert Barg	16	Chevrolet Camaro	4956	Richard Stevens, Ontario, Canada	T/12-3	180
26	Smokey Drolet / Rosemary Smith	59	BMW 2002	1991	Elsco Corporation, Jacksonville, Fla.	T/9-2	179
27	Innes Ireland / Mike Tillson / Howard Hanna	66	Lancia Fulvia Zagato	1600	Algar Enterprises, Inc., Rosemont, Pa.	P/8-2	179
28	Logan Blackburn / Gerald Truitt	62	MGB	1845	British Leyland Motor Corp., England	GT/9-4	178
29	George Drolsom / Harold Williamson	84	Porsche 911	1991	Dr. Harold Williamson, Tampa, Fla.	T/9-3	175
30	Serge Adams / Craig Fisher	93	Chevrolet Camaro	4956	Todco Racing Canada Ltd., Montreal, Canada	T/12-4	174
31	David McClain / Don Kerney	20	Chevrolet Camaro	4956	David H. McClain,Tampa, Fla.	T/12-5	174
32	John Colgate / Don Parks	99	MGB	1845	Gerry Racing Enterprise, Houston, Tex.	GT/9-5	172
33	Gregg Cameron / Ralph Kemmerer	73	Austin-Healey Sprite	1293	Arthur Tuckerman, Wanamassa, N.J.	P/7-3	170
34	Bill Brack / R. Craig Hill	36	MGC	2982	British Leyland Motor Corp., England	P/11-6	169
35	Armando DeAmbadgio / Sergio Trevale	41	Alfa Romeo GTJ	1290	Escuderia Mañana, Venezuela	T/7-1	167
36	Sam Posey / Bob Dini	38	Ferrari Dino	2400	N.A.R.T., Greenwich, Ct.	P/10-2	166
37	Merv Rosen / Dave Morrell	49	Porsche 906	1991	Dr. Merv Rosen, Waukeegan, Ill.	S/9-1	162
38	Chris Waldron / Ben Scott / Dean Donley	64	MGB	1798	Waldron Motors, Boca Raton, Fla.	GT/9-6	155
39	Richard Crebs / Ron Stricler / Robert Whitaker	85	Alfa Romeo GTA	1600	Richard Crebs, Altamonte Springs, Fla.	T/8-1	153

40	Walt Brown / Joe Marcus	60	Opel Rallye	1944	Jim Cooke Buick & Opel, Louisville, Ky.	T/9-4	152
41	Francis Grant / Deiter Oest	24	Ford GT40	4942	Auto Enterprises, Flourtown, Pa.	S/12-3	148
42	Umberto Maglioli / Hugh Kleinpeter / R. Beatty	57	Chevron BMW	1991	Raceco, Coral Gables, Fla.	S/9-2	143
43	Ray Heppenstall / Howard Brown	43	Heppenstall VW Spl.	1996	LeHigh Acres, Glenside, Pa.	P/9-3	142
44	Rusty Jowett / Bob Tullius	18	Chevrolet Camaro	4956	Wilton T. Jowett, Sr., Marlboro, Md.	T/12-6	140
45	Reggie Smith, Jr. / A.J. Lilly / Don Pickett	69	Lotus Europa	1470	John F. Howard, Plantation, Fla.	GT/8-1	130
46	Ron Polimeni / Robert Theall	98	Volvo 544	1798	George W. Sanderson, White Plains, N.Y.	T/9-5	128
47	Pedro Rodriguez / Chuck Parsons	26	Ferrari P1	3000	N.A.R.T., Greenwich, Ct.	DNF-t	163
48	Jim Gammon / Ray Mummery / Roger Houghton	63	MGB	1798	Waldron Motors, Boca Raton, Fla.	DNF-t	150
49	Brian Redman / Jo Siffert	31	Porsche 908	2996	Porsche System Eng., Stuttgart, Germany	DNF-s	133
50	Gregg Loomis / Peter Harrison / Jack Ryan	51	Porsche 911S	1991	RBM Motors, Griffin, Ga.	DNF-s	130
51	David Hobbs / Mike Hailwood	23	Ford GT 40	4942	J.W. Automotive Engineering Ltd., England	DNF-s	99
52	Hans Herrmann / Kurt Ahrens / Rolf Stommelen	28	Porsche 908	2996	Porsche System Eng., Stuttgart, Germany	DNF-s	97
53	Mark Donohue / Ronnie Bucknum	9	Lola Chevrolet Mk III	4956	Roger Penske Racing Ent., Philadelphia, Pa.	DNF-s	96
54	Maurice Carter / Nat Adams	19	Chevrolet Camaro	4956	Maurice Carter Chevrolet, Ontario, Canada	DNF-e	85
55	Jacques Duval / George Nicholas	50	Porsche 911T	1996	Grand Prix Motor Oil, Montreal, Canada	DNF-e	62
56	Larry Dent / Larry Bock	21	Chevrolet Camaro	4956	Laurel / Drover Racing, South Bend, Ind.	DNF-e	62
57	Charlie Rainville / Paul Pettey	7	Ford Mustang	4990	Argento Racing Org., Dearborn, Mich.	DNF-e	62
58	Ed Lowther / Robert Esseks	3	Chevrolet Corvette	7000	Robert D. Esseks, New York, N.Y.	DNF-s	55
59	Paul Sanford / Fred Opert	54	Porsche 911	1991	Fred Opert, Paramus, N.J.	DNF-t	53
60	Jo Bonnier / Ulf Norinder	14	Lola Chevrolet Mk III	4956	Sportscars Switzerland, Vandois, Switzerland	DNF-s	49
61	Randy Blessing / Don Cummings / Warren Stumes	88	Ford Shelby GT350	4742	Donald C. Cummings, Daytona Beach, Fla.	DNF-a	45
62	Ed Hugus / Chuck Dietrich	58	BMW 2002	1991	Elsco Corporation, Jacksonville, Fla.	DNF-e	36
63	Mike Rahal / Bill Stroh / Hugh Wise	48	Porsche 906	1991	Nationwide of Chicago Food, Glen Ellyn, Ill.	DNF-e	31
64	Don Madray / Herb Madray / G. Davis	6	Ford Mustang	4990	Herbert R. Madray, Ft. Lauderdale, Fla.	DNF-e	26
65	Nino Vaccarella / Lucien Bianchi	33	Alfa Romeo T33-3	2993	Autodelta SpA, Milan, Italy	DNF-e	17
66	Mario Casoni / Andrea de Adamich	32	Alfa Romeo T33-3	2993	Autodelta SpA, Milan, Italy	DNF-e	15
67	Scooter Patrick	10	Lola Chevrolet Mk III	4956	American Internat'l Racing, Los Angeles, Ca.	DNF-e	15
68	Bill Scott	68	Zink VSR	1584	HRH Corp., Annandale, Va.	DNF-t	13
69	Nanni Galli	34	Alfa Romeo T33-3	2993	Autodelta, SpA, Milan, Italy	DNF-s	2
70	Russ Shirley / Bill Boye	67	Beach 4B	1498	Competition Components, Clearwater, Fla.	Disq.–push start	
DNS	James Osbome / Erwin Dollinger	83	Porsche 911	1991	Kline Porsche, Indianapolis, Ind.	reserve	
DNS	Edward Hinchliff / Bill Clauson	92	Ford Mustang	4990	Haliff Racing Enterprises, Ypsilanti, Mich.	reserve	
DNS	Bruce Goldman / Al Lugo, Jr.	95	NSU	1000	Aztec Racing Ltd., Spring Valley, N.Y.	reserve	
DNS	Tony Adamowicz / Ray Cuomo / H. Wetanson	96	Porsche 911	1996	Herb Wetanson, Hewlett Bay Pk., N.Y.	reserve	
DNS	Mark Donohue / Ronnie Bucknum	97	Chevrolet Camaro	4956	Roger Penske Racing Ent., Philadelphia, Pa.	reserve	
DNS	Anatoly Arutunoff / Richard Irish	91	Fiat Abarth	2000	Anatoly Arutunoff, Bartlesville, Ok.	withdrew	
DNS	Fred Van Beuren / Raul PerezGama	8	Pontiac Firebird	5000	Fred Van Beuren, Mexico	accident	

Average Speed: 103.363 mph
Fastest Race Lap: #31 Jo Siffert 114.720 mph
Distance: 1,242.8 miles
Lap Leaders: **#31** 1-30, 42-58; **#9** 31-41, 59-64; **#25** 65-85, 98-114, 132-141, 180-182, 189-204; **#29** 86-97, 115-131, 142-179; **#27** 183-188; **#22** 205-239
Margin of Victory: 1 lap
Fastest Qualifier: #25 Chris Amon 116.835 mph
Attendance: 55,000 (est.)
Weather: Sunny and warm.

1969 HOURLY STANDINGS — TOP 10

POS.	1 HR.	2 HRS.	3 HRS.	4 HRS.	5 HRS.	6 HRS.	7 HRS.	8 HRS.	9 HRS.	10 HRS.	11 HRS.	Finish
1	31	9	9	25	25	29	29	29	25	25	22	22
2	30	31	29	29	29	25	25	25	27	22	25	25
3	29	25	25	9	28	31	27	27	22	11	29	27
4	25	29	28	28	27	27	22	22	11	29	27	44
5	9	28	31	27	31	22	11	11	29	44	44	29
6	28	27	27	31	22	11	44	44	44	27	11	11
7	27	23	23	22	11	44	30	30	37	30	30	30
8	22	22	22	11	44	45	37	37	5	37	45	45
9	48	14	11	44	45	30	45	45	45	45	37	37
10	44	11	44	45	37	37	5	5	46	5	5	5

1970

**1970 SEBRING WINNER —
Ferrari 512S**
Built and entered by Ferrari factory,
Italy. Chassis No. 1026; Engine: 5.0
liter, 12 cyl. Ferrari
**Drivers: Ignazio Giunti, Nino
Vaccarella, Mario Andretti**

19TH ANNUAL 12 HOURS OF SEBRING / MARCH 21, 1970

POS.	ST.	DRIVERS	NO.	MAKE	DISP.	ENTRANT	CLASS-POS.	LAPS
1	7	Ignazio Giunti / Nino Vaccarella / Mario Andretti	21	Ferrari 512S	4994	Ferrari SpA, Modena, Italy	S-1	248
2	15	Steve McQueen / Peter Revson	48	Porsche 908	2997	Solar Productions, Hollywood, Calif.	P-1	248
3	13	Masten Gregory / Toine Hezemans	33	Alfa Romeo T33-3	2993	Autodelta SpA, Milan, Italy	P-2	247
4	5	Pedro Rodriguez / Leo Kinnunen / Jo Siffert	15	Porsche 917	4494	J.W. Automotive Engineering, England	S-2	244
5	10	Henri Pescarolo / Johnny Servoz-Gavin	34	Matra-Simca 650	2999	Equipe Matra-Elf, Velizy, France	P-3	242
6	14	Mike Parkes / Chuck Parsons	22	Ferrari 312P	3000	N.A.R.T., Greenwich, Ct.	T-1	240
7	68	Gerard Larrousse / Gerhard Koch / Richard Attwood	46	Porsche 908	2997	Martini Racing Team, Germany	P-4	236
8	9	Piers Courage / Andrea de Adamich	31	Alfa Romeo T33-3	2993	Autodelta SpA, Milan, Italy	P-5	231
9	12	Rolf Stommelen / Nanni Galli	32	Alfa Romeo T33-3	2993	Autodelta SpA, Milan, Italy	P-6	230
10	25	Tony DeLorenzo / Dick Lang	1	Chevrolet Corvette	7000	Troy Promotions, Troy, Mich.	GT-1	219
11	28	Bob Johnson / B.R. Johnson / Jim Greendyke	3	Chevrolet Corvette	7000	Doug Bergen Racing, Marietta, Ohio	GT-2	214
12	8	Dan Gurney / Francois Cevert	35	Matra-Simca 650	2999	Equipe Matra-Elf, Velizy, France	P-7	213
13	43	Peter Gregg / Pete Harrison	53	Porsche 911	1991	Brumos Porsche Audi, Jacksonville, Fla	GT/U-2-1	205
14	33	Vince Gimondo / Chuck Dietrich	40	Chevrolet Camaro	5000	Takondo Racing, Orlando, Fla.	T-2	203
15	48	Jacques Duval / Bob Bailey / George Nicholas	52	Porsche 911	1991	Jacques Duval, Canada	GT/U-2-2	201
16	44	Robert Mitchell / Charlie Kemp	39	Chevrolet Camaro	5000	Robert S. Mitchell, Huntsville, Ala.	T-3	191
17	31	Bob Grossman / Don Yenko	9	Chevrolet Camaro	7000	Marlbank Racing Team, Ft. Lauderdale, Fla	GT-3	189
18	32	John Tremblay / Bill McDill	43	Chevrolet Camaro	4997	Bruce Behens Racing, Winter Park, Fla.	T-4	187
19	49	R. Smith / J. Guthrie / J. Kondratieff	73	Austin-Healey Sprite	1300	Ring Free Oil Team, Atlanta, Ga.	P/U-2-1	187
20	23	Jerry Thompson / John Mahler	2	Chevrolet Corvette	7000	Troy Promotions, Troy, Mich.	GT-4	187
21	46	Jim Corwin / Donna Mae Mims	91	Chevrolet Camaro	4956	Flem-Cor Enterprises, New Buffalo, Mich.	T-5	184
22	41	John Elliott / Don Gwynne, Jr.	92	Chevrolet Camaro	4956	Preston Hood Chevrolet, Ft. Walton Bch, Fla.	T-6	182
23	34	Mike Rahal / Hugh Wise / Werner Frank	50	Porsche 906	1991	Nationwide Food Brokers, Glen Ellyn, Ill.	S-3	181
24	47	Dr. V.P. Collins / Larry Wilson	37	Ford Mustang	4655	Collins-Wilson Racing, Houston, Tex.	T-7	175
25	55	John Belperche / Jim Gammon / Ray Mummery	57	MGB	1798	Waldron Motors, Boca Raton, Fla.	GT/U-2-3	175
26	57	Ben Scott / Lowell Lanier / Dave Houser	58	MGB	1798	Waldron Motors, Boca Raton, Fla.	GT/U-2-4	169
27	62	Paul Pettey / Roy Hallquist	18	Ford Mustang	5000	Paul Pettey, Litchfield, Ct.	T-7	162
28	57	Rod Kennedy / Bob Samm / Mike Tillson	80	Lancia Fulvia	1300	Texas Speed Museum, Austin, Tex.	T/U-2-1	157
29	40	Anatoly Arutunoff / Bill Pryor	54	Fiat Abarth Spyder	1980	Automobiles of Italy, Inc., Tulsa, Ok.	P*	166
30	36	Merv Rosen / Steve Behr	51	Porsche 906	1991	Porsche Audi, Waukeegan, Wisc.	S*	158
31	42	Carlos Fabre / Jose Luis	63	Chevron B8	1991	Carlos Fabre, Coyoacan, Mexico	S*	143
32	22	Gregg Young / Robin Ormes	26	Lola T-70 Chevy Mk III	5000	Randy's Auto Body, Clifton, N.J.	S*	114
33	60	Walt Brown / Joe Marcus / Jim Sandman	97	BMW 2002	1990	MCAS, Inc., Harrod's Creek, Ky.	T*	105
34	17	Hans Laine / Gijs Van Lennep	47	Porsche 908	2997	Racing Team AAAW, Finland	DNF-u	229
35	1	Mario Andretti / Arturo Merzario	19	Ferrari 512S	4994	Ferrari SpA, Modena, Italy	DNF-t	227
36	2	Jo Siffert / Brian Redman / Leo Kinnunen	14	Porsche 917	4494	J.W. Automotive Engineering, England	DNF-s	211
37	35	Dave Heinz / Or Costanzo	8	Chevrolet Corvette	7000	O. Costanzo, Tampa, Fla.	DNF-u	191
38	27	John Greenwood / Allan Barker	4	Chevrolet Corvette	7000	John Greenwood Auto Research, Troy, Mich.	DNF-u	159
39	4	Jacky Ickx / Peter Schetty	20	Ferrari 512S	4994	Ferrari, SpA, Modena, Italy	DNF-e	151

40	54	Jon Woodner / Dan O'Connor	56	MG Midget	1296	British Leyland Motors, Leonia, N.J.	DNF-u	122
41	26	Ray Heppenstall / T. Grant / Buzz Marcus	29	Ford GT 40	5000	Auto Enterprises, Flourtown Pa.	DNF-s	117
42	6	Ronnie Bucknum / Sam Posey	24	Ferrari 512S	4994	N.A.R.T., Greenwich, Ct.	DNF-t	92
43	56	Merle Brennan / Logan Blackburn	55	MGB	1867	British Leyland Motors, Leonia, N.J.	DNF-u	84
44	58	Robert Clark / Wayne Marsula	82	Lancia Fulvia	1584	General Plastics, Miami, Fla.	DNF-e	78
45	45	Bruce Jennings / Bob Tullius	77	Porsche 911T	1991	Bruce Jennings, Towson, Md.	DNF-a	78
46	67	Paul Spruell / Wilber Pickett	69	Alfa Romeo Spyder	1750	Scuderia Spruell, Winter Park, Fla.	DNF-u	75
47	21	Jim Baker / Clive Baker / Paul Richards	61	Chevron B16	1800	Ring Free Oil Team, Atlanta, Ga.	DNF-e	70
48	3	Kurt Ahrens / Vic Elford	16	Porsche 917	4494	Porsche Audi, Englewood Cliffs, N.J.	DNF-a	61
49	16	Luigi Chinetti, Jr. / Tony Adamowicz	23	Ferrari 312P	3000	N.A.R.T., Greenwich, Ct.	DNF-t	56
50	39	Jim Bandy / Fred Stevenson	67	Lotus 47	1600	Sport Motors, Grandview, Mo.	DNF-u	48
51	37	Joie Chitwood / M. Kearney	38	Chevrolet Camaro	4956	David McLain, Tampa, Fla.	DNF-u	47
52	30	Larry Bock / Larry Dent	41	Chevrolet Camaro	5000	Laurel Racing, South Bend, Ind.	DNF-e	40
53	24	Brian Robinson / Hugh Kleinpeter	62	Chevron B16	1800	Chevron Cars, Bolton, England	DNF-f	38
54	51	Ralph Meaney / Bill Bean	74	Porsche 911	1991	Ralph Meaney, Sherborn, Mich.	DNF-e	36
55	29	Bill Schumacher / Bill Petree	5	Chevrolet Corvette	7000	Wm. A Schumacher, Birmingham, Mich.	DNF-e	34
57	11	Hans Herrmann / Rudi Lins	17	Porsche 917	4494	Porsche Audi, Englewood Cliffs, N.J.	DNF-e	28
58	63	Robert Whitaker / Harvey Eckoff	87	Volvo 122S	1800	Robert Whitaker, Sanford, Fla.	DNF-e	25
59	20	Piers Forester / Andrew Hedges	30	Ford GT 40	4700	Trevor Graham, England	DNF-a	22
60	38	Josef Greger / Andreas Schmalback	49	Porsche 910	1991	Josef Greger, Dachau, Germany	DNF-k	22
61	50	Ray Cuomo / George Lisberg	36	Ford Mustang	4727	Ray Cuomo Racing, Commock, N.Y.	DNF-e	16
62	65	Robert Theall	86	Volvo 122S	1800	Sandy's Spares, White Plains, N.Y.	DNF-u	8
63	53	Bruce Morehead	7	American Motors AMX	6390	Bruce Morehead Racing, Tampa, Fla.	DNF-e	8
64	64	Bob Kilpatrick	60	MGB	1798	Herrington Motors, Warwick, N.Y.	DNF-a	7
65	52	Reggie Smith	59	BMC Roadster	1293	Waldron Motors, Boca Raton, Fla.	DNF-u	2
66	61	Del Taylor	79	Alfa Romeo GTV	1779	Del Taylor, Denver, Co.	DNF-e	2
66	19	Michael De Udy	27	Lola T-70 Chevy Mk III	5000	Grand Bahama Racing, London, England	DNF-a	1
67	66	Paul Fleming / Amos Johnson	88	Fiat 124	1438	Simone Fleming, Raleigh, N.C.	DNF-dq	47
68	18	Hans-Dieter Dechent / Gerhard Koch	45	Porsche 908	2997	Martini Racing Team, Germany	DNF-dq	31
DNS		Bill Harris / Bob Lewis	99	Austin-Healey Sprite	1293	William Harris, Jacksonville, Fla.	withdrew	
DNS		Bill Cooper / Norm Mosher	85	Opel Rallye	1970	HCAS Inc., Harrods Creek, Ky.	withdrew	
DNS		R. Kennedy / Bob Samm / M. Tillson	81	Lancia Fulvia	1300	Texas Speed Museum, Austin, Tex.	practice car	
DNS		John Bentley / Dave Roethel	12	Mustang Boss 302	5000	BRM Inc., Rockville, Md.	withdrew	
DNS		Harley Cluxton / Dr. Wilbur Pickett	25	Ferrari GTB	3300	Harley E. Cluxton III, New Orleans, La.	withdrew	

*Running at finish but not classified as finisher — not enough laps completed.

Average Speed: 107.029 mph
Distance: 1,289.6 miles
Margin of Victory: 22.1 seconds
Fastest Race Lap: #15 Siffert 122.537 mph
Fastest Qualifier: #19 Andretti 121.954 mph

Lap Leaders: #19 1-15, 18-22, 56-60, 65-79, 87-98, 121-227; #14 16-17, 25; #16 23-24; #15 26-55, 228-237; #20 61-64, 80-86, 99-120; #48 238; #21 239-248

Attendance: 67,000 (est.)
Weather: Sunny and warm.

1970 HOURLY STANDINGS — TOP 10

POS.	1 HR.	2 HRS.	3 HRS.	4 HRS.	5 HRS.	6 HRS.	7 HRS.	8 HRS.	9 HRS.	10 HRS.	11 HRS.	Finish
1	16	15	19	20	20	19	19	19	19	19	15	21
2	15	16	20	19	19	20	21	21	15	48	48	48
3	19	19	15	21	21	21	22	48	48	15	21	33
4	20	20	21	22	22	22	48	33	21	21	33	15
5	21	21	22	24	48	48	15	22	33	33	34	34
6	17	24	24	48	35	15	14	15	22	34	22	22
7	24	22	35	15	15	14	33	14	34	22	45	45
8	22	23	48	35	14	35	35	34	45	45	31	31
9	23	35	16	14	33	33	34	35	35	31	32	32
10	33	33	14	33	34	34	47	45	47	32	1	1

1971

**1971 SEBRING WINNER —
Porsche 917**
Built and entered by Porsche,
Stuttgart, Germany.
Chassis No. 917.020;
Engine: 5.0 liter, 12 cyl. Porsche
**Drivers: Vic Elford,
Gerard Larrousse**

20TH ANNUAL 12 HOURS OF SEBRING / MARCH 20, 1971

POS.	DRIVERS	NO.	MAKE	DISP.	ENTRANT	CLASS	LAPS
1	Vic Elford / Gerard Larrousse	3	Porsche 917	5000	Martini & Rossi Racing, Germany	S-1	260
2	Nanni Galli / Rolf Stommelen	33	Alfa Romeo T33	2993	Autodelta SpA, Milan, Italy	P-1	257
3	Andrea de Adamich / Henri Pescarolo	32	Alfa Romeo T33	2993	Autodelta SpA, Milan, Italy	P-2	248
4	Pedro Rodriguez / Jackie Oliver	2	Porsche 917K	4907	J.W. Automotive Engineering Ltd., England	S-2	248
5	Derek Bell / Jo Siffert	1	Porsche 917K	4907	J.W. Automotive Engineering Ltd., England	S-3	244
6	Mark Donohue / David Hobbs	6	Ferrari 512M	5000	Penske/White Racing, Newton Square, Pa.	S-4	243
7	John Greenwood / Dick Smothers	48	Chevrolet Corvette	7000	John Greenwood, Troy, Mich.	GTO-1	218
8	Luigi Chinetti, Jr. / George Eaton	21	Ferrari 312P	3000	N.A.R.T., Greenwich, Ct.	P-3	213
9	James Locke / Bert Everett	31	Porsche 911T	1991	Waterville Estates, Alton, NH	GTU-1	203
10	Dave Heinz / Bob Johnson	57	Chevrolet Corvette	7000	Dave Heinz Racing, Tampa, Fla.	GTO-2	199
11	Ash Tisdelle / Pete Kirill	39	Porsche 911S	1991	K&T Enterprises, Jacksonville, Fla.	TU-1	199
12	Harley Cluxton / Bob Grossman	24	Ferrari 365 GTB4	4400	N.A.R.T., Greenwich, Ct.	S-5	195
13	John Tremblay / Bill McDill	47	Chevrolet Camaro	7000	Bruce Behrens Racing, Winter Park, Fla.	TO-1	193
14	Peter Gregg / Hurley Haywood	59	Porsche 914/6	1991	Brumos Porsche Audi Corp., Jacksonville, Fla.	GTU-2	192
15	Bert Gafford / Houghton Smith	89	Chevrolet Camaro	5000	H. Houghton Smith, Montgomery, Ala.	TO-2	191
16	Ray Walle / Tom Davey / Tom Reddy	81	Porsche 911S	1991	Ray Walle Ent., Monmouth Jct., N.J.	GTU-3	187
17	Jacques Duval / George Nicholas / Bob Bailey	5	Porsche 914/6	1991	Jacques Duval, Quebec, Canada	GTU-4	187
18	Thomas Ciccone / Len Greenhalgh	19	Chevrolet Camaro	5000	Thomas T. Ciccone, Jr., Providence, R.I.	TO-3	183
19	C.C. Canada / Bob Christiansen	14	Chevrolet Camaro	5000	Boykin Auto Repair, Camden, S.C.	TO-4	183
20	John Hotchkis / Robert Kirby	40	Porsche 911S	1991	Bozzani Porsche, Inc., Monrovia, Calif.	GTU-5	180
21	Michael Walker / Daryl Springer	60	Porsche 911S	1991	Wheel Sport Ent., Jacksonville, Fla.	GTU-6	176
22	Bob Mitchell / Charlie Kemp	72	Chevrolet Camaro	5000	Robert R. Mitchell, Huntsville, Ala.	TO-5	158
23	Ron Goldleaf / Del Taylor / Bob Wheat	84	Alfa Romeo GTV	1600	Del Taylor, Denver, Col.	TU-2	148
24	John Elliott / Don Gwynne	63	Chevrolet Camaro	5000	Preston Hood Chevrolet, Ft. Walton Bch, Fla.	TO-6	142
25	Merv Rosen / Dick Jacobs / Russ Tyndall	74	Porsche 906	1991	Dr. Mervin Rosen, Waukegan, Ill.	S*	172
26	Don Yenko / Tony DeLorenzo	11	Chevrolet Corvette	7000	Troy Promotions, Inc., Troy, Mich.	GTO*	150
27	Tom Fraser / Jean Sage / Charles Reynolds	17	Chevron B-16	1800	Ring Free Oil Racing Team, Atlanta, Ga.	P*	141
28	Luis Sereix / Javier Garcia	42	Chevrolet Camaro	5000	Garcia Racing, Hialeah, Fla.	TO*	133
29	Steve Behr / Pete Conrad / John Buffum	29	Porsche 914/6	1991	Ralph Meaney, Inc., Sherborn, Mass.	GTU*	112
30	Richard Small / Robert Fordyce	66	Chevrolet Camaro	5000	Performance Automobile, S. Miami, Fla.	TO*	111
31	Ralph Meaney / Gary Wright / Forry Laucks	28	Porsche 914/6	1991	Ralph Meaney, Inc., Sherborn, Mass.	DNF-t	187
32	Peter Revson / Swede Savage	22	Ferrari 512M	5000	N.A.R.T., Greenwich, Ct.	DNF-k	169
33	Mike Rahal / Werner Frank / Hugh Wise	58	Porsche 906	1991	Nationwide Food Brokers, Glen Ellyn, Ill.	DNF-u	167
34	Hugh Kleinpeter / Tony Belcher	61	Lola T-210	1800	Promotional Advertising Corp., Miami, Fla.	DNF-u	161
35	John Oliver / John Maynard / Peter Flanagan	88	Chevrolet Camaro	5000	S-Car-Go Racing, Pompano Beach, Fla.	DNF-e	131
36	Mario Andretti / Jacky Ickx	25	Ferrari 312PB	2991	Ferrari Automobili, Modena, Italy	DNF-t	117
37	Ronnie Bucknum / Sam Posey	23	Ferrari 512S	5000	N.A.R.T., Greenwich, Ct.	DNF-e	114
38	Bobby Rinzler / Clive Baker	16	Chevron B-16	1800	Ring Free Oil Racing Team, Atlanta, Ga.	DNF-u	113
39	Cliff Gottlob / Ed Lowther	86	Chevrolet Corvette	7000	Cliff Gottlob, Arkansas City, Ks.	DNF-e	108

40	Manuel Garcia / Santiago Gonzalez	43	Chevrolet Nova	5000	Garcia Racing, Hialeah, Fla.	DNF-s	103
41	Paul Pettey / Tom Dutton	45	Ford Mustang	5000	Reventlow-Pettey Autos, Litchfield, Ct.	DNF-e	95
42	Manuel Quintana / John Belperche	38	Shelby GT500	4948	John P. Belperche, Orlando, Fla.	DNF-u	76
43	Larry Wilson / V.P. Collins	35	Chevrolet Camaro	5000	Collins-Wilson Racing Ent., Houston, Tex.	DNF-t	64
44	Anatoly Arutunoff / Wm. Pryor / Brian Goellnicht	54	Fiat Abarth	1994	Automobiles of Italy, Inc., Tulsa, Ok.	DNF-u	61
45	Vince Gimondo / Chuck Dietrich	71	Chevrolet Camaro	5000	Takondo Racing, Orlando, Fla.	DNF-e	61
46	Josef Greger / Hans Dieter Weigel	56	Porsche 907	1991	Josef Greger, Munich, Germany	DNF-u	53
47	Allan Barker / Eugene Harrington	50	Chevrolet Corvette	7000	John Greenwood, Troy, Mich.	DNF-e	50
48	Jerry Thompson / John Mahler	12	Chevrolet Corvette	7000	Troy Promotions, Inc., Troy, Mich.	DNF-e	42
49	Bob Gray / Terry Keller / Len Magner	46	Ford Mustang	5000	Sebring Racing Inc., Sebring, Fla.	DNF-b	39
50	Ben Scott / Lowell Lanier / Dave Houser	52	MGB	1892	Waldron Motors Racing, Boca Raton, Fla.	DNF-e	35
51	Masten Gregory / Gregg Young	20	Ferrari 512M	5000	Young America Racing Team, Wilton, Ct.	DNF-a	29
52	Nino Vaccarella / Toine Hezemans	34	Alfa Romeo T33	2993	Autodelta SpA, Milan, Italy	DNF-f	27
53	Jim Gammon / Dean Donley	51	MGB	1892	Waldron Motors Racing, Boca Raton, Fla.	DNF-e	25
54	Michael Keyser / Bruce Jennings	15	Porsche 911S	1991	Toad Hall Racing, Towson, Md.	DNF-e	23
55	Chuck Parsons / David Weir	26	Ferrari 512S	5000	N.A.R.T., Greenwich, Ct.	DNF-u	20
56	John Cordts	92	Chevrolet Camaro	5000	B.F. Goodrich Tire Co., Akron, Ohio	DNF-e	6
57	Janet Guthrie	18	Chevron B-16	1800	Ring Free Oil Racing Team, Atlanta, Ga.	DNF-e	1
DNS	Mike Rand / Randy Blessing	7	Ford Cobra	5000	Blessing Racing, Lakeland, Fla.	reserve	
DNS	Warren Drescher / Robert Luchette	53	Lotus-Cortina	1600	Marion E. Dickson, Akron, Ohio	reserve	
DNS	Juan Montalvo/Antonio Garcia/A. Gomez Mena	83	BMW 2002	1990	German Motors, Inc., West Palm Beach, Fla.	reserve	
DNS	Ron Polimeni / Robert Theall	78	Volvo 122S	2000	George W. Sanderson, E. White Plains, N.Y.	reserve	
DNS	Bobby Clark / Ray Kessler	55	Datsun 510	1600	Clearwater Datsun, Clearwater, Fla.	reserve	
DNS	William Schumacher / Robert Kiefer	10	Chevrolet Corvette	7000	Iroquois Racing Assn., Birmingham, Mich.	reserve	
DNS	Paul Fleming / Amos Johnson / Bill Barnes	9	Chevrolet Corvette	7000	Simone N. Fleming, Raleigh, N.C.	reserve	

*Unclassified Finisher—did not complete required number of laps
No. 1 Porsche penalized four laps for fueling infraction.

Average Speed: 112.50 mph
Fastest Race Lap: #1 Jo Siffert 124.418 mph
Distance: 1,352 miles
Lap Leaders: #6 1-20, 41-51, 59-60; **#1** 21-27; **#2** 30-40; **#25** 28-29, 52-58, 61-117; **#33** 118-148; **#3** 149-260
Margin of Victory: 3 laps
Fastest Qualifier: #6 Mark Donohue 123.440 mph
Attendance: 62,000 (est.)
Weather: Windy and cold.

1971 HOURLY STANDINGS — TOP 10

POS.	1 HR.	2 HRS.	3 HRS.	4 HRS.	5 HRS.	6 HRS.	7 HRS.	8 HRS.	9 HRS.	10 HRS.	11 HRS.	Finish
1	1	25	25	25	25	33	3	3	3	3	3	3
2	6	6	6	2	33	3	33	33	33	33	33	33
3	25	1	33	6	3	2	32	32	32	32	32	32
4	2	3	3	3	2	32	2	2	2	2	2	2
5	3	2	2	33	32	1	1	1	1	1	1	1
6	22	33	32	32	1	25	6	6	6	6	6	6
7	33	32	22	23	22	23	23	23	48	48	48	48
8	32	22	1	21	6	6	22	48	21	21	21	21
9	20	23	23	48	23	48	48	21	31	31	31	31
10	23	21	21	22	21	22	21	22	57	57	57	57

1972

**1972 SEBRING WINNER —
Ferrari 312PB**
Built and entered by Ferrari factory, Italy. Chassis No. 0882;
Engine: 3.0 liter, 12 cyl. Ferrari
**Drivers: Mario Andretti,
Jacky Ickx**

21ST ANNUAL 12 HOURS OF SEBRING / MARCH 25, 1972

POS.	ST.	DRIVERS	NO.	MAKE	DISP.	TEAM/SPONSOR	CLASS	LAPS
1	1	Mario Andretti / Jacky Ickx	2	Ferrari 312PB	2991	Ferrari, Modena, Italy	S3L-1	259
2	4	Ronnie Peterson / Tim Schenken	3	Ferrari 312PB	2991	Ferrari, Modena, Italy	S3L-2	257
3	9	Toine Hezemans / Nino Vaccarella	33	Alfa Romeo TT33	2992	Autodelta SpA, Milan, Italy	S3L-3	233
4	15	Dave Heinz / Bob Johnson	57	Chevrolet Corvette	7101	Dana English,Tampa, Fla.	GTO-1	221
5	26	Peter Gregg / Hurley Haywood	59	Porsche 911S	2495	Brumos Porsche Corp., Jacksonville, Fla.	GTU-1	215
6	8	Joakim Bonnier/Gerard Larrousse/R. Wisell	12	Lola T-280 Cosworth	3000	Ecurie Bonnier, Switzerland	S3L-4	213
7	11	Roman Pechman / Rudy Bartling / Milt Minter	39	Porsche 910	2300	B. Brezinka, Toronto, Canada	S3L-5	213
8	23	Luigi Chinetti, Jr. / Bob Grossman	22	Ferrari GTB/4	4400	N.A.R.T., Greenwich, Ct.	GTO-2	210
9	50	Daniel Muniz / Jose Luis	78	Porsche 914/6	2000	Daniel Muniz, Mexico	GTU-2	207
10	42	Vince Gimondo / Bill Dingman	17	Chevrolet Camaro	5000	Takondo Racing, Orlando, Fla.	SEDA-1	205
11	59	Bruce Jennings / Robert Beasley	77	Porsche 911S	1991	Bnuce Jennings, Towson, Md.	GTU-3	202
12	36	Erwin Kramer / Gunther Huber / Carlos Bolanos	28	Porsche 911S	2500	Porsche Kramer Racing Team, Germany	GTU-4	201
13	19	Tony Adamowicz / Sam Posey	21	Ferrari GTB/4	4400	N.A.R.T., Greenwich, Ct.	GTO-3	199
14	56	Peter Kirill / Russell Norburn	41	Porsche 911S	2500	Kirill Racing, Charlotte, S.C.	GTU-5	196
15	29	Robert Kirby / John Hotchkis	27	Porsche 914/6	2000	Bozzani Porsche Audi, Inc., Monrovia, Cal.	GTU-6	189
16	55	Dieter Oest / Mike Tillson / Al Holbert	69	Porsche 911T	1992	Holbert's Porsche-Audi, Warrington, Pa.	GTU-7	186
17	44	Bob Gray / Terry Keller	47	Chevrolet Corvette	7440	Sebring Racing, Inc., Sebring, Fla.	GTO-4	181
18	40	Robert Fisher / Bruce Ponder	38	Chevron B-16	1800	Hobby Car Enterprises, Lafayette, Cal.	S2L-1	176
19	48	Harry Ingle / Charles Reynolds	18	Ferrari GTB/4	4390	Ring Free Oil Team, Atlanta, Ga.	GTO-5	175
20	10	Nick Craw / Bill Barber	25	Chevron B-19	1800	Fred Opert, Upper Saddle River, N.J.	S2L-2	173
21	37	Merv Rosen / Jerry Schaub	74	Porsche 906	1991	Carousel Porsche-Audi, Hopkins, Minn.	S2L-3	172
22	16	Tom Waugh / Bob Beatty	56	Lola T-212 Cosworth	1790	Promotional Advertising Corp., Miami, Fla.	S2L-4	167
23	28	Bob Mitchell / Bob Christiansen	94	Chevrolet Camaro	5000	Bolus & Snopes, Ltd., Huntsville, Ala.	SEDA-2	166
24	21	Don Yenko / John Cordts	50	Chevrolet Corvette	7000	John Greenwood Racing, Troy, Mich.	GTO-6	163
25	46	Hector Rebaque / Guillermo Rojas	58	Porsche 914/6	1991	Brumos Porsche Audi, Jacksonville, Fla.	GTU-8	152
26	45	John Tremblay / David Ellis-Brown	10	Chevrolet Camaro	5000	C.C. Canada Lumber Co., Inc., Poland, N.Y.	SEDA-3	146
27	34	John Buffum / John Fitzpatrick	24	Ford Escort	1800	Libra International Racing, S. Burlington, Vt.	TU-1	97
28	35	Robert Stoddard / Joe Hines / Frank Harmstead	68	Porsche 914/6	1991	H & S Imports Racing, Statesboro, Ga.	GTU*	146
29	61	Craig Ross / Jacques Groleau	73	Datsun 240Z	2394	Ross Racing Ltd., Clearwater, Fla.	GTU*	121
30	2	Clay Regazzoni / Brian Redman	4	Ferrari 312PB	2991	Ferrari, Modena, Italy	DNF-f	215
31	25	John Greenwood / Dick Smothers	48	Chevrolet Corvette	7000	John Greenwood Racing, Troy, Mich.	DNF-e	179
32	47	Michael Summers / Bob McClure	9	Chevrolet Camaro	5000	Endurance Promotions, Inc., Syracuse, N.Y.	DNF-u	145
33	43	Manuel Garcia / Robert Cao	44	Chevrolet Nova	4956	Larrauri Racing, Coral Gables, Fla.	DNF-k	137
34	54	Neil Potter / Oran Ansley / Bill Hood	46	Ford Mustang	4727	Sebring Racing, Inc., Sebring, Fla.	DNF-e	130
35	6	Vic Elford / Helmut Marko	32	Alfa Romeo TT33	2992	Autodelta SpA, Milan, Italy	DNF-e	128
36	3	R. Stommelen/P. Revson/A. de Adamich	31	Alfa Romeo TT33	2992	Autodelta SpA, Milan, Italy	DNF-t	117
37	24	Tony DeLorenzo / Jerry Thompson	11	Ford Mustang	5000	Troy Promotions Inc., Troy, Mich.	DNF-e	116
38	31	Mike Keyser / Jurgen Barth	16	Porsche 911S	2500	Toad Hall Racing, Towson, Md.	DNF-e	102

39	58	Ralph Noseda/Jorge Garcia/Mark Livingston	42	Chevrolet Camaro	5000	Garcia Racing, Hialeah, Fla.	DNF-e	92
40	51	Houghton Smith / Bert Gafford	89	Chevrolet Camaro	5000	Rinzler Motoracing, Inc., Atlanta, Ga.	DNF-s	91
41	12	Hugh Kleinpeter / Tony Belcher	52	Chevron B-21 Cosworth	1790	Promotional Advertising Corp., Miami, Fla.	DNF-k	85
42	39	Gary Belcher / Jeff Stevens	37	Chevrolet Camaro	5000	Gary Belcher, Davie, Fla.	DNF-t	84
43	17	Rodolfo Junco / Fred Van Beuren	26	Chevron B-19	1998	Fred Opert, Upper Saddle River, N.J.	DNF-e	76
44	60	V.P. Collins / Roberto Gonzalez / Jack Beall	35	Chevrolet Camaro	5000	Dr. V.P. Collins, Houston, Tex.	DNF-e	76
45	57	George Stone / Russ Poole	76	Porsche 911T	1991	Silverstone Racing Team, Rockville, Md.	DNF-e	64
46	20	Anatoly Arutunoff / Brian Goellnicht	54	Fiat Abarth	2000	Automobile International Inc., Tulsa, Ok.	DNF-s	57
47	18	David Hobbs / Skip Scott	1	Ferrari GTB/4	4400	Kirk F. White Motor Racing, Ardmore, Pa.	DNF-t	53
48	49	David McClain / Dave White	19	Porsche 914/6	1991	David H. McClain, Tampa, Fla.	DNF-s	51
49	27	John Elliott / Bill McDill	80	Chevrolet Camaro	5000	Preston Hood Chevrolet, Ft. Walton Bch., Fla	DNF-e	50
50	7	Derek Bell / G. Van Lennep	7	Mirage Cosworth M6	2993	Gulf Research Racing, England	DNF-t	48
51	5	Nanni Galli / Andrea de Adamich	34	Alfa Romeo TT33	2992	Autodelta SpA, Milan, Italy	DNF-o	37
52	53	Manuel Quintana / John Belperche	30	Ford Shelby GT350	4948	Florida Tire Co., Key Biscayne, Fla.	DNF-a	33
53	22	Tom Nehl / Jim Fitzgerald	8	Chevrolet Camaro	5000	Automotive Engineering Ent., Jacksonville, Fla.	DNF-e	31
54	33	James Locke / Bob Bailey	61	Porsche 911S	2354	James N. Locke, Alton, N.H.	DNF-a	23
55	38	Lee McDonald / Bert Everett	70	Porsche 914/6	1991	Lee McDonald-Algar Porsche Audi, Rosemont, Pa.	DNF-e	22
56	13	Charlie Kemp / Oscar Koveleski	23	Chevrolet Corvette	7000	Rinzler Motoracing, Inc., Atlanta, Ga.	DNF-a	21
57	30	Roberto Quintanilla	97	Chevrolet Camaro	5000	Roberto Quintanilla, Jr., Mexico	DNF-a	20
58	41	Luis Sereix	43	Chevrolet Camaro	5000	Garcia Racing, Hialeah, Fla.	DNF-e	15
59	32	Josef Greger	63	Porsche 910 Spyder	1997	Josef Greger, Frankfurt, Germany	DNF-e	10
60	14	Roger McCaig	55	Lola T212 Cosworth	1780	Roger McCaig Racing, Ontario, Canada	DNF-a	7
61	52	Bill Bean	15	Porsche 911S	2500	Toad Hall Racing, Towson, Md.	DNF-e	5
DNS		Brad West / John Tunstall	45	Ford Shelby GT350	4727	T.C. Racing, Sarasota, Fla.	withdrew	
DNS		Juan Montalvo / Dr. John Pauley	84	BMW 2002	1991	Chem Air Spray Inc., Pahokee, Fla.	DNQ	
DNS		Bob Armstrong / Rod Bremner	67	Mazda R100	1964	Frossman Racing Service, Ontario, Canada	DNQ	
DNS		Eddie Johnson / Clay Young	79	Chevrolet Camaro	5000	Arrow Racing Team, Smyrna, Ga.	DNQ	
DNS		Bobby Clark / Ray Kessler	75	Datsun 510	1600	Clearwater Datsun, Clearwater, Fla.	DNQ	
DNS		Bob Fordyce / Richard Small	60	Chevrolet Camaro	5000	Robert Fordyce, Miami, Fla.	DNQ	
DNS		Don Baumgartner / Don Herman	53	Chevron B-8	1998	D.A. Baumgartner, Jr., Moreland Hills, Ohio	withdrew	
DNS		Ken Schumacher / Robert Keifer	29	Chevrolet Corvette	7000	Iroquois Racing, Michigan	engine	
DNS		Richard Crebs / Bill Jobe	51	Alfa Romeo GTV	2000	Richard Crebs, Dallas, Tex.	withdrew	

*Not classified as a finisher — not enough laps completed

Average Speed: 111.508 mph
Fastest Race Lap. #3 Ronnie Peterson 2:30.80 = 121.717 mph
Distance: 1,346.8 miles
Lap Leaders: #2 1-63, 211-259; #4 64-210.
Margin of Victory: 2 laps
Attendance: 58,000 (est.)
Fastest Qualifier: #2 Mario Andretti 123.630 mph
Weather: Sunny and warm

1972 HOURLY STANDINGS — TOP 10

	GRID	POS.	1 HR.	2 HRS.	3 HRS.	4 HRS.	5 HRS.	6 HRS.	7 HRS.	8 HRS.	9 HRS.	10 HRS.	11 HRS.	Finish
#2	2:31.14	1	2	2	4	4	4	4	4	4	4	4	2	2
#4	2:33.04	2	4	4	2	2	2	2	2	2	2	2	3	3
#31	2:33.86	3	3	3	3	3	3	33	3	3	3	3	4	33
#3	2:35.37	4	31	32	33	33	33	32	33	33	33	33	33	57
#34	2:35.92	5	33	33	32	32	32	3	57	57	57	57	57	59
#32	2:37.61	6	32	26	31	31	57	57	48	48	59	59	59	12
#7	2:40.67	7	26	52	26	57	59	59	59	59	39	39	12	39
#12	2:41.78	8	52	31	52	12	12	12	12	39	12	12	39	22
#33	2:42.75	9	34	57	57	59	39	39	39	12	22	22	22	78
#25	2:51.27	10	12	12	12	52	22	48	22	22	78	78	78	17

1973

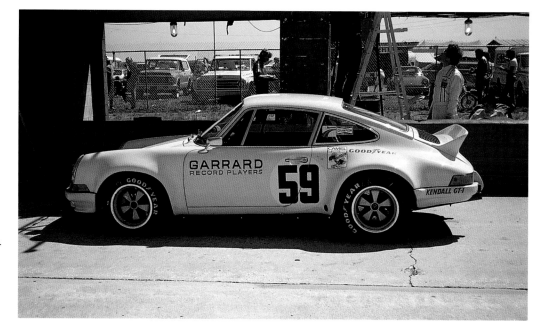

**1973 SEBRING WINNER —
Porsche Carrera RS**
Built by Porsche / Entered by Dr.
Dave Helmick and Peter Gregg.
Chassis No. 9113600865; Engine:
2.8 liter, 6 cyl. Porsche
**Drivers: Peter Gregg, Hurley
Haywood, Dave Helmick**

22ND ANNUAL 12 HOURS OF SEBRING / MARCH 24, 1973

POS.	ST.	DRIVERS	NO.	MAKE	ENTRANT / TEAM	CLASS	LAPS
1	4	Peter Gregg / Hurley Haywood / Dave Helmick	59	Porsche Carrera	Dr. Dave Helmick, Miami, Fla.	GTO-1	226
2	5	Michael Keyser / Milt Minter	1	Porsche Carrera	Toad Hall Racing, Towson, Md.	GTO-2	225
3	9	Ron Grable / John Greenwood / Mike Brockman	50	Chevrolet Corvette	John Greenwood Racing, Troy, Mich.	GTO-3	219
4	7	Gray Egerton / Elliott Forbes-Robinson	81	Porsche Carrera	Far West Racing, Costa Mesa, Calif.	GTO-4	217
5	10	Vince Gimondo / Bill Dingman	17	Chevrolet Camaro	Vince Gimondo, Orlando, Fla.	TO-1	212
6	22	Dan Moore / David McCullogh	37	Ford Mustang	Dan Moore, Dallas, Tex.	TO-2	210
7	44	Don Lindley / Steve Behr / Brian Goellnicht	27	Porsche 911S	Don Lindley, Tulsa, Ok.	GTU-1	209
8	23	George Stone / Mike Downs	76	Porsche 911S	Silverstone Racing, Rockville, Md.	GTU-2	209
9	18	Tim Chitwood / Joie Chitwood / Bob Nagel	24	Chevrolet Camaro	T.C. Racing, Tampa, Fla.	TO-3	208
10	43	Dieter Oest / Mike Tilson / Harry Bytzek	91	Porsche 911S	Holbert's Porsche-Audi, Warrington, Pa.	GTU-3	198
11	32	Phil Currin / Danny Fortin / Bill Johnson	99	Chevrolet Corvette	Phil Currin, Gainesville, Fla.	GTO-5	197
12	27	Luis Sereix / Tony Lilly / Dave Yoder	42	Chevrolet Camaro	Garcia Racing, Miami, Fla.	TO-4	193
13	36	Bruce Jennings / Bob Beasley	77	Porsche 911S	Bruce Jennings, Towson, Md.	GTU-4	193
14	57	Don Parish / Dave Calisey / Edwin Taylor	89	Porsche 911S	Thomas Barrick, Lawton, Okla.	GTU-5	193
15	19	Bob Bergstrom / Jim Cook	82	Porsche 911S	Bob Bergstrom, Woodland Hills, Calif.	GTU-6	191
16	6	Wilbur Pickett / Bill Bean	94	Chevrolet Corvette	Leldon Blackwell, St. Petersburg, Fla.	GTO-6	186
17	55	George Garcia / Vic Shinn	41	Chevrolet Corvette	George Garcia Racing, Miramar, Fla.	GTO-7	188
18	56	Klaus Selbert / Siegfried Glage	84	Porsche 911	Airport Motorsports, Ferguson, Md.	GTU-7	186
19	14	Jim Greendyke / Bob Johnson	49	Chevrolet Corvette	John Greenwood Racing, Troy, Mich.	GTO-8*u	182
20	53	Jim Grob / Juan Montalvo	114	BMW 2002	Jim Grob Racing, Ft. Lauderdale, Fla.	TU-1	180
21	45	Scott Chapman / John McLaren / Bill Hood	61	Chevrolet Corvette	Sebring Racing Inc., Sebring, Fla.	GTO-9	179
22	21	Ray Kessler / Jim Fitzgerald	9	Chevrolet Camaro	Ray Kessler, Inc., Holly Hill, Fla.	TO-5*u	178
23	40	David McClain / Dave White	67	Porsche 914/6	David H. McClain, Tampa, Fla.	GTU-7	177
24	26	Terry Keller / Bob Gray / Neil Potter	47	Chevrolet Corvette	Sebring Racing Inc., Sebring, Fla.	GTO-10	175
25	70	Dieter Oest / Don Heth / Dave Olimpi	92	Porsche 911S	Holbert's Porsche-Audi, Warrington, Pa.	GTU-8	174
26	61	Ray Walle / Richard Schuck	90	Mazda RX-2	Z & W Mazda, Princeton, N.J.	TU-2	173
27	62	Marc Davis / R. Melville / Bob Beatty	33	Alfa Romeo GTV	RaceCo. of Coral Gables, Fla.	TU-3*u	165
28	68	Dick Bauer / Jim DeStafeno / Nick Engels	3	Chevrolet Corvette	Perf. Associates, Emerson, N.J.	GTO-11*u	159
29	65	Whitt Diggett / Amos Johnson	00	AMC Gremlin	Levi's Team Highball, Raleigh, N.C.	TO-6	154
30	54	Don Parish / Ron Jones / John Hulen	85	Porsche 914/6	Donald Parish, Indianapolis, Ind.	GTU-9	154
31	50	Jacques Groleau / Craig Ross / Bill Shaw	74	Datsun 240Z	J.G. Racing, Tampa, Fla.	GTU-10	153
32	52	Manuel Quintana / Reinaldo Almeida	78	Ford Mustang	Manuel Quintana, Miami, Fla.	TO-7	150
33	42	Robert Christiansen / G. Myers / J. Tremblay	71	Chevrolet Camaro	Robert Christiansen, Huntsville, Ala.	TO-8*u	148
34	15	Javier Garcia / R. Almeida	57	Ford Mustang	Garcia Racing, Miami, Fla.	TO-9*u	148
35	25	James Lynch / Toby Milne	86	Porsche 911	James Lynch, Glenville, N.C.	GTU-11	148
36	48	Kirby Stumpff / Dick Vreeland / James Pirie	80	Ford Shelby	J. Kirby Stumpff, Ft. Lauderdale, Fla.	GTO-12	137
37	46	Eddy Johnson / Clay Young	7	Chevrolet Camaro	Eddie Johnson, Smyrna, Ga.	TO-10	132
38	35	Tony Ansley / Ron Connelly / Steve Avera	97	Chevrolet Corvette	Ansley Racing Ent., Miami, Fla.	GTO-13	131
39	58	Jack Baldwin / Bobby Clark	175	Datsun 510	Davis Racing, Sebring, Fla.	TU-4	130
40	72	Roberto Boza / Daniel Hernandez / Jose Romero	32	Ford Shelby	Roberto Auto Electric, Miami, Fla.	GTO-14	127
41	24	George Dickinson / Ed Wachs / Ernst Pultz	95	Porsche 911	G.W. Dickinson, Palatine, Ill.	GTU-12*u	125
42	12	Ron Goldleaf / John Tunstall	69	Chevrolet Corvette	WGB Niagara Wines, New York	GTO-15*u	124

43	64	Bob Lapp / Mike Meldeau	88	Datsun 240Z	Bob Lapp, Orlando, Fla.	GTU-13	124
44	67	Dennis Dallmeyer / Nick Dunn	30	Chevrolet Camaro	Dallmeyer Racing, Key West, Fla.	TO-11*u	124
45	47	Alberto Naon / A. Garcia / John Freyre	72	Chevrolet Camaro	Alberto Naon, Miami, Fla.	TO-12	123
46	31	Bert Gafford / John Belperche	83	Chevrolet Camaro	Houghton Smith, Delray Beach, Fla.	TO-13	121
47	1	Tony DeLorenzo / Steve Durst	11	Chevrolet Corvette	Troy Promotions, Troy, Mich.	GTO-16*e	113
48	37	Ralph Noseda / Ray Mummery / Rich Small	29	Chevrolet Camaro	Ralph H. Noseda, Miami, Fla.	TO-14	113
49	2	Dave Heinz / Jerry Thompson	5	Chevrolet Corvette	Race Ent. and Dev.,Tampa, Fla.	GTO-17	110
50	8	John Greenwood / Don Yenko	48	Chevrolet Corvette	John Greenwood Racing, Troy, Mich.	GTO-18*e	105
51	20	Tom Nell / Rich Dagiel / Joe Pirrotta	40	Chevrolet Corvette	Pironell Racing, Caledonia, Wisc.	GTO-19*e	104
52	71	Paul Fleming / Roger Mandeville	138	Mazda RX-2	PDF Racing, Raleigh, N.C.	TU-5*u	102
53	34	Sam Miller / Rob Hey	87	Ford Mustang	Miller/Hey, Atlanta, Ga.	TO-15*u	91
54	60	Dean Donley / Ben Scott	2	MGB	Dean Donley, Ft. Lauderdale, Fla.	GTU-14*u	81
55	33	Klaus Bytzek / Rudy Bartling	46	Porsche 911S	Bytzek Automotive, Toronto, Canada	GTU-15*u	80
56	39	John Elliott / Bill McDill	0	Chevrolet Camaro	Byron Cook Racing, Fla.	TO-16*u	80
57	3	Ike Knupp / Bob Tullius	34	Chevrolet Corvette	Murray Racing Team, Toledo, Ohio	GTO-20*e	74
58	69	Loren Pearson / Mike Spencer / Brian Taylor	98	Ford Shelby	Loren Ross, Topeka, Ks.	GTO-21*u	71
59	13	Jef Stevens / Peter Sherman	62	Chevrolet Corvette	Jef Stevens Racing, Coconut Grove, Fla.	GTO-22*e	53
60	30	Joe Rodriguez / Bob McClure	19	Chevrolet Camaro	Davis Racing, Sebring, Fla.	TO-17*u	50
61	11	John Buffum / Bert Everett	25	Ford Escort	Libra Int'l. Racing, Burlington, Vt.	TU-6*u	48
62	51	Manuel Garcia	44	Chevrolet Nova	Larrauri Racing, Hialeah, Fla.	TO-18*u	44
63	66	Bob Mitchell / Jim Williams	110	Dodge Colt	Bolus & Snopes, Jackson, Miss.	TU-7*u	43
64	41	Bill Schumacher / Richard Hay	54	Chevrolet Corvette	Iroquois Racing, Birmingham, Mich.	GTO-23*u	37
65	29	Marc Dancose	70	Porsche 911S	Marc Dancose, Montreal, Canada	GTU-16*u	30
66	63	Tom Kuenz	75	Porsche 912	Tom Kuenz, Pompano Beach, Fla.	GTU-17*u	23
67	38	Russ Boykin	14	Chevrolet Camaro	C.C. Canada Lumber, Poland, N.Y.	TO 19*u	22
68	49	Bob Lillquist	4	Porsche 911S	Western Sizzlin' Steak Houses, Augusta, Ga.	GTU-18*u	19
69	28	Ed Fleming	28	Chevrolet Camaro	Ed Fleming, Northville, Mich.	TO-20*e	17
70	16	Gene Felton	8	Chevrolet Camaro	Automotive Engineering, Jacksonville, Fla.	TO-21*e	6
71	17	Alex Davidson	6	Chevrolet Corvette	Alex Davidson, Liverpool, N.Y.	GTO-24*e	3
72	59	Charlie Cook	26	Chevrolet Nova	Wayne Alexander, Smyrna, Ga.	TO-22*e	2
DNS		L. Oliva / Ronald Pelimeni	176	Volvo 122S	Laurence Oliva, Mamaroneck, N.Y.	DNQ	
DNS		Sam Posey / Harley Cluxton	21	Ferrari Daytona	Grand Touring Cars, Glenview, Ill.	withdrew	
DNS		Steve Coleman / Dennis Shaw	169	Opel Manta	Performance Engineering, Raleigh, N.C.	withdrew	
DNS		S. Peters / Hoyt Overbagh	122	Ford Pinto	Mark IV Racing, Daytona Beach, Fla.	DNQ	
DNS		Dave Wolin / Gerry Cohen	188	Ford Pinto	Dave Wolin, Ft. Walton Beach, Fla.	DNQ	
DNS		Jack Swanson / Brad West	111	Austin America	Jeffrey Brooks, St. Petersburg, Fla.	DNQ	

*Not running at finish

Average Speed: 97.854 mph
Distance: 1,175.2 miles
Margin of Victory: 1 lap
Lap Leaders: **#11** 1-26, 30-44, 61-73, 79-85; **#34** 74-78; **#5** 27-29, 45-60; **#59** 86-226.
Total Purse: $30,000
Winner's Share: $8,150
Fastest Qualifier: #11 Tony DeLorenzo 106.960 mph
Fastest Race Lap: Milt Minter (unofficial)
Attendance: 20,000 (est.)
Weather: Sunny and warm

1973 HOURLY STANDINGS — TOP 10

GRID		POS.	1 HR.	2 HRS.	3 HRS.	4 HRS.	5 HRS.	6 HRS.	7 HRS.	8 HRS.	9 HRS.	10 HRS.	11 HRS.	Finish
#11	2:55.13	**1**	11	11	**59**	11	**59**	**59**	**59**	**59**	**59**	**59**	**59**	**59**
#5	2:58.01	**2**	34	**59**	11	5	81	81	81	1	1	1	1	1
#34	2:59.42	**3**	**59**	34	5	**59**	11	1	1	81	50	50	50	50
#59	3:01.08	**4**	81	94	34	48	48	11	50	50	81	81	81	81
#1	3:01.09	**5**	94	5	81	81	1	50	76	76	76	76	17	17
#94	3:02.40	**6**	48	81	48	50	50	76	37	37	17	17	37	37
#81	3:02.43	**7**	50	48	50	34	5	37	82	17	37	37	27	27
#48	3:03.17	**8**	49	69	49	49	76	48	24	27	27	27	24	76
#50	3:05.52	**9**	17	50	69	40	82	27	17	24	24	24	76	24
#10	3:05.58	**10**	40	49	40	1	37	82	27	57	91	91	82	91

1975

1975 SEBRING WINNER — BMW CSL
Built and entered by BMW factory,
Germany. Chassis No. 2275984;
Engine: 3.0 liter, 6 cyl. BMW
**Drivers: Brian Redman, Allan
Moffat, Sam Posey, Hans Stuck**

23RD ANNUAL 12 HOURS OF SEBRING / MARCH 21, 1975

POS.	ST.	DRIVERS	NO.	MAKE	ENTRANT / TEAM	CLASS	LAPS
1	4	Brian Redman / Allan Moffat / Sam Posey / Hans Stuck	25	BMW CSL	BMW Motorsport	O-1	238
2	10	George Dyer / Jacques Bienvenue	30	Porsche Carrera	Dyer Motor Racing	O-2	235
3	6	John Graves / John O'Steen / Dave Helmick	43	Porsche Carrera	Ecurie Escargot	O-3	231
4	17	J.C. Bolanos / Michel Jourdain / Gustavo Bolanos	91	Porsche Carrera	Bolanos Racing	O-4	230
5	24	G.W. Dickinson / Bill Webbe / Harry Theodoracopulos	4	Porsche Carrera	G.W. Dickinson	O-5	221
6	67	Milt Minter / Eppie Wietzes	111	Ferrari Boxer	N.A.R.T	O-6	215
7	13	Bob Harmon / Jon Woodner	5	Porsche Carrera		O-7	213
8	34	Diego Febles / Hiram Cruz	68	Porsche Carrera	Diego Febles Racing	O-8	211
9	25	Harry Jones / Marcel Mignot	87	Ferrari Daytona	Jones Motorsports	O-9	209
10	40	Tony Garcia / Albert Naon / John Freyre	44	Porsche 911S	Montura Ranch Estates	U-1	209
11	35	George Drolsom / Bob Nagel	34	Porsche 911S		U-2	207
12	5	Al Holbert / Elliott Forbes-Robinson	14	Porsche Carrera	Holbert's Porsche-Audi	O-10	204
13	7	Michael Keyser / Billy Sprowls / Andres Contreras	1	Porsche Carrera	Toad Hall Racing	O-11*a	200
14	12	Mike Callas / Jim Cook / Adrian Gang	79	Porsche Carrera		O-12	200
15	41	Rusty Bond / George Rollin / John Belperche	60	Porsche 911		U-3	200
16	29	Mike Tillson / Dieter Oest	92	Porsche Carrera	Oest-Tillson Racing	O-13*u	198
17	30	David McClain / Dave White	67	Porsche 911		U-4	198
18	38	Bob Speakman / John Maffucci	84	Datsun 240Z		U-5	197
19	48	Ray Walle / Tom Reddy	90	Mazda RX-3	Ray Walle Mazda	U-6	195
20	52	Bill Arnold / Wiley Doran	72	Chevrolet Corvette		O-14	183
21	61	Bruce Mabrito / Jack Steel	29	Datsun 240Z		U-7	180
22	58	Bill Scott / Harry MacDonald / Bill Neuhoff	82	AMC Gremlin	Bill Scott Racing	O-15	180
23	49	Dennis Stefl / Bob Fordyce	86	Chevrolet Corvette		O-16	176
24	23	Vince Gimondo / John Tremblay	17	Chevrolet Camaro		O-17	171
25	9	Charlie Kemp / Carson Baird	23	Porsche Carrera	Armorall Racing Team	O-18*a	167
26	21	Bob Christiansen / Gary Myers	73	Chevrolet Camaro		O-19*t	165
27	22	John Orr / Bill Jobe	32	Chevrolet Corvette	E.F. Miller & Co.	O-20	163
28	60	Armando Ramirez / Camilo Mutiz / Mauricio DeNarvaez	45	Porsche 911S	Delta Racing	U-8*a	152
29	68	Bill Schmid / Doc Bundy	914	Porsche 914	Holbert's Porsche-Audi	U-9	151
30	56	Luis Garcia, Jr. / Jose Arzeno / Armando Gonzalez	31	BMW 2002		U-10	151
31	37	Spencer Buzbee / Craig Ross / William Frates	46	Datsun 240Z	Buzbee Tropical Fish	U-11*u	143
32	18	Bob Beasley / Bruce Jennings	8	Porsche Carrera		O-21*u	132
33	20	John Carusso / Dick Vreeland / Luis Sereix	48	Chevrolet Corvette		O-22	132
34	51	Robert E. Davis / Tico Almeida / Joseph DeGirolamo	27	Chevrolet Corvette		O-23	132
35	62	Roberto Boza / Diosdado Diaz / Eduardo Garrid	38	Chevrolet Camaro		O-24*u	128
36	44	Terry Wolters / Jack Swanson	18	Chevrolet Camaro		O-25*u	126
37	57	Jacques Groleau / A.J. Brent / John Sweeney	47	Datsun 240Z		U-12	124
38	66	Larry Parker / Bob Lamay / Paul Morgan	61	Ford Pinto		U-13	114
39	1	Hans Stuck / Sam Posey	24	BMW CSL	BMW Motorsport	O-26*r	102

Pos.	Grid	Drivers	No.	Make	Team	Class	Laps
40	69	Ford Smith / Clay Young / Bennett Aiken	12	Chevrolet Corvette		O-27*u	102
41	27	John Tunstall / Joe Jenkins	54	Porsche Carrera	Southpoint Porsche	O-28*s	97
42	64	Ron Oyler / Guy Church	58	Renault R12	Professional Paint & Body	U-14	95
43	8	Mo Carter / Tony DeLorenzo	88	Chevrolet Camaro		O-29*t	93
44	63	Nick Craw / Russ Norburn	66	BMW 2002	Miller & Norburn	O-30*t	82
45	39	Burt Greenwood / Scott Voeltz / Dana English	76	Chevrolet Corvette	Kidd-America Racing	O-31*a	67
46	15	Roberto Quintanilla / David Loring	33	Porsche Carrera		O-32*u	67
47	46	Bonky Fernandez / Mandy Gonzalez / Gustavo Chevres	28	Lotus Elan Roadster		U-15*t	62
48	36	Scott Chapman / William Hood / Bob Dumont	62	Chevrolet Corvette		O-33*e	57
49	69	Neil Potter / Bob Gray / Terry Keller	49	Ford Mustang		O-34*u	54
50	55	Bob Punch / Tom Waugh / Elliott Mendenhall	63	Porsche 911	Doell Enterprises	U-16*u	53
51	43	Charles Gano / Mike Williamson / Jerry Parson	56	Chevrolet Camaro		O-35*u	52
52	28	John Hotchkis / Robert Kirby / Len Jones	51	Porsche 914/6	Johnson-Bozzoni Porsche-Audi	U-17*u	51
53	2	Peter Gregg / Hurley Haywood	59	Porsche Carrera	Brumos Porsche-Audi	O-36*s	50
54	54	John Hulen / Ron Coupland / Dave Causey	85	Porsche 914/6		U-18*u	46
55	33	Sergio Tabe / Jose Marron / Fidel Martinez	95	Porsche Carrera		O-37*b	45
56	3	John Greenwood / Jerry Thompson	75	Chevrolet Corvette	John Greenwood / Spirit of Sebring	O-38*f	42
57	42	Alf Gebhardt / Bruno Beilcke / Sepp Grinbold	10	BMW 2002		U-19*t	38
58	45	John Hastings / Glenn Bunch	40	Jaguar XKE		O-39*a	34
59	11	Tim Chitwood / Joie Chitwood	26	Chevrolet Camaro	Chitwood Racing	O-40*e	33
60	65	Pedro Vazquez / Manuel Quintana / Don Yenko	50	Porsche 911S		U-20*e	29
61	47	Henry Simon / Kirby Stumpff / Augusto Molina	55	Ford Mustang		O-41*u	20
62	59	Dr. Arthur Mollin / Arthur Riley	53	Volvo 142		U-21*u	19
63	32	Ralph Noseda / Ray Mummery	77	Chevrolet Camaro		O-42*e	17
64	53	Marty Hinze / Bob Grossman	57	Pantera		O-43*u	16
65	26	Dale Kreider / Bob DeMarco	22	Chevrolet Corvette		O-44*u	16
66	50	Tony Ansley	9	Chevrolet Corvette		O-45*u	16
67	31	Juan Montalvo	69	Ford Escort		U-22*u	8
68	14	Ludwig Heimrath	74	Porsche Carrera		O-46*u	5
69	16	Daniel Muniz	2	BMW CSL		O-47*k	3
DNS		Javier Garcia / M. Garcia	15	Chevrolet Corvette	Garcia Racing	withdrew	
DNS		Philip Dann	03	Opel GT	Ozone Industries	withdrew	
DNS		Neal Sullivan / Brit Wootten	83	Mini Cooper	P.P.C. Racing	withdrew	
DNS		Dean Donley / Ben Scott	39	MGB		withdrew	
DNS		Anthony Vinas / Miguel Perez	99	Chevrolet Camaro		withdrew	
DNS		H. Theodoracopulos / Skip Barber	3	Mercury Capri RS	Ippocampos Racing	drive shaft	
DNS		Amos Johnson / Dennis Shaw	71	AMC Gremlin	Levis Team Highball	withdrew	

*Not running at finish

Average Speed: 102.64 mph
Fastest Qualifier: #24 Hans Stuck 110.914 mph
Distance: 1,237.6 miles
Fastest Lap: #24 Hans Stuck 110.638 mph
Margin of Victory: 3 laps
Lap Leaders: #75 1-11; #24 12-67; #25 68-238.
Total Purse: $30,000
Attendance: 22,000 (est.)
Winner's Share: $6,650
Weather: Partly cloudy and warm

1976 HOURLY STANDINGS — TOP 10

	GRID	POS.	1 HR.	2 HRS.	3 HRS.	4 HRS.	5 HRS.	6 HRS.	7 HRS.	8 HRS.	9 HRS.	10 HRS.	11 HRS.	Finish
#24	2:48.78	1	24	24	24	25	25	25	25	25	25	25	25	25
#59	2:50.32	2	59	59	25	24	24	30	30	30	30	30	30	30
#75	2:51.38	3	25	25	14	30	1	1	1	1	1	1	91	43
#25	2:51.63	4	75	75	30	1	30	91	91	91	91	91	43	91
#14	2:54.91	5	14	14	1	14	14	43	43	43	43	43	4	4
#43	2:55.75	6	43	1	111	8	8	8	4	4	4	4	1	111
#1	2:55.88	7	1	30	33	91	91	4	5	14	111	111	111	5
#3	2:55.90	8	30	43	8	5	43	5	8	5	68	5	5	68
#88	2:56.17	9	79	111	91	111	111	68	14	111	34	68	68	87
#23	2:56.31	10	91	91	5	4	4	111	68	68	5	87	44	44

219

1976

**1976 SEBRING WINNER —
Porsche Carrera RSR**

Built by Porsche / Entered by
George Dickinson / Holbert's
Porsche-Audi. Chassis No.
4609056; Engine: 3.0 liter, 6 cyl.
Porsche
**Drivers: Al Holbert,
Michael Keyser**

24TH ANNUAL 12 HOURS OF SEBRING / MARCH 20, 1976

POS.	ST.	DRIVERS	NO.	MAKE	ENTRANT / TEAM	CLASS	LAPS
1	3	Al Holbert / Michael Keyser	14	Porsche Carrera	G.W. Dickinson / Holbert's Porsche-Audi	O-1	230
2	5	John Gunn / Carson Baird	11	Porsche Carrera	Dallas Heyser / SL-1	O-2	228
3	13	Roberto Quintanilla / Roberto Gonzalez	30	Porsche Carrera	John McClelland	O-3	227
4	10	Bob Hagestad / Jerry Jolly	56	Porsche Carrera	Spirit of Colorado / Hagestad Porsche	O-4	224
5	15	Diego Febles / Hiram Cruz	58	Porsche Carrera	Diego Febles Racing	O-5	222
6	17	Mauricio DeNarvaez / Albert Naon / John Freyre	44	Porsche Carrera	Mauricio DeNarvaez	O-6	221
7	2	Peter Gregg / Hurley Haywood	59	BMW CSL	BMW Motorsport	O-7	217
8	6	Jim Busby / Carl Shafer	61	Porsche Carrera	Brumos Porsche-Audi	O-8	210
9	19	David McClain / Dave White	67	Porsche 911S	Havatampa Cigar	U-1	209
10	34	Mike Tilson / Dieter Oest	92	Porsche Carrera	Oest-Tilson Racing	O-9	208
11	16	J.C. Bolanos / Billy Sprowls / E. Lopez	91	Porsche Carrera	Adams Apple	O-10	206
12	33	Charles Mendez / David Cowart	07	Porsche 911T	Charles Mendez, Jr.	U-2	206
13	42	Hans Berner / Willy Goebbels / Fritz Hochreuter	50	Porsche 911S		U-3	200
14	50	John Hotchkis / Robert Kirby / Leonard Jones	51	Porsche 914/6	Max Dial Porsche-Audi	U-4	198
15	35	Bruce Jennings / Bob Beasley	77	Porsche 911S		U-5*e	195
16	14	Tim Chitwood / Vince Gimondo	06	Chevrolet Camaro	Chitwood Racing	O-11	191
17	44	Carlos Moran / Bob Fine / Jamsal	45	Porsche 911S		U-6	185
18	31	Terry Keller / Bob Gray	7	Chevrolet Corvette		O-12	185
19	37	Bill Arnold / Carl Thompson	72	Chevrolet Corvette		O-13*u	182
20	49	Luis Sereix / Ignacio Gonzalez / Gus Robayna	78	Chevrolet Camaro		O-14	178
21	18	Hugh Kleinpeter / Ron Goldleaf	86	Pantera	H.I. Kleinpeter	O-15	176
22	25	John Thomas / Jim Cook	87	Porsche 914/6	R. Mandella	U-7	174
23	72	John Tunstall / Chuck Wade	52	Porsche Carrera	Starbrite	O-16	173
24	45	Ray Mummery / Jack Refenning / George Van Arsdale	27	Porsche 911S		U-8	170
25	65	Tom Davey / Tom Reddy	90	Mazda Cosmo	Ray Walle Mazda	U-9(s)	168
26	69	Anatoly Arutunoff / Jose Marina / Jack May	8	Lotus Europa	Automobiles International	U-10	162
27	63	Bart Hartman / Mark Domiteaux / Don Flores / Tom Turner	3	Austin Marina		U-11	159
28	67	Walter Johnston / Paul Spruell / Jan Petersen	38	Alfa Romeo Alfetta		U-12 (s)	158
29	4	Javier Garcia / George Garcia	15	Chevrolet Corvette	Garcia Brothers Racing	O-17	157
30	40	Pedro Vazquez / John Emig / Ray Gage	5	Porsche 911S		U-13	150
31	7	Don Yenko / Jerry Thompson / Richard Bostyan	19	Chevrolet Corvette	Richard Bostyan	O-18*u	144
32	75	Hal Sahlman / Steve Southard / Alex Job	54	Porsche 914/6		U-14	141
33	57	Dave Smith / Don Herman	81	Chevrolet Corvette		O-19	139
34	54	Tom Ross / Jim Weber	82	Ford Mustang		O-20	138
35	60	George Shafer / A.H. Crookston / Dick Scott	99	Datsun 240Z		U-15*e	129
36	68	Bruno Beilcke / Sepp Grinbold / Alf Gebhardt	03	BMW 2002		U-16*e	126
37	24	Herb Jones / Steve Faul	41	Chevrolet Camaro	Jones Industries Racing	O-21	113
38	58	Neil Potter / William Boyer	49	Ford Mustang		O-22	112
39	66	Charles Kleinschmidt / Jack Andrus	55	MGB		U-17*u	110
40	70	George Drolsom / Bob Nagel	34	Porsche 911S		U-18*t	106
41	12	John O'Steen / Dave Helmick	43	Porsche Carrera	Ecurie Escargot	O-23*e	102
42	53	Nick Craw / John Morton / Joe Peacock	64	BMW 2002	Miller & Norburn	U-19*e	102
43	27	Juan Montalvo / Jim Grob	31	Ford Escort		U-20	102
44	36	Tony Lilly / Frank Marrs	22	Lotus Europa		U-21*e	97
45	41	Eddie Johnson / Clay Young / Gene Felton	47	Chevrolet Camaro		O-24*k	96
46	61	Ron Oyler / Ken Braun / Guy Church	08	Renault 12	Stiles Construction	U-22*u	91

47	9	David Hobbs / Benny Parsons		24	BMW CSL	BMW Motorsport	O-25*u	90
48	22	Mike Meldeau / Bill McDill		68	Chevrolet Camaro		O-26*u	79
49	29	Richard Stone / Greg Gillingham / Frank Fine		21	Ford Shelby		O-27*u	78
50	30	Bob Hindson / Frank Carney / Dick Davenport		42	Porsche 911S	Bob Hindson Racing	U-23*a	77
51	51	Mike Williamson / L.P. Pleasants / Charles Gano		96	Chevrolet Camaro		O-28*u	74
52	55	Jim Alspagh / William McVey		97	Chevrolet Corvette		O-29*s	64
53	8	Jim Trueman / Bobby Rahal		05	Chevrolet Monza	Red Roof Inns	O-30*s	63
54	38	Ford Smith / Bennett Aiken		12	Chevrolet Camaro	Paul Bowden Racing	O-31*e	62
55	26	Rusty Bond / Ren Tilton		60	Porsche 911S	Rusty Bond	U-24*t	58
56	56	Bill Scott / Milt Minter		02	VW Scirocco		U-25*t	54
57	48	Bud Wamsley / Guy Thomas		29	Chevrolet Corvette		O-32*e	51
58	71	Manuel Quintana / Luis Mendez / Ahmed Valhuerdi		46	Ford Shelby		O-33*u	50
59	73	Clark Howey / David Crabtree		73	Chevrolet Corvette	Howey Farms	O-34*u	47
60	21	Wiley Doran / Gary Belcher		39	Chevrolet Corvette		O-35*e	46
61	59	Steve Bond / Dale Kreider		04	Pontiac Astre		O-36*u	46
62	39	Terry Wolters / Wayne Miller / Giuseppe Castellano		18	Chevrolet Camaro		O-37*u	39
63	11	Steve Behr / Janet Guthrie		66	Chevrolet Monza	Big Apple Racing / Champale	O-38*t	38
64	1	Mike Brockman / John Greenwood		76	Chevrolet Corvette	Levitt Racing / Spirit of Sebring	O-39*u	36
65	28	Armando Gonzales / Bonky Fernandez		26	Lotus Elan		U-26*u	28
66	52	Aubrey Bowles		17	Porsche 911S		U-27*u	21
67	23	R.V. Shulnberg / Bud Sherk		40	Chevrolet Corvette		O-40*u	11
68	62	Luis Mendez		63	BMW 2002		U-28*u	11
69	47	Tico Almeida / Pepe Romero		36	Chevrolet Camaro		O-41*u	10
70	43	William Frates		01	Datsun 240Z	William Frates	U-29*a	6
71	32	Tony Ansley		9	Chevrolet Corvette		O-42*e	6
72	74	Don Nooe		79	Ford Shelby		O-43*e	2
73	20	Ralph Noseda		71	Chevrolet Camaro		O-44*e	1
74	46	Dennis Stefl		33	Chevrolet Corvette		O-45*e	1
75	64	Skip Grenier		75	Mazda RX-2		U-30*u	0
DNS		Rick Mancuso / Burt Greenwood		37	Chevrolet Corvette		accident	
DNS		Harry Theodoracopulos / M. Jourdain		2	Chevrolet Monza		steering arm	
DNS		Bob Bergstrom / Bill Show		4	Honda Civic	C.A.C.I.	withdrew	
DNS		Larry Flynn / Larry Bock		93	Chevrolet Camaro	J.E. Logan	withdrew	
DNS		Jim Logan / Bobbie Johnson		83	BMW CSL		withdrew	
DNS		Brian Goellnicht / Louis McAlpine		10	Ferrari Dino		withdrew	

*Not running at finish
(s) = Showroom Stock

Average Speed: 99.667 mph
Fastest Qualifier: #76 Greenwood 111.470 mph
Distance: 1,196 miles
Fastest Lap: #76 Greenwood 109.658 mph
Margin of Victory: 2 laps
Total Purse: $32,500
Lap Leaders: #76 1-15; #24 16-63; #14 64-71, 157-230; #61 72-122; #56 123-156.
Winner's Share: $5,000
Attendance: 24,000 (est.)
Weather: Sunny and warm

1976 HOURLY STANDINGS — TOP 10

GRID		POS.	1 HR.	2 HRS.	3 HRS.	4 HRS.	5 HRS.	6 HRS.	7 HRS.	8 HRS.	9 HRS.	10 HRS.	11 HRS.	Finish
#76	2:47.93	1	24	24	24	61	61	61	61	14	14	14	14	14
#59	2:50.60	2	14	14	14	30	30	56	14	56	11	11	11	11
#14	2:54.29	3	61	56	61	56	56	14	56	11	56	56	30	30
#15	2:55.65	4	30	61	56	11	11	11	11	30	30	30	56	56
#11	2:56.97	5	56	66	58	24	14	30	30	61	58	58	58	58
#61	2:57.69	6	43	58	30	14	58	58	58	58	44	44	44	44
#19	2:57.94	7	66	30	11	58	44	44	44	44	61	61	61	59
#05	2:58.73	8	11	43	44	44	87	87	87	67	77	59	59	61
#24	2:59.30	9	15	44	67	67	67	67	67	77	67	67	67	67
#56	2:59.68	10	58	11	87	87	24	77	77	87	92	92	92	92

1977

1977 SEBRING WINNER —
Porsche Carrera RSR
Built by Porsche / Entered by
George Dyer Racing, CA.
Chassis No. 4609048;
Engine: 3.0 liter, 6 cyl. Porsche
Drivers: George Dyer,
Brad Frisselle

25TH ANNUAL 12 HOURS OF SEBRING / MARCH 19, 1977

POS.	ST.	DRIVERS	NO.	MAKE	ENTRANT / TEAM	CLASS	LAPS
1	7	George Dyer / Brad Frisselle	30	Porsche Carrera	George Dyer Racing	O-1	234
2	11	Diego Febles /Hiram Cruz	58	Porsche Carrera	Diego Febles Racing	O-2	229
3	1	Jim Busby / Peter Gregg	61	Porsche 934	Brumos Racing	O-3	229
4	4	Gary Belcher / John Gunn	09	Porsche 934	Belcher Racing	O-4	228
5	2	Ted Field / Danny Ongais / Hurley Haywood	0	Porsche 934	Vasek Polak / Interscope Racing	O-5	218
6	19	Klaus Bytzek / Rudy Bartling	9	Porsche Carrera	Bytzek Racing	O-6	217
7	16	Tom Frank / Carl Shafer	24	Porsche Carrera	Executive Industries	O-7	214
8	51	Fritz Hochreuter / Gerhard Hirsch / Rainer Brezinka	50	Porsche 911S		U-1	203
9	69	Ray Mummery / Jack Refenning / Joe Hamilton	27	Porsche 911S	Miami Auto Racing	U-2	203
10	17	Charles Mendez / David Cowart	07	Porsche Carrera	Morrison's, Inc.	O-8	197
11	43	Phil Francis / Eugenio Matienzo / Tom Nowling	78	Chevrolet Camaro		O-9	196
12	31	Wiley Doran / Jim Barnett / Charles Pelz	39	Chevrolet Corvette	Wiley Doran	O-10	194
13	41	B. Nylander / Gary Nylander / Michael Hammond	11	Porsche 911S	Motoring Enthusiasts	U-3	191
14	56	M.L. Speer / Windle Turley	70	Porsche 911S		U-4	188
15	27	Rusty Bond / Ren Tilton	60	Porsche 911S	R&R Racing	U-5	187
16	24	Bill Arnold / Billy Hagan	72	Chevrolet Corvette	Bill Arnold Racing	O-11	185
17	10	John Morton / Bob Carradine	65	Ferrari Daytona	Modena Sports Cars	O-12	184
18	29	Bob Bergstrom / Jim Cook	01	Porsche 911	Sports Ltd. Racing	U-6	183
19	35	Gary Mesnick / Dana Roehrig / David Panaccione	06	Porsche 911T		U-7	182
20	61	Anatoly Arutunoff / Jose Marina / Brian Goellnicht	7	Lancia Stratos	Hallet Motor Racing Circuit	U-8	178
21	39	Sam Fillingham / K.P. Jones / Mike Williamson	49	Chevrolet Corvette	Fillingham Racing	O-13	175
22	6	Jim Trueman / Jerry Thompson / Don Yenko	05	Chevrolet Monza	Red Roof Inns	O-14*u	172
23	3	Rick Mancuso / Burt Greenwood / John Greenwood	76	Chevrolet Corvette	Mancuso Chevrolet	O-15	167
24	32	Robert Kirby / John Hotchkis	51	Porsche 914/6	Kirby-Hotchkis Racing	U-9*u	164
25	60	Tom Ross / Paul Tavilla	82	Ford Mustang		O-16	161
26	49	Tony Ansley / Charlie Gano / Ron Connelly	94	Chevrolet Corvette		O-17*u	160
27	47	Clark Howey / Dale Koch / David Crabtree	73	Chevrolet Corvette	Howey Farms	O-18*a	157
28	37	John Hulen / Ron Coupland / Dave Causey	85	Porsche 914/6		U-10	157
29	14	Dick Smothers / Milt Minter / Bob Bondurant	64	Ferrari Daytona	Ramsey Ferrari	O-19*a	151
30	40	Bill Freeman / Paul Newman	2	Porsche 911S		U-11	150
31	44	Hans Berner / Willy Goebbels	10	Porsche Carrera		O-20*u	148
32	72	Jorge de Cardenas / Juan Montalvo / Tony Garcia	98	Porsche 911S	Conrad Racing	U-12*u	145
33	55	Terry Wolters / L.P. Pleasants	08	Porsche 911S	Busch Beer	U-13*	144
34	62	Neil Potter / William Boye	44	Ford Mustang		O-21	142
35	42	Jack Swanson / Wayne Miller	18	Chevrolet Camaro	Terry Wolters	O-22	138
36	33	Mike Tilson / David Olimpi	92	Porsche Carrera	Mike Tilson Motor Racing	O-23*u	135
37	22	Mauricio DeNarvaez / Alberto Naon	46	Porsche Carrera	Mauricio DeNarvaez	O-24*u	130
38	45	Tim Chitwood / Vince Gimondo / Joie Chitwood, Jr.	17	Chevrolet Nova	Chitwood Racing	A-1*t	128
39	8	Javier Garcia / Jack Baldwin / George Garcia	15	Chevrolet Corvette	Javier Garcia	O-25*a	125

40	38	Bruce Jennings / Bill Bean	77	Porsche 911S		U-14*u 123
41	63	Paul Bowden / Jimmy Tumbleston / Ken LaGrow	31	Chevrolet Camaro		O-26*t 122
42	58	Bill King / Jon Lehew	22	Datsun 240Z	Angel's Auto World	U-15*u 120
43	26	Carm Solomone / Fred Lang	80	Chevrolet Camaro	Carmon Solomone	O-27*u 116
44	66	Ronald Oyler / Carlos Muratti / Martinas Smit	03	Renault R-12		U-16 109
45	12	Hugh Kleinpeter / Jef Stevens	86	Pantera		O-28*t 93
46	59	Vince DiLella / Manuel Cueto	20	Porsche 914/4		U-17*u 93
47	53	George Shafer / Dick Scott	99	Datsun 240Z		U-18*u 89
48	64	Mark Leuzinger / Dave Redszus / Mike Vanderwerff	4	Pantera		O-29*u 89
49	48	Hal Sahlman / Preston Henn / Steve Cook	54	Porsche 914/6		U-19*u 81
50	34	Chip Mead / Tom Bagley	71	Porsche 911S	The Foreign Exchange	U-20*t 77
51	13	Bob Beasley / George Stone	8	Porsche Carrera		O-30*e 74
52	25	Harry Jones / Michael Keyser	1	Ferrari Daytona		O-31*t 66
53	50	Tico Almeida / Rene Rodriguez / Manuel Quintana	36	Chevrolet Camaro		O-32*u 62
54	21	John Carusso / Luis Sereix / Emory Donaldson	48	Chevrolet Corvette	Autodyne	O-33*u 59
55	5	Rick Hay / Phil Currin / Rob Hoskins	68	Chevrolet Corvette		O-34*e 53
56	18	Ralph Noseda / Rich Small / Jeff Loving	66	Chevrolet Camaro		O-35*u 49
57	23	Dave White / Dave McClain	67	Porsche 911S	Havatampa Cigars	U-21*a 48
58	52	Bonky Fernandez / Manuel Godinez / Juan Ferrer	29	Lotus Elan		U-22*u 47
59	46	Rick Thompkins / Jim Fitzgerald	55	Chevrolet Corvette	Rick Thompkins	O-36*u 45
60	71	Marty Hinze / Bob Davis	95	Chevrolet Corvette		O-37*e 42
61	20	Herb Jones / Steve Faul	41	Chevrolet Camaro	Jones Ind. Racing	O-38*u 39
62	65	Gene Budd / Walter Johnston	28	Alfa Romeo Alfetta		U-23*e 38
63	15	Dave Heinz / R.V. Shulnburg	40	Chevrolet Corvette		O-39*t 38
64	54	Pedro Vazquez, Jr. / Bill Wolfe	54	Porsche 911S		U-24*u 35
65	57	Rollie Walriven / Slim Helson	37	Chevrolet Camaro		O-40*u 35
66	67	Charles Kleinschmidt / Guido Levetto	52	MGB/GT		U-25*u 33
67	68	Louie McAlpine / Ernie Smith	26	Alfa Romeo Alfetta GT	Alpha South	U-26*u 26
68	28	Jim Boros	88	Porsche 911S		O-41*a 24
69	9	John Paul Sr.	38	Porsche Carrera	John Paul Sr.	O-42*e 13
70	70	Don Nooe	79	Ford Shelby GT350		O-43*u 10
71	36	Richard Bostyan / Gene Felton	19	Chevrolet Corvette		O-44*u 9
72	30	John Tunstall	57	Porsche Carrera		O-45*s 2
DNS		Dale Kreider / Bob DeMarco	04	Pontiac Astre		withdrew
DNS		Bob Christianson / Ossie DeLay	75	Chevrolet Camaro		withdrew
DNS		Les Delano / John Barringer	83	Porsche 911S		withdrew
DNS		Danny Ongais / Ted Field	00	Porsche 934	Interscope Racing	withdrew

*Not running at finish

Average Speed: 101.322 mph
Fastest Quaiifier: #61 Peter Gregg 112.094 mph
Distance: 1,216.8 miles
Lap Leaders: #0 1-11; #61 12-152; #30 153-234.
Margin of Victory: 5 laps
Fastest Lap: #61 Peter Gregg 111.801 mph
Total Purse: $35,000
Attendance: 27,000 (est.)
Winner's Share: $6,400
Weather: Sunny and warm

1977 HOURLY STANDINGS — TOP 10

	GRID	POS.	I HR.	2 HRS.	3 HRS.	4 HRS.	5 HRS.	6 HRS.	7 HRS.	8 HRS.	9 HRS.	10 HRS.	II HRS.	Finish
#61	2:47.00	1	61	61	61	61	61	61	61	61	30	30	30	30
#0	2:47.61	2	76	9	9	9	9	30	30	30	61	58	61	58
#76	2:49.48	3	68	58	24	30	30	9	9	58	58	61	58	61
#09	2:50.07	4	9	24	7	7	7	7	7	9	9	9	9	9
#68	2:54.56	5	0	46	30	9	46	58	58	9	0	0	0	0
#05	2:55.29	6	30	7	46	46	58	9	9	51	9	9	9	9
#30	2:55.44	7	24	30	76	64	9	46	51	0	51	24	24	24
#15	2:55.79	8	46	86	48	58	1	51	46	24	24	50	50	50
#38	2:58.49	9	58	64	9	15	60	77	0	7	50	27	27	27
#65	2:58.79	10	7	9	58	1	86	0	77	64	27	7	7	7

1978

1978 SEBRING WINNER —
Porsche 935
Built by Porsche / Entered by Dick
Barbour Racing, San Diego, CA.
Chassis No. 9307700910; Engine:
3.0 liter, 6 cyl. Porsche
Drivers: Brian Redman, Charles
Mendez, Bob Garretson

26TH ANNUAL 12 HOURS OF SEBRING / MARCH 18, 1978

POS.	ST.	DRIVERS	NO.	MAKE	ENTRANT / TEAM	CLASS	LAPS
1	5	Brian Redman / Charles Mendez / Bob Garretson	9	Porsche 935	Barbour Performance	X-1	240
2	3	Bob Hagestad / Hurley Haywood	95	Porsche 935	Bob Hagestad	X-2	240
3	8	Hal Shaw Jr. / Tom Spalding	13	Porsche 935	Ore-House / Vail / Hal Shaw	X-3	239
4	10	John Paul, Sr. / Bonky Fernandez	33	Porsche Carrera	J.L.P. Racing	O-1	233
5	16	Steve Earle / Bob Akin / Rick Knoop	32	Porsche Carrera	Earle & Akin Racing Assoc.	X-4	225
6	25	Francisco Romero / Ernesto Soto	77	Porsche 911	Bill Scott Racing	U-1	219
7	72	Chiqui Soldevila / Luis Gordillo	42	Porsche 911S	El Sol Racing	U-2	213
8	18	Kenper Miller / Walt Bohren	25	BMW CSL	KWM Racing	O-2*u	211
9	21	Gene Felton / Vince Gimondo	96	Buick Skylark	Unicure	A-1	209
10	52	William Koll / David Hamren / Dennis Sherman	62	Porsche 914/6	William J. Koll	U-3	209
11	45	Cliff Gottlob / Danny Terrill	03	Chevrolet Corvette	Cliff Gottlob	O-3	199
12	58	Steve Cook / Bill Cooper / Ron Southern	99	Datsun 240Z	Robert Bondurant	U-4	198
13	15	Diego Febles / Alec Poole	58	Porsche Carrera	Diego Febles Racing	O-4*u	197
14	48	Terry Keller / Robert Gray / Nort Northam	57	Chevrolet Corvette	Sebring Racing Ind.	O-5	197
15	41	Ron Case / Dave Panaccione / Jack Rynerson	36	Porsche 911	Ron Case	U-5	196
16	42	Fritz Hochreuter / Rudy Bartling / Rainer Brezinka	50	Porsche 911	Fritz Hochreuter	U-6	189
17	12	Luis Sereix / Lyn St. James / Phil Currin	48	Chevrolet Corvette	Autodyne	O-6	186
18	30	Dave White / J. Dana Roehrig / Gary Mesnick	01	Porsche 911	Roehrig Racing Inc.	U-7	185
19	34	Dave Sloyer / Jim Fitzgerald	92	Plymouth Volare	Dave Sloyer / Road Atlanta	A-2	184
20	13	Michael Callas / Peter Papke / Jim Cook	79	Porsche Carrera	Rennsport Porsche Works	O-7	182
21	39	Rusty Bond / Ren Tilton	89	Porsche 911	Barrick Motor Racing	U-8	181
22	64	Stephen Bond / Philip Dann	05	Chevrolet Monza	Saltwater Band	X-5	181
23	40	John Hulen / Ron Coupland / Nick Engels	85	Porsche 914	John Hulen	U-9	174
24	31	Don Whittington / Russ Boy	93	Porsche 934	Whittington Brothers	X-6	172
25	55	M.L. Speer / Windle Turley	70	Porsche 911	Race Car Inc.	U-10	168
26	35	John Higgins / Tim Cooper / James King	71	Porsche 911	Foreign Exchange Racing	U-11	168
27	46	Joseph Hamilton / Chuck Wade / Ron Collins	88	Porsche 911	Hamilton House Racing	U-12	167
28	23	David Cowart / Nick Craw / Giuseppe Castellano	07	Porsche Carrera	Morrison's Inc.	O-8*s	165
29	62	Steve Southard / Jim Trueman	00	Porsche 914	Red Roof Inns Inc.	U-13*u	164
30	68	C.H. Kleinschmidt / Lee Culpepper / Bill Koch	52	MGB	Native Tan	U-14	160
31	67	Vince DiLella / Manuel Cueto	21	Porsche 914	DiLella Racing	U-15	152
32	33	John Hotchkis / Robert Kirby / Dennis Aase	51	Porsche 911	Wynn's International	U-16*u	142
33	50	Robert LaMay / Dick Valentine / Larry Parker	14	Ford Mustang	Robert LaMay	O-9*u	140
34	36	Werner Frank / Roger Schramm	91	Porsche Carrera	Framm Promotions / W. Frank	O-10	140
35	57	Terry Wolters / Wayne Miller	08	Porsche 911S	Terry Wolters	U-17*u	219
36	56	Bruno Beilcke / Sepp Grinbold / Alf Gebhardt	35	BMW 2002	Team Beilcke	U-18	123
37	76	George Garcia / Danny Villarchao	12	Chevrolet Corvette	George Garcia	O-11	122
38	1	David Hobbs / Milt Minter / Tom Klausler	2	BMW 320i	McLaren North America	X-7	119
39	54	Alfred Cosentino / Jim Downing	61	Mazda RX-3	Faza Squadra	U-19	116
40	73	Gary Belcher / Doc Bundy	09	Porsche 935	Belcher Racing	X-8*u	115
41	28	M.F. Meldeau / Bill McDill	38	Chevrolet Camaro	Meldeau Tire Co.	X-9	113
42	74	Kenneth LaGrow / Jimmy Tumbleston	17	Chevrolet Camaro	Kenneth LaGrow	X-10	112

43	69	H. David Redzsus / Merv Rosen	02	BMW 2002	H. David Redzsus	U-20	111
44	66	George Drolsom / Hugh Davenport	34	Porsche 911S	Drolsom Racing Inc.	U-21*e	98
45	32	Bob Speakman / John Maffucci	84	Datsun 240Z	Worldparts	U-22*	98
46	43	Tim Chitwood / Sam Fillingham / K.P. Jones	47	Chevrolet Nova	Tim Chitwood	A-3*t	90
47	67	Pedro Vazquez / Ron Oyler	87	Porsche 911	Pedro Vazquez	O-12*u	83
48	6	R.V. Shulnburg / Dave Heinz / Michael Keyser	06	Chevrolet Corvette	Shulnburg Scrap Metal	X-11*u	83
49	7	Clif Kearns / Marty Hinze / Steve Behr	28	Porsche 935	Desperado Racing	X-12*e	79
50	14	Tom Frank / Bob Bergstrom	24	Porsche Carrera	Executive Ind.	O-13*t	77
51	19	Mauricio DeNarvaez / Albert Naon	46	Porsche Carrera	Mauricio DeNarvaez	O-14*u	76
52	49	Ray Mummery / Jack Refenning / Tom Sheehy	27	Porsche 911S	Miami Auto Racing	U-23*u	70
53	75	Gene Rutherford / Tom Wallace / Kathy Wallace	0	Oldsmobile Cutlass	Chesrown Olds	A-4*s	66
54	71	Bill Freeman / Bob Harmon / Byron Leydecker	3	Porsche Carrera	Bill Freeman Racing	O-15*u	62
55	37	Clark Howey / Dale Koch	73	Chevrolet Camaro	Howey Farms	X-13*e	50
56	63	Mark Leuzinger / Mike Van Der Werff	4	Pantera	B.R. Racing Team	O-16*u	48
57	2	Dick Barbour / Rolf Stommelen / Manfred Schurti	6	Porsche 935	Barbour Performance	X-14*s	47
58	20	Javier Garcia	11	Chevrolet Corvette	Javier Garcia	X-15*u	46
59	27	Herb Jones / Steve Faul	41	Chevrolet Camaro	Jones Ind. Racing	X-16*u	45
60	22	Frank Thomas / Lee Mueller / Paul May	76	Porsche 911	Quality Inn	U-24*e	43
61	47	Anatoly Arutunoff / Brian Goellnicht / Jose Marina	19	Lancia Stratos	Hallett Motor Racing Circuit	U-25*u	34
62	17	Bob Beasley / Bruce Jennings	8	Porsche Carrera	Robert Beasley	O-17*u	30
63	44	Gary Steele / Jim Gaeta / Bob Zulkowski	45	Porsche 911	Vann's Auto Body Shop	U-26*e	28
64	26	Richard Bostyan / Jerry Thompson / Don Yenko	20	Chevrolet Corvette	Bostyan Racing Ent.	0-18*u	26
65	38	Mandy Gonzalez / Hiram Cruz / Manuel Villa	30	BMW CSL	Aro-Mandy Racing	O-19*u	25
66	53	Herb Adams / Pat Bedard	80	Oldsmobile Cutlass	Herb Adams Assoc.	A-5*s	21
67	11	Hugh Kleinpeter / Jef Stevens	86	Pantera	Team Pantera	X-17*e	17
68	9	Rick Thompkins / Randy Blessing	04	Chevrolet Corvette	Rick Thompkins	O-20*u	15
69	4	Peter Gregg	59	Porsche 935	Brumos Porsche	X-18*a	11
70	29	Hoyt Overbagh	23	Chevrolet Monza	Overbagh Motor Racing	O-21*e	8
71	51	Rod Bremner	78	Triumph TR7	Ashley-Abingdon Motors	U-27*u	7
72	59	Ted Schumacher	49	Triumph GT6	Schumacher Racing	U-28*u	7
73	70	Ludwig Heimrath	7	Porsche 935	Heimrath Racing	X-19*e	6
74	60	Manuel Quintana	40	Ford Mustang	Quintana Racing	X-20*e	5
75	24	Dale Kreider	1	Chevrolet Corvette	Dale Kreider Racing	X-21*e	4
76	61	Joaquin Lopez	54	Chevrolet Camaro	Raul Garcia	X-22*u	2
DNS		Ralph Tolman / Rick Hurst	98	Saab Turbo	The Racing Team	withdrew	
DNS		Bill Harris / Charley Gano	43	Ford Pinto	Harris Engineering	withdrew	
DNS		Ernie Smith / Gene Budd	26	Alfa Romeo Veloce	Eleven Tenths Racing	withdrew	
DNS		Neil Potter / William Boyer	39	Ford Mustang	Neil Potter	withdrew	

*Not running at finish

Average Speed: 103.978 mph
Total Purse: $62,850
Distance: 1,248 miles
Winner's Share: $8,550
Margin of Victory: 92 seconds
Lap Leaders: #2 1; #95 2-50, 53-137, 150-153; #09 51-52; #9 138-143, 154-240; #13 144-149.
Fastest Qualifier: #2 David Hobbs, 120.205 mph
Fastest Lap: #2 David Hobbs, 121.141 mph
Attendance: 35,000 (est.)
Weather: Sunny and warm

1978 HOURLY STANDINGS — TOP 10

GRID		POS.	1 HR.	2 HRS.	3 HRS.	4 HRS.	5 HRS.	6 HRS.	7 HRS.	8 HRS.	9 HRS.	10 HRS.	11 HRS.	Finish
#2	2:35.73	1	95	95	95	95	95	95	9	9	9	9	9	9
#6	2:37.60	2	9	13	9	13	9	13	13	13	13	13	13	95
#95	2:40.58	3	24	9	33	9	13	9	95	33	95	95	95	13
#59	2:42.01	4	58	09	13	09	09	58	33	58	33	33	33	33
#9	2:45.27	5	13	33	24	33	33	33	58	95	58	32	32	32
#06	2:48.10	6	09	25	09	58	58	25	25	32	25	25	25	77
#28	2:50.78	7	06	58	58	25	25	32	32	25	32	58	77	42
#13	2:51.99	8	33	24	25	32	32	09	77	77	77	77	58	25
#04	2:53.62	9	25	46	32	46	77	77	42	96	96	42	42	96
#33	2:55.91	10	36	79	79	77	91	91	96	42	42	96	96	62

1979

27TH ANNUAL 12 HOURS OF SEBRING / MARCH 17, 1979

POS.	ST.	DRIVERS	NO.	MAKE	ENTRANT / TEAM	CLASS	LAPS
1	9	Bob Akin / Rob McFarlin / Roy Woods	9	Porsche 935	Dick Barbour Racing, San Diego, CA	X-1	239
2	4	Charles Mendez / Brian Redman / Paul Miller	5	Porsche 935	Busch Beer Racing, Tampa, FL	X-2	238
3	7	Bob Garretson / Gary Belcher / Bob Bondurant	3	Porsche 935	Dick Barbour Racing, San Diego, CA	X-3	235
4	1	Dick Barbour / Rolf Stommelen / Rick Mears	6	Porsche 935	Dick Barbour Racing, San Diego, CA	X-4	234
5	16	Bonky Fernandez / Tato Ferrer / Chiqui Soldevila	38	Porsche Carrera	Boricua Racing, San Juan, PR	O-1	233
6	14	Hal Shaw Jr. / Norm Ridgely	13	Porsche 935	Hal Shaw Racing, Vail, CO	X-5	231
7	28	Horst Kroll / Rudy Bartling	69	Porsche Carrera	Bytzek Automotive, Canada	O-2	230
8	20	Tony Garcia / Juan Montalvo / Alberto Vadia	54	Porsche Carrera	Montura Ranch Estates, Miami, FL	O-3	229
9	27	Lance Van Every / Ash Tisdelle	98	Porsche Carrera	Van Every Racing, Charlotte, NC	O-4	226
10	23	H. Espinosa / Francisco Lopez / Jorge Cortes	37	Porsche Carrera	Honorato Espinosa, Colombia	O-5	219
11	42	Rusty Bond / Ren Tilton	60	Porsche 911	E.J. Pruitt & Sons, Jensen Beach, FL	U-1	219
12	32	Jim Trueman / John Higgins / Chip Mead	39	Porsche 911	Barrick Motor Racing, Dayton, OH	U-2	215
13	39	Roger Mandeville / Amos Johnson / Jim Downing	77	Mazda RX-7	Roger Mandeville, Spartanburg, SC	X-6	213
14	21	David Cowart / Kenper Miller / David McClain	07	Porsche Carrera	Morrison's, Tampa, FL	O-6	205
15	15	Francisco Romero / Ernesto Soto	89	Porsche Carrera	Hector Huerta, Caracas, Venezuela	O-7	201
16	47	Peter Welter / Richard Aten / Jack Refenning	33	Porsche 911	Peter Welter, Vero Beach, FL	U-3	198
17	33	Bonnie Henn / Lyn St. James / Janet Guthrie	2	Ferrari Daytona	Thunderbird Swap Shop, Ft. Lauderdale, FL	O-8	194
18	36	Walt Bohren / James Besmer	70	Mazda RX-7	Walt Bohren Racing, Flemington, NJ	X-7	193
19	18	Roger Schramm / Werner Frank	91	Porsche Carrera	Framm Promotions, Rockford, IL	O-9	192
20	59	Robert Kirby / Wayne Baker / Thomas Winters	51	Porsche 914/4	Personalized Porsche, San Diego, CA	U-4	188
21	56	Terry Wolters / Bob Buchler / Nort Northam	08	Porsche 911	Moran Construction, Orlando, FL	U-5	182
22	19	William Koll / James Cook / Dennis Aase	62	Porsche 914/6	Koll Motor Sports, San Marcos, CA	U-6	182
23	58	David Deacon / Reagan Riley / Hank Franczak	93	Porsche 914/6	Deacon Racing, Atlanta, GA	U-7	179
24	3	John Paul / Al Holbert	18	Porsche 935	JLP Racing, Lawrenceville, GA	X-9*t	176
25	61	Jack Swanson / Dick Gauthier	52	Chevrolet Camaro	Ours & Hours Racing, Sarasota, FL	O-10	158
26	2	Preston Henn / Peter Gregg / Hurley Haywood	09	Porsche 935	Thunderbird Swap Shop, Ft. Lauderdale, FL	X-10*e	157
27	40	Jeff Loving / Richard Small / Ralph Noseda	66	Chevrolet Camaro	Sunset Racing, Miami, FL	O-11*u	148
28	12	Mauricio DeNarvaez / Albert Naon	46	Porsche Carrera	DeNarvaez Racing, Colombia	O-12*u	147
29	30	Dave White / Robert Overby	01	Porsche 911	Roehrig Racing, Tampa, FL	U-8	147
30	72	Ford Smith / Jimmy Tumbleston / Neil Potter	12	Chevrolet Camaro	Ford Smith Racing, Decatur, GA	O-13*e	139
31	53	Bruce Jennings / Bob Beasley	71	Porsche 911	Bruce Jennings, Parkton, MD	U-9*u	136
32	50	George Van Arsdale / Kent Murry	44	Porsche 911	SUD Porsche Racing, Ft. Lauderdale, FL	U-10	131
33	66	J. Dana Roehrig / J. Kurt Roehrig	02	Porsche 911	Roehrig Racing, St. Petersburg, FL	U-11	128
34	49	Guy Thomas / Milton Moise / Tom Nehl	53	Chevrolet Camaro	Guy F. Thomas, Jacksonville, FL	X-11	122
35	5	Ted Field / Danny Ongais	00	Porsche 935	Interscope Racing, Newport Beach, CA	X-12*s	120
36	24	Bill McDill / Tom Frank	43	Chevrolet Camaro	Meldeau Tire Racing, Winter Park, FL	X-13	118
37	57	Steve Faul / Herb Jones / Fred Lang	81	Chevrolet Corvette	Jones Ind. Racing, Ft. Myers, FL	O-14*u	116
38	67	Billy Hagan / Hoyt Overbagh / Ron Reed	29	Chevrolet Monza	Stratagraph, Lafayette, LA	O-15*u	115
39	46	Rainer Brezinka / Gary Hirsch / Fritz Hochreuter	50	Porsche 911	R & H Racing, Ontario, Canada	U-12*u	109

40	68	Mike Ramirez / Manuel Villa Prieto / Luis Gordillo	75	Porsche 911	Mike Ramirez, Guaynabe, PR	U-13*e	108
41	44	Ron Case / Dave Panaccione	36	Porsche 911	Case Racing, Lakeland, FL	U-14*u	106
42	6	Bill Whittington / Don Whittington	94	Porsche 935	Whittington Brothers, Ft. Lauderdale, FL	X-14*a	104
43	35	Bill Scott / Pierre Honegger	72	Porsche 911	Z&W Racing, Princeton, NJ	U-15*u	99
44	13	Dale Whittington / R.D. Whittington / Milt Minter	92	Porsche 934	Whittington Brothers, Ft. Lauderdale, FL	O-16*s	94
45	65	Dave Yerger / Dario Orlando / Del Russo Taylor	88	Alfa Romeo GTV	Day Enterprise Racing, Orlando, FL	U-16*u	90
46	37	John Hulen / Ron Coupland / Bob Speakman	85	Porsche 914/6	John E. Hulen, Indianapolis, IN	U-17*u	82
47	17	Craig Carter / Murray Edwards / Dick Valentine	56	Chevrolet Camaro	Peerless Racing, Indianapolis, IN	O-17*e	81
48	29	Charlie Kemp / Kees Nierop / Carson Baird	23	Ford Cobra II	Kemp Motoracing, Jackson, MS	X-15*e	80
49	41	Ray Mummery / Tom Sheehy / Luis Sereix	27	Porsche 911	Miami Auto Racing, Miami, FL	U-18*u	80
50	10	Ricardo Londono / George Garces / John Gunn	97	Porsche 935	Ricardo Londono, Miami, FL	X-16*u	77
51	55	Anatoly Arutunoff / Jose Marina / Danny Sullivan	8	Lancia Stratos	Automobiles International, Tulsa, OK	U-19*e	75
52	63	George Drolsom / Mark Greb / John Maffucci	34	Porsche 911	Drolsom Racing, Jacksonville, FL	U-20*t	75
53	51	Tico Almeida / Rene Rodriguez / Pepe Romero	03	Chevrolet Corvette	Motorcito Racing, Miami, FL	O-18*e	73
54	38	Hiram Cruz / Juan Lopez / Mandy Gonzalez	31	Porsche 911	Hiram Cruz, Miami, FL	U-21*a	66
55	22	Diego Febles / Phil Currin	58	Porsche Carrera	Diego Febles Racing, Rio Piedras, PR	U-22*u	64
56	34	Bob Bergstrom / Brad Frisselle	79	Mazda RX-7	Sports Ltd. Racing, Woodland Hills, CA	O-20*e	61
57	71	Rick Thompkins / Dave Heinz	04	Chevrolet Corvette	Rick Thompkins, Ft. Myers, FL	O-21*t	49
58	70	Steve Bond / Phil Dann	95	Chevrolet Monza	Ozone Industries, St. Petersburg, FL	O-22*u	37
59	62	Pete Kirill / Gerry Wellik / Carl Shafer	22	Chevrolet Camaro	Oftedahl Racing, Jacksonville, FL	U-23*u	34
60	45	Bob Zulkowski / Gerard Raney	25	Porsche 914/6	Metal Craft Racing, Pleasanton, CA	X-17*f	29
61	54	Ken LaGrow / Bill Boyer	17	Chevrolet Camaro	Kenneth LaGrow, Lake Placid, FL	U-24*e	25
62	31	Darrel Overstreet / Dwight Mitchell	16	Porsche 914/6	Overstreet Racing, Sacramento, CA	X-18*f	23
63	11	Clif Kearns / Gianpiero Moretti	28	Porsche 935	Desperado Racing, Elsinore, CA	U-25*u	19
64	43	Bill Bean	61	Mazda RX-3	Bill Bean, Ormond Beach, FL	X-19*e	17
65	8	Ludwig Heimrath	7	Porsche 935	Heimrath Racing, Ontario, Canada	U-26*e	12
66	60	J.F. Tremblay	57	Datsun 240Z	J.F. Tremblay, Winter Park, FL	U-27*u	11
67	52	Steve Southard	40	Porsche 914/6	Performance Specialists, Columbus, OH	U-28*u	9
68	64	Manuel Quintana	67	Porsche 911	Quintana Racing, Key Biscayne, FL	O-23*e	8
69	48	Sam Fillingham	48	Chevrolet Corvette	Fillingham Racing, Tampa, FL	O-24*e	8
70	25	Carl Shafer	21	Chevrolet Camaro	Oftedahl / Shafer Farms, Wyoming, IL	O-25*u	4
71	26	Alf Gebhardt	15	BMW CSL	Bavarian Motors, Tulsa, OK,	O-26*k	0
72	69	Mark Leuzinger	4	Pantera	B.R. Racing Team, Rockford, IL		
DNS		Danny Ongais / Ted Field	0	Porsche 935	Interscope Racing, Newport Beach, CA	backup car	
DNS		Josele Garza / Bill McVey	14	Porsche Carrera	Precision School Racing, Tampa, FL	withdrew	
DNS		Mike Williamson / Wayne Miller	87	Chevrolet Corvette	U-Mo Racing, Tampa, FL	withdrew	
DNS		Bob Lee / Rick Kump	90	American Motors AMX	Bob's Speed Products, Ft. Lauderdale, FL	withdrew	
DNS		Ken Williams / Wiley Doran	76	Datsun 240Z	Assoc. Speed & Performance, Houston, TX	withdrew	
DNS		Tim Chitwood / Joie Chitwood	47	Chevrolet Nova	Chitwood Racing, Tampa, FL	withdrew	

*Not running at finish

Average Speed: 103.446 mph
Total Purse: $56,000
Distance: 1,242.8 miles
Winner's Share: $10,000
Margin of Victory: 1 lap + 74.17 seconds
Attendance: 40,000 (est.)
Fastest Qualifier: #6 Rolf Stommelen 118.453 mph
Weather: Partly cloudy and warm
Fastest Lap: #6 Rolf Stommelen 117.629 mph
Lap Leaders: #6 1-5, 36-41; #09 6-35; #18 42-173; #9 174-239

1978 HOURLY STANDINGS—MOSLER

	GRID	POS.	1 HR.	2 HRS.	3 HRS.	4 HRS.	5 HRS.	6 HRS.	7 HRS.	8 HRS.	9 HRS.	10 HRS.	11 HRS.	Finish
#6	2:38.03	1	09	18	18	18	18	18	18	18	9	9	9	9
#09	2:39.91	2	18	09	6	09	09	09	09	9	18	5	5	5
#18	2:40.19	3	6	6	00	00	00	9	9	5	5	6	6	3
#5	2:44.43	4	3	3	09	3	3	07	5	09	3	3	3	6
#00	2:45.92	5	97	00	3	9	9	69	07	3	6	38	38	38
#94	2:46.23	6	28	97	9	07	07	5	69	07	38	07	69	13
#3	2:50.17	7	00	9	07	38	89	38	38	69	07	69	13	69
#7	2:50.50	8	9	92	89	89	69	89	3	38	69	13	54	54
#9	2:51.38	9	94	46	38	69	38	98	98	6	13	54	98	98
#28	2:51.49	10	13	38	69	98	5	3	6	98	54	98	60	37

1980

**1980 SEBRING WINNER —
Porsche 935 K3**
Built by Porsche / Entered by Dick
Barbour Racing, San Diego, CA.
Chassis No. 9308900024;
Engine: 2.8 liter, turbocharged 6
cyl. Porsche
**Drivers: Dick Barbour, John
Fitzpatrick**

28TH ANNUAL 12 HOURS OF SEBRING / MARCH 22, 1980

POS.	ST.	DRIVERS	NO.	MAKE	ENTRANT / TEAM	CLASS	LAPS
1	1	Dick Barbour / John Fitzpatrick	6	Porsche 935 K3	Dick Barbour Racing, San Diego, Calif.	X-1	253
2	7	Ted Field / Danny Ongais	0	Porsche 935	Interscope Racing, Newport Beach, Calif.	X-2	250
3	3	Don Whittington / Bill Whittington / Dale Whittington	93	Porsche 935	Whittington Brothers Racing, Ft. Lauderdale, Fla.	X-3	247
4	11	Preston Henn / John Paul / Al Holbert	09	Porsche 935	Thunderbird Swap Shop, Ft. Lauderdale, Fla.	X-4	239
5	5	Bob Akin / Roy Woods / Skeeter McKitterick	05	Porsche 935	Charles Mendez, Tampa, Fla.	X-5	232
6	21	Bob Tullius / Bill Adam	44	Triumph TR8	Group 44, Winchester, Va.	O-1	230
7	6	Bob Garretson / Bobby Rahal / Kees Nierop	9	Porsche 935 K3	Dick Barbour Racing, San Diego, Calif.	X-6	227
8	9	Ludwig Heimrath / Johnny Rutherford / Carlos Moran	07	Porsche 935	Ludwig Heimrath, Ontario, Canada	X-7	224
9	40	Roger Mandeville / Jim Downing / Brad Frisselle	77	Mazda RX-7	Mandeville Racing, Spartanburg, S.C.	U-1	222
10	2	Bruce Leven / Peter Gregg / Hurley Haywood	86	Porsche 935	Bayside Disposal Racing, Seattle, Wash.	X-8	220
11	24	Luis Mendez / Jaime Rodriguez / Ernesto Soto	68	Porsche Carrera	Porsche Montecarlo, Dominican Republic	O-2*u	216
12	28	Werner Frank / James Brolin	03	Porsche 934	Toyota Village, Elgin, Ill.	O-3	213
13	35	Roger Schramm / Rudy Bartling	92	Porsche Carrera	Framm Promotions, Rockford, Ill.	O-4	213
14	59	Mike Ramirez / Manuel Villa / Luis Gordillo	95	Porsche 911	Mike Ramirez, Puerto Rico	U-2	212
15	34	Sam Posey / George Alderman / Fred Stiff	96	Datsun 240Z	NTS Racing, Hockessin, Del.	U-3	211
16	18	Honorato Espinosa / Jorge Cortes	37	Porsche Carrera	Botero Racing, Colombia	O-5	211
17	50	Mark Welch / Tom Winters / Jim Cook	81	Mazda RX-7	Trinity Racing, Westminster, Calif.	U-4	210
18	76	George Drolsom / Bill Johnson / Rob Hoskins	34	Porsche 911	Drolsom Racing, Jacksonville, Fla.	U-5	206
19	49	Rick Borlase / Don Kravig / Michael Hammond	56	Porsche 911	Rick Borlase, Las Vegas, Nev.	O-6	205
20	71	Gary Hirsch / Ray Brezinka / Peter Aschenbrenner	22	Porsche 914/6	R & H Racing, Ontario, Canada	U-6	205
21	33	Lance Van Every / Ash Tisdelle	98	Porsche 911	Van Every Racing, Charlotte, N.C.	O-7	194
22	72	Bob Lee / Rick Kump / Jim Leo	90	AMC AMX	Bob's Speed Products, Ft. Lauderdale, Fla.	O-8	191
23	26	Tony Garcia / Albert Naon / Terry Herman	54	Porsche Carrera	Montura Racing, Miami, Fla.	O-9*e	187
24	74	Klaus Bitterauf / James Moxley / Vicki Smith	87	Porsche 911	Der Klaus Haus, Ft. Lauderdale, Fla.	U-7	185
25	60	Juan Lopez / Jose Arzeno	31	Porsche 911	Lopez Brothers, Dominican Republic	U-8	179
26	43	Mauricio DeNarvaez / Ricardo Londono	46	Porsche Carrera	DeNarvaez Enterprises, Colombia	O-10*	177
27	4	Gianpiero Moretti / Giorgio Pianta / Renzo Zorzi	30	Porsche 935	Electrodyne / Moretti, Italy	X-9*e	176
28	78	Vince DiLella / Manuel Cueto	24	Porsche 914/6	DiLella Racing, Hialeah, Fla.	U-9*u	172
29	30	Bill Ferran / Rusty Bond / Jack Refenning	60	Porsche Carrera	Bill Ferran, Ormond Beach, Fla.	O-11	172
30	14	David Cowart / Kenper Miller / Derek Bell	25	BMW M-1	Red Lobster Racing, Tampa, Fla.	X-10	172
31	10	Maurice Carter / Craig Carter / Murray Edwards	80	Chevrolet Camaro	All Canadian / Peerless Racing, Canada	X-11*u	167
32	61	Warwick Henderson / Bob Copeman / J. Humphreys	49	Porsche Carrera	Tortilla Flats Racing, Stockton, Calif.	O-12	166
33	64	Wayne Baker / Dan Gilliland / Jeffrey Scott	57	Porsche 914/4	Personalized Porsche, San Diego, Calif.	U-10	163
34	63	Bruce Nesbitt / Alan Johnson	78	Mazda RX-2	Revolution Wheels, Chicago, Ill.	U-11	162
35	68	Ray Ratcliff / M.L. Speer / Terry Wolters	08	Porsche 911	Moran Construction, Dallas, Tex.	U-12*u	161
36	47	Russ Boy / Tom Hunt	99	Chevrolet Corvette	National Jets, Ft. Lauderdale, Fla.	O-13	160
37	62	Robert Kirby / Fred Baker / Michael Sherwin	51	Porsche Carrera	Kilby-Hitchcock Racing, Los Angeles, Calif.	O-14*u	153
38	38	Bob Bergstrom / Pat Bedard	79	Mazda RX-7	Sports Ltd. Racing, Woodland Hills, Calif.	U-13	148
39	48	Herb Adams / Jerry Thompson	88	Pontiac Fire-Am	Herb Adams, Carmel, Calif.	O-15*u	146
40	54	Bard Boand / Robert Kivela / Raymond Irwin	84	Chevrolet Corvette	Bard Boand Racing, Barrington, Ill.	O-16	140
41	77	Kenneth LaGrow / Bill Boyer / Jack Turner	27	Chevrolet Camaro	Holley & LaGrow, Lake Placid, Fla.	X-12	138
42	19	Mandy Gonzalez / Diego Febles / Chiqui Soldevila	58	Porsche 934	Coco Lopez, San Juan, P.R.	O-17	135
43	28	John Casey / Stephen Dietrich / Lee Mueller	82	Mazda RX-7	Trinity Racing, Westminster, Calif.	U-14*x	123
44	37	Pierre Honegger / M. Hutchins / Walt Bohren	73	Mazda RX-7	Z & W Enterprises, Princeton, N.J.	U-15*u	118
45	41	James Mullen / Paul Fassler / Craig Siebert	06	Porsche Carrera	Fassler-Mullen Racing, Needham, Mass.	O-18*u	108

46	39	Joe Cotrone / Emory Donaldson / Phil Currin	40	Chevrolet Corvette	Joe Cotrone, Plantation, Fla.	O-19	106
47	25	Bob Young / Bob Lazier	21	Chevrolet Camaro	Oftedahl Trucking, Colorado Springs, Co.	O-20*u	101
48	8	Jim Busby / Bruce Jenner / Rick Knoop	3	BMW M-1	Jim Busby Industries, Laguna Beach, Calif.	X-13*t	100
49	15	Ralph Kent Cooke / Lyn St. James	55	Porsche 935	Condor Racing, Los Angeles, Calif.	X-14*e	87
50	51	Chris Doyle / Charles Guest / Mike Meyer	70	Mazda RX-7	Chris Doyle, Jupiter, Fla.	U-16*u	87
51	52	Lou Statzer / Amos Johnson / Dennis Shaw	7	Spirit AMX	Caribbean AMC / Jeep, Raleigh, N.C.	X-15*e	84
52	42	Jamsal / Carlos Pineda	32	Porsche Carrera	Scorpio Racing, El Salvador	O-21*t	80
53	20	Dave Heinz / Bob Nagel	10	Chevrolet Camaro	Oftedahl Trucking, Tampa, Fla.	O-22*e	74
54	22	Bonky Fernandez / Tato Ferrer / Ulrich Lange	38	Porsche Carrera	Boricua Racing, San Juan, P.R.	O-23*u	73
55	70	Bob Zulkowski / Dennis Brisken / Gary Nylander	23	Porsche 914/6	Metalcraft Racing, Pleasanton, Calif.	U-17*u	73
56	75	Bruce Jennings / Bill Bean / Tom Ashby	71	Porsche 911	Bruce Jennings, Parkton, Md.	U-18*u	69
57	46	David Deacon / Peter Moennick	83	Porsche Carrera	David Deacon, Toronto, Canada	O-24*e	63
58	53	Alf Gebhardt / Bruno Beilcke	15	BMW CSL	Bavarian Motors, Tulsa, OK	O-25*u	63
59	63	George Garcia / Vic Shinn / Daniel Vilarchao	14	Chevrolet Corvette	George Garcia, Miramar, Fla.	O-26*u	63
60	16	Buzz Marcus / Bob Harmon / Marty Hinze	4	Porsche 935	Dick Barbour Racing, San Diego, Calif.	X-16*a	52
61	13	Randolph Townsend / John Morton	13	Porsche 935	Andial Racing, Rancho Santa Fe, Calif.	X-17*u	52
62	79	Del Taylor / Janis Taylor / Dave Cavenaugh	35	Alfa Romeo Alfetta	Del Taylor, Deerfield Beach, Fla.	U-19*u	51
63	17	R.V. Shulnburg / Michael Keyser / Tim Morgan	50	Chevrolet Corvette	Shulnburg Scrap Metal, Tampa, Fla.	X-18*u	49
64	12	Charles Mendez / Brian Redman / Paul Miller	5	Porsche 935	Charles Mendez, Tampa, Fla.	X-19*u	49
65	57	Herb Jones / Steve Faul / Kent Combs	41	Buick Skylark	Jones Ind. Racing, Ft. Myers, Fla.	O-27*e	43
66	66	George Shafer / Craig Shafer / Al Crookston	66	Datsun 240Z	George Shafer, Somerset, Pa.	U-20*u	37
67	31	Ernesto Soto / Luis Rodriguez	89	Porsche Carrera	Hector Huerta Racing, Venezuela	O-28*u	35
68	23	Tico Almeida / Rene Rodriguez / Gabriel Riano	02	Chevrolet Corvette	T & R Racing, Miami, Fla.	X-20*e	33
69	45	Ralph Noseda	65	Chevrolet Camaro	Jeffrey Loving, Miami, Fla.	O-29*u	28
70	44	John Carusso	48	Chevrolet Corvette	Dynasales, Hollywood, Fla.	O-30*e	28
71	69	Ford Smith / Bruce Jernigan	12	Chevrolet Camaro	Performance Marine, Decatur, GA	O-31*e	28
72	56	Anatoly Arutunoff	8	Lancia Stratos	A.I. Honda, Tulsa, OK	U-21*u	23
73	58	John Hulen / Ron Coupland	85	Porsche 914/6	John E. Hulen, Indianapolis, IN	U-22*k	20
74	67	Tim Chitwood	17	Chevrolet Nova	Tim Chitwood, Tampa, Fla.	O-32*e	19
75	32	Robert Overby	28	Porsche 911	Hamilton House Racing, Sarasota, Fla.	O-33*u	12
76	73	Carlos Ramirez	74	Mazda RX-7	Z&W Enterprises, Princeton, N.J.	U-23*u	8
77	36	Vince Muzzin	61	Chevrolet Corvette	Tim Morgan, Northville, Mich.	O-34*e	5
78	27	Nobuhide Tachi	62	Dome Celica Turbo	Tom's / Dome / Kegel Ent., Japan	X-21*e	5
79	55	Dave Panaccione	36	Porsche 911 Sportomatic	Case Racing, Lakeland, Fla.	U-21*u	4
DNS		Bruce Leven / Hurley Haywood	53	Porsche 935	Bruce Leven, Seattle, Wash.	backup car	
DNS		Mark Trumbull / Peter Flanagan	45	Datsun 510	Magic Engineering, West Newton, Mass.	DNQ	
DNS		John Ellerman / D. Londono	39	BMW 2002	John Ellerman, Miami, Fla.	DNQ	
DNS		Manuel Quintana+ / F. Garcia	67	Porsche 911	Quintana Racing, Key Biscayne, Fla.	accident	

+ Killed in practice accident
* Not running at finish

Average Speed: 109.520 mph
Total Purse: $53,375
Distance: 1,315.60 miles
Winner's Share: $14,950
Margin of Victory: 3 laps
Lap Leaders: #6 1-4, 6-62, 146-253; #86 63-145; #93 5.
Fastest Qualifier: #6 John Fitzpatrick, 121.517 mph
Attendance: 40,000 (est.)
Fastest Lap: #93 Bill Whittington, 123.962 mph
Weather: Sunny and warm

1980 HOURLY STANDINGS — TOP 10

	GRID	POS.	1 HR.	2 HRS.	3 HRS.	4 HRS.	5 HRS.	6 HRS.	7 HRS.	8 HRS.	9 HRS.	10 HRS.	11 HRS.	Finish
#6	2:34.06	1	6	6	6	86	86	86	6	6	6	6	6	6
#86	2:34.97	2	86	9	86	6	6	6	86	0	0	0	0	0
#93	2:36.84	3	30	86	9	9	9	0	0	86	93	93	93	93
#30	2:39.75	4	93	93	09	0	0	93	93	93	09	09	09	09
#05	2:41.53	5	9	09	0	09	05	25	9	9	30	05	05	05
#9	2:42.00	6	09	0	05	05	93	9	30	30	9	44	44	44
#0	2:43.57	7	3	07	07	93	30	30	09	09	44	9	9	9
#3	2:44.56	8	0	5	78	07	25	07	07	07	05	77	77	07
#07	2:45.28	9	4	3	25	30	54	09	44	44	07	68	07	77
#80	2:46.09	10	80	05	54	25	09	44	05	05	46	07	68	86

1981

1981 SEBRING WINNER —
Porsche 935
Built by Porsche / Entered by
Bruce Leven / Bayside Racing,
Redmond, WA. Chassis No.
9307700909; Engine: 3.2 liter, tur-
bocharged 6 cyl. Porsche
Drivers: Hurley Haywood,
Al Holbert, Bruce Leven

29TH ANNUAL 12 HOURS OF SEBRING / MARCH 21, 1981

POS.	ST.	DRIVERS	NO.	MAKE	ENTRANT / TEAM	CLASS	LAPS
1	3	Hurley Haywood / Al Holbert / Bruce Leven	86	Porsche 935	Bayside Disposal Racing, Seattle, Wash.	X-1	245
2	10	Roy Woods / Ralph Kent Cooke / Skeeter McKitterick	90	Porsche 935 K3	Cooke Woods Racing, Los Angeles, Calif.	X-2	242
3	12	Marty Hinze / Milt Minter / Bill Whittington	2	Porsche 934/35 K3	Marty Hinze Racing, Davie, Fla.	X-3	240
4	2	Howard Meister / Rolf Stommelen / Harald Grohs	3	Porsche 935	Andial / Meister Racing, Rancho Santa Fe, Calif.	X-4	233
5	19	Chuck Kendall / Pete Smith / Dennis Aase	58	Porsche Carrera	Charles Kendall, Flintridge, Calif.	O-1	218
6	5	Gianpiero Moretti / Charles Mendez / Mauricio DeNarvaez	30	Porsche 935	Momo / Electrodyne, Italy	X-5*k	213
7	61	Timothy Selby / Earl Roe	23	Porsche Carrera	Roe / Selby Racing, Jonesboro, IN	O-2	212
8	40	M.L. Speer / Eddy Joosen / Dirk Vermeersch	73	Mazda RX-7	Z & W Enterprises, Princeton, NJ	O-3	212
9	47	Lee Mueller / Walt Bohren	98	Mazda RX-7	Kent Racing, Lynwood, Calif.	U-1	211
10	41	Bob Tullius / Bill Adam	44	Triumph TR8	Group 44, Winchester, VA	O-4	208
11	77	Mike Ramirez / Luis Gordillo / Manuel Villa	67	Porsche 911	Pennzoil of PR, San Juan, P.R.	U-2	208
12	26	Rene Rodriguez / Tico Almeida / Miguel Morejon	04	Porsche Carrera	T & R Racing, Miami, Fla.	O-5	203
13	23	Albert Naon / Tony Garcia / Hiram Cruz	54	Porsche Carrera	Montura Racing, Miami, Fla	O-6	203
14	16	Mandy Gonzalez / Bonky Fernandez / Juan Cochesa	35	Porsche 934	H.S.M. Racing, San Juan, P.R.	O-7	199
15	58	Jim Downing / Irv Hoerr / Scott Hoerr	50	Mazda RX-7	Downing / Maffucci Racing, Atlanta, GA	U-3	196
16	44	Al Cosentino / Bob Speakman	49	Mazda RX-7	Faza Squadra, Daytona Beach, Fla.	U-4	190
17	4	Bob Garretson / Bobby Rahal / Brian Redman	9	Porsche 935 K3	Garretson Enterprises, Mountain View, Calif.	X-6*a	190
18	32	Dwight Mitchell / Ray Ratcliff / Bill Cooper	45	Porsche 914/6	Autosport Technology, Carmichael, Calif.	U-5*t	189
19	48	Sam Posey / Fred Stiff	28	Datsun 280ZX	NTS Racing, Skillman, NJ	O-8*s	187
20	42	John Kelly / Pat Bedard	4	Triumph TR8	Group 44, Winchester, VA	O-9	187
21	35	George Alderman / John McComb	32	Datsun 240Z	Alderman Datsun, Hockessin, Del.	U-6*s	186
22	65	Bruce Jennings / Bill Bean / Tom Ashby	77	Porsche 911	Bruce R. Jennings, Parkton, Md.	U-7	185
23	37	R.J. Valentine / Maurice Carter	68	Chevrolet Corvette	USA Racing, Braintree, Mass.	X-7	182
24	43	Fred Flaquer / Joe Gonzalez / Angelo Dominguez	05	Porsche Carrera	Miguel Morejon Carol City, Fla.	O-10	182
25	70	Anatoly Arutunoff / Jose Marina	31	Lancia Stratos	Hallet Racing Circuit, Hallet, OK	U-8	177
26	69	Jamsal / Eduardo Barrientos / Guillermo Valiente	84	Porsche 934/35	Scorpio Racing, El Salvador	X-8	177
27	15	David Cowart / Kenper Miller	25	BMW M-1	Red Lobster Racing, Tampa, Fla.	O-11	176
28	59	Steve Dietrich / Tom Winters / Hugh McDonough	81	Mazda RX-7	Trinity Racing, Westminster, Calif.	U-9	174
29	33	George Shafer / J. Craig Shafer / Al Crookston	83	Chevrolet Camaro	George R. Shafer, Somerset, PA	X-9	173
30	53	George Drolsom / Rob Hoskins / Buzz Marcus	34	Porsche 924T	Drolsom Racing, Jacksonville, Fla.	O-12	165
31	50	Kathy Rude / Divina Galica	92	Mazda RX-7	Kent Racing, Seattle, Wash.	U-10*u	160
32	55	Doug Lutz / Dave Panaccione	15	Porsche Carrera	D.L. Performance Eng., Trenton, NJ	O-13	155
33	60	Jack Swanson / Tom Cripe / Van McDonald	52	Porsche 911	Ours & Hours Racing, Sarasota, Fla.	U-11	154
34	36	Bob Gregg / Bob Young / Joe Varde	43	Porsche Carrera	Bob Gregg Racing, Newport Beach, Calif.	O-14*u	153
35	63	Klaus Bitterauf / James Moxley / Jim Leo	88	Porsche 911	Klaus Bitterauf, Boynton Beach, Fla.	U-12	150
36	20	Billy Hagan / Terry Labonte	41	Chevrolet Camaro	Stratagraph, Lafayette, Lou.	X-10*u	144
37	24	Jack Refenning / Ren Tilton / Peter Welter	24	Porsche 934	Jack Refenning, Pompano Beach, Fla.	O-15*u	139
38	45	John Higgins / Chip Mead / Bill Johnson	39	Porsche 911	The Foreign Exchange, Dayton, OH	U-13	136
39	49	Jack Dunham / Tom Sheehy / Luis Sereix	66	Mazda RX-7	Dunham Racing, Coral Springs, Fla.	U-14	136
40	62	John Morton / Tom Klausler	02	Ford Mustang GTP	Firestone Tire & Rubber, Akron, OH	X-11	133
41	1	John Fitzpatrick / Jim Busby	1	Porsche 935 K3	John Fitzpatrick Racing, San Diego, Calif.	X-12*t	129
42	57	Bob Lee / Vicki Smith / Tom Marx	60	AMC AMX	Bob's Speed Products, Ft. Lauderdale, Fla	O-16	128
43	28	William Koll / Jeff Kline	62	Porsche 911	Kegel Enterprises, Carlsbad, Calif.	U-15*u	121
44	7	Ted Field / Danny Ongais	0	Porsche 935 K3	Interscope Racing, Newport Beach, Calif.	X-13*e	117
45	56	Fritz Hochreuter / Rainer Brezinka / Gary Hirsch	53	Porsche Carrera	Fritz Hochreuter, Ontario, Canada	O-17*u	114

46	46	Kenneth LaGrow / Jack Turner	27	Chevrolet Camaro	La Grow / Holley, Lake Placid, Fla.	X-14*a	114
47	25	Jim Mullen / Michael Zimicki	7	Mazda RX-7	Loud Car Racing, Beverly Farms, MA	U-16*u	112
48	18	Preston Henn / John Gunn / Gary Belcher	09	Porsche 935 K3	T-Bird Swap Shop, Ft. Lauderdale, Fla.	X-15*u	107
49	14	Alf Gebhardt / Marc Surer	14	BMW M-1	BMW Challenge Team, Tulsa, OK	O-18*e	106
50	39	Wayne Baker / Robert Overby / Dan Gilliland	57	Porsche 914/6	Personalized Autohaus, San Diego, Calif.	U-17*u	96
51	75	Del Russo Taylor / Rex Ramsey	72	Alfa Chevron GTP	Vince Thompson, Ft. Lauderdale, Fla.	X-16	96
52	13	Chris Cord / Jim Adams	20	Chevrolet Monza	Chris Cord Racing, Beverly Hills, Calif.	X-17*u	94
53	22	D.G. Cummings / Tom Juckette	97	Chevrolet Monza	The Cummings Marque, Ormond Beach, Fla.	X-18*e	94
54	51	Roger Mandeville / Amos Johnson	55	Mazda RX-7	Mandeville Racing, Spartanburg, SC	U-18*t	89
55	27	John Carusso / Russ Boy / Rex Ramsey	93	Chevrolet Corvette	Sanyo / Russ Boy, Plantation, Fla.	O-19*u	89
56	30	Bill McDill / Bob Whitaker	48	Chevrolet Camaro	Meldeau Tire Stores, Maitland, Fla.	X-19*u	85
57	52	Nort Northam / Chiqui Soldevila	29	Porsche Carrera	Bill Ferran, Ormond Beach, Fla.	O-20*u	84
58	91	Jim Cook / John Casey / Bob Bergstrom	82	Mazda RX-7	Trinity Racing, Westminster, Calif.	U-19*u	74
59	67	Jimmy Tumbleston / Robert Dumont / Ford Smith	12	Chevrolet Camaro	Performance Marine Racing, Lake Placid, Fla.	O-21*e	63
60	8	Bob Akin / Derek Bell / Craig Siebert	5	Porsche 935 K3	Bob Akin Motor Racing, Ossining, NY	X-20*u	62
61	72	Pierre Honegger / Pierre Dieudonne / Jean-Paul Libert	75	Mazda RX-7	Z&W Enterprises, Princeton, NJ	U-20*f	60
62	11	Ludwig Heimrath / Ludwig Heimrath Jr.	07	Porsche 934/35	Heimrath Porsche, Ontario, Canada	X-21*u	57
63	66	Doug Grunnet / Jim Burt / Steve Paquette	16	Mazda RX-7	Corp Racing Ltd., Streator, Ill.	U-21*u	50
64	17	David Deacon / Mike Freberg / Rudy Bartling	40	BMW M-1	David Deacon Racing, Ontario, Canada	O-22*u	47
65	9	Don Whittington / Bill Whittington / Dale Whittington	94	Porsche 935 K3	Whittington Brothers, Ft. Lauderdale, Fla.	X-22*u	43
66	6	John Paul / John Paul Jr.	8	Porsche 935	JLP Racing, Atlanta, GA	X-23*s	40
67	31	Lance Van Every	79	Porsche Carrera	Van Every Racing, Charlotte, NC	X-23*u	27
68	76	Rick Borlase	56	Porsche Carrera	Rick Borlase, Las Vegas, Nev.	X-24*u	27
69	38	Angelo Pallavicini	03	Porsche 934	Angelo Pallavicini, Switzerland	O-25*u	23
70	64	Al Levenson	89	Chevrolet Corvette	Vette Brakes, Daytona Beach, Fla.	O-26*w	21
71	78	Joe Cotrone / Kal Showket	42	Chevrolet Corvette	Cotrone Racing Ent., Plantation, Fla.	O-27*u	20
72	29	Jeffrey Loving	85	Chevrolet Camaro	Sunrise Auto Parts, Miami, Fla.	O-28*e	18
73	73	C. C. Canada	61	Chevrolet Corvette	Sharkskin Racing, Camden, SC	O-29*u	15
74	71	Ron Case	38	Porsche 911 Sportomatic	Case Racing, Lakeland, Fla.	U-22*a	2
75	34	Chris Doyle	70	Mazda RX-7	Doyle Racing, Jupiter, Fla.	U-23*u	10
76	74	P. Aschenbrenner	21	Porsche 914/6	Alps Restoration, Ontario, Canada	U-24*u	6
77	54	John Lino	13	Chevrolet Corvette	Garcia Racing, Miramar, Fla.	O-30*e	2
78	68	Janis Taylor	37	Alfa Romeo GTV	Vince Thompson, Deerfield Beach, Fla.	U-25*e	1
DNS		Pierre Honegger / Ernesto Soto	74	Mazda GTP	Z&W Enterprises, Princeton, NJ		withdrew
DNS		Tim Chitwood / Joe Varde	10	Chevrolet Camaro	T.C. Racing, Tampa, Fla.		withdrew
DNS		John Gunn / Paul Canary	22	McLaren M-12GT	Paul Canary, Delavan, Wisc.		withdrew
DNS		Danny Ongais / Ted Field	00	Porsche 935	Interscope Racing, Newport Beach, Calif.		backup car
DNS		Doc Bundy / Paul Miller	36	Porsche 924 Turbo	Herman-Miller P.A., Summit, NJ		accident
DNS		Chris Cord / Jim Adams	19	Chevrolet Monza	Chris Cord Racing, Beverly Hills, Calif.		backup car

*Not running at finish
1 full-course caution for 10 minutes

Average Speed: 106 mph
Distance: 1,274 miles
Margin of Victory: 3 laps + 2 min. 46.2 seconds
Fastest Qualifier: #1 John Fitzpatrick, 125.912 mph
Fastest Lap: #8 John Paul Jr., 125.950 mph
Weather: Sunny and warm

Total Purse: $58,025
Winner's Share: $12,650
Lap Leaders: #86 1, 22-39, 69-84, 199-245; #1 2-21, 40-68, 112-121; #3 85-102; #0 103-111; #90 122-197; #2 198.
Attendance: 47,000 (est.)

1981 HOURLY STANDINGS — TOP 10

GRID	POS.	1 HR.	2 HRS.	3 HRS.	4 HRS.	5 HRS.	6 HRS.	7 HRS.	8 HRS.	9 HRS.	10 HRS.	11 HRS.	Finish
#1 2:28.67	1	86	1	86	3	1	1	90	90	90	86	86	86
#3 2:29.88	2	1	86	3	86	0	90	30	30	2	90	2	90
#86 2:30.81	3	3	3	0	0	30	30	2	2	86	30	90	2
#9 2:34.36	4	0	30	1	1	90	2	86	86	30	2	30	3
#30 2:34.67	5	90	90	9	30	1	86	35	32	3	3	3	58
#8 2:35.65	6	30	9	90	90	86	35	32	3	32	58	58	30
#0 2:35.81	7	07	0	30	9	2	32	3	4	4	98	98	23
#5 2:35.83	8	9	5	2	2	35	0	45	43	45	23	23	73
#94 2:36.80	9	25	35	5	09	32	43	4	45	58	73	73	98
#90 2:36.84	10	20	09	09	35	7	4	43	58	73	67	67	44

1982

1982 SEBRING WINNER —
Porsche 935
Built and entered by JLP Racing, Atlanta, GA. Chassis No. JLP-3; Engine: 2.8 liter, turbocharged 6 cyl. Porsche
Drivers: John Paul Jr., John Paul Sr.

30TH ANNUAL 12 HOURS OF SEBRING / MARCH 20, 1982

POS.	ST.	DRIVERS	NO.	MAKE	DISP.	ENTRANT / SPONSOR	CLASS	LAPS
1	6	John Paul Jr. / John Paul Sr.	18	Porsche 935	3.2	JLP Racing, Atlanta, GA	P-1	244
2	1	Bobby Rahal / Jim Trueman / Mauricio DeNarvaez	46	Chevrolet March 82G	5.7	Garretson Development, Mtn. View, CA	P-2	244
3	13	M.L. Speer / Terry Wolters / Charles Mendez	8	Porsche 935	3.0	JLP Racing, Atlanta, GA	P-3	237
4	20	Diego Febles / Tato Ferrer / Chiqui Soldevila	50	Porsche Carrera RSR	3.0	Diego Febles Racing, San Juan, PR	O-1	235
5	3	Bruce Leven / Hurley Haywood / Al Holbert	86	Porsche 935	3.2	Bayside Disposal Racing, Seattle, WA	P-4	231
6	26	Roger Mandeville / Jeff Kline / Amos Johnson	38	Mazda RX-7	2.3	Mandeville Racing, Spartanburg, SC	U-1	224
7	9	Ray Ratcliff / Grady Clay / Skeeter McKitterick	9	Porsche 935	3.0	Garretson Development, Mtn. View, CA	P-5	224
8	27	Rainer Brezinka / Rudy Bartling / Fritz Hochreuter	39	Porsche Carrera RSR	3.0	R&H Racing, Toronto, Canada	O-2	221
9	66	John Morton / Tom Klausler	01	Ford Mustang	5.0	Marketing Corp., El Segundo, CA	O-3	219
10	23	Tico Almeida / Ernesto Soto / Rene Rodriguez	05	Porsche Carrera	3.2	T&R Racing, Miami, FL	O-4	218
11	60	Earl Roe / Tim Selby	26	Porsche Carrera	2.5	Roe / Selby Racing, Jonesboro, IN	O-5	212
12	5	Bob Akin / Derek Bell / Craig Siebert	5	Porsche 935 K3	3.0	Akin Motor Racing, Ossining, NY	P-6	212
13	29	Jim Downing / Tom Waugh / John Maffucci	63	Mazda RX-7	2.3	Jim Downing, Atlanta, GA	U-2	209
14	34	Doug Lutz / Dave Panaccione	75	Porsche Carrera	3.0	D&L Performance, Trenton, NJ	O-6	205
15	42	Milt Minter / John Bauer	02	Ford Mustang	5.0	Marketing Corp., El Segundo, CA	O-7	194
16	53	Jim Fowells / Ray Mummery / John Carruso	27	Mazda RX-7	2.3	Scuderia Rosso, Miami, FL	U-3	194
17	62	Paul Goral / Nort Northam / Jim Burt	61	Porsche 911	2.5	Paul Goral, Miami, FL	U-4	189
18	4	Ted Field / Danny Ongais	00	Porsche 935 K3	3.0	Interscope Racing, Newport Beach, CA	P-7*e	187
19	32	Joe Crevier / Paul Fassler / Bob Zeigel	21	BMW M-1	3.5	Crevier & Associates, Placentia, CA	O-8	187
20	7	Ralph Cooke / Jim Adams / David Hobbs	7	Chevrolet Lola T-600	5.6	Cooke Racing, Los Angeles, CA	P-8*e	184
21	50	Dudley Davis / Henry Godfredson / Charles Lloyd	77	Porsche 911S	2.5	Dudley Davis, Golden Valley, MN	U-5	184
22	46	Vicki Smith / Klaus Bitterauf / Scott Flanders	78	Porsche 911	2.5	Der Klaus Haus, Ft. Lauderdale, FL	U-6	183
23	30	Jim Busby / Doc Bundy / James Brolin	58	Porsche 924 Carrera GTR	2.0	Brumos Racing / BFG, Jacksonville, FL	O-9	175
24	45	John Rynerson / Van McDonald / H. McDonald	68	Porsche 911	2.5	John Rynerson, Bradenton, FL	U-7	168
25	40	Gary Wonzer / Bill Bean / Chuck Grantham	42	Porsche 911	2.5	Gary Wonzer, Ft. Myers, FL	U-8*u	164
26	17	Janet Guthrie / Desire Wilson / Bonnie Henn	6	Ferrari 512 BB/LM	5.0	NART / T-Bird Swap Shop, Ft. Lauderdale, FL	P-9*e	163
27	10	Marty Hinze / Bill Whittington / Don Whittington	16	Porsche 935	3.0	T-Bird Swap Shop, Ft. Lauderdale, FL	P-10*u	151
28	11	Preston Henn / Dale Whittington / Randy Lanier	09	Porsche 935	3.0	T-Bird Swap Shop, Ft. Lauderdale, FL	P-11*u	146
29	65	George Shafer / J. Craig Shafer / Al Crookston	88	Chevrolet Camaro	5.7	Shafer Concrete, Somerset, PA	O-10	144
30	67	Tom Buckley / Peter Aschenbrenner / Gene Rutherford	07	Porsche 914/6	2.0	Road Runner Racing, Hiawassee, GA	U-9	142
31	31	Don Cummings / Irwin Ayres	97	Chevrolet Monza	5.7	Cummings Marque, Ormond Bch., FL	P-12	141
32	38	Bard Boand / Richard Anderson / Brian Utt	94	Chevrolet Corvette	5.7	Bard Boand, Barrington, IL	O-11	138
33	57	Darin Brassfield / Jerry Brassfield / Bill Cooper	4	Pontiac Firebird	6.0	Oftedahl Racing, San Jose, CA	O-12*u	135
34	54	Uli Bieri / Jean-Pierre Silte / Herman Lausberg	93	Porsche 911S	2.5	Uli Bieri, Ontario, Canada	U-10	127
35	33	Jack Dunham / Luis Sereix	66	Mazda RX-7	2.3	Dunham Trucking, Coral Springs, FL	U-11*a	124
36	37	George Drolsom / Bill Johnson / Tom Davey	34	Porsche 924 Carrera GTR	2.0	Drolsom Racing, Jacksonville,-FL	O-13*u	119
37	35	Angelo Pallavicini / Neil Crang / John Sheldon	03	Porsche 935	3.0	Angelo Pallavicini, Switzerland	P-13*u	119
38	51	Ron Reed / Mike Langlinais	96	Datsun 240Z	2.5	Bon Temps Racing, Lafayette, LA	U-12*u	119
39	14	Tony Garcia / Albert Naon / Fred Stiff	54	BMW M-1	3.5	Montura Racing, Miami, FL	O-14*e	116

40	64	Bill McDill / Mike Meldeau / Tom Juckette	81	Chevrolet Camaro	5.7	Meldeau Tire World, Maitland, FL	P-14	104
41	25	Ed Pimm / Walt Bohren / Doug Carmean	51	Mazda RX-7	2.3	Red Roof Inns, Dublin, OH	U-13*u	103
42	49	Bruce Jernagan / Bill Boyer	20	Chevrolet Camaro	5.7	Fuchs-Whitaker, Ft. Lauderdale, FL	P-15*e	90
43	18	Jamsal / Eduardo Barrientos	84	Porsche 934	3.0	Scorpio Racing, El Salvador	O-15*t	77
44	8	David Cowart / Kenper Miller	25	BMW March 82G	3.5	Red Lobster Racing, Tampa, FL	P-16*e	72
45	44	Kenneth LaGrow / Bill Boyer / Jack Turner	69	Chevrolet Monza	5.7	Kenneth LaGrow, Lake Placid, FL	P-17*u	68
46	52	Billy Hagan / Gene Felton	44	Chevrolet Camaro	5.7	Stratagraph, Lafayette, LA	O-16*e	63
47	47	Ron Case / Michael Barry / Angelo Pizzagelli	30	Porsche 911	2.5	Case Racing, Lakeland, FL	U-14*u	62
48	12	Carson Baird / Tom Pumpelly / Chip Mead	65	Ferrari 512 BB/LM	5.0	Prancing Horse Farms, Lorton, VA	P-18*u	59
49	63	Del Taylor / Wayne Dassinger	74	Buick Chevron B23 GTP	3.5	Mark Wagoner, Deerfield Bch., FL	P-19*e	52
50	36	Luis Gordillo / Manuel Prieto / Mandy Gonzalez	40	Porsche Carrera RSR	3.0	Manuel Villa, San Juan, PR	O-17*u	56
51	19	Tom Winters / Robert Overby / Bob Bergstrom	79	Porsche 924 Carrera GTR	2.0	ProMotion / Whitehall, Tucson, AZ	O-18*u	55
52	58	Bob Raub / Tony Brassfield / Carl Shafer	10	Pontiac Firebird	6.0	Oftedahl Racing, San Jose, CA	O-19*e	52
53	28	Luis Mendez / R. Sanchez	87	Mazda RX-7	2.3	R. Sanchez Racing, Miami, FL	U-15*u	50
54	59	Raoul Garcia / Armando Fernandez	23	Chevrolet Camaro	5.7	Superior Racing, Miami, FL	P-20*e	38
55	22	Jim Cook / Jim Mullen	82	Mazda RX-7	2.3	Trinity Racing, Westminster, CA	U-16*s	36
56	55	Tim Lee / Al White / Craig Pearce	15	Mercury Capri	2.0	Tim Lee, Tampa, FL	U-17*u	36
57	43	Fomfor / Guillermo Valiente	53	BMW CSL	3.0	Fomfor Racing, El Salvador	O-20*u	27
58	16	Phil Currin / John Carusso	48	Chevrolet Corvette	5.7	Sanyo, Plantation, FL	P-21*e	26
59	56	Ned Skiff / Jim Leo	3	Renault R-12	1.7	Ned Skiff, Ft. Lauderdale, FL	U-18*u	26
60	24	Ash Tisdelle / Lance Van Every	19	Porsche Carrera RSR	3.2	Van Every Racing, Charlotte, NC	O-22*u	23
61	61	Paul Miller	36	Porsche 924 Carrera GTR	2.0	Herman / Miller, Summit, NJ	O-23*e	23
62	21	Hershel McGriff	45	Chevrolet Camaro	5.7	Stratagraph, Lafayette, LA	P-21*e	21
63	48	Bob Lee / Brian Erikson	60	AMC AMX	4.3	Bob's Speed Products, Ft. Lauderdale, FL	O-24*u	18
64	41	Jeffrey Loving	71	Chevrolet Camaro	5.7	Sunrise Auto Parts, Miami, FL	O-25*e	14
65	2	John Fitzpatrick	2	Porsche 935 K3	3.2	John Fitzpatrick Racing, England	P-22*a	7
66	39	Hoyt Overbagh	29	Oldsmobile Starfire	4.2	Oberdorfer Research, Colonial Hts., VA	O-26*e	7
67	15	Dennis Aase	11	BMW M-1	3.5	Kendall Racing, Flintridge, CA	O-27*a	1
DNS		Ted Field / Danny Ongais	0	Porsche 935 K3	3.0	Interscope Racing, Newport Beach, CA	withdrew	
DNS		Bill McVey / David Deacon	28	Chevrolet Camaro	5.7	McVey Racing Ent., Port Charlotte, FL	withdrew	
DNS		Anatoly Arutunoff / Jose Marina	31	Lancia Stratos	2.5	Hallet Motor Racing, Hallet, OK	withdrew	
DNS		Mark Williamson / Charles Gano	57	Chevrolet Corvette	5.7	Capricorn Motor Racing, Orlando, FL	withdrew	
DNS		Tim Chitwood / Joe Varde	17	Chevrolet Camaro	5.7	Tim Chitwood, Tampa, FL	withdrew	
DNS		Werner Frank / Ken Madren	22	Porsche 934	3.0	Toyota Village Inc., Atlanta, GA	withdrew	
DNS		Rick Borlase / Michael Hammond	56	Porsche Carrera	3.2	Borlase Plumbing, Las Vegas, NV	withdrew	

*Not running at finish

Average Speed: 105.401 mph
Total Purse: $65,000
Distance: 1,268.2 miles
Winner's Share: $15,880
Margin of Victory: 2 min. 28.27 seconds
Lap Leaders: #00 1-2, 49-62, 71-87; #2 3-5; #86 6-23, 25-41; #5 24; #46 42-47; #16 88-143; #18 48, 63-70,144-244
Fastest Qualifier: #46 Bobby Rahal, 127.289 mph
Fastest Race Lap: #2 John Fitzpatrick, 121.173 mph
Attendance: 63,000 (est.)
Weather: Sunny and warm

1982 HOURLY STANDINGS — TOP 10

GRID		POS.	1 HR.	2 HRS.	3 HRS.	4 HRS.	5 HRS.	6 HRS.	7 HRS.	8 HRS.	9 HRS.	10 HRS.	11 HRS.	Finish
#46	2:27.06	1	86	46	**18**	00	16	16	16	**18**	18	18	18	18
#2	2:30.23	2	46	**18**	00	16	00	00	00	00	00	46	46	46
#86	2:32.39	3	00	00	86	86	8	**18**	18	8	46	8	8	8
#0	2:33.87	4	**18**	86	16	8	7	8	8	46	8	50	50	50
#00	2:34.32	5	5	5	8	**18**	**18**	46	46	50	7	86	86	86
#5	2:36.05	6	9	16	7	7	50	50	50	05	50	05	05	38
#18	2:36.14	7	8	8	50	50	46	86	05	7	86	00	9	9
#7	2:38.27	8	65	9	05	46	05	05	7	86	38	38	38	39
#25	2:38.60	9	16	7	9	05	86	54	86	16	05	7	39	01
#9	2:39.23	10	7	03	65	03	66	7	38	38	9	9	01	05

1983

1983 SEBRING WINNER —
Porsche 934

Built by Porsche / Entered by
Wayne Baker, San Diego, CA.
Originally 911
Chassis No. 90030; Engine: 2.8 liter,
turbocharged 6 cyl. Porsche
Drivers: Wayne Baker,
Jim Mullen, Kees Nierop

31ST ANNUAL 12 HOURS OF SEBRING / MARCH 19, 1983

POS.	ST.	DRIVERS	NO.	MAKE	DISP.	ENTRANT / SPONSOR	CLASS	LAPS
1	14	Wayne Baker / Jim Mullen / Kees Nierop	9	Porsche 934	3.2	Personalized Autohaus, San Diego, CA	O-1	231
2	6	Bob Akin / Dale Whittington / John O'Steen	5	Porsche 935 K3	3.0	Bob Akin Motor Racing, Ossining, NY	P-1	231
3	7	Hurley Haywood / Al Holbert	86	Porsche 935	3.2	Bayside Disposal Racing, Redmond, WA	P-2*k	229
4	20	Don Courtney / Luis Sereix / Brent O'Neill	61	Chevrolet Monza	5.7	Vista Racing, Miami, FL	O-2	227
5	47	Reggie Smith / Lyn St. James / Drake Olson	22	Aston Martin Nimrod	5.4	Nimrod Racing, England	P-3	224
6	31	Jack Dunham / Jeff Kline / Jon Compton	66	Mazda RX-7	2.3	Mike Meyer Racing, W. Palm Beach, FL	U-1	224
7	40	Luis Gordillo / Manuel Prieto / Chiqui Soldevila	65	Porsche Carrera	3.2	Manuel Villa, San Juan, PR	O-3	224
8	22	Joe Varde / Jack Baldwin / John Casey	82	Mazda RX-7	2.3	Trinity Racing, Westminster, CA	U-2	223
9	41	John Morton / Tom Klausler	01	Ford Mustang	5.0	MRKS Corp. of America, Northville, MI	O-4	222
10	38	Al Leon / Paul Gilgan / Wayne Pickering	35	Porsche Carrera RSR	3.2	Pegasus Racing, Dallas, TX	O-5	222
11	5	Ralph Cooke / Jim Adams / Josele Garza	10	Chevrolet Lola T-600	5.7	Cooke Racing, Beverly Hills, CA	P-4*e	221
12	9	Don Whittington / Bill Whittington	94	Porsche 935 K3	3.2	Henn's Swap Shop Racing, Ft. Lauderdale, FL	P-5	218
13	10	Skeeter McKitterick / Milt Minter	3	Cosworth Grid S1 Plaza	3.3	Grid Motor Racing, Encino, CA	P-6	216
14	79	Peter Welter / Tom Burdsall / Nort Northam	37	Mazda RX-7	2.3	Burdsall / Welter, Vero Beach, FL	U-3	216
15	68	Tim Selby / Earl Roe	23	Porsche 911	2.4	Roe / Selby Racing, Jonesboro, IN	U-4	210
16	61	Ray Brezinka / Rudy Bartling / Roger Schramm	83	Porsche Carrera RSR	3.0	R & H Racing, Ontario, Canada	O-6	204
17	23	Lee Mueller / Terry Visger	92	Mazda RX-7	2.3	Kent Racing, Westminster, CA	U-5	204
18	46	Jim Downing / John Maffucci / Chuck Ulinski	63	Mazda RX-7	2.3	RGP 500 Racing, Atlanta, GA	U-6	204
19	69	Paul Goral / Larry Figaro / Peter Uria	11	Porsche 911	2.5	Paul Goral, Hialeah, FL	U-7	202
20	25	Armando Gonzalez / Hiram Cruz	69	Porsche 934	3.2	Hiram Cruz Racing, Puerto Rico	O-7	201
21	16	Pete Halsmer / Rick Knoop	7	Mazda RX-7	2.6	Racing Beat, Anaheim, CA	O-8*b	199
22	62	M.H.Shaefer / Doug Zitza / Jack Refenning	90	Porsche 911S	2.4	901 Shop, Pompano Beach, FL	U-8	198
23	56	Juan Lopez / Luis Mendez	06	Porsche 934	3.2	Juan Lopez, Santo Domingo, DR	O-9	192
24	39	Jamsal / Eduardo Barrientos / Eduardo Galdamez	89	Porsche Carrera	3.0	Taca El Salvador, El Salvador	O-10	188
25	60	Jim Fowells / Ray Mummery / Steve Potter	27	Mazda RX-7	2.3	Scuderia Rosso, Miami, FL	U-9	185
26	15	Carl Shafer / Carlos Ramirez / Mike Meldeau	14	Pontiac Trans-Am	6.0	Oftedahl Racing, Wyoming, IL	O-11	185
27	48	Jack Rynerson / Van McDonald / Chris Wilder	68	Porsche 911S	2.5	Jack Rynerson, Bradenton, FL	U-10	183
28	52	Dave Heinz / Jerry Thompson / Paul Gentilozzi	57	Chevrolet Camaro	5.7	Dave Heinz Imports, Tampa, FL	O-12	181
29	64	Bob Lee / Timothy Lee / Gary Myers	03	Ford Maverick	3.5	Bob's Speed Products, Ft. Lauderdale, FL	O-13	180
30	73	C.W. Bryant / Alex Priest / Mike Guido	91	BMW 2002	2.0	Bryant & Graham Racing, Boca Raton, FL	U-11	178
31	58	John Higgins / James King / Chip Mead	93	Porsche 911	2.5	Foreign Exchange, Dayton, OH	U-12*e	175
32	66	Ron Case / Craig Case / Dave Pannacione	30	Porsche 911	2.5	Case Racing, Lakeland, FL	U-13	173
33	30	Jim Cook / Steve Dietrich / Al Bacon	60	Mazda RX-7	2.3	Team Morrison, Los Alamitos, CA	U-14*e	168
34	42	Doug Carmean / Don Herman	51	Mazda RX-7	2.3	Red Roof Inns, Amlin, OH	U-15	167
35	50	Deborah Gregg / Kathy Rude / Bonnie Henn	58	Porsche 924 Carrera GTR	2.0	Brumos Racing, Jacksonville, FL	O-14	165
36	45	Phil Byrd / Fred Baker / Robert Kirby	96	Porsche Carrera RSR	3.2	Weld Fixturing, Waterford, WI	O-15	162
37	57	Gary Wonzer / Bil Bean / Buzz Cason	42	Porsche 911	2.5	Gary Wonzer, Ft. Myers, FL	O-16	162
38	77	Ned Skiff / Jim Leo	95	Renault R-12	1.6	Ned Skiff, Ft. Lauderdale, FL	U-17*e	159
39	37	Lance Van Every / Ash Tisdelle	19	Porsche Carrera RSR	3.2	Van Every Racing, Charlotte, NC	O-16*e	153
40	51	Ronnie Bucknum / John Bright	02	Ford Mustang	5.0	MRKG Corp. of America, Northville, MI	O-17*e	153
41	11	Billy Hagan / Gene Felton / Sam Moses	4	Chevrolet Camaro	5.7	Stratagraph, Lafayette, LA	O-18	153
42	71	Vince Di Lella / Manolo Cueto	04	Porsche 911	2.5	Di Lella Racing, Hialeah, FL	U-18	152
43	43	Tom Winters / Bob Bergstrom / Peter Dawe	79	Porsche 924 Carrera GTR	2.0	Whitehall / Promotion, Tucson, AZ	O-19	148
44	21	M.L. Speer / Ken Madren / Ray Ratcliff	24	Porsche 935	3.0	Pegasus III Racing, Dallas, TX	P-7*u	145
45	44	Hoyt Overbagh / Pete Kirill / Paul Romano	49	Chevrolet Monza	5.7	OMR Engines, Colonial Heights, VA	O-20*e	145
46	18	Paul Fassler / Steve Pope	13	Pontiac Trans-Am	6.0	Oftedahl Racing, Needham, MA	O-21*e	142
47	59	Carmen Lista / David Marks / Roy Newsome	18	Chevrolet Camaro	5.7	Diehl Hi-Pro, Tampa, FL	O-22	140

Pos	#	Drivers	Car#	Car	Liters	Team	Class	Laps
48	78	Timothy Lee / Al White / Irwin Ayes	76	Mercury Capri	2.0	Hi Fi Hospital, Tampa, FL	U-19	140
49	82	Doug Lutz / Mike Brummer / Larry Connor	15	Porsche Carrera RSR	3.2	DL Performance Engineering, Trenton, NJ	O-23	139
50	29	Paul Miller / Jim Busby / Ron Grable	36	Porsche 924 Carrera GTR	2.0	Herman & Miller P&A, Morristown, NJ	O-24*e	132
51	76	Robert Gottfried / Tom Turner / Don Flores	87	Porsche 911	2.4	Don Flores, Jacksonville, FL	U-20	131
52	4	Marty Hinze / Randy Lanier / Terry Wolters	16	Chevrolet March 83G	5.7	Hinze Fencing, Davie, FL	P-8*e	128
53	36	Karl Keck / Bill McDill / Robert Whitaker	33	Chevrolet Corvette	5.7	Karl Keck, Melbourne, FL	O-25	128
54	33	Robert Overby / Don Bell / Chris Doyle	29	Chevrolet Camaro	5.7	Overby's, Jacksonville, FL	O-26*e	127
55	80	Cameron Worth / Alan Crouch / Janis Taylor	75	Ford Pinto	2.4	Bryant & Graham Racing, Pompano Beach, FL	U-21	127
56	1	John Paul, Jr. / Derek Bell / Michael Andretti	09	Porsche 935	3.2	Henn's Swap Shop Racing, Ft. Lauderdale, FL	P-9*e	125
57	28	Steve Shelton / Tom Shelton	8	Ferrari 512BB	5.0	Shelton Ferrari, Ft. Lauderdale, FL	P-10*x	120
58	2	Bob Tullius / Bill Adam	44	Jaguar XJR-5	5.3	Group 44, Winchester, VA	P-11*e	95
59	55	George Drolsom / Steve Cohen / Bill Gellis	34	Porsche 924 Carrera GTR	2.0	Drolsom Racing, Jacksonville, FL	O-27*e	94
60	24	Tom Nehl / Nelson Silcox / Patty Moise	26	Chevrolet Camaro	5.7	Centurion Leasing, Jacksonville, FL	O-28*t	92
61	12	Victor Gonzalez / Drake Olson	21	Aston Martin Nimrod	5.4	Nimrod Racing, England	P-12*e	86
62	13	Tico Almeida / Ernesto Soto	05	Porsche Carrera RSR	3.2	T&R Racing, Miami, FL	P-13*a	82
63	72	Santiago Londono / Carlos Munoz / Hugo Gralia	99	Porsche Carrera	3.0	Londono Bridge Racing, Miami, FL	O-29*a	81
53	36	Paul Canary / Jim Sanborn	20	Pontiac Firebird	6.0	Paul Canary Racing, Delavan, WI	O-30*t	78
65	67	Dick Gauthier / Tom Cripe / Ron Collins	52	Porsche 911	2.5	TFC Racing, Sarasota, FL	U-22*u	67
66	17	Pierre Honegger / Walt Bohren	77	Mazda GTP	2.6	Z & W Enterprises, Princeton, NJ	P-14*x	61
67	54	Marcus Opie / Tim Morgan / Grant Bradey	64	Chevrolet Corvette	5.7	Marcus Opie, Rogers City, MI	O-31*e	59
68	63	Klaus Bitterauf / Vicki Smith / Scott Flanders	78	Porsche 911	2.4	Der Klaus Haus, Ft. Lauderdale, FL	U-23*t	59
69	19	Fomfor / Arnoldo Kreysa	28	BMW M-1	3.5	Air Florida/Team El Salvador	O 32*a	58
70	26	Roger Mandeville / Amos Johnson / Danny Smith	38	Mazda RX-7	2.3	Mandeville Auto/Tech., Spartanburg, SC	U-24*k	56
71	75	Reynaldo Fernandez / Daniel Vilarchao	54	Chevrolet Camaro	5.7	Daniel Vilarchao, Miami Lakes, FL	O-33*a	56
72	32	J. Craig Shafer / George Shafer / Joseph Maloy	6	Chevrolet Camaro	5.7	Shafer Motor Racing, Somerset, PA	O-34*b	55
73	49	Del Taylor	74	Buick Chevron B23 GTP	3.5	Mark Wagoner, Boca Raton, FL	P-15*e	53
74	34	Don Cummings / Craig Rubright / Charles Gano	12	Chevrolet Monza	5.7	The Cummings Marque, Ormond Beach, FL	P-16*e	50
75	83	David Cowart / Kenper Miller / Mauricio DeNarvaez	25	Porsche March 82G	3.0	Red Lobster Racing, Tampa, FL	P-17*a	46
76	84	Jack Griffin	31	Porsche 914/4	2.0	Pegasus Racing, Dallas, TX	U-25*a	38
77	27	Kikos Fonseca / Tato Ferrer	50	Porsche Carrera	3.2	Latino Racing, San Juan, PR	O-35*e	36
78	65	Bobby Diehl / Roy Newsome	08	Mazda RX-7	2.3	Diehl Hi-Pro Ent., Tampa, FL	U-26*t	26
79	3	John Gunn / Ricardo Londono	39	Chevrolet Phoenix JG-1	5.7	Holly Racing, Miami, FL	P-18*e	26
80	35	Uli Bieri	40	BMW M-1	3.5	Bieri Racing, Toronto, Canada	O-36*a	21
81	81	Fred Flaquer / Gustavo Londono	07	Porsche Carrera RSR	3.2	Londono Bridge Racing, Miami, FL	O-37*e	21
82	76	Billy Dingman	17	Chevrolet Corvette	5.7	Dingman Brothers Racing, Winter Park, FL	P-19*e	11
83	8	Bill Whittington	47	Chevrolet March 83G	6.0	Pepe Romero, Miami, FL	P-20*t	8
84	74	Bill Nelson	62	Pontiac Firebird	6.0	Bill Nelson, Sarasota, FL	O-38*e	1
DNS		Anatoly Arutunoff	80	Lancia Stratos	2.4	Hallet Motor Racing, Hallet, OK		withdrew
DNS		Marty Hinze / Randy Lanier / Terry Wolters	2	Porsche 935	3.2	Hinze Fencing, Davie, FL		withdrew
DNS		Raul Garcia / Eugenio Matienzo	53	Chevrolet Camaro	5.7	Superior Racing Team, Miami, FL		withdrew
DNS		Danny Ongais / Ted Field	00	Chevrolet Lola T-600	6.0	Interscope Racing, Santa Ana, CA		withdrew
DNS		George Alderman / Carson Baird	32	Datsun 280SX	2.8	Alderman Datsun, New Castle, DE		withdrew

*Not running at finish
23 laps run under full-course caution.

Average Speed: 91.273 mph
Distance: 1,097.25 miles
Total Purse: $87,050
Winner's Share: $20,900
Fastest Qualifier: #09 John Paul, Jr. 2:23.96 = 118.779 mph
Fastest Lap: #47 Bill Whittington, 119.790 mph

Lap Leaders: #44 1, 10, 22-26, 41-42, 51-74; #47 2-9; #86 11-21, 27-40, 43-50, 207-220; #16 75-86, 91-94, 96-108, 117, 121-122; #5 87-90, 95, 109-116, 118-120, 123-163; #7 164-198; #3 199-206; #9 221-231
Margin of Victory: 94.802 seconds
Attendance: 56,500 (est.)
Weather: Sunny and warm

1983 HOURLY STANDINGS — TOP 10

GRID		POS.	1 HR.	2 HRS.	3 HRS.	4 HRS.	5 HRS.	6 HRS.	7 HRS.	8 HRS.	9 HRS.	10 HRS.	11 HRS.	Finish
#09	2:23.96	1	86	86	44	16	16	5	5	5	7	7	86	9
#44	2:25.59	2	44	44	86	44	5	16	7	7	3	3	3	5
#39	2:25.68	3	3	16	16	5	86	86	86	86	86	86	9	86
#16	2:26.65	4	5	5	5	09	7	7	3	3	9	9	5	61
#10	2:26.99	5	16	77	7	86	09	09	9	61	61	61	61	22
#5	2:28.45	6	10	7	09	7	24	3	61	9	5	5	65	66
#86	2:28.49	7	77	09	21	21	3	24	63	63	65	65	22	65
#47	2:29.12	8	94	25	24	05	9	9	65	65	82	22	66	82
#94	2:29.13	9	7	21	05	24	19	8	19	19	66	66	82	01
#3	2:30.88	10	13	05	9	9	36	61	16	66	22	82	10	35

1984

**1984 SEBRING WINNER —
Porsche 935**
Built by Porsche / Owned by Joest
Racing / Entered by DeNarvaez
Ent., Colombia. Chassis No. not re-
corded; Engine: 3.0 liter, turbo-
charged 6 cyl. Porsche
**Drivers: Mauricio DeNarvaez,
Hans Heyer, Stefan Johansson**

32ND ANNUAL 12 HOURS OF SEBRING / MARCH 24, 1984

POS.	ST.	DRIVERS	NO.	MAKE	DISP.	ENTRANT / SPONSOR	CLASS	LAPS
1	16	Mauricio DeNarvaez / Hans Heyer / Stefan Johansson	48	Porsche 935	3.2t	DeNarvaez Enterprises, Colombia	P-1	263
2	64	Randy Lanier / Bill Whittington / Marty Hinze	57	Chevrolet March 83G	5.7	Blue Thunder Racing, Davie, FL	P-2	261
3	5	A.J. Foyt / Bob Wollek / Derek Bell	6	Porsche 935	3.2t	Henn's Swap Shop Racing	P-3	258
4	12	Wayne Baker / Jim Mullen / Tom Blackaller	9	Porsche 935	3.2t	Hino Truck, San Diego, CA	P-4	258
5	3	Bob Akin / John O'Steen / Hans Stuck	5	Porsche 935	3.0t	Akin Motor Racing, Ossining, NY	P-5	256
6	6	John Graham / Hugo Gralia / Preston Henn	14	Porsche 935	3.0t	John Fitzpatrick Racing, England	P-6	246
7	10	John Morton / Tony Garcia / Tony Adamowicz	45	Chevrolet Lola T-600	5.7	Conte Racing, Los Angeles, CA	P-7	244
8	15	Billy Hagan / Gene Felton / Terry Labonte	4	Chevrolet Camaro	5.7	Stratagraph, Lafayette, LA	O-1	243
9	36	Jack Baldwin / Ira Young / Robert Reed	76	Mazda RX-7	2.3	Malibu Grand Prix, Malibu, CA	U-1	238
10	34	George Alderman / Carson Baird / Lew Price	32	Datsun 280ZX	2.8	Alderman Nissan, New Castle, DE	U-2	234
11	1	Brian Redman / Pat Bedard	04	Jaguar XJR-5	5.4	Group 44, Winchester, VA	P-8	234
12	52	Ren Tilton / Blake Pridgen / Rusty Bond	7	Porsche 911	2.8	E.J. Pruitt & Sons, Jensen Beach, FL	U-3	234
13	32	Al Bacon / Charles Guest	17	Mazda RX-7	2.3	Al Bacon Racing, Kingsport, TN	U-4	222
14	62	Van McDonald / Dennis Defranceschi	51	Porsche 911	2.8	Chris Wilder, Boynton Beach, FL	U-5	222
15	55	John Higgins / James King / Howard Cherry	71	Porsche 911	2.8	THR Foreign Car, Dayton, OH	U-6	221
16	49	Tim Selby / Earl Roe	23	Porsche 914/6	3.0	Roe / Selby Racing, Jonesboro, KY	U-7	221
17	25	Roger Mandeville / Amos Johnson / Danny Smith	38	Mazda RX-7	2.3	Mandeville Auto Tech, Spartanburg, SC	O-2	221
18	65	Luis Mendez / Chiqui Soldevila / Cristobal Marte	68	Porsche Carrera	3.0	Luis Mendez Racing, Santo Domingo,DR	O-3	217
19	40	Don Marsh / Ron Pawley / Kelly Marsh	93	Mazda RX-7	2.3	Mid-O Racing, Columbus, OH	U-8	216
20	68	Tico Almeida / Miguel Morejon	05	Porsche 935	3.2t	Hi-Tech Racing, Miami, FL	P-9	216
21	42	Tim Morgan / Pete Morgan / Charles Bair	62	Chevrolet Corvette	5.7	Tim Morgan, Royal Oak, MI	O-4	215
22	38	John Jellinek / Stefan Edlis / Tom Brennan	28	Porsche 924 Carrera GTR	2.0t	Budweiser Racing, Waukegan, IL	U-9	212
23	67	Tom Shelton / Steve Shelton / Claude Ballot-Lena	97	Ferrari 512BB	5.0	Tide & Mosler Racing, Ft.-Lauderdale, FL	P-10	211
24	66	Lee Mueller / Terry Visger / John Casey	82	Mazda RX-7	2.3	Trinity Racing, Westminster, CA	U-10	208
25	35	Dave White / George Drolsom / Jerry Kendall	10	Porsche 924 Carrera GTR	2.0t	Dave White Racing, Tampa, FL	U-11	202
26	53	Ron Case / Dave Panaccione	0	Porsche 911	3.0	Case Racing, Lakeland, FL	U-12*u	186
27	60	George Hulse / Jerry Kennedy / Mike Cheung	01	Porsche Carrera	3.0	THR Foreign Car, Dayton, OH	O-5	183
28	33	Craig Allen / George Schwarz / Andre Schwarz	21	Pontiac Firebird	6.0	Oftedahl Racing,-Alberta, Canada	O-6*u	181
29	58	William Boyer / Steve Roberts	26	Chevrolet Camaro	5.7	Steve Roberts, Avon Park, FL	O-7	181
30	23	Diego Montoya / Brian Goellnicht / Michael Roe	43	BMW M-1	3.5	Walker Brown Racing, Miami, FL	O-8	180
31	69	Uli Bieri / Man Gysler / Angelo Pallavicini	40	BMW M-1	3.5	Bieri Racing, Ontario, Canada	O-9	177
32	37	George Shafer / Craig Shafer / Joe Maloy	67	Chevrolet Camaro	5.7	Shafer Concrete, Somerset, PA	O-10	170
33	28	Lance Van Every / Ash Tisdelle	09	Porsche Carrera RSR	3.2	Van Every Racing, Charlotte, NC	O-11*u	169
34	19	Frank Jellinek / Paul Fassler / Jerry Molnar	46	Pontiac Firebird	6.0	Classic Motor Car, N. Hampton, NH	O-12*u	167
35	20	Phil Currin / Steve Gentile / Jim Cook	99	Chevrolet Corvette	5.7	Comp Fiberglass, Gainesville, FL	O-13	161
36	27	David Cowart / Kenper Miller	25	Porsche March 82G	3.2t	Red Lobster Racing, Tampa, FL	P-11*s	158
37	80	Bill Gardner / Jim Durovy	94	Pontiac Firebird	6.0	Tangent Racing, Atlanta, GA	O-14	149
38	7	John Kalagian / John Lloyd	15	Chevrolet Lola T-600	6.0	Kalagian / Ardisana, Folly Beach, SC	P-12*e	148
39	47	Frank Rubino / Joe Rodriguez / David Leira	13	Mazda RX-7	2.3	Rubino Racing, Coconut Grove, FL	U-13*u	146
40	50	Karl Keck / Robert Whitaker / Bill Wessel	83	Chevrolet Corvette	5.7	K & P Racing, Melbourne, FL	O-15	138
41	79	Bob Lee / Gary Myers / Bill Julian	90	Buick Skyhawk	3.5	Bob's Speed Products, Ft. Lauderdale, FL	O-16*u	137
42	74	Larry O'Brien / Mike Van Steenberg	31	Mazda OVS-1	2.3	Import Service Center, Lakeland, FL	P-13*a	137
43	2	Sarel Van der Merwe / Graham Duxbury / Tony Martin	00	Porsche March 84G	3.2t	Kreepy Krauly Racing, South Africa	P-14*e	134
44	9	Claude Ballot-Lena / Hurley Haywood / Al Holbert	86	Porsche 935	3.2t	Bayside / Lowenbrau, Seattle, WA	P-15*e	123
45	57	Dennis Krueger / Tom Hendrickson / Rick Kinner	60	Mazda RX-7	2.3	Roserace / Morrison, Portland, OR	U-14*u	114
46	4	Bob Tullius / Doc Bundy	44	Jaguar XJR-5	5.4	Group 44, Winchester, VA	P-16*s	114

47	11	Gary Belcher / Jean Rondeau / John Gunn	41	Chevrolet Rondeau 382	5.7	Silver Lake Plantation, Miami, FL	P-17*u	109
48	45	Clay Young / Doug Grunnet / Jim Burt	84	Pontiac Fiero	2.5	Dole Racing, Smyrna, GA	U-15*u	105
49	70	Dale Kreider / Roy Newsome / Bobby Diehl	11	Chevrolet Camaro	5.7	Kreider Racing, St. Petersburg, FL	O-17*u	103
50	31	M.L. Speer / Jack Griffin	24	Porsche 935	3.2t	Pegasus Racing, Dallas, TX	P-18*t	96
51	26	Ken Murray / Russ Boy / Dick Valentine	88	Chevrolet Camaro	5.7	Motorsports Marketing, Ft. Lauderdale, FL	O-18*u	95
52	51	Luis Gordillo / Eduardo Salguero / Manuel Prieto	95	Porsche Carrera	3.0	Pennzoil de P.R., San Juan, PR	O-19*t	71
53	59	John Hofstra / Peter Uria / Mick Robinson	69	Porsche 911	2.8	George Shafer, Plantation, FL	U-16*u	69
54	48	Jim Fowells / Ray Mummery / Steve Potter	27	Mazda RX-7	2.3	Scuderia Rosso, Miami, FL	U-17*f	65
55	61	Max Welti / Fomfor / Willy Valiente	18	BMW Sauber C-7	3.5	Team Fomfor Racing, El Salvador	P-19*u	63
56	43	Whitney Ganz / Gene Hackman	55	Mazda RX-7	2.3	Preston & Son, Laguna Nigel, CA	U-18*u	59
57	8	Al Leon / Art Leon	2	Chevrolet March 84G	5.7	Leon Brothers Racing, Dallas, TX	P-20*e	56
58	24	Tom Winters / Bob Bergstrom	79	Porsche 924 Carrera GTR	2.0t	Whitehall / Promotion, Lansing, MI	U-19*u	52
59	75	Buzz Cason / Peter Uria	42	Porsche 911	2.8	Gary Wonzer, Ft. Myers, FL	U-20*u	49
60	14	Ken Madren / M.L. Speer	3	Buick March 84G	4.2	Pegasus Racing, Dallas, TX	P-21*e	44
61	56	Worth Williams / Jimmy Leeward	35	Porsche Carrera RSR	3.0t	G & H Development, Dallas, TX	O-20*u	43
62	18	Billy Dingman / Walt Bohren	47	Chevrolet Corvette	5.7	Dingman Brothers Racing, Winter Park, FL	O-21*u	43
63	39	Alfredo Mena / Jim Trueman	58	Porsche 924 Carrera GTR	2.0t	El Salvador Racing, Coconut Grove, FL	U-21*e	40
64	73	Tim Chitwood	30	Chevrolet Monte Carlo	5.4	Tim Chitwood, Tampa, FL	P-22*u	38
65	78	Klaus Bitterauf / Vicki Smith	78	Porsche 911	2.8	Der Klaus Haus, Ft. Lauderdale, FL	U-22*u	37
66	17	Don Courtney / Brent O'Neill	61	Cosworth Argo JM-16	5.4	Deco Sales, Hialeah, FL	P-23*u	36
67	29	Kikos Fonseca / Jamsal / Diego Febles	85	Porsche Carrera	3.0	Latino Racing, Costa Rica	O-22*e	32
68	30	Jack Dunham / Paul Lewis	66	Mazda RX-7	2.3	Mike Meyer Racing, W. Palm Bch., FL	U 23*e	25
69	54	Ron Coupland / John Hulen	64	Porsche Carrera	3.0t	John Hulen, Indianapolis, IN	O-23*e	25
70	72	Larry Figaro / Fernando Sabino	22	Pontiac Firebird	6.0	Walter Johnston, Jupiter, FL	O-24*e	25
71	13	Marty Hinze	16	Chevrolet March 83G	5.7	Marty Hinze Racing, Davie, FL	P-24*u	22
72	41	Jeffrey Loving / Richard Small	77	Chevrolet Camaro	5.7	Sunrise Auto Parts, Miami, FL	O-25*e	20
73	81	Vince DiLella / Manolo Cueto	03	Porsche 911	2.8	DiLella Racing, Hialeah, FL	U-24*u	19
74	22	John Maffucci	63	Mazda Argo JM-16	2.3	RGP 500 Racing, Atlanta, GA	P-25*a	17
75	71	Paul Canary	20	Chevrolet Corvette	5.7	Paul Canary Racing, Delavin, WI	O-26*u	17
76	46	Peter Welter	37	Mazda RX-7	2.3	Vero Racing, Vero Beach, FL	U-25*s	16
77	63	Rick Borlase / Mike Hammond	56	Porsche 934	3.0t	Downing / RGP Racing, Atlanta, GA	O-27*u	12
78	44	John McComb	33	Jaguar XJS	5.4	John McComb, Milford, PA	O-28*u	6
79	76	Paul Goral	49	Porsche 935	3.2t	Paul Goral, Miami, FL	P-26*e	5
80	21	Elliott Forbes-Robinson	87	Porsche 924 Carrera GTR	2.0t	Performance Motorsports, Dallas, TX	U-26*f	4
81	77	Hoyt Overbagh	52	Chevrolet Camaro	5.7	OMR Engines, Petersburg, VA	O-29*u	4
DNS		Paul Canary / Eppie Wietzes	8	Chevy McLaren	6.0	Paul Canary Racing, Delavin, WI	withdrew	
DNS		Jimmy Tumbleston / Bob Dumont	19	AMC Spirit	2.5	Signal 12 Racing, Lake Placid, FL	withdrew	
DNS		Dan Nooe / Gale O'Doski	53	Chevrolet Corvette	5.7	Dan Nooe, Lakeland, FL	withdrew	
DNS		C.W. Bryant / Rick Burr / Mike Graham	91	BMW 2002	2.0	B&G Racing, Deerfield Bch., FL	withdrew	
DNS		Richard Habersin / Bob Murray	65	Chevrolet Camaro	5.7	Richard Habersin, Miami, FL	withdrew	
DNS		Robert Amar / Ashmeed Mohammed	92	Toyota Corolla	1.8	Amar Racing Team, Trinidad	withdrew	
DNS		Alfredo Sesana / Jorge Cortes	98	Chevrolet Monza	5.7	Sesana Racing, Colombia	withdrew	
DNS		Donald Flores / Tom Turner	34	Lotus Europa	2.5	Florco Design, Atlantic Bch., FL	withdrew	

*Not running at finish

Average Speed: 106.364 mph
Total Purse: $92,950
Distance: 1,278.18 miles
Winner's Share: $22,200
Margin of Victory: 2 laps
Fastest Lap: #04 Brian Redman 122.563 mph

Fastest Qualifier: #04 Brian Redman 125.902 mph
Attendance: 52,500 (est.)
Lap Leaders: #04 1; #44 2-3, 5-60, 62-69; #00 4; #6 61, 76-175; #45 70-75; #5 176-219, 223-226; #48 220-222, 227-263
Weather: Partly cloudy and cool

1984 HOURLY STANDINGS — TOP 10

	GRID	POS.	1 HR.	2 HRS.	3 HRS.	4 HRS.	5 HRS.	6 HRS.	7 HRS.	8 HRS.	9 HRS.	10 HRS.	11 HRS.	Finish
	#04	2:18.96	1	44	44	45	6	6	6	6	5	5	48	48	48
	#00	2:19.67	2	15	45	6	5	5	5	5	57	57	5	57	57
	#5	2:20.08	3	04	6	5	15	15	57	57	48	48	57	6	6
	#44	2:21.29	4	5	04	11	57	57	15	48	6	6	6	9	9
	#6	2:21.65	5	45	5	15	48	48	48	9	9	9	9	5	5
	#14	2:22.94	6	6	14	9	14	9	9	15	4	4	45	14	14
	#15	2:24.11	7	86	15	48	9	14	14	4	76	45	4	4	45
	#2	2:25.17	8	14	00	57	44	46	00	14	14	76	14	45	4
	#86	2:25.22	9	9	9	4	46	44	05	76	45	14	76	76	76
	#45	2:25.78	10	4	48	14	4	05	32	32	32	32	32	32	32

1985

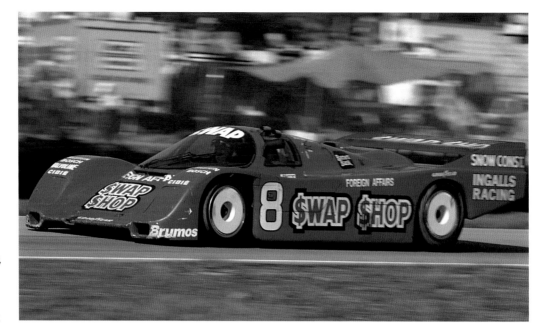

1985 SEBRING WINNER —
Porsche 962
Built by Porsche / Entered by
Preston Henn Swap Shop Racing,
Ft. Lauderdale, FL. Chassis No.
104; Engine: 2.8 liter, turbo-
charged 6 cyl. Porsche
Drivers: A.J. Foyt, Bob Wollek

33RD ANNUAL 12 HOURS OF SEBRING / MARCH 23, 1985

POS.	ST.	DRIVERS	NO.	MAKE	DISP.	ENTRANT / SPONSOR	CLASS	LAPS
1	13	A.J. Foyt / Bob Wollek	8	Porsche 962	3.2t	T-Bird Swap Shop Racing, Ft. Lauderdale, Fl.	P-1	281
2	2	Al Holbert / Derek Bell / Al Unser, Jr.	14	Porsche 962	3.2t	Holbert Racing / Lowenbrau, Warrington, Pa.	P-2	277
3	12	Pete Halsmer / Rick Knoop / Dieter Quester	68	Porsche 962	2.8t	Busby / B.F. Goodrich, Newport Beach, Calif.	P-3	268
4	3	Bob Tullius / Chip Robinson	44	Jaguar XJR-5	6.0	Group 44, Winchester, Va.	P-4	259
5	18	Jim Downing / John Maffucci	63	Mazda Argo JM16	1.3	Downing / RGP 500, Atlanta, Ga.	L-1	253
6	49	Wally Dallenbach / John Jones	65	Ford Mustang	5.4	Roush Protofab, Livonia, Mich.	O-1	251
7	10	Al Leon / Art Leon / Skeeter McKitterick	2	Porsche March 85G	3.2t	Leon Brothers Racing, Atlanta, Ga.	P-5	250
8	46	Chuck Kendall / John Hotchkis / Bob Kirby	11	Porsche 935	3.2	Kendall Racing, La Canada, Calif.	P-6	240
9	40	Les Delano / Andy Petery / Patty Moise	90	Pontiac Firebird	5.7	Road Circuit Tech., Greenwich, Ct.	O-2	239
10	41	Peter Uria / Mike Schaefer / Larry Figaro	09	Porsche Carrera	3.0	901 Shop, Plantation, Fl.	O-3	237
11	34	Don Courtney / Brent O'Neill / Mike Hackney	61	Chevrolet Monza	5.7	Team USA / Deco Sales, Hialeah, Fl.	O-4	231
12	31	Jamsal / Kikos Fonseca / Alfredo Mena	89	Porsche 934	3.0t	Scorpio Racing, El Salvador	O-5	219
13	32	Danny Smith / Tom Waugh	53	Mazda RX-7	1.3	Mandeville Auto Tech., Spartanburg, S.C.	O-6*u	218
14	33	Tom Burdsall / Pete Weller / Nick Nicholson	37	Mazda Tiga GT285	1.3	Aerex Manufacturing, Vero Beach, Fl.	L-2	216
15	61	Gary Auberlen / Pete Jauker / Adrian Gang	56	Porsche 911	2.8	S P Racing, Torrance, Calif.	U-1	209
16	23	Kelly Marsh / Ron Pawley / Don Marsh	93	Mazda Argo JM16	1.3	Mid-O / Rusty Jones, Columbus, Ohio	L-3	205
17	51	Paul Goral / R. Wilson	31	Porsche 935	3.2t	Goral Racing, Miami, Fl.	P-7	204
18	57	Rainer Brezinka / J.M. Centano / Fritz Hochreuter	39	Porsche Carrera	3.0t	R&H Racing, Toronto, Canada	O-7*u	202
19	53	Tom Kendall / Bart Kendall / Max Jones	00	Mazda RX-7	1.3	Kendall Racing, La Canada, Calif.	U-2	202
20	28	Rick Borlase / Michael Hammond / Jim Torres	58	Porsche 934	3.0t	Coin Operated Racing, Las Vegas, Nv.	O-8*s	198
21	59	Larry O'Brien / Mike Van Steenburg	34	Mazda OVS-1	1.3	Import Service Center, Lakeland, Fl.	L-4	184
22	69	Bob Lee / Bill Julian / Jeff Hudlett	98	Buick Skyhawk	4.2	Bob's Speed Products, Pompano Beach, Fl.	O-9	182
23	22	Dick Silver / Don Herman / Fred Baker	20	Porsche 935	3.2t	Spirit of Cleveland, Cleveland, Ohio	P-8	182
24	30	Roger Mandeville / Logan Blackburn	38	Mazda RX-7	1.3	Mandeville Auto Tech., Spartanburg, S.C.	O-10*t	180
25	73	Jack Griffin / Bobby Hefner / Skip Winfree	35	Porsche 911	2.8	Team Dallas, Dallas, Texas	U-3	178
26	6	Jim Busby / John Morton / Jochen Mass	67	Porsche 962	2.8t	Busby / B.F. Goodrich, Laguna, Calif.	P-9*s	175
27	8	John Kalagian / John Lloyd / Tommy Grunnah	15	Chevy March 84G	5.7	Kalagian Racing, Folly Beach, S.C.	P-10*t	170
28	55	Ron Case / Dave Panaccione	36	Porsche 911	2.8	Case Racing, Lakeland, Fl.	U-4	165
29	39	Karl Keck / Bill Wessel / Squeak Kennedy	83	Chevrolet Corvette	5.7	K&P Racing, Melbourne, Fl.	O-11*s	158
30	16	Mauricio DeNarvaez / David Cowart / Kenper Miller	43	Porsche 935	3.2t	DeNarvaez Enterprises, Colombia	P-11*e	157
31	47	Roy Newsome / Bill McVey / Dale Kreider	02	Mazda RX-7	1.3	RNGC Racing, St. Petersburg, Fl.	U-5	148
32	29	Craig Shafer / George Shafer / Joe Maloy	88	Chevrolet Camaro	5.7	Shaferacing, Somerset, Pa.	O-12*e	145
33	21	Dave Heinz / Jim Trueman / Jerry Thompson	55	Chevrolet Corvette	5.7	Dave Heinz Imports, Tampa, Fl.	O-13*u	134
34	45	John Higgins / Chip Mead / James King	78	Porsche Carrera	2.8t	Tokina Zoom Lenses, Dayton, Ohio	O-14*e	128
35	14	Preston Henn / Bob Wollek / Don Whittington	7	Porsche 935	3.2t	T-Bird Swap Shop Racing, Ft. Lauderdale, Fl.	P-12	121
36	70	Don Nooe / Jim Stricklin / Tim Stringfellow	85	Chevrolet Corvette	5.7	Don Nooe, Lakeland, Fl.	O-15*u	118
37	38	Paul Lewis / Scott Pruett / Joe Varde	42	Mazda RX-7	1.3	Mike Meyer / Daffy, Malibu, Calif.	U-6*u	117
38	37	Ken Bupp / Guy Church / E.J. Generotti	81	Chevrolet Camaro	5.7	CRT Contracting Corp., Ft. Lauderdale, Fl.	O-16*u	116
39	27	Jack Baldwin / Jeff Kline	76	Mazda RX-7	1.3	Malibu Grand Prix, El Segundo, Calif.	U-7*e	114

40	4	Randy Lanier / Bill Whittington	1	Chevrolet March 84G	5.7	Blue Thunder Racing, Ft. Lauderdale, Fl.	P-13*e	114
41	43	Luis Gordillo / Rolando Falgueras / Manuel Villa	45	Porsche Carrera	2.8t	Pennzoil of P R, San Juan, P.R.	O-17*u	111
42	58	Steve Zwiren / Mike Teamey / Rob Peters	54	Mazda RX-7	1 3	Zwiren Racing, Denville, N.J.	U-8	111
43	60	William Boyer / Steve Roberts / John Barben	25	Chevrolet Camaro	5.7	Steve Roberts Jr., Avon Park, Fl.	O-18	109
44	11	Don Bell / Mike Brockman / Tommy Riggins	01	Buick Argo JM16	4.5	Stauffer Classics, Rolling Hills, Calif.	P-14*t	105
45	44	Del Taylor / John Hays / Ravid Albanese	22	Pontiac Firebird	5.7	Walter Johnston, Boca Raton, Fl.	O-19*u	101
46	65	Cameron Worth / Foko Gritzalis	75	Mazda RX-3	1.2	Pettit Wholesale, Lighthouse Pt., Fl.	U-9*u	91
47	48	Darin Brassfield / Arie Luyendyk / J. Brassfield	29	Chevrolet March 85G	5.7	DeAtley Motorsports, Los Gatos, Calif.	P-15*a	90
48	35	John McComb / Rick Mancuso / Fred Fiala	51	Ferrari 512 BB	5.0	Mosler Racing, Milford, Pa.	O-20*t	88
49	67	Bob Whitaker / Ed Crosby / Jeff Hudlett	05	Chevrolet Camaro	5.7	Bob Whittiker, Sanford, Fl.	P-16*u	76
50	17	Marty Hinze / Milt Minter / Art Yarosh	16	Porsche 935	3.2t	Marty Hinze Racing, Davie, Fl.	P-17*s	70
51	20	Werner Frank / Dave White / Jerry Kendall	26	Porsche 935	3.2t	Toyota Village, Tampa, Fl.	P-18*e	68
52	42	Al Bacon / Charlie Guest / Bobby Akin Jr.	17	Mazda RX-7	1.3	Al Bacon Racing, Kingsport, Tn.	U-10*u	67
53	1	Bob Akin / Hans Stuck / Jim Mullen	5	Porsche 962	3.2t	Bob Akin Motor Racing, Ossining, N.Y.	P-19*s	66
54	26	Tom Winters / Bob Bergstrom / E. Forbes-Robinson	79	Porsche 924 Carrera	2.0t	Whitehall / Fabcar, Lansing, Mich.	U-11*e	65
55	66	Carlos Munoz / Louis Lopez / Herman Galeano	49	Porsche 911	3.0	Conrad Racing, Miami, Fl.	U-12*u	65
56	19	Walt Bohren / Steve Millen	47	Pontiac Firebird	6.0	Dingman Brothers Racing, Orlando, Fl.	O-21*e	63
57	54	Austin Godsey / Paul Gentilozzi / Kent Hill	74	Porsche 924 Carrera	2.0t	Whitehall / Willard, Lansing, Mich.	U-13*e	59
58	24	Bill Gelles / Steve Cohen	21	Ferrari 512 BB	5.0	Gopher Motion, Chappaqua, N.Y.	O-22*e	54
59	36	Amos Johnson / Jack Dunham	71	Mazda RX-7	1.3	Team Highball, Raleigh, N.C.	U-14*t	48
60	63	Dennis Wagoner / Ken Knott	13	Mazda RX-7	1.3	Rubino Racing, Miami, Fl.	U-15*u	46
61	72	John Hofstra / Charles Slater / Mick Robinson	69	Porsche Carrera	3.0t	Gary Wonzer, Ft. Myers, Fl.	O 23*u	45
62	62	Drake Olson / Steve Potter	08	Mazda RX-7	1.3	Simms - Romano, Gainesville, Fl.	U-16*u	44
63	25	Lance Van Every / Ash Tisdelle	95	Porsche 935	3.2	Van Every Racing, Charlotte, N.C.	P-20*u	42
64	68	Tom Hunt / Jim Shelton	60	Mazda RX-3	1.2	Tom Hunt, Plantation, Fl.	U-17*s	40
65	5	Ken Madren / Wayne Pickering / John Paul, Jr.	3	Buick March 84G	3.5t	Royal Crown Cola, Roswell, Ga.	P-21*a	38
66	56	Don Cummings / Craig Rubright	70	Chevrolet Corvette	5.7	Ormond Racing Assoc., Ormond Beach, Fl.	O-24*	37
67	7	Brian Redman / Hurley Haywood	04	Jaguar XJR-5	5.4	Group 44, Winchester, Va.	P-22*e	36
68	50	Buz McCall / Pancho Carter	50	Chevrolet Camaro	5.7	Monty Trainer's Restaurant, Miami, Fl.	O-25*e	34
69	9	Carson Baird / Terry Labonte	4	Chevrolet Corvette GTP	5.8	Lee Racing, New Castle, Del.	P-23*e	27
70	52	Chris Gennone / Hoyt Overbagh	92	Chevrolet Camaro	5.7	OMR Engines, Petersburg, Va.	O-26*e	27
71	15	George Schwarz / Frank Jelinski	12	Ford Gebhardt JC843	5.4	Gebhardt Motorsports, W. Germany	P-24*a	22
72	64	Rick Habersin / Art Habersin	66	Chevrolet Camaro	5.7	Habersin Camera Shop, Miami, Fl.	O-27*t	22
73	71	Tom Cripe	48	Porsche 934	3.0t	Gary Wonzer, Ft. Myers, Fl.	O-28*w	9
74	74	John Bossom	32	Triumph TR8	3.5	KJJ Enterprises, Ontario, Canada	O-29*u	0
DNS		Carlos Catter / Hector Coco	80	Chevrolet Camaro	5.7	Carlos Catter, Hialeah, Fl.	withdrew	
DNS		Charles Morgan / Bill Alsup	6	Buick Royale/Argo	4.2	Morgan Performance, Conway, Ark.	withdrew	
DNS		Carlos Munos / Joe Gonzalez	77	Chevrolet Camaro	5.7	Tortuga Racing, Miami, Fl.	withdrew	

*Not running at finish

Average Speed: 113.787 mph
Fastest Lap: #14 Al Holbert, 128.916 mph
Distance: 1,365.66 miles
Total Purse: $100,925
Fastest Qualifier: #5 Hans Stuck, 131.574 mph

Winner's Share: $23,200
Margin of Victory: 4 laps
Attendance: 58,000 (est.)
Lap Leaders: #3 1-3; #5 4-24; #04 25-29; #67 30-175; #8 176-281.
Weather: Sunny and warm

1985 HOURLY STANDINGS — TOP 10

	GRID	POS.	1 HR.	2 HRS.	3 HRS.	4 HRS.	5 HRS.	6 HRS.	7 HRS.	8 HRS.	9 HRS.	10 HRS.	11 HRS.	Finish
#5	2:12.97	1	5	67	67	67	67	67	67	8	8	8	8	8
#14	2:16.31	2	3	5	68	8	8	8	8	14	14	14	14	14
#44	2:17.10	3	67	1	15	15	15	15	15	68	68	68	68	68
#1	2:17.42	4	04	8	8	14	14	14	14	44	44	44	44	44
#3	2:17.67	5	44	68	5	7	7	68	68	63	63	63	63	63
#67	2:19.42	6	2	15	2	43	63	63	63	65	65	65	65	65
#04	2:19.47	7	15	29	43	63	43	65	65	67	2	2	2	2
#15	2:20.30	8	7	2	65	65	65	44	44	89	89	11	11	11
#4	2:22.08	9	68	44	63	2	68	11	11	15	11	90	90	90
#2	2:23.14	10	8	43	7	68	2	53	53	90	90	09	09	09

1986

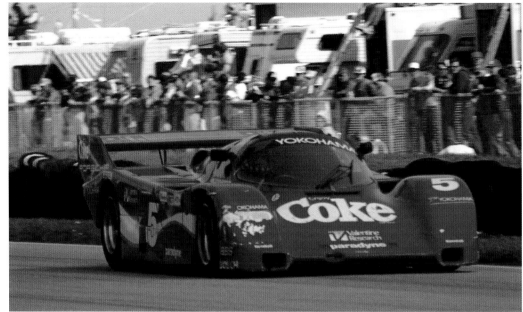

**1986 SEBRING WINNER —
Porsche 962**
Built by Porsche / Entered by Bob
Akin, Ossining, NY. Chassis No.
113; Engine: 3.2 liter, turbo-
charged 6 cyl. Porsche
**Drivers: Bob Akin, Hans Stuck,
Jo Gartner**

34TH ANNUAL 12 HOURS OF SEBRING / MARCH 22, 1986

FIN.	ST.	DRIVERS	NO.	MAKE	DISP.	TEAM	CLASS	LAPS
1	4	Bob Akin / Hans Stuck / Jo Gartner	5	Porsche 962	3.2t	Bob Akin Racing / Coke, Ossining, N.Y.	P-1	287
2	6	John Morton / Darin Brassfield / Jim Busby	67	Porsche 962	3.2t	Busby / BF Goodrich, Newport Beach, Calif.	P-2	279
3	2	Al Holbert / Derek Bell / Al Unser Jr.	14	Porsche 962	3.2t	Holbert Racing / Lowenbrau, Warrington, Pa.	P-3	269
4	20	Bruce Jenner / Scott Pruett	7	Ford Mustang	6.0	Roush Racing / 7-Eleven, Livonia, Mich.	O-1	265
5	21	Bill Elliott / Ricky Rudd	50	Ford Mustang	6.0	Roush / Folgers / Motorcraft, Livonia, Mich.	O-2	265
6	25	Jim Rothbarth / Mike Meyer / Jeff Kline	66	Mazda Royale RP40/JM16	1.3	STS - Mike Meyer Racing, West Palm Beach, Fla.	L-1	246
7	36	Ron Grable / John Heinricy / Bobby Carradine	88	Chevrolet Corvette	5.7	Morrison-Cook Motorsports, Albany, Ga.	O-3	245
8	32	Roger Mandeville / Danny Smith	38	Mazda RX-7	1.3	Mandeville Auto Tech, Spartanburg, S.C.	U-1	240
9	18	Jim Downing / John Maffucci / John O'Steen	63	Mazda Argo JM19	1.3	Downing / Certified Brakes, Atlanta, Ga.	L-2	238
10	38	Lance Van Every / Ash Tisdelle / Rusty Bond	92	Chevrolet Camaro	5.7	Van Every Racing, Charlotte, N.C.	O-4*s	233
11	37	Rick Borlase / Jim Torres / Michael Hammond	58	Porsche 934	2.8t	Rick Borlase, Las Vegas, NV.	O-5	231
12	29	Les Delano / J. Nightingale / Patty Moise	90	Chevrolet Camaro	5.0	Road Circuit Tech, Greenwich, Ct.	O-6	230
13	48	Tom Kendall / Bob Reed / John Hogdal	75	Mazda RX-7	1.3	C C R / Malibu, El Segundo, Calif.	U-2	226
14	65	Jack Griffin / Bobby Hefner / Skip Winfree	35	Porsche 911	3.0t	Team Dallas, Dallas, Texas	U-3*t	225
15	31	Marty Hinze / Jack Newsum / Tom Blackaller	16	Porsche 935	3.2	MHR Racing, Ft. Lauderdale, Fla.	P-4	222
16	64	Peter Uria / Larry Figaro / Jack Refenning	78	Porsche 911	3.0t	901 Racing, Plantation, Fla.	U-4	220
17	34	Brent O'Neill / Steve Shelton / Don Courtney	61	Buick Argo JM16	3.0	Deco Sales, Miami, Fla.	L-3	219
18	68	Hernan Galeano / Christian Jacobs / Pedro Cardenas	45	Porsche 911	3.0	Turbo Concepts, Miami, Fla.	U-5	209
19	23	Chris Marte / Tim Coconis	62	Ford Mustang	6.0	Roush Racing, Livonia, Mich.	O-7*a	200
20	35	Ron Canizares / William Jacobson / Howard Katz	29	Mazda Tiga GT285	1.3	Ares Sports, New York, N.Y.	L-4	198
21	60	Ray Brezinka / Rudy Bartling / John Centano	39	Porsche 911	3.0	R & H Racing, Ontario, Canada	U-6	197
22	28	John Higgins / Chip Mead / Howard Cherry	42	Porsche Fabcar 85L	3.0	White / Allen Porsche, Dayton, Ohio	L-5	184
23	54	Paul Corazzo / Ed Flemke / Tom Hessert	22	Mazda Royale RP40/JM16	1.3	Team 22 / Sherri Cup, Wethersfield, Ct.	L-6*e	181
24	14	Charles Morgan / Logan Blackburn	6	Buick Tiga GT286	3.0	Morgan Performance, Conway, Ark.	L-7*e	181
25	47	Kikos Fonseca / Luis Mendez / Jamsal	34	Porsche 934	3.0t	Latino Racing, Dominican Republic	O-8*u	174
26	56	Lanny Hester / Maurice Hassey	64	Ford Mustang	6.0	Raintree Corporation, Brentwood, Tenn.	O-9	173
27	69	Del Russo Taylor / Mick Hackney / Arvid Albanese	26	Pontiac Firebird	5.7	Bob's Speed Products, Boca Raton, Fla.	O-10	172
28	13	Tommy Byrne / Wally Dallenbach Jr.	02	Chevrolet Camaro	5.8	Spirit Racing, Basalt, Co.	O -11*k	171
29	41	Don Knowles / Robert McConnell / Tommy Morrison	87	Chevrolet Corvette	5.7	Morrison-Cook Motorsports, Albany, Ga.	O-12*t	171
30	53	Al Bacon / Bill Scott / Dennis Krueger	17	Mazda RX-7	1.3	Al Bacon Racing, Kingsport, Tenn.	U-7*u	168
31	66	Gary Auberlen / Peter Jauker / Cary Eisenlohr	54	Porsche 911	3.0	SP Racing, Redondo Beach, Calif.	U-8	168
32	49	Roy Newsome / Tom Burdsall / Pete Welter	37	MazdaTiga GT285	1.3	Burdsall / Newsome Racing, Vero Beach, Fla.	L-8*u	162
33	33	Costas Los / Dudley Wood	99	Cosworth Tiga GT285	1.7t	RB Promotions, England	P-5*u	160
34	71	John Hofstra / Charles Slater / Mickey Robinson	21	Porsche 911	3.0	Gary Wonzer, Ft. Myers, Fla.	U-9	160
35	73	Luis Mendez / Mauricio DeNarvaez	60	Porsche 911	3.0	Latino Racing, Dominican Republic	U-10*t	159
36	58	Reed Kryder / Tom Palmer / Todd Morici	57	Nissan 280ZX	2.8t	Kryder Racing, Canal Fulton, Ohio	U-11	157
37	39	Ken Bupp / Guy Church / E.J. Generotti	31	Chevrolet Camaro	5.7	CRT Contracting, Ft. Lauderdale, Fla.	O-13*u	156
38	44	Chuck Kendall / Paul Lewis / Max Jones	11	Mazda Lola T616	1.3	Kendall Racing, La Canada, Calif.	L-9*e	153
39	1	John Paul Jr. / Whitney Ganz / Ken Madren	46	Buick March 85G	3.5t	Conte Racing / RC Cola, Calif.	P-6*e	151
40	51	Bill Boyer / Buzzy Roberts / Mike Rand / B. Unser	85	Pontiac Firebird	6.0	Highlands County Racing, Sebring, Fla.	O-14	151

41	55	Amos Johnson / Dennis Shaw / Jack Dunham	71	Mazda RX-7	1.3	Team Highball, Raleigh, N.C.	U-12*u	150
42	27	Pancho Carter / Buz McCall / Tom Sheehy / Walt Bohren	30	Chevrolet Camaro	5.7	Buz McCall / Skoal Bandit, Boca Raton, Fla.	O-15*s	147
43	15	Tommy Riggins / Elliott Forbes-Robinson	47	Pontiac Firebird	5.7	Dingman Brothers Racing, Orlando, Fla.	0-16*s	147
44	8	Brian Redman / Hurley Haywood / Vern Schuppan	04	Jaguar XJR-7	6.0	Group 44, Winchester, Va.	P-7*e	146
45	46	Rick Moore / Hoyt Overbagh / Chris Genome	9	Chevrolet Camaro	6.0	OMR Engines, Petersburg, Va.	0-17*t	145
46	5	Drake Olson / A.J. Foyt	8	Porsche 962	3.2t	Henn's Swap Shop Racing, Ft. Lauderdale, Fla.	P-8*s	141
47	67	Tom Hunt / Jim Shelton	89	Mazda RX-7	1.3	Team Hunt Racing, Plantation, Fla.	U-13*x	140
48	45	Jim Fowells / David Cowart / Kenper Miller	27	Mazda Argo JM19	1.3	MSB Racing, Pittsford, N.Y.	L-10*e	136
49	61	Dave Fuller / Squeak Kennedy	82	Chevrolet Corvette	7.5	K&P Racing, Daytona Beach, Fla.	P-9*e	127
50	70	Paul Romano / Jim Freeman / Jim Nelson	08	Mazda RX-7	1.3	Simms-Romano Ent., Gainesville, Fla.	U-14	125
51	30	Roger Andrey / Bob Herlin / Rick Mancuso	01	Ferrari Alba AR2	3.0	Gaston Andrey Racing, Framingham, Mass.	L -11*k	123
52	43	George Shafer / Joe Maloy / Bill McVey	83	Chevrolet Camaro	5.7	Shafer Racing, Somerset, Pa.	O-18*u	114
53	9	Bob Tullius / Chip Robinson / Claude Ballot-Lena	44	Jaguar XJR-7	6.0	Group 44, Winchester, Va.	P-10*e	106
54	26	Kelly Marsh / Ron Pawley	93	Mazda Argo JM16	1.3	Rusty Jones Co., Dublin, Ohio	L-12*a	102
55	62	Bob Lee / Bill Julian / Tim Lee / Jim Saxon	96	Buick Skyhawk	4.2	Bob's Speed Products, Ft. Lauderdale, Fla.	O-19*e	97
56	57	Tom Nehl / Jim Fortin / Scott Gaylord	25	Chevrolet Camaro	5.0	Lucas Truck Service, Jacksonville, Fla.	O-20*e	96
57	74	Gary Wonzer / Miguel Pagan / Bruce Dewey / Tom Cripe	48	Porsche Carrera	3.0	Gary Wonzer, Ft. Myers, Fla.	O-21	94
58	63	Chauncey Wallace / Van McDonald / Kevin Bruce	41	Mazda RX-7	1.3	Lion Rampart, West Palm Beach, Fla.	U-15*t	90
59	50	Ron Case / Dave Panaccione	36	Porsche 924 Carrera	2.0t	Case Racing, Lakeland, Fla.	U-16*e	83
60	17	Chris Cord / Dennis Aase	98	Toyota Celica T	2.1t	All American Racers / Toyota, Santa Ana, Calif.	O-22*t	73
61	19	Terry Labonte / Phil Parsons / Benny Parsons	28	Oldsmobile Calais	5.0	Tex Ent. / US Tobacco, Charlotte, N.C.	O-23*a	67
62	40	Frank Rubino / Ray Mummery	13	Mazda Argo JM19	1.3	Outlaw Racing Team, Coral Gables, Fla.	L-13*a	65
63	42	Dave Heinz / Don Yenko / Steve Zwiren	51	Chevrolet Corvette	5.7	Dave Heinz Imports, Tampa, Fla.	0-24*t	65
64	12	Jack Baldwin / Jim Miller	76	Chevrolet Camaro	5.0	Peerless Racing, Indianapolis, In.	0-25*f	57
65	16	Carlo Facetti / Martino Finotto / Ruggero Melgrati	80	Ferrari Alba AR6	3.0	Gaston Andrey Racing, Framingham, Mass.	L-14*t	41
66	22	Jerry Kendall / Dave White / Werner Frank	05	Porsche 935	3.2t	Jerry Kendall, St. Petersburg, Fla.	P-11*u	40
67	76	Carlos Munoz / Carlos Migoya / Luis Albiza	73	Chevrolet Camaro	5.0	Eurospec Imports, Miami, Fla.	O-26*a	40
68	11	Jim Adams / John Hotchkis / John Kalagian	00	Porsche March 84G	3.2t	Hotchkis Racing / Wynn's, Pasadena, Calif.	P-12*e	38
69	3	Bob Wollek / Paolo Barilla	86	Porsche 962	3.2t	Bayside Racing / Bridgestone, Redmond, Wash.	P-13*e	36
70	59	Carlos Ruesch	24	Mazda RX-7	1.3	Global Racing, Ft. Lauderdale, Fla.	U-17*u	28
71	75	Bill Gardner / John Greene / Steve Noffke	69	Chevrolet Monza	5.7	Rick Balderson, Atlanta, Ga.	O-27*e	28
72	52	Craig Rubright	55	Chevrolet Corvette	5.7	Bud Light Corvette, Clearwater, Fla.	O-28*a	27
73	72	Jeffrey Loving	77	Chevrolet Camaro	5.7	Sunrise Racing, Miami, Fla.	O-29*f	16
74	7	Gianpiero Moretti	0	Porsche 962	3.2t	Momo / Joest Racing, Germany	P-14*e	10
75	10	Jim Mullen	4	Chevrolet Corvette GTP	6.0	Lee Racing, New Castle, Del.	P-15*e	9
76	24	Bob Bergstrom	72	Oldsmobile Toronado	5.7	Whitehall-Rocketsports, Lansing, Mich.	O-30*t	9
DNS		David Hobbs / John Watson	12	BMW March 86G GTP	3.5t	BMW North America, Westwood, N.J.	fire damage	
DNS		Bobby Rahal / John Watson	18	BMW March 86G GTP	3.5t	BMW North America, Westwood, N.J.	accident	
DNS		John Andretti / Davy Jones	19	BMW March 86G GTP	3.5t	BMW North America, Westwood, N.J.	withdrew	
DNS		Jim Busby / Oscar Larrauri	68	Porsche 962	3.2t	Busby / BF Goodrich, Newport Beach, Calif.	accident	
DNS		Bob Henderson / Timothy Lee	56	Chevrolet Camaro	5.7	Hi-Fi Hospital, Tampa, Fla.	withdrew	
DNS		Skeeter McKitterick / Bill Koll	79	Chevrolet Alba	3.0	Whitehall Rocketsports, Lansing, Mich.	withdrew	
DNS		F. Tomlinson / John Finger	91	Mazda RX-7	1.3	Foreign Matter Racing, Charlotte, N.C.	withdrew	

*Not running at finish

Average Speed: 115.852 mph
Fastest Lap: #14 Derek Bell, 130.707 mph
Distance: 1,394.82 miles
Total Purse: $171,500
Margin of Victory: 8 laps
Winner's Share: $38,300

Fastest Qualifier: #46 Whitney Ganz, 133.134 mph
Attendance: 60,000 (est.)
Lap Leaders: #14 1-26, 81-89, 104-116, 119-134; #8 27-31, 50-55, 101-103;
#86 32-35; **#46** 36-40; **#67** 41-48, 56-57; **#5** 49, 58-80, 90-100, 117-118, 135-287
Weather: Sunny and mild, cold at night

1988 HOURLY STANDINGS—TOP 10

	GRID	POS.	1 HR.	2 HRS.	3 HRS.	4 HRS.	5 HRS.	6 HRS.	7 HRS.	8 HRS.	9 HRS.	10 HRS.	11 HRS.	Finish
#46	2:11.41	1	14	14	5	5	14	5	5	5	5	5	5	5
#14	2:12.33	2	8	5	14	8	5	14	14	14	67	67	67	67
#86	2:12.71	3	86	8	8	14	8	46	67	67	14	14	14	14
#5	2:13.84	4	5	04	44	44	46	67	7	7	7	7	50	7
#8	2:14.18	5	04	44	04	46	67	8	50	50	50	50	7	50
#67	2:16.04	6	44	46	46	67	50	04	56	66	66	66	66	66
#0	2:17.56	7	46	67	67	50	7	7	66	88	88	88	38	88
#04	2:18.80	8	67	86	93	04	04	50	04	38	38	38	88	38
#44	2:19.02	9	76	93	50	93	44	61	8	63	63	92	63	63
#4	2:22.19	10	02	50	7	7	6	75	88	92	92	63	92	92

1987

**1987 SEBRING WINNER —
Porsche 962**
Built by Porsche / Entered by
Bayside Motorsports, Redmond,
WA. Chassis No. 121; Engine: 3.2
liter, turbocharged 6 cyl. Porsche
**Drivers: Jochen Mass,
Bobby Rahal**

35TH ANNUAL 12 HOURS OF SEBRING / MARCH 21, 1987

POS.	ST.	DRIVERS	NO.	MAKE	DISP.	ENTRANT / SPONSOR	CLASS	LAPS
1	2	Jochen Mass / Bobby Rahal	86	Porsche 962	3.0t	Bayside / Budweiser, Seattle, Wash.	P-1	298
2	1	Al Holbert / Chip Robinson	14	Porsche 962	3.0t	Holbert Racing / Lowenbrau, Warrington, Pa.	P-2	296
3	6	Brian Redman / Chris Kneifel / Elliott Forbes-Robinson	8	Porsche 962	3.0t	Primus Motorsports, Chicago, Ill.	P-3	293
4	4	John Winter / Sarel Van der Merwe / Danny Ongais	0	Porsche 962	3.0t	Joest Racing / Sachs, Germany	P-4	281
5	15	Greg Pickett / Tommy Riggins	28	Chevrolet Camaro	5.5	Protofab Racing / Yokohama, Indianapolis, Ind.	O-1	281
6	8	Bob Akin / James Weaver / Steve Shelton	5	Porsche 962	2.8t	Bob Akin Motoracing, Ossining, NY	P-5	280
7	5	Darin Brassfield / Bob Wollek / Wally Dallenbach Jr.	67	Porsche 962	3.0t	Busby / B.F. Goodrich, Newport Beach, Calif.	P-6	275
8	18	Bruce Jenner / Bobby Akin	22	Ford Mustang	6.0	Roush Racing, Livonia, Mich.	O-2	274
9	16	Chris Cord / Juan Fangio II	98	Toyota Celica T	2.1t	All American Racers / Toyota, Santa Ana, Calif.	O-3	267
10	36	John Higgins / Charles Monk / Howard Cherry	42	Porsche Fabcar 85L	3.0	MMG / White Allen, Dayton, Ohio	L-1	265
11	40	Charles Morgan / Jim Rothbarth	05	Mazda Argo JM16	1.3	R M Racing, St. Louis, Mo.	L-2	261
12	13	Steve Durst / Mike Brockman / Tony Belcher	09	Pontiac Fiero GTP	3.0	Ball Bros. Racing, Cherry Hill, N.J.	L-3	261
13	41	Jerry Clinton / Morris Clement / Stan Barrett	65	Ford Mustang	6.0	Grey Eagle Racing / Budweiser, St Louis, Mo.	O-4	256
14	21	Jim Downing / John Maffucci / John O'Steen	63	Mazda Argo JM19	1.3	Jim Downing / Certified Brakes, Atlanta, Ga.	L-4	253
15	29	Scott Schubot / Linda Ludemann / Lance Jones	19	Mazda Tiga GT285	1.3	S & L Racing, West Palm Beach, Fla.	L-5*f	252
16	26	Paul Gentilozzi / Irv Hoerr / Tom Winters	74	Oldsmobile Toronado	6.0	Whitehall Rocketsports, Lansing, Mich.	O-5	251
17	43	Al Bacon / Bob Reed	17	Mazda RX-7	1.3	Al Bacon Racing, Kingsport, Tenn.	U-1	245
18	54	Gary Auberlen / Bill Auberlen / Karl Durkheimer	54	Porsche 911	3.0	SP Racing, Rolling Hills, Calif.	U-2	244
19	11	Jack Baldwin / Eppie Wietzes	76	Chevrolet Camaro	6.0	Peerless / Hendrick, Indianapolis, IN	O-6*e	243
20	67	Peter Uria / Larry Figaro / Kyle Rathbun / Jack Refenning	89	Porsche 911	3.0	901 Racing, Plantation, Fla.	U-3	243
21	42	T. Morrison / Stuart Hayner / Don Knowles / Bob McConnell	87	Chevrolet Corvette	5.7	Morrison-Cook Motorsport, Albany, Ga.	O-7	241
22	30	Buz McCall / Walt Bohren / Paul Dallenbach	30	Chevrolet Camaro	5.7	Skoal Bandit Racing, Boca Raton, Fla.	O-8	241
23	24	Tim McAdam / Scott Overby / Chip Mead	43	Porsche Fabcar 85L	3.0	MMG / Classic Shine, Greenwich, Ct.	L-6	238
24	46	Tom Kendall / Bart Kendall / Max Jones	75	Mazda RX-7	1.3	C. Cunningham Racing, El Segundo, Calif.	U-4	236
25	34	Mandy Gonzalez / Manuel Villa / Luis Gordillo	35	Porsche Royale RP40	3.0	Diman Racing, San Juan, P.R.	L-7	235
26	19	Brent O'Neill / John Lloyd	61	Buick Argo JM19	3.0	Performance Tech, Miami, Fla.	L-8	230
27	72	Guy Church / Tom Hunt / E.J. Generotti	84	Mazda RX-7	1.3	Guy Church, Ft. Lauderdale, Fla.	U-5	226
28	63	Dick Greer / Mike Mees / John Finger	82	Mazda RX-7	1.3	Aspen Inn, Columbus, Ohio	U-6	225
29	68	Miguel Morejon / Hernan Galeano	46	Porsche 911	3.0	Turbo Concepts, Miami, Fla.	U-7	224
30	49	Amos Johnson / Dennis Shaw	71	Mazda RX-7	1.3	Delta Bldg. Supplies, Raleigh, NC	U-8	217
31	22	Lyn St. James / Tom Gloy	11	Ford Mustang	6.0	Roush Racing, Livonia, Mich.	O-9	213
32	74	Bill Boyer / Buzzy Roberts	85	Pontiac Firebird	5.7	Highlands Racing, Sebring, Fla.	O-10	211
33	70	Charles Slater / David Duttinger / Rudy Bartling	00	Porsche 911	3.0	S Squared Engineering, Ft. Lauderdale, Fla.	U-9	209
34	31	Ken Bupp / Guy Church / Del Taylor	81	Chevrolet Camaro	5.0	Sentry Bank Equipment, Ft. Lauderdale, Fla.	O-11*u	205
35	32	George Petrilak / Dave Rosenberg / Bruce MacInnes	23	Buick Argo JM19	3.0	Motion Promotion, Ft. Salonga, NY	L-9	201
36	62	Dennis Chambers / Chaunce Wallace	68	Mazda RX-7	1.3	Chambers Racing, Gregenacres, Fla.	U-10	201
37	66	Paul Romano / Vance Swifts / John Drew	08	Mazda RX-7	1.3	Simms Romano Enterprises, Gainesville, Fla.	U-11	188
38	57	Ron Case / Bruce Dewey / Buzz Cason / Nort Northam	52	Mazda Lola T616	1.3	Gary Wonzer, Ft. Myers, Fla.	L-10	186
39	9	Scott Pruett / Pete Halsmer	4	Ford Mustang GTX Spl.	6.5	Roush Racing / Applicon, Livonia, Mich.	P-7*t	179
40	10	Martino Finotto / Ruggero Melgrati / Piero Silva	80	Ferrari Alba AR6	3.0	Gaston Andrey Racing, Framingham, Mass.	L-11*t	177
41	64	Craig Rubright / Garrett Jenkins / Roy Newsome	24	Chevrolet Corvette	5.8	CAR Enterprises, Clearwater, Fla.	O-12	165
42	69	Bob Lee / Gary Myers / Tim Lee	90	Buick Skyhawk	5.0	Bob's Speed Products, Boca Raton, Fla.	O-13*u	161

43	73	Henry Brosnaham / Glen Cross / Jim Johnson	50	Chevrolet Camaro	5.7	Henry A. Brosnaham, Valrico, Fla.	O-14	158
44	17	Roger Andrey / David Loring / Willy Lewis	25	Ferrari Tiga GT286	3.0	Gaston Andrey Racing, Framingham, Mass.	L-12	145
45	71	Paul Goral / Rusty Bond / Larry Figaro	44	Porsche 911	2.8	Goral Racing, Miami, Fla.	U-11*u	140
46	59	Carlos Munoz / Carlos Catter / Joe Gonzalcz	49	Pontiac Firebird	5.7	Catters Racing Team, Hialeah, Fla.	O-15*u	136
47	3	Price Cobb / Vern Schuppan	16	Porsche 962	3.0t	Dyson Racing, Pleasant Valley, NY	P-8*a	123
48	61	Steve DePoyster / Bob Schader / Jim Kurz / Mike Jocelyn	60	Mazda RX-7	1.3	Schaderacing, Boulder, CO	U-12*t	114
49	98	Greg Hobbs / Gary Robinson / David Hobbs	31	BMW Gebhardt 853	2.0	Gebhardt Racing, Tulsa, OK	L-13*e	110
50	53	Eduardo Dibos / Keith Rinzler	96	Mazda Tiga GT287	1.3	Hessert Racing Cherry Hill, NJ	L-14*u	93
51	55	Doug Mills / Richard Oakley	47	Mazda RX-7	1.3	Cumberland Valley Racing, Hagerstown, Md.	U-13*t	90
52	50	Bill Wink / Bill Martin / Don Erickson / Tim Evans	56	Chevrolet Camaro	5.7	Bill Wink Racing, Birmingham, Mich.	O-16*e	87
53	23	Skeeter McKitterick / Ted Boady / Paul Lewis	79	Oldsmobile Alba AR5	3.0	Whitehall Rocketsports, Lansing, Mich.	L-15*u	86
54	14	Jerrill Rice / Willy T. Ribbs	99	Toyota Celica T	2.1t	All American Racers, Santa Ana, Calif.	O-17*e	84
55	33	Uli Bieri / Angelo Pallavacini	40	Ferrari Alba AR2	3.0	Bieri Racing, Ontario, Canada	L-15~e	76
56	52	Craig Shafer / Joseph Maloy / George Shafer	83	Chevrolet Camaro	5.7	Shafer Racing, Somerset, Pa.	O-18*a	76
57	37	Dave Heinz / Bob Young	51	Chevrolet Corvette	6.0	Quality Motorsports, Tampa, Fla.	O-19*e	75
58	7	A.J. Foyt / Danny Sullivan / Hurley Haywood	1	Porsche 962	3.0t	A.J. Foyt Enterprises / Columbia Crest, Houston, TX	P-9*a	73
59	60	Mark Altman / Gary Altman / Tim Selby	13	Porsche 914/6	3.0	Altman Bros. Motor Racing, Uniontown, Pa.	U-14*t	71
60	25	Finley Tomlinson / Terry Loebel / Richard Morgan	9	Mazda Tiga GT285	1.3	Finco Racing, Charlotte, NC	L-16*e	57
61	38	Roger Mandeville / Kelly Marsh	38	Mazda RX-7	2.0	Mandeville Auto Tech, Spartanburg, SC	O-20*e	56
62	35	Frank Jellinek / John Grooms	36	Mazda Royale RP40/JM16	1.3	Erie Scientific Racing, Portsmouth, NH	L-17*e	54
63	56	Del Taylor / Mark Montgomery	26	Pontiac Firebird	5.2	Bob's Speed Products, Boca Raton, Fla.	O-21*u	45
64	51	Scott Gaylord / Luis Albiza	91	Oldsmobile Calais	5.0	Lucas Truck Service, Lakewood, CO	O-22*e	38
65	47	Harold Shafer / Tom Nehl / Robert Peters	12	Buick Somerset	5.8	Centurion Auto Trans., Jacksonville, Fla.	O-23*x	36
66	12	Don Bell / Jeff Kline	01	Pontiac Fiero GTP	3.0	Pontiac / AT&T, Rolling Hills, Calif.	L-18*e	31
67	20	Bob Lappalainen	77	Chevrolet Camaro	6.0	Brooks Racing, Pittsford, NY	O-24*x	25
68	65	Jeffrey Loving / Richard Small	72	Chevrolet Camaro	5.8	Sunrise Racing, Miami, Fla.	O-25*u	23
69	58	Dick Murray / Terry Visger	15	Pontiac Fiero	3.0	Murray Racing, Chandler, Ariz.	U-15*e	20
70	45	Tom Juckette	70	Chevrolet Camaro	5.8	Hi-Tech Coatings, Maitland, Fla.	O-26*u	19
71	44	Gene Felton	21	Chevrolet Camaro	6.0	OMR Engines, Marietta, Ga.	O-27*e	10
72	39	John Heinricy	88	Chevrolet Corvette	5.8	Morrison-Cook Motorsport, Albany, Ga.	O-28*e	9
73	27	Steve Philips	29	Buick Tiga GT286	3.0	Aries Sports, Palisades, NY	L-19*k	8
74	48	Art Pilla	04	Porsche 944	2.3t	Dave White Racing, Tampa, Fla.	O-29*e	7
DNS		Reed Kryder / Barry Kassel / Paul Thomas	57	Nissan 300ZX	3.0	Kryder Racing, Canal Fulton, Ohio	withdrew	
DNS		Ron Case / Vicki Smith / Peter Uria	53	Mazda Lola T616	1.3	Gary Wonzer, Ft. Myers, Fla.	withdrew	
DNS		Tim Evans / Andy Pilgrim / Doug Goad	18	Pontiac PAS Spl.	3.0	Prototype Automotive, Farmington, Mich.	withdrew	
DNS		Frank DelVecchio / Chris Thompson	39	Chevrolet Camaro	5.0	Gary English, Trumbull, Ct.	DNQ	
DNS		Mike Graham / Rick Burr / C. Bryant	41	BMW 325	2.0	B & G Racing, Pompano Beach, Fla.	DNQ	
DNS		Rudy Bartling / F. Hochreuter / Warner Frank	78	Porsche 911S	2.8	Fritz Hochreuter, Toronto, Canada	withdrew	
DNS		Vince Gimondo / Ken Grostic / Terry Watters	3	Oldsmobile Calais	5.0	Vince Gimondo, Orlando, Fla.	withdrew	
DNS		Jim Stricklin / Don Nooe / Tim Stringfellow	10	Chevrolet Corvette	5.0	Don Nooe, Bartow, Fla.	DNQ	
DNS		Ash Tisdelle / Lance Van Every	92	Chevrolet Camaro	5.0	Van Every Racing, Charlotte, NC	withdrew	

*Not running at finish
6 full-course caution periods totaling 2 hours and 31 minutes.

Average Speed: 101.859 mph
Fastest Lap: #14 Robinson, 118.368 mph
Distance: 1,224.78 miles
Total Purse: $268,200
Fastest Qualifier: #14 Chip Robinson, 120.331 mph
Winner's Share: $41,800

Margin of Victory: 2 laps + 1 min. 53.7 sec.
Attendance: 65,000 (est.)
Lap Leaders: #86 1-4, 65-68, 258-298; #16 5-26;
#14 27-64, 69-257
Weather: Sunny and warm

1987 HOURLY STANDINGS — TOP 10

	GRID	POS.	1 HR.	2 HRS.	3 HRS.	4 HRS.	5 HRS.	6 HRS.	7 HRS.	8 HRS.	9 HRS.	10 HRS.	11 HRS.	Finish
#14	2:02.96	1	14	14	14	14	14	14	14	14	14	14	86	86
#86	2:03.76	2	86	16	86	86	86	86	86	86	86	86	14	14
#16	2:04.98	3	0	86	16	16	0	0	8	8	8	8	8	8
#0	2:06.71	4	16	8	0	0	16	8	0	0	0	0	28	0
#67	2:06.91	5	1	67	8	8	8	5	5	5	5	5	0	28
#8	2:07.59	6	8	1	67	28	28	28	28	67	28	28	5	5
#1	2:09.14	7	67	0	5	5	5	67	67	28	22	22	22	67
#5	2:09.53	8	5	5	1	67	67	22	22	22	67	67	67	22
#4	2:13.88	9	99	99	28	28	98	25	42	76	42	98	98	98
#80	2:14.96	10	28	28	98	76	22	42	76	42	98	42	42	42

1988

**1988 SEBRING WINNER —
Porsche 962**
Built by Porsche / Entered by
Bayside Motorsports, Redmond,
WA. Chassis No. 121; Engine: 3.2
liter, turbocharged 6 cyl. Porsche
**Drivers: Klaus Ludwig,
Hans Stuck**

36TH ANNUAL 12 HOURS OF SEBRING / MARCH 19, 1988

POS.	ST.	DRIVERS	NO.	MAKE	DISP.	ENTRANT / SPONSOR	CLASS	LAPS
1	4	Klaus Ludwig / Hans Stuck	86	Porsche 962	3.0t	Havoline / Bayside, Seattle, Wash.	P-1	318
2	9	John Winters / Frank Jelinski / Paolo Barilla	0	Porsche 962	3.0t	Joest Racing / Sachs, Germany	P-2	309
3	2	Price Cobb / James Weaver	16	Porsche 962	3.0t	Dyson / Blaupunkt, Pleasant Valley, NY	P-3	307
4	7	A.J. Foyt / Hurley Haywood / Rob Dyson	1	Porsche 962	3.0t	Foyt Ent. / Copenhagen, Houston, TX	P-4	304
5	8	John Hotchkis / Jim Adams / John Hotchkis Jr.	10	Porsche 962	3.0t	Hotchkis Rcg / Wynn's, Pasadena, Calif.	P-5	303
6	19	Wally Dallenbach Jr. / John Jones	5	Chevrolet Corvette	5.8	ProtoFab / Polyvoltac, Indianapolis, IN	O-1	289
7	3	Jan Lammers / Davy Jones / Danny Sullivan / John Nielsen	61	Jaguar XJR-9	6.0	TWR / Castrol Jaguar, Valparaiso, IN	P-6	283
8	15	Deborah Gregg / Lyn St. James	6	Lincoln-Mercury XR4Ti	2.5t	Roush / Mac Tools / Stroh's, Livonia Mich.	O-2	282
9	22	Tom Hessert / David Loring	9	Buick Tiga GT286	3.0	Essex Racing / Tarmax, Cherry Hill, NJ	L-1	282
10	30	Andy Petery / Les Delano / Craig Carter	33	Mercury Capri	6.0	Rico Camera / Roush, Livonia, Mich.	O-3	278
11	18	Scott Pruett / Pete Halsmer	11	Lincoln-Mercury XR4Ti	2.5	Mac Tools / Stroh's, Livonia, Mich.	O-4	275
12	21	John Morton / P.J. Jones	76	Mazda RX-7	1.9	CCR, El Segundo, Calif.	O-5	273
13	37	Uli Bieri / Paul Guaitamacchi / Angelo Pallavicini / Martino Finotto	40	Ferrari Tiga GT286	3.0	Gaston Andrey Rcg, Framingham, Mass.	L-2	269
14	29	Jim Downing / Howard Katz / Hiro Matsushita	63	Mazda Argo JM19	1.9	Panasonic Mazda, Atlanta, Ga.	L-3*e	268
15	43	Amos Johnson / Dennis Shaw	71	Mazda RX-7	1.3	Team Highball, Raleigh, NC	U-1	267
16	28	Roger Mandeville / Don Marsh / Kelly Marsh	38	Mazda RX-7	1.9	Mandeville Auto Tech, Spartanburg, SC	O-6	266
17	50	Bart Kendall / Tom Frank	75	Mazda RX-7	1.3	CCR, El Segundo, Calif.	U-2	265
18	16	Martino Finotto / Ruggero Melgrati / Guido Dacco	80	Ferrari Alba AR6	3.0	Gaston Andrey Rcg, Framingham, Mass.	L-4	264
19	12	Steve Durst / Mike Brockman / Jeff Kline	09	Pontiac Spice GTP	4.5	Jiffy Lube Firebird, Cherry Hill, NJ	P-7	262
20	59	Dick Greer / Matt Minich / John Finger / Mike Meese	82	Mazda RX-7	1.3	Aspen Inn, Columbus, Ohio	U-3	261
21	40	George Petplak / Rex McDaniel / Scott Livingston	23	Buick Argo JM16	3.0	Di-Tech Buick, Ft. Salonga, NY	L-5	259
22	27	Terry Visger / Paul Lewis / Jon Woodner	55	Pontiac Spice	3.0	Huffaker Racing, Los Angeles, Calif.	L-6	251
23	61	Jack Broomall / Tim Evans / Garth Ullom	53	Dodge Daytona	2.1t	Team Shelby, Birmingham, Ala.	U-4	250
24	39	Ash Tisdelle / Lance Van Every / Nort Northam	94	Chevrolet Camaro	5.7	Ash Tisdelle, Orlando, Fla.	O-7	232
25	54	Jack Refenning / Rusty Bond / Fred Baker	20	Porsche 911	3.2	Martinelli-Scott, Pompano Beach, Fla.	U-5	232
26	44	Bill Jacobson / John Schneider / Jim Brown	19	Mazda Tiga GT287	1.3	Essex Racing, Cherry Hill, NJ	L-7*t	229
27	26	Charles Morgan / Don Bell	01	Pontiac Spice Fiero	2.7	AT&T / Spice Engineering, Atlanta, Ga.	L-8	229
28	46	Craig Rubright / Kermit Upton	84	Chevrolet Camaro	6.0	Car Ent., Clearwater, Fla.	O-8	229
29	62	Peter Uria / Larry Figaro / Skip Winfree	89	Porsche 911	3.2	901 Racing, Plantation, Fla.	U-6	226
30	33	Buz McCall / Paul Dallenbach / Jack Baldwin	03	Chevrolet Camaro	5.7	Skoal Bandit Racing, Boca Raton, Fla.	O-9*s	225
31	48	Bill Auberlen / Adrian Gang / Gary Auberlen	54	Porsche 911	3.0	S P Racing, Rolling Hills, Calif.	U-7	224
32	49	Al Bacon / Bob Reed / Amos Johnson	17	Mazda RX-7	1.3	Al Bacon Performance, Kingsport, Tenn.	U-8	217
33	60	Rudy Bartling / Ray Brezinka / Fritz Hochreuter	90	Porsche 911	3.0	Rudy Bartling, Canada	U-9	217
34	35	Howard Cherry / Charles Monk / Lorenzo Lamas / Jack Newsum	42	Porsche Fabcar 85L	3.2	MMG/Lamas Motorsports, Dayton, OH	L-9	212
35	41	Del Russo Taylor / Bob Lee / Gary Myers / Mark Montgomery	92	Pontiac Firebird	5.0	Bob's Speed Products, Boca Raton, Fla.	O-10	205
36	52	Steve Roberts / Kurt Roehrig	7	Pontiac Firebird	5.7	Highlands Race Team, Sebring, Fla.	O-11	197
37	57	Kal Showket / Neil Hannemann	00	Dodge Daytona	2.4t	Full Time Racing, Birmingham, Ala.	U-10	183
38	38	Greg Walker / Scott Lagasse / King Smith	69	Chevrolet Corvette	5.8	Greg Walker Rcg, Ormond Beach, Fla.	O-12	174
39	14	Whitney Ganz / Doc Bundy / Bill Cooper	49	Buick March 86G	3.0t	H P Racing, Laguna Hills, Calif.	P-8*f	173

40	51	Ken Bupp / Guy Church / Bob Peters	81	Chevrolet Camaro	5.7	Sentry Bank Equip., Ft. Lauderdale, Fla.	O-13	168
41	58	Henry Brosnaham / Kent Keller	12	Chevrolet Camaro	5.7	Spirit of Brandon, Brandon, Fla.	O-14*t	161
42	56	Paul Romano / W. McVey / Robert Seaman / William Hornack	18	Mazda RX-7	1.3	Simms-Romano, Gainesville, Fla.	U-11	161
43	6	Sarel Van der Merwe / Elliott Forbes-Robinson	22	Chevy Lola Corvette GTP	3.0t	Hendrick Motorsports, Charlotte, NC	P-9*e	151
44	45	Dan Ripley / Alan Freed / Keith Rinzler	50	Pontiac Fiero	3.0t	Marco Polo, New York, NY	U-12*e	145
45	65	Tom Kendall / Max Jones	02	Chevrolet Beretta	3.0	C&C, Detroit, Mich.	U-13*e	145
46	1	Chip Robinson / Al Holbert	14	Porsche 962	3.0t	Holbert Racing / Miller, Warrington, Pa.	P-10*e	142
47	32	Richard McDill / Tom Juckette / Bill McDill	26	Pontiac March 84G	6.0	Hi-Tech Racing, Maitland, Fla.	P-11*t	142
48	25	Jean Louis Ricci / Claude Ballot-Lena / Skeeter McKitterick	97	Spice Pontiac Fiero	3.0	Whitehall Motorsports, Lansing, Mich.	L-10*k	141
49	13	Gianpiero Moretti / Michael Roe	30	Buick March 86G	3.0t	Buick Momo, Italy	P-12*e	135
50	17	Greg Pickett / Tommy Riggins	2	Chevrolet Corvette	5.8	Protofab, Indianapolis, IN.	O-15*e	126
51	90	Scott Schubot / Linda Ludemann / Jim Miller	4	Buick Spice SE88P	3.0	S & L Racing, West Palm Beach, Fla.	L-11*e	117
52	42	Bobby Brown / Billy Hagan / Ron Nelson	06	Buick Tiga GT286	3.0	Brown Racing, Dayton, Ohio	L-12*e	102
53	55	Luis Mendez / Kikos Fonseca	68	Porsche 911	3.0	Latino Racing, Dominican Republic	U-14*t	100
54	23	Chris Cord / Dennis Aase	98	Toyota Celica T	2.1t	All American Racing, Santa Ana, Calif.	O-16*e	99
55	63	Bill Bean / Gary Wonzer / Mike Cooper	57	Mazda Lola T616	1.3	Gary Wonzer, Ft. Myers, Fla.	L-13*u	93
56	53	Luis Sereix / Daniel Urrutia	41	Chevrolet Camaro	5.7	Ferrea Racing, Hialeah, Fla.	O-17*x	88
57	34	Lon Bender / Albert Naon Jr.	72	Ford Tiga GT287	3.3	Roy Baker Racing, Los Angeles, Calif.	P-13*t	81
58	24	John Gunn	39	Chevrolet Phoenix JG-2	5.0	Phoenix Race Cars, Sebring, Fla.	P-14*e	63
59	47	Richard Oakley / Doug Mills	47	Mazda RX-7	1.3	Cumberland Valley, Hagerstown, Md.	U-15*e	37
60	5	Martin Brundle	60	Jaguar XJR-9	6.0	TWR / Castrol Jaguar, Valparaiso, IN	P-15*e	31
61	64	Dorsey Schroeder / Bruce MacInnes	07	Dodge Daytona	2.4	Full Time Racing, Birmingham, Ala.	U-16*e	25
62	10	Jim Rothbarth	15	Porsche 962	3.0	Kalagian Racing, St. Louis, Mo.	P-16*a	21
63	21	Willy T. Ribbs	99	Toyota Celica T	2.1t	All American Racing, Santa Ana, Calif.	O-18*e	16
64	11	Tom Gloy	31	Buick March 86G	4.5	Momo Racing, Italy	P-17*e	2
65	36	Chip Mead	48	Porsche Fabcar 85L	3.2	Lamas Motorsports, Malibu, Calif.	L-14*f	2
DNS		Paul Goral / Brian Cameron	58	Mazda Lola T616	1.3	Wonzer Racing, Ft. Myers, Fla.		withdrew
DNS		S. Kennedy / Carl Keck	45	Chevrolet Corvette	5.8	K & P Racing, Daytona Beach, Fla.		withdrew
DNS		Bob Copeman* / Joe Philips	51	Porsche 911	3.0	H P Motorsports, Mt. View, Calif.		accident
DNS		Phil Mahre / Steve Mahre	96	BMW URD	3.0	URD Junior's Team, Yakima, Wash.		withdrew
DNS		Tim McAdam / Chip Mead	8	Chevrolet Fabcar	5.7	Fabcar Racing, Greenwich, Ct.		withdrew
DNS		Mike Guido / M. Graham	46	BMW 325	3.0	Red Line Racing, Pompano Beach, Fla.		DNQ
DNS		C. Wallace / Warren Newell	66	Chevrolet Camaro	5.7	Wallace Engineering, W. Palm Beach, Fla.		DNQ

*Killed in practice accident
*Not running at finish
2 full-course caution periods totaling 37 minutes.

Average Speed: 108.782 mph
Total Purse: $260,900
Distance: 1,306.98 miles
Winner's Share: $53,000
Margin of Victory: 9 laps + 21.53 seconds
Lap Leaders: #16 1-29, 61, 88-128, 139-158 #14 36; #86 30-35, 37-60, 62-87, 129-138, 159-318

Fastest Qualifier: #4 Chip Robinson, 127.721 mph
Fastest Race Lap: #16 Price Cobb, 122.569 mph
Attendance: 61,500 (est.)
Weather: Partly cloudy and cool

1988 HOURLY STANDINGS — TOP 10

	GRID	POS.	1 HR.	2 HRS.	3 HRS.	4 HRS.	5 HRS.	6 HRS.	7 HRS.	8 HRS.	9 HRS.	10 HRS.	11 HRS.	Finish
#14	1:55.84	1	16	86	86	16	86	86	86	86	86	86	86	86
#16	1:55.86	2	14	16	16	86	16	16	16	16	0	0	0	0
#60	1:55.98	3	61	0	61	0	61	61	61	61	16	16	16	16
#86	1:56.11	4	86	61	0	61	0	0	0	0	10	10	1	1
#61	1:56.40	5	0	1	1	1	1	1	1	1	1	1	10	10
#22	1:58.86	6	1	22	30	30	10	10	10	10	5	5	5	5
#1	2:02.36	7	60	30	10	10	22	22	5	5	6	6	61	61
#10	2:03.04	8	22	10	80	5	2	5	80	80	61	61	6	6
#0	2:03.65	9	30	2	5	80	5	80	76	76	9	9	9	9
#15	2:04.78	10	10	5	98	2	80	76	11	09	63	63	63	33

1989

**1989 SEBRING WINNER —
Nissan GTP ZXT**
Built and entered by
Electramotive, El Segundo, CA.
Chassis No. 8801; Engine: 3.0 liter,
turbocharged 6 cyl. Nissan
**Drivers: Geoff Brabham, Chip
Robinson, Arie Luyendyk**

37TH ANNUAL 12 HOURS OF SEBRING / MARCH 18, 1989

POS.	ST.	DRIVERS	NO.	MAKE	DISP.	TEAM / SPONSOR	CLASS-POS.	LAPS
1	1	Geoff Brabham / Chip Robinson / Arie Luyendyk	83	Nissan GTP-ZXT	3.0t	Electramotive Engineering, El Segundo, Calif.	P-1	330
2	3	Price Cobb / John Nielsen	61	Jaguar XJR-9	6.0	TWR / Castrol Jaguar Racing, Valparaiso, IN	P-2	328
3	6	James Weaver / Dominic Dobson	86	Porsche 962C	3.0t	Texaco Havoline / Bayside, Redmond, Wash.	P-3	320
4	10	Gianpiero Moretti / Massimo Sigala / M. Roe / Derek Bell	30	Porsche 962C	3.0t	Momo / Gebhardt Racing, Italy	P-4	317
5	7	Jean-Louis Ricci / Frank Jelinski / Bob Wollek	0	Porsche 962C	3.0t	Joest Racing / Blaupunkt, Germany	P-5	315
6	9	John Hotchkis /James Adams /John Hotchkis	10	Porsche 962	3.0t	Wynn's / Hotchkis, Pasadena, Calif.	P-6	300
7	19	Dan Marvin / Bob Lesnett	55	Spice Pontiac Firebird	3.0	Huffaker Racing, Santa Clara, Calit.	L-1	292
8	17	Wally Dallenbach / Dorsey Schroeder	11	Mercury Cougar XR7	6.0	Stroh's Light / Roush, Livonia, Mich.	O-1	292
9	18	Tom Hessert / Charles Morgan	9	Buick Spice SE88	3.0	Essex Racing, Cherry Hill, NJ	L-2	290
10	15	Pete Halsmer / Bob Earl	16	Mercury Cougar XR7	6.0	Stroh's Light / Roush, Livonia, Mich.	O-2	289
11	8	Costas Los / Jeff Kline	33	Spice Pontiac Firebird	5.0	Monoceran / Spice USA, Atlanta, Ga.	P-7	285
12	25	Roger Mandeville / Kelly Marsh	38	Mazda RX-7	1.9	Mandeville Auto Tech., Spartanburg, SC	O-3	284
13	26	Andy Petery / Les Delano / Craig Carter	90	Mercury Capri	6.0	Road Circuit Tech, Greenwich, CT	O-4	282
14	4	Jan Lammers / Davy Jones	60	Jaguar XJR-9	6.0	TWR / Castrol, Valparaiso, IN	P-8	281
15	38	George Robinson / Bart Kendall / Johnny Unser	74	Pontiac Fiero	3.0	Huffaker Racing, Santa Clara, Calif.	U-1	278
16	46	Dick Greer / Mike Mees / John Finger	82	Mazda RX-7	1.3	Aspen Inn, Columbus, OH	U-2	273
17	36	Amos Johnson / Dennis Shaw / Paul Lewis	71	Mazda RX-7	1.3	Team Highball, Raleigh, NC	U-3	272
18	30	Reggie Smith / Michael Row / Monte Shallat	19	Buick Tiga GT286	3.0	Essex Racing, Cherry Hill, NJ	L-3	270
19	42	Peter Uria / Jack Refenning / Fred Baker	89	Porsche 911	3.2	901 Racing, Plantation, Fla.	U-4*m	268
20	12	Steve Durst / Mike Brockman / Jay Cochran	09	Buick Spice SE88P	4.5	Jiffy Lube, Medford Lakes, NJ	P-9*m	263
21	27	J. Higgins / Lorenzo Lamas / Charles Monk / Chip Mead	43	Porsche Fabcar	3.0	Motorsports Marketing, Dayton, OH	L-4	254
22	48	Jay Kjoller / Patrick Mooney / Steve Volk	72	Porsche 911	3.2	Ohio Diagnostics, Toledo, OH	U-5	248
23	23	Buz McCall / Max Jones	03	Chevrolet Camaro	5.5	Skoal Bandit Racing, Boca Raton, Fla.	O-5	246
24	21	Jim Downing / Howard Katz / John O'Steen	63	Mazda Argo JM19	1.3	Mazda / Downing Racing, Atlanta, Ga	L-5	246
25	13	Scott Schubot / Linda Ludemann / Tom Blackaller	4	Buick Spice SE88P	3.0	S&L / Quaker State, West Palm Beach, Fla.	L-6	245
26	47	Reed Kryder / John Gimble / Frank Delvecchio	57	Nissan 300ZX	2.8	Kryderacing, Canal Fulton, OH	U-6	245
27	31	Ken Bupp / Rob Peters	18	Chevrolet Camaro	5.0	Sentry Bank Equipment, Ft Lauderdale, Fla.	O-6	244
28	34	Lance Stewart / Ron Cortez	87	Mazda RX-7	1.3	Mazda / Firestone, Irvine, Calif.	U-7	243
29	39	Bob Leitzinger / Chuck Kurtz / Butch Leilzinger	95	Nissan 240SX	3.0	Fastcolor Auto Art, State College, PA	U-8	228
30	51	Alex Job / Chris Kraft / Rusty Bond	62	Porsche 911	3.2	Alex Job Racing, Orlando, Fla.	U-9	225
31	29	Carlos Bobeda / Al Rocca / Tomas Lopez	12	Mazda Tiga GT 286	1.3	Canada Shoes, Mexico	L-7	225
32	41	Al Bacon /Bob Reed	17	Mazda RX-7	1.3	Al Bacon Performance, Kingsport, TN	U-10	216
33	16	John Morton / Steve Millen	75	Nissan 300ZX	3.0t	Nissan / CCR, El Segundo, Calif.	O-7*e	215
34	22	Uli Bieri / Paulo Guatamachi / Martino Finotto	40	Ferrari Tiga GT 286	3.0	Bieri Racing, Ontario, Canada	L-8*m	193
35	40	Chaunce Wallace / Luis Sereix / F. DeLesseps / H. Requot	47	Chevrolet Camaro	5.0	Lion Rampant Racing, W. Palm Beach, Fla.	O-8	189
36	52	Mike Graham / D. Russell / Allan Crouch	48	BMW 325i	3.4	Redline Racing, Ft. Lauderdale, Fla.	U-11*m	187
37	5	John Andretti / Bob Wollek / Derek Bell	67	Porsche 962C	3.0t	Miller / Busby, Newport Beach, Calif.	P-10*s	184
38	43	Charles Bair / Marcus Opie / Peter Morgan / Tim Morgan	44	Chevrolet Corvette	3.0	Thomas Sapp, Royal Oak, Ml	O-9*k	171
39	11	Chris Cord / Drake Olson / Steve Bren	98	Toyota 88C	2.1t	All American Racers, Santa Ana, Calif.	P-11*m	149

40	44	Richard McDill / Bill McDill	53	Chevrolet Camaro	6.0	Hi-Tech Coatings, Maitland, Fla.	O-10*t	146
41	49	Guy Church / E.J. Generotti / L. D'Agostino	22	Mazda RX-7	1.3	Florida Fixtures, Ft. Lauderdale, Fla.	U-12*e	141
42	24	Brent O'Neill / Steve Shelton	25	Buick Argo JM19	3.0	Performance Tech, Miami, Fla.	L-9*k	137
43	20	Richard Andison / Hunter Jones / John Jones	2	Chevrolet Corvette	5.5	Powell Equipment, Canada	O-11*t	116
44	45	Rudy Bartling / Ray Brezinka / Fritz Hochreuter	50	Porsche 911	3.0	F. Hochreuter, Ontario, Canada	U-13*m	115
45	32	Luis Mendez / M. Gonzalez / Tato Ferrer	68	Porsche 911	3.5t	Mendez Racing, Dominican Republic	U-14*t	101
46	53	Charles Slater / Ken Brady / Norm Dupont	45	Porsche 911	3.2	Symbiosis Corp., Ft. Lauderdale, Fla.	U-15*e	93
47	28	Kenny Hendrick	05	Oldsmobile Toronado	4.5	Park Auto Bake, Chino, Calif.	O-12*k	90
48	50	Juan Carlos Negron / Chiqui Soldevila / Luis Gordillo	7	Mazda RX-7	1.3	Seven Up, Miami, Fla.	U-16*k	72
49	37	Del Taylor / Mark Montgomery	12	Pontiac Firebird	6.0	Bob's Speed Products, Boca Raton, Fla.	O-13*a	58
50	33	Daniel Urrutia	46	Chevrolet Camaro	5.7	Team Gulfwind, Pompano Beach, Fla.	O-14*e	20
51	35	Bill Bean	58	Mazda Lola T616	1.3	Gary Wonzer Realty, Ft. Myers, Fla.	L-10*m	19
52	2	Arie Luyendyk	84	Nissan GTP-ZXT	3.0t	Electramotive Engineering, El Segundo, Calif.	P-12*s	14
53	14	John Gunn	39	Chevrolet Phoenix JG-9	5.0	Phoenix Race Cars, Sebring, Fla.	P-13*e	10
DNS		Joe Varde / Tommy Riggins	07	Dodge Daytona	2.4	Full Time Racing, Birmingham, Ala.		withdrew
DNS		Willy Ribbs / Juan Fangio	99	Toyota Eagle HF89	2.1t	All American Racers, Santa Ana, Calif.		suspension
DNS		Kal Showket / Neil Hannemann	00	Dodge Daytona	2.4	Full Time Racing, Birmingham, Ala.		accident

*Not running at finish
1 full-course caution for 29 minutes.

Average Speed: 112.742 mph
Total Purse: $267,025
Distance: 1,356.30 miles
Winner's Share: $47,200
Margin of Victory: 2 laps

Lap Leaders: #83 1-69, 74-88, 99-330; #61 70-73, 89-98.
Fastest Qualifier: #83 Geoff Brabham 127.747 mph
Attendance: 75,000 (est.)
Fastest Lap: #83 Arie Luyendyk, 123.530 mph
Weather: Clear and warm

1989 HOURLY STANDINGS—TOP 10

	GRID	POS.	1 HR.	2 HRS.	3 HRS.	4 HRS.	5 HRS.	6 HRS.	7 HRS.	8 HRS.	9 HRS.	10 HRS.	11 HRS.	Finish
#83	1:55.82	1	83	83	83	83	83	83	83	83	83	83	83	83
#84	1:55.97	2	61	61	61	67	67	67	61	61	61	61	61	61
#61	1:55.99	3	60	60	67	61	61	61	86	86	30	86	86	86
#60	1:58.82	4	67	67	10	98	10	86	30	30	86	30	30	30
#67	1:58.94	5	33	86	30	30	98	10	67	0	0	0	0	0
#86	2:00.04	6	10	33	98	10	30	30	0	10	10	10	10	10
#0	2:00.47	7	98	0	86	86	86	0	10	75	55	55	55	55
#33	2:02.06	8	86	10	63	0	0	11	11	55	11	11	11	11
#10	2:03.06	9	0	30	0	11	11	33	75	03	03	9	9	9
#30	2:03.40	10	30	98	11	63	63	16	16	11	75	16	16	16

1990

**1990 SEBRING WINNER —
Nissan GTP ZXT**
Built and entered by Nissan Performance Technology, Vista, CA. Chassis No. 8801; Engine: 3.0 liter, turbocharged 6 cyl. Nissan
Drivers: Derek Daly, Bob Earl

38TH ANNUAL 12 HOURS OF SEBRING / MARCH 17, 1990

POS.	ST.	DRIVERS	NO.	MAKE	DISP.	TEAM / SPONSOR	CLASS	LAPS
1	3	Derek Daly / Bob Earl	83	Nissan GTP-ZXT	3.0t	Nissan Performance, Vista, Calif.	P-1	301
2	1	Chip Robinson / Geoff Brabham / Derek Daly	84	Nissan GTP-ZXT	3.0t	Nissan Performance, Vista, Calif.	P-2	301
3	11	Davy Jones / Jan Lammers / Andy Wallace	61	Jaguar XJR-12	6.0	TWR / Castrol, Valparaiso, IN	P-3	301
4	13	John Hotchkis / James Adams / John Hotchkis, Jr.	10	Porsche 962	3.0	Hotchkis / Wynn's, Pasadena, Calif.	P-4	292
5	5	Kevin Cogan / John Paul, Jr.	67	Nissan GTP-ZXT	3.0t	Busby / BFGoodrich, Newport Beach, Calif.	P-5	286
6	20	Robby Gordon / Calvin Fish / Lyn St. James	15	Mercury Cougar XR7	6.0	Whistler Radar / Roush, Livonia, Mich.	O-1	278
7	18	Tom Hessert / Charles Morgan	8	Buick Spice SE89P	3.0	Cherry Hill Cars / Essex, Cherry Hill, NJ	L-1	273
8	19	Dorsey Schroeder / Max Jones	11	Mercury Cougar XR7	6.0	Whistler Radar / Roush, Livonia, Mich.	O-2	270
9	23	Bob Lesnett / David Rocha / Bruce Qvale	55	Spice Pontiac	3.0	Huffaker / Firestone, Los Angeles, Calif.	L-2	266
10	29	David Loring / Butch Leitzinger / Chuck Kurtz	95	Nissan 240SX	2.9	Fast Color Auto Art, State College, PA	U-1	262
11	8	Bob Wollek / John Winter / Henri Pescarolo	0	Porsche 962C	3.0t	Joest Racing, Germany	P-6*a	261
12	16	Martino Finotto / Paolo Guaitamacchi / Ruggero Melgrati	80	Ferrari Spice SE89P	3.0	Bieri Racing, Ontario, Canada	L-3	261
13	32	Al Bacon / Lance Stewart / John Finger	37	Mazda MX-6	1.3	Mazda Motorsports, Irvine, Calif.	U-2	248
14	14	Raul Boesel / Hans Stuck	17	Porsche 962C	3.0t	BFGoodrich / Dauer, Germany	P-7*a	246
15	35	Dick Greer / Mike Mees / John Hogdal	82	Mazda RX-7	1.3	Greer Racing, Columbus, OH	U-3	240
16	15	Tomas Lopez / Fermin Velez / Richard Piper	32	Buick Spice SE90P	3.0	Canada Shoes / Minolta, Atlanta, GA	L-4	239
17	34	Peter Uria / Jim Pace / Bob Dotson	71	Mazda RX-7	1.3	Peter Uria Racing, Plantation, Fla.	U-4	232
18	7	Bernard Jourdain / Tom Kendall / Albert Naon, Jr.	33	Chevrolet Spice SE90P	6.0	Spice USA, Atlanta, GA	P-8*m	222
19	28	Brent O'Neill / Jean Delamoussaye / Pepe Romero	25	Buick Argo JM19B	3.0	Performance Tech, Miami, Fla.	L-5	221
20	31	Kal Showket / Don Knowles / Neil Hannemann	00	Dodge Daytona	2.4	Full Time Racing, Birmingham, Ala.	U-5	215
21	40	Reed Kryder / Alistair Oag / Frank DelVecchio	57	Nissan 300ZX	3.0	Kryderacing, Canal Fulton, OH	U-6*a	215
22	33	Kelly Marsh / Al Bacon	38	Mazda MX-6	1.3	Mazda Motorsports, Irvine, Calif.	U-7	210
23	17	Pete Halsmer / E. Forbes-Robinson / John Morton	1	Mazda RX-7 4 rotor	2.6	Mazda Motorsports, Irvine, Calif.	O-3*a	209
24	41	Gary Burnett / Gary Smith / Albert Ruiz	22	Chevrolet Camaro	6.0	Carolina Racing Engines, Ft. Lauderdale, Fla.	O-4	202
25	10	Drake Olson / Juan Fangio II	98	Toyota Eagle HF89	2.1	All American Racers, Santa Ana, Calif.	P-9*s	199
26	26	Uli Bieri / John Graham / David Tennyson	40	Ferrari Tiga GT287	3.0	Bieri Racing, Ontario, Canada	L-6	195
27	43	Anthony Puleo / Kent Painter / Raymond Irwin	87	Chevrolet Camaro	5.7	Powertron, St. Augustine, Fla.	O-5	195
28	6	Rocky Moran / Willy T. Ribbs	99	Toyota Eagle HF89	2.1	All American Racers, Santa Ana, Calif.	P-10*s	185
29	39	Julian Gutierriz / Juan Vento / Luis Gordillo	09	Pontiac Fiero	3.0	Huffaker Racing, Los Angeles, Calif.	U-8	170
30	44	David Russell, Jr. / Mike Robinson / Bill Weston / John Hofstra	70	Mazda RX-7	1.3	Rising Sun Racing, Ft. Lauderdale, Fla.	U-9	154
31	9	Rene Herzog / Hurley Haywood / Scott Schubot	2	Porsche 962	3.0t	Shapiro / Alucraft, Switzerland	P-11*k	151
32	25	Howard Katz / Ferdinand DeLesseps / Jay Cochran	9	Buick Spice SE89P	3.0	Essex Racing, Cherry Hill, N.J.	L-7*k	150
33	48	Henry Brosnahan / S. Burgner / R. McElheny / Angel Figueras	04	Chevrolet Camaro	5.7	Spirit of Brandon, Brandon, Fla.	O-6*m	142
34	22	Jim Downing / Amos Johnson / John O'Steen	63	Mazda RX-7 4 rotor	2.6	Mazda Motorsports, Irvine, Calif.	O-7*e	137
35	30	Mike Davies / Stu Hayner	07	Dodge Daytona	2.4	Full Time Racing, Birmingham, Ala.	U-10*e	103
36	49	E.J. Generotti / Mark Montgomery	29	Chevrolet Camaro	5.5	Overbagh Racing, Chesterfield, VA	O-8*m	102
37	21	Ken Knott / Marty Hinze / Kenper Miller	79	Spice Pontiac SE89P	3.0	Whitehall Motorsports, Lansing, Mich.	L-8*e	98
38	45	Don Arpin / Rex Ramsey / Mark Montgomery	12	Pontiac Firebird	5.7	General Kinetics, Ft. Lauderdale, Fla.	O-9*m	91
39	37	Craig Rubright / Kermit Upton	21	Chevrolet Camaro	5.7	Budweiser, Clearwater, Fla.	O-10*a	86
40	2	Bob Wollek / Dominic Dobson / Sarel Van der Merwe	86	Porsche 962C	3.0t	Bayside / Texaco-Havoline, Seattle, Wash.	P-12*e	65

41	24	George Robinson / Johnny Unser / Paul Dallenbach	74	Ford Mustang	6.0	74 Hunting Ranch, San Antonio, TX	O-11*m	61
42	4	Price Cobb / John Nielsen	60	Jaguar XJR-12	6.0	TWR / Castrol, Valparaiso, IN	P-13*e	56
43	47	Louis D'Agostino / Steve Kelton	90	Mazda RX-7	1.3	Florida Fixtures, Plantation, Fla.	U-11*e	49
44	42	Rudy Bartling / Werner Frank	50	Porsche 911	3.0	Rudy Bartling, Ontario, Canada	U-12*e	45
45	12	Bill Adam / Scott Harrington	23	Porsche 962 DR-1	3.0t	DSR Motorsports, Canada	P-14*a	39
46	44	Michael Graham / Cameron Worth	48	BMW 325i	3.0	Redline Imported, Pompano Beach, Fla.	U-13*m	31
47	27	George Sutcliffe / Richard Jones	01	Pontiac Spice SE87P	3.0	Race Craft Int'l, Lakeland, Fla.	L-9*e	24
48	36	Bill Bean	58	Mazda Lola T616	1.3	Gary Wonzer Realty, Ft. Myers, Fla.	L-10*a	14
49	38	Chris Kraft	26	Porsche 911	3.0	Border Cantina, Lighthouse Pt., Fla.	U-14*a	14
DNS		Scott Schubot / Linda Ludemann	4	Buick Spice SE88P	3.0	S&L Racing, West Palm Beach, Fla.	fire damage	
DNS		Scott Pruett / James Weaver	16	Porsche 962C	3.0t	Dyson Racing, Pleasant Valley, NY	withdrew	
DNS		Jack Boxstrom / Dale Kreider	15	Pontiac Firebird	5.7	Sun Bank, Sebring, Fla.	accident	
DNS		Chet Fillip / Ron Cortez	20	Consulier GTP	2.4	Consulier Ind., Riviera, Fla.	withdrew	
DNS		Rick Titus / Bruce MacInnes	91	Consulier GTP	2.4	Consulier Ind., Riviera, Fla.	withdrew	
DNS		J. Negron / Daniel Urrutia	77	Mazda RX-7	1.3	JC Racing, Miami, Fla.	accident	
DNS		Richard McDill / Bill McDill	53	Chevrolet Camaro	5.7	HighTech Racing, Maitland, Fla.	withdrew	

*Not running at finish
6 full-course caution periods totaling 2 hours and 58 minutes.

Average Speed: 102.993 mph
Total Purse: $288,050
Distance: 1,237.1 miles
Winner's Share: $60,500
Margin of Victory: 1 min. 27.8 secs.
Lap Leaders: #86 1-16, 20-21, 33-42; #84 17-19, 69-78, 89-104; #17 22, 43-68; #67 23-32; #83 79-88, 105-113, 123-138, 142-162, 183-231, 255-301; #0 114-122, 139-141, 163-182, 232-254.

Fastest Qualifier: #84 Chip Robinson 127.808 mph
Fastest Lap: #84 Geoff Brabham 124.774 mph
Attendance: 78,000 (est.)
Weather: Partly cloudy and warm

1990 HOURLY STANDINGS — TOP 10

	GRID	POS.	1 HR.	2 HRS.	3 HRS.	4 HRS.	5 HRS.	6 HRS.	7 HRS.	8 HRS.	9 HRS.	10 HRS.	11 HRS.	Finish
#84	1:55.76	1	67	17	84	84	83	83	83	83	0	83	83	83
#86	1:56.35	2	86	86	83	83	0	0	0	0	83	0	84	84
#16	1:56.36	3	99	61	61	0	61	33	61	61	61	84	61	61
#83	1:56.65	4	60	60	0	61	33	61	84	84	84	61	10	10
#60	1:56.81	5	33	83	99	99	10	84	33	33	10	10	0	67
#67	1:57.63	6	17	99	98	98	98	98	98	10	33	67	67	15
#99	1:58.75	7	0	67	33	33	84	10	10	98	67	15	15	8
#33	1:59.36	8	83	0	17	10	99	15	15	67	15	8	8	11
#0	2:00.13	9	61	33	10	15	15	11	67	15	8	11	11	55
#2	2:00.54	10	10	10	15	11	2	8	1	8	11	55	55	95

1991

**1991 SEBRING WINNER —
Nissan NPT-90**
Built and entered by Nissan
Performance Technology, Vista,
CA. Chassis No. 9003; Engine: 3.0
liter, turbocharged 6 cyl. Nissan
**Drivers: Geoff Brabham,
Derek Daly, Gary Brabham**

39TH ANNUAL 12 HOURS OF SEBRING / MARCH 16, 1991

POS.	ST.	DRIVERS	NO.	MAKE	DISP.	TEAM / SPONSOR	CLASS	LAPS
1	1	Geoff Brabham / Derek Daly / Gary Brabham	83	Nissan NPT-90	3.0t	Nissan Performance, Vista, Calif.	P-1	298
2	3	Chip Robinson / Bob Earl / Julian Bailey	84	Nissan NPT-90	3.0t	Nissan Performance, Vista, Calif.	P-2	297
3	2	Bob Wollek / Bernd Schneider / Massimo Sigala	6	Porsche 962C	3.0t	Joest Porsche Racing, Germany	P-3	296
4	6	John Winter / Henri Pescarolo / Frank Jelinski	7	Porsche 962C	3.0t	Joest Porsche Racing, Germany	P-4	295
5	5	John Nielsen / Davy Jones / Raul Boesel	3	Jaguar XJR-12	6.5	Bud Light / TWR Jaguar Racing, Valparaiso, IN	P-5	284
6	7	Brian Bonner / Scott Sharp / Jeff Kline	4	Chevrolet Spice SE89P	6.0	Applebee's / Milner, Winchester, Va.	P-6	283
7	21	Charles Morgan / Jim Pace	8	Buick Kudzu DG-1	3.0	Miller Genuine Draft / Essex, Cherry Hill, NJ	L-1	280
8	26	Robby Gordon / Max Jones	15	Ford Mustang	6.0	Whistler / Roush Racing, Livonia, Mich.	O-1	279
9	11	John Hotchkis / James Adams / Chris Cord	10	Pontiac Spice SE90P	6.0	Wynn's / Hotchkis, Pasadena, Calif.	P-7	278
10	9	Gianpiero Moretti / Stanley Dickens / Helmuut Mundas	30	Porsche 962C	3.0	Momo / Gebhardt Racing, Italy	P-8	277
11	17	Steve Millen / Jeremy Dale / Johnny O'Connell	75	Nissan 300ZX	2.7t	Nissan / CCR, El Segundo, Calif.	O-2	277
12	20	Price Cobb /John O'Steen / Brian Redman	63	Mazda RX-7 4 rotor	2.6	Mazda Motorsports, Irvine, Calif.	O-3	275
13	22	Dorsey Schroeder / John Fergus	12	Ford Mustang	6.0	Whistler / Roush Racing, Livonia, Mich.	O-4	271
14	23	Pete Halsmer / Calvin Fish / John Morton	62	Mazda RX-7 4 rotor	2.6	Mazda Motorsports, Irvine, Calif.	O-5	270
15	19	Almo Coppelli / Jay Hill	33	Buick Spice SE89P	3.0	Hawaiian Tropic/Spice USA, Atlanta, GA	L-2	265
16	37	Andy Pilgrim / R.K. Smith	92	Chevrolet Corvette ZR-1	5.7	EDS / Mobil / Goodyear, Albany, GA	O-6	260
17	31	Bob Leitzinger / David Loring	95	Nissan 240SX	3.0	Fastcolor Auto Art, State College, PA	U-1	257
18	4	Juan Fangio II / Willy T. Ribbs	99	Toyota Eagle Mk II	2.1t	All American Racers, Santa Ana, Calif.	P-9*m	256
19	30	Jim Stevens / Jim Jaeger / Don Walker	90	Ford Mustang	6.0	Portland Supply / Roush, Livonia, Mich.	O-7	250
20	41	Alex Job / Chris Kraft / Jack Refenning	26	Porsche 911	3.2	Border Cantina, Plantation, Fla.	U-2	247
21	27	Andy Evans / George Robinson / Carlos Bobeda	18	Buick Spice SE89P	3.0	Carlos Bobeda Racing, Northridge, Calif.	L-3	236
22	43	Brad Hoyt / Leighton Reese	69	Mazda RX-7	2.6	North Coast Racing, Minneapolis, Minn.	U-3	234
23	39	Dick Greer / Al Bacon / Peter Uria / Mike Mees	82	Mazda RX-7	2.6	Greer Racing, Columbus, OH	U-4	232
24	24	Mike Dow / David Tennyson / Ken Knott	54	Buick Spice SE89P	3.0	HDF Motorsports, Costa Mesa, Calif.	L-4	227
25	12	John Paul, Jr. / James Weaver	24	Porsche 962	3.0t	Shapiro Motorsports, Ft. Lauderdale, Fla.	P-10*s	218
26	40	Reed Kryder / Frank DelVecchio / Joe Danaher	57	Nissan 240SX	3.0	Kryderacing, Canal Fulton, OH	U-5	207
27	16	Parker Johnstone / Doug Peterson	48	Acura Spice SE9OP	3.0	Acura / Comptech, Rancho Cordova, Calif.	L-5*m	204
28	42	H. Brosnaham / S. Roberts / B. Scolo / P. Mazzacane / R. Andison	04	Chevrolet Camaro	5.9	Spirit of Brandon, Brandon, Fla.	O-8	166
29	10	Tim McAdam / Jeff Purner / Fred Phillips	5	Chevrolet Spice SE89P	6.0	Applebee's / Milner, Winchester, VA	P-11*m	165
30	14	Martino Finotto / Ruggero Melgrati / Fermin Velez	80	Ferrari Spice SE89P	3.0	Bieri Racing, Ontario, Canada	L-6*a	147
31	35	H. Espinosa / R. Wilson / F. Solano / F. Lopez	37	Mazda MX-6	2.6	Botero Racing, Colombia	U-6*m	140
32	28	Uli Bieri / John Graham	40	Ferrari Alba AR2	3.0	Bieri Racing, Ontario, Canada	L-7*a	138
33	33	Scott Lagasse / Don Knowles / Stuart Hayner	91	Chevrolet Corvette ZR-1	5.7	EDS / Mobil / Goodyear, Albany, GA	O-9*k	134
34	25	Tom Hessert / Costas Los	09	Buick Kudzu DG-1	3.0	Cherry Hill Cars / Essex, Cherry Hill, NJ	L-8*e	128
35	46	E.J. Generotti / Paul Tavilla / Guy Church	94	Mazda RX-7	2.6	Florida Fixtures, Ft. Lauderdale, Fla.	U-7*a	113
36	34	Richard McDill / Bill McDill	53	Chevrolet Camaro	6.0	TIC Financial System, Maitland, Fla.	O-10*e	112
37	45	Jay Kjoller / Patrick Mooney / Steve Volk	72	Porsche 911	3.2	Jay Kjoller Motorsports, Lambertville, Mich.	U-8*e	108
38	44	David Russell, Jr. / Mike Graham / Cameron Worth	41	BMW 325i	2.8	Redline Import, Pompano Beach, Fla.	U-9*m	103
39	8	Rocky Moran / Andy Wallace	98	Toyota Eagle Mk II	2.1t	All American Racers, Santa Ana, Calif.	P-12*m	82

40	29	Tommy Johnson / Rob Robertson / John Sheldon	29	Buick Tiga GT288	3.0	R J Racing, Orlando, Fla.	L-9*t	82
41	32	Anthony Puleo / John Annis / Tom Panaggio / Tom Walsh	87	Chevrolet Camaro	6.0	Powertron, St. Augustine, Fla.	O-11*a	75
42	15	Hurley Haywood / Wayne Taylor	21	Porsche 962	3.0t	Alucraft, Switzerland	P-13*m	70
43	38	Butch Leitzinger / Chuck Kurtz	96	Nissan 240SX	2.7	Fastcolor Auto Art, State College, PA	U-10*e	52
44	18	Johnny O'Connell	76	Nissan 300ZX	2.7t	Nissan / CCR, El Segundo, Calif.	O-12*m	33
45	13	Craig Carter	05	Chevrolet Fabcar	6.0	Milner Racing, Winchester, VA	P-14*t	23
46	36	Rob Peters	52	Chevrolet Camaro	5.9	Bupp Racing, Ft. Lauderdale, Fla.	O-13*e	3
DNS		Hoyt Overbagh / Oma Kimbrough	06	Chevrolet Camaro	5.8	Hitex Corp, Tyrone, PA	DNQ	
DNS		Davy Jones / Kenny Acheson	2	Jaguar XJR 12	6.5	Bud Light / TWR Jaguar, Valparaiso, IN	accident	
DNS		Jeremy Dale / Steve Millen	77	Nissan 300ZX	2.7t	Nissan / CCR, El Segundo, Calif.	practice car	
DNS		Don Beckett / Scott Lieb	17	Chevrolet Corvette	5.8	Beckett Racing, Tampa, Fla.	DNQ	

7 full-course caution periods totaling 3 hours 14 minutes.
*Not running at finish

Average Speed: 91.626 mph
Total Purse: $306,650
Distance: 1,102.6 miles
Winner's Share: $62,500
Margin of Victory: 1 lap + 90.89 seconds
Lap Leaders: #6 1-5, 9-40, 44-64, 73-80; #7 6-8; #84 41-43, 142-145, 164-190, 202-203, 244, 282-291; #83 65-72, 81-141, 146-163, 191-201, 204-243, 245-281, 292-298.
Fastest Qualifier: #83 Geoff Brabham 121.354 mph
Fastest Lap: #6 Bob Wollek 119.870 mph
Attendance: 82,000 (est.)
Weather: Cloudy, rain

1991 HOURLY STANDINGS — TOP 10

GRID		POS.	1 HR.	2 HRS.	3 HRS.	4 HRS.	5 HRS.	6 HRS.	7 HRS.	8 HRS.	9 HRS.	10 HRS.	11 HRS.	Finish
#83	1:49.76	1	6	6	84	83	83	84	84	83	83	83	83	83
#6	1:50.27	2	7	84	83	84	84	83	83	84	84	84	84	84
#84	1:50.68	3	84	83	7	99	99	99	7	7	7	7	6	6
#99	1:52.60	4	83	7	6	7	7	7	6	6	6	6	7	7
#3	1:53.50	5	3	3	99	4	30	4	4	4	4	99	4	3
#7	1:52.43	6	99	99	3	6	4	6	99	99	99	4	99	4
#4	1:54.88	7	98	4	4	30	6	10	30	8	8	8	15	8
#98	1:56.31	8	4	98	98	24	80	30	8	30	33	10	3	15
#30	1:56.50	9	30	30	30	3	33	15	10	33	10	15	8	10
#5	1:57.08	10	48	24	24	33	63	8	33	10	15	3	10	30

1992

1992 SEBRING WINNER —
Toyota Eagle Mk III
Built and entered by All American
Racers, Santa Ana, CA. Chassis No.
004; Engine: 2.1 liter, turbocharged
4 cyl. Toyota
Drivers: Juan Fangio II,
Andy Wallace

40TH ANNUAL 12 HOURS OF SEBRING / MARCH 21, 1992

POS.	ST.	DRIVERS	NO.	MAKE	DISP.	TEAM/SPONSOR	CLASS	LAPS
1	5	Juan Fangio II / Andy Wallace	99	Toyota Eagle Mk III	2.1t	All American Racers, Santa Ana, Calif.	P-1	360
2	2	Geoff Brabham / Derek Daly / Arie Luyendyk / Gary Brabham	83	Nissan NPT-91A	3.0t	Nissan Performance, Vista, Calif.	P-2*s	355
3	7	Gianpiero Moretti / M. Sigala / Oscar Larrauri / B. Schneider	30	Porsche 962C	3.2t	Momo / Joest Racing, Germany	P-3	345
4	10	Davy Jones / David Brabham	2	Jaguar XJR-12D	6.5	Bud Light / TWR, Valparaiso, IN	P-4	338
5	20	Howard Katz / Jim Downing / Tim McAdam	36	Mazda Kudzu DG-1	2.6	Downing Atlanta, Atlanta, GA	L-1	314
6	15	Charles Morgan / Tommy Riggins	45	Buick Kudzu DG-1	3.4	Scandia Motorsports, Redmond, WA	L-2	308
7	19	Darin Brassfield / G. Robinson / Paul Gentilozzi / Irv Hoerr	51	Oldsmobile Cutlass	6.0	Olivetti / Rocketsports, Lansing, Mich.	S-1	302
8	22	David Loring / John Paul, Jr.	96	Nissan 240SX	3.0	Fastcolor Auto Art, State College, PA	U-1	301
9	24	Bob Leitzinger / Butch Leitzinger / Chuck Kurtz	95	Nissan 240SX	3.0	Fastcolor Auto Art, State College, PA	U-2	297
10	6	P.J. Jones / Rocky Moran	98	Toyota Eagle Mk III	2.1t	All American Racers, Santa Ana, Calif.	P-5	294
11	18	Jeremy Dale / John Morton / Steve Millen	76	Nissan 300ZX	3.0t	Nissan / CCR, El Segundo, Calif.	S-2	285
12	28	Dick Greer / Al Bacon / Peter Uria / Mike Mees	82	Mazda RX-7	2.6	Wendy's Race Team, Columbus, Ohio	U-3	278
13	37	Jack Lewis / Bill Ferran / Joe Cogbill	73	Porsche 911	3.2	Jack Lewis Ent., Atlanta, GA	U-4	276
14	41	Sam Shalala / Bill Sargis / Andre Toennis / Dan Pastorini	58	Porsche 911	3.2	Pro-Technik Inc., Houston, TX	U-5	266
15	25	Luis Sereix / Daniel Urrutia / Jorge Polanco / John Josey	22	Chevrolet Camaro	6.0	J&B Motorsports, Hialeah, Fla.	S-3	259
16	32	Richard McDill / Bill McDill / Tom Juckette	35	Chevrolet Camaro	6.2	Martini & Rossi, Maitland, Fla.	S-4	252
17	13	Costas Los / Ruggero Melgrati / Parker Johnstone	48	Acura Spice SE88P	3.0	Comptech Racing, La Costa, Calif.	L-3*e	250
18	26	John Fergus / Don Walker / Neil Hannemann	0	Dodge Daytona	2.4	Infinity/Full Time Racing, Birmingham, Ala.	U-6	249
19	30	Gary Smith / Gene Whipp / Albert Ruiz	23	Pontiac Grand Prix	5.9	Gary Smith, Ft. Lauderdale, Fla.	S-5*m	248
20	48	Mel Butt / Ron Zitza / Tommy Johnson / Robert Robertson	6	Buick Tiga GT287	3.0	MAB Racing, Orlando, Fla.	L-4	245
21	39	Joe Pezza / Jack Refenning / Butch Hamlet	26	Porsche 911	3.2	Alex Job Racing, Plantation, Fla.	U-7*e	240
22	38	Kent Painter / Robert Borders / Ed Delong	21	Chevrolet Camaro	5.8	Western Chemical, Ft. Collins, CO	S-6	238
23	36	Oma Kimbrough / M. Montgomery / R. McElheny / Hoyt Overbagh	29	Chevrolet Camaro	5.8	OMR Engines, Tyrone, PA	S-7	238
24	1	Chip Robinson / Bob Earl / Arie Luyendyk	84	Nissan NPT-91A	3.0t	Nissan Performance, Vista, Calif.	P-6*e	227
25	4	John Winter / Frank Jelinski / Bernd Schneider	7	Porsche 962C	3.2t	Torno / Joest Racing, Germany	P-7*e	221
26	14	Andy Evans / Fermin Velez / Jay Cochran	44	Buick Kudzu DG-2	3.4	Scandia Motorsports, Redmond, WA	L-5*s	221
27	33	J. Annis / Louis Beall / Dick Downs / L. Schumacher / Bob Deeks	12	Chevrolet Lumina	5.5	John Annis, Tampa, Fla.	S-8	208
28	31	Eduardo Dibos / Juan Dibos / Raul Orlandini	34	Mazda MX-6	2.6	Alberti Motorsports, Peru	U-8	199
29	17	Paul Gentilozzi / Irv Hoerr / Jack Baldwin	41	Oldsmobile Cutlass	6.5	Olivetti / Rocketsports, Lansing, Mich.	S-9*e	185
30	47	Rudy Bartling / Ahmad Khodkar / Ray Brezinka	39	Porsche 911	3.2	Fischbach Hi-Tech, Ontario, Canada	U-9*e	183
31	40	Paul Mazzacane / Brad Shinder / C. Edwards / P. Argetsinger	67	Chevrolet Camaro	5.8	Mazkar Racing, Miami, Fla.	S-10	154
32	42	Duke McLaughlin / Frank DelVecchio / Joe Danaher	57	Nissan 240SX	3.0	Kryderacing, Canal Fulton, Ohio	U-10*s	139
33	16	John Morton / Johnny O'Connell	75	Nissan 300ZX	3.0t	Nissan / CCR, El Segundo, Calif.	S -11*e	117
34	11	Wayne Taylor / F. Migault / Hugh Fuller / David Tennyson	4	Chevrolet Spice SE90P	6.3	Applebee's / Milner, Winchester, VA	P-8*s	111
35	49	Dale Kreider / John Gooding / Nort Northam	25	Oldsmobile Cutlass	4.5	Kreider Racing, St Petersburg, Fla.	S-12*m	104
36	34	Art Cross / Bobby Scolo	54	Chevrolet Camaro	5.8	Art Cross Racing, Tampa, Fla.	S-13*s	72
37	43	David Duda / Mike Speakman	80	Nissan 300ZX	2.8	David Duda, Baltimore, MD	U-11*m	68
38	35	Bob Schader / Steve Mahre / Phil Mahre	55	Mazda MX-6	2.6	GTE Mobilnet / Brix, Boulder, CO	U-12*m	60
39	12	Parker Johnstone / Dan Marvin	49	Acura Spice SE91P	3.0	Comptech Racing, La Costa, Calif.	L-6*e	55

40	23	Gene Felton / Jerry Nadeau	65	Chevrolet Beretta	6.5	Waxoyl, Sebring, Fla.	S-14*s	48
41	21	Hurley Haywood / Bobby Carradine	59	Porsche Gunnar 966	3.0t	Brumos Porsche, Jacksonville, Fla.	P-9*e	45
42	44	Don Arpin / Rob Vining / Edward Davin	8	Chevrolet Camaro	5.8	General Kinetics, Ft. Lauderdale, Fla.	S-15*m	42
43	8	Gary Brabham	1	Nissan NPT-91A	8.0t	Nissan Performance, Vista, Calif.	P-10*w	20
44	29	Henry Camferdam	9	Mazda MX-6	2.6	Support Net Racing, Indianapolis, IN	U-13*m	11
45	16	Jim Pace / Barry Waddell	15	Chevrolet Lumina	5.5	Tim Banks, Owensboro, KY	S-16*s	9
46	27	Rob Wilson	37	Mazda MX-6	2.6	Botero Racing, Colombia	U-14*e	8
47	3	Perry McCarthy	5	Chevrolet GTP RM-1	6.5	Applebee's / Milner, Winchester, VA	P-11*t	7
48	45	Heinz Wirth	40	Ford Alba AR2	3.0	Bieri Racing, Ontario, Canada	L-7*e	3
DNS		Price Cobb / Pete Halsmer	77	Mazda RX-792P	5.2	Mazda Motorsports, Charlotte, NC	exhaust	
DNS		Geoff Brabham / Chip Robinson	11	Nissan NPT-91A	3.0	Nissan Performance, Vista, Calif.	backup car	

*Not running at finish
2 full-course cautions for 26 minutes

Average Speed: 110.724 mph
Total Purse: $325,650
Distance: 1,332.6 miles
Winner's Share: $70,500
Margin of Victory: 5 laps + 41.85 seconds
Lap Leaders: #98 1-3; #84 4-15, 25-27, 126-145, 149-171, 174-190, 205-225; #30 29; #83 16-19, 28, 53-66, 77-125, 146-148, 172-173, 191-204, 226-251; #99 20-24, 30-52, 67-76, 252-360.
Fastest Qualifier: #99 Juan Fangio II, 123.328 mph
Fastest Race Lap: #83 Geoff Brabham, 121.47 mph
Attendance: 95,000 (est.)
Weather: Clear and warm.

1992 HOURLY STANDINGS — TOP 10

	GRID	POS.	1 HR.	2 HRS.	3 HRS.	4 HRS.	5 HRS.	6 HRS.	7 HRS.	8 HRS.	9 HRS.	10 HRS.	11 HRS.	Finish
#84	2:01.47*	1	99	83	83	83	84	84	84	83	99	99	99	99
#83	2:01.47*	2	83	84	84	84	83	83	83	99	83	83	83	83
#5	2:01.77*	3	84	99	99	99	99	99	99	30	30	30	30	30
#99	1:48.00	4	30	7	30	30	30	7	30	84	2	2	2	2
#98	1:49.44	5	2	30	7	7	7	30	7	2	36	36	36	36
#30	1:50.33	6	7	4	4	4	2	2	2	7	48	51	45	45
#1	1:51.75	7	4	2	44	2	48	48	48	48	84	45	96	51
#2	1:52.95	8	49	49	45	48	36	36	36	36	96	96	51	96
#4	1:53.27	9	48	44	2	76	51	51	51	51	51	95	95	95
#7	1:54.79	10	41	45	41	36	76	76	41	96	45	48	98	98

*qualified in rain

1993

**1993 SEBRING WINNER —
Toyota Eagle Mk III**
Built and entered by All American
Racers, Santa Ana, CA. Chassis No.
004; Engine: 2.1 liter, turbocharged
4 cyl. Toyota
**Drivers: Juan Fangio II,
Andy Wallace**

41ST ANNUAL 12 HOURS OF SEBRING / MARCH 20, 1993

POS.	ST.	DRIVERS	NO.	MAKE	DISP.	TEAM/SPONSOR	CLASS	LAPS
1	1	Juan Fangio II / Andy Wallace	99	Toyota Eagle Mk III	2.1t	All American Racers, Santa Ana, Calif.	P-1	230
2	5	Gianpiero Moretti / Derek Bell / John Paul Jr.	30	Nissan NPT-90	3.0t	Momo Racing, Miami, Fla.	P-2	228
3	2	P.J. Jones / Rocky Moran	98	Toyota Eagle Mk III	2.1t	All American Racers, Santa Ana, Calif.	P-3*m	217
4	9	Steve Millen / Johnny O'Connell / John Morton	1	Nissan 300ZX	3.0t	Cunningham Nissan, El Segundo, Calif.	S-1	217
5	14	Parker Johnstone / Dan Marvin / Ruggero Melgrati	49	Acura Spice SE91P	3.0	Acura, Rancho Cordova, Calif.	L-1	216
6	11	Tom Kendall / John Fergus	11	Ford Mustang Cobra	6.5	Roush Racing, Livonia, Mich.	S-2	216
7	17	Walter Rohrl / Hans Stuck / Hurley Haywood	59	Porsche 911 Turbo LM	3.2t	Brumos Porsche, Jacksonville, Fla.	V-1	214
8	12	Paul Gentilozzi / Dorsey Schroeder / Calvin Fish	31	Oldsmobile Cutlass	6.5	Olivetti Oldsmobile, Lansing, Mich.	S-3	214
9	15	Bob Earl / Bob Schader / Jeremy Dale	9	Acura Spice AK93	3.0	Motorola / Brix Racing, Boulder, CO	L-2	213
10	8	Darin Brassfield / Scott Pruett	51	Oldsmobile Cutlass	6.5	Olivetti Oldsmobile, Lansing, Mich.	S-4	213
11	4	David Tennyson / Hugh Fuller / Steve Fossett / Francois Migault	19	Chevrolet Spice SP92	6.3	Spice USA, Atlanta, GA	P-4	210
12	6	James Adams / Chris Cord	20	Porsche 962	3.2t	Wynns, Anaheim, Calif.	P-5	205
13	16	Jim Downing / Tim McAdam / Howard Katz	63	Mazda Kudzu DG-2	2.3	Downing / Bel-Ray Oil, Atlanta, GA	L-3	204
14	23	John Heinricy / Stuart Hayner / Andy Pilgrim	94	Chevrolet Corvette	5.7	Morrison / Mobil, Columbus, GA	V-2	202
15	25	Jim Minneker / Ron Nelson / Andy Pilgrim / Boris Said	93	Chevrolet Corvette	5.7	Morrison / Mobil, Columbus, GA	V-3	200
16	22	Dick Greer / Al Bacon / Peter Uria / Mike Mees	82	Mazda RX-7	2.6	Wendy's Race Team, Kingsport, TN	U-1	200
17	45	Ronny Meixner / Enzo Calderari / Luigino Pagotto	28	Porsche Carrera 2	3.5	Cigarette Racing, Germany	V-4	199
18	29	Butch Hamlet / Charles Slater / Bill Ferran	26	Porsche 911	3.2	Alex Job Racing, Hialeah, Fla.	U-2	199
19	33	Jochen Rohr / John O'Steen / Rich Moskalik / Dave White	01	Porsche Carrera 2	3.5	Rohr Engineering, Germany	V-5	197
20	37	Chris Hodgetts / Dave Donohue / Dieter Quester	0	BMW M-5	3.5	Ed Arnold Racing, Valley Forge, PA	V-5	195
21	39	Mike Peters / Oliver Kuttner / Justin Bell	48	Porsche Carrera 2	3.5	Champion Porsche, Pompano Beach, Fla	V-7	194
22	18	Richard McDill / Bill McDill / Tom Juckette	35	Chevrolet Camaro	5.7	Hi-Tech Coating, Maitland, Fla.	S-5	194
23	26	Andras Petery / John Macaluso / Tommy Schweitz	90	Pontiac Firebird	6.5	Apple Motorsports, Greenwich, CT	S-6	192
24	21	Daniel Urrutia / Gene Whipp / Luis Sereix	22	Chevrolet Camaro	6.5	Southern Racing Chassis, Ft. Lauderdale, Fla	S-7	190
25	28	Kent Painter / Bruce Trenery / Andrew Osman	21	Chevrolet Camaro	6.2	Fantasy Junction, Ft. Collins, CO	S-8	186
26	34	Reed Kryder / Guy Kuster	57	Nissan 240SX	6.2	Kryderacing, Canal Fulton, Ohio	U-3	186
27	24	Eddie Sharp Sr. / Eddie Sharp Jr. / Dick Downs	2	Oldsmobile Cutlass	5.7	Alert Bumper Inc. / Sharp, Largo, Fla.	S-9	183
28	10	John Morton / Tommy Riggins	76	Nissan 300ZX	3.0t	Cunningham Nissan, El Segundo, Calif.	S-10*m	182
29	3	John Winter / Manuel Reuter / Chip Robinson	7	Porsche 962C	3.0t	Joest Racing, Germany	P-6*a	180
30	42	Sam Shalala / Mike Sheehan / A. Lazzaro / G. Spreng / P. Favre	42	Porsche Fabcar	3.0	ZZ Pro-Technik Racing, Sugarland, TX	L-4	180
31	41	Vito Scavone / Teny Martel / Rich Hayward	45	Porsche 944 Turbo	2.5t	Antica AB, Canada	V-8	179
32	43	Frank Beard / Haas Fogle / Ernie Lader / Curt Catallo	58	Porsche 911	3.0	ZZ Pro-Technik Racing, Sugarland, TX	U-9	177
33	19	Don Knowles / Bob Leitzinger	95	Nissan 240SX	3.0	Fastcolor Auto Art, State College, PA	U-5	174
34	32	John Annis / Louis Beall / Kenper Miller	87	Chevrolet Camaro	5.7	John Annis, Tampa, Fla.	S-11	173
35	38	C.L. Hicks / Ron Zitza / Tommy Johnson / Mel Butt	91	Porsche 911	3.2	Team Casual Motorsport, Winter Park, Fla.	U-6	169
36	20	Eduardo Dibos / Bill Auberlen	24	Mazda MX-6	2.3	Dibos Racing / Team Peru, Peru	U-7	166
37	13	Wayne Taylor / Jeff Andretti / Morris Shirazi / James Weaver	5	Chevrolet Spice SE91P	6.3	Auto Toy Store, Ft. Lauderdale, Fla.	P-7*m	165
38	44	John Jones / Neil Jamieson / Jeff Lapcevich	40	Ford Alba AR-2	3.0	Bieri Racing, Canada	L-5	165
39	30	M. Montgomery / Oma Kimbrough / H. Overbagh / R. McElheny / Bob Hundredmark	50	Chevrolet Camaro	5.7	Hooters, Gainesville, Fla.	S-12*m	136

40	47	Robert Borders / Gary Smith / Mark Kennedy	32	Pontiac Grand Prix	5.7	Carolina Racing, Plant City, Fla.	S-13*m	121
41	31	Paul Mazzacane / Peter Argetsinger / Chester Edwards	67	Chevrolet Camaro	5.7	Kendall Oil, Miami, Fla.	S-14	112
42	40	L. Heimrath / Tom Rathbun / B. Hubbard / Ken McKinnon	16	Porsche 944 Turbo	2.5t	Champion Porsche, Pompano Beach, Fla	V-9*a	111
43	27	Steve Sirgany / Cliff Rassweiler / James Lee	12	Alfa Romeo Phoenix	2.8	Auto Volante, Miami, Fla.	L-6*m	98
44	46	Domenico DeLuca / Bill Weston	70	Mazda MX-6	2.3	Domenico DeLuca, Hollywood, Fla.	U-8*e	93
45	7	Dennis Aase / B. Carradine / Chip Hanauer / Jay Cochran	66	Porsche Gunnar 966	3.2t	Jeannette / Diet Coke, Riviera Beach, Fla.	P-8*a	47
46	36	Lance Stewart / Rob Wilson / Ed Hubbard	15	Porsche 944 Turbo	2.5t	Champion Porsche, Pompano Beach, Fla.	V-10*m	42
47	35	Andreas Fuchs / Philippe De Craene	41	Porsche Carrera 2	3.5	Bernt Motorsport, Germany	V-11* k	32
DNS		John Winter / Manuel Reuter	6	Porsche 962C	3.2t	Joest Racing, Germany	practice car	
DNS		Ed Arnold / David Donohue	54	Dodge Stealth Turbo	2.5t	Ed Arnold Racing, Valley Forge, PA	withdrew	

*Not running at finish

5 hours 55 min. of caution laps including 1 hour 9 min. red flag

Average Speed: 70.699 mph
Total Purse: $304,250
Distance: 851 miles
Winner's Share: $42,000
Margin of Victory: 2 laps + 1 min. 17 seconds
Lap Leaders: #99 1, 38, 76-90, 107-183, 192, 209-230; #98 2-14, 16-37, 39-75, 91-106, 184-191, 193-208; #30 15-18;
Fastest Qualifier: #99 Juan Fangio II, 125.500 mph
Fastest Race Lap: #98 P.J. Jones, 120.215 mph
Attendance: 86,000 (est.)
Weather: Rain

1993 HOURLY STANDINGS — TOP 10

	GRID	POS.	1 HR.	2 HRS.	3 HRS.	4 HRS.	5 HRS.	6 HRS.	7 HRS.	8 HRS.	9 HRS.	10 HRS.	11 HRS.	Finish
#99	1:46.13	1	98	98	98	98	98	98	98	98	**99**	**99**	**99**	**99**
#98	1:47.12	2	**99**	**99**	**99**	**99**	**99**	**99**	**99**	**99**	98	98	30	30
#7	1:50.51	3	30	30	30	30	30	30	30	30	30	30	98	98
#19	1:52.75	4	19	7	7	7	7	7	7	7	7	7	49	1
#30	1:51.74	5	7	19	19	19	19	19	19	19	19	49	1	49
#20	1:56.80	6	49	5	5	49	49	49	49	49	49	19	59	11
#66	1:57.22	7	66	49	1	5	1	1	5	1	9	1	7	59
#51	1:57.62	8	5	66	49	1	5	5	1	5	1	59	11	31
#1	1:58.76	9	20	1	20	9	51	51	59	51	59	9	9	9
#76	1:59.44	10	11	20	51	59	9	9	51	9	5	11	31	51

1994

**1994 SEBRING WINNER —
Nissan 300 ZX**
Built and entered by Clayton
Cunningham Racing, El Segundo,
CA. Chassis No. 07; Engine: 3.0 li-
ter, turbocharged 6 cyl. Nissan
**Drivers: Steve Millen, Johnny
O'Connell, John Morton**

42ND ANNUAL 12 HOURS OF SEBRING / MARCH 19, 1994

POS.	ST.	DRIVERS	NO.	MAKE	DISP.	TEAM / SPONSOR	CLASS	LAPS
1	4	Steve Millen / Johnny O'Connell / John Morton	75	Nissan 300ZX	3.0t	Nissan / Clayton Cunningham, El Segundo, CA	S-1	327
2	8	Derek Bell / Andy Wallace / James Weaver	9	Chevrolet Spice SE89	5.0	Auto Toy Store, Ft. Lauderdale, FL	W-1	322
3	6	Jim Downing / Wayne Taylor / Tim McAdam	63	Mazda Kudzu DG-3	1.9	Famous Amos / Danka / Downing, Atlanta, GA	W-2	314
4	2	Andy Evans / Ross Bentley / Butch Leitzinger	44	Chevrolet Spice HC89	5.0	AGFA Film / Perry Ellis / Scandia, Redmond, WA	W-3	309
5	19	Mark Sandridge / Joe Varde / Nick Ham	49	Porsche 911 RSR	3.8	Sandridge Gourmet Salads, Westfield Center, OH	U-1/E2-1	305
6	14	Jim Pace / Butch Hamlet / Barry Waddell	95	Nissan 240SX	3.0	Fastcolor Auto Art / Leitzinger, State College, PA	U-2	305
7	20	Ornulf Wirdheim / F. Konrad / F. De Lesseps / Charles Mendez	99	Porsche 911 Turbo	3.6t	Konrad Racing, Germany	S-2 / E1-1	299
8	23	Jochen Rohr / Jeff Purner / John O'Steen	01	Porsche 911 RSR	3.8	Rohr Corp. / Northland Porsche, Cincinnati, OH	U-3 / E2-2	298
9	48	Enzo Calderari / Lilan Keller / Renato Mastropietro	37	Porsche 911 RSR	3.8	Calderari Racing, Switzerland	U-4	293
10	31	Scott Lagasse / Ken Schrader	20	Chevy Consulier Intruder	5.0	Consulier Industries, Riviera Beach, FL	W-4	289
11	12	Hans Stuck / Walter Rohrl / Hurley Haywood	59	Porsche 911 Turbo	3.6t	Brumos Porsche, Jacksonville, FL	S-3 / E1-2	287
12	35	Gustl Spreng / Ray Mummery	69	Porsche Carrera	3.6	Gustl Spreng Racing, Daytona Beach, FL	S-4 / E1-3	283
13	24	Charles Slater / Peter Uria / Joe Cogbill	26	Porsche 911	3.4	Alex Job Racing, Orlando, FL	U-5	280
14	30	Jerry Churchill / Randy Churchill	71	Oldsmobile Cutlass	5.0	National Semi-Trailer Corp., Dearborn, MI	S-5	277
15	26	Erik Van Vliet / Antonio Hermann / Maurizo Sala	00	Porsche 911 RSR	3.8	Konrad Racing, Germany	U-6	267
16	9	Irv Hoerr / T. Riggins / R.K. Smith / Darin Brassfield	6	Oldsmobile Cutlass	6.0	GTE Mobilnet / Brix Racing, Boulder, CO	S-6*m	265
17	46	Oliver Kuttner / Dieter Quester / Pete Halsmer	36	BMW Argo Pegasus	2.3	Nature's Choice / Kuttner, Charlottesville, VA	W-5	259
18	13	Eduardo Dibos / Bill Auberlen / Les Lindley	4	Mazda RX-7	1.3	Team Peru / Lima, Peru	U-7	255
19	29	Sam Shalala / Mycroft Karos / Ron Kerr / Bill Ferran	58	Porsche 911	3.6	Pro Technik Racing, Houston, TX	U-8	254
20	40	Bruce Trenery / Jeffrey Pattinson / Andrew Osman	51	Oldsmobile Cutlass	5.8	Fantasy Junction, Martinez, CA	S-7	253
21	10	Joseph Hamilton / Tony Kester / Stan Cleva	11	Mazda Tiga SC86	1.9	Black Swan / Auto Tech, Canada	W-6*m	252
22	38	Reed Kryder / Frank Delvecchio / Joe Danaher	57	Nissan 240SX	2.8	Kryderacing, Canal Fulton, OH	U-9	241
23	44	Vito Scavone / Derek Oland / John McAulay	81	Porsche 944 Turbo	3.0t	Vito Scavone, Canada	U-10	237
24	36	C. Wagner / D. Russell, Jr. / Kenneth Brady / Steve Mott	09	Mazda RX-7	1.3	Charles Wagner, Ft. Lauderdale, FL	U-11	237
25	27	Doc Bundy / David Murry	12	Lotus Esprit S4	2.2t	Lotus USA, Atlanta, GA	U-12	231
26	39	Tom Curren / Bob Borders / Bill Julian / Gene Harry	23	Oldsmobile Cutlass	5.7	Curren Motorsports, Orlando, FL	S-8	224
27	33	Art Cross / Buzzy Roberts / Bobby Dumont	04	Chevrolet Camaro	5.8	Art Cross, Tampa, FL	S-9	218
28	41	Lorin Hicks / Mel Butt / Ron Zitza	91	Porsche 911	3.6	Mel Butt, Orlando, FL	U-13	207
29	34	Bob Hundredmark / Peter Hanson / Ken Fengler / D. King	21	Oldsmobile Cutlass	5.8	Bob Hundredmark, Jacksonville, FL	S-10	198
30	25	Jack Lewis / John Bourassa / Jack Refenning	73	Porsche 911	3.6	Jack Lewis Enterprises, Atlanta, GA	U-14*m	194
31	37	K. McKinnon / Charles Coker, Jr. / Flip Groggins / Hugh Johnson	68	Porsche 944 Turbo	2.5t	Tweeks Ltd., Hartsville,SC	U-15	194
32	7	Tommy Riggins / Scott Pruett / Price Cobb	5	Oldsmobile Cutlass	6.0	Uniden / Brix Racing, Boulder, CO	S-11*m	190
33	28	M. Montgomery / Oma Kimbrough / Hoyt Overbagh / T. Ministri	50	Chevrolet Camaro	5.8	Hooters, Gainesville, FL	S-12	186
34	18	John Heinricy / Andy Pilgrim / Stu Hayner	94	Chevrolet Corvette	5.7	Mobil 1 / Morrison Mtrs., Albany, GA	S-13	185
35	17	Geoff Boss / Andy Boss / Glenn Straub	96	Nissan 240SX	3.0	Fastcolor Auto Art / Leitzinger, State College, PA	U-16*m	178
36	21	Jim Minneker / Del Percilla / Jeff Nowicki / Andy Pilgrim	93	Chevrolet Corvette	5.7	Mobil 1 / Morrison Mtrs., Albany, GA	S-14*m	165
37	42	Gary Smith / Timothy Spurr / Steven Goldin	03	Chevrolet Camaro	5.8	Carolina Racing Engines, Ft. Lauderdale, FL	S-15*m	129
38	3	Butch Leitzinger / Paul Gentilozzi	76	Nissan 300ZX	3.0t	Nissan / Clayton Cunningham, El Segundo, CA	S-16*m	121
39	22	Paul Debban / John Macaluso / Hugh Fuller	45	Buick Kudzu DG-2	4.5	AGFA Film / Perry Ellis / Scandia, Richmond, WA	W-7*e	114

40	1	Bob Schader / Jeremy Dale / Ruggero Melgrati	2	Oldsmobile Spice AK93	5.0	Motorola / Brix Racing, Boulder, CO	W-8*m	91
41	16	Bill Adam / John Paul, Jr. / Victor Gonzalez	72	Porsche 911 Turbo	3.2t	Champion / H.H. Brown, Pompano Beach, FL	S-17*m	91
42	32	Linda Pobst / Leigh O'Brien / Kat Teasdale	19	Chevrolet Camaro	5.8	O'Brien Motorsports, Orlando, FL	S-18	91
43	11	John Jones / Neil Jamieson / Jeff Lapcevich	10	Buick Tiga FJ94	4.5	Premdor / Toronto, Canada	W-9*t	68
44	47	John Annis	87	Chevrolet Camaro	5.8	Annis Racing, Tampa, FL	S-19*m	13
45	15	Richard McDill / Tom Juckette / Bill McDill	35	Chevrolet Camaro	5.8	Hi-Tech Coating, Orlando, FL	S-20*m	8
46	43	Henry Taleb	08	Nissan 300ZX	3.0	Saeta Racing, Ecuador	U-17*e	6
47	5	Andy Wallace	22	Toyota Spice SE90	4.0	Screaming Eagles Racing, Hollywood, CA	W-10*e	5
48	45	Leigh Miller	0	Porsche 944 Turbo	3.0t	Go Vacations / Champion Porsche, W. Palm Bch, FL	U-18*f	4
DNS		Roger Mandeville / Henry Camferdam	8	Mazda Hawk MD3R	1.9	Support Net Racing, Indianapolis, IN		withdrew

*Front row starting positions reserved for WSC cars.

Average Speed: 100.63 mph
Total Purse: $288,500
Distance: 1,209.9 miles
Winner's Share: $47,300
Margin of Victory: 5 laps + 49.315 seconds
Lap Leaders: #2 1-19, 34-40, 45-62, 68, 76-83; #9 20-21, 23-33, 69-75, 90-160, 176-182, 201-202; #75 22, 161-175, 183-200, 203-327; #44 41-42; #6 43-44, 63-67, 84-89.
Fastest Qualifier: *#76 Paul Gentilozzi 110.039 mph
Fastest Race Lap: #44 Andy Evans 107.992 mph
Attendance: 90,000 (est.)
Weather: Partly cloudy and warm

1994 HOURLY STANDINGS — TOP 10

	GRID	POS.	1 HR.	2 HRS.	3 HRS.	4 HRS.	5 HRS.	6 HRS.	7 HRS.	8 HRS.	9 HRS.	10 HRS.	11 HRS.	Finish
#2*	2:01.37	1	9	2	2	9	9	**75**	**75**	**75**	**75**	**75**	**75**	**75**
#44*	2:01.82	2	2	9	6	**75**	**75**	9	9	9	9	9	9	9
#76	2:01.04	3	44	6	9	6	6	6	44	63	63	63	63	63
#75	2:01.98	4	6	**75**	**75**	63	63	63	63	44	44	44	44	44
#22	2:02.01	5	**75**	63	63	44	44	44	95	95	95	49	49	49
#63	2:02.15	6	59	59	76	45	95	95	49	49	49	95	95	95
#5	2:02.22	7	63	76	45	76	49	49	99	99	99	99	99	99
#9	2:02.94	8	76	95	36	36	96	99	01	01	01	01	01	01
#6	2:03.59	9	36	45	44	95	99	01	37	37	37	37	37	37
#11	2:07.32	10	95	36	95	49	01	37	6	20	20	20	20	20

*Front row reserved for WSC cars only.

1995

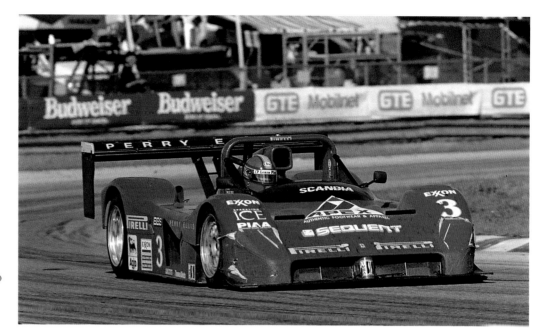

**1995 SEBRING WINNER —
Ferrari 333SP**
Built by Ferrari / Entered by
Scandia Motorsports, Redmond,
WA. Chassis No. 003; Engine: 4.0
liter, V-12 Ferrari
**Drivers: Andy Evans, Fermin
Velez, Eric Van de Poele**

43RD ANNUAL 12 HOURS OF SEBRING / MARCH 18, 1995

POS.	ST.	DRIVERS	NO.	MAKE	DISP.	TEAM/SPONSOR	CLASS	LAPS
1	4	Andy Evans / Fermin Velez / Eric Van de Poele	3	Ferrari 333SP	4.0	Scandia / Pirelli / Apex One, Redmond, WA	W-1	260
2	7	Derek Bell / Andy Wallace / Jan Lammers	9	Chevrolet Spice	5.0	Auto Toy Store, Ft. Lauderdale, FL	W-2	260
3	8	Jim Downing / Butch Hamlet / Jim Pace	63	Mazda Kudzu DG-3	1.9	Downing Atlanta / Danka, Atlanta, GA	W-3*a	256
4	1	Michele Alboreto / Mauro Baldi / Eric Van de Poele	33	Ferrari 333SP	4.0	Scandia / Pirelli, Redmond, WA	W-4	256
5	12	Steve Millen / Johnny O'Connell / John Morton	75	Nissan 300 ZX	4.5	Clayton Cunningham Racing, El Segundo, CA	GT1-1	255
6	21	Bill Adam / Hans Stuck	74	Porsche 911 Turbo	3.6t	Champion / STP, Pompano Beach, FL	GT1-2	253
7	2	Jeremy Dale / Jay Cochran / Fredrik Ekblom	2	Oldsmobile Spice BDG02	5.0	Brix Racing / Motorola, Boulder, CO	W-5	245
8	18	Franz Konrad / Antonio Hermann / Ernst Schuster	00	Porsche 962 Spyder	3.0t	Konrad Racing, Germany	LM-1	244
9	11	Irv Hoerr / R.K. Smith / Brian DeVries	4	Oldsmobile Cutlass	5.0	Brix Racing, Boulder, CO	GT1-3	244
10	15	Rick Sutherland / Stanley Dickens / John Graham	6	Oldsmobile Spice AK93	5.0	Power Macintosh Racing, Los Gatos, CA	W-6	244
11	24	John Fergus / Neto Jochamowitz	72	Porsche 911 Turbo	3.3t	Champion / H.H. Brown / STP, Pompano Beach, FL	GT1-4	242
12	30	Charles Slater / Joe Cogbill / Bill Auberlen	26	Porsche 911	3.6	Alex Job Racing, Plantation, FL	GT2-1	241
13	28	Rob Wilson / Henry Taleb / Jean Pierre Michelet	93	Nissan 240SX	2.8	Mobil 1 / Team Ecuador, Ecuador	GT2-2	240
14	34	Jorge Trejos / Dennis Aase / Martin Snow	55	Porsche 911 RSR	3.8	Team Costa Rica	GT2-3	240
15	42	Larry Schumacher / Jeff Purner / Andy Pilgrim	02	Porsche 911 RSR	3.8	Rohr Corp., Cincinnati, OH	GT2-4	239
16	14	Darin Brassfield / Calvin Fish / Mark Dismore	5	Oldsmobile Cutlass	5.0	Brix Racing, Boulder, CO	GT1-5	234
17	37	Jack Lewis / Hal Kelley / Dave White / J. Bourassa	73	Porsche 911	3.6	Jack Lewis Ent., Atlanta, GA	GT2-5	232
18	38	Lloyd Hawkins / David Murry / Shawn Hendricks	86	Porsche 968 Turbo	3.8t	Crescent City Motorsports, New Orleans, LA	GT2-6	229
19	40	Dan Lewis / Tommy Johnson / John Sheldon	18	Mazda MX-6	1.3	Hooters, Ft. Myers, FL	GT2-7	228
20	41	Dieter Quester / John Paul, Jr.	12	BMW M3	3.0	PTG / Valvoline, Winchester, VA	GT2-8	228
21	33	Art Pilla / Charles Mendez / Kenper Miller	17	Porsche 911 Turbo	3.4t	Barrett Ent., Ridgewood, N.J.	GT1-6	227
22	3	Elton Julian / Massimo Sigala / Fabrizio Barbazza	50	Ferrari 333SP	4.0	Euromotorsports Racing, Indianapolis, IN	W-7	226
23	16	Oliver Kuttner / Juan Gac / J.C. Carbonell	37	BMW Argo Pegasus	4.9	Nature's Choice/Pegasus Racing, Charlottesville, VA	W-8	225
24	44	Bo Roach / Cort Wagner	99	Porsche 911 RSR	3.8t	Konrad Racing, Germany	GT2-9	225
25	17	Roger Schramm / Steve Petty / Stu Hayner	91	Chevrolet Camaro	5.0	RVO Motorsports, Rockford, IL	GT1-7	224
26	31	Chuck Cottrell / Mike Holt / L. Miller / Eric Van Cleef	0	Buick Kudzu DG-3	4.2	Redline Oil, Franktown, CO	W-9	223
27	32	David Donohue / Pete Halsmer	13	BMW M3	3.0	PTG / Valvoline, Winchester, VA	GT2-10	222
28	36	Dick Greer / Al Bacon / Peter Uria	82	Mazda RX-7	1.3	Wendy's Race Team, Columbus, OH	GT2-11	221
29	57	Andy Strasser / Kevin Wheeler / D. Defranchesci	52	Porsche 911 RSR	3.2	Auto Sport South, Pompano Beach, FL	GT2-12	216
30	10	Christophe Bouchut / Jurgen Lassig / Giovanni Lavaggi	10	Porsche Spyder K8	3.0t	Kremer Racing, Germany	LM-2	215
31	51	Tim Vargo / Jack Refenning / Mike Peters	27	Porsche 911	3.8	Champion / STP, Pompano Beach, FL	GT2-13	214
32	50	Gustl Spreng / Ray Mummery	69	Porsche 911 Turbo	3.2t	Spreng Racing, Daytona Beach, FL	GT1-8*m	212
33	39	Mel Butt / Jim Higgs / Ron Zitza	64	Chevrolet Camaro	5.7	Mel Butt, Orlando, FL	GTI-9	212
34	6	Wayne Taylor / Gianpiero Moretti / Didier Theys	30	Ferrari 333SP	4.0	MOMO / Danka, Miami, FL	W-10	211
35	45	Andelo Cilli / Bruce Barkelew / Gerry Jackson	25	Porsche 911 RSR	3.6	Chronoswiss / Alex Job Racing, Orlando, FL	GT2-14*a	209
36	35	Tom Curren/David Rankin/Billy Bies/Pat Patterson/Jim Hildock	62	Oldsmobile Cutlass	6.0	Curren Motorsports, Orlando, FL	GT1-10	205
37	5	Rob Dyson / James Weaver / Butch Leitzinger	16	Ford R & S Mk 3	5.0	Dyson Racing, Pleasant Valley, NY	W-11	201
38	60	Danny Marshall/John Biggs/Weldon Scrogham/Steve Marshall	08	Porsche 911 RSR	3.6	G&W Motorwerkes, Danville, VA	GT2-15	200

39	22	Rob Morgan / Charles Morgan	47	Oldsmobile Cutlass	5.2	TCBY, Charles Morgan, Conway, AR	GT1-11*m	195
40	47	Gary Smith / Jon Leavy / Ron Lowenthal / Luis Sereix	42	Chevrolet Camaro	5.7	Carolina Racing Engines, Ft. Lauderdale, FL	GT1-12	186
41	53	Robert Hundredmark / Gene Harry / Steve Pfeffer	23	Oldsmobile Cutlass	5.0	Robert Hundredmark, Jacksonville, FL	GT1-13	179
42	13	Andras Petery / Tommy Riggins / Craig Carter	90	Chevrolet Camaro	5.7	Landstar / Riggins, Jacksonville, FL	GT1-14	173
43	23	Luis Mendez / Scott Hoerr	67	Ford Mustang	5.7	Luis Mendez, Dominican Republic	GT1-15*m	165
44	58	John Annis / Louis Beall / David Donavon / Ed Scolaro	87	Chevrolet Camaro	5.7	Stone Turtle, Tampa, FL	GT1-16	163
45	52	Bill Ferran / Simon Gregg / Scott Tyler	60	Porsche 911	3.6	Vito Scavone, Canada	GT2-16*m	159
46	29	Richard McDill / Bill McDill / Tom Juckette	53	Chevrolet Camaro	5.7	Hi-Tech Coating, Winter Park, FL	GT1-17	157
47	56	Reed Kryder / Frank Del Vecchio	57	Nissan 240SX	2.8	Kryderacing, Canal Fulton, OH	GT2-17	155
48	49	Ralph Thomas / Douglas Campbell / Amos Johnson	88	Mazda RX-7	1.3	Douglas Campbell, Highlands, NC	GT2-18	154
49	26	Jochen Rohr / Hurley Haywood / John O'Steen	01	Porsche 911 Turbo	3.6t	Rohr Corp./American Signature, Cincinnati, OH	GT1-18*m	142
50	63	Art Cross / Squeak Kennedy / Craig Conway	71	Chevrolet Camaro	5.7	Art Cross, Tampa, FL	GT1-19	141
51	55	Mark Montgomery / Hoyt Overbagh / Mauro Casadei / Steve Goldin / D. Kicak	92	Chevrolet Camaro	5.7	Superfuels, Gainesville, FL	GT1-20	139
52	61	Bill Cooper / Scott Maxwell / Chris McDougall	06	Chevrolet Corvette ZR-1	6.3	DRM Corvette Team U.S.A., Plymouth, MN	GT1-21*m	121
53	54	Bruce Trenery/Jeffery Pattinson/Grahame Bryant/Buddy Norton	51	Chevrolet Cannibal Spl.	5.0	Fantasy Junction Racing, Martinez, CA	W-12	99
54	25	Roger Mandeville / Henry Camferdam	8	Mazda Hawk MD3R	1.9	Support Net Racing, Indianapolis, IN	W-13*s	91
55	59	Vito Scavone / Derek Oland / Alan Jones	84	Porsche 944 Turbo	2.5t	Vito Scavone, Canada	GT2-19*m	91
56	9	Craig T. Nelson / Dan Clark / Ross Bentley	44	Lexus Spice SE90	4.0	Screaming Eagles / Slick 50, Hollywood, CA	W-14*e	88
57	46	Doug Frazier / Sam Shalala / Jim Matthews / Dan Pastorini	58	Porsche 911	3.6	Pro Technik Racing, Houston, TX	GT2-20*e	88
58	64	Tim Banks / Don Arpin / Tim Hubman / Erik Van Vliet	77	Chevrolet Camaro	5.7	Tim Banks, Owensboro, KY	GT1-22	86
59	20	Don Bell / Tom Volk / Paul Debban	7	Chevrolet Spice HC89	5.0	North Coast Seal / Bobby Brown, Lexington, OH	W-15*n	81
60	27	Ruggero Melgrati / Martino Finotto / John Finger	80	Ferrari 308 GTS	3.0	Ruggero Melgrati, Italy	GT2-21*m	74
61	19	Peter Lockhart / Chris Smith / Robbie Buhl	98	Ford Chevron B71	4.0	Chevron Motorsports, Laconia, NH	W-16*e	70
62	48	Rudy Bartling / Ernie Lader / Amad Kodkar / Ray Brezinka	39	Porsche 911	3.2	Ray Brezinka, Ontario, Canada	GT2-22*m	70
63	62	Charles Coker Jr.	68	Porsche 968 Turbo	3.0t	Tweeks / Hendricks Porsche, Hartsville, SC	GT2-23*e	30
64	43	Richard Raimist / Karl Singer	78	Porsche 911	3.8	Richard Raimist, La Jolla, CA	GT2-24*m	20
DNS		Steve Sirgany / Carlos Moran	41	Alfa Romeo Phoenix	2.8	Auto Volante, Miami, FL	mechanical	
DNS		Robert Gottfried / Butch Brickell	83	Chevrolet Banshee KNI-1	5.0	Banshee Racing, Jacksonville, FL	withdrew	
DNS		Luis Sereix / Daniel Urrutia	11	Ford Mustang	5.7	Drivers Alert, Ft. Lauderdale, FL	mechanical	

6 full-course cautions for 4 hours, 21 minutes,
including one hour 15 minute red flag.

Average Speed: 80.04 mph
Fastest Qualifier: #33 Michele Alboreto 1:54.597 = 116.233 mph
Distance: 962 miles
Fastest Race Lap: #50 Elton Julian 1:58.029 = 112.853 mph
Margin of Victory: 86.59 seconds
Total Purse: $300,275
Weather: Warm, intermittent rain
Winner's Share: $48,000
Attendance: 92,000 (est.)
Lap Leaders: #3 1-19, 24-39, 43-49, 127-131, 147, 169-171, 173-201, 203-260;
#50 20-23; **#2** 40-42, 51-67; **#33** 68-69, 92-104, 114-126, 133-146, 148-168;
#30 50, 70-90, 105-113; **#9** 91, 132, 172, 202

1995 HOURLY STANDINGS — TOP 10

	GRID	POS.	1 HR.	2 HRS.	3 HRS.	4 HRS.	5 HRS.	6 HRS.	7 HRS.	8 HRS.	9 HRS.	10 HRS.	11 HRS.	Finish
#33	1:54.59	1	3	2	30	33	33	33	3	3	3	3	3	3
#2	1:55.22	2	2	3	9	30	3	3	9	9	9	9	9	9
#50	1:55.42	3	50	9	33	9	9	9	63	63	63	63	63	63
#3	1:55.69	4	33	33	63	3	30	63	75	75	75	33	33	33
#16	1:55.94	5	9	30	3	63	63	75	10	33	33	75	75	75
#30	1:56.58	6	30	63	75	75	75	10	33	74	74	74	74	74
#9	2:00.62	7	63	75	74	74	10	74	74	4	4	4	4	2
#63	2:01.20	8	10	10	10	10	74	72	4	72	72	00	00	00
#44	2:01.69	9	74	74	5	72	01	4	00	6	00	6	6	4
#10	2:02.63	10	6	5	00	01	72	30	72	00	6	2	2	6

x = rain

YEAR	SANCTION	CIRCUIT	ST.	FIN.	% FIN.	LDRS.	LD. CHGS.	MILES	MARGIN	AVG.	CAUTIONS	FASTEST QUALIFIER	FASTEST RACE LAP
1995	IMSA	3.70	64	45	70.3	6	23	962.0	86.5 Sec.	80.04x	6/4:21	Michele Alboreto 116.23	Elton Julian 112.853
1994	IMSA	3.70	48	30	62.5	5	19	1,209.9	5 Laps	100.63	0	Paul Gentilozzi 110.04	Andy Evans 107.992
1993	IMSA	3.70	47	34	72.3	3	12	851.0	2 Laps	70.69x	5/5:55	Juan Fangio II 125.50	P.J. Jones 120.215
1992	IMSA	3.70	48	23	47.9	5	20	1,332.0	5 Laps	110.72	2/0:26	Juan Fangio II 125.50	Geoff Brabham 121.465
1991	IMSA	3.70	46	23	54.3	4	18	1,102.6	1 Lap	91.63x	7/3:14	Geoff Brabham 121.35	Bob Wollek 119.870
1990	IMSA	3.70	49	24	48.9	6	19	1,237.1	87.8 Sec.	102.99	6/2:58	Chip Robinson 127.81	Geoff Brabham 124.774
1989	IMSA	4.11	53	31	58.5	2	4	1,356.3	2 Laps	112.74	1/0:29	Geoff Brabham 127.75	Arie Luyendyk 123.530
1988	IMSA	4.11	65	37	57.0	3	9	1,306.9	9 Laps	108.78	2/0:37	Chip Robinson 127.72	Geoff Brabham 122.569
1987	IMSA	4.11	74	38	51.3	3	6	1,224.8	2 Laps	101.85	6/2:31	Chip Robinson 120.33	Price Cobb 118.368
1986	IMSA	4.86	76	28	36.8	6	16	1,394.8	8 Laps	115.85	1/0:24	Whitney Ganz 133.13	Chip Robinson 130.707
1985	IMSA	4.86	74	27	36.4	5	4	1,365.6	4 Laps	113.78	0	Hans Stuck 131.57	Derek Bell 128.916
1984	IMSA	4.86	81	33	40.7	7	11	1,278.2	2 Laps	106.36	2/0:21	Brian Redman 125.90	Al Holbert 122.563
1983	IMSA	4.75	84	41	48.8	8	23	1,097.2	94 Sec.	91.27	5/1:28	John Paul Jr. 118.78	Brian Redman 119.790
1982	IMSA	5.20	67	28	41.7	7	11	1,268.2	121 Sec.	105.40	0	Bobby Rahal 127.29	B. Whittington 121.173
1981	IMSA	5.20	78	33	42.3	6	10	1,274.0	3 Laps	106.04	1/0:10	John Fitzpatrick 125.91	John Paul Jr. 125.930
1980	IMSA	5.20	79	34	43.0	3	4	1,315.6	3 Laps	109.52	0	John Fitzpatrick 121.52	John Fitzpatrick 123.962
1979	IMSA	5.20	72	29	40.2	4	4	1,242.8	1 Lap	103.46	0	Rolf Stommelen 118.45	B. Whittington 117.629
1978	IMSA	5.20	76	35	46.0	5	7	1,248.0	92 Sec.	103.98	1/0:12	David Hobbs 120.25	Rolf Stommelen 118.972
1977	IMSA	5.20	72	29	40.2	3	2	1,216.8	5 Laps	101.40	0	Peter Gregg 112.09	Rolf Stommelen 111.801
1976	IMSA	5.20	75	34	45.3	5	5	1,196.0	2 Laps	99.62	0	John Greenwood 111.47	Peter Gregg 109.658
1975	IMSA	5.20	69	30	43.4	3	2	1,237.0	3 Laps	102.64	0	Hans Stuck 110.91	John Greenwood 110.638
1973	IMSA	5.20	72	39	54.1	4	7	1,175.2	1 Lap	97.85	0	Tony DeLorenzo 106.96	Hans Stuck
1972	SCCA	5.20	61	29	47.5	2	2	1,341.6	2 Laps	111.80	0	Mario Andretti 123.63	Milt Minter* 121.717
1971	SCCA	5.20	57	24	42.1	6	9	1,352.0	3 Laps	112.86	0	Mark Donohue 123.44	Ronnie Peterson 124.418
1970	SCCA	5.20	68	28	41.1	7	15	1,289.6	22.1 Sec.	107.03	0	Mario Andretti 121.95	Jo Siffert 122.537
1969	SCCA	5.20	70	46	65.7	6	13	1,242.8	13 Laps	103.36	0	Chris Amon 116.83	Jo Siffert 114.720
1968	SCCA	5.20	68	36	52.1	3	6	1,232.0	11 Laps	102.51	0	Hans Herrmann 110.51	Jo Siffert 110.769
1967	SCCA	5.20	58	35	59.3	3	5	1,237.6	12 Laps	102.13	0	Mario Andretti 111.43	Jo Siffert 111.032
1966	SCCA	5.20	64	30	46.8	4	4	1,185.8	12 Laps	98.07	0	Dan Gurney 107.22	Scooter Patrick 106.900
1965	SCCA	5.20	66	43	65.1	3	4	1,019.2	4 Laps	84.72x	0	Mike Spence 105.41	Mike Spence 104.410
1964	ARCF	5.20	66	40	60.6	6	14	1,019.2	1 Lap	92.73x	0	Mario Andretti	Dan Gurney 104.410
1963	ARCF	5.20	65	42	64.6	4	6	1,112.8	1 Lap	90.93	0	Jim Hall	Dan Gurney 100.410
1962	ARCF	5.20	65	37	56.9	4	7	1,086.8	10 Laps	89.14	0	Dan Gurney	Jim Hall 97.805
1961	ARCF	5.20	65	40	61.5	3	4	1,092.0	9 Laps	90.71	0	John Surtees	John Surtees 97.200
1960	ARCF	5.20	65	41	63.0	5	2	1,019.2	2 Laps	84.92	0	Jim Hall	John Surtees 97.400
1959	ARCF	5.20	65	48	73.8	7	7	977.6	1 Lap	81.46x	0	John Surtees	John Surtees 94.996
1958	ARCF	5.20	65	41	63.0	2	2	1,040.0	1 Lap	86.76	0	John Surtees	Pedro Rodriguez 92.857
1957	ARCF	5.20	65	38	58.4	2	1	1,024.4	1 Lap	85.36	0	Pedro Rodriguez	Stirling Moss 93.600
1956	ARCF	5.20	59	24	41.0	2	7	1,008.8	2 Laps	84.07	0	Stirling Moss	Juan Fangio 92.500
1955	AAA	5.20	80	49	61.2	2	2	946.4	24.5 Sec.	78.86	0	Stirling Moss	Mike Hawthorn* 92.500
1954	AAA	5.20	59	25	42.4	5	9	868.4	4 Laps	72.96	0	Stirling Moss	Alberto Ascari* 89.500
1953	AAA	5.20	51	34	66.6	3	5	899.6	1 Lap	74.96	0	Jean Behra	John Fitch*
1952	AAA	5.20	32	17	53.1	2	1	754.0	5 Laps	62.83	0	Stirling Moss	Bill Spear*

* = unofficial

12 HOURS OF SEBRING WINNING CAR DATA SUMMARY

YEAR	NO.	MAKE / TYPE	CHASSIS NO.	OWNER/TEAM (COUNTRY)	ENGINE	CYL.	COLOR	TIRE	AVG.	Q.POS.	LAPS LED	% OF RACE
1995	3	Ferrari 333SP	003	Scandia Motorsports (USA)	4.0 Ferrari	12	red	PI	80.04+r	4		53.0
1994	75	Nissan 300ZX	07	Clayton Cunningham (USA)	3.0t Nissan	6	red/blue	YO	100.63	4		48.6
1993	99	Toyota Eagle Mk II	004	All American Racers (USA)	2.1t Toyota	4	white	GY	70.69r	1		50.8
1992	99	Toyota Eagle Mk III	004	All American Racers (USA)	2.1t Toyota	4	white	GY	110.73	1		40.8
1991	83	Nissan NPT-90	9003	Nissan Performance Tech. (USA)	3.0t Nissan	6	blue/red	GY	91.63r	1		61.0
1990	83	Nissan ZXT GTP	8801	Nissan Performance Tech. (USA)	3.0t Nissan	6	blue/red	GY	102.99	3		50.1
1989	83	Nissan ZXT GTP	8801	Electramotive (USA)	3.0t Nissan	6	blue/red	GY	112.7+	1		95.7
1988	86	Porsche 962	121	Bruce Leven / Bayside (USA)	3.0t Porsche	6	white/black	GY	108.78	4		71.1
1987	86	Porsche 962	121	Bruce Leven / Bayside (USA)	3.2t Porsche	6	white/red	GY	101.85	2		16.4
1986	5	Porsche 962	113	Bob Akin (USA)	3.2t Porsche	6	red/white	YO	115.85	4		83.6
1985	8	Porsche 962	104	Preston Henn (USA)	3.2t Porsche	6	orange	GY	113.78	13		37.7
1984	48	Porsche 935	n/a	Reinhold Joest (Germany)	3.0t Porsche	6	white/blue	GY	106.36	16		13.7
1983	9	Porsche 934	91190030	Wayne Baker (USA)	2.8t Porsche	6	yellow	FS	91.27	14		4.7
1982	18	Porsche 935	JLP-3	John Paul Sr. (USA)	2.8t Porsche	6	blue/yellow	GY	105.40	4		45.1
1981	86	Porsche 935	930770909	Bruce Leven (USA)	2.8t Porsche	6	white/blue	GY	106.04	4		33.4
1980	6	Porsche 935K3	930890024	Dick Barbour (USA)	2.8t Porsche	6	white/blue	GY	109.52	1		66.7
1979	9	Porsche 935	930770959	Dick Barbour (USA)	2.8t Porsche	6	blue/yellow	GY	103.46	9		27.6
1978	9	Porsche 935	930770910	Dick Barbour (USA)	2.8t Porsche	6	blue/yellow	GY	103.98	5		38.7
1977	30	Porsche Carrera RSR	4609048	George Dyer (USA)	3.0 Porsche	6	white	GY	101.40	7		35.0
1976	14	Porsche Carrera RSR	4609056	George Dickinson (USA)	3.0 Porsche	6	blue/yellow	GY	99.62	3		35.6
1975	25	BMW CSL	2275984	BMW Factory (Germany)	3.0 BMW	6	white/red	DL	102.6+	4		71.8
1973	59	Porsche Carrera RS	9113600865	Dr. Dave Helmick (USA)	2.8 Porsche	6	yellow	GY	97.85	4		62.4
1972	2	Ferrari 312P	082	Ferrari Factory (Italy)	3.0 Ferrari	12	red	FS	111.80	1		43.4
1971	3	Porsche 917	917.020	Martini Racing Team (Germany)	5.0 Porsche	12	silver/blue	FS	112.66	3		48.4
1970	21	Ferrari 512S	1026	Ferrari Factory (Italy)	5.0 Ferrari	12	red	FS	107.03	7		4.0
1969	22	Ford GT40	1075	John Wyer (England)	4.9 Ford	8	blue/orange	FS	103.36	(12)*		14.6
1968	49	Porsche 907 (short tail)	907.023	Porsche Factory (Germany)	2.2 Porsche	8	white/green	FS	102.51	(1)*		88.9
1967	1	Ford Mk IV	J4	Ford Factory (USA)	7.0 Ford	8	yellow	FS	102.13	(1)*		95.7
1966	1	Ford X-1 (roadster)	110	Shelby American (USA)	7.0 Ford	8	red	GY	98.07	(5)*		0.4
1965	3	Chaparral 2A	001	Jim Hall (USA)	5.4 Chevrolet	8	white/brown	FS	84.72r	(1)*		91.3
1964	22	Ferrari 275P	0812	Ferrari Factory (Italy)	3.3 Ferrari	12	red	DL	92.73	(5)*		9.8
1963	30	Ferrari 250P	0810	Ferrari Factory (Italy)	3.0 Ferrari	12	red	DL	90.39			34.4
1962	23	Ferrari 250TR	0792	SSS Republica de Venezia (Italy)	3.0 Ferrari	12	dark red	DL	89.14			52.9
1961	14	Ferrari 250TR	0792	Ferrari Factory (Italy)	3.0 Ferrari	12	red	DL	90.71			41.4
1960	42	Porsche RS60	718042	Joakim Bonnier (Sweden)	1.6 Porsche	4	silver	EN	84.92			30.6
1959	7	Ferrari 250TR	0766	Ferrari Factory (Italy)	3.0 Ferrari	12	red	EN	81.46r			65.0
1958	14	Ferrari 250TR	0704	Ferrari Factory (Italy)	3.0 Ferrari	12	red	PI	86.76			89.8
1957	19	Maserati 450S	4501	Maserati Factory (Italy)	4.5 Maserati	8	red	PI	84.07			52.0
1956	17	Ferrari 860 Monza	0604M	Ferrari Factory (Italy)	3.4 Ferrari	6	red	EN	84.07			97.8
1955	19	Jaguar D	XKD406	Briggs Cunningham (USA)	3.4 Jaguar	6	dark green	DL	79.30			4.1
1954	56	OSCA MT-4b	1137	Briggs Cunningham (USA)	1.5 OSCA	4	white	PI	72.80			80.3
1953	57	Cunningham C4R	5216	Briggs Cunningham (USA)	5.4 Chrysler	8	white/blue	FS	74.96			80.3
1952	9	Frazer Nash LMR	421100160	Duke Donaldson (USA)	2.0 Bristol/BMW	6	silver	DL	62.80			64.8

t = turbocharged
n/a = information not available.
r = heavy rains slowed average speed.
x = set fastest race lap.

All Sebring winners since 1963 had rear engines except 1975, '94.
Tire Codes: DL = Dunlop; GY = Goodyear; FS = Firestone; EN = Englebert; PI = Pirelli; YO = Yokohama.
*(Qualify Position) Le Mans type start. Cars were lined up according to engine displacement prior to 1964.

MAJOR MANUFACTURER PARTICIPATION AT SEBRING

Country groupings: **ITALY** (Alfa Romeo, Ferrari, Fiat, Lancia, Maserati, OSCA) · **ENGLAND** (Aston Martin, Austin-Healey, Jaguar, Lotus, MG, Triumph) · **GERMANY** (BMW, Porsche) · **JAPAN** (Mazda, Nissan/Datsun, Toyota) · **UNITED STATES** (AMC, Chevrolet-Corvette, Chevrolet-Camaro, Chevrolet-Other, Ford-Mustang, Ford-Other, Pontiac, Mercury, Oldsmobile) · **OTHER** (Renault–France, Volvo–Sweden)

YEAR	ALFA ROMEO	FERRARI	FIAT	LANCIA	MASERATI	OSCA	ASTON MARTIN	AUSTIN-HEALEY	JAGUAR	LOTUS	MG	TRIUMPH	BMW	PORSCHE	MAZDA	NISSAN/DATSUN	TOYOTA	AMC	CHEVROLET-Corvette	CHEVROLET-Camaro	CHEVROLET-Other	FORD-Mustang	FORD-Other	PONTIAC	MERCURY	OLDSMOBILE	RENAULT (France)	VOLVO (Sweden)
52	–	3	–	–	–	–	1	–	4	–	8	–	–	–	–	–	–	–	–	–	–	–	–	–	1	–	–	–
53	–	3	–	–	2	3	2	–	10	–	6	–	–	–	–	–	–	–	–	–	–	–	–	–	–	–	–	–
54	–	3	–	4	2	6	2	4	11	–	4	1	–	3	–	–	–	–	–	–	–	–	–	–	–	–	–	–
55	–	11	1	–	3	6	–	10	7	2	2	1	–	7	–	–	–	–	–	–	–	1	–	–	–	–	3	–
56	–	8	–	–	5	1	2	4	9	2	3	–	–	4	–	–	–	–	5	–	–	–	–	–	–	–	1	–
57	3	9	–	–	7	1	–	3	6	4	3	3	–	6	–	–	–	–	4	–	–	–	–	–	–	–	3	–
58	3	13	4	–	2	2	3	3	5	4	–	3	–	7	–	–	–	–	3	–	–	–	–	–	–	–	–	–
59	4	11	4	2	1	4	2	3	3	5	3	2	–	7	–	–	–	–	–	–	–	–	–	–	–	–	–	–
60	7	10	1	–	4	4	–	4	–	3	3	–	–	8	–	–	–	–	5	–	–	–	–	–	–	–	–	–
61	5	13	2	–	6	2	2	3	–	–	2	2	–	7	–	–	–	–	5	–	–	–	–	–	–	–	–	–
62	5	11	1	–	3	3	–	1	1	2	3	1	–	6	–	–	–	–	7	–	–	–	1	–	–	–	–	–
63	1	11	–	–	–	2	–	3	4	2	2	5	–	4	–	–	–	–	7	–	–	–	–	–	–	–	–	1
64	4	11	–	–	–	–	–	3	–	3	3	2	–	10	–	–	–	–	5	–	–	–	–	–	–	–	3	3
65	4	9	–	–	–	–	–	3	2	3	4	4	–	9	–	–	–	–	4	–	–	–	2	–	–	–	2	1
66	3	5	–	–	–	–	–	2	1	1	4	5	–	12	–	–	–	–	3	–	–	–	10	–	–	–	2	–
67	2	7	–	1	–	1	–	3	1	–	3	4	–	13	–	–	–	–	4	–	–	–	10	–	–	–	1	1
68	–	1	–	2	–	–	–	1	1	1	3	3	–	13	–	–	–	3	5	10	–	8	4	–	2	–	1	–
69	5	4	–	2	–	–	–	3	–	1	6	–	2	18	–	–	–	–	4	9	–	2	3	–	–	–	–	1
70	5	6	2	2	–	–	–	1	–	1	4	–	1	15	–	–	–	1	6	8	–	3	2	–	–	–	–	2
71	4	8	1	–	–	–	–	–	–	–	2	–	–	16	–	–	–	–	6	12	1	2	1	–	–	–	–	–
72	4	7	1	–	–	–	–	–	–	–	–	–	–	18	–	1	–	–	5	12	1	2	2	–	–	–	–	–
73	–	–	–	–	–	–	–	–	–	–	1	–	1	19	2	3	–	1	18	15	2	4	4	–	–	–	–	–
75	–	1	–	–	–	–	–	–	–	1	1	–	6	27	1	4	–	1	11	8	–	2	–	–	–	–	1	1
76	1	–	–	–	–	–	–	–	–	–	3	–	5	25	2	1	–	–	13	10	2	2	3	1	–	–	1	–
77	2	3	–	1	–	–	–	–	–	–	1	1	–	33	–	2	–	–	13	8	2	2	–	–	–	–	1	–
78	–	–	–	1	–	–	–	–	–	–	1	2	5	39	1	2	–	–	9	5	3	2	–	–	–	2	–	–
79	1	–	–	1	–	–	–	–	–	–	–	–	1	45	4	–	1	–	4	9	2	–	1	–	–	–	–	–
80	1	–	–	1	–	–	–	–	–	–	–	1	3	42	8	2	1	2	8	6	1	–	–	1	–	–	–	–
81	1	–	–	1	–	–	–	–	–	–	–	2	3	38	13	2	–	1	6	6	2	1	–	–	–	–	–	–
82	–	2	–	1	–	–	–	–	–	–	–	–	5	30	7	1	–	1	2	7	2	2	–	1	–	1	1	–
83	–	1	–	–	–	–	2	–	1	–	–	–	3	36	10	–	–	–	3	6	3	2	2	4	1	–	1	–
84	–	1	–	–	–	–	–	–	3	–	–	–	2	31	11	1	–	–	5	7	1	–	–	5	–	–	–	–
85	–	2	–	–	–	–	–	–	2	–	–	1	–	27	13	–	–	–	5	7	1	1	–	3	–	–	–	–
86	–	–	–	–	–	–	–	–	2	–	–	–	–	19	9	1	1	–	6	7	1	4	–	3	–	1	–	–
87	–	–	–	–	–	–	–	–	–	–	–	–	–	15	10	–	2	–	4	11	–	4	–	6	–	2	–	–
88	–	–	–	–	–	–	–	–	2	–	–	–	–	12	8	–	2	–	4	6	1	–	–	6	3	–	–	–
89	–	–	–	–	–	–	–	–	2	–	–	–	1	11	7	5	1	–	2	5	–	–	–	4	3	–	–	–
90	–	–	–	–	–	–	–	–	2	–	–	–	1	8	8	5	2	–	–	5	–	1	–	2	2	–	–	–
91	–	–	–	–	–	–	–	–	1	–	–	–	1	7	6	7	2	–	2	4	–	3	–	–	–	–	–	–
92	–	–	–	–	–	–	–	–	1	–	–	–	–	6	5	9	2	–	–	7	1	–	–	1	–	3	–	–
93	–	–	–	–	–	–	–	–	–	–	–	–	1	13	3	5	2	–	2	6	–	1	–	2	–	3	–	–
94	–	–	–	–	–	–	–	–	–	–	1	–	–	15	2	6	–	–	2	6	–	–	–	–	–	6	–	–
95	–	5	–	–	–	–	–	–	–	–	–	–	2	23	3	3	–	–	1	9	–	1	–	1	–	5	–	–
TOTAL	65	180	17	18	35	35	16	54	82	40	71	42	43	704	133	61	15	10	198	211	26	49	48	39	12	23	21	10
BEST O/A FINISH	3	1(10x)	10	2	1	1	2	3	1	4	6	6	1	1(17x)	6	1(4x)	1(2x)	12	3	3	4	4	1(3x)	7	6	7	15	23

This chart shows participation by major international automotive manufacturers at the 12 Hours of Sebring with a minimum of ten entries. Not included are the many limited production makes (Cobra, D-B, Arnolt-Bristol, Cunningham, etc.) and special racing chassis entries (March, Lola, Elva, Matra, Spice, Chevron, etc.). This chart generally does not credit manufacturers for engines used in special racing chassis entries other than their own.

INDEX OF WINNING DRIVERS

Bostyan, Richard	1976, 77, 78	
Bott, Frank	1953, 54, 57, 58, 60	
Bouchut, Christophe	1995	
Bourassa, John	1994, 95	
Bowden, Paul	1977	
Bowers, R.	1961	
Bowles, Aubrey	1976	
Bowman, Bill	1967	
Boy, Russ	1978, 80, 81, 84	
Boye, Bill	1968, 69, 77	
Boyer, Bill	1976, 79, 80, 82, 84, 85, 86, 87	
Boykin, Russ	1973	
Boynton, Ted	1955, 56, 57	
Boza, Roberto	1973, 75	
Brabham, David	1992	
Brabham, Gary	1991, 92	
Brabham, Geoff	1989, 90, 91, 92	
Brack, Bill	1969	
Bradey, Grant	1983	
Bradley, Francis	1961	
Bradley, W.	1960	
Brady, Kenneth	1989, 94	
Braniff, Carlos	1955	
Brassfield, Darin	1982, 85, 86, 87, 92, 93, 94, 95	
Brassfield, Jerry	1982, 85	
Brassfield, Tony	1982	
Braun, Ken	1976	
Bremner, Rod	1978	
Bren, Steve	1989	
Brennan, Merle	1964, 65, 70	
Brennan, Tom	1984	
Brent, A.J.	1975	
Brero, Lou	1956, 57	
Brewster, William	1954, 55, 56	
Brezinka, Rainer	1977, 78, 79, 80, 81, 82, 83, 85, 86, 88, 89, 92, 95	
Briggs, T.	1958	
Bright, John	1983	
Brisken, Dennis	1980	
Brocken, Karl	1954, 55, 56	
Brooker, Brad	1967	
Brockman, Mike	1973, 76, 85, 86, 88, 89	
Brolin, James	1980, 82	
Brooks, Tony	1956, 58	
Broomall, Jack	1988	
Brosnaham, Henry	1987, 88, 90, 91	
Brown, Bob	1966, 70	
Brown, Bobby	1988	
Brown, G.	1965	
Brown, H.	1958	
Brown, Howard	1969	
Brown, Jim	1988	
Brown, Walt	1969, 70	
Browne, Gordon	1963	
Bruce, Kevin	1986	
Brumby, John	1958	
Brummer, Mike	1983	
Brundage, Hubert	1952, 53, 54, 55, 56	
Brundage, I.	1952	
Brundage, James Lewis	1954	
Brundle, Martin	1988	
Bryant, C.W.	1983	
Bryant, Grahame	1995	
Bucher, Robert	1961	
Buchler, Bob	1979	
Buckley, Tom	1982	
Buckman, William	1966, 67	
Bucknum, Ronnie	1963, 64, 66, 68, 69, 70, 71, 83	
Budd, Gene	1977	
Bueb, Ivor	1956, 57, 58, 59	
Buffum, John	1971, 72, 73	
Buhl, Robbie	1995	
Bulgari, Gianni	1964	

Bunch, Glenn	1975	
Bundy, Doc	1975, 78, 82, 84, 88, 94	
Bunker, Art	1957, 58	
Bupp, Ken	1985, 86, 87, 88, 89	
Burdsall, Tom	1983, 85, 86	
Burgner, Steve	1990	
Burnett, Gary	1990	
Burns, Bobbie	1959	
Burns, Robert	1956	
Burr, Tim	1967	
Burroughs, Ben	1961	
Burt, Jim	1981, 82, 84	
Busby, Jim	1976, 77, 80, 81, 82, 83, 85, 86	
Bushell, John	1965	
Bussinello, Roberto	1964, 65, 66, 67	
Butt, Mel	1992, 93, 94, 95	
Buzbee, Spencer	1975	
Buzzetta, Joe	1961, 64, 65, 66, 67, 69	
Byrd, Phil	1983	
Byrne, Herb	1966	
Byrne, Tommy	1986	
Byron, Red	1956, 59	
Bytzek, Harry	1973	
Bytzek, Klaus	1973, 77	

C

Calderari, Enzo	1993, 94	
Caldwell, Ray	1967	
Calisey, Dave	1973	
Callahan, Skip	1959	
Callas, Mike	1975, 78	
Calhoun, James	1961	
Cameron, Gregg	1969	
Cameron, John	1968	
Camferdam, Henry	1992, 95	
Campbell, Bill	1967	
Campbell, Don	1963	
Campbell, Douglas	1995	
Campbell, Frank	1959	
Canada, C.C.	1971, 81	
Canary, Paul	1983, 84	
Canfield, Randy	1968	
Canizares, Ron	1986	
Cannon, John	1963, 64, 65, 67	
Cantrell, Ed	1963, 64	
Cao, Robert	1972	
Capriles, Armando	1968, 69	
Carbonell, J.C.	1995	
Cardenas, Jorge de	1977	
Cardenas, Pedro	1986	
Cardwell, Claude	1968	
Carlisle, Cris	1963	
Carlson, Glen	1961	
Carmean, Doug	1982, 83	
Carney, Frank	1976	
Carpenter, W.K.	1954	
Carradine, Bobby	1977, 86, 92, 93	
Carraras, Abelardo	1958	
Carroll, Morris	1952, 53	
Carter, Craig	1979, 80, 87, 89, 91, 95	
Carter, Mo	1969, 75, 80, 81	
Carter, Pancho	1985, 86	
Carusso, John	1975, 76, 80, 81, 82	
Carveth, Rod	1959	
Casadei, Mauro	1995	
Case, Craig	1983	
Case, Ron	1978, 79, 81, 82, 83, 84, 85, 86, 87	
Casey, John	1980, 81, 83, 84	
Casner, Lloyd	1959	
Cason, Buzz	1983, 84, 87	
Casoni, Mario	1969	
Cassel, Chuck	1961, 62, 63, 64, 65	
Castellano, Giuseppe	1976, 78	
Castellotti, Eugenio	1954, 56	

Catallo, Curt	1993	
Catter, Carlos	1987	
Cattini, Remo	1959	
Causey, Dave	1960, 61, 75, 77	
Cavenaugh, Dave	1980	
Cella, Leo	1967	
Centano, John	1985, 86	
Ceresole, Paul	1952, 53, 55, 58	
Cevert, François	1970	
Chamberlain, Jay	1957, 58, 59, 60	
Chambers, Dennis	1987	
Chapman, Colin	1957, 58, 59	
Chapman, Harry	1955	
Chapman, Scott	1973, 75	
Cherry, Howard	1984, 86, 87, 88	
Cheung, Mike	1984	
Chevres, Gustavo	1975	
Chinetti, Jr., Luigi	1970, 71, 72	
Chitwood, Joie	1968, 70, 73, 75, 77	
Chitwood, Tim	1973, 75, 76, 77, 78, 80, 84	
Christiansen, Bob	1971, 79, 73, 75	
Christianson, Norm	1953, 54, 55	
Christy, John	1959, 64	
Church, Guy	1975, 76, 85, 86, 87, 88, 89, 91	
Churchill, Jerry	1994	
Churchill, Randy	1994	
Ciccone, Thomas	1971	
Cicurel, Richard	1952, 54	
Cilli, Angelo	1995	
Clarens, William	1963	
Clark, Bobby	1973	
Clark, Dan	1995	
Clark, Grant	1963, 64	
Clark, Jim	1964	
Clark, Robert	1970	
Clarke, Beau	1952, 53	
Clarke, Peter	1965	
Class, Howard	1953	
Clay, Grady	1982	
Clement, Morris	1987	
Cleva, Stan	1994	
Cline, Richard	1968	
Clinton, Jerry	1987	
Cluxton, Harley	1971	
Cobb, Price	1987, 88, 89, 90, 91, 94	
Cochesa, Juan	1981	
Cochran, Jay	1989, 90, 92, 93, 95	
Coconis, Tim	1986	
Cogan, Kevin	1989	
Cogbill, Joe	1992, 94, 95	
Cohen, Steve	1983, 85	
Cohn, Arthur	1968	
Coker, Jr., Charles	1994, 95	
Colby, George	1952, 53, 54	
Cole, Robert	1963	
Coleman, Linley	1962, 63, 66	
Colgate, John	1959, 60, 61, 62, 63, 64, 69	
Collins, Myke	1952	
Collins, Peter	1953, 54, 56, 57, 58	
Collins, Ron	1978, 83	
Collins, Vince	1970, 71, 72	
Colombosian, R.	1966	
Combs, Kent	1980	
Comito, Lou	1957, 58, 59, 60, 61	
Compton, Jon	1983	
Cone, Nick	1962, 63, 64, 65	
Conley, Austin	1953, 54, 55	
Connell, Alan	1960, 61, 62	
Connelly, Ron	1973, 77	
Connor, Larry	1983	
Conrad, Pete	1971	
Constantine, George	1958, 60, 61, 62	
Consten, Bernard	1965, 66	
Contreres, Andres	1975	
Conway, Craig	1995	

Cook, Bill	1953, 55
Cook, Charlie	1973
Cook, Hobart	1952
Cook, James	1957, 59
Cook, Jim	1973, 75, 76, 77, 78, 79, 80, 81, 82, 83, 84
Cook, Steve	1977, 78
Cooke, Ralph Kent	1980, 81, 82, 83
Cooper, Bill	1978, 81, 82, 88, 95
Cooper, Jackie	1955
Cooper, Mike	1988
Cooper, Tim	1978
Copeman, Bob	1980
Coppelli, Almo	1991
Corazzo, Paul	1986
Cord, Chris	1981, 86, 87, 88, 89, 91, 93
Cordts, John	1971, 72
Corrigan, Pat	1962
Cortes, Jorge	1979, 80
Cortez, Ron	1989
Corwin, Jim	1968, 70
Cosentino, Al	1978, 81
Costanzo, Or	1967, 68, 69, 70
Costley, Ed	1960
Costner, Al	1966
Cotrone, Joe	1980, 81
Cottrell, Chuck	1995
Coupland, Ron	1975, 77, 78, 79, 80, 84
Courage, Piers	1970
Courtney, Don	1983, 84, 85, 86
Cowart, Dave	1976, 77, 78, 79, 80, 81, 82, 83, 84, 85, 86
Cowdin, Charles	1955
Crabtree, David	1976, 77
Cracaft, Leech	1955, 56
Craene, Philippe de	1993
Crang, Neil	1982
Craw, Nick	1972, 75, 76, 78
Crawford, Ed	1955, 56, 57, 58, 60, 67
Crawford, Ray	1955, 56
Crebs, Richard	1969
Crevier, Joe	1982
Cripe, Tom	1981, 83, 85, 86
Crise, Red	1957
Cronkite, Walter	1959
Crookston, Al	1976, 80, 81, 82
Croquer, Pancho	1955
Crosby, Ed	1985
Cross, Art	1992, 94, 95
Cross, Glen	1987
Crouch, Alan	1983, 89
Crouzet, Francois	1956
Crowder, George	1958
Cruz, Hiram	1975, 76, 77, 78, 79, 81, 83
Cueto, Manuel	1977, 78, 80, 83, 84
Cuevas, John	1958, 60
Cullen, Don	1957
Culpepper, Lee	1978
Cumming, Tony	1952, 53
Cummings, Don	1969, 81, 82, 83, 85
Cunningham, Briggs	1952, 53, 54, 55, 56, 57, 58, 59, 60, 61, 62, 63, 64, 65, 66
Cunningham, David	1957, 58, 60, 61
Cuomo, Ray	1957, 58, 59, 60, 61, 62, 63, 65, 66, 70
Curren, Tom	1994, 95
Currin, Phil	1973, 77, 78, 79, 80, 82, 84
Curtis, Franklin	1954
Cussino, Lanzo	1959

D

Dacco, Guido	1988
Dagavar, Fred	1952, 53, 54, 55
D'Agostino, Louis	1989, 90
Daigel, Rich	1973
Daigh, Chuck	1955, 59, 60, 62

Dale, Jeremy	1991, 92, 93, 94, 95
Dallenbach, Paul	1987, 88, 90
Dallenbach, Wally	1985, 86, 87, 88, 89
Dallmeyer, Dennis	1973
Dalton, John	1958, 59, 64
Daly, Derek	1990, 91, 92
Daly, James	1954
Danaher, Joe	1991, 92, 94
Dancose, Marc	1973
Dann, Phil	1978, 79
Dassinger, Wayne	1982
Davenport, Dick	1976
Davenport, Hugh	1978
Davey, Tom	1971, 76, 82
Davidson, Alex	1973
Davies, Mike	1990
Davin, Edward	1992
Davis, Bob	1977
Davis, C.J.	1954
Davis, Colin	1962
Davis, Don	1955, 56
Davis, Dudley	1982
Davis, G.	1969
Davis, Marc	1973
Davis, Newton	1962, 64, 65
Davis, Robert	1955
Davis, Robert E.	1975
Dawe, Peter	1983
Deacon, David	1979, 80, 81
DeAmbadgio, Armando	1969
Debban, Paul	1994, 95
Dechent, Hans-Dieter	1970
Decker, Sherman	1959, 61, 65, 66
Dee, Marvin	1961
Deeks, Bob	1992
Defranceschi, Dennis	1984, 95
DeGirolamo, Joseph	1975
Delamoussaye, Jean	1990
Delano, Les	1985, 86, 88, 89
DeLong, Ed	1992
DeLorenzo, Tony	1968, 69, 70, 71, 72, 73, 75
DeLuca, Domenico	1993
Del Vecchio, Frank	1989, 90, 91, 92, 94, 95
DeMarco, Bob	1975
DeNarvaez, Mauricio	1975, 76, 77, 78, 79, 80, 81, 82, 83, 84, 85, 86
Dennis, John	1961
Dent, Larry	1969, 70
Deponte, George	1953
DePoyster, Steve	1987
Derujinsky, Gleb	1954, 55
Deserti, Bruno	1965
Deshon, Ralph	1953
DeStafeno, Jim	1973
Devaney, Charles	1953, 54
DeVries, Brian	1995
Dewey, Bruce	1986, 87
Diaz, Diosdado	1975
Diaz, Jim	1964
Dibley, Hugh	1964, 68
Dibos, Eduardo	1987, 92, 93, 94
Dibos, Juan	1992
Dickens, Stanley	1991, 95
Dickinson, George	1973
Dieas, Leland	1965
Diehl, Bobby	1983, 84
Diehl, Ed	1963
Diehl, Milton	1965
Dietrich, Charles	1958, 59, 62, 64, 69, 70, 71
Dietrich, Stephen	1980, 81, 83
Dietrich, Suzy	1967
Dieudonne, Pierre	1981
Diggett, Whitt	1973
DiLella, Vince	1977, 78, 80, 83, 84
Dini, Bob	1969
Dingman, Billy	1972, 73, 83, 84

Dismore, Mark	1995
Dittmore, Jim	1968
Doane, Richard	1958
Dobson, Dominic	1989, 90
Dominguez, Angelo	1981
Domiteaux, Mark	1976
Domizi, Dave	1968
Donaldson, Emory	1977, 80
Donavon, David	1995
Donley, Dean	1969, 71, 73
Donner, Bob	1961, 62, 63
Donohue, Dave	1993, 95
Donohue, Mark	1962, 63, 65, 66, 68, 69, 71
Doran, Wiley	1975, 76, 77
Dorey, Fritz	1960
Döry, Anton von	1959, 60
Döry, Pedros von	1960
Dotson, Bob	1990
Dow, Michael	1989, 91
Downing, Jim	1978, 78, 80, 81, 82, 83, 85, 86, 87, 88, 89, 90, 92, 93, 94, 95
Downs, Dick	1992, 93
Downs, Mike	1969, 73
Doyle, Chris	1980, 81, 83
Dressel, J.H. "Hap"	1956, 57
Drew, John	1987
Dreyfus, Rene	1955
Drolet, Smokey	1959, 67, 69
Drolsom, George	1967, 69, 75, 76, 78, 79, 80, 81, 82, 83, 84
Droulers, J.	1957
Duda, David	1992
D'Udy, Michael	1968, 70
Duke, Geoff	1953
Dumont, Bob	1975, 81
Dumont, Bobby	1994
Duncan, Dale	1953, 56, 57, 58
Dungan, Dick	1957, 60
Dunham, Jack	1981, 82, 83, 84, 85, 86
Dunn, Nick	1973
Dupont, Norm	1989
Durant, Ross	1960, 61, 62, 63
Durbin, Ralph	1957, 58, 59, 60, 61
Durkheimer, Karl	1987
Durovy, Jim	1984
Durst, Steve	1973, 87, 88, 89
Dusinberrie, Bob	1961
Duttinger, David	1987
Dutton, Tom	1971
Duval, Jacques	1966, 68, 69, 70, 71
Duxbury, Graham	1984
Dyer, George	1975, 77
Dyson, Rob	1987, 95

E

Eager, Allen	1961
Eager, William	1953, 54, 55
Earl, Bob	1989, 90, 91, 92, 93
Earle, Steve	1978
Easton, Rex	1952
Eaton, George	1971
Eckoff, Harvey	1970
Edlis, Stefan	1984
Edwards, Chester	1992, 93
Edwards, Murray	1979, 80
Edwards, Sterling	1955
Egerton, Gray	1973
Ehrman, Gus	1952, 54, 55, 56, 57, 58, 59
Eisenlohr, Cary	1986
Ekblom, Fredrik	1995
Elford, Vic	1968, 69, 70, 71, 72
Elliott, Bill	1986
Elliott, John	1971, 72, 73
Ellis-Brown, David	1972
Emig, John	1976

Name	Years
Enever, Roger	1967
Engelin, Gunnar	1964
Engels, Nick	1974, 78
Engeman, Liane	1967, 68, 69
English, Dana	1975
Ennis, Bob	1965, 66
Ensley, Jack	1955, 56, 57
Entwistle, William	1959
Erickson, Don	1987
Erickson, Ernie	1955, 56, 57, 59, 60, 61
Erikson, Brian	1982
Escott, Colin	1960
Espinosa, Honorato	1979, 80, 91
Esseks, Robert	1969
Evans, Andy	1991, 92, 94, 95
Evans, C.W.	1960
Evans, Tim	1987, 88
Eve, William	1964
Everett, Bert	1968, 71, 72, 73

F

Name	Years
Fabre, Carlos	1970
Facetti, Carlo	1962, 86
Falgueras, Rolando	1985
Fanelli, Henry	1954
Fangio, Juan Manuel	1954, 56, 57
Fangio II, Juan Manuel	1987, 90, 91, 92, 93
Farago, Paul	1953
Fassler, Paul	1980, 82, 83, 84
Faul, Steve	1976, 77, 78, 79, 80
Favré, Philippe	1993
Favreau, Francois	1968
Febles, Diego	1975, 76, 77, 78, 79, 80, 82, 84
Feld, Jim	1954, 55
Felton, Gene	1973, 76, 77, 78, 82, 83, 84, 87, 92
Fengler, Ken	1994
Fenner, H.	1956
Fergus, John	1991, 92, 93, 95
Fergus, Robert	1952, 55
Ferguson, Joe	1952
Ferguson, R.	1958
Ferguson, Rick	1995
Fernandez, Armando	1982
Fernandez, Bonky	1975, 76, 77, 78, 79, 80, 81
Fernandez, Juan	1957, 59
Fernandez, Reynaldo	1983
Ferran, Bill	1980, 92, 93, 94, 95
Ferrer, Juan	1977, 80, 82, 83, 89
Ferrier, Nadege	1957
Fiala, Fred	1985
Field, Ted	1977, 79, 80, 81, 82
Figaro, Larry	1983, 84, 85, 86, 87, 88
Figueras, Angel	1990
Fillingham, Sam	1977, 78, 79
Fine, Bob	1976
Fine, Frank	1976
Finger, John	1987, 88, 89, 90, 95
Finotto, Martino	1986, 87, 88, 89, 90, 91, 95
Fish, Calvin	1990, 91, 93, 95
Fisher, Craig	1966, 68, 69
Fisher, Robert	1972
Fitch, John	1953, 54, 56, 57, 58, 59, 60, 61, 62, 63, 65, 66
Fitzgerald, Jim	1972, 73, 77, 78
Fitzpatrick, John	1972, 80, 81, 82
Flaherty, Jack	1959, 60, 61, 62, 63
Flanagan, Peter	1971
Flanders, Scott	1982, 83
Flaquer, Fred	1981, 83
Fleming, Ed	1973
Fleming, Paul	1970, 73
Flemke, Ed	1986
Flemming, Bob	1963
Flemming, Tom	1959, 64
Flockhart, Ron	1958
Flores, Don	1976, 83
Flynn, Chet	1955, 56, 57, 58
Fogle, Haas	1993
Fogle, Robert	1968
Foitek, Karl	1968
Follmer, George	1966, 68
Fomfor	1982, 83, 84
Fonseca, Kikos	1983, 84, 85, 86, 88
Forbes-Robinson, Elliott	1956, 57
Forbes-Robinson, Elliott, Jr.	1973, 75, 84, 85, 86, 87, 88, 90
Fordyce, Robert	1971, 75
Forester, Piers	1970
Forlong, Duncan	1958
Forno, James	1960
Fortin, Danny	1973
Fortin, Jim	1986
Fossett, Steve	1993
Foulgoc, M.	1957
Fowells, Jim	1982, 83, 84, 86
Fowler, Howard	1955, 60
Foyt, A.J.	1963, 64, 66, 67, 84, 85, 86, 87, 88
Francis, Phil	1977
Franczak, Hank	1979
Frank, Tom	1977, 78, 79, 88
Frank, Werner	1970, 71, 78, 79, 80, 85, 86, 90
Fraser, Tom	1971
Frates, William	1975, 76
Frazier, Doug	1995
Freberg, Mike	1981
Freed, Alan	1988
Freeman, Bill	1977, 78
Freeman, Jim	1986
Frère, Paul	1957
Frescobaldi, Piero	1963
Freyre, John	1973, 75, 76
Friedmann, Thomas	1955
Frisselle, Brad	1977, 79, 80
Fritts, Bill	1960
Froines, Steve	1966
Frost, Bill	1958
Fry, Harry	1958
Fuchs, Andreas	1993
Fuerhelm, Duane	1965
Fuller, Bill	1962
Fuller, Dave	1986
Fuller, F.	1958
Fuller, Hugh	1992, 93, 94
Fulp, John "Buck"	1960, 61, 62, 63, 64, 65, 66

G

Name	Years
Gac, Juan	1995
Gaeta, Jim	1978
Gafford, Bert	1971, 72, 73
Gage, Ray	1976
Galdamez, Eduardo	1983
Galeano, Herman	1985, 86, 87
Galica, Divina	1981
Galli, Nanni	1967, 69, 70, 71, 72
Galtes, Jorge	1958
Gamble, Fred	1960
Gammino, Mike	1964, 65
Gammon, Jim	1968, 69, 70, 71
Gang, Adrian	1975, 85, 88
Gano, Charles	1975, 76, 77, 83
Ganz, Whitney	1984, 86, 88
Garant, Sylvain	1968
Garces, George	1979
Garcia, A.	1973
Garcia, Javier	1971, 73, 76, 77, 78
Garcia, George	1972, 73, 76, 77, 78, 80
Garcia, Jr., Luis	1975
Garcia, Manuel	1971, 72, 73
Garcia, Raoul	1982
Garcia, Tony	1973, 75, 77, 79, 80, 81, 82, 84
Gardner, Bill	1984, 86
Gardner, Frank	1966
Gardner, Jim	1960
Garretson, Bob	1978, 79, 80, 81
Garrid, Eduardo	1975
Gartner, Jo	1986
Garton, Mike	1968
Gary, Robert	1954, 56, 57, 60, 61
Garz, Al	1953, 54, 55
Garza, Josele	1983
Gates, Charles "Bud"	1961, 63, 65, 66
Gatta	1954
Gatz, Bob	1956
Gauthier, Dick	1979, 83
Gaylord, Scott	1986, 87
Gebhardt, Alf	1975, 76, 78, 79, 80, 81
Gegen, Bob	1952, 53
Geitner, Gil	1957, 58, 59, 60
Gelder, Ed	1961
Gelles, Bill	1983, 85
Gendebien, Olivier	1957, 58, 59, 60, 61, 62
Generotti, E.J.	1985, 86, 87, 89, 90, 91
Gennone, Chris	1985, 86,
Gentile, Steve	1984
Gentilozzi, Paul	1983, 85, 87, 92, 93, 94
Gerber, Dan	1964, 65
German, Jack	1954, 55
Gilbert, R.	1957
Gilgan, Paul	1983
Gilliland, Dan	1980, 81
Gillingham, Greg	1976
Gilmartin, E. Richard	1966
Gimble, John	1989
Gimondo, Vince	1969, 70, 71, 72, 73, 75, 76, 77, 78
Ginther, Richie	1957, 58, 59, 60, 61, 63, 64, 65
Giubardo, Joseph	1954, 55
Giunti, Ignazio	1970
Glage, Siegfried	1973
Glemser, Dieter	1966
Gloy, Tom	1987, 88
Godfredson, Henry	1982
Godinez, Manuel	1977
Godsey, Austin	1985
Goebbels, Willy	1976, 77
Goellnicht, Brian	1971, 72, 73, 77, 78, 84
Goetz, Peter	1965
Goldich, Bob	1954, 56, 57
Goldin, Steven	1994, 95
Goldleaf, Ron	1971, 73, 76
Goldman, Max	1956, 57, 58, 59, 60, 61
Goldschmidt, Alfred Erwin	1953, 54
Gonzalez, Mandy	1975, 76, 78, 79, 80, 81, 82, 83, 87, 89
Gonzalez, Ignacio	1976
Gonzalez, Joe	1981, 87
Gonzalez, Luis	1955
Gonzalez, Roberto	1972, 76
Gonzalez, Santiago	1956
Gonzalez, Santiago	1971
Gonzalez, Victor	1983, 94
Gooding, Jon	1992
Goral, Paul	1982, 83, 84, 85, 87
Gordillo, Luis	1978, 79, 80, 81, 82, 83, 84, 85, 87, 89, 90
Gordon, Jack	1960, 62, 63
Gordon, Robby	1990, 91
Gorstead, K.	1962
Gottfried, Robert	1983
Gottlob, Cliff	1971, 78
Gougleman, Paul	1955
Grable, Ron	1973, 83, 86

Grady, Henry	1961		
Graham, Ed	1963		
Graham, James	1954		
Graham, John	1984, 90, 91, 95		
Graham, Mike	1989, 90, 91		
Gralia, Hugo	1983, 84		
Grandsire, Henri	1968		
Grant, Allen	1965		
Grant, Francis	1969, 70		
Grant, Jerry	1962, 63, 64, 65, 66, 68		
Grantham, Chuck	1982		
Graves, John	1975		
Gray, Bob	1971, 72, 73, 75, 76, 78		
Gray, Harry	1952, 53, 54		
Gray, Raymond	1967		
Gray, Walt	1953, 54, 55		
Greb, Mark	1979		
Greendyke, Jim	1970, 73		
Greene, John	1986		
Greenhalgh, Len	1971		
Greenspun, Gene	1956, 57		
Greenwood, Burt	1975, 77		
Greenwood, J.	1952		
Greenwood, John	1970, 71, 72, 73, 75, 76, 77		
Greer, Dick	1987, 88, 89, 90, 91, 92, 93, 95		
Greger, Josef	1970, 71, 72		
Greger, Sepp	1967, 68		
Gregg, Bob	1981		
Gregg, Deborah	1983, 88		
Gregg, Peter	1965, 66, 67, 69, 70, 71, 72, 73, 75, 76, 77, 78, 79, 80		
Gregg, Simon	1995		
Gregory, Masten	1953, 55, 56, 57, 58, 61, 66, 70, 71		
Grenier, Skip	1976		
Grier, Bob	1952, 55, 57		
Griffin, Jack	1983, 84, 85, 86		
Griffith, Pat	1954		
Grimm, Ernie	1962		
Grinbold, Sepp	1975, 76, 78		
Gritzalis, Foko	1985		
Grob, Jim	1973, 76		
Groggins, Flip	1994		
Groggins, Phil	1967		
Grohs, Harald	1981		
Groleau, Jacques	1972, 73, 75		
Grooms, John	1987		
Grossman, Bob	1954, 59, 60, 61, 62, 63, 64, 65, 66, 67, 68, 69, 70, 71, 72, 75		
Grunnah, Tommy	1985		
Grunnet, Doug	1981, 84		
Guaitamacchi, Paolo	1988, 89, 90		
Guest, Charles	1980, 84, 85		
Guichet, Jean	1962, 64, 67		
Guido, Mike	1983		
Gunn, John	1968, 76, 77, 79, 81, 83, 84, 88, 89		
Gurney, Dan	1958, 59, 60, 61, 62, 63, 64, 65, 66, 70		
Guthrie, Janet	1967, 68, 69, 70, 71, 76, 79, 82		
Gutierriz, Julian	1990		
Guy, Gene	1967		
Gwynne, Don	1970, 71		
Gysler, Matt	1984		
H			
Haas, Carl	1957, 58, 59, 62		
Habersin, Art	1985		
Habersin, Rick	1985		
Hackman, Gene	1984		
Hackney, Mike	1985, 86		
Haenelt, B.	1964		
Hagan, Billy	1968, 77, 79, 81, 82, 83, 84, 88		
Hagan, Paul	1961		
Hagestad, Bob	1976, 78		
Hailwood, Mike	1969		
Hall, Bob	1963		
Hall, Chuck	1954, 60, 61, 62		
Hall, Jim	1959, 60, 61, 62, 63, 64, 65, 66, 67		
Hallock, Tom	1957		
Halquist, Roy	1970		
Halsmer, Pete	1983, 85, 87, 88, 89, 90, 91, 94, 95		
Ham, Nick	1994		
Hamilton, Duncan	1956		
Hamilton, Joseph	1977, 78, 94		
Hamlet, Butch	1992, 93, 94, 95		
Hamlett, Jim	1953		
Hammil, George	1962		
Hammond, Michael	1977, 80, 83, 85, 86		
Hamren, David	1978		
Hanauer, Chip	1993		
Hanks, Sam	1955		
Hanna, Howard	1954, 55, 58, 59, 61, 62, 63, 64, 65, 66, 69		
Hanna, Robert	1959		
Hannaway, Bret	1954, 55		
Hannemann, Neil	1988, 90, 92		
Hanrioud, Jean	1968		
Hansgen, Walt	1952, 53, 54, 55, 56, 57, 59, 60, 61, 62, 63, 64, 65, 66		
Hanson, Peter	1994		
Hanstein, Huschke von	1955, 57, 58, 59		
Harmon, Bob	1975, 78, 80		
Harmstead, Frank	1972		
Harper, Peter	1961, 62		
Harrington, Eugene	1971		
Harrington, Scott	1990		
Harris, William	1968		
Harrison, Pete	1960, 68, 69, 70		
Harry, Gene	1994, 95		
Hartman, Bart	1976		
Haskell, Isabell	1955, 56, 58		
Hassan, Charles	1952, 53, 56, 57		
Hassey, Maurice	1986		
Hastings, John	1975		
Hawkins, Lloyd	1995		
Hawkins, Paul	1961, 65, 66, 68		
Hawthorn, Mike	1955, 56, 57, 58		
Hay, Richard	1973, 77		
Hays, John	1985		
Hayes, Charlie	1962, 63, 64		
Hayes, Fred	1959, 60		
Hayner, Stuart	1987, 90, 91, 93, 94, 95		
Hayward, Rich	1993		
Haywood, Hurley	1971, 72, 73, 75, 76, 77, 78, 79, 80, 81, 82, 83, 84, 85, 86, 87, 88, 90, 91, 92, 93, 94, 95		
Heavlin, Ken	1954		
Hedges, Andrew	1962, 65, 66, 67, 68, 69, 70		
Hefner, Bobby	1985, 86		
Heftler, Roger	1965		
Heimrath, Ludwig	1961, 62, 66, 75, 78, 79, 80, 81, 93		
Heimrath, Jr., Ludwig	1981		
Heinricy, John	1986, 87, 93, 94		
Heinz, Dave	1968, 69, 70, 71, 72, 73, 77, 78, 79, 80, 83, 85, 86, 87		
Helborn, William	1957, 58, 61		
Helmick, Dave	1973, 75, 76		
Helson, Slim	1977		
Henderson, Warwick	1980		
Hendrick, Kenny	1989		
Hendricks, Jim	1954		
Hendricks, Shawn	1995		
Hendrickson, Tom	1984		
Henn, Bonnie	1979, 82, 83		
Henn, Preston	1977, 79, 80, 81, 82, 84, 85		
Heppenstall, Ray	1963, 67, 68, 69, 70		
Herbert, P.	1955		
Herlin, Bob	1986		
Herman, Don	1976, 83, 85		
Herman, Terry	1980		
Hermann, Antonio	1994, 95		
Hernandez, Daniel	1973		
Herrmann, Hans	1956, 57, 60, 61, 63, 66, 67, 68, 69, 70		
Herzog, Rene	1990		
Herzog, Victor	1954		
Hessert, Jr., Edmund	1963		
Hessert, Tom	1986, 88, 89, 90, 91		
Hester, Lanny	1986		
Heth, Don	1973		
Heuer, Harry	1963, 64		
Heuss, L.	1958		
Hey, Rob	1973		
Heyer, Hans	1984		
Hezemans, Toine	1970, 71, 72		
Hicks, Lorin	1993, 94		
Hildock, Jimmy	1995		
Higgins, John	1978, 79, 81, 83, 84, 85, 86, 87, 89		
Higgs, Jim	1995		
Hill, Craig	1965, 66, 69		
Hill, Graham	1960, 61, 63, 64, 65, 66		
Hill, Jay	1991		
Hill, Kent	1985		
Hill, Logan	1953		
Hill, Phil	1953, 54, 55, 56, 57, 58, 59, 61, 62, 63, 64, 65, 66		
Hindson, Bob	1976		
Hines, Joe	1972		
Hinkle, Jack	1958		
Hinze, Marty	1975, 77, 78, 80, 81, 82, 83, 84, 85, 86, 90		
Hirsch, Dave	1952		
Hirsch, Gary	1977, 79, 80, 81		
Hissom, Ronnie	1961, 62, 63, 64, 65		
Hitchcock, Thomas	1964		
Hivley, Howard	1955, 56, 57, 59		
Hobbs, David	1968, 69, 71, 72, 76, 78, 82, 87		
Hobbs, Gene	1959		
Hobbs, Greg	1987		
Hochreuter, Fritz	1976, 77, 78, 79, 81, 82, 85, 88, 89		
Hodgetts, Chris	1993		
Hoerr, Irv	1981, 87, 92, 94, 95		
Hoerr, Scott	1981, 95		
Hoffman, Dick	1968		
Hoffman, John	1961		
Hofstra, John	1984, 85, 86, 90		
Hogdal, John	1986, 90		
Hopkirk, Paddy	1961, 63, 64, 65, 66, 67, 68, 69		
Horn, Don	1960, 61		
Hornack, William	1988		
Holbert, Al	1972, 75, 76, 79, 80, 81, 82, 83, 84, 85, 86, 87, 88		
Holbert, Bob	1958, 59, 60, 61, 62, 63, 64		
Hollander, Bruce	1968		
Holquist, Richard	1963, 64, 65, 66		
Holt, Mike	1995		
Honegger, Pierre	1979, 80, 81, 83		
Hood, Bill	1972, 73, 75		
Horchler, Dave	1968		
Hoskins, Rob	1977, 80, 81		
Hotchkis, John	1971, 72, 75, 76, 77, 78, 85, 86, 88, 89, 90, 91		
Hotchkis, Jr., John	1988, 89, 90		
Houghton, Roger	1969		
Houser, Dave	1970, 71		

Howey, Clark	1976, 77, 78
Hoyt, Brad	1991
Hubbard, Bernadette	1993
Hubbard, Ed	1993
Huber, Gunther	1972
Hubman, Tim	1995
Hudlett, Jeff	1985
Hudson, Skip	1958, 61, 64, 65
Hufstaeder, Gib	1969
Hughes, Jim	1960
Hugus, Ed	1956, 57, 58, 59, 60, 61, 62, 64, 65, 66, 67, 69
Hulen, John	1973, 75, 77, 78, 79, 80, 81
Hulette, Don	1962
Hull, Dave	1965
Hulse, George	1984
Hulsey, Bud	1960
Humphreys, John	1980
Hundredmark, Bob	1993, 94, 95
Hunt, Evans	1954
Hunt, George	1954, 56
Hunt, Jim	1959
Hunt, Tom	1980, 85, 86, 87
Huntoon, George	1952, 53, 54, 55, 56
Hurtley, H.	1958
Hurtubise, Jim	1963
Hutchins, Mark	1980
Huth, Malte	1968

I

Ickx, Jacky	1968, 69, 70, 71, 72
Ingle, Harry	1972
Ireland, Innes	1962, 63, 66, 69
Irish, Dick	1952, 53, 54, 55
Irwin, Raymond	1980, 90

J

Jackson, Gerry	1995
Jackson-Moore, Roy	1955, 56, 57, 58, 59
Jacobs, Christian	1986
Jacobs, Dick	1971
Jacobs, Jake	1962
Jacobson, Allan	1961
Jacobson, Bill	1986, 88
Jaeger, Jim	1991
Jamieson, Neil	1993, 94
Janis, Conrad	1954
Jamsal	1976, 80, 81, 82, 83, 84, 85, 86
Jauker, Peter	1985, 86
Jelinski, Frank	1985, 88, 89, 90, 92
Jellinek, Frank	1984, 87
Jellinek, John	1984
Jenkins, Garrett	1987
Jenkins, Joe	1975
Jenner, Bruce	1980, 86, 87
Jennings, Bruce	1962, 64, 65, 66, 67, 68, 69, 70, 71, 72, 73, 75, 76, 77, 78, 79, 80, 81
Jeffords, Jim	1957, 58, 59, 60
Jernigan, Bruce	1980, 82
Jett, Paul	1967
Job, Alex	1976, 89, 91
Jobe, Bill	1975
Jocelyn, Mike	1987,
Jochamowitz, Neto	1995
Johansson, Stefan	1984
Johns, R.	1957
Johnson, Alan	1967, 68, 80
Johnson, Amos	1970, 73, 79, 80, 81, 82, 83, 84, 85, 86, 87, 88, 89, 90, 95
Johnson, Bob R.	1970
Johnson, Bill	1973, 80, 81, 82
Johnson, Bob	1961, 62, 64, 65, 67, 68, 70, 71, 72, 73
Johnson, Delmo	1960, 62, 63, 64, 65

Johnson, Eddie	1973, 76
Johnson, Hugh	1994
Johnson, Jim	1960, 61
Johnson, Jim	1987
Johnson, Tommy	1991, 92, 93, 95
Johnston, James	1959
Johnston, Sherwood	1953, 54, 55, 56
Johnston, Walter	1976, 77
Johnstone, Parker	1991, 92, 93
Jolly, Jerry	1976
Jones, Alan	1995
Jones, Davy	1988, 89, 90, 91, 92
Jones, Harry	1975, 77
Jones, Herb	1976, 77, 78, 79, 80
Jones, Hunter	1989
Jones, John	1985, 88, 89, 93, 94
Jones, K.P.	1977, 78
Jones, Lance	1987
Jones, Leonard	1975, 76
Jones, Max	1985, 86, 87, 88, 89, 90, 91
Jones, P.J.	1988, 92, 93
Jones, Richard	1990
Jones, Ron	1973
Joosen, Eddy	1981
Jopp, Peter	1961, 63
Jordan, William	1959
Jordan, Dave	1963, 64, 65, 66, 68
Josey, John	1992
Jourdain, Bernard	1990
Jourdain, Michel	1975
Jowett, Wilton	1967, 68, 69
Juckette, Tom	1981, 82, 87, 88, 92, 93, 94, 95
Julian, Bill	1984, 85, 86, 94
Julian, Elton	1995
Junco, Rodolfo	1972

K

Kalagian, John	1984, 85, 86
Kaplan, Jake	1953, 54, 55, 56, 57, 58, 59, 60, 61
Karber, L.	1957
Karmer, J.	1958
Karos, Mycroft	1994
Kaser, Jim	1964
Kater, Hans	1967
Katskee, Loyal	1955, 56
Katz, Howard	1986, 88, 89, 90, 92, 93
Kearns, Clif	1978, 79
Kearny, Donald	1964, 70
Keck, Harold	1964
Keck, Karl	1983, 84, 85
Keeley, Jim	1952
Keenan, Dale	1968
Keith, Peter	1965
Keith, Rowland	1955, 57
Keller, Kent	1988
Keller, Lilan	1994
Keller, Terry	1971, 72, 73, 75, 76, 78
Kelley, Hal	1995
Kellner, Dana	1963
Kelly, T.J.	1967
Kelly, John	1967, 81
Kelton, Steve	1990
Kemmerer, Ralph	1969
Kemp, Charlie	1970, 71, 72, 75, 79
Kendall, Bart	1985, 87, 88, 89
Kendall, Chuck	1981, 85, 86
Kendall, Jerry	1984, 85, 86
Kendall, Tom	1985, 86, 87, 88, 90, 93
Kennedy, Bob	1952, 54, 57, 58
Kennedy, Jerry	1984
Kennedy, Mark "Squeak"	1985, 86, 93, 95
Kennedy, Rod	1970
Kerney, Don	1969, 70
Kerr, Ron	1994

Kessinger, Charles	1958, 60
Kessler, Bruce	1956, 57, 58, 59
Kessler, Ray	1973
Kester, Tony	1994
Keyser, Michael	1971, 72, 73, 75, 76, 77, 78, 80
Khodar, Ahmad	1992
Kicak, David	1995
Kilborn, John	1956, 61, 62
Kilpatrick, Bruce	1970
Kimberly, Bill	1958, 60, 63
Kimberly, Jim	1953, 55, 56, 57, 58
Kimbrough, Oma	1992, 93, 94
Kinchloe, William	1952, 56, 57, 58
King, Bill	1977
King, Dan	1994
King, James	1978, 83, 84, 85
Kingham, Bob	1962, 65, 66, 67
Kingham, Dick	1962
Kinne, Buel	1955
Kinner, Rick	1984
Kinnunen, Leo	1970
Kirby, Robert	1967, 68, 71, 72, 75, 76, 77, 78, 79, 80, 83, 85
Kirill, Pete	1971, 72, 79, 83
Kirtley, Bill	1965, 66
Kite, Harry	1956
Kivela, Robert	1980
Kjoller, Jay	1989, 91
Klass, Guther	1965, 66, 67
Klausler, Tom	1978, 81, 82, 83
Kleinpeter, Hugh	1967, 68, 69, 70, 71, 72, 76, 77, 78
Kleinschmidt, Charles	1976, 77, 78
Kline, Jeff	1981, 82, 83, 85, 86, 87, 88, 89, 91
Kneeland, William	1963
Kneifel, Chris	1987
Knoop, Rick	1978, 80, 83, 85
Knott, Ken	1985, 90, 91
Knowles, Don	1986, 87, 90, 91, 93
Knudsen, Ralph	1953
Knupp, Ike	1973
Koch, Bill	1978
Koch, Dale	1977, 78
Koch, Gerhard	1970
Kodkar, Amad	1995
Koehne, George	1960
Kohler, Terry	1966
Kolb, Charles	1959, 60, 62, 63, 64, 66, 67, 69
Koll, Bill	1978, 79, 81
Kondracki, Richard	1967, 68
Kondratieff, Judy	1970
Konrad, Franz	1994, 95
Koster, Fritz	1953, 55
Koveleski, Oscar	1965, 72
Kraft, Chris	1989, 90, 91
Kramarsky, Wynn	1959
Kramer, Erwin	1972
Kravig, Don	1980
Kreider, Dale	1975, 76, 78, 84, 85, 92
Kreysa, Arnoldo	1983
Kroll, Horst	1966, 68, 79
Krueger, Dennis	1984, 86
Kryder, Reed	1986, 89, 90, 91, 93, 94, 95
Kuenz, Tom	1973
Kuhn, R.	1959
Kulok, Larry	1952, 54
Kumnick, Roy	1963
Kump, Rick	1980
Kunstle, Jean	1958
Kunstle, Pierre	1957
Kunz, Harold	1955, 58, 59
Kurtz, Charles	1958, 59, 61
Kurtz, Chuck	1989, 90, 91, 92

Kurz, Jim	1987
Kuster, Guy	1993
Kuttner, Oliver	1993, 94, 95
Kwech, Horst	1968

L

Labonte, Terry	1981, 84, 85, 86
Lader, Ernie	1993, 95
Lagasse, Scott	1988, 91, 94
LaGrow, Ken	1977, 78, 79, 80, 81, 82
Laine, Hans	1970
Lamas, Lorenzo	1988, 89
LaMay, Bob	1975, 78
Lammers, Jan	1988, 89, 90, 95
Lane, David	1961, 65
Lang, Dick	1969, 70
Lang, Fred	1977, 79
Lange, Skip	1959
Lange, Ulrich	1980
Langlinais, Mike	1982
Lanier, Lowell	1970, 71
Lanier, Randy	1982, 83, 84, 85
Lansing, Steve	1952, 54
Lapcevich, Jeff	1993, 94
Lapp, Bob	1973
Lappalainen, Bob	1987
Larrauri, Oscar	1992
Larrousse, Gérard	1969, 70, 71, 72
Lassig, Jurgen	1995
Latta, Arthur	1966
Laucks, Forry	1971
Laughton, Frank	1961
Laureau, Gerard	1956, 59
Lausberg, Herman	1982
Lavaggi, Giovanni	1995
Lawrence, Ted	1964
Layman, Paul	1964
Lazier, Bob	1980
Lazzaro, Anthony	1993
Leavens, Abe	1957
Leavens, Ed	1959, 60, 61
Leavy, Jon	1995
Lee, Bob	1980, 81, 82, 83, 84, 85, 86, 87, 88
Lee, James	1993
Lee, Tim	1982, 83, 86, 87
Leeward, Jimmy	1984
Lehew, Jon	1977
Leibensperger, Ray	1953
Leira, David	1984
Leitzinger, Bob	1989, 90, 91, 92, 93
Leitzinger, Butch	1989, 91, 92, 94, 95
Lennep, Gijs Van	1967, 70, 72
Leo, Jim	1980, 81, 82, 83
Leon, Al	1984, 85
Leon, Art	1983, 84, 85
Lerch, Peter	1963
Lesko, Ken	1954
Leslie, Ed	1962, 64, 65, 69
Lesnett, Bob	1989, 90
Lesseps, Ferdinand de	1989, 90, 94
Leuzinger, Mark	1977, 78, 79
Leven, Bruce	1980, 81, 82
Levenson, Al	1981
Levetto, Slim	1977
Levy, Ruth	1958
Lewis, Dan	1995
Lewis, Jack	1992, 94, 95
Lewis, Marshall	1953
Lewis, Paul	1984, 85, 86, 87, 88, 89
Lewis, Willy	1987
Leydecker, Byron	1978
Libert, Jean-Pierre	1981
Lieb, Frank	1959
Liebl, George	1967
Lilley, Leon	1960, 63

Lillquist, Bob	1973
Lilly, Tony	1968, 69, 73, 76
Lindley, Don	1973
Lindley, Les	1994
Linge, Herbert	1955, 56, 57, 58, 63, 64, 65
Lino, John	1981
Lins, Rudi	1969, 70
Linton, Otto	1952, 53, 54, 55, 57, 58, 64
Lisberg, George	1970
Lista, Carmen	1983
Litchie, Spencer	1962
Livingston, Mark	1972
Livingston, Scott	1988
Lloyd, Bill	1953, 54, 55, 56, 58
Lloyd, Charles	1982
Lloyd, John	1984, 85, 87
Locke, Jim	1968, 69, 71, 72
Lockhart, Peter	1995
Loebel, Terry	1987
Londono, Gustavo	1983
Londono, Ricardo	1979, 80, 83
Londono, Santiago	1983
Longworth, Robert	1953
Loomis, Gregg	1968, 69
Lopez, E.	1976,
Lopez, Francisco	1979, 91
Lopez, Juan	1978, 79, 80, 83
Lopez, Louis	1985
Lopez, Tomas	1989, 90
Loring, David	1975, 87, 88, 90, 91, 92
Los, Costas	1986, 89, 91, 92
Lott, B.	1958
Love, Bill	1958
Lovely, Pete	1956, 57, 58, 59, 60, 61
Loving, Jeff	1977, 79, 81, 82, 84, 86, 87
Lowenthal, Ron	1995
Lowther, Ed	1962, 63, 64, 65, 66, 67, 68, 69, 71
Lozano, Ignacio	1957
Lucas, Jean	1956, 57, 59
Ludemann, Linda	1987, 88, 89
Ludwig, Klaus	1987
Luis, Jose	1970, 72
Lumkin, John	1960
Lund, Tiny	1964
Lunken, Ed	1953, 55, 57, 59
Lutz, Doug	1981, 82, 83
Luyendyk, Arie	1985, 89, 92
Lynch, James	1973

M

MacDonald, Harry	1975, 82
MacGrotty, Ross	1966
MacInnes, Bruce	1987, 88
McAdam, Tim	1987, 91, 92, 93, 94
McAfee, Ernie	1955
McAfee, Jack	1953, 55, 56, 57, 59
McAlpine, Louie	1977
McArthur, Sandy	1955, 57, 59
McAulay, John	1994
McCaig, Roger	1972
McCall, Buz	1985, 86, 87, 88, 89
McCarthy, Dean	1960
McCarthy, Perry	1992
McClain, Dave	1965, 67, 68, 69, 72, 73, 75, 76, 77, 79
McCluggage, Denise	1958, 59, 60, 61, 62, 63, 67
McClure, Bob	1972, 73
McClure, George	1958, 63
McComb, John	1968, 81, 84, 85
McConnell, Bob	1986, 87
McCullogh, David	1973
McDaniel, Rex	1988
McDaniel, Richard	1968
McDill, Bill	1970, 71, 72, 73, 76, 78, 79, 81, 82, 83, 88, 89, 91, 92,

	93, 94, 95
McDill, Richard	1988, 89, 91, 92, 93, 94, 95
McDonald, Gary	1952
McDonald, Dave	1963, 64
McDonald, Lee	1972
McDonald, Van	1981, 82, 83, 84, 86
McDonough, Hugh	1981
McDougall, Chris	1995
McElheny, Robert	1990, 92, 93
McFarlin, Rob	1979
McGee, Jim	1955
McGriff, Hershel	1982
McKelvy, W.S.	1964
McKemie, William	1966
McKenna, Traver	1954, 55
McKinnon, Ken	1993, 94
McKinsley, Bob	1953
McKitterick, Skeeter	1980, 81, 82, 83, 85, 87, 88
McKnought, Don	1953, 54, 55
McLaren, Bruce	1961, 62, 63, 65, 67
McLaren, John	1973
McLaughlin, Duke	1992
McLaughlin, William	1964
McLean, Bob	1966
McNamara, William	1967
McNeill, Archibald	1959, 63, 66
McQueen, Steve	1962, 70
McVey, Bill	1976, 85, 86, 88
Mabrito, Bruce	1975
Mac, Roger	1965, 66
Macaluso, John	1993, 94
Mackenzie, Gordon	1955
Macklin, Lance	1954, 55, 56
Madray, Don	1969
Madray, Herb	1969
Madren, Ken	1983, 84, 85, 86
Maffucci, John	1975, 78, 79, 82, 83, 84, 85, 86, 87
Maggiacomo, Jocko	1962, 63, 64
Maglioli, Claudio	1968, 69
Maglioli, Umberto	1955, 64, 65, 67, 69
Maggs, Tony	1965
Magner, Len	1971
Magwood, Gary	1967
Mahler, John	1970, 71
Mahre, Phil	1992
Mahre, Steve	1992
Mairesse, Willy	1961, 62, 65
Makinen, Timo	1965, 66, 67
Makins, Rees	1953, 54, 59, 60
Malle, Jean	1958
Maloy, Joe	1983, 84, 85, 86, 87
Mancuso, Rick	1977, 85, 86
Mandeville, Roger	1973, 79, 80, 81, 82, 83, 84, 85, 86, 87, 88, 89, 95
Manley, Frank	1961, 62, 65
Manton, Peter	1966
Manzon, Robert	1954
Marcotulli, Mauricio	1956
Marcus, Buzz	1970, 80, 81
Marcus, Joe	1969, 70
Marina, Jose	1976, 77, 78, 79, 81
Markelson, Alan	1957, 58
Marko, Helmut	1972
Marks, David	1983
Marron, Jose	1975
Marrs, Frank	1976
Marsh, Don	1984, 85, 88
Marsh, Kelly	1984, 85, 86, 87, 88, 89, 90
Marshall, Danny	1995
Marshall, George	1956
Marshall, John (Miles Collier)	1953, 54
Marshall, Steve	1995
Marsula, Wayne	1970
Marte, Chris	1984, 86

Martel, Terry	1993	Mills, Doug	1987, 88
Martin, B.	1958	Milne, Toby	1973
Martin, Bill	1987	Milo, Richard	1958
Martin, Edwin	1958, 59	Mims, Donna Mae	1966, 67, 68, 69, 70
Martin, M. Barry	1965	Ministri, Tom	1994
Martin, Tony	1984	Minneker, Jim	1993, 94
Martinez, Fidel	1975	Minter, Milt	1972, 73, 75, 76, 77, 78, 79, 81, 82, 83, 85
Martinez, Ray	1958		
Marvin, Dan	1989, 92, 93	Mitchell, Dwight	1979, 81
Marx, Tom	1981	Mitchell, Robert	1970, 71, 72, 73
Mass, Jochen	1985, 87	Mitter, Gerhard	1965, 66, 67, 68, 69
Mastandra, Noberto	1968, 69	Mnich, Matt	1988
Masterson, John	1960	Moennick, Peter	1980
Mastropietro, Renato	1994	Moffatt, Allan	1968, 75
Matienzo, Eugenio	1977	Moffett, George	1954
Matsushita, Hiro	1988	Moise, Milton	1979
Matthews, Jim	1995	Moise, Patty	1983, 85, 86
Maxwell, Scott	1995	Molina, Augusto	1975
May, Jack	1976	Mollin, Arthur	1968, 75
May, Leo	1961	Molnar, Jerry	1984
May, Paul	1978	Monk, Charles	1987, 88, 89
Maynard, John	1971	Monroe, F.	1958
Mazzacane, Paul	1991, 92, 93	Montalvo, Juan	1973, 75, 76, 77, 79
Mazzi, Robert	1960	Montgomery, Mark	1987, 88, 89, 90, 92, 93, 94, 95
Mead, Chip	1977, 79, 81, 82, 83, 85, 86, 87, 88, 89		
		Montoya, Diego	1984
Means, Arch	1959	Mooney, Patrick	1989, 91
Meaney, Ralph	1970, 71	Moore, Ben	1961, 66
Mears, Rick	1979	Moore, Dan	1972
Mees, Mike	1987, 88, 89, 90, 91, 92, 93, 95	Moore, Fred	1959
		Moore, John	1968
Meister, Howard	1981	Moore, Rick	1986
Meixner, Ronny	1993	Moran, Carlos	1976, 80
Meldeau, Mike	1973, 76, 78, 82, 83	Moran, Charles	1953, 57, 58, 59
Melgrati, Ruggero	1986, 87, 88, 90, 91, 92, 93, 94, 95	Moran, Rocky	1990, 91, 92, 93
		Morehead, Bruce	1970
Melville, R.	1973	Morehouse, Wade	1952, 53
Mena, Alfonso	1956, 57, 58, 59	Morejon, Miguel	1981, 84, 87
Mena, Alfredo	1984, 85	Moretti, Gianpiero	1979, 80, 81, 86, 88, 89, 91, 92, 93, 95
Mendenhall, Elliott	1975		
Mendez, Charles	1976, 77, 78, 79, 80, 81, 82, 94, 95	Morewood, A.	1958
		Morewood, Palmer	1955
Mendez, Luis	1976, 80, 82, 83, 84, 86, 88, 89, 95	Morgan, Charles	1986, 87, 88, 89, 90, 91, 92, 95
		Morgan, David	1960, 61, 62, 63, 64, 65, 66, 67, 68
Menditeguy, Carlos	1956		
Mercader, G.	1956	Morgan, Paul	1975
Mercader, M.	1959	Morgan, Pete	1984, 89
Merello, Fausto	1968	Morgan, Richard	1987
Merino, Victor	1957, 62, 63, 64	Morgan, Rob	1995
Merwe, Sarel Van der	1984, 87, 88, 90	Morgan, Tim	1980, 83, 84, 89
Merzario, Arturo	1970	Morici, Todd	1986
Mesnick, Gary	1977, 78	Morley, Don	1963
Meyer, Mike	1980, 86	Morrell, Dave	1969
Michaels, Dave	1954, 55	Morrell, Frank	1962, 63, 65
Michelet, Jean Pierre	1995	Morrison, Tommy	1986, 87
Michy, Maurice	1957	Morton, Jack	1954
Middleton, Jay	1959	Morton, John	1964, 76, 77, 80, 81, 82, 83, 84, 85, 86, 88, 89, 90, 91, 92, 93, 94, 95
Mieres, Roberto	1959		
Migault, Francois	1992, 93		
Mignot, Marcel	1975		
Migoya, Carlos	1986	Moser, Silvio	1965
Miles, Ken	1957, 58, 59, 62, 63, 64, 65, 66	Moses, Sam	1983
		Moskalik, Rich	1993
Millen, Steve	1985, 89, 91, 92, 93, 94, 95	Moss, Stirling	1954, 55, 56, 57, 58, 59, 60, 61, 62
Miller, Alan	1957		
Miller, E.C.	1955	Motschenbacher, Lothar	1968, 69
Miller, Frank	1955	Mott, Steve	1994
Miller, Jim	1986, 88	Mouat, R.	1967
Miller, Kenper	1978, 79, 80, 81, 82, 83, 84, 85, 86, 90, 93, 95	Moxley, James	1980, 81
		Mueller, Albert	1967
Miller, Leigh	1994, 95	Mueller, Lee	1978, 80, 81, 83, 84
Miller, Paul	1979, 80, 82, 83	Mull, Ed	1957
Miller, Ralph	1956	Mull, John	1957
Miller, Sam	1973	Mullen, Jim	1980, 81, 82, 83, 84, 85, 86
Miller, Wayne	1976, 77, 78	Mummery, Ray	1968, 69, 70, 73, 75, 76, 77, 78, 79, 82, 83, 84, 86, 94, 95
Milliken, Bill	1958, 60		

Munari, Sandro	1967
Mundas, Helmut	1991
Muniz, Daniel	1972, 75
Munoz, Carlos	1983, 85, 86, 87
Muratti, Carlos	1977
Murphy, B.	1955
Murphy, Jim	1968
Murray, Dick	1987
Murray, Ken	1984
Murry, David	1994, 95
Murry, Kent	1979
Musso, Luigi	1954, 56, 57, 58
Mutiz, Camilo	1975
Muzzin, Vince	1980
Myers, Gary	1973, 75, 83, 84, 87, 88

N

Nadeau, Jerry	1992
Nagel, Bob	1965, 67, 73, 75, 76, 80
Namerow, Norman	1963
Naon, Alberto	1973, 75, 76, 77, 78, 79, 80, 81, 82
Naon, Jr., Albert	1988, 90
Neerpasch, Jochen	1968
Negron, Juan Carlos	1989
Nehl, Tom	1972, 73, 79, 83, 86, 87
Nelson, Bill	1983
Nelson, Craig T.	1995
Nelson, Ed	1968
Nelson, Jim	1986
Nelson, Ron	1988, 93
Nesbitt, Bruce	1980
Nethercutt, Jack	1959
Netterstrom, Jim	1969
Neuhoff, Bill	1975
Neumann, Johnny von	1958
Newcomer, Eitum	1962
Newman, Allen	1961
Newman, Paul	1977
Newsome, Roy	1983, 84, 85, 86, 87
Newsum, Jack	1986, 88
Nicholas, George	1969, 70, 71
Nicholson, Nick	1985
Niday, Cal	1955
Nielsen, John	1988, 89, 90, 91
Nierop, Kees	1979, 80, 83
Nightingale, Jeremy	1986
Nile, Jack	1953
Noffke, Steve	1986
Nooe, Don	1976, 77, 85
Norburn, Russ	1972, 75
Norcross, J.	1952
Norinder, Ulf	1960, 69
Norris, John	1965
Norris, M.	1958
Northam, Nort	1978, 79, 81, 82, 83, 87, 88, 92
Norton, Buddy	1995
Norwood, John	1955, 59,
Noseda, Ralph	1964, 68, 72, 73, 75, 76, 77, 79, 80
Novoa, Ruben	1968
Nowicki, Jeff	1994
Nowling, Tom	1977
Nylander, Bobbee	1977
Nylander, Gary	1977, 80

O

O'Brien, Larry	1984, 85
O'Brien, Leigh	1994
O'Brien, Robert	1952
O'Brien, Tom	1960, 61, 64, 65
O'Connell, Johnny	1991, 92, 93, 94, 95
O'Connor, Dan	1970
O'Connor, Pat	1957

O'dell, Dan	1958
O'dell, Don	1959
O'Hare, Frank	1952
O'Neill, Brent	1983, 84, 85, 86, 87, 89, 90
O'Shea, Paul	1953, 55, 57, 58, 59
O'Steen, John	1975, 76, 83, 84, 86, 87, 89, 90, 91, 94, 95
O'Sullivan, Tony	1960, 61
Oag, Alistair	1990
Oakes, Jane	1955
Oakes, Sidney	1955
Oakley, Richard	1987, 88
Oest, Dieter	1969, 72, 73, 75, 76
Oker, Robert	1957, 58
Oland, Derek	1994, 95
Olimpi, David	1973, 77
Oliver, Jackie	1969, 70
Oliver, John	1971
Olson, Drake	1983, 85, 86, 89, 90
Olthoff, Bob	1961, 62, 63
Ongais, Danny	1977, 79, 80, 81, 82, 87
Opert, Fred	1966, 67, 69
Opie, Marcus	1983, 89
Orlandini, Raul	1992
Orlando, Dario	1979
Ormes, Robin	1969, 70
Orr, James	1954
Orr, John	1975
Osborne, Ray	1954
Osman, Andrew	1993, 94
Oulette, Jean	1966
Overbagh, Hoyt	1978, 79, 82, 83, 84, 85, 86, 92, 93, 94, 95
Overby, Robert	1979, 80, 81, 82, 83
Overby, Scott	1987
Overstreet, Darrel	1979
Owen, Buell	1967
Oyler, Ron	1975, 76, 77, 78

P

Pabst, Augie	1958, 60, 61, 62, 64, 66
Pace, Jim	1990, 91, 92, 94, 95
Pagan, Miguel	1986
Pagotto, Luigino	1993
Painter, Kent	1990, 92, 93
Palivka, Jerry	1962
Pallavicini, Angelo	1981, 82, 84, 87, 88
Palmer, Tom	1986
Panaccione, David	1977, 78, 79, 80, 81, 82, 83, 84, 85, 86
Panaggio, Tom	1991
Panch, Marvin	1962
Panks, John	1955
Papke, Peter	1978
Paquette, Steve	1981
Parish, Don	1973
Parker, Larry	1975, 78
Parkes, Mike	1963, 64, 66, 70
Parkinson, Jim	1959, 60, 61, 62, 63, 64
Parkinson, Ralph	1956
Parks, Don	1969
Parnell, Reg	1953, 54, 56
Parson, Jerry	1975
Parsons, Benny	1976, 86
Parsons, Chuck	1969, 70, 71
Parsons, Don	1961
Parsons, Phil	1986
Parsons, Ray	1964
Pastorini, Dan	1992, 95
Patrick, Scooter	1965, 66, 67, 68, 69
Patterson, Allan	1953, 54
Patterson, Dean	1958, 60
Patterson, Pat	1995
Pattinson, Jeffrey	1992, 95
Patton, N.	1952
Paul, Jr., John	1981, 82, 83, 85, 86, 90, 91,

	92, 93, 94, 95
Paul, Sr., John	1977, 78, 79, 80, 81, 82
Pauley, Jim	1954, 55, 56, 57
Pauly, John	1967
Pawley, Ron	1984, 85, 86
Payne, Tom	1958, 60, 61, 62, 65
Peacock, Joe	1976
Pearce, Craig	1982
Pearsall, Randy	1952, 53
Pearson, Loren	1973
Pease, Al	1964, 65
Peck, George	1961
Pechman, Roman	1972
Pederra, Luis	1957
Pelz, Charles	1977
Pendleton, Bill	1966
Penn, Al	1960
Penn, John	1955
Pennybacker, E.	1957
Penske, Roger	1961, 62, 63, 64
Percilla, Del	1994
Perdisa, Cesare	1955, 56
Perkins, Larry	1964, 66
Perrier, Henri	1959
Pescarolo, Henri	1970, 71, 90, 91
Peters, Mike	1993, 95
Peters, Rob	1985, 87, 88, 89, 91
Petersen, Jan	1976
Peterson, Doug	1991
Peterson, J.E.	1956, 57
Peterson, Ronnie	1972
Petery, Andy	1985, 88, 89, 93, 95
Petree, Bill	1970
Petrilak, George	1987, 88
Pettey, Paul	1969, 70, 71
Pettey, Steve	1995
Pezza, Joe	1992
Pfaff, Bob	1958, 59
Pfeffer, Gene	1995
Philips, Steve	1987
Phillips, Fred	1991
Pianta, Giorgio	1980
Pickard, Brad	1965
Pickering, Michael	1967, 68
Pickering, Ray	1959
Pickering, Wayne	1983, 85
Pickett, Don	1968, 69
Pickett, Greg	1987, 88
Pickett, Wilbur	1967, 69
Piggott, Pat	1962
Pilette, Teddy	1963
Pilgrim, Andy	1991, 93, 94, 95
Pilla, Art	1987, 95
Pimm, Ed	1982
Pineda, Carlos	1980
Pinto, Raefele	1968, 69
Piper, David	1963, 64, 65, 67, 68
Piper, Richard	1990
Pipin, Fred	1968
Pirie, James	1973
Pirrotta, Joe	1973
Pizzagalli, Angelo	1982
Pleasants, L.P.	1976, 77
Pobst, Linda	1994
Polanco, Jorge	1992
Pollack, W.	1957
Polimeni, Ron	1969
Polo, Julio	1955, 56
Poltronieri, Mario	1959
Pon, Ben	1964, 65
Ponder, Bruce	1972
Pons, Jean	1955
Pons, Louis	1955
Poole, Alec	1967, 78
Poole, Candy	1955
Poole, George	1972

Pope, Steve	1983
Portago, Alfonso de	1954, 55, 56, 57
Posey, Sam	1966, 68, 69, 70, 71, 72, 75, 80, 81
Potter, Neil	1972, 73, 75, 76, 77, 79
Potter, Steve	1983, 84, 85
Price, Lew	1984
Price, R.	1961
Pridgen, Blake	1984
Priest, Alex	1983
Priolo, Massimo	1962
Proctor, Peter	1960, 61, 62
Pruett, Scott	1985, 86, 87, 88, 93, 94
Pruyn, Lance	1965
Pryor, William	1967, 70, 71
Publicker, Robert	1959, 60, 61, 62, 63
Puleo, Anthony	1990, 91
Pultz, Ernst	1973
Pulver, Peter	1962, 64, 65
Pumpelly, Tom	1982
Punch, Bob	1975
Purner, Jeff	1991, 94, 95

Q

Quackenbush, Don	1953
Quester, Dieter	1985, 93, 94, 95
Quintana, Manuel	1971, 72, 73, 75, 76, 77, 78, 79
Quintanilla, Roberto	1972, 75, 76
Qvale, Bruce	1990

R

Rabe, George	1955
Rahal, Bobby	1976, 80, 81, 82, 87
Rahal, Ed	1959
Rahal, Mike	1969, 70, 71
Raimist, Richard	1995
Rainville, Charlie	1957, 58, 59, 60, 61, 62, 64, 65, 68, 69
Ramirez, Armando	1975
Ramirez, Carlos	1980, 83
Ramirez, Mike	1979, 80, 81
Ramos, Paul	1952
Ramsey, Rex	1981, 90
Rand, Bill	1955
Rand, F.	1962
Rand, George	1959
Rand, Mike	1986
Raney, Gerard	1979
Rankin, David	1995
Rappaport, Lew	1958
Rashin, Jack	1961
Rassweiler, Cliff	1993
Ratcliff, Ray	1980, 81, 82, 83
Rathbun, Kyle	1987
Rathbun, Tom	1993
Rathmann, Jim	1958
Raub, Bob	1982
Reardon, Ray	1961
Rebaque, Hector	1961, 72
Reddy, Tom	1971, 75, 76
Redman, Brian	1968, 69, 70, 72, 75, 78, 79, 80, 81, 84, 85, 86, 87, 91
Redszus, Dave	1977, 78
Reed, Bob	1984, 86, 87, 88, 89
Reed, George	1956, 57, 58, 59, 60, 61, 62, 63, 64, 65
Reed, Ron	1979, 82
Reese, Leighton	1991
Refenning, Jack	1976, 77, 78, 79, 80, 81, 83, 86, 87, 88, 89, 91, 92, 94, 95
Regazzoni, Clay	1972
Requot, H.	1989
Reuter, Manuel	1993
Reventlow, Lance	1957, 59
Revson, Peter	1966, 68, 70, 71, 72

Reynolds, Charles	1971, 72
Rhodes, John	1967
Riano, Gabriel	1980
Ribbs, Willy T.	1987, 88, 90, 91
Ricci, Jean-Louis	1988, 89
Rice, Jerrill	1987
Richards, Paul	1959, 60, 62, 63, 64, 65, 67, 68, 69, 70
Richardson, Bob	1960, 61, 62, 63
Rickert, Chuck	1961
Ridgely, Norm	1970
Riggins, Tommy	1985, 86, 87, 88, 92, 93, 94, 95
Riley, Art	1963, 64, 65, 75
Riley, Peter	1960, 61
Riley, Reagan	1979
Rinzler, Bobby	1971
Rinzler, Keith	1987, 88
Ripley, Dan	1988
Ripley, Millard	1958, 61, 65, 66,
Rivera, Miguel	1958
Rix, Lonnie	1959
Roach, Bo	1995
Robayna, Gus	1976
Roberts, Glen "Fireball"	1963
Roberts, J.	1957, 58
Roberts, Steve "Buzzy"	1984, 85, 86, 87, 88, 91, 94
Robertson, George	1961, 62, 64, 65
Robertson, Rob	1991, 92
Robinson, Brian	1970
Robinson, Chip	1985, 86, 87, 88, 89, 90, 91, 92, 93
Robinson, Gary	1987
Robinson, George	1989, 90, 91, 92
Robinson, Mickey	1984, 85, 86, 90
Robson, Richard	1965, 66, 67, 68
Rocca, Al	1989
Rocha, David	1990
Rodgers, Alton	1961, 62, 63, 64, 65
Rodgers, Johnnie	1952, 53
Rodgers, Rajah	1966, 67, 68
Rodriguez, Gary	1968
Rodriguez, Jaime	1980
Rodriguez, Joe	1973
Rodriguez, Joe	1984
Rodriguez, Pedro	1959, 60, 61, 62, 63, 64, 65, 66, 67, 68, 69, 70, 71
Rodriguez, R.	1967, 69
Rodriguez, Rene	1977, 79, 80, 81, 82
Rodriguez, Ricardo	1959, 60, 61, 62
Roe, Earl	1981, 82, 83, 84
Roe, Michael	1984, 88, 89
Roehrig, Dana	1977, 78, 79
Roehrig, Kurt	1979, 88
Rohlfs, Warren	1959
Rohr, Jochen	1993, 94, 95
Röhrl, Walter	1993, 94
Rojas, Guillermo	1972
Rolland, Jean	1965
Rollason, Rob	1959
Rollin, George	1975
Romano, Paul	1983, 86, 87, 88
Romero, Francisco	1978, 79
Romero, Pepe	1973, 76, 79, 90
Rondeau, Jean	1984
Rosales, Rafael	1957, 62, 63
Rosen, Merv	1969, 70, 71, 72, 78
Rosenberg, Dave	1987
Rosenberger, A.	1955
Rosinski, Jose	1964
Ross, Alan	1958, 61, 62
Ross, Craig	1972, 73, 75
Ross, Tom	1976, 77
Rossler, R.G.	1964
Roth, Rolf	1960
Rothbarth, Jim	1986, 87, 88

Rothschild, Mike	1953, 54, 55, 56, 57, 58, 59, 60, 62, 63, 65, 66, 67
Rubin, Bob	1959
Rubin, R.	1957
Rubino, Frank	1984, 86
Rubirosa, Porfiro	1954, 55, 56, 58
Rubright, Craig	1983, 85, 86, 87, 88, 90
Ruby, Lloyd	1957, 66, 67, 68
Rudd, Ricky	1986
Rude, Kathy	1981, 83
Rudkin, Henry	1954
Ruesch, Carlos	1986
Ruiz, Albert	1990, 92
Russell, Jr., David	1989, 90, 91, 94
Russo, Giacomo	1966
Rutan, Bill	1955, 56
Rutherford, Gene	1978, 82
Rutherford, Johnny	1980
Rutman, Bill	1959
Ruttman, Troy	1956
Ryan, Jack	1964, 65, 66, 67, 68, 69
Ryan, John	1955, 56
Ryan, Peter	1961, 62
Rynerson, Jack	1978, 82, 83

S

Sabino, Fernando	1984
Sage, Jean	1969, 71
Sahlman, Hal	1976, 77
Said, Bob	1953, 54, 55, 58, 66
Said, Boris	1993
Saidel, Ray	1959
St. James, Lyn	1978, 79, 80, 83, 87, 88, 90
Sala, Giancarlo	1962
Sala, Maurizio	1994
Salguero, Eduardo	1984
Salo, Fred	1966
Sales, Carlos	1961
Salvadori, Roy	1954, 56, 57, 58, 59
Salyer, Ralph	1963
Samm, Bob	1970
Samm, Robert	1959
Samson, Andre	1968
Samuelson, R.W.	1955
Sanborn, Jim	1983
Sanderson, George	1952
Sanderson, Ninian	1958
Sandman, Jim	1970
Sandridge, Mark	1994
Sandro Sala, Maurizio	1994
Sanesi, Consalvo	1964
Sanford, Paul	1969
Santander, Sergio	1982
Sargis, Bill	1992
Sarle, Chuck	1952, 53
Saunders, Jack	1965
Savage, Swede	1971
Saxon, Jim	1986
Scarfiotti, Lodovico	1963, 64, 66, 68
Scarlatti, Giorgio	1957, 60
Scatchard, Thomas	1952, 53
Scavone, Vito	1993, 94, 95
Schade, Bill	1959
Schader, Bob	1987, 92, 93, 94
Schaefer, Mike	1985
Schaub, Jerry	1972
Schmalback, Andreas	1970
Schechter, Roy	1960
Schell, Harry	1954, 55, 56, 57, 58
Schenken, Tim	1972
Scherer, Fred	1955
Schlesser, Jo	1964, 65
Schetty, Peter	1970
Schmid, Bill	1975
Schmidt, John	1954, 55
Schmidt, Oliver	1962

Schneider, Bernd	1991, 92
Schneider, John	1988
Schoenfield, Walter von	1953
Schott, Charles	1952, 53, 54
Schrader, Ken	1994
Schrafft, George	1952, 53, 54, 59
Schramm, Roger	1978, 79, 80, 83, 95
Schroeder, Dorsey	1988, 89, 90, 91, 93
Schroeder, Frank	1960
Schubot, Scott	1987, 88, 89, 90
Schuck, Richard	1973
Schumacher, Bill	1970, 73
Schumacher, Larry	1992, 95
Schumacher, Ted	1978
Schuppan, Vern	1986, 87
Schurti, Manfred	1978
Schuster, Ernst	1995
Schutz, Udo	1966, 67, 69
Schwarz, Andre	1984
Schwarz, George	1984, 85
Schweitz, Tommy	1993
Scolaro, Ed	1995
Scolo, Bob	1991, 92
Scott, Bill	1969, 75, 76, 79, 86
Scott, Ben	1968, 69, 70, 71, 73
Scott, Dick	1976, 77
Scott, Jeffrey	1980
Scott, Norman	1955, 56, 57, 58
Scott, Robert	1964
Scott, Robert "Skip"	1965, 66, 68, 72
Scott-Brown, Archie	1956, 58
Scrogham, Weldon	1995
Seaman, Robert	1988
Sears, John	1960, 62
Seaverns, Bud	1960, 61
Seeley, Bill	1967
Segura, Fernando	1954
Seidel, Wolfgang	1958
Selbert, Klaus	1973
Selby, Tim	1981, 82, 83, 84, 87
Sellers, Kenneth	1965, 66
Sereix, Luis	1971, 72, 73, 75, 76, 77, 78, 79, 81, 82, 83, 88, 89, 92, 93, 95
Serena, Fabrizio	1960, 61, 62
Servoz-Gavin, Johnny	1970
Sesslar, Don	1959, 61, 62, 63, 64
Sevadvian, Ed	1965
Shaefer, M.H.	1983
Shafer, Carl	1976, 77, 79, 83
Shafer, Craig	1980, 81, 82, 83, 84, 85, 87
Shafer, George	1976, 77, 80, 81, 82, 83, 84, 85, 86, 87
Shafer, Harold	1987
Shakespare, John	1955
Shalala, Sam	1992, 93, 94, 95
Shallett, Monte	1989
Shantz, Edgar	1966
Sharp, Jr., Eddie	1993
Sharp, Sr., Eddie	1993
Sharp, Hap	1959, 60, 61, 62, 63, 64, 65, 66, 68
Sharp, Scott	1991
Shaw, Bill	1973
Shaw, Dennis	1980, 86, 87, 88, 89
Shaw, Graham	1964, 65
Shaw, Jr., Hal	1978, 79
Shaw, Robert	1966
Sheehan, Mike	1993
Sheehy, Tom	1978, 79, 81, 86
Shelby, Carroll	1954, 55, 56, 57, 58, 59, 60
Sheldon, John	1982, 91, 95
Shelton, Jim	1985, 86
Shelton, Steve	1983, 84, 86, 87, 89
Shelton, Tom	1983, 84
Sheppard, Joe	1956, 57, 59, 60, 62

Sherk, Bud	1976		Spross, Fred	1960		Taylor, F.	1961
Sherman, C.	1958		Sprowls, Billy	1975, 76		Taylor, Janis	1980, 81, 83
Sherman, Dennis	1978		Spruell, Paul	1970, 76		Taylor, Wayne	1991, 92, 93, 94, 95
Sherman, Peter	1973		Spurr, Timothy	1994		Tchkotoura, Zourab	1964
Sherwin, Michael	1980		Spychiger, Tommy	1963		Teamey, Mike	1985
Shields, Jim	1953		Starr, Malcolm	1968		Teasdale, Kat	1994
Shinder, Brad	1992		Statzer, Lou	1980		Tennyson, David	1990, 91, 92, 93
Shinn, Vic	1973, 80		Stear, L.W. "Luke"	1958, 60, 61		Terrill, Danny	1978
Shirazi, Morris	1993		Steel, Jack	1975		Tharin, Whit	1967
Shirley, Russ	1969		Steele, Gary	1978		Theall, Robert	1969, 70
Showket, Kal	1981, 88, 90		Stefl, Dennis	1975, 76		Theodoli, Flippo	1961, 62, 63, 64
Shulnberg, R.V.	1976, 77, 78, 80		Steinemann, Rico	1967, 68		Theodoracopulos, Harry	1961, 62, 75
Siebert, Craig	1980, 81, 82		Stetson, Hal	1955, 57, 58		Theys, Didier	1995
Siegmund, Laszlo	1967		Stevens, Jef	1963, 64, 72, 73, 77, 78		Thiele, Alfonso	1958, 59, 62
Siffert, Jo	1966, 67, 68, 69, 70, 71		Stevens, Jim	1991		Thiem, Doug	1963
Sigala, Massimo	1989, 90, 92, 95		Stevens, Rick	1969		Thirion, Gilberte	1957
Signore, Jay	1962		Stevenson, Fred	1970		Thomas, Frank	1978
Silcox, Nelson	1983		Stewart, Jackie	1966		Thomas, Guy	1976, 79
Silte, Jean-Pierre	1982		Stewart, Lance	1989, 90, 93		Thomas, John	1976
Silva, Piero	1987		Stewart, Phil	1955, 56, 57		Thomas, Ralph	1995
Silver, Dick	1985		Stiff, Fred	1980, 81, 82		Thompkins, Rick	1977, 78, 79
Simon, Henry	1975		Stiles, Phil	1952, 53, 54, 56, 57, 58, 59		Thompson, Carl	1976
Simpson, James	1952, 53, 54		Stimpson, J.	1954		Thompson, Dick	1952, 55, 57, 58, 59, 60, 61,
Simson, Cyril	1961		Stoddard, Chuck	1964, 65			62, 63, 64, 65, 66, 67, 68
Singer, Karl	1995		Stoddard, Robert	1972		Thompson, Jerry	1968, 69, 70, 71, 72, 73, 75,
Sirgany, Steve	1993		Stommelen, Rolf	1967, 68, 69, 70, 71, 72, 78,			76, 77, 78, 80, 83, 85
Skiff, Ned	1982, 83			79, 81		Thorpe, LeRoy	1955
Slater, Charles	1985, 86, 87, 89, 93, 94, 95		Stone, George	1972, 73, 77		Tidwell, Ted	1965
Slottag, Jack	1966		Stone, Richard	1976		Tillson, Mike	1969, 70, 72, 73, 75, 76, 77
Sloyer, Dave	1978		Storr, G.	1957		Tilton, Ren	1976, 77, 78, 79, 81, 84
Small, Rich	1971, 73, 77, 79, 84, 87		Straehle, Paul-Ernst	1962		Timmins, Paul	1954
Smit, Martinas	1977		Strasser, Andy	1995		Tisdelle, Ash	1971, 79, 80, 82, 83, 84, 85,
Smith, Chris	1995		Straub, Glenn	1994			86, 88
Smith, Danny	1983, 84, 85, 86		Stricklin, Jim	1985		Titterington, Desmond	1956
Smith, Dave	1976		Stricler, Ron	1969		Titus, Jerry	1963, 68
Smith, Ernie	1977		Stringfellow, Tim	1985		Todd, John	1962
Smith, Everet	1962		Stroh, Bill	1969		Todd, W.B.	1962
Smith, Ford	1975, 76, 79, 80, 81		Stubbs, Arnold	1953		Toennis, Andre	1992
Smith, Gary	1990, 92, 93, 94, 95		Stück, Hans	1975, 84, 85, 86, 88, 90, 93,		Toland, Richard	1954, 55, 58, 59, 62, 63, 64,
Smith, Houghton	1971, 72			94, 95			65
Smith, King	1988		Stumes, Warren	1969		Tomaso, Alejandro de	1956, 58, 59
Smith, M.D.	1967		Stumpff, Kirby	1973, 75		Tomlinson, Finley	1987
Smith, Pete	1981		Sturgis, William	1960, 61		Torco, Lou	1953
Smith, R.K.	1991, 94		Sullivan, Danny	1979, 87, 88		Torruellas, Jorge	1964
Smith, Jr., Reggie	1969, 70, 83, 89		Summers, Michael	1968, 72		Torpy, Daniel	1968
Smith, Rosemary	1969, 70		Surer, Marc	1981		Torres, Jim	1985, 86
Smith, Vicki	1980, 81, 82, 83, 84		Surtees, John	1963, 64		Tower, Charlemagne	1960
Smith, William	1956		Sutcliffe, George	1990		Towle, E.	1955
Smothers, Dick	1969, 71, 72, 77		Sutcliffe, Peter	1966		Townsend, Randolph	1980
Smyth, Phil	1953		Sutherland, Hugh	1959		Trejos, Jorge	1995
Snow, Martin	1995		Sutherland, Rick	1995		Tremblay, John	1969, 70, 71, 72, 73, 75, 79
Solano, Felipe	1991		Swanson, Art	1960, 61, 62, 63, 65, 66		Trenery, Bruce	1993, 94, 95
Soldevila, Chiqui	1978, 79, 80, 81, 82, 83, 84,		Swanson, Jack	1975, 77, 79, 81		Trevale, Sergio	1969
	89		Swartz, H.	1963		Trintignant, Maurice	1957
Soler-Roig, Alex	1969		Sweeney, John	1975		Trips, Wolfgang von	1956, 57, 58, 59, 61
Solomone, Carm	1977		Sweikert, Bob	1956		Trueman, Jim	1976, 77, 78, 79, 82, 84, 85
Soto, Ernesto	1978, 79, 80, 82, 83		Swifts, Vance	1987		Truitt, Gerald	1968, 69
Soulas, Rene	1953		Sylvia, Earl	1968		Tucker, Edward	1961
Southard, Steve	1976, 78, 79					Tullius, Bob	1963, 65, 66, 68, 69, 70, 73,
Southern, Ron	1978		**T**				80, 81, 83, 84, 85, 86
Sparacino, Peter	1954		Tabe, Sergio	1975		Tumbleston, Jimmy	1977, 78, 79, 81
Spalding, Tom	1978		Tachi, Nobuhide	1980		Tunstall, John	1973, 75, 76, 77
Spaulding, G.	1958		Taleb, Henry	1994, 95		Turley, Windle	1977, 78
Speakman, Bob	1975, 78, 79, 81		Tallakson, Dave	1958		Turner, Billy	1967
Speakman, Mike	1992		Tamburo, Vince	1961		Turner, Jack	1980, 81, 82
Spear, Bill	1952, 53, 54, 55, 56		Tannlund, Chuck	1965		Turner, Tom	1976, 83
Speer, M.L.	1977, 78, 80, 81, 82, 83, 84		Taramazzo, Gigi	1968		Tweedale, Art	1958, 59, 62
Spence, Mike	1967		Taruffi, Piero	1954, 55, 56, 57		Tyler, Scott	1995
Spencer, Lew	1960, 62, 63, 64, 65		Tattersall, Art	1964		Tyndall, Russ	1971
Spencer, Mike	1973		Tavano, Sergio	1962		
Spitler, Steven	1952, 53, 56, 57		Tavilla, Paul	1977, 91		**U**
Spoerry, Dieter	1967, 68		Taylor, Anita	1967		Ulinski, Chuck	1983
Spreng, Gustl	1993, 94, 95		Taylor, Brian	1973		Ullom, Garth	1988
Springer, Daryl	1971		Taylor, Del Russo	1970, 71, 79, 80, 81, 82, 83,		Ullrich, Hal	1953, 54, 55, 56, 57
Sprinzel, Ed	1961			85, 86, 87, 88, 89		Underwood, Don	1954
Sprinzel, John	1960		Taylor, Edwin	1973		Underwood, Lake	1959, 64, 65, 66

Note

This index includes only those drivers who have driven in the 12 Hours of Sebring. It does not include drivers who entered but did not drive, support races, or the 1950 Sam Collier six-hour race.

OTHER SEBRING RACE WINNERS

In addition to the famous 12-hour classic held every March, Sebring International Raceway has hosted many other racing events over the past five decades. A three-hour race held the day after the 1957 12 Hours of Sebring was the first of many supporting events.

America's first Formula One World Championship race took place at Sebring in December of 1959. The following year marked the beginning of supporting events the day before the 12 hours. The first ever SCCA Trans-Am race was held at Sebring in 1966, and was repeated the following year, then incorporated with the 1968 12 hour. The SCCA Continental series raced at Sebring in 1969 and 70, utilizing the shorter 2.2-mile circuit. These two events were held at the end of the year.

In the fall of 1987 and 1988, Sebring hosted SCCA professional races. The fall races were revived beginning in 1992, featuring primarily IMSA events.

YEAR	RACE	WINNER (CAR)
1957	3 Hr. GT	David Cunningham (Ferrari)
1959	USGP F1	Bruce McLaren (Cooper T51)
	Formula Junior	Walt Hansgen (Stanguellini)
	2 Hr. Compact	Hansgen/Crawford (Jaguar)
1960	Under 1 liter GT	Paul Richards (Fiat Abarth)
	Formula Junior	Jim Hall (Elva)
1961	Under 1 liter GT	Harry Washburn (Fiat Abarth)
	Formula Junior	Charlie Kolb (Gemini)
1962	Under 1 liter GT	Bruce McLaren (Fiat Abarth)
	Formula Junior	Pat Pigott (Lotus)
1963	Under 1 liter GT 3 Hr.	Hans Herrmann (Fiat Abarth)
	Formula Junior	Dave Morgan (Lotus)
1964	Touring Sedans 2 Hr.	Charlie Rainville (Volvo)
	Stock Car 250km	Augie Pabst (Ford Fairlane)
	Motorcycles	Frank Scurria (Norton)
1965	Touring Sedans 3 Hr.	Jim Clark (Lotus Cortina)
1966	4 Hr. Trans-Am	Jochen Rindt (Alfa Romeo)
1967	4 Hr. Trans-Am	Jerry Titus (Ford Mustang)
1968	Under 2 liter Trans-Am	Bert Everett (Porsche 911)
	2 Hr. Formula Vee	Hugh Kleinpeter (Beach)
1969	SCCA Continental	David Hobbs (Surtees TS5)
1970	SCCA Continental	Mark Donohue (Lola T190)
1971	Super Vee	Harry Ingle (Zink)
1972	Super Vee	Gregor Kronegard (Lola)
1973	Formula Ford	Bertil Roos (Ford)
1975	3 Hr. Sedan	Nick Craw (BMW)
	VW Cup	Howdy Holmes (Lola)
1976	3 Hr. Sedan	Gene Felton (AMC Gremlin)
1977	3 Hr. Sedan	Walt Bohren (Mazda RX-2)
1978	3 Hr. Sedan	Roger Mandeville (Mazda RX-3)
1979	3 Hr. Sedan	Dennis Shaw (AMC Spirit)
1980	200km Sedan	Jim Downing (Mazda RX-3)
1981	200km Sedan	Roger Mandeville (Mazda RX-3)
1982	200km Sedan	Irv Pearce (AMC Spirit)
1983	200km Sedan	Amos Johnson (Mazda GLC)
1984	200km Sedan	Tommy Archer (AMC-Alliance)
1985	Firehawk 6 Hr.	Flanders/Gunnell (Chevy Camaro)
	Firehawk 1 Hr. Compact	Karl Hacker (VW Golf)
1986	Firehawk 6 Hr.	Goad/Goad (Pontiac Firebird)

YEAR	RACE	WINNER (CAR)
1987	Firehawk 3½ Hr. GS	Bayley/Pilgrim (Pontiac Firebird)
	Firehawk 3½ Hr. S/T	Schroeder/DeBrecht (Shelby Charger)
	SCCA Racetruck	Bobby Archer (Jeep)
	6 Hr. Street Stock	Bakeracing (Corvette)
	VW Cup	Alan Pope (VW Golf)
	Sports Renault	Mike Davies (Renault)
1988	Firehawk 4 Hr. GS	Goad/Hayner (Pontiac Firebird)
	Firehawk 4 Hr. S/T	Earwood/DeBrecht/Ullom (Dodge Daytona)
	SCCA Racetruck	Jeff Krosnoff (Nissan)
	4 Hr. Street Stock	Heinricy/Knowles (Camero)
	USA Stockcar	Joe Nemechek (Chevrolet)
	Formula Atlantic	Scott Harrington (Swift DB-4)
1989	Firehawk 4 Hr. GS	Wright/Heinricy (Chevy Camaro)
	Firehawk 4 Hr. S/T	Showket/Dale (Dodge Daytona)
1990	Firehawk 4 Hr. GS	Varde/Wallace (Chevy Camaro)
	Firehawk 4 Hr. S/T	Hacker/Hacker (Oldsmobile Quad 442)
1991	Firehawk 4 Hr. GS	Ham/Tosi (Porsche 944S)
	Firehawk 4 Hr. S/T	Cord/Jones (Toyota MR-2T)
1992	Firehawk 4 Hr. GS	Moskalik/Ham (Porsche 944S2)
	Firehawk 4 Hr. S/T	Hacker/Hacker (Oldsmobile Achieva)
	30-min. Barber Saab	Robert Amren (Saab)
	30-min. Intl. Sedan	Chuck Hemmingson (2) (Oldsmobile)
	12 Hr. Firehawk	Hawkins/Murry (Porsche 944 S2)
	USAC F2000	Chris Simmons (Van Dieman RF92)
1993	Firehawk 4 Hr. GS	Hawkins/Murry/Earwood (Porsche 944S2)
	Firehawk 4 Hr. S/T	Pobst/Schwartzott (Honda Prelude)
	30-min. Barber Saab	Kenny Brack (Saab)
	12 Hr. Firehawk	Murry/Hendricks/Reuter (Porsche 944S2)
	30-min. Supercar	Hans Stuck (Porsche 911T)
	30-min. Intl. Sedan	Chuck Hemmingson (Oldsmobile)
1994	Firehawk 6 Hr.	Murray/Hawkins (Porsche 968)
	100km Supercar	Peter Farrell (Mazda RX-7)
	30-min. Barber Saab	Hans DeGraaff (Saab)
	12 Hr. Firehawk	Hawkins/Said/O'Steen/Murry (Porsche 944S2)
	30-min. Supercar	David Donohue (BMW)
1995	30-min. Supercar	Sean Roe (Corvette)
	30-min. Barber Dodge	Barry Waddell (Dodge)
	30-min. Ferrari Challenge	Peter Sachs (Ferrari 355)
	Street Stock 4 Hr.	Farrell/Candia (Mazda RX-7)

UNITED STATES F1 GRAND PRIX SEBRING /DECEMBER 19, 1959

POS.	QUAL.	DRIVER	NO.	CAR	ENTRANT	LAPS
1	10	Bruce McLaren	9	Cooper T51 Climax	Cooper Car Co., Ltd.	42
2	5	Maurice Trintignant	6	Cooper T45 Climax	R.R.C. Walker Racing Team	42
3	4	Tony Brooks	2	Ferrari Dino 240	Scuderia Ferrari	42
4	2	Jack Brabham	8	Cooper T51 Climax	Cooper Car Co., Ltd.	42nr
5	9	Innes Ireland	10	Lotus 16 Climax	Team Lotus	39
6	6	Wolfgang Von Trips	4	Ferrari Dino 246	Scuderia Ferrari	38n*
7	16	Henry Blanchard	17	Porsche RSK (F2)	Blanchard Automobile Co.	38
8	11	Roy Salvadori	12	Cooper T45 Maserati	High Efficiency Motors	24nr
9	7	Cliff Allison	3	Ferrari Dino 246	Scuderia Ferrari	23nr
10	19	Rodger Ward	1	Kurtis Kraft Offy (Midget)	Leader Cards Inc.	21nr
11	14	Alessandro de Tomaso	14	Cooper T45 OSCA	Alessandro de Tomaso	14nr
12	8	Phil Hill	5	Ferrari Dino 246	Scuderia Ferrari	9nr
13	17	Frederico D'Orey	15	Tech Mec F415 Maserati	Gordon Pennington, Jr.	7nr
14	15	George Constantine	16	Cooper T45 Climax	Mike Taylor	6nr
15	3	Harry Schell	19	Cooper T45 Climax	Harry Schell	6nr
16	1	Stirling Moss	7	Cooper T51 Climax	R.R.C. Walker Racing Team	5nr
17	12	Graham Hill	11	Lotus 16 Climax	Team Lotus	2nr
18	13	Bob Said	18	Connaught D-type	Connaught Engineering Co.	1nr
DNS	18	Phil Cade	22	Maserati 250F	Phil Cade	—

*Penalized one lap

Distance: 218.4 miles
Average Speed: 98.87 mph
Fastest Race Lap: Trintignant 101.13 mph
Fastest Qualifier: Moss
Attendance: 17,000 (est.)
Weather: Partly cloudy and cool

Start of the 1959 United States Grand Prix

1ST PALM BEACH SHORES ROAD RACE

January 3, 1950

POS	DRIVER	HOMETOWN	NO.	MAKE/MODEL	DISP.	CLASS	LAPS
1	George Huntoon	Miami, FL	44	Ford Duesenberg Spl.	4588	C-1	50
2	Briggs Cunningham	Green Farms, CT	50	Cadillac Healey Spl.	5442	B-2	50
3	George Rand	Delray Beach, FL	21	Ferrari 166 Inter	1955	E-1	49
4	Leslie Johnson	Walthamstow, England	45	Jaguar XK120	3442	C-2	49
5	Phil Walters	New York, NY	34	Healey Silverstone	2443	D-1	48
6	Sam Collier	Everglades, FL	42	Jaguar XK120	3442	C-3	47
7	Steve Lansing	New York, NY	26	MG TC	1250/s	E-2	47
8	John Fitch	White Plains, NY	17	MG TC	1250	F-1	46
9	Dick Haynes	Detroit, MI	1	Fiat 1100 coupe	1088	G-1	46
10	Alden Johnson	Worcester, MA	14	MG TC	1250	F-2	46
11	Logan Hill	Riverside, CT	41	Jaguar XK120	3442	C-4	46
12	Fritz Koster	New York, NY	18	HRG Aerodynamic	1496	F-3	45
13	John Bentley	New York, NY	25	MG TC	1250/s	E-3	45
14	George Maginnis	Miami, FL	9	MG TC	1250	F-4	45
15	Jack Rutherford	Palm Beach, FL	38	Healey Silverstone	2443	D-2	45
16	E. E. McIntosh	West Palm Beach, FL	10	MG TC	1250	F-5	45
17	Phil Stiles	Palm Beach, FL	15	HRG Aerodynamic	1496	DNF	44
18	Paul Ceresole	Concord, MA	27	BMW 328	1971	DNF	39
19	Bill Milliken	New York, NY	33	Bugatti T51	2270/s	DNF	33
20	Otto Linton	Philadelphia, PA	19	Fiat 1100S coupe	1088/s	DNF	25
21	Perry Boswell	Baltimore, MD	5	Cisitalia Offenhauser	1484	DNF	22
22	Tom Wisdom	Chicago, IL	36	Healey Silverstone	2443	DNF	20
23	George Roberts	Lantana, FL	62	Ford Special	4517	DNF	19
24	Paul Farrago	Detroit, MI	2	Cisitalia coupe	1098	DNF	17
25	Bill Spear	Manchester, NH	46	Jaguar XK120	3442	DNF	15
26	Fred Wacker	Chicago, IL	8	MG TC	1250	DNF	12
27	Perry Fina	New York, NY	37	Danese Alfa Romeo MM	2443	DNF	11
28	Gus Ehrman	Greenwich, CT	11	MG TC	1250	DNF	11
29	Tony Pompeo	New York, NY	35	Danese Alfa Romeo MM	2443	DNF	10
30	Zora Duntov	New York, NY	60	Allard J2 Ardun Ford	4517	DNF	8
31	Harry Heim	Baltimore, MD	22	MG TC	1250/s	DNF	7
32	George Weaver	Boston, MA	49	Kurtis Kraft Mercury	4700	DNF	3
33	Miles Collier	Tampa, FL	40	Ford Riley Spl.	4517	DISQUALIFIED	
34	Tom Cole	New York, NY	51	Allard J2 Cadillac	5442	DISQUALIFIED	
DNS	Kenneth Stone	Miami, FL	6	MG TC			
DNS	Karl Brocken	Milwaukee, WI	12	MG-TC			
DNS	Henry Donnachie	Washington, DC	16	MG TC			
DNS	Bob Gegen	Miami, FL	20	Bugatti T38/44			
DNS	R. Provins	Miami, FL	23	Triumph conv.			
DNS	Perk Frazer	Delray Beach, FL	24	MG TC			
DNS	Red Byron	Atlanta, GA	32	Austin A-90 Atlantic			
DNS	Jim Kimberly	Chicago, IL	43	Jaguar XK120			
DNS	Mike Vaughn	Atlanta, GA	47	Lagonda Rapide			

Note: Lap totals are somewhat questionable due to timing equipment failure during race.
s = supercharged

Circuit: 2.1 miles
Time of Race: 1:54.40
Distance: 50 laps (105 miles)
Average Speed: 57.4 mph
Leaders: #51 1-2; #44 3-50
Weather: Cloudy, cool, windy, light rain.
Est. Attendance: 19,000

2ND PALM BEACH SHORES ROAD RACE

December 8, 1951

2-HOUR RIVIERA BEACH TROPHY RACE

POS	DRIVER	HOMETOWN	NO.	MAKE/MODEL	DISP.	CLASS	LAPS
1	John Fitch	White Plains, NY	1	Ferrari 340 America	4100	2-1	56
2	Fred Wacker	Chicago, IL	8	Allard J2 Cadillac	5424	2-2	55
3	Briggs Cunningham	Palm Beach, FL	2	Ferrari 166 Inter	1995	4-1	54
4	Bill Spear	Palm Beach, FL	11	Ferrari 166 MM	1995	4-2	54
5	Phil Stiles	Palm Beach, FL	99	Ford Riley	1517	2-3	54
6	George Huntoon	Palm Beach, FL	6	Alfa Romeo Monza 8C	2576	3-1	53
7	David Viall	Alexandria, VA	39	MG Lester Spl.	1462	6-1	51
8	Paul O'Shea	Water Mill, NY	5	Fitch-O'Shea Spl.	2214	4-3	49
9	Alfons Koster	Sayeville, NY	37	HRG Aerodynamic	1496	6-2	47
10	Sherwood Johnston	Winchester, MA	74	Jaguar XK120	3442	3-2	46
11	Jack Rutherford	Palm Beach, FL	34	Porsche 356 Coupe	1486	6-3	45
12	Phil Walters	West Palm Beach, FL	7	Healey Cadillac	5424	DNF	16
13	Bob O'Brien	Hackensack, NJ	9	Jaguar XK120 Spl.	3442	DNF	14
14	Tom Cole	New York, NY	4	Chrysler Allard J2	5424	DNF	4
DNS	Joe Grossheim	Miami, FL	3	MG TD Ford 60	2214		
DNS	R.W. Scott	Dallas, TX	10	Allard J2 Cadillac	5424		

Winner's Average Speed: 60.6 mph
Leaders: #7 1-14; #1 15-56.Leaders: #7 1-14; #1 15-56.

2-HOUR A.O. EDWARDS AND KIWANIS TROPHY RACE

POS	DRIVER	HOMETOWN	NO.	MAKE/MODEL	DISP.	CLASS	LAPS
1	Alfons Koster	Sayeville, NY	37	HRG Aerodynamic	1496	M-1	53
2	Phil Stiles	Palm Beach, FL	29	HRG Aerodynamic	1496	M-2	53
3	Bob Samuelson	Dallas, TX	41	MG TC	1250	M-3	53
4	Briggs Cunningham	Palm Beach, FL	30	Porsche 356 Coupe	1486	C-1	53
5	J.S. Grier	Coral Gables, FL	21	MG TC	1250	C-2	50
6	Peter Iselin	New York, NY	26	MG TD	1250	C-3	50
7	Bob Gegen	Miami, FL	35	MG TD	1250	M-4	48
8	Lon Parkes	Boston, MA	28	MG TD	1250	C-4	46
9	George Schrafft	Palm Beach, FL	59	Crosley Le Mans Spl.	726	DNF	45
10	Max Hoffman	New York, NY	40	Glockler Porsche Spyder	1488	DNF	24
11	David Vial	Alexandria, VA	39	Lester MG	1462	DNF	20
12	Tony Pompeo	New York, NY	33	Siata	1395	DNF	11
13	Bill Lloyd	Green Farms, CT	32	MG Offenhauser	1490	DNF	10
14	Jim Cunningham	Houston, TX	38	MG TC	1250	DNF	9

M = Modified

C = Catalog (stock)

Circuit: 1.9-mile street course

Leaders: #40 1-24; #37 25-30, 34-40, 44-53; #41 31-33, 41-43.

Est. Attendance: 15,000

Weather: Partly cloudy, warm.

ONE-HOUR HOFFMAN TROPHY STOCK JAGUAR RACE won by John Fitch.

15-LAP PALM BEACH CUP RACE won by Peter Dillnut.

VERO BEACH ENDURANCE RACE

March 8, 1952 / Vero Beach Airport

12-HOUR ENTRANTS

POS	DRIVERS	NO.	CAR MAKE/MODEL	DISP.	CLASS-POS	INDEX	LAPS
1	Jim Kimberly / Marshall Lewis	5	Ferrari 340 America	4100	2-1	5	245
2	Tom Cole / Paul O'Shea	9	Allard J2X Cadillac	5424	2-2	7	239
3	Bill Spear / Phil Walters	31	Ferrari 166 MM	1995	4-1	2	237
4	J.G. Bennett / Charles Moran	36	Ferrari 212 Export	2562	4-2	6	234
5	Briggs Cunningham	32	Ferrari 166 Inter	1995	4-3	4	233
6	Rowland Keith / Robert Wilder	16	Allard J2 Ardun Ford	4517	3-1	9	227
7	John Bentley / Karl Brocken	57	Porsche 356 Coupe	1486	6-1	3	226
8	Dick Cicurel / E. McDonald	14	Jaguar XK120	3442	3-2	8	225
9	George Huntoon / Bob Gegen	73	Siata Crosley	870	7-1	1	208
10	Sherwood Johnson / John Scott	24	Jaguar XK120 Spl.	3442	3-3		204
11	Frank O'Hare / F.F. Allen	46	MG MkII Spl.	1250	6-2		198
12	Dick Irish	63	Siata Ford V8-60	1400	6-3		193
13	Frank Bott / Rees Makins	47	Cisitalia Coupe	1050	6-4		166
14	Fred Wacker	8	Allard J2X Cadillac Hydramatic	5424	2-3		123
15	Bob O'Brien	29	Jaguar XK120	3442	3-4		123
16	Fritz Koster	41	Porsche 356 Coupe	1486	6-5		93
17	Ken Ahr / George Lenz	12	Jaguar XK120	3442			DNF
18	Oscar Babcock	18	Jaguar XK120	3442			DNF
19	Joe Price / Dick Dorn	52	Morris Austin Spl.	2660			DNF
20	Ed Lunken	33	Aston Martin DB2	2500			DNF
21	Colby Whitmore / John Fitch	23	Jaguar Spl.	3442			DNF
22	Bob Said	55	Bandini Cisitalia	1050			DNF
23	Otto Linton	75	Siata Crosley	725			DNF
24	George Schraft	71	Crosley Le Mans Spl.	725			DNF

6-HOUR ENTRANTS

POS	DRIVERS	NO.	CAR MAKE/MODEL	DISP.	CLASS-POS	INDEX	LAPS
1	Byron King	17	Jaguar XK120	3442	3-1	2	122
2	George Rand / Steve Lansing	19	Jaguar XK120	3442	3-2	8	120
3	James Simpson / George Colby	34	Ferrari 166 MM	1995	3-3	3	120
4	LeRoy Thorpe / Bill Lloyd	43	MG Offenhauser	1484	4-1	4	120
5	Fritz Koster / Joe Koster	42	HRG Offenhauser	1484	4-2	6	110
6	Art Cheatam	15	Jaguar XK120	3442	3-4	9	108
7	Charles Hassan	72	Bandini Crosley	867	4-3	1	107
8	Norman Patten	49	MG TD	1250	4-4	7	107
9	T.R. Culler	56	MG TD	1250	4-5	5	102
10	Ernie Kreidner	50	MG TD	1250	4-6		87
11	Paul Ceresole	45	Cisitalia Spyder	1050	4-7		45
12	Kurt Hildebrand / Bob Ballinger	48	Nardi Fiat Spyder	1100			DNF
13	Lester Flink / Lewis Flink	54	MG TD	1250			DNF
DNS	John Mays	76	Crosley Hot Shot	725			

Circuit: 3.25-mile airport
Fastest Lap: #23 John Fitch 2:34.0
Winner's Average: 66.3 mph
Weather: Clear and warm
Est. Attendance: 12,000
ONE HOUR RACE won by Paul O'Shea.
6-hour cars were flagged off the course during the 12-hour event.

MACDILL SIX HOUR COLLIER MEMORIAL

MacDill Air Force Base / Tampa, Florida February 21, 1953

POS	DRIVERS	NO.	MAKE	INDEX	CLASS	LAPS
1	John Fitch	1	Cunningham C4R	6	B-1m	120
2	Bill Spear / Phil Hill	10	Ferrari 340 Mexico	4	C-1m	119
3	Jim Kimberly / George Huntoon	5	Ferrari 225S	2	C-2m	119
4	Sherwood Johnston	24	Jaguar XK120C	5	C-3m	117
5	Bob Gegen / David Hirsch	311	Jaguar XK120C	10	C-4m	116
6	Henry Wessells / Jim Carson	28	Jaguar XK120C	9	C-5m	114
7	Fred Warner	9	Allard J2 Cadillac	16	B-2m	114
8	Briggs Cunningham	72	OSCA M14	1	F-1	113
9	Ed Lunken / Charles Hassan	70	Ferrari 166 MM	12	E-1	107
10	Charles Moran / J.G. Bennett	50	Ferrari 212 Export	13	D-1	106
11	Colby Whitmore / Art Cheatham	40	Jaguar Spl.	22	C-6m	106
12	Karl Brocken	94	Porsche 356 Coupe	7	F-2	105
13	Otto Linton	75	Siata 208S	14	E-2	105
14	M.R.J. Wyllie / John Sabel	45	Jaguar XK120	25	C-7m	104
15	Robert Ryberg / J. Hugus	35	Jaguar XK120	18	C-1p	104
16	Rees Makins / Frank Bott	93	OSCA MT4	3	G-1	103
17	Daniel Whitz / R. Edmison	47	Jaguar XK120	21	C-2p	102
18	Fred Procter / Alfons Koster	97	Porsche 1500 Super	15	F-3	102
19	Roger Wing / Steve Spitler	26	Jaguar XK120 Spl.	28	C-8m	100
20	Robert Keller / Paul Farago	100	Siata Spyder	8	G-2	98
21	William Lloyd / LeRoy Thorpe	95	Offenhauser Lester MG	19	F-4	96
22	Paul Ceresole	11	Cisitalia Spyder	17	G-3	95
23	Max Goldman	98	Porsche 1500 Super	29	F-5	94
24	Don Bridges	33	Jaguar XK120	31	C-3p	91
25	Paul Gougelman	109	Nardi Spyder	11	H-1	89
26	Robert Fergus / Frankie Watts	55	MG-TC	23	F-1p	89
27	Clyde Carver / James Franklin	62	Jaguar XK120	33	C-4p	89
28	L. Rainwater / Dick Richmond	85	MG TD	24	F-2p	88
29	Robert Gary / Robert Nelson	88	MG TC	30	F-3p	87
30	K. Hildebrand / Bud Seaverns	64	MG TD	26	F-4p	86
31	Fred Allen	69	MG TD	27	F-5p	85
32	Ernest Von Kreidner	112	Crosley Le Mans	20	H-2	79
33	George Schrafft	111	Palm Beach Crosley Spl.	32	H-3	70
34	Lewis Flink	90	Siata Spyder	34	F-6p	68
35	George Sanderson	108	Crosley Hot Shot	35	G-4	39
	Phil Walters	2	Cunningham C4R		DNF	
	Bob Holbert	74	MG TD		DNF	
	Fred Wacker	8	Allard J2X Cadillac		DNF	
	Phil Stiles	4	Cunningham C4RK Coupe		DNF	
	Frank Larson	46	Jaguar XK120		DNF	
	Claude Haycraft	110	Austin		DNF	
	Bill Victor	43	Jaguar XK120		DNF	
	E.J. Koster	67	Maserati A6GCS		DNF	
	Donald MacNaughton	39	Nash Healey		DNF	
	Ted Boynton	7	Frazer Nash LMR		DNF	
	James Harbour	65	MG TD		DNF	
	John Negley	19	Allard J2 Chrysler		DNF	
	Robert Blackwood	31	Jaguar XK120C		DNF	
	James Simpson	91	OSCA MT4 1100		DNF	
	E.J. Tobin	73	BMW		DNF	
	James Brundage	3	Allard J2 Lincoln		DNF	
	Kenneth Ahr	116	Siata Spyder		DNF	
	Jack Ensley	22	Allard J2X Cadillac		DNF	
	Bill Fleming	96	Porsche 1500 America		DNF	
	Arthur Feuerbacher	14	Jaguar XK120C		DNF	
	Richard Meagher	37	Jaguar XK120		DNF	
	James MacCabe	115	Renault 1063		DNF	
	Jacic Morton	83	HRG Aerodynamic		DNS	

m = modified   p= production
Circuit: 4.1-mile, concrete airport runways
Leaders: #2 1-32; #1 33-93, 108-120; #10 94-107.

Est. Attendance: 70,000.
Weather: Clear and warm.
50-mile race for production sports cars won by Ernie Erickson in a Jaguar XK120.

FIA SPORTS CAR WORLD CHAMPIONS

MANUFACTURERS

1953	Ferrari	1978		Porsche
1954	Ferrari	1979		Porsche
1955	Mercedes-Benz	1980		Lancia
1956	Ferrari	1981		Porsche
1957	Ferrari	1982		Porsche
1958	Ferrari	1983		Porsche
1959	Aston Martin		C2	Alba
1960	Ferrari	1984		Porsche
1961	Ferrari		C2	Alba
1962	Ferrari	1985		Rothman's Porsche
1963	Ferrari		C2	Spice Engineering
1964	Ferrari	1986		Brun Motorsport
1965	Shelby Cobra			Porsche
1966	Ford		C2	Ecurie Ecosse
1967	Ferrari	1987		Silk Cut Jaguar
1968	Ford (P,S);		C2	Spice Engineering
	Porsche (GT)	1988		Silk Cut Jaguar
1969	Porsche		C2	Spice Engineering
1970	Porsche	1989		Sauber Mercedes
1971	Porsche		C2	Chamberlain
1972	Ferrari			Engineering
1973	Matra-Simca	1990		Sauber Mercedes
1974	Matra-Simca	1991		Silk Cut Jaguar
1975	Alfa Romeo	1992		Peugeot Talbot
1976	Porsche			
1977	Porsche			

DRIVERS

The World Challenge for Endurance Drivers included a wide variety of sports car endurance events in North America, Europe and Central and South America. The 12 Hours of Sebring was part of this driving championship.

1978	John Paul Sr.
1979	Don Whittington
1980	John Paul Sr.
1981	Bob Garretson

The FIA began to recognize driver championships in addition to manufacturer titles in 1982. There were no Group C events in the United States, somewhat diminishing the importance of this title. Below are the champions.

1982	Jacky Ickx		1988	Martin Brundle
1983	Bob Wollek			(C2) Gordon Spice /
1984	Stefan Bellof			Ray Bellm
1985	Hans Stuck		1989	Jean Louis Schlesser
	(C2) Gordon Spice			(C2) Nick Adams /
1986	Derek Bell			Fermin Velez
	(C2) Gordon Spice /		1990	Jean Louis Schlesser/
	Ray Bellm			Mauro Baldi
1987	Raul Boesel		1991	Teo Fabi
	(C2) Gordon Spice /		1992	Derek Warwick/
	Fermin Velez			Yannick Dalmas

IMSA SPORTS CAR MANUFACTURER CHAMPIONSHIPS

1971	GT	Chevrolet	1980	GT	Porsche	1986	GTP	Engine: Porsche	1991	GTP	Nissan
	GTU	Porsche		GTO	Porsche		GTP	Chassis: Porsche		GTP-L	Acura
				GTU	Mazda		GTP-L	Engine: Mazda		GTO	Mazda
1972	GT	Chevrolet					GTP-L	Chassis: Argo		GTU	Nissan
	GTU	Porsche	1981	GT	Porsche		GTO	Ford			
				GTO	BMW		GTU	Mazda	1992	GTP	Toyota
1973	GT	Porsche		GTU	Mazda					GTP-L	Acura
	GTU	Porsche				1987	GTP	Porsche		GTS	Nissan
			1982	GTP	Porsche		GTP-L	Pontiac		GTU	Nissan
1974	GT	Porsche		GTO	Chevrolet		GTO	Toyota			
	GTU	Porsche		GTU	Mazda		GTU	Mazda	1993	GTP	Toyota
										GTP-L	Acura
1975	GT	Porsche	1983	GTP	Engine: Porsche	1988	GTP	Porsche		GTS	Oldsmobile
	GTU	Datsun		GTP	Chassis: March		GTP-L	Pontiac		GTU	Nissan
				GTO	Porsche		GTO	Lincoln-Mercury			
1976	GT	Porsche		GTU	Mazda		GTU	Chevrolet	1994	WSC	Oldsmobile
	GTU	Datsun								GTS	Nissan
			1984	GTP	Engine: Porsche	1989	GTP	Nissan		GTU	Nissan
1977	GT	Porsche		GTP	Chassis: March		GTP-L	Buick		EGT 1	Porsche
	GTU	Porsche		GTO	Chevrolet		GTO	Mercury		EGT 2	Porsche
				GTU	Mazda		GTU	Mazda			
1978	GT	Porsche							1995	WSC	Ferrari
	GTO	Porsche	1985	GTP	Engine: Porsche	1990	GTP	Nissan		GT-1	Oldsmobile
	GTO	Porsche		GTP	Chassis: Porsche		GTP-L	Buick		GT-2	Porsche
				GTP-L	Engine: Mazda		GTO	Mercury			
1979	GT	Porsche		GTP-L	Chassis: Argo		GTU	Mazda			
	GTO	Porsche		GTO	Ford						
	GTU	Datsun		GTU	Mazda						

MAJOR U.S. SPORTS CAR CHAMPIONS

Year	Org	Class	Champion
1951	SCCA	Ntl. Points	John Fitch
1952	SCCA	Ntl. Points	Sherwood Johnston
1953	SCCA	Ntl. Points	Bill Spear
1954	SCCA	Ntl. Points	Jim Kimberley
1955	SCCA	Ntl. Points	Sherwood Johnston
1956	SCCA	Ntl. Points	Walt Hansgen
1957	SCCA	Ntl. Points	Walt Hansgen
1958	USAC	USRRC	Dan Gurney
1959	USAC	USRRC	Augie Pabst
1960	USAC	USRRC	Carroll Shelby
1961	USAC	USRRC	Ken Miles
1962	USAC	USRRC	Roger Penske
1963	SCCA	USRRC	Bob Holbert
1964	SCCA	USRRC	Jim Hall
1965	SCCA	USRRC	George Follmer
1966	SCCA	USRRC	Chuck Parsons
	SCCA	Can-Am	John Surtees
1967	USAC	SCCA	Mark Donohue
	SCCA	Trans-Am	Jerry Titus
	SCCA	Can-Am	Bruce McLaren
1968	SCCA	Trans-Am	Mark Donohue
	SCCA	Can-Am	Dennis Hulme
1969	SCCA	Trans-Am	Mark Donohue
	SCCA	Can-Am	Bruce McLaren
1970	SCCA	Trans-Am	Parnelli Jones
	SCCA	Can-Am	Dennis Hulme
1971	SCCA	Trans-Am	Mark Donohue
	IMSA	GT	Peter Gregg / Hurley Haywood
	SCCA	Can-Am	Peter Revson
1972	SCCA	Trans-Am	George Follmer
	IMSA	GT	Hurley Haywood
	SCCA	Can-Am	George Follmer
1973	IMSA	GT	Peter Gregg
	IMSA	GTU	Bob Bergstrom
	SCCA	Trans-Am	Peter Gregg
	SCCA	Can-Am	Mark Donohue
1974	IMSA	GT	Peter Gregg
	IMSA	GTU	Walt Maas
	SCCA	Trans-Am	Peter Gregg
	SCCA	Can-Am	Jackie Oliver
1975	IMSA	GT	Peter Gregg
	IMSA	GTU	Bob Sharp
	SCCA	Trans-Am	John Greenwood
1976	IMSA	GT	Al Holbert
	IMSA	GTU	Brad Frisselle
	SCCA	Trans-Am I	Jocko Maggiacomo
	SCCA	Trans-Am II	George Follmer
1977	IMSA	GT	Al Holbert
	IMSA	GTU	Walt Maas
	SCCA	Trans-Am I	Bob Tullius
	SCCA	Trans-Am-II	Ludwig Heimrath
	SCCA	Can-Am	Patrick Tambay
1978	IMSA	GT	Peter Gregg
	IMSA	GTO	Dave Cowart
	IMSA	GTU	Dave White
	SCCA	Trans-Am I	Bob Tullius
	SCCA	Trans-Am II	Greg Pickett
	SCCA	Can-Am	Alan Jones
1979	IMSA	GT	Peter Gregg
	IMSA	GTO	Howard Meister
	IMSA	GTU	Don Devendorf
	SCCA	Trans-Am I	Gene Bothello
	SCCA	Trans-Am II	John Paul Sr.
	SCCA	Can-Am	Jacky Ickx
1980	IMSA	GT	John Fitzpatrick
	IMSA	GTO	Luis Mendez
	IMSA	GTU	Walt Bohren
	SCCA	Trans-Am	John Bauer
	SCCA	Can Am	Patrick Tambay
1981	IMSA	GT	Brian Redman
	IMSA	GTO	Dave Cowart
	IMSA	GTU	Lee Mueller
	SCCA	Trans-Am	Eppie Wietzes
	SCCA	Can-Am	Geoff Brabham
1982	IMSA	GT	John Paul Jr.
	IMSA	GTO	Don Devendorf
	IMSA	GTU	Jim Downing
	SCCA	Trans-Am	Elliott Forbes-Robinson
	SCCA	Can-Am	Al Unser Jr.
1983	IMSA	GTP	Al Holbert
	IMSA	GTO	Wayne Baker
	IMSA	GTU	Roger Mandeville
	SCCA	Trans-Am	David Hobbs
	SCCA	Can-Am	Jacques Villeneuve
1984	IMSA	GTP	Randy Lanier
	IMSA	GTO	Roger Mandeville
	IMSA	GTU	Jack Baldwin
	SCCA	Trans-Am	Tom Gloy
	SCCA	Can-Am	Michael Roe
1985	IMSA	GTP	Al Holbert
	IMSA	GTPL	Jim Downing
	IMSA	GTO	John Jones
	IMSA	GTU	Jack Baldwin
	SCCA	Trans-Am	Wally Dallenbach, Jr.
	SCCA	Can-Am	Rick Miaskiewicz
1986	IMSA	GTP	Al Holbert
	IMSA	GTPL	Jim Downing
	IMSA	GTO	Scott Pruett
	IMSA	GTU	Tom Kendall
	SCCA	Trans-Am	Wally Dallenbach, Jr.
	SCCA	Can-Am	Horst Kroll
1987	IMSA	GTP	Chip Robinson
	IMSA	GTPL	Jim Downing
	IMSA	GTO	Chris Cord
	IMSA	GTU	Tom Kendall
	SCCA	Trans-Am	Scott Pruett
1988	IMSA	GTP	Geoff Brabham
	IMSA	GTPL	Tom Hessert
	IMSA	GTO	Scott Pruett
	IMSA	GTU	Tom Kendall
	SCCA	Trans-Am	Hurley Haywood
1989	IMSA	GTP	Geoff Brabham
	IMSA	GTPL	Scott Schubot
	IMSA	GTO	Pete Halsmer
	IMSA	GTU	Bob Leitzinger
	SCCA	Trans-Am	Dorsey Schroeder
1990	IMSA	GTP	Geoff Brabham
	IMSA	GTPL	Tomas Lopez
	IMSA	GTO	Dorsey Schroeder
	IMSA	GTU	Lance Stewart
	SCCA	Trans-Am	Tom Kendall
1991	IMSA	GTP	Geoff Brabham
	IMSA	GTPL	Parker Johnstone
	IMSA	GTO	Pete Halsmer
	IMSA	GTU	John Fergus
	SCCA	Trans-Am	Scott Sharp
1992	IMSA	GTP	Juan Fangio II
	IMSA	GTPL	Parker Johnstone
	IMSA	GTS	Steve Millen
	IMSA	GTU	David Loring
	SCCA	Trans-Am	Jack Baldwin
1993	IMSA	GTP	Juan Fangio II
	IMSA	GTPL	Parker Johnstone
	IMSA	GTS	Tom Kendall
	IMSA	GTO	Charles Morgan
	IMSA	GTU	Butch Leitzinger
	SCCA	Trans-Am	Scott Sharp
1994	IMSA	WSC	Wayne Taylor
	IMSA	GTS	Steve Millen
	IMSA	GTO	Joe Pezza
	IMSA	GTU	Jim Pace
	SCCA	Trans-Am	Scott Pruett
1995	IMSA	WSC	Fermin Velez
	IMSA	GT-1	Irv Hoerr
	IMSA	GT-2	Jorge Trejos
	SCCA	Trans-Am	Tom Kendall

PHOTO CREDITS

Courtesy of Brian Cleary
All memorabilia photos throughout book;
143, 144, 145, 157.

Courtesy of Darrell Dean
Front cover (bottom), 62 (bottom), 63, 80, 91, 97, 98, 105, 108, 113,
139, 141.

Courtesy of Dave Friedman
Front cover (top), 7, 58, 62, 64 , 66 (top), 68, 70, 71, 74, 78 (bottom),
79, 83, 85, 86, 89, 92, 93, 95, 96 (bottom), 101, 104, 112 (top).

Courtesy of Bill Foster collection
(photos by Jess Woods)
13-23, 25-29, 33-44, 48, 50, 51 (top), 52, 54 (top), 55.

Courtesy of Geoffrey Hewitt
8, 147, 155, 163.

Courtesy of Jim LaTourette
6, 78 (top).

Courtesy of Tedd Liggett
120, 121, 122, 138.

Courtesy of Pete Lyons
(photos by Ozzie Lyons) 30-31.

Courtesy of Bill Oursler
107, 125, 129, 130, 131, 133.

Courtesy of Porsche Cars North America
(photos by Hal Crocker) 115, 117, 124.

Courtesey of Chuck Segert
2-3, 46, 51 (bottom).

Courtesy of James Sitz
45.

Courtesy of Denis Tanney
164.

Courtesy of Bill Warner
67 (Claude Haycraft), 88, 102.

Courtesy of Jerry Wyszatycki
161, 164, 165.

**All other photos and memorabilia from
the collection of the author.**

APPENDIX WINNING CAR PHOTO CREDITS:

1950 Ken Breslauer collection

1952 Ken Breslauer collection

1953 Ken Breslauer collection

1954 Bill Foster collection

1955 Bill Foster collection

1956 Bill Foster collection

1957 Bill Foster collection

1958 Bill Foster collection

1959 Dave Friedman

1960 Courtesy Porsche North America

1961 Dave Friedman

1962 Dave Friedman

1963 Dave Friedman

1964 Ken Breslauer collection

1965 Dave Friedman

1966 Dave Friedman

1967 Dave Friedman

1968 Dave Friedman

1969 Ken Breslauer collection

1970 Dave Friedman

1971 Leonard Turner

1972 Ken Breslauer collection

1973 Darrell Dean

1975 Hal Crocker

1976 Tedd Liggett

1977 Bill Oursler

1978 Geoffrey Hewitt

1979 Geoffrey Hewitt

1980 Bill Oursler

1981 Bill Oursler

1982 Bill Oursler

1983 Leonard Turner

1984 Hal Crocker/Courtesy of Porsche Cars NA

1985 Tedd Liggett

1986 Brian Cleary

1987 Geoffrey Hewitt

1988 Brian Cleary

1989 Jerry Johnson

1990 Geoffrey Hewitt

1991 Geoffrey Hewitt

1992 Ken Breslauer

1993 Jerry Johnson

1994 Jerry Johnson

1995 Denis Tanney.

BIBLIOGRAPHY

Adams, Dick
"Noon 'til Midnight." *Speed Age*
(August 1952): 56.

Adams, Dick
"Sebring Grand Prix." *Speed Age* (June 1953):
35-38.

Bagnall, Bill
"Vero Beach." *Road and Track* (May-June
1952): 15-17, 24.

Bartley, D.M.
"Regatta on the Runways." *Speed Age*
(June 1959): 8-11.

Bentley, John
"Sebring was my Jinx." *Speed Age*
(July 1957): 18-19, 57.

Bentley, Ruth Sands
"Flashback on Florida." *Autosport*
(March 20, 1953): 368-70.

Bentley, Ruth Sands
"Ferraris Win in Florida." *Autosport*
(April 4, 1958): 428-33.

Bentley, Ruth Sands
"Porsche One-Two At Sebring." *Autosport*
(April 1, 1960): 428-32.

Biro, Pete
"Sebring: Cobra vs. Ferrari." *Motor Trend* (July
1964): 58-61.

Blume, Budd
"Sebring- A Full Report." *On the Grid*
(June 1960): 5-24.

Bochroch, Al
"Ferrari Wins Again." *Sports Car*
(May, 1962): 4-8.

Bochroch, Al
"Sebring." *Road & Track* (June 1968): 27-32.

Bochroch, Al
"'69 Sebring 12 Hours." *Road & Track*
(June 1969): 41-44.

Bochroch, Al
"The Red Cars are Back." *Road & Track*
(June 1970): 98-101.

Brady, Jack
"Sebring: Grand Prix of the U.S." *Road &
Track* (March 1960): 24-28.

Braillon, Didier
"Sebring: Blast from the Past." *Grand Prix
International* (March 1983): 62-81.

Brown, Stanley
"Sebring: Death, Victory Ride Bumpers Apart."
The Miami Herald
(March 28, 1966): 4E.

Buffington, Betsy
"Sebring Race: Spectacle of Speed, Color."
The Miami Herald (February 2, 1962): 8E.

Cahier, Bernard
"Sebring '57." *Road & Track* (June 1957):
14-17, 54.

Cahier, Bernard
"Sebring." *Road & Track* (June 1958):
28-31.

Cahier, Bernard
"Sebring '59." *Road & Track* (June 1959):
48-51.

Callahan, Bill
"Sebring Summary." *Motorsport*
(March 1951): 5-7, 24-25.

Callahan, Bill
"Sebring International." *Motorsport*
(June 1952): 17, 26.

Callahan, Bill
"Sebring Summary." *Motorsport* (June 1954):
16-18.

Callahan, Bill
"Sebring Sidelights." *Motorsport*
(July-August 1955): 6-11.

Callahan, Bill
"Sebring Sequel." *Motorsport*
(Aug-Sept 1956): 14-19, 33.
Callahan, Bill
"Vero Beach." *Motorsport* (June 1952):
12-13, 25.

Christy, John
"Sebring '58- Twelve Tough Hours." *Sports
Cars Illustrated* (June 1958): 18-21.

Christy, John
"Storm Over Sebring." *Sports Cars Illustrated*
(June 1959): 20-23, 80.

Christy, John
"Sebring '62." *Sports Car Graphic*
(June 1962): 20-25, 67, 70.

Christy, John
"Sebring '63." *Sports Car Graphic*
(June 1963): 18-26, 82.

Christy, John
"Sebring '65." *Sports Car Graphic*
(June 1965): 26-31, 64-68.

Christy, John
"Sebring '61 The Twelve Toughest Hours."
Sports Car Graphic (June 1961): 12-15,
66-67, 77.

Ciampa, George R. "Assault on Sebring."
Sports Car (May 1971): 18-19.

Ciampa, George R. "Sebring 72." *Sports Car*
(May 1972): 32-24.

Cipnic, Dennis "Sebring." *Road & Track* (July
1967): 61-64.

Cooper, Jeff "12 Hours at Sebring."
Road & Track (June 1955): 17-21.

Cooper, Jeff "Sixth Sebring," *Road & Track*
(June 1956): 13-17.

Cooper, Jeff "Sebring." *Motor Sports* (June
1958): 70-73, 81.

Crow, James T. "Ferrari, Ferrari, Ferrari..."
Road & Track (June 1963): 60-64.

Crow, James T. "1965 Sebring 12 HR."
Road & Track (June 1965): 42-47.

Cumberford, Robert "Sebring, 1954."
Road and Track (May 1954): 41-45.

Cumberford, Robert "Pilgrimage: Sebring."
Automobile (March 1994): 108-10.

Culley, Laura "History Lesson." *On Track*
(April 17, 1992): 40-49.

Culley, Laura "Withstanding Water."
On Track (April 9, 1993): 49-56.

Czaja, Bruce "Sebring Sees BMW Blitzkrieg."
AutoWeek (March 29, 1975): 10-11.

Czaja, Bruce "Holbert, Keyser Win 24th
Annual Sebring Classic." *AutoWeek*
(March 27, 1976): 1, 8.
Czaja, Bruce "Friselle and Dyer Hang On to
Win." *AutoWeek* (March 26, 1977): 1, 16-17.

Dechert, Peter "Sebring 1956." *Sports Car*
(May-June 1956): 13-18.

Dechert, Peter "Sebring Commentary."
Sports Car (May 1958): 2-4.

Dixon, Dick "Sebring 12-Hour." *Auto*
(June 1952): 28-29.

Economaki, Chris "Ferraris Wipe Sebring Slate
Clean." *National Speed Sport News* (March 26,
1958): 3.

Economaki, Chris "Miles and Ruby Claim
Sebring for Ford." *National Speed Sport News*
(March 30, 1966): 3.

Economaki, Chris "Gregg and Haywood Win
Sebring." *National Speed Sport News*
(March 28, 1973): 1, 3.

Fitch, John "12 Hours at Sebring." *Esquire*
(November 1953): 82-3, 131.

Fitch, John "The Florida International
Twelve- hour Grand Prix of Endurance."
Autosport (March 1954): 29-34.

Fitch, John "Florida Speed Festival." *Motorsport*
(March 1952): 28-31, 46.

Finefrock, Bill "Porsche, Camaro Win Sebring
Honors." *Competition Press/AutoWeek*
(April 13, 1968): 1, 16.

Fishback, Jere M. "Old Sebring Never Dies..." *AutoWeek* (March 22, 1982): 30, 39.

Ford, Tom "12 Hours of Sebring." *Speed Age* (July 1987): 25-28.

Gardner, John "Akin for a Win." *Florida Motor Sports* (July 1986): 12-18.

Gardner, John "The More Things Change..." *Florida Motor Sports* (June 1987): 10-17.

Gardner, John "Trivial Pursuit." *Florida Motor Sports* (May 1988): 16-23.

Gardner, John "Something Special." *Florida Motor Sports* (July 1989): 16-21.

Girdler, Allan "Sebring's Majority." *Road & Track* (June 1971): 47-50.

Given, Kyle "Specter From Another Era." *Car and Driver* (June 1970): 48-50, 89.

Grant, Gregor "The Sixth Sebring." *Autosport* (April 5, 1957): 432-33.

Grant, Gregor "Ferrari Win at Sebring." *Autosport* (March 27, 1959): 398-401, 406).

Grant, Gregor "Sebring 12 Hours." *Autosport* (March 30, 1962): 442-448.

Grant, Gregor "Ferrari Field Day." *Autosport* (March 27, 1964): 410-414.

Grant, Gregor "Ford 1-2-3 at Sebring." *Autosport* (April 1, 1966): 494-500.

Grant, Gregor "A Ford one-two at Sebring." *Autosport* (April 7, 1967): n/a.

Grant, Gregor "Sebring Afterthoughts." *Autosport* (December 25, 1959): n/a.

Harrison, Bob "Ponycars give Sebring its Only Real Race." *Car Life* (July 1968): 35-37.

Horsley, Fred "Sebring." *Motor Trend* (July 1954): 22-25, 67.

Halland, William "OSCA the Giant Killer." *Speed Age* (July 1954): 37.

Hirsch, Randy "12 Hours of Sebring." *Auto Racing* (June 1967): 18-21.

Hogg, Tony "Cobra at Sebring." *Road & Track* (June 1964): 30-35.

Howell, Glenn "A Tale of Two Teams." *Formula* (June 1977): 24-27.

Howell, Glenn "Brian Comes Back with a Bang." *AutoWeek* (March 31, 1978): 1, 16-18.

Huntoon, George "Sam Collier Memorial Grand Prix." *Road and Track* (March 1951): 4-7.

Ingram, Jonathan "Revenge of the 935s..." *On Track* (April 23, 1984): 28-36.

Ingram, Jonathan "Franco-American." *On Track* (April 15, 1985): 20-29.

Ingram, Jonathan "Three Wheelin'." *On Track* (April 14, 1986): 58-65.

Ingram, Jonathan "Sebring Tradition." *On Track* (April 13, 1987): 14-21.

Ingram, Jonathan "Porsche Parade." *On Track* (April 4, 1988): 16-24.

Ingram, Jonathan "Stormed Bastion." *On Track* (April 6, 1989): 38-45.

Jerome, John "Sebring 1963." *Car and Driver* (June 1963): 27-34.

Jones, Robert F. "Racy Red Beasts and King Kong, Too." *Sports Illustrated* (March na, 1972): 26-27.

Kidd, Al "Debut at Sebring." *Motor Trend* (June 1956): 34-35, 50.

Kovacik, Bob "Sebring '67." *Sports Car Graphic* (June 1967): 31-33, 82-84.

Kovacik, Bob "Sebring." *Sports Car Graphic* (June 1968): 22-25.

Kowaleski, Tom "Barbour Porsches Dominate Sebring." *AutoWeek* (April 2, 1979): 1, 20-21.

Kowaleski, Tom "Sebring Sidelights." *Road & Track* (August 1979): 58-60.
Lane, Joseph J. "Sebring Grand Prix of Endurance." *Road and Track* (May-June 1952): 30-31.

Lane, Joseph J. *Sebring 1956 Lap Charts.* Sebring, Fla.: Automobile Racing Club of Florida, 1956.

Lane, Joseph J. *Sebring 1958 Lap Charts.* Sebring, Fla.: Automobile Racing Club of Florida, 1958.

Lane, Joseph J. *Sebring 1962 Official Records.* Sebring, Fla.: Automobile Racing Club of Florida, 1962.

Lane, Joseph J. *Sebring 1963 Official Records.* Sebring, Fla.: Automobile Racing Club of Florida, 1963.

Lane, Joseph J. *Sebring 1964 Official Records.* Sebring, Fla.: Automobile Racing Club of Florida, 1964.

Lane, Joseph J. *Sebring 1965 Official Records.* Sebring, Fla.: Automobile Racing Club of Florida, 1965.

Lane, Joseph J. *Sebring 1966 Official Records.* Sebring, Fla.: Automobile Racing Club of Florida, 1966.

Lane, Joseph J. *Sebring 1967 Official Records.* Sebring, Fla.: Automobile Racing Club of Florida, 1967.

Lane, Joseph J. *Sebring 1968 Official Records.* Sebring, Fla.: Automobile Racing Club of Florida, 1968.

Lightowler, G.M. "Sebring Grand Prix of Endurance." *Speed Age* (June 1955): 71-76.

Long, Gary "Sebring: Survival of the Slowest." *The Miami Herald* (March 21, 1983): 3D.

Lovell, Bill "History is Bunk." *AutoWeek* (March 28, 1988): 50-52.

Lovell, Bill "A Kinder and Gentler Race." *AutoWeek* (March 27, 1989): 57-59.

Lovell, Bill "Undertired and undeterred." *AutoWeek* (March 31, 1986): 50-53.

Lovell, Bill "Same Old Sebring." *AutoWeek* (March 30, 1987): 58-59.

Lovell, Bill "The Best Laid Plans..." *AutoWeek* (March 26, 1990): 48-50.

Lovell, Bill "Lights out at Sebring." *AutoWeek* (March 30, 1992): 48-49.

Ludvigsen, Karl "Ferrari Takes the Twelve-Hour!" *Car and Driver* (June 1961): 25-28.

Ludvigsen, Karl "Chevies Stretch Three Ways at Sebring." *Corvette News* (Vol. 11, No. 5 1968): 4-7.

Lyons, Ozzie "Sebring- America's Longest Race Separates the Men from the Boys." *Auto Sportsman* (July 1953): 41-43.
Lyons, Pete "The 12 Hours of Sebring." *Auto Racing* (June 1970): 28-35.

Lyons, Pete "Porsche's Marvelous Monster." *Road & Track* (June 1971): 51-54.

Lyons, Pete "The Last Annual 12 Hours of Sebring." *Road & Track* (July 1972): 58-62.

Mandel, Leon "12 Hrs of Sebring." *Car & Driver* (June 1969): 43-45, 93.

Mandel, Leon "Andretti/Ickx Win Sebring." *Competition Press/AutoWeek* (April 15, 1972): 1, 20-23.

McCutcheon, Bill "Sebring Revisited." *Auto Age* (September 1955): 33-37.

McNamara, Jerry "Endurance at a Record Pace - Sebring '61." *Motor Trend* (June 1961): 72-77.

Mims, Donna Mae "Corvettes At Sebring." *On the Grid* (July 1962): 11-14.

Moses, Sam "Day and Night, A.J. Was Just Right." *Sports Illustrated* (April na, 1985): 24-26.

Muldoon, Tony "Sebring 1971." *Sports Car* (May 1971): 20-23.

O'Reilly, Don "The Sports Car's Big Year." *Speed Age* (April 1950): 12-13.

Oursler, Bill "Dark Horses Win Sebring." *National Speed Sport News* (March 28, 1984): 6, 15.

Potter, Steve "Hanging In There." *On Track* (April 12, 1982): 12-14.

Purdy, Ken "The Spectacle of Sebring." *The Saturday Evening Post* (March 26, 1960) 29-30, 114-16.

Putnam, Pat "No Tickets Necessary to Die at Sebring." *The Miami Herald* (March 29, 1966): 2-D.

Rosien, Arthur H. "Sebring: Impressions." *Sports Car* (May, 1960): 3-8.

Rosien, Arthur H. "Sebring Sidelights." *Sports Car* (May 1961): 3-10.

Rubin, Daniel R. "12 Hours of Racing." *True* (June 1953): 44-45.

Rudeen, Kenneth "Sebring Comes of Age." *Sports Illustrated* (March 26, 1956): 23, 66.

Rudeen, Kenneth "Fantastico for Fangio." *Sports Illustrated* (April 1, 1957): 14-15, 50.

Schmidt, Gerald "Sedans at Sebring." *Foreign Car Guide* (June 1966): 14-17.

Scott, Jeff "The 12 Hours of Sebring." *Auto Racing* (June 1969): 24-27, 48

Scott, Jeff "Sebring: Cradle of Big-Time Sports Car Racing." *Competition Press/AutoWeek* (April 3, 1971): 14.

Shattuck, Dennis "Sebring '60." *Road & Track* (June 1960): 20-23.

Shattuck, Dennis "Eight for Ferrari." *Road & Track* (July 1961): 78-84.

Silverman, Ron "Nissan Domination!" *Formula* (June 1989): 54-56.

Smiley, John "Porsches in Paradise Lost." *Competition Press/AutoWeek* (April 14, 1973): 1, 22-28.

Smith, Steve "Sebring 1964." *Car and Driver* (June 1964): 27-32.

Smith, Steve "Sebring 1965." *Car and Driver* (June 1965): 28-34.

Smith, Steve "Sebring 1966." *Car and Driver* (June 1966): 30-36.

Tanner, Hans "Sixth Sebring." *Motor Racing* (May 1957): 118-19.

Teissedre, Jean-Marc *24 Heures du Mans.* Le Mans, France. Automobile Club de L'Ouest, 1993.

Thoms, Wayne "A Sebring Adventure." *Sportscar Graphic* (July-August 1959): 24-33.

Troy, Lane "Sebring Twelve Hours." *Speed Age* (June 1956): 62-65.

Turner, Betty Jo "The Sebring/Camel 12 Hour: No Margin for Error." *Porsche Panorama* (May 1973) 4-7.

Turner, Betty Jo "The 12 Hours of Sebring." *Porsche Panorama* (May, 1978): 4-10.

Turner, Betty Jo "The Twelve Hours of Sebring." *Porsche Panorama* (May 1980): 4-12.

Turner, Betty Jo "12 Hours of Sebring." *Porsche Panorama* (May 1981): 4-16.

Turner, Betty Jo "12 Hours of Sebring." *Porsche Panorama* (May 1983): 6-15.

Turner, Betty Jo "The 12 Hours of Sebring." *Porsche Panorama* (May 1986): 4-11.

Turner, Betty Jo "Sebring Sundown." *Porsche Panorama* (May 1989): 28-31.

Typond, Don "Sebring- Next Year Bigger and Better." *Sports Cars Illustrated* (July 1960) 43-44, 80.

Ulmann, Alec *The Sebring Story.* Philadelphia. Chilton Book Company, 1969.

Unknown "Twelve American Hours." *The Autocar* (March 20, 1953): 378-79.

Unknown "Sebring 1959: A Saga of Speed and Storm." *Foreign Cars Illustrated* (June 1959): 4-7, 34-38.

Unknown "Palm Beach Shores Road Race." *Road and Track* (February 1952): 4-5.

Vincent, Joe "Ford Stomps Foes in Tragic Sebring." *Competition Press/AutoWeek* (April 16, 1966): 1, 9-10.

Yates, Brock "While Ferrari's Away The Fords Will Play." *Car and Driver* (June 1967): 26-32.

Walker, Rob "My Visit to Sebring." *Motor Sport* (July 1954) 379-82.

Wallace, Bill "Sebring 12-Hour." *On Track* (April 16, 1981): 8-10.

Warren, Cameron A. "Sebring 1966." *Road & Track* (June 1966): 96-100.

Weil, Ernest "The Florida International Twelve-hour Grand Prix." *Autosport* (March 1955): 35-37.

Weil, Ernest "The Florida International Twelve-hour Grand Prix." *Autosport* (March 1956): 67-69.

West, Ted "Sebring - A Race Right Down to the Wyer!" *Sports Car Graphic* (June 1969): 34-37, 62.

West, Ted "A very Special One." *Sports Car Graphic* (June 1970): 59-62.

Whitlock, Joe "Sebring 1971." *Sports Car Graphic* (June 1971): 80-84.

Wick, Justus "The Red Parade." *Sports Car* (May 1963): 6-9.

Wilder, Bob "Palm Beach, 1950." *Sports Car* (February, 1950): 7-12.

Windridge, Pinkie "Sing a Song of Sebring." *Sports Car* (May June 1957): 9-11.

Wright, Alfred "Long Push for a Champion." *Sports Illustrated* (December 21, 1959): na.

Wyer, John "First Act in Florida." *The Motor* (April 15, 1953): 353-355.

Yeager, Mark "A Most Unlikely Combination." *Formula* (May 1978): 22-25.

Zack, Frank J. "Florida Handicap Endurance Race." *Sports Car* (March-April 1952): 18-21.

Zuckert, Sherrie "Sebring 1964." *Car and Driver* (June 1964): 28-32, 80-81.

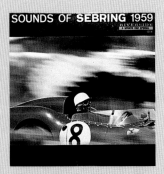

ACKNOWLEDGMENTS

The author wishes to thank the many people who assisted in compiling statistical data and photographs for this history of America's great sports car race. Most notably, the assistance of Jerry Johnson, Dave Friedman and Bill Foster made this project possible.

Assisting in photography: Bill Foster, Dave Friedman, Darrell Dean, James Sitz, Geoffrey Hewitt, Jim LaTourette, Bill Oursler, Tedd Liggett, Jerry Wyszatycki, Brian Cleary, Jerry Johnson, Tim Johnson, Hal Crocker, Leonard Turner, Bruce Clarke, Pete Lyons, Denis Tanney and Bill Warner.

Assisting in research: Jerry Johnson, Debra Goodrich, Dale Miller, Paul Crumlish and Janos Wimpffen.

Special thanks also to the following individuals and organizations who provided help along the way: Charles Earwood, The Type House, Impressions of Miami, Tres Stephenson, Mark Raffauf, Dick Greene, Betty Jo Turner, Jack Middleton, Lynn Myfelt, Bob Breslauer, Stan Durrance, Porsche Cars North America, Lou Tallon and my wife, Barbra.

ABOUT THE AUTHOR

Ken Breslauer is Communications Director and Track Historian at Sebring International Raceway. He graduated from the University of West Florida with a degree in journalism and was a sportswriter before joining Sebring in 1985. A respected motorsports historian, Ken founded *Auto Racing Memories* magazine in 1981 and has written numerous articles on racing history. He served as editor and publisher of the International Motor Sports Association Yearbook from 1989 through 1995. In addition, he is the promoter of the "Day Before the 500" auto racing memorabilia show held every May in Indianapolis, as well as several other antique and collectibles shows. A Florida native, he lives in St. Petersburg with his wife, Barbra.